Studies in *PERSONNEL* and
INDUSTRIAL PSYCHOLOGY

Studies in PERSONNEL and INDUSTRIAL PSYCHOLOGY

Edited by   EDWIN A. FLEISHMAN

*Department of Industrial Administration
and Department of Psychology*
YALE UNIVERSITY

1961

THE DORSEY PRESS, INC.

HOMEWOOD, ILLINOIS

———————

First Printing, July, 1961
Second Printing, February, 1962

Library of Congress Catalogue Card No. 61-15060

PRINTED IN THE UNITED STATES OF AMERICA

PREFACE

THIS BOOK is designed for use as either a basic or supplementary text in personnel and industrial psychology courses. The book developed, in part, out of my own experiences in teaching such courses at Yale University. First of all, I felt the need, as have many of my colleagues, for an up-to-date readings book for students in these courses. Many developments in the last ten years are not adequately reflected in the older readings books or even in more recent primary texts. Secondly, I noted that my students were often stimulated by assigned readings and this was reflected in the level of the class discussion. Such readings provide a special appreciation of the scientific aspects of industrial psychology as well as a critical regard for the methods and concepts used to investigate human behavior in industrial settings.

In undertaking this task, it seemed to me that a book in industrial psychology could be developed to include many of the advantages of both a primary text and a readings book. I have attempted to do this by integrating review and discussion articles, within particular areas, with articles emphasizing, in depth, key empirical studies. For each of the nine major sections, I have written introductory material showing the relevance of each article to the important issues in the field and to the theme of that Section, providing (hopefully) additional coherence to that area.

I have also tried to provide a balanced coverage of the field of personnel and industrial psychology. Many of our excellent texts have devoted proportionately more space to the "traditional" aspects of this field (such as selection, training, or work methods) than to the social, motivational, attitudinal aspects. Other texts have emphasized the latter. While it is difficult to say what is a "balanced view," a conscious attempt has been made here to give expanded treatment to the social-motivational aspects without minimizing developments in the more "hardheaded" areas. This is reflected, for example, in the extended treatment of the motivation, leadership, communication, and organizational areas. Also, I have included research from related disciplines as well as from military and educational settings which I felt particularly appropriate for industrial psychology.

The up-to-date character of this work is reflected in the fact that 55 of the 66 articles were published in 1950 or later (42 of these are 1955 or later). Of the other 11 articles, only one goes back as far as 1939. (This doesn't mean that the "classic" studies are ignored since they are reviewed in the light of more recent work.) There was considerable turnover in selected articles from the beginning to the end of this venture as more useful articles appeared or other unknown, but relevant, articles were uncovered. Actually, one article published as late as April, 1961, was inserted at the galley proof stage because of its timeliness. Since each article was selected with a view to its relation with other articles in that section, many excellent articles originally included had to be dropped to minimize overlap and to keep the book to manageable size.

I have tried to keep the undergraduate student firmly in mind. As a consequence I have done a good deal of editing here and there for which I hope the authors will forgive me. In a number of cases, complicated tabular material, analysis of variance tables, or involved descriptions of advanced statistical techniques were omitted or simplified. In no case did this seem to detract from the value of the article or to lose any essential information. Sometimes paragraphs were inserted to summarize the material omitted, especially in the case of elaborate tables and statistical tests. Similarly, in several cases articles were shortened, discussion sections abbreviated, or exposition simplified. In all such cases I preferred this course to substituting less relevant articles for those I considered more essential.

There is, of course, a mixture of styles and level of technical sophistication and I have made no attempt to control this. I believe this has more advantages than disadvantages; while it makes for some unevenness, it also creates a certain freshness and relief from boredom. It also gives the student additional exposure to the varieties of sources in this field and to the various "personalities" of the different journals.

As I have tried to make clear, it is not my purpose merely to present a "collection" of readings, although most instructors may prefer to use the book as a supplementary readings text. And there is enough flexibility in coverage to allow the instructor to select articles of his choice. Similarly, the text may be useful at the graduate level if the instructor wishes to focus more in depth on problem issues. However, it is my feeling that the book can be used successfully as a primary text. I hope some instructors will be tempted to try. I hope that those who do will let me know their reactions (as well as those of their students) to such a course.

I am indebted to the following publishers for providing special permission to reprint the articles from their journals: American Psychological Association, Inc. (*Journal of Applied Psychology, Journal of Consulting Psychology, American Psychologist*), American Management Association, Inc. (*Personnel, General Management Series*), National Institute of Industrial Psychology (*Occupational Psychology*), Personnel Psychology, Inc. (*Personnel Psychology*), American Society of Training Directors, Inc. (*Journal of American Society of Training Directors*), Journal Press (*Journal of Social Psychology*), Harvard University Graduate School of Business Administration (*Harvard Business Review*), Tavistock Publications, Ltd. (*Human Relations*), American Association for the Advancement of Science (*Science*), Bell Laboratories, Inc. (*Bell Laboratories Record*), American Sociological Association (*Sociometry*). In addition, a number of articles are drawn from government publications and others are based on manuscripts not yet published elsewhere. In all cases the original source of the individual articles is acknowledged on the title page of each article. Special permission to reprint was also obtained from each author and I am grateful to them; I hope they are pleased with the final product.

I am also indebted to Mrs. Carolyn Talalay, who typed the manuscript portions of the book and helped with the numerous details of getting the permissions of the authors and publishers.

EDWIN A. FLEISHMAN

New Haven, Connecticut
June, 1961

TABLE OF CONTENTS

SECTION ONE: PERSONNEL SELECTION

SECTION TWO: PERFORMANCE APPRAISAL

SECTION THREE: TRAINING EMPLOYEES AND MANAGERS

Section One

PERSONNEL SELECTION

Introduction

THIS SECTION describes the application of scientific methods in the selection of employee and management personnel. The basic problem is that of improving decisions made at the hiring stage. Essentially, the person doing the hiring is making a prediction of an applicant's probable success on a particular job. Put another way, he is trying to match individual differences in people to differences in the requirements of particular jobs. The adequacy with which he can do this depends on his knowledge of how to assess the relevant individual differences, on the accuracy of his information regarding the requirements of the jobs in question and on the validity of the assessment procedures used.

Many personnel procedures are used to assist the personnel department in making hiring decisions. These include job descriptions, application blank information, interviews, psychological test data, and employment references. Often these are used unsystematically and without knowledge of their actual usefulness in particular job situations. The readings in this section describe specific research studies aimed at evaluating or improving such procedures.

The first article, by Rothe, describes one of the first steps in setting up a personnel selection program. This step, usually called *job analysis*, involves an analysis of the operations and requirements of the job for which we wish to select people. In "Matching Men to Job Requirements," Rothe describes a method developed for supervisory jobs.

A second step in the hiring process is that of *recruitment*, which involves attracting suitable applicants to the company. It is surprising how little systematic information is actually known about the relative importance of various factors in attracting applicants. Yet many companies have enormous recruiting campaigns which even may include full-page magazine advertisements or visits by company executives to college campuses. The second article in this section, "What Applicants Look for in a Company" by Jurgensen, describes one of the few studies on this subject.

Perhaps, no personnel technique is so widely used (and misused) as the employment interview. It is here that the applicant may have his first personal contact with the company. Thus, the employment interview has a public relations function. It also has the function of informing the applicant about the company. But its principle function is to allow the interviewer to seek information about the interviewee from which he can make a prediction about probable job success. Despite its widespread use, the interview is seldom evaluated systematically. When such evaulations have been made, the results have been disappointing. The article by McMurry, "Validating the Patterned Interview," reviews some of these studies, points up the limitations of the usual interview procedure, and provides evidence of the kind of interview which may have value.

There are many specific questions about the value of different hiring procedures which can be answered only by research. The article by Weitz, "Job Expectancy and Survival," shows how research provided an answer to a puzzling question: Is later turnover among insurance agents related to the kind of concept of the job originally provided when they were hired?

Practically every organization uses an application blank in its employment procedure. Essentially, this is an attempt to make use of the applicant's personal history in placing him in the job. The report by Fleishman and Berniger, "Using the Application Blank to Reduce Office Turnover," demonstrates the kind of improvement which can be made through a statistical, follow-up approach to application blank data. Incidentally, this study, along with the previous one by Weitz, shows two ways of reducing turnover by appropriate hiring techniques.

Another frequently used employment tool is the letter of recommendation from previous acquaintances, employers, teachers, co-workers, etc. Some attempt has been made to systematize these references by means of a questionnaire sent to those persons familiar with the applicant. But how useful is such information? We know such information is used, but what does research show about its value? Mosel and Goheen have made several studies in this area. Their report, "The Validity of the Employment Recommendation Questionnaire in Personnel Selection," investigates the extent to which such recommendations, in a variety of skilled occupations, actually correlate with later job performance.

Psychological tests are often used in personnel selection and placement and their use is increasing. Sometimes they are misused, as are the interview and application blank. However, many tests and testing programs have been subjected to a great deal of statistical and experimental scrutiny. The article by Hay, entitled "The Validation of Tests," reviews the principles and procedures involved in developing and evaluating testing programs for employees.

The final two articles in this section deal with *management* selection. Although it is a field of tremendous recent interest, this area is not as well developed as is the area of *employee* selection. One reason is that the criteria of management success are not so well agreed on. Another reason is that what is effective in a leadership position depends somewhat on situational factors. The two articles described depart from traditional selection techniques and represent two recent developments which look promising in this area. Weitz's article, "Selecting Supervisors with Peer Ratings," shows how evaluations made by associates proved successful in predicting performance of men after they became assistant managers in insurance agencies. This study confirms other findings from a variety of different organizations where this technique has been used. The title of Bass's article, "The Leaderless Group Discussion as a Leadership Evaluation Instrument," is self-explanatory. Bass describes the method and reviews the encouraging results of research by him and others who have used this approach.

1. Matching Men to Job Requirements*

Harold F. Rothe

IN ALL PSYCHOLOGICAL evaluations of personal characteristics and their relation to jobs, the first step is to obtain an accurate picture of the job in question, namely a job description. From the psychologist's point of view, many job descriptions, at least of supervisory jobs, suffer because of the non-specific and non-operational definitions. What meaning can a psychologist attach to such descriptions as: "Responsible to the General Manager for the following functions"; "Supervises the work of Department 12"; "Responsible for personnel and costs"; etc.? After reading such descriptions one may readily raise the question, "Just what does he do?"

Detailed interviews with many hundreds of supervisors led to the establishment of six basic operations, or clusters of operations, that an industrial leader performs. These are in approximate chronological order:

(1) plans an activity,
(2) decides to do, or not to do, a certain thing,
(3) organizes a group of persons to carry out the plans that have been decided upon,
(4) communicates the program to the organization,
(5) leads the organization toward the established goal, and
(6) analyzes the progress toward the goal.

These six operations are, of course, not as specific and rigorous as an experimental psychologist would desire. On the other hand they have the advantages of being common to many industrial and even non-industrial leadership positions, and also of being readily further refined into more specific operations. The key to the entire technique described here lies in the breakdown of these six clusters into their components.

It is interesting to note that other writers have developed essentially the same operations. Flanagan[1] has described an evaluation system in which "critical incidents" of leadership behavior are classified in six areas:

(1) proficiency in handling administrative detail,
(2) proficiency in supervising personnel,
(3) proficiency in planning and directing action,
(4) proficiency in (military) occupational specialty,

* From *Personnel Psychology*, Vol. 4, 1951, pp. 291–301.
[1] J. C. Flanagan, "A New Approach to Evaluating Personnel," *Personnel*, Vol. 26, 1949, pp. 35–42.

(5) acceptance of organizational responsibility, and

(6) acceptance of personal responsibility.

Although Flanagan writes chiefly of the behavior of the person on the job, he points out that it is possible to develop job requirements from this behavior. Shuman[2] writes that the functions of management are planning, making decisions, and coordinating—this latter by communicating. He adds to these the bearing of responsibility and the giving of orders that are in consequence of that responsibility.

BREAKDOWN OF THE BASIC OPERATIONS

Six basic managerial operations have been isolated. These are, to recapitulate briefly: (1) plan, (2) decide, (3) organize and delegate, (4) communicate, (5) lead, (6) analyze.

Three of these operations are "intellectual," namely plan, communicate, and analyze. These involve the ability to analyze problems, to think logically, to express one's self, and to analyze numerical values. The other three are predominantly personality characteristics, namely decide, organize, and lead.

The planning required by a supervisory job may be very simple, or it may be very complex. If the type of work is highly standardized, a great deal of control information is available, and plans must be made for only a few specific jobs and for only a few days ahead; then relatively little ability for planning is required. But if the situation is unstandardized, there is very little guiding information, and plans must be made for a year ahead, covering many unrelated functions; then an extremely high degree of planning ability is required by the job. A foreman of a shipping department might need the simpler level of ability and the general manager of the plant might need the extreme degree at the other end of the scale.

Similarly for communicating, some jobs require only a low level of the ability for self-expression, and other jobs require an extremely high degree. The number of contacts in which to express the message, the method of communication (face-to-face talks, written memos, speeches, etc.), the specificity or the abstractness of the subject, and the objective to be attained by the communication—all influence the demands of the job so far as the complexity of this ability is required.

In our culture, plans and progress are generally expressed in numerical terms and hence some ability for handling arithmetical problems is required by most supervisory jobs. The type of arithmetical operation involved, the method of reporting, and the extent of deduction from numbers all tend to make a job simple or complex in the numerical area.

The making of decisions is treated as a personality characteristic. Most

[2] R. B. Shuman, *The Management of Men* (Norman: University of Oklahoma Press, 1948).

persons can make decisions, but they cannot all make stable, mature decisions. Maturity is required in order to make highly complex decisions. Some understanding of the behavior of persons is required by many jobs, since decisions are often made in a social situation. The ability to stand pressure and tensions in the situation is also often required if sound decisions are to result from the situation. The ability to switch rapidly from one task to another, or from one part of a task to another part (versatility) is often required if stable decisions are to be made.

It is noteworthy that the making of decisions, as used in this system, is concerned with the making of stable or "reliable" decisions, but not necessarily correct or "valid" decisions. That is, the factor of decisions is defined in non-intellectual terms, and is not the same as planning.

The organizing of a collection of persons into a group pursuing a goal is an activity characterized chiefly by the delegating away, the retaining, or the accepting of responsibility. Some persons find it difficult to accept responsibility for the work of others. Some persons find it difficult to delegate anything. It appears quite likely that both of these difficulties arise because of insecurity feelings, and hence the factor of organizing is defined in personality terms. Complex jobs involve the supervision of many persons, covering many types of work, and supervised "indirectly," (i.e., through "layers" of subordinate supervisors). Simpler supervisory jobs involve few subordinates, few jobs, direct supervisory contacts, and the reception of fairly close supervision from above.

The amount of leadership or social aggressiveness required by a job varies with the integrity of the groups involved, the aggressiveness of the members of the groups, the type of work skills possessed by the membership, and the degree of pressure upon the group or groups for achievement. Thus a supervisor over six filing clerks would not need much leadership ability, but the works manager of an automotive parts plant would require a great deal.

JOB COMPLEXITY PROFILES

For any supervisory job each of the six factors just described is analyzed into its constitutents. The final result is a rating, on a scale of sixteen steps, of the complexity of the job in question. The person on the job may then be "evaluated" by a psychologist, and his qualifications may be tested and/or rated on the same six factors and again on a scale of sixteen steps. This permits an immediate comparison of the person's qualifications with the job's requirements.

In the system described by Gaiennie[3] a total "job" score and a "person" score were determined. In the system described here a job profile and a man profile are made, but usually there is no attempt made to get

[3] L. R. Gaiennie, "An Approach to Supervisory Organization Control in Industry," *Personnel Psychology*, Vol. 3, 1950, pp. 41-52.

a total single score. There are, of course, some occasions when a total score is desirable, as Gaiennie has pointed out. There are also reasons for not turning profiles into single scores, as is evident in much psychological test work.

In the light of various researches on job evaluation systems, it is to be expected that the six factors in terms of which supervisory jobs are analyzed here would be inter-correlated fairly highly.[4] These inter-correlations have been determined in one plant for 58 jobs ranging from foreman through factory manager, and they are shown in Table 1. The inter-correlations range from .94 to .18; the median r is .73.

The question might be raised, "Why use six factors that are fairly highly correlated?" Why not use only one or two factors? There are two main reasons for using six factors. The chief one is that executives who receive reports of the qualifications of their subordinates often prefer a detailed analysis of assets and liabilities, and not merely a single statement that the man does or does not measure up to the demands of a job. The six factors described in this article provide a convenient framework for writing reports about individuals. The second reason is the belief that an analysis of requirements is more accurate than a summary in one or two broad terms. Since psychologists can analyze a person and also a job into six reasonably discrete categories, it is probably best to use them, so long as each might be contributing something at least partially different. Inter-correlations of about .73, although fairly high, still leave room for each factor to contribute something different.

TABLE 1

INTER-CORRELATION OF JOB COMPLEXITY ANALYSIS ELEMENTS FOR 58
SUPERVISORY POSITIONS IN ONE MANUFACTURING ORGANIZATION

	P	C	A	L	D	D
Plan.................	.94	.55	.83	.67	.79
Communicate..........		.58	.74	.56	.73
Analyze..............			.18	.52	.42
Lead................				.71	.85
Delegate.............					.86
Decide..............					

THE USE OF COMPLEXITY PROFILES

Complexity profiles, and the written "evaluation" of the persons who are profiled, are used by management in a variety of ways. One use is to study the strong and weak points of individuals to ascertain areas that

    [4] D. J. Chesler, "Reliability of Abbreviated Job Evaluation Scales," Journal of Applied Psychology, Vol. 32, 1948, pp. 622–28; C. H. Lawshe, Jr. and G. A. Satter, "Studies in Job Evaluation: I. Factor Analyses of Point Ratings for Hourly-Paid Jobs in Three Industrial Plants," Journal of Applied Psychology, Vol. 38, 1944, pp. 189–98, and subsequent papers; N. Locke, "Few Factors or Many?—An Analysis of a Point System of Classification," Personnel, Vol. 26, 1949, pp. 442–48.

need further development through training and counselling. A second use is as a guide in planning promotions. This application is shown in Figure 1 where the profile of one person is compared with the profiles for three jobs.[5] The man in question has superior qualifications (assuming adequate job knowledge) for his present position as section supervisor. He has adequate qualifications for a position as general supervisor, but he is not yet ready—and he may never be ready—for a position as superintendent.

Another illustration of this application is shown in Figure 2, where three foremen are compared with the requirements for a higher job. Mr. Brown has superior qualifications for his present job, and is doing an excellent piece of work on that job. He is the first foreman considered for promotion. Mr. Black meets his job requirements nicely, and is doing a good job. Mr. White is slightly below his job requirements. But Mr. White is handling his job fairly well, and he is on the most difficult job. Although his job record is not outstanding he is the best qualified for the general foreman's position of these three men, all of whom have roughly equal job knowledge. Thus the man with the least impressive job performance is actually the best candidate for promotion.

A more complete application takes the form of an organization study such as is illustrated in Figure 3. Here is one section of a large company. This section is not a profitable section. A man-job study shows that this department has generally poor foremen. In actuality these foremen each supervised an average of twelve men. Thus there is a high supervisory overhead. The foremen's jobs have been deskilled to the point where the jobs are small and the job requirements are low. Even at that, the men of these jobs are still lower, presenting a sorry picture. With information of this type available, and readily seen at a glance, management has some information for taking steps to better the situation.

CONCLUSIONS

This paper has presented some of the details of a system for matching the demands of supervisory jobs with the qualifications of incumbents on those jobs or candidates for those jobs. The purpose of this article has been to present more complete details of the system used in analyzing job requirements, and to illustrate the applications of a technique of this type to management problems on an executive and supervisory level. With slight variations in breakdown of factors the system is useful for staff and sales personnel and positions.

It is believed that this type of technique represents a distinct advance in the application of psychological methods to the management of key per-

---

[5] In making the profiles, the order of the six operations has been changed from the order previously listed in this article. The three "intellectual" characteristics are listed first, and then the three "personality" characteristics. Thus strengths and weakness of ability or personality may be seen at a glance.

FIGURE 1

COMPARISON OF QUALIFICATIONS OF ONE CANDIDATE WITH REQUIREMENTS OF THREE JOBS

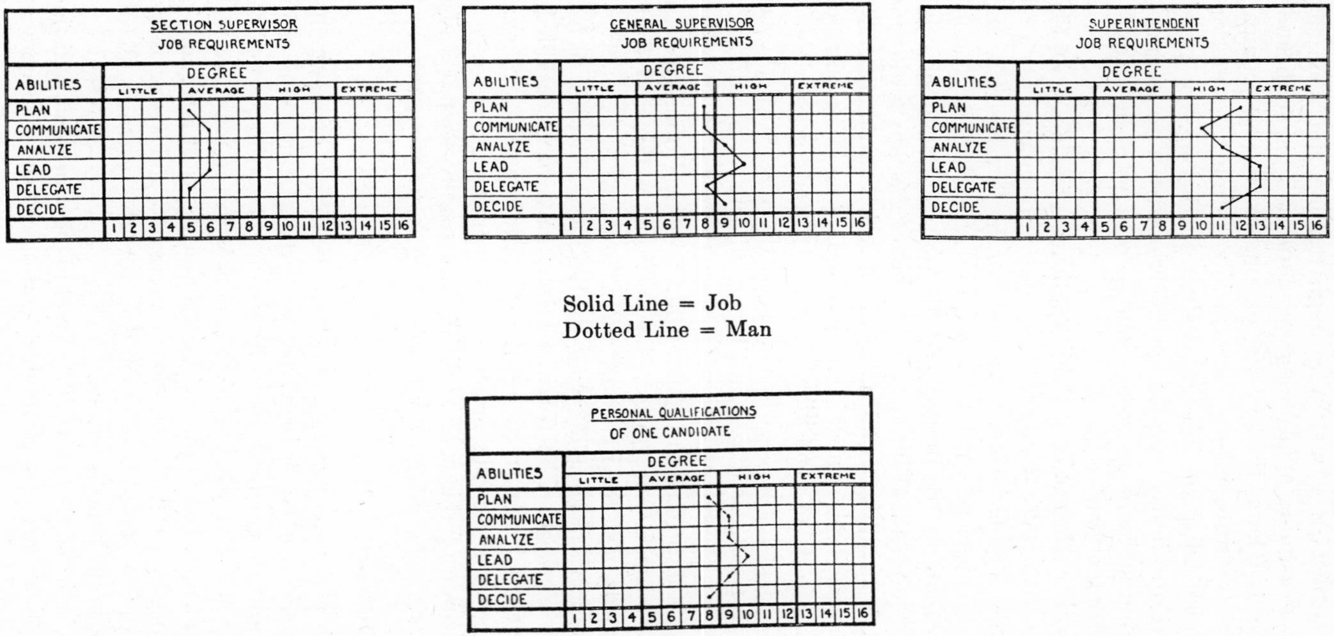

Solid Line = Job
Dotted Line = Man

FIGURE 2

COMPARISON OF THE QUALIFICATIONS OF THREE CANDIDATES WITH REQUIREMENTS
OF ONE JOB

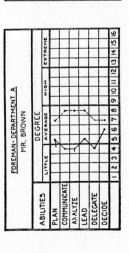

Solid Line = Job
Dotted Line = Man

FIGURE 3

JOB-MAN COMPLEXITY ANALYSIS ORGANIZATION CHART OF ONE DIVISION
OF A COMPANY

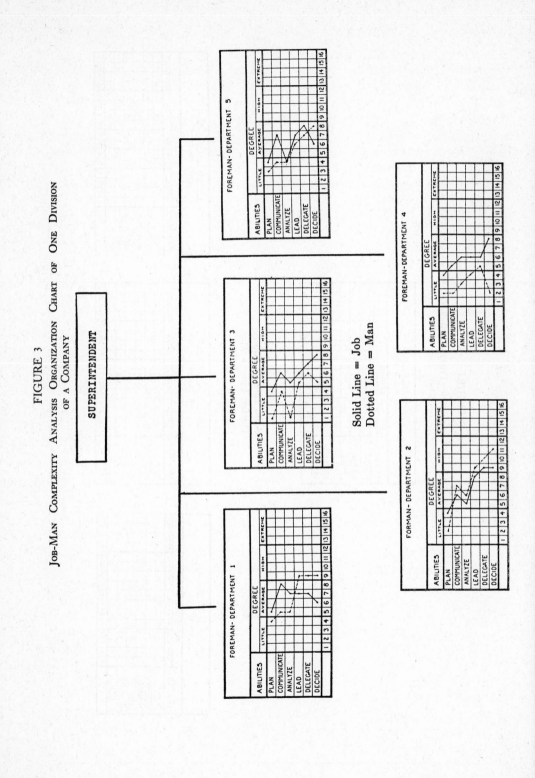

Solid Line = Job
Dotted Line = Man

sonnel. Without a technique of this kind a psychologist must use a rather vague opinion about job requirements and then recommend, or not recommend, a person for a job based upon that concept of the job. In many instances the psychologist's evaluation of a man, using test norms for various kinds of workers, is far more refined than is his concept of the job the man holds, or will hold.

Thus a psychologist may test and interview an applicant for a position as purchasing agent. On an intelligence test, for example, he may have available only norms for the general population. If his techniques are more refined he will have norms for purchasing agents. Suppose now that this applicant is slightly below the average purchasing agent in intelligence. Is he, or is he not, recommended for that position?

The answer to this question obviously lies in knowing how much intelligence (or any other ability) the specific job requires. Norms of people are not enough. Norms of jobs must be developed. This means that jobs must be analyzed into operating aspects and these aspects must be quantified. A technique such as the one described in this article does do just that.

2. What Job Applicants Look for in a Company*

Clifford E. Jurgensen

ALL OF US HAVE heard persons say, "Company X is the best company to work for in the whole state." Similarly, we have heard persons say "I wouldn't work for company Y if it were the last place on earth." Applicants frequently state in their interview for employment, "I would like a job here because everyone says it's a good place to work." These opinions which people have toward any company are important to that company, and are particularly important in the case of a public utility. They do much to establish and maintain good or poor public relations; and they make it easy or hard to build up an adequate pool of job applicants from which to select satisfactory employees.

What are the factors by which persons decide whether a job is a "good" job or a company is a "good" company? Discussion with executives, supervisors, union officials, employees, and job applicants frequently emphasizes the importance of the following ten factors:

---

* From *Personnel*, Vol. 25, 1949, pp. 352–55.

1. *Advancement* (Opportunity for promotion)
2. *Benefits* (Vacation, sick pay, insurance, etc.)
3. *Company* (Employment by company you are proud to work for)
4. *Co-Workers* (Fellow workers who are pleasant, agreeable, and good working companions)
5. *Hours* (Good starting and quitting time, good number of hours per day or week, day or night work, etc.)
6. *Pay* (Large income during year)
7. *Security* (Steady work, no layoffs, sureness of being able to keep your job)
8. *Supervisor* (A good boss who is considerate and fair)
9. *Type of Work* (Work which is interesting and which you like)
10. *Working Conditions* (Comfortable and clean—no objectionable noise, heat, cold, odors, etc.)

Few persons would deny that all these factors are important, but many disagreements arise regarding their *relative* importance. When executives are asked to rank these factors in order of their importance to workers, they frequently disagree widely. Many lengthy discussions and conferences have been held in an attempt to reconcile the opinions of various individuals. Little experimental data are available, however, and most of these are based on exceedingly small numbers of cases or are based on specialized or minority groups which cannot be considered representative of typical workers.

HOW DO APPLICANTS RATE THESE FACTORS?

In 1945 the Minneapolis Gas Company decided to obtain data on what job applicants said they wanted rather than what executives thought they wanted. Since that time each job applicant has been given a questionnaire containing the ten job factors listed above and asked to rank the factors in order of their importance to him. Each applicant was told that there were no right or wrong answers, and that he was to answer according to what he thought rather than what he believed others might think. Applicants were not asked to sign their names, although for research purposes they were requested to give their sex, marital status, number of dependents, age, salary, extent of education, and main occupation.

Table 1 gives the average (mean) rank assigned the 10 job factors by 3,345 men and 378 women applicants. Factors are listed in order of their importance to men applicants. Inasmuch as the factor considered to be most important by the applicant was given a rank of one and the factor considered least important given a rank of 10, the smaller the average given in Table 1, the more important the factor was considered to be.

It will be noted that these factors fall into three rather distinct groups so far as men applicants are concerned. Security, advancement, and type of work are considered most important. Company, pay, co-workers, and supervisor are considered to be of intermediate importance. Hours, working conditions, and benefits are least important. Data obtained from women applicants can likewise be classified into three groups. Type of work stands alone as being most important. Benefits stand alone as being least important. The remaining factors were considered to be fairly close to each other.

In general, women were less interested than men in security, advancement, company, pay, and benefits; and were more interested than men in type of work, co-workers, supervisor, hours, and working conditions. These differences form a definite pattern. Women were more interested in short-range or temporary factors which increase the pleasantness of work; whereas men were more interested in the factors of most im-

TABLE 1

Average (Mean) Ranks Assigned Job Factors by Applicants

Job Factor	3,345 Men	378 Women
Security	3.3	4.6
Advancement	3.6	4.8
Type of work	3.7	2.8
Company	5.0	5.4
Pay	6.0	6.4
Co-workers	6.0	5.4
Supervisor	6.1	5.4
Hours	6.9	6.1
Working conditions	7.1	5.8
Benefits	7.4	8.2

portance from a long-range viewpoint of a lifetime of work to support themselves and their families.

SIGNIFICANCE OF FINDINGS

The emphasis given security is not surprising, for the importance of security has generally been stressed by management, unions, and psychologists. These data indicate that such emphasis is well deserved. The high rank of advancement will also be expected by many readers.

The great emphasis placed by these applicants on type of work is surprising to many persons. Data show that type of work increased in importance as the job level increased, and that persons who worked on the least pleasant job were those who were least interested in type of work. It would appear that management and unions have both erred considerably in neglecting to emphasize the importance of type of work.

The emphasis placed on the company is also surprising to many. It would appear that most companies could derive considerable benefit from increased attempts to "sell" the company to employees. House organs, bulletin boards, employee induction manuals, and other communication lines can be used to give information to employees and increase their pride in their company.

The fact that pay and co-workers are tied for fifth position is of considerable interest. There is considerable discrepancy between the importance pay is usually believed to have and the position actually assigned it by applicants. The fact that a pay increase is usually the first demand of any union might be interpreted to mean that these data are incorrect. However, this viewpoint is not supported by the fact that unionization has frequently taken place first in those companies paying the highest wage rates and the most intense labor strife has often been in those same companies and industries. Pay obviously is not a panacea which will solve all controversies.

From the employee viewpoint, several reasons may explain the emphasis which has frequently been given pay. All employees would like to secure more pay than they have secured in the past, and if they believe they can get more, they may try to do so. Further, demands for greater pay are often made in substitution of the demands for other wants which may be either conscious or unconscious. The demand for higher pay is given further emphasis when employees are on strike.

Not only do the foregoing reasons apply, but additional reasons enter into the picture. No group of employees strikes against an employer unless there is intense feeling on both sides, and frequently there is a desire to hit the opponent in a sensitive spot. The pocketbook is such a sensitive spot, and so employees frequently emphasize a pay increase even though the basic reasons for the strike are far removed from the question of wages. Striking employees may also overemphasize pay increases in order to arouse public sympathy in their favor. Sympathy is particularly easy to arouse if the public is made to believe that the workers are grossly underpaid. Use of this technique has often resulted in serious public misconceptions regarding wages paid in particular industries.

IMPLICATIONS FOR MANAGEMENT

In summary, it appears that the relative importance of pay has often been overemphasized. This is not to say that pay is unimportant or that substandard wages will not result in employee discontent. It does mean, however, that other factors are of equal or greater importance and should be emphasized more in the future than they have been in the past.

The fact that the job factor, co-workers, is tied in rank with pay and that these are closely followed in importance by the supervisor is further evidence that man does not live by bread alone. It would appear well worthwhile for management to give greater consideration to the personalities and backgrounds of employees who work together and to increase their efforts along the line of supervisory training.

Hours of work and working conditions were factors which obtained low ranks relative to the amount of effort generally expended toward their improvement. Considering the enormous improvement in hours of work and in working conditions during the past decade or so, it would appear that the point of diminishing returns has been reached and that time might more profitably be devoted to factors currently considered more important by the average job applicant. Unions seem to be currently overemphasizing these factors on the basis of what workers wanted a generation ago rather than what they want today.

Benefits were relegated by job applicants to the last position. It would thus appear worthwhile for management and unions to review reasons for emphasizing benefits. There certainly is no justification for emphasizing benefits on the basis of the desires of job applicants, although emphasis may be warranted by employee need or other conditions.

In conclusion, too much emphasis has often been given factors which, according to this study, are considered relatively unimportant by applicants. There would seem to be an excellent opportunity to devise principles and procedures that would result in greater job satisfaction on the part of employees, and consequently in improved quality of work, increased quantity of output, and lower costs.

3. Validating the Patterned Interview*

Robert N. McMurry

DURING RECENT years several studies have been conducted on the value of the patterned interview as a selection instrument. It constitutes a relatively new technique and has not been so widely used as employment tests. Its approach to selection problems is primarily *clinical*, as contrasted to weighted application blanks and tests, which are psychometric procedures. It is designed to measure the applicant's chief character traits (his stability, industry, ability to get along with others, loyalty, perseverance, self-reliance, and emotional maturity) and his motivation (his incentives to stay on the job and work). It bases its predictions relative to the applicant's suitability on a very simple premise: The best basis for judging what a person will do in the future is to know what he has done in the past.

The patterned interview reviews the applicant's work record; his service record; his schooling; his early environment; his present financial situation; his domestic situation; and his health. In short, the patterned interview is principally a fact-finding procedure, combining information obtained from the applicant with data received from schools

* From *Personnel*, Vol. 23, 1947, pp. 2–11.

and previous employers. Once the relevant facts about the interviewee have been assembled, the evaluation of his qualifications can proceed on a systematic basis. It is the purpose of this article to consider the contribution which the patterned interview can make to selection work.

It has been traditional to question the value of the interview as a device to predict job success. Until recently, many textbooks on industrial psychology have stated categorically that the interview is dangerously unreliable as a selection instrument. These statements were based on several "experiments" (the most recent of which was conducted a number of years ago) in which groups of interviewers, usually sales managers, were asked to evaluate the qualifications of applicants and rank them in the order of their desirability. After this, comparisons were made of the interviewers' ratings. Almost universally in these experiments, little agreement was found among the rankings.

HOLLINGWORTH'S AND OTHER STUDIES

Typical of such experiments was the study reported by H. L. Hollingworth[1] in which 57 applicants for sales positions were interviewed individually by 12 different sales managers. These interviewers were allowed to conduct the interviews in whatever fashion they wished, but at the conclusion were required to rate each applicant with respect to his "suitability for the position in question." These ratings were then cast into such form that it was possible to assign each interviewee a rank ranging from 1 to 57 for the job. The results showed marked disagreement among the interviewers. One applicant, for example, was placed first by one interviewer and fifty-third by another. Other applicants showed similar discrepancies in rank. As the interviewers were sales managers of considerable experience, the extent of their disagreement was held to be rather disquieting.

In another study, reported by Walter Dill Scott,[2] six sales managers interviewed 36 applicants. When the results were summarized, it was found that in the case of 28 of the 36 applicants the managers disagreed as to whether the individual should be in the upper or the lower half of the group.

In the third study, conducted by A. J. Snow,[3] an advertisement for a truck salesman was inserted in a paper, and 12 applicants were selected on the basis of the letters received. They were interviewed individually by six sales managers and by a psychologist to determine their fitness for the position. While there was fair agreement among the interviewers as

---

[1] *Judging Human Character* (New York: D. Appleton & Co., 1923), p. 268.

[2] "The Scientific Selection of Salesmen," *Advertising & Selling*, Vol. 25, No. 5–6, 1915, pp. 94–96.

[3] "An Experiment in the Validity of Judging Human Ability," *Journal of Applied Psychology*, Vol. 8, 1924, pp. 339–46.

NK-BELT COMPANY STUDY

The first study to be reported was made at the plant of the Link-Belt ompany, in Chicago, beginning in February, 1943. All interviews were nducted by members of the company's employment staff, following ining in the patterned interview procedure. For purposes of validation

---

TELEPHONE CHECK

Name of Contract _____ Position _____

Company _____

1. Was Mr._____ employed by your company? What were the dates of his employment? From_____ 19__ to_____ 19__

. What was the nature of his work? _____

. He states that he was earning $_____ at the time he left. Is this correct? Yes_____ No, $_____

How was he in handling detail? Good:_____ Fair:_____ Poor:_____

How did he accept supervision? _____

How would you characterize his willingness and capacity for hard work? _____

How well did he get along with other people? _____

Did he lose much time from the job? _____

What were his reasons for leaving? _____

Would you rehire? (If not, why not?) Yes_____ No_____

As far as you know, did he have any financial trouble—have his income garnisheed or assigned? No_____ Yes,_____

Did he have any domestic trouble which interfered with his work? No_____ Yes,_____

Did he have any drinking or gaming habits which affected his work? No_____ Yes,_____

Checked by_____

Date_____

---

to the two best and the two worst candidates, in the other cases the agreement was slight indeed. The average deviation of the judges was somewhat over three places; and, inasmuch as there were only 12 possible places, this deviation was serious. When a comparison was made between the judgments of the sales managers and those of the psychologist, it was discovered that he did practically as well as any of the experienced sales executives.

INADEQUACY OF THE EXPERIMENTS

These and similar studies have long been cited as demonstrating that the interview is of little value as a selection device. Nevertheless, when the controls employed in these studies are carefully scrutinized, the "experiments" themselves become subject to question. To begin with, the only criterion used in choosing the interviewers was the fact that they were sales managers. It does not necessarily follow that a man automatically qualifies as an interviewer because he is a sales manager. He may be very successful in sales management, but not because of any particular skill in selecting his staff.

Second, in two of the three experiments summarized, no job specifications were established to serve as guides to the interviewers. In fact, there is no evidence that in these two cases the participating sales managers were even selecting men for the same kind of work.

Third, none of these men had an organized plan to follow in the course of his interview. Each was permitted to ask whatever came to mind, and it is probable that an individual interviewer's questions even varied somewhat from applicant to applicant.

Fourth, it is to be presumed that none of these interviewers had had any careful or organized training in the techniques of conducting an interview or a plan—i.e., a series of clinical concepts—as an aid in interpreting the findings.

Fifth, no attempt was made to insure that the intellectual capacity of the several interviewers was sufficient to enable them all successfully to comprehend the intangibles of human behavior.

Sixth, neither was any attempt made to check the tendency of raters to be seriously biased or to suffer from emotional maladjustments which might interfere with the objectivity of their judgments. It was naïvely assumed that since the men were sales managers, no other measure of their qualifications was required.

In view of the almost total absence of any control on the manner in which the interviews were conducted, or on the qualifications of the interviewers, it is not at all surprising that the resulting rankings of the applicants showed a high degree of unreliability.[4]

---

[4] Editor's note: However, the interviews studied in these experiments were actually in use in these companies, and are typical of many employment interviews in use today.

LIMITATIONS OF USUAL INTERVIEW PROCEDURE

The interview has several basic weaknesses. Its value depends on the competence and training of the person who conducts it. If he has no plan to follow, no standards for the job for which he is hiring, and has received no training in the techniques of conducting the interview and interpreting the information obtained, or if he is opinionated, or emotionally maladjusted, few valid judgments can be expected from him. Many may have to operate without job specifications, without an organized interview procedure, without training in interviewing techniques, and without a plan for the interpretation of the findings. As a result, their judgments to tend, in many cases, to lack both reliability and validity.[5] Nevertheless, some of these conditions can be remedied.

DOMESTIC AND SOCIAL SITUATION

Married   Single   Widowed   Divorced   Separated   Date of marriage
_____
                                          Are he and his wife compatible

Living with wife?   Yes   No   (If no) Specify   Dependents: Number

Ages   What plans do you have for your children?   What difficulties or
Do dependents provide adequate motivation?

serious arguments have you had with your wife?
_____
                              Financial   Social   Personal?

Have you been married previously?   Yes   No   (If yes) How many times?

When and what was the reason for end of marriage or marriages?   Death   Divorce

Separation   (Unless death) What were the reasons?
Do his domestic difficulties indicate immaturity?

Of what lodges and clubs are you a member?   Officer?
                                          Does he show leadership?

What do you do for recreation?   What hobbies do you have?
        Does his recreation show maturity   Will his hobbies help his work?

To what extent do you and your wife entertain?
                                          Does he seem socially well-adjusted?

When did you last drink intoxicating liquor?   To what extent?   (Doesn't drink)
                        Is this sensible drinking?

What types of people, racial or religious groups or nationalities do you actively dislike?
                        Is he biased?

EXCERPT FROM PATTERNED INTERVIEW FORM

---

[5] Editor's note: Errors of "halo effect," "leniency," "bias," etc., which reduce the value of the interview will be discussed in a later section on rating techniques.

One of the principal criticisms leveled at the intervie findings are highly subjective. While there is no d viewers' judgments must, of necessity, be subjective, that they must lack reliability and validity *simply bec jective.* Subjective judgments are not necessarily wron is provided by the diagnosis of the physician. It must jective. Nevertheless, taking physicians' judgments a right much more frequently than they are wrong.[6]

ADVANTAGES OF PATTERNED INTERVIEW

The *patterned* interview endeavors to overcome t ordinary employment interview in several ways: F works from definite job specifications; he knows w requires. Second, he has a plan; he knows what qu he has been trained in the techniques of conducti he knows how to put the candidate at ease, how t how to extract pertinent information. Fourth, p he has checked with outside sources (previous em and already knows a great deal about the applica telephone check form, used in contacting previous ing page.) Fifth, he has a series of "yardsticks" for ating the information obtained from the candidat

HOW STUDIES WERE CONDUCTED

In assessing the worth of the patterned interv the true proof of the pudding lies in the eating. validity (and, indirectly, of its reliability) as a be found in the results of carefully controlled conducted to test the extent to which intervie *mate job success* of candidates (not merely com that these studies had maximum objectivity, the following basis: The interviewer judged tions at the time of employment, indicating of his prediction. In the cases reported here candidates were rated either as "1" (an out (a good one); as "3" (a fair or marginal o factory one who would normally be rejected *all* applicants were employed—the "4's" (th well as those rated "1," "2," or "3." In this sentative cross-section of applicants was inc procedure permitted an evaluation of the means not only of predicting success but

---

[6] Editor's note: As with the interviewer, the ph to be right if he has additional objective indices o

it was possible to use both length of service and foremen's ratings as measures of job success. These ratings were made by supervision as of the time the final validation study was made—i.e., one and a half years after the men and women had been initially employed. Supervisors were not shown the interviewers' evaluations at the time.

Two sets of correlations were run: first, between the length of service of those who had left the company and interviewers' initial ratings; and, second, between foremen's ratings on those still employed and the interviewers' initial ratings. The findings of the relationship between interviewers' ratings and length of service on 587 cases are shown in Table 1.

TABLE 1

COMPARISON OF INTERVIEW RATINGS WITH LENGTH OF SERVICE
(Employees Who Left before May 1, 1944)

Length of Service	INTERVIEWERS' RATINGS		
	1	2 or 3	4
1 year and over.....................	33	128	3
	(45.8%)	(28.9%)	(4.3%)
6 months to 1 year..................	20	129	4
	(27.8%)	(29.0%)	(5.7%)
3 months to 6 months...............	8	65	7
	(11.1%)	(14.6%)	(10.0%)
2 months to 3 months...............	6	45	7
	(8.3%)	(10.1%)	(10.0%)
1 month to 2 months...............	4	38	7
	(5.6%)	(8.5%)	(10.0%)
1 week to 1 month..................	1	26	14
	(1.4%)	(5.7%)	(20.0%)
Less than one week.................	0	14	28
	(0.0%)	(3.2%)	(40.0%)
	72	445	70
Total.......................	(100.0%)	(100.0%)	(100.0%)

The Pearson coefficient of correlation in Table 1 is .43 ± .02.

Table 2 depicts the relationship between interviewers' initial ratings and those made by foremen one and one-half years later with 407 cases still on the job.

Foremen's ratings were made on the following basis: The foremen were asked to divide the men into two equal groups: above-average and below-average, taking into consideration their productivity, their attitudes toward supervision, and their general over-all desirability as employees. They were next asked to indicate who in the above-average group were outstanding with respect to their characteristics, and similarly they were asked to indicate who in the below-average group were clearly unsatisfactory. This provided a fourfold grouping of the employees in terms of their over-all worth. When possible, two or more such ratings were attained independently, comparisons were then made between these ratings, and where disagreements existed the foremen were asked to discuss the individual cases and reach an agreement on the man's or woman's true worth. In this way, a forced distribution of the ratings and a reasonably reliable consensus were obtained.

TABLE 2

COMPARISON OF INITIAL INTERVIEW SCORE WITH SUCCESS RATING
(Men and Women Combined)

		INTERVIEWERS' RATINGS			
		1	2	3	4
FOREMEN'S SUCCESS-ON-THE-JOB RATING	Outstanding.......	6 (35.3%)	8 (47.1%)	3 (17.6%)	
	Above Average....	2 (1.2%)	88 (53.0%)	75 (45.2%)	1 (.6%)
	Below Average.....		13 (6.6%)	175 (88.8%)	8 (4.6%)
	Very Poor........			4 (14.8%)	23 (85.2%)

In Table 2, as may be seen, the relationship is unusually close. The Pearson coefficient of correlation is $.68 \pm .02$.

WHITE MOTOR–AERO-MAYFLOWER STUDY

The second study was conducted for the White Motor Company in cooperation with the Aero-Mayflower Company in Indianapolis, from February to August, 1946. Here predictions were made relative to the probable success of men being considered for positions as truck drivers. A group of 108 men who met the company's preliminary standards for employment as truck-driver trainees were interviewed, and ratings were made of their qualifications. These interviews were conducted by a trained psychologist, independent of the company's employment department. The job success of these 108 men was then carefully followed over an 11-week period as the men passed through the training course and went out on the road as drivers. At the end of this time a study was made of the correlation between the interviewer's initial ratings and the men's subsequent success as indicated by their length of service. The findings are shown in Table 3; here the biserial coefficient correlation is $.61 \pm .11$.

Specifically, it may be seen that those rated "1" by the interviewer had roughly seven and one-half chances in 10 of being successful, as indicated by still being on the job at the end of the study; of those rated "2," roughly four out of 10 were still on the job (an improvement over the average of the group as a whole); of those rated "3," only two and one-half out of 10 were still on the job (appreciably below average); and of those rated "4"—i.e., the ones who would ordinarily have been rejected—fewer than one and one-half out of 10 were on the job at the

TABLE 3

COMPARISON OF DRIVER INTERVIEW RATINGS WITH PASS-FAIL CRITERION

	INTERVIEWERS' RATINGS			
	1	2	3	4
Still in Service (Successful)............	6	15	12	2
	(75.0%)	(38.5%)	(26.1%)	(13.3%)
Left Service Any Reason (Failures).....	2	24	34	13
	(25.0%)	(61.5%)	(73.9%)	(86.7%)
Total No. Originally Interviewed.......	8	39	46	15
	(100%)	(100%)	(100%)	(100%)

conclusion of the study. Put in other terms, those rated "4" had better than eight and one-half chances out of 10 of failing. Had the company hired only those rated "1," it would have more than halved its turnover; had it hired only the "1's" and "2's," it still would have reduced its turnover by 12 per cent.

YORK KNITTING MILLS, LTD.

The third study was conducted in a plant of the York Knitting Mills, Ltd., in Canada, in January, 1946, under the supervision of J. J. Carson and Dr. H. C. Grant, of the firm of J. D. Woods and Gordon, Ltd., of Toronto. Here the interviewing of 84 applicants was done by members of the company's regular employment department, using a patterned interview procedure, following careful training by Mr. Carson and Dr. Grant. Here the interviewers' judgments were correlated with supervisors' ratings. These findings are shown in Table 4; here the Pearson coefficient of correlation is .61 ± .05.

TABLE 4

SUCCESS OF PREDICTIVE RATINGS ON 84 APPLICANTS
HIRED SINCE JANUARY 2, 1946

SUPERVISORS' RATINGS	INTERVIEWERS' PREDICTIVE RATINGS				
	1	2	3	4	5
	Excellent	Above Average	Average	Below Average	Definitely Unsuitable
1 Excellent.................1	1				
2 Above Average............		6			1
3 Average..................		2	31	5	5
4 Below Average............			9	13	8
5 Definitely Unsuitable........					3

CONCLUSION

The foregoing findings indicate that the patterned interview, if carefully conducted, has value in predicting the subsequent job success and stability of persons employed in two factory occupations and as truck drivers. While several of the validities are not exceptionally high, allowance must also be made for some unreliability in the criteria where they consist of supervisors' ratings. In every case, however, the validities are of sufficient magnitude to justify the assumption that the interview has definite merit as a selection instrument.

Earlier workers have maintained that the interview is notoriously unreliable. Findings reported here support the conviction that a properly conducted and evaluated *planned* interview is a statistically reliable selection instrument. The "true" reliability of a predictive variable is equal to or greater than its "true" validity—i.e., accuracy of prediction may approach, but cannot surpass, the accuracy of the instrument used in making the prediction. It follows from this statistical axiom that patterned interview validities of .43, .61, and .68, with probable errors as low as ±.02, are evidence that the reliability of those interviews was at or above such limits. These studies demonstrate that the interview can be a reliable and valid selection instrument.

4. Job Expectancy and Survival*

Joseph Weitz

IN AN INVESTIGATION[1] of job satisfaction of life insurance agents, we found that those agents who said the manager misrepresented the job or job possibilities during the hiring interview were more likely to terminate than those who did not agree with this statement. From other data, we also found that new agents having a realistic job concept were more likely to survive than those whose job expectancy was not as accurate.

From these two pieces of information, the hypothesis was made that when potential agents are given a clear picture of their job duties, they are more likely to survive on the job.

* From *Journal of Applied Psychology*, Vol. 40, No. 4, 1956, pp. 245–47.

[1] J. Weitz and R. C. Nuckols, "Job Satisfaction and Job Survival," *Journal of Applied Psychology*, Vol. 39, 1955, pp. 294–300.

PROCEDURE

This study was done in one insurance company. A questionnaire was devised asking for the approximate amount of time spent in each of a number of different job activities such as collecting, servicing, prospecting, selling, etc. These questionnaires were sent to all agents of the company with a request that they be completed and returned to the Life Insurance Agency Management Association. The results for each question were tallied and the median number of hours was computed for each activity. All length of service groups were combined since we were interested in an approximate composite picture.

From the results of this questionnaire, a booklet was made up consisting of a brief introduction stating that the hours shown for each activity in the booklet were approximate but should give the applicant a fair idea of how he would be spending his time if he were hired for the job. The rest of the booklet consisted of sketches showing an agent engaged in each of the various activities, a brief description of the activity, and the approximate number of hours agents currently employed spent in each activity.

The company supplied us with a list of their districts (offices), the number of agents in each office, the number of terminators per district, and the number of open debit weeks[2] for the preceding year. Matches were made by district, taking into account the geographical location of the district, the termination rate, and the number of open debit weeks.

With juggling, we were able to obtain quite good matches. The termination rate in each group was the same and the average number of open debit weeks was 43 and 48.

By flipping a coin, we decided which group was to be the experimental group and which the control. It turned out that the group with 52 districts was the experimental, and the control group would be that containing 51 districts. All applicants in the experimental group would receive the job description booklet, no one in the control group would receive the booklet.

The mechanics of this for the experimental group was as follows:

All applications for the job of agent go to the home office. In the case of those persons filing an application in any of the experimental districts, the home office would send the following letter to the prospective agent:

We finally received your application for employment as an agent with our company and want you to know how pleased we are that you are considering a career with company X. It is our feeling that the life insurance business offers a fine career to the man who is qualified for it. Because of this, our responsibility for bringing into our company men who have the best chance of succeeding is serious and of prime importance.

Very likely you are uncertain as to whether you should enter the life insurance business. Similarly, we are also uncertain as to whether you should or not. To the end of fulfilling our responsibility as stated above, and helping you make your decision, we would like you to read the enclosed booklet. We are sending this to your home so that you can study it at your leisure and to give you the opportunity of discussing it with your family.

The booklet describes the job of X company's agent. The company wants

---

[2] A district is composed of a number of debits. A debit includes a specified number of policy holders living in a particular geographical area (several blocks or miles) in which the agent is to collect premiums and sell. Each agent has his own debit. If an agent terminates, his debit is "open" until a new agent is hired in that district for that particular debit. The length of time the debit is open is measured in what is called "open debit weeks." Of course, some agents may be hired for new debits.

you to know in advance, insofar as it is possible, exactly the kind of work our agents do. Frankly, if this is not the kind of work you want to do, we want you to find it out now rather than later. If it is the kind of work you want to do, well and good. You can discuss further the possibility of a position with the manager who took your application. Either way, your action will be based on a clear concept of our job, which we feel very deeply is the proper way to make a decision.

Our best wishes go to you for a successful future, whether it be with our company or another organization.

Sincerely,

This letter was accompanied by a copy of the booklet.

This procedure, of course, was not carried out with applicants in the control districts.

RESULTS

The study continued for six months, starting in May and ending in October. Two hundred and twenty-six agents were hired during this period in the experimental group and 248 in the control. Nineteen per cent of the agents in the experimental group terminated during this period, whereas 27% of the control group terminated. This is significant beyond the 5% level using a one-tail test.

More significant perhaps is the fact that the differences in termination rate for the two groups held up month after month. That is to say, if we determine the percentage of termination for each group hired in each month and exposed until October, we obtain the results shown in Table 1.

TABLE 1

TERMINATION RATE FOR PERSONS HIRED IN EACH MONTH OF THE STUDY

	EXPERIMENTAL			CONTROL		
HIRED IN	N Hired	N Terminated through October	Per Cent Terminated	N Hired	N Terminated through October	Per Cent Terminated
May	41	13	32	45	21	47
June	32	11	34	39	19	49
July	28	7	25	32	10	31
August	50	9	18	37	8	22
September	44	2	5	42	4	10
October	31	1	3	53	5	9

As might be expected, the monthly termination rate decreases as the last month (October) of the study is approached. The reason, of course, is that there is less exposure of the men hired later in the study; that is to say, they have a shorter time in which to quit. For each month, however, it can be seen that a higher proportion of the control group terminated. Over all, there was a reduction in termination of about 30%, a meaningful statistic to a company.

In order to check on the possibility that giving a clear picture of the job to prospective agents might make it more difficult to hire a man, the proportion of open debit weeks (how long it takes to fill a vacancy) was determined for the experimental and control groups. You might expect that if it were more difficult to hire a man who was given a clear picture of the job, the experimental group would have a higher proportion of open debit weeks. This was not the case. The experimental group had 7.8% open debit weeks while the control group had 8.9% open debit weeks for the six-month period of the study. While this difference is not significant, it is opposed to the expected direction. We can conclude that the booklet certainly did not slow up the hiring procedure.

If we examine the termination rate in the two groups of agents unaffected by the booklet, that is, those hired before the start of the study, we find that there is no significant difference. There were 796 agents on the job in the experimental districts and 706 in the control districts as of the end of April. We determined the termination rate of these "on-the-job" agents during the six months of the study and found that in the experimental group 27% terminated, and 28% terminated in the control group. This would lend more weight to any differences we find in the groups of agents involved in the study since apparently our earlier matches held up. All in all it appeared that something was effective.

DISCUSSION

The reason we say it appeared that *something* was effective, rather than the job description booklet, is this. The home office contact, via the letter accompanying the booklet, may have been part of the reason the system worked. This procedure perhaps created a favorable impression and resulted in higher survival in the experimental group.

This variable could be controlled in further studies by issuing the booklet at the point of application (but would the manager issue the booklet?), or by having the home office send out a "public relations" letter to applicants without mentioning the job description.

There are always many things you would like to do to "purify" your findings. One must not, however, in industrial work, purify to the point of sterilization.

CONCLUSION

We feel that this study shows that giving prospective agents a realistic concept of the job and having this description come from an "executive" source will reduce termination. We further found that this procedure will not make it more difficult to hire new agents.

5. Using the Application Blank to Reduce Office Turnover*

Edwin A. Fleishman and Joseph Berniger

THOUGH THE application blank, in one form or another, is omnipresent in business and industry, all too often it is used in a superficial and unsystematic manner. In many employment situations, for example, the personnel interviewer either merely scans the blank for items he considers pertinent or uses the information only as a point of departure for the employment interview. As a result, much of the wealth of information in the application blank is going to waste, or worse, is often improperly used. In actual fact, however, there is sufficient evidence to indicate that, properly validated and used, the application blank can markedly increase the efficiency of the company's selection procedures.

The rationale for using the application blank (though this is seldom verbalized explicitly) is that the applicant's personal history, such as his previous experience and interests, is predictive of his future success on the job. And, indeed, it does seem reasonable to assume that such data as previous employment history, specific skills, education, financial status, marital record, and so forth, reflect a person's motives, abilities, skills, level of aspiration, and adjustment to working situations.

A number of assumptions can be made from such information. For example, the fact that an applicant has held a similar job indicates the likelihood of his transferring some of his training to the new job. Similarly, what he has done successfully before is likely to reflect his basic abilities in that area, as well as his interest in and satisfaction derived from these activities. Such personal history items as age, number of dependents, years of education, previous earnings, and amount of insurance have also been found to correlate with later proficiency on the job, earnings, length of tenure, or other criteria of job success. It should be emphasized, however, that the items found to be predictive of success in one job may not be the same for another, similar job—even in the same company. Furthermore, even for the same job, some items on the application blank may be more predictive of one particular aspect of job performance than of other aspects (for example, turnover, accidents, or earnings).

---

* From "One Way To Reduce Office Turnover," *Personnel*, Vol. 37, 1960, pp. 63–69.

Hand in hand with this consideration is the fact that, in personnel selection, the application blank is usually reviewed as a whole by an employment interviewer, a procedure that obviously involves a great deal of subjective judgment on his part. Consequently, the success of the form in predicting job performance depends not only upon the accuracy of the job description used as a reference, but also upon the skill of the interviewer and, most importantly, on his knowledge of the validity of individual items in relation to certain jobs and criteria. Unfortunately, however, it is this last critical point that most organizations fail to check out with empirical data. In this article, we shall endeavor to point out that such data are not difficult to obtain and may materially help the employment interviewer in arriving at better hiring decisions.

DESIGN OF THE STUDY

The study outlined here describes the way in which the potential value of the routine application blank used at Yale University was enhanced through appropriate research methods. The purpose of the study was to develop a way of scoring the application blank to select clerical and secretarial employees who were most likely to remain on the job. In other words, it was designed to explore the possibility of using the blank as part of a selection program aimed at reducing turnover.

The first step in the study was to find out which items in the application blank actually differentiated between short-tenure and long-tenure employees who had been hired at about the same time. For this purpose, 120 women office employees, all of whom had been hired between 1954 and 1956, were studied. Half of these, designated the "long tenure" group, were women whose tenure was from two to four years and who were still on the job. The other 60 employees had terminated within two years and accordingly were designated the short-tenure group. Of this group, 20 per cent had terminated within six months and 67 per cent within the first year. The sample excluded known "temporaries" and summer employees. The women studied had all been hired as "permanent" employees, and all who had left had done so voluntarily.

The application blank in question is similar to those used in most organizations. It takes up four pages and includes approximately 40 items —personal data, work history, education, interests, office skills, and the like. The original application blanks of the employees in both the short- and long-tenure groups were examined and the responses to the individual items were then compared to determine which, if any, differentiated the employees who terminated from those who stayed and, if so, which items were the best predictors of tenure.

A preliminary review suggested the ways in which to classify the answers to the various items. The next step was to tally the responses for each group and then convert them to percentages to facilitate comparisons. Some examples of items that did and did not differentiate be-

TABLE 1

How Item-Responses by Long- and Short-Tenure Office Employees Compared

	PERCENTAGE OF		
APPLICATION BLANK ITEMS	SHORT-TENURE GROUP	LONG-TENURE GROUP	WEIGHT ASSIGNED TO RESPONSE
Local address			
Within city................39	62	+2
Outlying suburbs............50	36	−2
Age			
Under 20..................35	8	−3
21–25....................38	32	−1
26–30.................... 8	2	−1
31–35.................... 7	10	0
35 and over...............11	48	+3
Previous Salary			
Under $2,000..............31	30	0
$2,000–3,000..............41	38	0
$3,000–4,000..............13	12	0
Over $4,000.............. 4	4	0
Age of children			
Preschool..................12	4	−3
Public school...............53	33	−3
High school or older..........35	63	+3

tween the two groups are shown in Table 1. As the table shows, local address, for instance, was a good differentiator, but previous salary was not. Certain responses to the question of age also distinguished between the two groups, as did "reason for leaving last employment," "occupation of husband," and "number of children."

WEIGHTING THE ITEMS

Since some items were found to be better predictors of tenure than others, it seemed reasonable to assign them more weight in the actual hiring procedure—the next step in our study. Thus, items that did not discriminate were weighted zero (i.e., they were not counted). Others were weighted negatively (they counted against the applicant), and still others, positively (in favor of the applicant). For example, an address in the suburbs was more characteristic of short-tenure employees, and so this response was scored negatively. An address in the city, on the other hand, was scored positively. Similarly, "age over 35" received a positive weight, but "under 30" received a negative weight.

Next, the size of the weight was determined. Items that showed a bigger percentage difference between the long- and short-tenure groups were given a higher weight. For example, "age under 20" was weighted −3, whereas "age 26–30" was weighted only −1. (Though there are more precise methods for assigning weights,[1] we found that the simple

[1] See, for example, W. H. Stead and C. L. Shartle, *Occupational Counseling Techniques* (New York: American Book Company, 1940).

but systematic procedure described above yielded comparable results.)

An applicant's total score is, of course, obtained by adding or subtracting the weights scored on each item on the application blank. In our first sample, we found that total scores ranged from −17 to 27, the average score for the short-tenure group being −2.3, while that for the long-tenure group was 8.9—a difference of 11.2, which is highly significant statistically. The correlation between the total scores made by these employees and their subsequent tenure was .77.

This correlation was, of course, misleading and spuriously high since we had calculated it from the very sample from which we had determined the weights for the individual items in the first place. To obtain an unbiased estimate of the validity of our scoring procedure, we had to try it out, therefore, on an independent sample of employees.

THE CROSS-VALIDATION STUDY

Accordingly, the application blanks of a second random sample of short- and long-tenure girls, hired during the same period, were drawn from the files. Again, the short-tenure group consisted of girls who had left within two years and the long-tenure group was composed of those who were still on the job after two years or more. The scoring system developed on the first sample was then applied to the application blanks of this second group (85 clerical and secretarial employees).

The range of scores for this sample was −10 to 21, and the correlation with subsequent tenure was .57. This confirmed that the weighted blank did possess a high degree of validity for predicting tenure. The average score for the short-tenure group was −0.7, while that of the long-tenure group was 6.3. Again, this was a statistically significant difference. A recheck was also made on the individual items, which showed, in general, that those items which differentiated in the first sample did so in the second sample as well.

We had, then, a selection instrument that indicated the probability of an applicant's staying with the organization or not, but the question of how to use it in reaching the actual hiring decision still remained. Of course, such factors as the relative importance of turnover in the organization, the number of available applicants during a hiring period, and other selection procedures in use have to be taken into account here. It is desirable, nonetheless, to set a score on the application blank that does the best job of differentiating between "long-" and "short-" tenure risks at the time of employment. In other words, what is needed is a cut-off score that will maximize correct hiring decisions; or—to put it another way—a score that will minimize both the number of people hired who will turn out to be short-tenure employees and the number rejected who would have actually remained on the job.

To establish our cut-off score, we used the method of "maximum differentiation." In other words, we tabulated the percentage of employees reaching or exceeding each score point in the range, −10 to 21. We then calculated the differences between the percentages obtained in the two groups at each score point to find the point of greatest differentiation.

TABLE 2

OBTAINING A CUTTING SCORE BY USING "MAXIMUM DIFFERENTIATION"

| | PERCENTAGE OF SUBJECTS AT OR ABOVE A GIVEN SCORE | | |
| | A | B | |
TOTAL SCORE	PERCENTAGE OF LONG-TENURE EMPLOYEES	PERCENTAGE OF SHORT-TENURE EMPLOYEES	INDEX OF DIFFEREN-TIATION (A MINUS B)
21	4	0	4
20	4	0	4
19	4	0	4
18	12	0	12
17	16	0	16
16	20	0	20
15	20	0	20
14	24	0	24
13	24	3	21
12	28	3	25
11	32	5	27
10	36	8	28
9	40	10	30
8	40	14	26
7	44	15	29
6	48	17	31
CUTTING SCORE 5	60	20	40 POINT OF
4	68	22	46 GREATEST
3	72	27	45 DIFFER-
2	72	32	40 ENTIATION
1	72	39	33
0	80	42	38
−1	80	46	34
−2	80	54	26
−3	84	66	18
−4	92	68	24
−5	92	76	16
−6	92	85	7
−7	96	90	6
−8	96	94	2
−9	100	98	2
−10	100	100	0

The result is shown in Table 2, from which it will be seen that in our case the difference between the two groups reached its maximum at a score of +4. This told us that applicants scoring 4 points or more were most likely to stay on the job two years or more, whereas those scoring less than 4 could be considered potential short-tenure employees.

Figure 1 shows the degree of success that would have been achieved if this cutting score of +4 had been used on our second sample of 85 employees. The shaded areas represent the percentage of correct hiring decisions, and the unshaded areas, the percentage of incorrect hiring decisions. As may be seen, the personnel interviewer would have hired two out of three of the employees who stayed more than two years, and rejected approximately four out of five of those who had left before that time.

Finally, to facilitate routine scoring, we constructed a cardboard template for each page of the application blank.[2] In the template are windows,

FIGURE 1

PERCENTAGES OF CORRECT HIRING DECISIONS THAT WOULD HAVE BEEN OBTAINED
THROUGH USING CUTTING SCORE

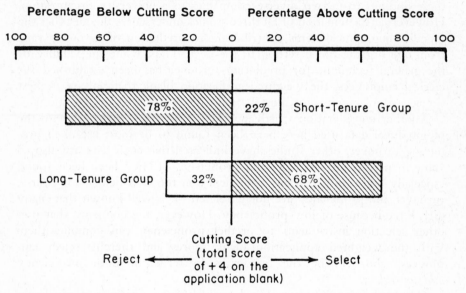

which expose only the responses to be scored. The weights for each response are printed on the template next to the appropriate window.

An interesting offshoot of our study was the picture it yielded of the woman office worker most likely to be the best long-tenure risk at Yale University. We arrived at it by using the application blank items that differentiated between long- and short-tenure employees in both our original and our cross-validation samples. Here is a profile of the typical long-tenure woman office employee at Yale:

She is 30 years old or over, has a local address rather than a suburban one, is married (but not to a student), or is a widow. Her husband is most likely to be an executive or a professional man. She may have one or two children, but if she does they are of high school age or over. At least one member of her family has been employed at Yale. She herself is not employed at the time of

---

[2] W. F. Wood, "A New Method for Reading the Employment Questionnaire," *Journal of Applied Psychology*, Vol. 31, 1947, pp. 9–15.

application. She has had a business, secretarial school, or college education, and can often speak more than one language. If she can type, she does so at a speed of 50–60 words per minute. Usually, she cannot take shorthand—but if she does, it is at a relatively high rate of speed. She does not list more than one outside interest aside from work, and that one indicates that she is most interested in organizations and people. Finally, she spent at least two years at her last job.

The findings of our study bear out those obtained in previous studies at the Prudential Life Insurance Company[3] and the Minnesota Mining and Manufacturing Company,[4] both of which showed that a high degree of predictability of turnover among female office employees was achieved from a weighted application blank. Our study extends the generality of these findings from two diverse companies to a university organization. However, an examination of all three studies underscores the fact that the specific biographical items contributing to prediction of turnover vary from one organizational setting to the next. Thus, while the validity of the general technique for predicting turnover has been established for clerical employees, the weighted application blank that will work best for a particular company must be tailor-made for that organization.

Another consideration worth mentioning, perhaps, is that though the biographical data used here have been found to be most useful in predicting turnover, other studies have indicated that such data are also of value in predicting accidents and proficiency. (They have been found especially useful in predicting proficiency in the sales field.)[5] Of course, turnover and proficiency are not unrelated—it is well known that many girls leave because of low proficiency. However, the company that uses other selection instruments to predict proficiency can combine them with the weighted application blank scores and thereby select employees who will be the best risks in terms of both proficiency *and* tenure.

One final point: The research described in this article is relatively inexpensive. Indeed, most companies have file drawers literally bulging with application blank data that are well suited to the kind of analysis described here.

---

[3] P. H. Kreidt and M. S. Gadel, "Prediction of Turnover Among Clerical Workers," *Journal of Applied Psychology*, Vol. 37, 1953, pp. 338–40.

[4] W. K. Kirchner and M. D. Dunnette, "Applying the Weighted Application Blank Technique to a Variety of Office Jobs," *Journal of Applied Psychology*, Vol. 41, 1957, pp. 206–8.

[5] "The AI-4-48 In Use: A Selection Study" (Hartford, Conn.: Life Insurance Agency Management Association, 1951).

6. The Validity of the Employment Recommendation Questionnaire in Personnel Selection*

James N. Mosel and Howard W. Goheen

ALTHOUGH IT CONTINUES to be a staple device in the selection procedures of many organizations, the employment recommendation questionnaire (ERQ) has received almost no empirical study. Known variously as reference check, voucher, "perif," and recommendation form, this device attempts to utilize the judgments and information of persons familiar with the applicant as an aid in personnel selection. Letters of recommendation and telephone checks represent other approaches to the same end. Scott et al.,[1] in their periodic surveys of company personnel practices, have noted an increase in the use of structured, standardized questionnaires and a decline in the use of open-ended testimonial letters and narrative recommendations. In a survey conducted by the writers,[2] the great majority of companies (76 per cent) felt that their selection procedures would suffer if ERQ replies were not available.

In general, four kinds of information are obtainable by ERQ: (*a*) employment history, (*b*) evaluations of the applicant's personality and "character," (*c*) evaluations of the applicant's job ability, and (*d*) attitude toward rehiring. The first kind of information is used to verify statements made in the application for employment. The remainder are used primarily to appraise the applicant's employability, and thus to predict job success. It is felt by many that while the employment interview and application blank tell *what* the applicant did, the ERQ may in addition tell *how well* he did it.

Yet there have been very few attempts to ascertain the reliability and

---

* From *Personnel Psychology*, Vol. II, 1958, pp. 481–90. The studies reported here are from a program of studies conducted by the U.S. Civil Service Commission under the direction of the writers. The opinions expressed in this article are those of the writers and publication does not necessarily imply endorsement by the Civil Service Commission or the Department of the Army.

[1] W. D. Scott, R. C. Clothier, and W. R. Spriegel, *Personnel Management* (5th ed.; New York: McGraw-Hill, 1954).

[2] J. N. Mosel and H. W. Goheen, "Use of 'ERQ' in Hiring," *Personnel Journal*, Vol. 36, 1958, pp. 338–40.

validity of recommendation data in employee selection. The present writers[3] have summarized the existing research in another article. The scant evidence on validity is almost exclusively confined to studies of letters of recommendations, not structured questionnaires. In their survey of company practices, the writers found no company who reported any systematic research on the effectiveness of the ERQ.

PROCEDURE

In all, ERQ's on 1,193 civil-service employees in 12 skilled occupations were studied. These ERQ's had been submitted prior to employment by previous employers, supervisors, personnel managers, co-workers and acquaintances. The names of these references had been obtained from information contained in the application for employment (Civil Service Form 57).

On the average there were about four ERQ's sent out on each applicant, and of these an average of 56 per cent returned completed, 23 per cent returned incomplete, 18 per cent failed to return, and three per cent returned unopened.[4]

The criterion of job proficiency consisted of total scores from specially devised performance ratings made by present supervisors. The number and nature of the elements rated varies somewhat according to the characteristics of the job. Considerable care was taken to train supervisors in making the ratings and to provide favorable conditions for rating. The reliability of the ratings appeared quite acceptable. The correlations of .86 between the independent ratings of two supervisors in the case of 40 equipment repairmen and .93 in the case of 25 carpenters were typical.

The ERQ studied was specifically designed for trades and skilled occupations (Civil Service Form 1800a). In addition to evaluative items, this form requests information concerning certain objective facts of employment history, data on the respondent's relation to the applicant, how knowledge of the applicant was obtained, and comments on national loyalty. It also provided the respondent with the job title and specific option or specialty for which the applicant was applying.

The content of this ERQ had been determined by the judgment of job experts and the desires of examiners. In actual practice this ERQ is interpreted "clinically," but to provide a quantitative evaluation of its content, an objective scoring system was employed in the present study. Analysis was confined to the five evaluative items which presumedly

---

[3] J. N. Mosel and H. W. Goheen, "The Employment Recommendation Questionnaire: A Review" (Unpublished manuscript).

[4] These figures are fairly representative of the return rate of federal ERQ's. Other results on 16,093 ERQ's sent out on applicants for 22 professional and semi-professional jobs revealed that 64 per cent returned complete, 13 per cent returned incomplete, 20 per cent failed to return, and three per cent returned undelivered.

reflect the applicant's character and the quality of his previous job performance. These items and their scoring system were as follows:

Item 1: Rating on *occupational ability.* Based on sum of four-point ratings on four equally weighted elements: skill, carefulness, industry, and efficiency.

Item 2: Four-point rating on *character and reputation.* Score based on values assigned to rating intervals.

Item 3: "Is applicant specially qualified in any particular branch of trade in which he seeks employment? (Yes, No) If yes: give branch." Scored by assigning weight of zero to a "no" reply, 3 to "yes," and two additional points if branch mentioned corresponded to the option for which the applicant was applying.

Item 4: "Would you employ him in a position of the kind he seeks?" Scored by assigning weight of zero to "no," and 5 to "yes."

Item 5: "Has applicant ever been discharged from any employment to your knowledge? If yes: Why?" A weight of zero was assigned to "no" or if reason was "reduction in force." Other reasons, as identified by content analysis, were given negative weights ranging from 1 to 10, depending upon seriousness of the reason for discharge. Weights for seriousness were determined by scaling reasons on the basis of a consensus of job specialists' judgment.

RESULTS

Validity of ERQ Total Scores. By summing the scores from each item, an objective total score was obtained for each ERQ. These total scores were then averaged for each worker and correlated with performance ratings for each trade. Table 1 shows the results.

TABLE 1

CORRELATION OF MEAN ERQ SCORES WITH SUPERVISORS' PERFORMANCE RATINGS

(Data from 1,117 Employees in 12 Skilled Trades)

TRADE	N	r
Carpenter	51	.01
Equipment repairman	40	.23
Machinist	100	.24*
Machine operator	108	−.10
Ordanceman-torpedo	125	−.01
Radio mechanic	107	.29**
Aviation metalsmith	94	.24*
Highlift fork operator	108	.21*
Auto mechanic	98	.09
Painter	70	.07
Ordnanceman	100	.10
Printer	116	.11

* Significant .05 level.
** Significant at .01 level.

It will be seen that the ERQ scores show no consistent or sizable relationship with present job success. There are significant correlations in four trades (radio mechanic, machinist, aviation metalsmith, highlift fork operator), but the coefficients are all in the .20's. In all other cases the correlations are so low that the true relationships cannot be considered as significantly greater than zero.

Discrimination Power of Items. To determine the extent to which specific items in the ERQ were bringing out individual differences among applicants, analysis was made of the response to each category of the separate items. The combined data from five trades (carpenter, equipment repairman, machinist, machine operator, ordnanceman-torpedo) are representative of the general situation and are displayed in Table 2.

TABLE 2

PERCENTAGE DISTRIBUTION OF RESPONSES TO EACH ERQ ITEM
(Data from 855 ERQ's on 400 Workers in Five Trades)

ITEM	PER CENT OF RESPONSES
1. Rating on occupational ability	
Outstanding	32.4
Good	59.2
Satisfactory	8.0
Poor	0.4
2. Rating on character and reputation	
Outstanding	45.1
Good	49.4
Satisfactory	4.8
Poor	0.7
3. "Is applicant specially qualified in any particular branch. . . . ?"	
Yes; branch corresponded	71.1
Yes; branch did not correspond	14.2
No	14.7
4. "Would you employ him. . . . ?"	
Yes	97.5
No	2.5
5. "Has applicant ever been discharged. . . . ?"	
No	99.1
Yes	0.9

It is quite evident that on the whole discrimination is poor. There is considerable skewness toward the favorable responses for all items, although Item 3 suffers less than the others. Items 4 and 5 are especially insensitive. It appears that these items are detecting only the extreme cases; they may nevertheless have some value for this very purpose despite the fact that they provide little discriminatory information about the great majority of applicants.

Analysis of Items 1 and 2. To determine the validity of respondent judgments of occupational ability and character, correlational analysis against the criterion of job proficiency was made of Item 1 (occupational ability rating) and Item 2 (character rating). The mean of an applicant's ratings from his various respondents constituted his score for each item. Table 3 gives the correlations between each item and the criterion.

While the character ratings tend to show greater across-trade validity than do ability ratings, neither item appears to have any appreciable value if used as an independent predictor. The superiority of the character ratings brings to mind the finding of Rundquist and Bittner[5] that personality ratings provided a less contaminated measure of ability than did ability ratings, and thus were more predictable. In this connection it is also interesting to note the finding by Sleight and Bell[6] to the effect that personnel officials place greatest value on personality information in letters of recommendation.

The correlations of Item 1 for machinist and mechanic and painter and Item 2 for ordnanceman-torpedo, painter, radio mechanic, carpenter,

TABLE 3

CORRELATION OF RESPONDENT RATINGS ON OCCUPATIONAL ABILITY (ITEM 1)
AND CHARACTER (ITEM 2) WITH SUPERVISORS' PERFORMANCE RATINGS
(Data from 807 Employees in 9 Skilled Trades)

TRADE	N	ITEM 1	ITEM 2
Carpenter	51	.09	.33*
Equipment repairman	40	.10	.23
Machinist	100	.21*	.11
Ordnanceman-torpedo	125	.03	.24**
Radio mechanic	107	.05	.23*
Auto mechanic	98	.16	.16
Painter	70	.16	.23*
Ordnanceman	100	.15	.09
Printer	116	.04	.03

* Significant at .05 level.
** Significant at .01 level.

and auto mechanic are possibly acceptable as item validities go, and might make a small contribution to a battery in which they were unique. The two items are not, however, entirely independent of each other. Their intercorrelations in three samples were .42 (radio mechanics), .42 (auto mechanics), and .43 (painters). In these same samples the two items gave multiple correlations of .29, .27, and .31, respectively, with the criterion. These coefficients are slightly higher than those obtained when the most predictive item is used alone.

In examining Items 1 and 2, the question arises whether such ratings are not to a considerable extent influenced by the amount and kind of occupational experience and training which the applicant has had. It would seem reasonable that references might judge an applicant in terms of his work history, rather than the quality of his performance in that work. Inasmuch as one presumed value of the ERQ is that it reflects

[5] E. A. Rundquist and R. H. Bittner, "Using Ratings to Validate Personnel Instruments, A Study in Method," *Personnel Psychology*, Vol. 1, 1948, pp. 163–83.

[6] R. D. Sleight and Grace D. Bell, "Desirable Content of Letters of Recommendation," *Personnel Journal*, Vol. 32, 1954, pp. 421–22.

how well the applicant has performed in the past rather than *what* he performed, this question is indeed pertinent.

It was possible to obtain evidence on this question in five trades through the use of ratings on experience and training. Part of the hiring process for these workers involved scoring the Civil Service Commission's application blank (Form 57) on the quantity, level, recency, and pertinency of past experience and training (a procedure technically known as the "unassembled examination").[7] These ratings were made by experienced examiners using a standardized rating schedule which assigns predetermined rational weights to the various elements of experience. These weights are then combined into a total score. The correlations between such experience ratings and the judgment of references on Items 1 and 2 are displayed in Table 4.

TABLE 4

CORRELATION OF RESPONDENT RATINGS ON OCCUPATIONAL ABILITY (ITEM 1)
AND CHARACTER (ITEM 2) WITH EXPERIENCE RATINGS
(Data from 400 Employees in Five Trades)

TRADE	N	ITEM 1	ITEM 2
Carpenter	51	.10	.06
Equipment repairman	40	.21	.11
Machinist	76	−.10	−.07
Machine operator	108	.00	.00
Ordnanceman-torpedo	125	.12	.02

None of these coefficients is statistically significant. Apparently, then, respondent appraisals on Items 1 and 2 are independent of applicant experience and training as rated by these procedures.

Analysis of Item 3.   Data from three trades (radio mechanic, painter, and auto mechanic) gave a representative picture of the validity of Item 3. Table 5 shows the mean criterion scores of employees receiving scores of zero ("no") and 5 ("yes" with branch named corresponding to option applied for). To bring out more clearly any relationship which might exist, only those employees whose ERQ's were unanimously "yes" or "no" were used. (However, the total number of employees available in each trade was larger than in the previous analysis since it was possible to include those who had to be omitted from previous analyses because of incomplete ERQ's.)

---

[7] For a more detailed description of these methods, see W. P. Lehman, "Evaluating Education and Experience: II. Examination Processes Preliminary to Rating," *Personnel Administration*, Vol. 9, 1947, p. 4 ff.; R. Pollock, "Evaluating Education and Experience: III. Rating Methods," *Personnel Administration*, Vol. 9, 1947, p. 7 ff.; for discussion of rationale, see J. N. Mosel, "The Validity of Rational Ratings on Experience and Training," *Personnel Psychology*, Vol. 5, 1952, pp. 1–10; C. I. Mosier, "Rating of Training and Experience in Public Personnel Selection," *Educational Psychological Measurement*, Vol. 6, 1946, pp. 313–29.

TABLE 5

MEAN CRITERION SCORES OF "YES" AND "NO" GROUPS ON ERQ ITEM 3

"Is applicant specially qualified for any particular branch of the trade in which he seeks employment?"

| | "YES" GROUP | | "NO" GROUP | | | CRITICAL |
TRADE	N	Mean	N	Mean	D_m	RATIO
Radio mechanic...........19		6.60	116	5.90	.446	1.57
Auto mechanic...........45		6.38	57	5.98	.730	0.55
Painter..................34		5.82	112	5.87	.219	0.23

These results reveal no statistically significant difference between the criterion means of the two groups; none of the critical ratios reached even the .05 level of confidence. Apparently respondent judgments regarding the applicant's qualifications for the particular branch of the trade in which he seeks employment have no bearing on subsequent job performance.

A further check was made on 116 printers in which the mean of respondent replies to Item 3 was used as the score. The correlation with the criterion was .05, thus supporting the above finding.

SUMMARY AND CONCLUSIONS

Evidence is presented on the validity of a widely used but little studied personnel selection instrument—the employment recommendation questionnaire (ERQ). This device obtains judgments and information by mail from persons familiar with the applicant. The ERQ's studied were objectively scored, and the score for each applicant was the average of his scores from all respondents reporting on him. Validity was studied for 12 skilled jobs against the criterion of performance ratings, and for three professional jobs against the results from intensive field investigations.

Results show that ERQ's for the trades positions had practically no value in predicting later supervisory ratings. Evaluations by references on the applicant's character manifested slightly higher validity than did those on occupational ability, although the correlations varied considerably from job to job. For certain jobs both of these ratings showed sufficient promise to warrant their inclusion as items in a group of other predictors.

Item discrimination in general was very poor, with the possible exception of judgments on the applicant's special qualifications for the particular branch of the trade for which he was applying. This latter item, however, showed no validity.

It should be noted that these results have been obtained for the conventional type of ERQ item, scored objectively according to "face value," and combined on an average-respondent basis. No provision was made for possible inter-respondent differences in validity. (This will be the subject of a later paper.) Consequently, these findings do not reject the possibility of developing empirically a more effective ERQ built around other types of items.

7. The Validation of Tests*

Edward N. Hay

LET US BEGIN with an understanding of what *validity* is. A test is valid if it will actually measure the thing which it is supposed to measure. An arithmetic test is a measure of how much you know about arithmetic. In this case the validity is quite obvious. This is because the test contains exactly the same kinds of items that were in your course in arithmetic. When you come to tests of mechanical or clerical "aptitude," however, the situation is not so clear. To begin with, you need to be sure you know what "aptitude" is and what relation it bears to success in your business.

After all, the only purpose of testing job applicants is to try to improve your chances of getting the best ones. "Best ones" means those who, after employment, prove to be the best workers. In other words, the test should *predict* which applicants will become the best workers after a period of training and experience. Consequently, a test is valid if it is efficient in prediction. Or, it is more accurate to say that a test is valid *to the extent that* it will predict who will be the better workers.

It is essential that any test which you use eventually be validated in the situation in which you use it. It may well be that a test will be valid for another employer but not for you, perhaps because of differences in the type of work you do. This article is based on the assumption that you wish to validate tests which you are using in order to make certain that they are actually "doing the job" in your employment office. This is, of course, a very practical problem. While there is some assurance that the test will be valid for you if your conditions are like those of the employment office in which the test was first developed, you can never be sure. Consequently, sooner or later, you must face the problem of whether the test is in fact valid for *you.*

SUGGESTIONS FOR TESTING

Before getting more deeply into our subject of validation it might be well to review briefly some of the considerations that should be kept in

* From *Personnel*, Vol. 29, 1953, pp. 500–507.

mind in adopting tests for employment purposes. To begin with, unless you have a very skillful psychologist, well trained in test construction, you had better depend on tests which you can purchase from reliable sources. In selecting such tests use the same judgment you would use in buying anything else. For example, find out who is using the tests and get from them some statement of their proven value. Use tests sponsored by reputable people. Ordinarily a test should not be used which has not been validated already in a situation somewhat similar to your own.

Since expense is important in business and industry it is essential to select tests which will do the job you want done in the least possible time. As an example, some clerical tests require more than an hour for administration. This is far too long. Other tests are available which have proven their value and which require 15 minutes or less. In selecting tests for brief administration it is, of course, unwise to sacrifice predictiveness, or validity, of the test. In other words, no saving in time will compensate for any material loss in the ability of the test to do the job you want done.

BEGIN WITH A JOB ANALYSIS

To begin with, let us assume that you want to make a careful study in order to decide what kind of tests you should use in a given employment situation. There is no test of completely general application. It is advisable, therefore, to begin with a detailed study of the job for which you are going to test.

The first thing to do is to write a brief description of the job. Next, study every detailed motion and write down a list giving the the sequence of operations being performed. Sometimes it is advisable to list not only the operations themselves but, with each operation, a list of the hand and eye movements necessary in the performance of that operation.

THE JOB PSYCHOGRAPH

On the basis of this operation and motion study it is now possible to list the psychological and physical requirements for each job. This is sometimes called a job profile or job psychograph. From a study of this list of physical and psychological requirements, tests may be selected—or designed—to measure these particular functions.[1]

Initially, the selection of tests should be based on the job psychograph. For example, if the operation analysis shows that finger dexterity seems to be involved, then it would obviously be wise to include in the experimental test battery a number of tests of such dexterities. In the battery from which tests were selected as described in "Predicting Success In Machine Bookkeeping"[2] there were 25 tests. Three of these were

---

[1] How this was done in one situation is described in detail in "Predicting Success in Machine Bookkeeping," *Journal of Applied Psychology,* December, 1943, p. 483.

[2] *Ibid.*

chosen for the final test battery, although many others could have been used to advantage. It is interesting to note that none of the dexterity tests "panned out." Probably this is because accuracy and quickness of perception are so important for success in clerical work that manual dexterities are relatively unimportant.

OTHER CONSIDERATIONS

It is usually desirable that tests have what is known as "face validity." That is, they should be tests that "look good" to the applicant. A test of matching the markings on butterfly wings might be a very good test of perception and be a satisfactory predictor of clerical success. But it would look like a silly thing to do and applicants would consider it foolish. Matching numbers, however, looks sensible to clerks.

In any experimental test situation it is usually possible to find a great many tests already available, and for sale, which can be tried out on the particular operation. Sometimes, however, it is necessary to develop special tests for the purpose. Developing tests is something beyond the powers of the average person and should be left to trained people. Many psychologists today are experienced in test construction.

One characteristic of tests should be mentioned. Some tests are a combination of different kinds of items. For this reason they are called "omnibus" tests. If such a test proves predictive of success, you still have to make a detailed analysis of the test to find out which items are effective. The other items are "dead wood" and might just as well be eliminated. Consequently, it is usually better to start with tests, each of which is comprised of only one kind of item. It is then possible to tell which test is doing the work.

Several tests are generally more dependable than a single test. This is because chance errors may affect a single test quite seriously in a given case, but are not likely to affect all tests equally at the same time and in the same way. In other words the errors will tend somewhat to average out if the battery consists of two or three or more tests. Practically, however, three or four tests is the usual limit of efficient test use. Beyond this the additional time and labor do not produce a commensurate additional increase in efficient prediction.

THE SAMPLE

A particular group of employees on whom we are going to try to validate a test is known as a "sample." Unnoticed variations in the characteristics of such groups who are being studied are a frequent cause of failure to validate. Some very peculiar sampling effects are encountered on occasion. In banks, for example, it is usual for bookkeepers to be allowed to go home after their accounts are posted and settled. Thus, there is an incentive for quick and accurate work. Likewise, there is a penalty for carelessness, since the bookkeeper must stay long enough to find her errors and correct them. If this policy of allowing the book-keepers to go home when their work is finished is faithfully adhered to, the incentive to work rapidly and accurately is very great. This was one of the conditions which probably accounts in part for the very high validity coefficients reported in "Predicting Success in Machine Bookkeeping," referred to earlier.

Failure to validate the same tests in another bank was thought to be due to the policy of management of loading on more work whenever girls began to get finished early. In consequence they quit working so hard and all the girls produced at about the same rate, making it impossible to tell which ones were fast and which were slow.

Sometimes the "small" sample provides too small a base upon which to get a satisfactory validation. A small sample is usually considered to be less than about 30 cases. However, the actual dividing point between a small and a large sample is determined to a considerable degree by the characteristics of the sample itself. For example, in laboratory experiments of an agricultural nature small samples are commonly used. This, however, is because the variables can be better controlled than is the case when working with people.

It is important to eliminate extraneous variables and to control the sample in such a way that only one variable is operating at a given time. For example, men and women differ enough in some attributes that it becomes necessary to separate the two sexes in analyzing the data. Often age is a factor too.

THE CRITERION

The most difficult part of test validation is the selection and use of the criterion.[3] Criterion is merely a short term for "measure of success." It is very important to select the right criterion when validating tests. In baseball batting the criterion of success is the season's average. In a machine shop the criterion is usually the number of pieces of acceptable accuracy which are turned out in a given time. In clerical work the criterion is usually expressed in the same way. However, many people consider accuracy paramount in clerical work and occasionally accuracy has been selected as a criterion. It is seldom as satisfactory as speed of production, however.

In many situations satisfactory production records are not available. It is then necessary to resort to some other "measure of success," or "criterion." One such measure is ratings by foremen or supervisors. Such ratings are sometimes notoriously undependable, however, and great skill is needed to secure ratings which will make it possible to validate the tests. One way of doing this is to rank the operators from best to poorest. If too many workers are involved this becomes a burdensome task.

---

[3] Editor's note: Section two of this text is devoted to a more detailed examination of this important problem.

Resort may then be had to assigning the employees to fifths or to "best quarter, middle half and lowest quarter." Paired comparison may also be used.

Most raters tend to give higher ratings to old employees than to newer ones. In a project at the Washington Gas Light Company several years ago, it was at first found impossible to validate the tests. However, when it was suggested that the ratings should be made in five-year age groups, it was found possible to secure a satisfactory validation coefficient. Under that method of rating, old employees were rated against old employees and newer ones against one another, but old ones were not rated against newer ones.

THE WORK SAMPLE AS CRITERION

Another type of criterion which is often effective is what is known as a "work sample." A work sample is a miniature task which is like the real task itself. Of course, work-sample criteria can usually be used only with experienced employees. Though it has never actually been put to the test, it is the writer's opinion that a work sample would be a much better criterion if some incentive or reward were given for high performance on the work sample and on the tests.

After the decision as to what criterion is to be used, the next problem is to collect the material itself. If your employees are paid on a piecework basis there will not be much difficulty in getting the production record. Production records achieved under piecework methods are not always as good criteria as might be expected. This is probably because, as is well known, piece-workers sometimes hold back in order not to incur the disapproval of their fellow workers. Under such conditions the best workers often do not produce very much more than the poorest ones. Thus there are many pitfalls in gathering accurate information. However it is done, care must be taken to see that the information is accurate.

An interesting case where validation was difficult to achieve involved 57 bookkeeping machine operators in a bank. The first criterion to be used was a record of production, and it showed no relationship with test scores. The second time a production record was also obtained but, in addition, ratings of employees were made by supervisors. These supervisors had worked with the employees, and in most cases for quite a long time, so that they knew their work pretty well. Again the production record showed no relation to the tests, but surprisingly enough the ratings yielded a fairly good correlation with test scores. Subsequent discussion revealed that the gathering of production records had not been carefully supervised. It was found, for example, that some operators subtracted lunch-hour time, while others did not. Some eliminated the time required to find and correct errors, while others included this in their total time. There undoubtedly were other inconsistencies, but these alone are sufficient to explain why the criterion of production did not produce a satisfactory correlation with the test scores, whereas the ratings did. So many "bugs" can creep into a validation experiment that it is necessary to watch every detail with the utmost care.

OTHER KINDS OF CRITERIA

Other criteria, which on occasion may be suitable, are number of promotions within a given period of time, job grade attained, and salary achieved after a given number of years. The choice of criterion depends on what you are trying to predict.

In many attempts to validate, the criterion which has been selected is the amount of material which has been learned in a given length of time. This is usually a poor criterion, because there may be great differences in the amount learned by different people in the same length of time, but in the end they may nevertheless all perform the task itself about equally well. In other words, there is not necessarily a very close relation between the amount of time it takes to learn the task and the eventual proficiency with which the task can be performed. Learning time, therefore, should usually be avoided as a criterion.

Sometimes success is dependent upon a number of factors; or, to put it another way, the criterion is "multiple." This creates a difficult situation. The best way to handle it, if it is possible to do so, is to measure each element of success separately and then test for it separately. It is, of course, not always possible to do this. Actually, a multiple measure of success can sometimes be made—that is, several different measures of success can be combined into a formula expressed as a consolidated measure. A test or battery of tests can then be validated against this multiple criterion.

Many tests which are satisfactory in differentiating the better workers from the poorer ones fall down entirely when used with inexperienced applicants. When this happens it is usually because the test itself embodies some function which is contained in the job and which can be done better by experienced workers than by inexperienced ones. One way to find out whether this is so is to give the tests to experienced employees and, simultaneously, to a group of inexperienced ones. Calculate the mean score for each group and then determine statistically whether there is a "significant difference" between the two. If there is, then the test is one which favors the experienced worker.

The final problem regarding the criterion is that of measuring its dependability. This is usually referred to as "reliability," and is expressed by a co-efficient of correlation between two measures of success of the same people. Many tests which have been validated in one situation have shown nothing in another situation because the criterion was unreliable. Technically, reliability means that two measures of the same thing will agree. If we take a record of the number of words per hour typed by Mary, Sally, and Joan, we would expect, if Mary is best and Sally is next best and Joan is the slowest at one time, that they would be in the same order the next time. If so, the measure is a reliable one.

VALIDATION METHODS

There are two principal ways of validating. In one method tests are given to present employees. The criterion is selected and used and comparison is made between test scores and criterion figures for all employees. This is sometimes unsuccessful because the poorest workers have already left or been released. The range of job performance is greatly reduced, and validation becomes more difficult as the range decreases. It is essential that the range of test scores and the range of criterion measures from high to low show a good spread. If one of the two variables—either the test score or the criterion score—has no range or has a very slight one, then it is obviously impossible to find any relationship between them. The fact that there is a wide range in each case does not assure that a relationship will be found. But without a good range, certainly no relationship exists.

The other method is to give tests to new employees but withhold test scores from interviewers. After the new employee has been at work long enough to measure his performance his name can be added to the validation group.

One difficulty with this method is that the entire validation group cannot usually be measured at one time and the criterion figures are therefore not always comparable.

A difficulty common to both methods is that of getting a large enough sample of employees doing exactly the same work. Another problem in all validity studies is that it is impossible to make small distinctions because of errors. Also, differences are less dependable when near the middle of the range than at the extreme. This is one reason why a restricted range is a serious handicap and why validation results become poorer the shorter the range of criterion scores as well as of test scores.

STATISTICAL METHODS IN VALIDATION

The most usual analysis of test results is to relate the scores on each test with the criterion measure. This is done by a process known as "correlation," a description of which will be found in any basic text on statistics. Unfortunately, business and industry present many situations in which correlation does not operate satisfactorily. This is too technical a matter to be discussed here, but usually better results are obtained, and with far less labor, by using "critical cutting scores" instead of resorting to correlation. A critical score is one which separates the best operators from the poorest ones. Since it will usually be found that two or more tests predict more efficiently than any single test, it then becomes important to determine the most efficient combination of cutting scores on the various tests, so that as many as possible of the good operators are selected by the tests, and the greatest number of poor operators are eliminated.

Finding multiple cutting scores is much easier than calculating the multiple co-efficient of correlation. The advantage, however, is even greater when *using* the tests because it is then necessary to deal only with the actual scores obtained by the applicant. In using multiple correlation, on the other hand, it becomes necessary to multiply each test score by a factor, add them together, and then compare the result with the cutting score in the multiple correlation formula.

The reasons why multiple correlation does not always work are technical, but the principal one is that, in most smaller samples found in industry and business, "regression is not rectilinear." This is one of the assumptions on which product-moment correlation is based and without which it should not be used. Better results are actually obtained in most cases with multiple cutting scores. Consequently, if the process is easier to use and predicts better, there seems little reason for using the more traditional method of correlation.

Multiple correlation is based on the assumption that a high score on one of the tests in the "battery" will offset a low score on another test. This is not always so, because a low score sometimes means a complete lack of some essential ability. Furthermore, with multiple correlation, the higher the score the more efficient the applicant is expected to be. This doesn't take account of the fact that excess ability often does not produce better performance. On the contrary, the employee is sometimes bored and gives a poorer performance. A case in point is where an employee is too intelligent for a simple task.

It should be repeated that tests should not be used for very long until they have been validated in the user's particular situation. It does not matter how often the tests have been validated elsewhere; the user should always look forward to validating them with his own group. In doing this, it is often a good idea to give two or three kinds of tests which are designed to accomplish the same purpose. This gives a comparison of the efficiency of different tests. It will often be found that the test which is currently in use will not do as good a job as some other test. Also, it may be possible to shorten the time by finding another test which is as valid as the test currently used but which requires less time for administration.

8. Selecting Supervisors with Peer Ratings*

Joseph Weitz

ONE PROBLEM constantly facing industry is the selection of supervisory personnel. This has been true for two reasons. One is the development of selection tests or procedures which are valid and secondly, perhaps even more important, is the determination of appropriate criteria for the evaluation of successful or unsuccessful supervisors. Usually the criteria consist of some kind of rating since in many instances production criteria are not meaningful.

The test procedures have ranged all the way from very short "personality" paper and pencil devises to a thorough clinical diagnosis. Frequently, a stereotype is set up of what good supervisory or managerial personnel should be with no relation to reality. Then the candidate is interviewed, Rorschached, Thematicappercepted, and generally analyzed until the selector comes out with a personality description of the candidate. Sometimes the selector even says whether or not this candidate would make a good supervisor. Very frequently, however, the paper picture is presented and top management is left to make up its own mind whether or not they want this kind of a man. Now, there is some question as to whether this paper picture itself is accurate and a further question as to whether the description is pertinent to the job that is to be done.

If any testing is done, it is rare indeed to have people selected without regard to the test results, put in a managerial position, subsequently rated in some way on their performance, and then their test results related to the performance ratings. While ratings are by no means perfect and we know considerable about their unreliability at the present time, this is one of the few criteria that is available to workers in this area. They do have the value of meaningfulness to top management.

The purpose of this study was to investigate the use of peer nominations (buddy ratings) in predicting supervisory competence.

PROCEDURE

This study developed from two different angles. One developed from the question as to whether or not there are identifiable characteristics of

---

* From *Personnel Psychology*, Vol. 11, 1958, pp. 25–35.

good and poor supervisory personnel which are recognizable to subordinates, and secondly can these characteristics be recognized in peers so that in effect they can identify potentially good supervisors. These then are the hypotheses to be tested in this study: (1) Good supervisors have certain identifiable characteristics which differentiate them from poor supervisors, and (2) these characteristics can be identified in potential supervisors by peers at the time they are all in the subordinate capacity.

Mann and Dent[1] have shown that subordinates can identify certain characteristics in their supervisors which differentiate those who are considered promotable from those who are considered unsatisfactory by top management. Some of the items which seemed pertinent were judgments concerning whether or not the supervisor was "good at handling people," "were the workers free to discuss job problems with the supervisor," "were they free to discuss personal problems with the supervisor," whether the "supervisor will go to bat when an employee has a complaint," whether the "supervisor uses general supervision," etc. The judgments by the subordinates on these characteristics and others showed significant differences when related to the criterion of promotability. This then would argue in favor of hypothesis one, that there are characteristics which differentiate good and poor supervisors. Further, it would appear that these characteristics can be identified by subordinates.

Hollander[2] showed in a review article that buddy ratings (peer nominations) were useful in predicting certain performance criteria in the military situation and further showed in another article[3] that the validity of peer nomination scores is not adversely affected by questions of friendship. Completing the questionnaire under what he calls an administrative set (that is, playing for keeps) rather than a "research" set does not appear to affect the validity of the peer nominations. With this information it was thought feasible to use buddy ratings as a selection device for supervisory personnel.

The present study was conducted in one life insurance company. This company is made up of 127 districts with a total of approximately 2,200 agents. In each district, there is a district manager and several assistant managers. Each assistant manager has from two to six men under him whom he supervises (median = 4). The task here was to select new assistant managers for replacement and expansion.

The study was started in January, 1956. The district manager in each district administered a fourteen-item questionnaire to each of his agents.

---

[1] Floyd C. Mann and James K. Dent, "The Supervisor: Member of Two Organizational Families," *Harvard Business Review*, Vol. 32, 1954, pp. 103–12.

[2] E. P. Hollander, "Buddy Ratings: Military Research and Industrial Implications," *Personnel Psychology*, Vol. 7, 1954, pp. 385–93.

[3] E. P. Hollander, "The Friendship Factor in Peer Nominations," *Personnel Psychology*, Vol. 9, 1956, pp. 425–47.

The manager was aware of the purpose of the study; the agents were told it was to study the development of agents and how they operate as a team. The questionnaire is shown in Appendix 1. It can be seen from the questionnaire that two kinds of items were used—those which were work-oriented and those which were socially-oriented. Some of the items used were similar to those described by Mann and Dent. Each man was to complete the questionnaire anonymously and send it in a self-addressed return envelope to the Research Division of the Life Insurance Agency Management Association. Cooperation was very good and from only two districts did we not receive any questionnaires. It is true that all agents did not complete all of the questions but a vast majority of them had at least one nomination for each item.[4]

After the questionnaires were returned, a tally was made of the first, second, and third place choices received by each man in the district for each item. A simple scoring system was used; that is, three points for a first place, two points for a second place, and one point for a third place. The total number of points for each man was computed for each item and these totals were then added for the district. Each man's total number of points on each item was then divided by the district total to give the proportion of the total vote he received on that item. This was necessary since there were a different number of votes in each district. Using this percentage score, the men were then ranked in terms of the proportion of the district vote which he received on each item.

Arrangements were made with the company to report to us any promotions made to assistant manager. These promotions were made without knowledge of the peer nominations. Six months after a man was promoted, we asked the home office regional supervisors (that is, top management people who visit the districts and have very close contact with the district operation) to complete a rating scale on each man promoted. This form is shown in Appendix 2. From the testing date in January through September, 1956, 100 men had been promoted and had been rated six months after promotion. This brought us through to March, 1957.

It will be recalled that the proportion of votes each man received in the district on each item was ranked within the district. For a final score on these men who were promoted, we counted the number of items on which they were either first, second, or third in rank in the district in terms of the proportion of votes they received. In other words, if a man received the most, second most or third most votes, for ex-

---

[4] In future work, we plan to request three nominations for each item and not give the alternative of nominating one or two. The instructions should also be modified for this kind of work group in another way. Instead of saying exclude *your* assistant manager, they should say exclude *assistant managers*. The author overlooked the possibility that some agents might choose an assistant manager other than his own in answering a question. Unfortunately, a few of the agents did just this and these votes had to be eliminated.

ample, on eight of the fourteen items, he would receive a score of eight. If a man was not in the top three ranks on any items, he would receive a score of zero. Thus, scores could range from zero to fourteen.

RESULTS

The score of each man was related to the rating given him by the regional supervisor; that is, excellent, good, fair or poor. Anyone who was returned to the job of an agent or left the company was combined with those who were rated poor.

The 100 cases were split into approximate thirds. This gave groupings of scores zero to three, four to nine, and ten to fourteen. The per cent rated good or excellent for each of these score groups is shown in Table 1. This gives a chi square of 10.08 which is beyond the .01 level

TABLE 1

RATINGS FOR EACH OF THREE THIRDS
($N = 100$)

SCORE	N	PER CENT GOOD OR EXCELLENT
10–14	33	76
4–9	28	54
0–3	39	39

of significance. Using all the scores without grouping, a biserial correlation was computed splitting the group of good and excellent vs. poor and fair ratings. The r_{bis} is .40 (significant beyond the .01 level). Since there is a possibility that all of the assumptions of the r_{bis} are not met, the data were tested with the Kolmogorov-Smirnov test.[5] The data were significant beyond the .01 level.

It should be remembered that the home office regional supervisors who made the ratings never saw the peer nominations. Consequently, it would appear that these nominations are useful in predicting the ratings for assistant manager. If this criterion of success on the job is acceptable and certainly it must have some meaningfulness to be this predictable, the buddy ratings would seem to be a valid procedure for selecting this type of supervisory personnel.

In order to see whether or not item weighting would add to the predictiveness of the score, the sample was split in half. The relationship between each item and the criteria was computed on the first half. Each of the items in this half was predictive of the criterion in the expected direction and there were no wide discrepancies in item discrimination. On the hold-out sample, strangely enough, each of the items actually

---

[5] Sidney Siegel, *Nonparametric Statistics for the Behavioral Sciences* (New York: McGraw-Hill Book Co., Inc., 1956).

showed greater discrimination. Again, there was very little difference between the differential prediction between the items. Consequently, it was felt that unit weighting was just about as good as any more elaborate weighting system.

We were interested in the intercorrelations of all items. They ranged from .47 to .96. For these correlations, a random sample ($N = 317$) of all agents was used (not just those promoted). The highest correlation was between Item 1 and Item 2. We thought we were getting at two different aspects of the job but obviously were not. As would be expected, the socially-oriented items clustered, and the work-oriented items clustered. The lowest correlations were between Items 9 and 4 (who is the best all-around agent, and who do you prefer to be with socially), Items 13 and 14 (who is best at programming, and who do you prefer to be with socially), Items 13 and 5 (who is best at programming, and who is most likely to cheer you up if you feel low), Items 3 and 5 (who would you prefer to have help you on your accounts and records, and who is most likely to cheer you up if you feel low). All of these correlated below .50.

Undoubtedly, the test could be cut down in length or perhaps improved by the addition of other items. There is unquestionably some halo as indicated by the correlations, yet each of the items seem to be predictive and the battery of items significantly predictive.

DISCUSSION

One might raise the question of whether or not the managers and assistant managers could do just as good a job of forecasting who the agents would pick for each of the items. If this were true, why bother asking the agents? On a questionnaire administered at the same time as the agents' questionnaire, we asked the assistant managers to predict who the agents would pick first, second and third on each of the items, and although no formal analysis was made it was found that this was a highly variable art. Some of the assistant managers could guess fairly accurately whereas others missed the boat completely. This analysis itself may lead to some fruitful hypothesis concerning excellence of supervision. How do good and poor supervisors differ with respect to knowing who their agents will choose?

The question of whether or not supervisory personnel could do just as well in selecting assistant managers as the peer ratings is not answered. Since 45% of those promoted were subsequently rated poor or fair or were demoted, it would militate against this supposition. The supervisory personnel in a district are consulted in any promotion and, in fact, their recommendations are given very heavy weight in the final decision. Why then should 45% of the agents promoted wind up being "poor" or "fair" if the persons responsible for making promotions could do as well or better than the peer nominations?

While this study answers some questions, it raises a number. No account was taken of length of service of the agent doing the choosing. Equal weight was given to the choices of new men as well as those on the job and in the district for a longer period of time. Had this factor been controlled, would it have changed the predictions? Further, if every agent had made three choices would this have improved the prediction? The analysis would certainly have been easier.

Another question which is unanswered in this study is how valuable is this procedure for predicting success or failure of assistant managers promoted to districts outside of the district in which the peer nominations occurred. There were some cases included in these data, but not a sufficiently large enough group to treat separately.

The question also arises as to what will happen when this company uses this technique for selection purposes. Due to the turnover of agents, if this technique were to be used for selection purposes, the peer nomination questionnaire would have to be administered about once every year. (We are already getting promotions of people who were not in the district when the questionnaire was administered.) If the agents knew that this questionnaire was "for keeps" and would have an effect on the promotions of their fellow agents, would this affect the validity of the procedure? Judging from Hollander's[6] study it would not. In view of the fact that the last item on the questionnaire asked, "Which agents would make the best assistant manager?" and these agents are not naive, it could be argued that they had some idea of the purpose of the present questionnaire. This also would lead one to believe that if the technique were used for promotional purposes it would not lose its validity. It may be of interest to know that this company is planning to use this procedure in selecting their assistant managers. It should be pointed out, however, that other evaluations will be made and that selection will not be based only on peer ratings. The author believes that these ratings should be used as additional information in the selection of supervisory personnel not as a panacea.

If we can generalize from this study, there is no reason to believe that this technique could not be used at other levels and in other work situations. Of course, the questions would have to be modified and the procedure tested to see if it were fruitful.

It would seem that both hypotheses are supported—that is: (1) There are certain identifiable characteristics which differentiate good and poor supervisory personnel, and (2) these characteristics can be identified in potential supervisors by peers at the time they are all in the subordinate position.

APPENDIX 1

For each question, please rank the top three agents in your office on the following items; exclude yourself, your assistant manager, your manager and clerical force. If, in your opinion, there are not as many as three people who

---

[6] E. P. Hollander, "The Friendship Factor in Peer Nominations," *op. cit.*

fulfill the requirements of a particular question, name only the top two or top one. However, wherever possible please rank the top three.

1. Who would you prefer to go to for help on a tough case?
   1st _____
   2nd _____
   3rd _____

2. Who would you prefer to have accompany you on a tough case?
   1st _____
   2nd _____
   3rd _____

3. If you needed help on your accounts and records, who would you prefer to have help you?
   1st _____
   2nd _____
   3rd _____

4. Who do you prefer to be with socially?
   1st _____
   2nd _____
   3rd _____

5. Who is most likely to cheer you up if you feel low?
   1st _____
   2nd _____
   3rd _____

6. Who is usually pulling most for both the district and the agents?
   1st _____
   2nd _____
   3rd _____

7. Who gets along best with his assistant manager?
   1st _____
   2nd _____
   3rd _____

8. Who gets along best with the manager?
   1st _____
   2nd _____
   3rd _____

9. Who is the best all-around agent in the office?
   1st _____
   2nd _____
   3rd _____

10. If you were going to be away for a week or two, which agent would you want to take over your debit?
    1st _____
    2nd _____
    3rd _____

11. With which agents in the office do you feel free to discuss your personal problems?
    1st _____
    2nd _____
    3rd _____

12. Which agents in the office are best at handling people?
    1st _____
    2nd _____
    3rd _____

13. Which agents are best at programming?

1st _____
2nd _____
3rd _____
14. Which agents would make the best assistant manager?
1st _____
2nd _____
3rd _____

APPENDIX 2

1. I believe that Assistant Manager _____ in
District _____ is performing his duties (check one)
Much better than I expected _____
Better than I expected   _____
As well as I expected   _____
Not as well as I expected   _____
Much poorer than I expected _____
2. As Assistant Manager (check one)
He is doing an excellent job _____
He is doing a good job   _____
He is doing a fair job   _____
He is doing a poor job   _____
Rater's name   _____

9. The Leaderless Group Discussion as a Leadership Evaluation Instrument*

Bernard M. Bass

AT THE BEGINNING of Cameron Hawley's novel "Executive Suite," Avery Bullard, President of the Tredway Corporation could not decide whom to choose as his successor from among his five vice-presidents.

An idea flashed. He would get them together tonight for one last look . . . He'd put some kind of proposition before them . . . anything . . . the possibility of building a new factory in North Carolina. It would hit them cold . . . He would toss out the idea and then sit back . . . watching, listening, judging. Then he would pick the man who showed up best. (p. 5)

As is suggested by this passage from the recent best-seller about executive life, the leaderless group discussion has a common sense basis as a leadership evaluation instrument. For the technique has high face validity.

---

* From *Personnel Psychology*, Vol. 7, 1947, pp. 470–77.

RATIONALE

The rationale underlying the leaderless group discussion, and other situational tests of leadership can be summarized as follows: *the more similar the problem in a new situation to one in an old situation, the more likely the same persons to attempt and be successful as leaders in both situations.*

The hypothesis is consistent with what we know about transfer of training. Also, when we average a series of seven test-retest studies of the leaderless group discussion in order of the similarity between test and retest, we obtain reliability coefficients or consistency correlations that increase from .39 to .90 as the similarity increases in conditions during the test and retest.

WHAT IS THE LEADERLESS GROUP DISCUSSION?

The basic scheme of the leaderless group discussion (LGD) is to ask several examinees, as a group, to carry on a discussion. No leader is appointed. Examiners do not enter the discussion once it begins but remain free to observe and note the performance of each examinee.

As yet, there has been no final standardization by all users of the technique of the size of the group, length of testing time, type of problem presented, directions, seating arrangement, number of raters and rating procedure. There is considerable evidence available on the effects of many of these variations to suggest which particular aspect of the LGD are most in need of standardization and what the final standardized LGD should be like.

Unless otherwise indicated, the results we shall describe are based on observers' ratings of the *amount of successful leadership displayed* in the discussion or else are inferences about the personalities of the candidates based on observations of this behavior.

According to 12 studies involving 1065 examinees ranging from administrative trainee candidates to ROTC cadets, rater agreement is high, especially where standardized behavior check lists are used. A median correlation of .82 exists between pairs of observer ratings for the 12 investigations.

WHAT IS THE VALIDITY OF THE LEADERLESS GROUP DISCUSSION?

As with most other personality variables, there is no absolute or "true" criterion upon which to validate ratings based on the leaderless group discussion. Rather, we must be content to demonstrate, by experimentation, consistencies between LGD performance and other measures where these other measures are indicative, by deduction and/or induction, of the tendency to be successful as a leader.

For example, suppose we deduce or discover experimentally elsewhere that, all other things being equal, the higher an individual's verbal aptitude, the more he will display successful leadership behavior. Then if

LGD performance correlates with scores on a verbal intelligence test, we may infer that the LGD performance is, partially, at least, a sample of leadership behavior.

Various relationships concerning individual differences in successful leader behavior can be derived by definition, postulate, and deduction. The relationships are shown in Figure 1.

According to Figure 1, if the LGD is a means of measuring successful leadership behavior, then: (1) LGD scores should correlate with

FIGURE 1

SOME RELATIONSHIPS CONCERNING INDIVIDUAL DIFFERENCES IN
SUCCESSFUL LEADER BEHAVIOR DERIVED BY DEFINITION, POSTULATE, AND DEDUCTION

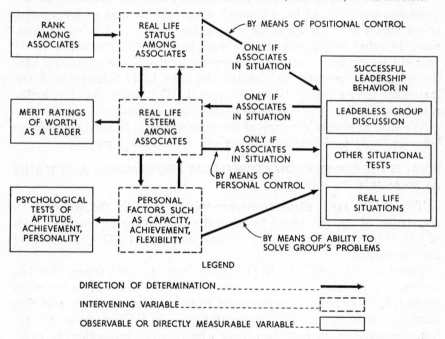

status as measured by rank, when the LGD is among associates of different rank; (2) LGD scores should correlate with esteem as estimated by merit ratings; (3) LGD scores should correlate with leadership performance in other quasi-real situations; (4) LGD scores should correlate with success in real-life leadership situations; and (5) LGD scores should correlate with personal characteristics, as measured by psychological tests and measurements, commonly associated with success as a leader. (Status refers to the worth of a person, according to his associates, due to the position he occupies. Esteem refers to the worth of a person, as a person, regardless of his position.[1]

---

[1] Editor's note: A detailed discussion of esteem, status, and the deductions mentioned is presented in, B. M. Bass, *Leadership, Psychology and Organizational Behavior* (New York: Harper & Brothers, 1960).

Each positive correlation between an LGD rating and another of these specified measures will provide experimental evidence of the "validity" of LGD performance. This rationale ignores situational variations and their important but not all-important effect on leader behavior. For we find that successful leaders in the LGD manage to exhibit success as a leader in a wide range of other situations. We therefore believe we are dealing with consistent individual differences in successful leadership behavior which are significant above and beyond the effects of situational variations.

Actually the LGD absorbs to some extent the effects of situational variations. For example, the problems on which and the participants with whom an individual is tested vary consistently with the problems and individuals on which and for whom the individual has high or low esteem, or on which or with whom he usually has been tested in other situations. In other words, we tend to correlate the LGD behavior of 18 year old female examinees with the esteem of the examinees among adolescent girls. If we were to correlate the same LGD behavior with the examinees' esteem among 35 year old men, LGD validity would undoubtedly be altered.

We shall now consider each of the expected and obtained correlations between LGD performance and the other mentioned variables.

WHAT IS THE CORRELATION BETWEEN LGD PERFORMANCE AND STATUS AS MEASURED BY RANK?

Two studies are available to answer this question. In the first study, a correlation of .88 was found between the rank in the company of each of 131 oil refinery supervisors and their success as LGD leaders among their associates.

In the second study, 180 ROTC cadets were retested among their associates a year after an original test. During the year, all cadets were promoted. Those who were promoted from cadet non-com to cadet first lieutenant or higher gained significantly more in LGD score on the retest, compared to the test, than those who received promotions to cadet second lieutenant only.

We conclude from the results that—as expected, if the LGD is a valid measure of successful leadership—performance in an initially leaderless discussion among associates of varying status is strongly related to status in real-life among these associates.

WHAT IS THE CORRELATION BETWEEN LGD PERFORMANCE AND ESTEEM AS ESTIMATED BY MERIT RATINGS?

Fourteen correlations are available between LGD performance and esteem as estimated by merit ratings. They involve a total of 1,495 cases varying from foreign service candidates to oil refinery supervisors. Only one of these published studies failed to obtain a significantly positive correlation between LGD scores and merit ratings. (In this one case, men of differing rank were tested together and most of the variance in LGD success was determined by rank.) The median correlation of .44 and the range from .29 to .68 for all these studies excepting the one where examinees varied in rank lead us to infer (as we also deduced) that esteem and LGD performance are moderately associated. We again conclude that LGD performance is valid as a measure of successful leadership.

WHAT IS THE CORRELATION BETWEEN LGD PERFORMANCE AND PERSONAL CHARACTERISTICS ASSOCIATED WITH LEADERSHIP?

According to Stogdill's[2] survey of over 100 empirical studies, leaders tend to surpass non-leaders in certain traits such as capacity, achievement, responsibility and participation. Similarly, we can deduce the existence of positive correlations between successful leadership and capacity, achievement and participation. Therefore, if performance in the LGD is associated with these personal factors, we will have another indirect indication of the validity of LGD performance as a measure of successful leadership behavior.

Published studies, involving a total of 2,361 test scores, report 17 correlations between LGD performance and various measures of capacity and achievement such as verbal aptitude tests, college grades, and intelligence tests. The median correlation is .30 and the range is from .17 to .57. These results tend to conform to expectations and lead us once more to conclude that the LGD is valid as a measure of successful leadership.

When we examine the correlations between LGD performance and various personality variables which approximate the "responsibility" and "participation" clusters of Stogdill, we infer that a consistency exists between Stogdill's conclusions concerning the relations between leadership in general and such personality traits as energy, flexibility of judgment, self-esteem and the tendency to participate, and our results concerning the relations between these traits and LGD performance. We find a median correlation of .30 and a range from .07 to .60 for the nine available correlations concerning these relationships. Some contradiction or lack of consistency appears when we consider such traits as responsibility, emotional stability, ascendency, and sociability especially when they have been measured by forced-choice rather than traditional personality inventories.

WHAT IS THE CORRELATION BETWEEN LGD PERFORMANCE AND LEADERSHIP PERFORMANCE IN OTHER QUASI-REAL SITUATIONS?

The median correlation is .60 and the range from .30 to .78 for the 16 available correlations between ratings of "leadership" or "desirability for

[2] R. M. Stogdill, "Personal Factors Associated with Leadership: A Survey of the Literature," *Journal of Psychology*, Vol. 25, 1948, pp. 31–75.

leadership positions" based on LGD performance and similar ratings based on other situational tests. These data concern over 2,000 examinees varying from OSS assessees to shoe factory management trainees. The correlations probably overestimate the relationships somewhat, for in many of the studies the same observers rated performance in the LGD and in the other situations.

However, we conclude that ratings in the LGD are associated with ratings of success as a leader in a wide variety of other situational tests and infer again that LGD ratings are valid as measures of successful leadership.

WHAT IS THE CORRELATION BETWEEN LGD PERFORMANCE AND LEADERSHIP PERFORMANCE IN REAL-LIFE SITUATIONS?

We find a median of .27 for seven correlations between LGD performance and real-life leadership performance. The most important result here is that while LGD ratings correlate with the tendency to hold leadership offices, ($r = .27, .36$) they appear to be associated primarily with the tendency in real-life to initiate structure among associates and subordinates ($r = .32$). On the contrary, according to the one study available on the relationship, a low negative correlation appears to exist between LGD performance and the tendency in real-life to be considerate of the welfare of subordinates and associates ($r = -.25$).[3] Two factorial analyses support the hypothesis that LGD performance is a function of the tendency to initiate and to be socially bold, as well as several other factors such as esteem, intellectualism, and verbality.

WHAT IS THE UTILITY OF THE LGD AS AN ASSESSMENT TECHNIQUE?

Since 1947, the LGD has gained widespread use in the United States. In 1951, Fields[4] reported that 44 out of 190 Civil Service Agencies were using some form of the LGD. Mandell[5] has published a manual on the procedure for use by the Federal Civil Service. The LGD is widely used by many industrial and business firms today—so widely used that it has prompted Meyer[6] to caution about the over-enthusiastic acceptance of the technique. In one West Coast city alone, the procedure has been used by a large bank, a department store, a canning and container concern, a petroleum company, and an airline. According to the 40-odd pub-

---

[3] A more detailed discussion of the factors of "initiation" and "consideration" is presented in, E. A. Fleishman, "Leadership Climate, Human Relations Training, and Supervisory Behavior," *Personnel Psychology*, Vol. 6, 1953, pp. 205–22.

[4] H. Fields, "An Analysis of the Use of the Group Oral Interview," *Personnel*, Vol. 27, 1951, pp. 480–86.

[5] M. Mandell, "The Group Oral Performance Test," U.S. Civil Service Commission, 1952 (Multilithed).

[6] C. A. Meyer, "The Group Interview Test: Its Weakness," *Public Personnel Review*, Vol. II, 1950, pp. 147–54.

lished reports available the LGD has been used profitably to assess examinees ranging from officer candidates to visiting teachers.

The wide variety of situations in which the LGD has been applied with profit probably is due to the almost universal requirement that the leader adequately communicate *verbally* with those he leads. Until individuals in "real-life" groups begin communicating with each other by means of telepathy or the passing of symbols printed on cards, it is probable that the LGD will provide one general means among several others (such as individual interviews and intelligence tests) for partially assessing the leadership potential of individuals for a wide range of situations.

Section Two

PERFORMANCE APPRAISAL

Introduction

AFTER INDIVIDUALS are selected and placed in jobs, it becomes important to evaulate how well they are performing. As we shall see, this is not as simple as it sounds. The development of adequate methods of measuring job proficiency is one of the most difficult problems in personnel psychology. Yet, such measures are essential as a basis for promotion and transfer, evaluation of the need for and results of training, estimating labor costs, determining wages, and for other purposes. Job proficiency measures are also important as "criterion measures" against which to validate tests and the other selection procedures described in the previous section.

It is desirable to make these measurements as objective as possible. Where the job allows for measurement of "units produced," "errors made," etc., the problem may not seem as difficult. However, even here people differ in their experience, in the quality of their machines, in the quotas they are given, etc., and steps must be taken to insure comparability of the measures taken. The article by Brogden and Taylor discusses some of the problems and procedures involved in obtaining dependable criteria of employee effectiveness. In "Measuring On-the-Job Performance—Applying Cost Accounting Concepts to Criterion Construction," they present a rationale for converting production units, errors, time consumed of other personnel, etc., into dollar units. They also show how a proper combination of performance indices may yield an over-all estimate of the employee's contribution to the effectiveness of the organization.

Often it is not possible or feasible to use direct measures of "on-the-job" performance in evaluating employee proficiency. The "job sample test," which involves many principles of achievement testing, is one approach to this problem. The article by Bresnard and Briggs, "A System Simulator for Measuring Job Proficiency" shows how this method was extended to a highly complex job.

The next three articles illustrate some developments in the field called "merit rating." This field has been the center of some controversy. Some critics feel it is unethical for one man to be in the position of rating another; others feel that ratings make for conformity in the organization. Still other criticisms emphasize that such ratings are frequently biased, difficult to make, or impossible to compare from one situation to the next. A general reply to such criticism is that ratings of subordinates have always been made, often in an unsystematic, slipshod, unrecorded, often impulsive, and frequently undefended way. Decisions to promote, dismiss, or retain employees are made every day. The shift to "merit rating" is an attempt to transfer haphazard judgments to ratings made in a more calm, deliberate, systematic manner which allows better comparisons among individuals. Furthermore, the supervisor does this at periodic intervals, and it is on the record for the subordinates to see and discuss with him. This is the aim, although many rating systems fall short of the mark. We are dealing here with the subjective area of human judgment. Such judgments are subject to error. However, many of these errors are systematic and are known, and much research has been done to reduce these tendencies in rating systems.

The articles chosen include the three major developments among merit-rating procedures. These are the *graphic-rating system*, the *forced choice system*, and the *critical incident technique*. Each system has its advantages and disadvantages and each is designed to overcome and minimize certain kinds of rating errors, such as halo and leniency. The article by Bittner, "Developing an Employee Merit Rating Procedure," gives a general, comprehensive overview of the area. He deals with such questions as how are ratings used, who should do the rating, how often should ratings be made, what are the different types of ratings, how can errors in rating be reduced, and what are the steps in training of raters. His article concludes with a description of the "forced choice" technique.

The next article, by Stockford and Bissel is entitled "Establishing a Graphic-Rating Scale." This study takes us through the steps of an actual research program in which a merit-rating program was developed and refined in a large company.

Perhaps no job has as many "expert opinions" expressed about it as the job of salesman. What makes a successful salesman? Obviously, there are many kinds of sales jobs, and there are no general answers. But, for a particular sales job, how does one identify the successful salesman? The first impulse is to say that one needs to simply examine how much he sells. Anyone in the sales field can answer that this is not the whole story. The study by Kirchner and Dunnette, "Using Critical Incidents to Measure Job Proficiency Factors," provides a more analytical approach to the problem of evaluating salesman performance. It also illustrates the recent approach to proficiency measurement called the "critical incident" technique.

Up to this point, we have emphasized the measurement and evaluation side of performance appraisal. Perhaps even more important is the problem of communicating the appraisal back to the employee so that: (*a*) he has "feedback" or "knowledge of results" of how his work is evaluated; (*b*) he develops some constructive approach to improving his performance; and (*c*) he is motivated to modify his behavior in the indicated directions. Thus, performance appraisal has a "personnel _development_" objective as well as an _evaluation_ objective. The trouble is that these two objectives may work against each other, unless the supervisor is skilled in how he communicates the appraisal during the appraisal interview. The final article in this section by Richards, entitled "Some New Insights into Performance Appraisal," discusses this problem and describes the very human problems involved in the superior-subordinate relationship of the appraisal interview. He also describes some research into this problem which shows the relation between the supervisor's behavior, the subordinate's attitudes, and the success of the appraisal interview.

10. Measuring On-the-Job Performance— Applying Cost Accounting Concepts to Criterion Construction*

Hubert E. Brogden and Erwin K. Taylor

IT IS GENERALLY agreed that the most important problem facing the industrial psychologist interested in test validation is devising adequate criteria of industrial efficiency. In spite of this, too little effort is usually expended in criterion development. The criteria used are too frequently those most immediately available rather than those which would be most desirable.

This article emphasizes the need for a common metric for sub-criterion variables, such that the measures obtained reflect the contribution of the individual to the objectives (or, usually to the overall efficiency) of the hiring organization. The principles to be discussed are pertinent to a number of possible common metrics. It is proposed in particular, however, that dollar units, determined on a cost accounting basis, will be found the most desirable units for many criterion purposes. For convenience this discussion will be confined to such monetary units—since the authors believe these to be most generally useful for criterion purposes. In addition, it is their opinion that the cost accounting criterion makes possible a more definitive solution of related problems in the area of personnel selection and differential placement.

The criterion problem under discussion in this article is the development of an overall index of an employee's value to the hiring organization.

THE MAJOR CRITERION PROBLEMS

To provide background for the discussion to follow, we will consider, briefly, some of the major criterion problems and indicate the relationship between these problems and the concept we are proposing. The principal problems encountered in criterion construction are, we believe, included in the following discussion.

1. Definition of the job. Before any type of criterion construction can be undertaken, the job involved must be defined in order to identify a

---

* From "The Dollar Criterion—Applying the Cost Accounting Concept to Criterion Construction," *Personnel Psychology*, Vol. 3, 1950, pp. 133–54.

group of workers homogeneous with respect to their job duties. The cost accounting concept may sometimes be relevant in shedding light on discrepancies between apparently similar jobs. This is particularly true where two jobs have common elements but where the relative importance of these elements are quite different in terms of their value to the organization.

2. *"What it is" that criterion elements should measure.* Definition of the nature of criterion elements is one of the basic problems in criterion construction. The solution to this problem is intimately related to the underlying logic of the cost accounting concept.

3. *Isolation of all essential sub-criterion elements.* There is probably no practical means of securing a criterion which will take *all* criterion elements into consideration. The writers believe that the cost accounting criterion procedures aid in judging which of the job elements are most essential.

4. *Devising means of measuring the sub-criterion variables' reliability.* The cost accounting concept proposed offers no solution to the problem of reliability.

5. *Avoiding inclusion of irrelevant factors (criterion contamination).* The approach under consideration bears indirectly on certain types of criterion contamination.

6. *Developing a procedure for combining sub-criterion measures.* This is the area in which the cost accounting criterion makes its major contribution.

7. *Developing equal scale units.* The procedure proposed aids in the solution of this problem.

8. *Meaningful units.* A direct solution to this problem is provided.

9. *Sponsor acceptability.* The procedure by its very nature should yield a criterion that is meaningful and fully acceptable to management.

10. *Demonstrable significance.* In addition to the foregoing the authors feel that a full consideration of criterion problems requires the introduction and discussion of the requirement that the criterion composite and its individual elements possess *demonstrable significance*.

In constructing predictor variables, the research investigator need not directly justify the use of any type of measure, since the responsibility for determining usefulness of the predictors rests on the criterion, and, of course, on the design of the research study.

In constructing criterion variables, however, it must be possible to demonstrate (by means other than the usual correlational techniques of validation studies) that the on-the-job behaviors measured do contribute to the objective of the sponsoring organization. If use of a criterion is justified only by showing its relationship to a better established criterion, the essential criterion problem will not have been solved. Justification of the second criterion is then required. This shift of responsibility cannot become an infinite regress. The criterion must, in the last analysis, be directly justifiable on logical grounds. To solve the criterion problem, it must be possible to show, as the authors would phrase it, that the criterion possesses demonstrable significance or, if you wish, "logical validity."

The Theoretical Significance of Cost Accounting Units to the Solution of the Criterion Problem

In discussing the theoretical significance of cost accounting units, two approaches are possible. It will be profitable, we believe, to consider both.

The first grew out of a search for a common denominator or a common metric for combining various sub-criterion measures which are apparently quite different in nature. Suppose that for a typing job, the number of pages of typed copy produced is one sub-criterion variable and number of errors is a second criterion element. How can these two be combined to give an overall measure of typing proficiency suited to the needs of a particular hiring organization? One possible solution was suggested by Otis[1] in the handling of two corresponding criterion elements obtained on key punch operators. In the given work situation, errors were found and corrected by a verifier. The total number of correctly punched cards could not be directly obtained. It was discovered, however, that something over 13 cards could be punched by the key punch operator while the verifier corrected a single error. To obtain an overall criterion measure, 13 times the number of erroneous cards was subtracted from the total number of cards punched.

In this instance the *time* required for two different work units was employed as a means of expressing both measures in comparable units. The time required to correct an error was found to be 13 times that required to punch an original card. The implicit and obvious assumption in this combining procedure is that man-hours required for a given production unit is a fundamental measure of the degree of contribution to the efficiency of the organization. If the principle illustrated in this example is carried further, the possibility of converting man-hours required into the cost of punching a card or correcting an error becomes obvious. Without taking the time to elaborate too far at this point, the reader will note that with conversion to monetary units it would be possible to make allowance for possible differences in salary between key punch operators and verifiers. While in this example such salary differences would probably be small, other cases could be cited where salary differences are greater and assume considerable importance. It would also be possible, for example, to obtain as a criterion measure the amount of supervisory time required by different workers in a given job assignment. Here, man-hours used as a common denominator would ob-

---

[1] Jay Otis in Stead, Shartle et al., *Occupational Counseling Techniques* (New York: American Book Co., 1940).

viously fail properly to weight card punching, errors in punching, and supervisory time required into a composite defensible as a measure of the effect of workers in that job on the overall efficiency of the organization.

It should also be apparent that monetary units allow the expression of a considerable variety of additional factors in the same metric. Material wastage, accidents, overhead, etc., can, where they are important factors, be expressed in dollar units and combined to give an overall evaluation. A logical basis is thus obtained for combining elements which were originally expressed in units having no obvious relation to each other.

The second approach to the cost accounting criterion grew out of the previously mentioned close relationship between this concept and the criterion problem, "What is it that the criterion should measure?" The authors believe that a definition of "what it is that the criterion should measure" must stress that the only functions of the criterion are: (1) to establish the basis for choosing the "best" battery from the experimental predictors, and (2) to provide an estimate of the validity of that battery. Logically, then, the question of "what it is that the criterion should measure" is subsidiary to the question of "what it is that the predictors should predict." Since, in practice, the predictors operate as selection instruments, the question can be rephrased again to ask "what is it that the selection process should accomplish?"

Since the selection instruments determine which of a group of applicants will be admitted to an organization, the characteristics measured by the instruments must be related to the general objective of that organization. The instruments contribute to that objective to the degree that they select those applicants who will contribute most to the general objective of the organization.

In statistical processing, a battery of selection instruments is chosen through validation data to provide numerical scores having as close agreement with the criterion scores as possible. The battery is evaluated according to the degree of that relationship. A perfect relationship indicates perfect validity. Disregarding considerations such as time and expense, the criterion should, then, constitute the most perfect predictor obtainable and should, theoretically at least, be capable of effecting selection of those applicants who would contribute most to the general objective of the organization.

This line of reasoning leads in the authors' opinion to a definite answer to the question of "what it is that the criterion should measure." *The criterion should measure the contribution of the individual to the overall efficiency of the organization.*

To say that the criterion should measure the contribution of the individual to the overall efficiency of the organization leads next to a definition of the objectives of the organization. The general objective of industrial firms is to make money. This statement carries no implication of an undesirable materialistic attitude. Even in the case of governmental agencies, and nonprofit organizations, it is desired to render service as efficiently as possible—and efficiency is measured in terms of monetary outlay. Monetary saving, being the objective of the organization, is the logical measure of the degree to which on-the-job activity of the individual contributes to or detracts from this overall objective. Only after we have succeeded in evaluating on-the-job performance in these terms can we be sure that our criterion measures conform to the objectives of the organization. It seems apparent that examination of the way in which a given employee affects overall efficiency requires that we determine the way in which his on-the-job activities produce objects or services of monetary value and the ways in which his errors, accidents, spoilage of materials, etc., result in monetary outlay.

While this article is not primarily concerned with the nature of or techniques required to identify the component variables of a composite criterion, it might be noted that cost accounting weights may be applied only to certain types of variables. Such variables must be expressed in units that can be evaluated in dollar terms. An object produced, an error or an accident can be evaluated in dollar terms; units of rating scales (as ordinarily constructed) cannot be so evaluated. It is believed, however, that unless criterion elements are of such a nature that they can be expressed in dollar units, their use as criterion measures cannot be directly justified and do not satisfy the requirement of logical face validity previously discussed.

This does not mean that the authors propose to leave important areas of job success unmeasured. In practice it is better to employ scales of questionable validity and approximate weighting than to ignore an important area of job success entirely.

The Relationship between the Cost Accounting Concept and Techniques of Criterion Construction

With this overall justification of the cost accounting concept, we will proceed to relate the general concept to techniques of criterion construction. In showing the relationship to these techniques, the concept can be further clarified. Techniques deriving from the cost accounting concept will be introduced in the course of this discussion.

As in the case of all criteria, the variables of a cost accounting criterion must be identified by means of some form of job analysis. In the development of cost accounting criteria, however, it is necessary in the analysis of the job to go beyond the mere identification of the component criterion variables and to determine the manner and extent to which the products or behaviors measured affect the efficiency of the organization. In this additional process, information basic to the construction of cost accounting criteria is obtained. Considerable attention will consequently be devoted to discussion of this phase of criterion construction.

Before proceeding to a discussion of this additional process, we should like to stress one point important in use of job analysis for identification of component criterion variables.

In job analysis for criterion purposes we believe that a clear-cut distinction must be made between the end products of a given job and the job processes that lead to these end products. It may be pertinent to such other legitimate objectives of job analysis as training or position classification, to study the exact sequence of operations in the production of the finished product. The skills needed, the tools used, and the methods employed may all be needed for this purpose. Such information does not, however, give a direct answer to the major question, "how much does the employee produce and how good is it?" The criterion problem centers primarily in the quantity, quality and cost of the finished product. While work sequences and such factors as skill undoubtedly do indirectly affect efficiency of the organization, any attempt to demonstrate such effect will lead, first of all, to a demonstration of the way in which skill affects productivity and finally to a *tracing out* of the effect of the objects produced to determine what happens in the organization as a consequence of the production of errors, accidents or finished products. Such factors as skill are latent; their effect is realized in the end product. They do not satisfy the logical requirements of an adequate criterion.[2]

A *tracing out* of the exact nature and importance of the *effect* of each sub-criterion variable on the efficiency of the organization is the essential step which differentiates the dollar criterion from the more conventional techniques. This technique will, in our opinion, be found useful to the technician in the early stages of criterion construction in which job analysis is ordinarily employed. Its usefulness lies in the possibility provided of obtaining an early estimate of the relative importance of the various criterion elements, and a selection of those elements of most importance in arriving at a practicable approximation to a measure of the total effect of the individual on the efficiency of the organization. Evaluation in dollar units is one of the two variables determining the importance of the given criterion element to overall value to the organization. The second variable is the standard deviation of the given component criterion measures. From cost accounting evaluation and such rough estimates of the standard deviation as can be made before actual criterion measurement, the relative importance of the various possible sub-variables can be estimated. On this basis an intelligent and more exact judg-

---

[2] It is recognized that the relationship between job-process and job-product vary widely from job to job. There are, thus, some situations in which, after establishing the existence of a high correlation, job processes (because they may be easier to observe than job products) may be substituted as a criterion. They satisfy the logical requirement of criterion variables, however, only because of their demonstrated relationship to job products.

ment can be made as to which elements it is necessary to evaluate in constructing the criterion for the actual validation study.

Let us illustrate the tracing out process by taking as an example the criterion variables resulting from actual analysis of the job of a carpenter laying underflooring. We will assume that the criterion variables isolated are: (1) square feet of lumber wasted, (2) damage to equipment, (3) time of other personnel consumed, (4) accidents, (5) quality of finished product, (6) errors in finished product and (7) square feet of underflooring laid for a given time unit.

To trace out the effect of square feet of lumber wasted on the efficiency of the organization, we need only determine the cost of lumber. Records might be kept or supervisors might be questioned regarding individual differences in wastage and the value of the lumber wasted. These estimates will provide a basis for deciding whether or not to include lumber usage as a sub-criterion variable. If it were found that the cost of lumber used varied considerably from carpenter to carpenter, the variable would be included as a criterion element. If the cost of lumber were so little as to be of no consequence or if the amount wasted were practically the same for all carpenters, no measures of this variable would need to be obtained in the actual validation study.

If the equipment were supplied by the company, it would be necessary to determine the cost of repair and replacement. If this amount were significant, it would then be necessary to estimate the extent of individual differences in such costs. The magnitude of these two factors would determine whether or not to include this as a criterion element.

In tracing out the effect of "time of other personnel consumed" we need only determine the salaries of the various individuals concerned. The actual component criterion variable, weighted in dollar terms, would be the total salary of all individuals concerned for the total amount of time wasted by the individual whose criterion score is being computed. Such a variable would, of course, receive negative weighting.

It is realized that some difficulties may arise in assigning responsibility for time consumed. It may also be true in the case of supervisors that their sole function is supervision and that their time can be utilized for no other useful purpose. No general rule can be given for handling problems such as these.

If overhead is an appreciable factor in the total cost of the product it should be considered in evaluating the dollar value of the contributions of the subjects of the criterion study. Overhead costs, it should be stressed, are not properly prorated equally to each subject. The overhead cost per object produced is much less for an efficient worker than for an inefficient worker.

To trace out the effects of accidents, an evaluation of the cost of repairing the resulting damage would be required. Time of other personnel lost because of the accident, damage paid by the company because of personal injury, etc., would also enter into the cost accounting evaluation. Individual differences in frequency of accidents may, however, be found to be too small to warrant its consideration as a criterion variable in the case of carpenters. In this particular instance, also, the reliability of any possible criterion variable would bear close inspection.

Evaluation of quality and errors in the finished product would require the most laborious "tracing out." Here it would be necessary to determine by observation of, or interviews with, follow-up workers, the additional amount of their time required because of errors or deficiencies in quality. Such a follow-up, if made with complete thoroughness, might involve a large number of different types of subsequent workers and might even lead to the effect of such errors or variations in quality on the final evaluation of the finished structure. In any event the errors, etc., would be classified, and the average additional labor entailed as their consequence, determined. It would be neither feasible nor theoretically desirable to trace the effect of each individual error, since in doing so we would be allowing individual differences in efficiency of follow-up workers differentially to influence the criterion estimates of different subjects of the validation study. It can be seen that such tracing out may become complex since inadequacies in laying the underflooring may not only increase the time requirements for subsequent operations but may cause inadequacies in these subsequent operations which would have to be evaluated in turn.

Deficiencies in the final structure would present a special problem involving salability of the structure and reputation of the construction company. Some overall arbitrary judgment would probably have to be made by the administrators with necessary background for such a judgment.

Square feet of underflooring completed within a given time unit can be converted to dollar units by determining units completed per time interval by all carpenters in that given job classification, and dividing this into total wages for the time involved. In effect, we thus determine the cost of laying a square foot of underflooring or its value to the organization.

Given the cost accounting evaluations of the individual criterion elements and the best available estimates as to individual differences, the importance of each criterion element can now be estimated as the product of these two figures. In the example under discussion it would probably be found that effect of equipment damage is negligible. Thus, this variable may well have been eliminated at the outset or at least after interviewing a construction supervisor. Lumber wasted may also be found unimportant because all workers use about the same amount. Quality of the finished product might possibly have too little significance to justify its evaluation. Whether or not these variables were included, the number of production units would probably be found most important.

It is believed that the tracing out of possible sub-criteria to their end effect on the efficiency of the organization will often lead to results at considerable variance with judgmental evaluations that the technician or management might have made without benefit of this additional information. In the case of the correction of punch-card errors referred to above, it took over 13 times as long, it will be recalled, to correct an error as to punch an original card. It is doubtful if a technician constructing a composite criterion would have judged errors to be so costly.

If the effect of such errors were traced further, it would be found, probably, that the number of errors escaping all checks is a function of the number of initial errors made. Such errors may in some organizations be extremely costly. Some may require effort equivalent to redoing a complete accounting job in addition to their effects on other scheduled work and on the reputation and morale of the organization. If the cost of correcting an initial error by a bank teller, for example, is 50¢ and one in every two hundred errors escaped initial detection and cost $100 on the average to find and correct, the total dollar weighting for each error would be one dollar instead of 50¢. In other words, the weighting would, on the average, be doubled. Experience with the cost of errors in statistical analysis suggests that such a finding would not be unusual.

A single clerical error, to cite an extreme example in another type of work, in the computation of the amount of lead ballast in a ship being sold by the government for scrap resulted in a loss of several hundred thousand dollars to the seller.

This general approach of evaluating importance, in cost accounting terms, leads to consideration of elements that are important to evaluation of overall efficiency but which would probably be generally ignored by usual methods. If, for example, a good IBM tabulator operator produced twice as many usable reports as a poor one, it should be noted that even if they are paid on a piecework basis, the rental of the machine is the same in both cases. In a cost accounting criterion, this cost would be taken into account along with many other such items. In the usual rating element or production record criteria, this factor would usually be ignored.

It may be helpful to list factors which will probably have to receive consideration in the proposed cost accounting type of employee evaluation. The following listing of such factors is not intended to be all-inclusive; a careful analysis of each job in relation to the organization will undoubtedly disclose factors peculiar to each.

1. Average value of production or service units.
2. Quality of objects produced or services accomplished.
3. Overhead—including rent, light, heat, cost depreciation or rental of machines and equipment.
4. Errors, accidents, spoilage, wastage, damage to machines or equipment through unusual wear and tear, etc.

5. Such factors as appearance, friendliness, poise, and general social effectiveness, where public relations are heavily involved. (Here, some approximate or arbitrary value would have to be assigned by an individual or individuals having the required responsibility and background.)

6. The cost of the time of other personnel consumed. This would include not only the time of the supervisory personnel but also that of other workers.

So far, we have considered briefly the relation of job analysis to the isolation of criterion variables and have discussed in some detail the nature and importance of the "tracing out" process to the construction of the cost accounting criterion. Given the criterion elements and the dollar weights obtained as a result of the "tracing out" process, the problems of technique of measurement for each criterion element and of combination of the measured elements still remain.

Both of these problems need only very brief consideration. Problems of technique of measurement, while of general importance to the criterion problem, bear no intimate relation to the concept of criterion construction under consideration. As we have indicated earlier, the measurements obtained must be in production unit form for ready application of the cost accounting procedures. Possible adaptations to rating measurement will be discussed later. Other important problems in technique of measurement, such as that of eliminating bias and that of obtaining adequate reliability, would be approached in the same manner as in any criterion construction problem.

The problem of weighting needs only brief consideration because its solution has in effect already been presented. Given the cost of production units, errors, etc., with all criterion units translated into dollar terms, the weighting problem is solved. All variables are expressed in a common denominator and may be directly summed to obtain an overall composite.

In the opinion of the authors, the most significant contributions of the cost accounting approach to criterion construction emerge in the combining of the criterion elements to yield an overall measurement of the workers' contribution to the effectiveness of the organization. Two distinct advantages of the cost accounting technique may be identified: (1) all measures are made in or translated into a single, meaningful metric—the dollar contribution to or detraction from the overall objective of the sponsoring organization; and (2) the resultant determination of the importance of each element in terms of its standard deviation. These two characteristics of the cost accounting approach completely solve the problem of combining criterion elements. The cost accounting units common to all elements make them directly additive; the reflection of importance directly as the standard deviation makes possible appropriate weighting by merely adding of raw score values of the several elements.

Significance of Cost Accounting Units to Related Selection and Classification Problems

It has been stressed in the introduction to this article that the cost accounting approach to the criterion problem makes its most significant contribution, not only in converting the criterion variables to units most meaningful and satisfactory to an industrial sponsor of validation research, but also in offering a sound theoretical solution to a number of important problems in this general area of selection and classification. The ways in which cost accounting units offer a solution to problems internal to criterion construction have already been considered.

An evident extension of the usefulness of dollar units in combining component criterion variables is suggested in obtaining an integration of training cost, turnover, and on-the-job productivity into a single index showing the total picture of the potential value of an applicant. In relating cost of training to other criterion measures, it is evident that the employee whose services are terminated during training represents a loss to the company equal to the cost of selection and training. For the remaining employees, cost of training would have to be prorated over the time spent in the assignments toward which the training was directed. Turnover or attrition assume importance, then, when selection and/or training is costly. Of course, efficiency during the on-the-job training or warm-up should be considered along with formal training.

In a follow-up study of applicants selected by a given battery of predictors, training, attrition and production on-the-job (expressed in dollar terms) could be readily and logically integrated into a single value showing the total value or loss to the organization for the entire period of employment of a given individual. Cost of training would simply be subtracted from the total dollar value of his productivity during the period of his employment.

Elsewhere,[3] one of the authors has shown how various statistical constants lend themselves to interpretations which should greatly aid the psychologist in convincing the sponsor of research studies of the appropriateness and adequacy of the criterion measures and the value of the resulting selection procedures. Thus, saving effected per selected individual is given by the mean of the criterion scores of the selected group minus the mean of the population of applicants. The coefficient $r_{xy}\sigma_y$ gives the increase in dollar saving per unit increase in standard (z) predictor scores. In this formula r_{xy} is the validity coefficient and σ_y is the standard deviation in dollar terms of the criterion.

The validity coefficient itself gives the ratio of dollars saved by use of the predictors to select a given number of workers to the saving that

[3] H. E. Brogden, "On the Interpretation of the Correlation Coefficient as a Measure of Predictive Efficiency," *Journal of Educational Psychology*, Vol. 37, 1946, pp. 65–76.

would have resulted if selection of the same number of workers could have been made on the criterion itself; that is, it gives the per cent of perfect prediction achieved by use of a given set of selector instruments.

Criterion measures expressed in dollar terms allow determination of the interrelations of the cost of testing, the selection ratio, the standard deviation of the dollar criterion and the validity coefficient. Equations and graphs showing these interrelations have been presented elsewhere.[4] When test administration is expensive, the advantage that is expected from a highly favorable selection ratio is sharply diminished. In general, the role of the selection ratio in saving effected by testing undergoes considerable reevaluation.

Possibly the most important of the several related problems to be considered in this section arises in connection with differential classification. Even though regression weights of members of a test battery for predicting success in several assignments have been adequately established, the relative importance of amount of production, number of errors, etc., in the several assignments must still be considered in deciding upon the disposition of any given applicant.

Even though an applicant's predicted criterion score is equally high in both of two assignments, it does not follow that his placement in either of the jobs will be equally profitable to the company. Obviously a man who could do equally well as a janitor or as a manager would contribute much more to the objectives of the organization in the latter capacity. If the criteria for these two jobs were expressed in dollar units, the monetary benefits of this placement would be accurately estimated. In general, the use of dollar units for the criteria of all jobs provides a common denominator which makes it possible to compare an applicant's potential contribution in each of the several positions for which he might be hired.

When the predicted dollar criterion scores taken as deviations from the mean of the applicant population are added for all selected individuals for a given job, this sum is an expression of the dollar saving realized as a result of the selection process.

The sum of such predicted criterion scores for the selected cases (when expressed as deviations from the mean of applicants) gives the total saving expected from one of the several jobs under consideration. Furthermore, sums obtained in this way for each of several assignments are in comparable units and are directly additive. Thus, a "sum of sums" will indicate the total saving resulting from differential placement into several assignments. If the total saving is divided by total assigned cases, the average saving per selected individual may be obtained. This index of average saving will serve to show advantages of differential placement

---

[4] H. E. Brogden, "When Testing Pays Off," Personnel Psychology, Vol. 2, 1949, pp. 171–83.

and may be used as a basis for determining optimal differential placement procedures.

Discussion

A number of investigators have published procedures for weighting sub-criterion variables into a composite. Horst[5] and Edgerton-Kolbe[6] both proposed weighting to give the most reliable and "most predictable" composite. Such procedures are believed by the authors to be unjustifiable unless the criterion measures involve only a single factor. Neither group nor specific factors can be neglected. Since such procedures provide the first principal axis of the configuration of criterion variables, some aspects of the job will most certainly be neglected or minimized. It might be noted in addition that in those situations where the supposition of a single factor would appear reasonable, weighting to provide the first principal axis would afford too little improvement over an equally weighted composite to justify the labor entailed.

Richardson[7] has proposed a weighting procedure which has since been used in combining the sub-criterion variables so that they contribute equally to the covariance of the overall composite. His procedure provides an interesting contrast to the above maximum reliability procedure. By Richardson's procedure the weights are large if the given criterion variable has low average correlation with the remaining sub-criterion variables; by the maximum reliability procedure, the weights are relatively small under these conditions.

We might stress here that weighting according to effect on overall efficiency as in use of dollar units is quite independent of the degree of correlation between the criterion elements. *If it costs 13 times as much to correct an error in card punching as to punch a card, the weights should be 13 and one regardless of whether the correlation between them is high and positive, negligible or high and negative.* If the correlation between two variables is very high, it may be considered expedient to obtain measures of one only and to employ it as a substitute for or as a predictor of the sum. If this is done, however, the substitute for the sum should be made to have the same dollar unit standard deviation as would the sum.

Toops[8] has proposed combining sub-criterion variables according to

---

[5] Paul Horst, "Obtaining a Composite Measure from a Number of Different Measures of the Same Attribute," *Psychometrika*, Vol. 1, 1936, pp. 53–60.

[6] H. A. Edgerton and L. E. Kolbe, "The Method of Minimum Variation for the Combination of Criteria," *Psychometrika*, Vol. 1, 1936, pp. 183–87.

[7] M. W. Richardson, "The Combination of Measures," in Paul Horst (ed.), *The Prediction of Personal Adjustment* (New York: Social Science Research Council, 1941), pp. 377–431.

[8] H. A. Toops, "The Selection of Graduate Assistants," *Personnel Journal*, Vol. 6, 1928, pp. 457–72.

"guessed beta's" or evaluations by qualified judges of the importance of each sub-criterion variable to overall on-the-job efficiency. His procedure attempts, in part at least, to achieve by pooled judgment the same end that would be achieved by cost accounting criteria—assignment to each element a weight proportionate to the extent of its contribution to overall efficiency. It is difficult, however, in requesting judgments as to importance of a criterion variable to overall efficiency to disentangle the effect of the standard deviation of the sub-criterion variables from the value or importance of a unit of production, an error of some other unit of measurement of a criterion variable. Guessed beta's in addition, are dependent upon the judgment of the person(s) doing the guessing.

These arguments will not be pressed too strongly, they are mentioned to emphasize the point that the obtained judgments are subjective and are not buttressed by analysis demonstrating the nature and importance of the ultimate effect on the organization of the individual production units, errors, etc., which enter into the final composite. When ratings are employed as criteria, it is probable that judgments such as that provided by guessed beta's will offer the most practicable rational basis for criterion combination.

It is suggested, however, that the procedure might be improved by explaining to the persons providing the judgment, how overall efficiency is best defined in terms of the effect on efficiency of operation of the organization, illustrating with a few examples the way in which various sub-criterion variables have their effect. In effect, then, an estimate would be obtained of the outcome of a cost accounting analysis.

Implications of the Cost Accounting Concept for Use of Ratings

Within the limited resources usually available for validation studies, it is doubtful that all phases of production, errors, accidents, etc., can be economically evaluated through direct observation. Limitations as to time of completion and the intangible nature of certain important sub-criterion variables may, together with the above consideration, require frequent use of ratings to evaluate a number of the sub-criterion variables involved.

Application of the cost accounting procedure to ratings presents certain special problems. With current rating procedures, the significance of the mean and standard deviation of the obtained ratings is questionable. It is probably more desirable, however, to include a rating with inaccurate scale units and weighting than to exclude any important criterion variable for lack of more objective evaluation procedure, since to exclude it entirely would be tantamount to estimating its weight as zero.

In many validation studies, ratings may have to be employed in evaluating all aspects of performance on the job. It is believed that the basic rationale of the proposed procedure does have implications, as yet quite untested, for procedures and format of such criterion ratings.

Briefly the reasoning is as follows. Criterion ratings are substitutes for direct observations of effectiveness expressed in dollar units. The adequacy of ratings is, consequently, a function of the accuracy with which they estimate the measures for which they are substitutes. An obvious approach to the problem would be to state explicitly the objectives in the directions to the raters and to have the ratings themselves made in terms of the monetary value of individual differences in the area being measured. The disadvantage of this approach is that it assigns two judgments to the rater: first, he must evaluate the performance of the employee on the behavior under consideration; and secondly, the rater must make a second judgment in assigning a monetary value on that behavior.

What appears to be a more promising technique is that of determining in the tracing out process the continuum on which critical behaviors in a given area occur and to have raters evaluate in terms of these behaviors. If the dollar value of these several steps had also been determined in the tracing out process, these values could then be centrally applied during statistical processing to the ratings. The latter would then put greater stress on recording of observations and less on value judgments on the part of the raters.

In the absence of research data on the effect of such a modification in rating format and procedure on reliability, intercorrelations, and ease of administration, no claim of advantage can be made. It would be desirable, where production records are to be obtained for validation purposes, to collect ratings by both the proposed and some conventional procedure in order that their comparative merits may be determined by showing the accuracy with which they predict the production records.

11. A System Simulator for Measuring Job Proficiency*

Guy G. Bresnard and Leslie J. Briggs

A PERFORMANCE test was developed to evaluate the proficiency of maintenance personnel[1] for the E-4 Fire Control System. This test consists of a

---

* From *Comparison of Performance upon the E-4 Fire Control System Simulator and upon Operational Equipment* (Lackland Air Force Base, Tex.: Air Force Personnel and Training Research Center, April, 1956), Development Report AFPTRC-TN-56-47.

[1] L. J. Briggs, G. G. Bresnard, and E. S. Walker, *An E-4 Fire Control System Performance Test: I. Functional Description* (Lowry Air Force Base, Colo.: Arma-

simulator device which is designed to permit rapid and accurate measurement of proficiency of students in performing a selected group of eight maintenance checks and adjustments. It requires the student to perform the actual series of behaviors required to accomplish these adjustments on operational equipment, but it offers certain conveniences and economies in testing not realized in testing on operational equipment.

First of all, such time-consuming but noncritical activities as unscrewing dust cover fasteners and lifting and carrying of test sets are eliminated. This is accomplished by use of lightweight synthetic components arranged as pull-out drawers in a vertical surface and by use of built-in synthetic test sets.

Second, cost of the simulator was kept low by creating circuitry to represent only those equipment functions essential to performance of the selected checks and adjustments. Thus, the functions of only certain portions of components are synthesized, other portions being represented only pictorially or structurally to provide realistic content.

A third convenient feature, for testing purposes, is that the circuitry in the simulator operates independently for each check and adjustment problem. Therefore, if the student leaves one adjustment out of tolerance, he can, nevertheless, immediately be tested in making the next adjustment with no necessity for interruption by the examiner to bring the simulator back to normal operation.

A fourth important characteristic is ease of maintenance. Since the simulator reproduces only some functions of operational equipment, and since those reproduced are independent of each other, the resulting simplified circuitry is much more free of malfunctions than is the operational equipment. In addition, the device operates from any standard 115-volt power supply, so that obtaining and maintaining of special power supplies required by operational equipment are eliminated.

A fifth feature of the test is safety for the student and avoidance of damage to equipment. The relatively unskilled students to be tested in early phases of training often damage test equipment and fire control components through carelessness and lack of knowledge. Although they must learn during training to observe safety precautions to protect themselves and the equipment, it appears desirable to test their maintenance performance under conditions free from such dangers or anxieties about them. The simulator contains no high voltages to endanger the unwary student, and the use of pull-out, lightweight synthetic components minimizes damage to the simulator because components and

ment Systems Personnel Research Laboratory, Air Force Personnel and Training Research Center, March, 1955), Technical Memorandum ASPRL-TM-55-8; E. S. Walker, *An E-4 Fire Control System Performance Test: II. Circuit Design* (unclassified title) (Lowry Air Force Base, Colo.: Armament Systems Personnel Research Laboratory, Air Force Personnel and Training Research Center, March, 1955), Technical Memorandum ASPRL-TM-55-9 (Contents CONFIDENTIAL).

test sets are not carried about and damaged by dropping as sometimes happens in testing with operational equipment. Also, adjusting a wrong potentiometer in the simulator will •not damage circuit components.

The E-4 simulator in its present form is shown in Figure 1. The device is 76" high, 26" wide, 98" long, and varies in depth along the sloping front surface. The front panel is painted gray, while the remaining structure is black. Each picture of a component is covered with 1/16" plexiglass and outlined in black.

Figure 1 shows that components are arranged roughly in three rows. In the bottom row are located all the standard test components required

FIGURE 1

THE E-4 FIRE CONTROL SYSTEM SIMULATOR

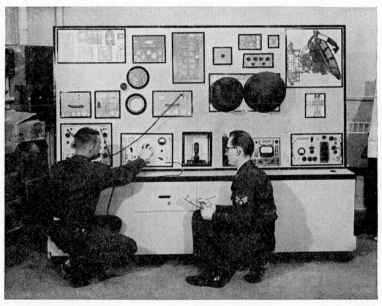

for the eight check and adjustment procedures and also the radar hand control (near the middle of the row). Just to the right of the hand control have been recessed the only two real (unsimulated) test sets used in the simulator. The other three items of test equipment consist of life-size pictures of standard test sets through which have been inserted real knobs and other controls. These are made realistic in operation by appropriate circuitry in the interior of the device. Knobs on the test equipment which are not used in proper performance of the eight test problems are made real and movable to afford normal opportunity to make errors in use of the test equipment. Such knobs have no circuitry behind them because they would not have an observable effect in the operational equipment. The irrelevant manipulation of them, however, may be recorded in the test situation.

In the top two rows of components (Figure 1) are located the simulated E-4 components. Those having handles or knobs are three-dimensional re-creations which can be pulled out like a drawer. For example, the component on the extreme left in the middle row has a handle and two jacks on the exterior for taking voltage readings. If interior adjustments are necessary, the student simply grasps the handle and pulls the drawer-like component out part way to gain access to the two potentiometers; he then performs screw-driver adjustments until the voltage reading on the voltmeter is correct.

The two large hats in Figure 1 cover three-dimensional simulations of equipment. These are like the hats on operational equipment, and are removed by the student in performing tests involving these components.

The rack shown at the left of the simulator in Figure 1 was built to hold the test leads and power cords required for the eight performance items. Use of the rack presents available leads and cords in a standard way and saves time by preventing tangling of cords.

Thus, in general, there is brought together in a convenient array and in a standard manner all the equipment needed to perform the test items on the simulator.[2]

Although intended primarily as a testing device, it is apparent that the simulator could be employed to give additional practice of maintenance procedures in the classroom. As a training device, it would be even more convenient were the eight circuits associated with the eight performance items separated physically into separate small trainers. This would entail only moderate increase in cost because of need for more power supplies and voltmeters.

Purpose

The physical characteristics of the simulator as discussed are immediately apparent upon examination of the device itself. However, two important measurement issues remain for examination. The purpose of this report is to consider these issues and to present data regarding the representativeness or relevance of the behaviors measured and regarding the efficiency of measurement by the device.

RELEVANCE OF BEHAVIORS MEASURED

Since the purpose of the test is to measure the proficiency with which students perform certain job-like maintenance activities, rather than to measure their knowledge about maintenance, it is necessary to demonstrate that the behaviors elicited and scored on the test device are essentially like behaviors required in maintenance of operational equip-

---

[2] The schematic drawings, showing how the simulated relationships among components and parts are accomplished to parallel relationships in E-4 equipment are presented in Walker, *op. cit.* (Contents are CONFIDENTIAL. Access to this report is limited to government agencies and their qualified contractors on a basis of a need for this information.), along with further details of the significance of each check and adjustment in E-4 operation.

ment. If, then, important behaviors required on operational equipment are listed in detail, and if these are shown to occur also on the simulator, the behavior elicited on the simulator may be considered relevant to the test purpose. In addition, the number and kind of errors made on the simulator should be similar to those observed in a test situation with operational equipment. This study was designed to obtain a comparison of behavior on the simulator with behavior on operational equipment.

EFFICIENCY OF MEASUREMENT

A second characteristic required of a performance test is efficiency in measurement. In the present context, this means that the test problems employed must yield performance data which adequately represent the larger set of job-like activities, of which test problems are a part. To obtain adequate sampling of the whole set of job-like activities, the number of test problems must be as large as possible in the test time available. Observations of behavior in each test problem situation must be detailed enough to permit a reasonable range of individual differences in proficiency. But testing students on operational equipment is a time-consuming process, at best. Often it is impossible to give more than one performance problem to each student in the time available. The convenient arrangement of equipment components on the simulator should permit faster performance of each test problem. Thus, in a given testing period, more problems and better measurement should be possible. This is the second point on which data will be presented.

Procedure

SUBJECTS

The subjects for the study were Air Force students who had just completed the phase of fire control maintenance training which involves instruction in the checks and adjustments built into the simulator. Several successive classes of such students were tested over a period of several weeks. The various classes were taught by a number of different instructors regularly assigned to teach this phase of the course. Subjects from these intact classes were assigned to two testing groups by use of a table of random numbers. One group was tested on the simulator, and the other on operational equipment (as it is set up on a maintenance test bench). There were 40 subjects in each of the two groups. A check showed that the mean Electronics Technician Aptitude Index scores, derived from tests in the Airman Classification Battery and keyed items from the Biographical Inventory, were equal for the two groups.

SELECTION OF PERFORMANCE ITEMS

The eight performance items presented by the simulator are described in detail elsewhere.[3] It was necessary, for the purposes of this study, to

---
[3] E. S. Walker, *ibid*.

administer only a few items, due to the limited time students could be spared from their normal classrooms for experimental testing. The detailed characteristics of the eight performance items were examined, and three items were selected as representative of the type of activities required in all. The problems chosen were:

1. The radar low-voltage power supply adjustments, involving a series of simple adjustments and use of a voltmeter.
2. The repetition rate adjustment, involving use of an oscilloscope and an audio oscillator.
3. The transmitter power and frequency check, involving use of a special radar test set.

Since the three problems chosen vary considerably in nature, in complexity, and in number of specific behaviors involved, it was thought that they should yield a considerable range in performance time and in proficiency of performance. This choice of problems was made to guard against an artificial restriction in error in results for the two groups.

TEST PROCEDURES

Each subject was tested in a special test room containing both the simulator and the operational equipment. Two independent test records were made of each subject's performance; one was made by the "examiner" and one by the "recorder." After a subject entered the room, he was informed that he was to be given three experimental performance test items, either on the simulator or on the operational equipment, as predetermined by the use of the table of random numbers. He then listened to a 2-minute tape-recorded set of directions. The two recordings, one for each equipment, represented all the assistance or orientation given to subjects. After hearing the directions, the subject was given the three test items. Although two independent observers made records of each subject's performance, the record of the examiner was used for data presented herein. (The second record was used only for a separate study of inter-observer agreement. The amount of agreement was found to be high for the two experienced examiners who gathered data for this study.)

USE OF CHECK LISTS

In advance of this study, check lists were carefully prepared and edited by a procedure described in another report.[4] Briefly, these check lists were first developed for recording performance on each separate step in each check or adjustment procedure, as it is performed on operational equipment. These check lists were then checked against performance on the simulator, to make certain that no important step

---

[4] L. J. Briggs, G. G. Bresnard, and E. S. Walker, *op. cit.*

was left unprovided for in the construction of the device. It was ascertained that, with the exception of connecting power plugs to outlets, removing of dust covers, and carrying of equipment, the simulator provides opportunity to perform every operation required in all problems. (This fact, in itself, suggests the high degree of representativeness of the simulator, as does a visual comparison of synthetic and operational components and test sets.) The prepared check lists are, therefore, appropriate for use in recording performance of students on both operational equipment and upon the simulator.

SCORING PERFORMANCE

It was desired that every student complete all performance problems so that their performances could be compared. Consequently, an "error-correction" procedure was followed during testing. The student was allowed to proceed with each problem until he made an error. The error was called to his attention and recorded on the check list. He was shown how to correct his error, and then was asked to go right on. Actually, the examiner recorded errors in terms of their nature, such as an omitted step, an irrelevant behavior, a step performed incorrectly, or the student being "stuck" and having to be told the next step. Specific rules were followed as to the exact circumstances which define each kind of error. However, these circumstances will not be defined here, since data are presented only in terms of total errors for each problem and performance time required. Although the "error-correction" procedure results in time and error scores which could not be expected to be entirely independent of each other and of the procedure itself, it yields more specific information about a performance than would a simple notation of "pass" or "fail" for the problem. More important for the present purpose is the fact that exactly the same procedure was followed in testing the two groups of students.

Results and Discussion

Table 1 presents the mean number of errors made by each group on the three problems. It may be seen that the simulator group made

TABLE 1

MEAN ERROR SCORES FOR THE TWO GROUPS ON THE
THREE TEST PROBLEMS

(N = 40 for Each Group)

PROBLEM	OPERATIONAL EQUIPMENT GROUP	SIMULATOR GROUP
1.	5.08	5.58
2.	9.08	9.45
3.	5.48	4.03
Total errors	19.63	19.05

slightly more errors than the operational equipment group on the first two problems, but fewer errors on the third. The size of the difference on the third problem was large enough to yield a total error score which is slightly smaller for the simulator group. The difference between groups in total errors, however, is not statistically significant. The conclusion, therefore, is that no difference has been demonstrated in number of errors made in the two test situations. Some caution is indicated, however, by the finding that there were differences between the groups in the number of errors made to particular problems. However, these differences are not large.

Table 2 presents data on the time required to perform each problem by the two groups. Unlike the data for error scores, the means for the three

TABLE 2

MEAN TIME FOR PERFORMANCE OF THE THREE TEST PROBLEMS BY
THE TWO GROUPS
($N = 40$ for Each Group)

PROBLEM	OPERATIONAL EQUIPMENT GROUP	SIMULATOR GROUP
1	7.00	5.43
2	15.51	13.13
3	14.42	7.85
Total time	36.94	26.41

problems are consistent in direction but vary considerably in amount of difference between the two groups. Thus, while total performance time is significantly less for the simulator group, the amount of time saved on the simulator varies in amount, but not in direction, among the different problems.

One might ask whether the actual errors made occur on the same or on different single behaviors within each problem. To check this, the individual performance record sheets were again referred to, and the number of subjects in each group who made errors on each single behavior item within each problem was determined. Then the significance of the differences between groups in proportions missing each item was computed.

This analysis showed that the difference between groups in proportion of subjects missing individual items is significant (.10 level of confidence) in the case of only one item out of the total 25 on Problem 1. The corresponding figure for Problem 2 is two items. However, the results for Problem 3 are considerably different—8 out of 21 items are significant, again suggesting that Problem 3 is unlike the other two in how it is performed on the two equipments. In an attempt to explain this, the nature of the activity involved in these 8 items for Problem 3 was examined. These eight items were equally divided between those in which the direction of the difference favored the operational equipment group and those in which the difference favored the simulator group. This is an indirect suggestion that items on which significant differences occurred may have been due to differences in cues offered by the two equipments. An item-by-item inspection of the direction of the significant difference led to some interesting observations; and one rather curious one.

One item, missed more often by the operational equipment group, requires a student to turn the radar set on after some preliminary procedures. When this is done on operational equipment, loud blower noise begins. On the simulator, there is no auditory result of this switch setting. This lack of noise had been mentioned to the simulator group in their recorded instructions. This apparently led them to be more careful to perform this step when the proper time arrived. Four other items did not involve any such difference in noise or any other kind of indication, either before or after the step was performed. Performance of these steps seems to depend on carefulness and memory as to when they should be accomplished in the total problem sequence. In three of the four cases, the simulator group made the lesser number of errors, suggesting that possibly an extra effort was made to recall required steps in the proper order, perhaps in the mistaken belief that operational equipment gives a cue which the simulator does not. Finally, in the case of the remaining three items, the simulator group made more errors than the operational equipment group. Curiously enough, these three items required that dials be set very accurately; the error made then is not forgetting to do the act, but not doing it accurately enough. It may be supposed that the subjects thought, again falsely, that the simulator would respond in a *less real manner* to inaccurate settings than would normal equipment. The explanation for the differences between groups on these eight items for Problem 3, therefore, seems to reflect in only one case that something realistic (i.e., noise) was left out of the simulated situation, while in the other seven cases, the differences may reflect a set of beliefs or assumptions on the part of the subject about the nature of the simulator which are false. It is suggested, therefore, that more emphasis should be placed, in the directions to the student, upon the fact that the simulator *really* acts exactly like the operational equipment *except for making noise*.

Summary

Two groups of subjects, chosen by a table of random numbers, were given a performance test consisting of three check and adjustment procedures which are standard tasks in maintenance of the E-4 Fire Control System. All subjects had just completed normal training in the appropriate phase of the course. One group of subjects was tested on operational fire control equipment; the other group was tested on the E-4 procedural simulator.

In terms of total performance errors made, no difference was found between the two groups, suggesting that scores earned on the simulator are like those earned on operational equipment. This finding is based upon three problems which were considered quite unlike in some respects, but which, on the other hand, together may be representative of other groups of problems performable on the simulator. Since the direction and amount of error differences varied somewhat from problem to problem, however, allowance must be made for the possibility that error differences could be found with other samples of problems. For the present sample of problems, the conclusion is that there is a high degree of correspondence between proficiency measured on the two equipments.

In terms of time to perform, the simulator group required significantly less time than the operational equipment group. The amount of time saved, however, varied from problem to problem. On the average, the indication is that about one-third more problems could be given on the simulator than upon operational equipment in a given amount of testing time.

An examination of those individual behaviors, within one of the three problems, upon which there were significant group differences in number of subjects making errors, resulted in a suggestion for improving instructions to students performing on the simulator. This improvement, it is expected, would counteract any tendency on the part of subjects erroneously to attribute to the simulator features of operation different from those of operational equipment.

In general, it may be said that the E-4 Fire Control System Simulator, when used as a performance testing device, has the following desirable characteristics:

1. A 2-minute orientation is enough to enable students to begin performing maintenance tasks upon it. This, in itself, reflects the high degree of similarity between the simulator and the operational equipment.
2. The errors made on the simulator are closely similar in number and kind to those made on operational equipment. This suggests that the simulator proficiency measurements are representative of those obtained on operational equipment. The relevance of the simulator for the testing purpose it was intended to serve is thus supported.
3. An appreciable amount of time is saved in testing on the simulator, over that required to perform the same test problems on operational equipment. Practically, this means that reliability and representativeness of measurement can be increased through testing on more problems during a given amount of testing time.

4. The possibility of increasing the similarity between simulator and operational equipment performance is suggested by clearer instructions to the student regarding the fidelity with which the simulator represents normal equipment functions.

5. Some of the mentioned characteristics of the simulator are relevant to an evaluation of the simulator as a training device. However, these would only suggest its training value when used for intensive practice of procedures. Experimental data on the training values of the device are not now available.

12. Developing an Employee Merit Rating Procedure*

Reign Bittner

I SHOULD LIKE to consider for a moment this question: "Shall we or shall we not rate the people who work for us?" This is a question that perennially crops up to plague us. Almost every management publication we pick up has something to say on this question. And busy executives often spend valuable time discussing the pros and cons of it.

The fact of the matter is that there is only one answer to the question. Most certainly we *are* going to rate our people; we have no choice between rating and not rating. As long as two people are thrown together, each will make judgments about the other. Even if our population were reduced to the proverbial "last man on earth," he would form judgments about various aspects of his environment. And forming judgments about people or things is all that we mean by rating.

We do have a choice to make, however, as to _how_ we make our ratings. We can decide to indulge in making capricious judgments about people, with each rater giving full rein to his own standards and biases. Or we can choose to rate people according to an organized and systematic procedure which attempts to set up common standards of judgment which all raters can apply uniformly and without bias. Obviously, the latter choice is the wiser one. Having made this choice, then, it becomes necessary to accept some form of merit rating procedure, for _it_ is the tool that enables judgments to be formed systematically and on common bases.

* From *Personnel Psychology*, Vol. 1, 1948, pp. 403–32.

WHY MAKE MERIT RATINGS?

Let us assume that an adequate merit rating procedure will provide accurate and comparable measures of the effectiveness of our workers. But why should we be concerned about obtaining such measures, especially when they are accumulated at the expense of considerable time, effort, and money?

It is just good business to take periodic inventory of our people. We are most careful to keep close tabs on money, raw materials, machinery, and buildings employed in our enterprise. We know where we stand on these through periodic audits and inventories, but what about our people? No one would say that the people are unimportant; they furnish the know-how and skill that make it possible to carry on a business. No one would say that they are unimportant cost-wise; we often spend as much or more on people than we do on any one of the other items it takes to make an enterprise function. So it is just good business to take a periodic inventory of our peoples' weaknesses and strengths in order that we can make better use of them to our profit and theirs. We need answers to questions like these:

1. How are they doing on their jobs? Do they measure up to the standards we need to produce a high-quality product at a competitive price?
2. What are their weaknesses so we can help them improve?
3. What are their strengths so we can make full use of these?
4. Apart from just doing their job, do they fit in generally with our way of doing things?
5. Are they getting ahead as fast and as far as their ability will take them?

Answers to questions like these are needed if we are to handle our people wisely. A periodic inventory of our employees through merit ratings is a systematic way of getting these answers.

Problems in Developing a Merit Rating Procedure

PRELIMINARY PLANNING

Effective merit rating procedures cannot be purchased from a catalog; nor can they be "lifted" or borrowed from another friendly company. If *your* rating procedure is to be effective, it should be tailor-made to fit the problems in *your* organization. There is much more, too, in developing your merit rating procedure than selecting the merit rating form you wish to use. Too often we are so concerned about the particular form to use that we do not give these other problems the consideration they deserve. Actually, these problems should be faced before we worry about the rating form. So let us put them in their proper perspective by examining them before we think about the rating form itself.

What Are the Aims and Purposes? The first step in developing a merit rating procedure is to formulate its aims and purposes. Just what you seek to accomplish by means of merit ratings should be thought through carefully, for this will determine in great measure the form your procedure will take. The rating procedure is only a tool to help you achieve certain objectives, and the tool must be designed to do a specific job. This is such an obvious point that it is amazing how often it is overlooked. Frequently a merit rating system has been adopted because it looked good in some other company, but it may have been designed to accomplish an entirely different purpose from that desired by the borrowing concern.

I shall not attempt to specify what the purposes *should* be. These are a matter of individual concern for each company. It may be of interest, however, to note what *are* the purposes commonly found for industrial merit rating plans. A survey of 94 companies made by the Conference Board revealed the following list of purposes:

1. To help in deciding who should be promoted, demoted, or given a raise in pay.
2. To discover workers' weaknesses as a basis for planning training.
3. To uncover exceptional talents.
4. To furnish a basis for discharge of totally unfit employees.
5. To help top supervisors learn how each person is appraised by his foreman.
6. To help top supervisors judge the fairness, severity, or leniency with which supervisors judge their people.
7. To help in assigning work in accordance with workers' ability.
8. To serve as a check on employment procedures generally and interviews and tests specifically.
9. To stimulate people to improve.
10. To develop people's morale through stimulating confidence in management's fairness.

This is an impressive list of purposes, and it is doubtful if any one merit rating plan could accomplish them all well. In fact, in formulating the aims and purposes of your individual plan it is well to limit them to as few as possible.

Will People Be Told How They Rated? A merit rating program, in my opinion, is not complete without provision for reporting back to the ratee his supervisor's evaluation of him. My belief in the necessity for this is derived from two facts: (1) Workers want to know how they stand with the boss; and (2) many of the possible benefits of the merit rating program cannot be achieved without it.

People want to know how their work is regarded by those who exercise authority over their future status in the organization. The Conference Board recently asked workers in a number of companies to rank in importance 73 different factors that were presumed to be involved in worker morale. The white-collar workers chose as *fifth* in importance "the practice of informing you of your job status, including both successes and failures," and *eighth* in importance was "employee merit and performance rating." Only "job security," "type of work," "compensation," and "opportunities for advancement" ranked higher than the practice of informing you where you stand on the job. It should be noted, too, that informing people of their job status has a direct bearing on their feelings of security. <u>Feelings of insecurity are aggravated by lack of information about one's status.</u>

Reporting merit rating results back to the person rated makes possible certain outcomes of the rating program that are not achieved otherwise. Let's look at some of the major ones:

1. Job performance can be improved by letting the worker know his weaknesses and strengths and making definite plans with him to overcome his defects and to make capital of his strengths.
2. Grievances can be prevented by letting the worker understand the basis for actions which may be taken in the future and by clearing up misunderstandings about past actions that have affected him.
3. The supervisor and the worker can be brought into a closer personal relationship wherein each has a better understanding of the other, and the worker is made to feel that he is a person and not just a clock number.
4. Pent-up emotions which may be reflected in acts of aggression toward management may be relieved by providing opportunity for rebuttal and talking out the situation.

The report back to the ratee is best accomplished through an <u>interview</u>. The rater should sit down with the person he has rated and in an informal conversation explain how the person rates and why he has been rated that way. He should listen with sympathy to the person's side of the story. Throughout, his attitude should be one of helpfulness, and the interview should bring out definite suggestions and plans for the person's future development.

It must be recognized that if you decide to include a post-rating interview in your program—and I don't see how you can pass this up—it will have considerable effect on your plans. (The design of the merit rating form itself will very likely be affected.) The matter of time which the rater will be asked to devote to the program becomes of more concern, for good interviews take time. The choice of raters may be affected. The training program will certainly be affected. So it is an important point to consider early in the development of a merit rating program. Failure to build your program in the light of the demands of the post-rating interview may result in its emasculation.

Who Should Rate? A question that needs to be answered in formulating a rating system is "Who should rate?" There are three possibilities to choose from. Persons can be rated by: ① their superiors; ② their peers, i.e., others of equal rank; ③ their subordinates.

It is almost universal practice for ratings to be made by superiors. There is some experimental evidence that people actually prefer to be rated by superiors. Army officers, at least, felt this way. When 1,800 of them were asked whether they would prefer to be rated by men of equal rank, 78 per cent said "No." When asked if they would prefer to be rated by men of lower rank, 77 per cent said "No." Thus the practice of having ratings made by superiors has support on the basis that it is common practice and that what experimental evidence we have indicates people prefer it that way.

It is _uncommon_ for ratings to be made by peers or subordinates. Despite this, it is highly probable that ratings made by a person's peers or subordinates will more accurately reflect his real competence than will a rating made by his superior. There are at least three reasons for this. In the first place, a man's peers and subordinates are usually in closer contact with what he does hour-by-hour and day-by-day than is his superior. In the second place, a man naturally tries to present only his best side to his superior, but his peers and subordinates see him as he is. Finally, using peers and subordinates as raters makes it possible to get a number of judgments, the average of which will be a more reliable measure than a single measure alone. It is well, then, to consider this possibility in deciding who should make the ratings, particularly in the case of rating supervisors.

The general rule in deciding who should rate is that the rater should be the person or persons in closest contact with the ratee's work. In setting up the rating program, it is well that the best-qualified raters from this point of view be selected and *definitely named* as the raters for certain individuals. If this is not done, it will be found that some supervisors will insist on rating all those under them even though subordinate supervisors are much more capable of rating employees down the line.

Allied with the question of who should rate is that of whether more than one person should rate an individual. Much has been published in the literature on ratings about the increase in reliability of ratings when ratings made by several raters are averaged. On this assumption, rating systems have been set up requiring that each person be rated by several raters. However, one highly important thing has sometimes been forgotten. The reliability of ratings will be increased by averaging the ratings made by several raters *only if the raters are equally competent to make the ratings.* Averaging a rating made by a rater unfamiliar with the ratee's work with a rating made by a rater who really knows the person's work merely lessens the validity of the one good one. The old adage that "Two heads are better than one" holds good only when both heads have something in them. In summary, the principle to apply here is to get as many ratings on each person as you have raters who are familiar with the person's work.

A final point on who should rate is the question of whether ratings should be reviewed or endorsed by the supervisor next up the line. Again the answer depends on whether the reviewer or endorser is familiar enough with the person's work to make him a competent judge.

I know of only one experiment where the effect of endorsements on the validity of ratings was studied. This was a study of the ratings of Army officers, where it is the practice for ratings to be reviewed and endorsed by the officer at the next higher level of command. It was found that, on the average, endorsements produced increases in the validity of the ratings. This gain was greatest when the endorsers had intimate knowledge of the ratee's performance, and there was actually a loss in validity when endorsers were far removed organizationally from the ratee.

How Often to Rate?   The question of whether to rate annually, semi-annually, quarterly or at other intervals must be decided. This is largely a question of practicability, though the frequency of ratings may have an indirect effect upon the validity of the ratings. If ratings are required too frequently, raters have a tendency to feel that they are being unduly burdened by this extra work. As a result, they may tend to race through them in a slipshod manner, thus reducing their validity.

Periodic ratings made at intervals of six months are, in my opinion, generally frequent enough. Ratings made annually may be frequent enough for supervisors and other long-service employees. It might be noted here that 74 per cent of Army officers preferred semi-annual to annual ratings.

Special ratings should also be made at critical times during the employee's service:

1. *New Employee or Old Employee on New Job.* A special rating, say at the end of three months, should be made for a new employee or an old employee who is on a new job. If you have a union shop or office, this special rating for the new employee should be just before the end of the probationary period.
2. *Termination.* A special rating should be made at the time an employee is terminated. This rating should include a statement whether the supervisor would or would not rehire the employee.
3. *Transfer.* A special rating should be made at the time of transfer by the person's old supervisor.

Will Raters Have Time to Carry Out the Program?   One consideration in setting up a merit rating program that is often overlooked is that of the demands the system makes on the rater's time. It is all well and good for us who are in the personnel business to say that nothing is more important than taking this periodic inventory of our personnel assets and liabilities and that surely no one should begrudge the time spent on it. The fact remains, though, that merit rating is in competition with many other things for the rater's time, and the accomplishment of these other things has a more direct bearing in the rater's mind on his bread and butter. This presents a dilemma, because an adequate merit rating plan requires the rater to devote considerable time to it if the results are to be worth while. In my experience, many raters are either unwilling to give the required time or just don't have the time to give. This is more true, I think, of factory supervisors than of office supervisors or the higher levels of supervisory personnel.

Several ways in which this problem can be attacked may be mentioned:

1. Have top management take an active interest in the merit rating program and give it unqualified support. This will go a long way toward insuring that merit ratings are not unduly handicapped in the competition for the rater's time.
2. Include in the merit rating plan a systematic way of freeing the rater from his other duties for sufficient time in which to make out his ratings.
3. Stagger the distribution of the merit rating forms so that the rater completes a few each week until he is finished.

Personally, I feel that the first two ways are preferable. The last method —staggering the distribution of rating forms—has the disadvantage of spreading the ratings over a considerable period of time, which may become irksome to the rater. Also, it does not allow the ratings to be consistent with respect to the period covered. Finally, it may lead to less reliable and valid discriminations among the individuals in the group rated because of changes in the rater's standards and the occurrence of incidents which will take on too much importance in determining his rating for certain individuals.

DEVELOPING THE RATING FORM

The development of the rating form is fraught with many problems, some of which are highly technical. There are many pitfalls to trap the unwary. Let's take a look at some of these.

What Traits to Measure? It is the usual practice to start off by deciding what traits or worker characteristics we desire to measure. The number of traits—dependability, intelligence, initiative, etc.—included in rating forms varies widely. A survey of rating forms in 18 companies not long ago showed that a total of 35 supposedly different traits were being used. The greatest number on any one form was 19, the smallest number was four, and the average was 10. What is the maximum or minimum number of traits that should be included? This cannot be decided arbitrarily. I am willing to say, however, that the company which had 19 traits was kidding itself if it thought it was getting meaningful ratings on each of these separate traits.

A thoroughgoing analysis of the jobs to be covered by the rating procedure should be the basis for developing a preliminary list of traits. We must know what is required of a person in doing a job before we can measure whether he meets these requirements. Since it is impracticable to develop a separate rating scale for each job, we want to pick out for our general scale the important requirements that are common to many jobs. Thus analysis and comparison of the jobs will set the stage for the selection of traits.

The traits to be included finally should be selected on the basis of the following criteria:

1. *Observability.* Can the rater actually observe this trait in action? Is the worker's possession of this trait clearly evident to the rater in what the worker does? These are the questions to be answered in considering whether a trait is observable.

2. *Universality.* Is the trait under consideration an important characteristic in successful performance of all the jobs to be rated? Obviously, it should be if the rating procedure is to be generally applicable. It is unlikely, too, that the trait could even be observed when the job does not call it into play.

3. *Distinguishability.* Is the trait under question clearly distinguishable as meaning something different from another trait with a different name? Do they overlap so much in meaning that ratings on the two would be nothing more than two ratings on the same basic characteristic?

Selecting traits that meet these criteria is not an easy task. It always requires an experimental study to give us the correct answer. Let me illustrate by citing a few examples of such studies:

1. In a study of a 12-trait rating scale applied to over 1,100 men in industry, a factor analysis showed that only two traits were really being measured. These were called "ability to do present job" and "quality of performance on the job." This result was due to the great overlapping or inability of the raters to distinguish between the traits.

2. In a study of a 10-trait rating scale applied to 2,000 Army officers, factor analysis revealed that only three traits were being measured—namely, "sense of duty," "physical and mental endurance and ability," and "leadership." It was also found that "ability to obtain results" correlated .90 with the total score on the 10 traits, and four of the 10 traits predicted the total score almost perfectly with a correlation of .97.

3. In another study of a 13-trait rating scale applied to Army Air Force officers, factor analysis showed that only four traits were being measured —namely, "sense of duty," "physical and mental stability and endurance," "leadership," and "judgment and common sense."

4. In developing a new Army rating scale, 900 behavior items—statements like "can't take suggestions," "resents criticism"—were rated by a group of officers on observability and universality, and it was necessary to throw out 600 of them as being not observable, not universally applicable, or both.

The import of these and similar studies is that only a few traits will be included in the rating scale if the three criteria—observability, universality, and distinguishability—are observed in selecting them. Add more if you like, but you end up with essentially the same result (and often misleading results) at the cost of considerably more effort. A few companies have recognized this and applied it in their rating procedure. At least one company I know rates on only two traits—"ability to do present job" and "promotability."

What Type of Rating Form? The type of rating form or chart is another question that must be decided. There are three basic types from which to choose:

1. General trait scale; where general traits like "dependability" are defined and the rater is asked to mark on a scale the degree to which the person possesses this trait.
2. Behavior check list; where a number of statements of specific activities involved in doing the job are given and the rater is asked to check simply whether the person does them, or he may be asked to estimate how well the person does them.
3. Ranking; where the rater is asked to list his people in rank order from "best" down to "poorest" on over-all ability or some other defined characteristic.

Personally, I am not willing to recommend any one type. I do not feel that any one of them is sufficiently better than the others to warrant its being adopted universally. There is one thing, though, that I should like to make clear. The choice of the type of form should be dictated to a large extent by the purpose of your rating procedure. If the major purpose of your procedure is to have a form that will serve as a basis for a constructive interview with the worker, then I recommend the Behavior Check List type. This type gives the rater something concrete to talk about in the interview rather than abstract things like "initiative" and "dependability." If the major purpose is to obtain a measure of over-all job performance for administrative use, then one of the other types *may be* preferable.

Should Traits Be Weighted? Another problem in connection with developing the rating form is that of whether the traits should be given different weights in computing the total score. There is so much misinformation kicking around on the weighting of traits that I should like to try to clear some of it up.

Let us assume that we have four traits each rated on a scale of 1 to 10, and we decide that Trait A should have the least weight, Trait B should have twice the weight of A, Trait C should have three times the weight of A, and Trait D, which is the most important, should have five times the weight of A. Now we are glibly told by many writers on merit rating that all you have to do to have your traits weighted in this way is to multiply A by 1, B by 2, C by 3, and D by 5. But this just isn't so.

Let us assume, on the other hand, that you decide to let your four traits have equal weight in the total score. Then we are often told that all you do is to see that the scale for each trait has the same maximum value —say, ranging from 1 to 10—and then they each have the same weight in the total score. But this isn't so, either.

The facts are that the true weight of a trait is a function of the variability of the ratings on that trait. By variability is meant the extent to which the ratings in a group of people scatter over the trait scale—in technical parlance, the standard deviation. This is a mathematical problem in statistics, and the reason many people do not understand this is that they have not been statistically trained.

For the hypothetical case, let's assume for simplicity that you have only two traits, A and B, each with a scale ranging from 1 to 10. You decide to weight trait A 10 times trait B, so you multiply all ratings on trait A by 10 and add these values to the rating on trait B. Now in the most extreme case, let's assume that in your group of ratees every man was given a rating on trait A of 5, or "average"; the ratings do not scatter over the whole scale from 1 to 10. You now multiply each man's trait A rating by 10, the weight you decided to give trait A, and each man gets 50. Then you add this to his trait B rating to arrive at his total score. It is not too difficult to see now that adding a constant 50 to every man's trait B score does not have an effect at all on his standing in relation to other men in the group. The man's standing in the group is determined completely by his standing in relation to the other men on trait B. Thus trait A has a weight of zero as far as its effect on relative standing of the men in the group on the basis of their total scores is concerned. And it is the effectiveness of a trait in determining a man's standing relative to other men in the group that is the true weight of the trait. Since the variability or standard deviation of the scores on trait A was zero, its weight was also zero. As the standard deviation becomes larger, its weight also increases.

An actual case of the effectiveness of weighting is reported by Tiffin. A 12-trait scale where all traits were presumably weighted equally was applied to several thousand workers. Analysis of the true weights showed that "health" got 22 per cent more weight in the total score than did "productivity" and 19 per cent more weight than "over-all job performance."

A study of a 13-trait scale applied to 3,000 Army Air Force officers where the various traits were given different weights attacked the matter from another point of view. The question to be answered here was: "Does it make any difference what arbitrary weights the individual traits are given as far as their effect on determining a man's standing in the total group is concerned?" Various combinations of arbitrary weights were applied to the traits, and the total scores computed for the men. These scores were then compared by means of correlation statistics, and it was found that regardless of the arbitrary weights applied to the individual traits a man's relative standing in the group was still essentially the same. (The correlations were as high as .99.) It was concluded that arbitrary weighting in this case was useless and thus not worth the extra computational labor involved. In addition, it was grossly misleading, for it led people to believe that the traits had weights which they manifestly did not have.

What is the meaning of all this? Let me summarize some points to keep in mind about weighting of traits:

1. The real weight of a trait is not the same as the numerical factor you multiply the trait by in computing a total rating score.
2. The real weight of a trait depends upon its variability or standard deviation.

3. To determine the real weight of a trait, you must apply the scale to a group of men and then analyze the variability of the ratings on each individual trait.
4. Only after the real weights have been established by analyzing the ratings made, can you determine the multiplying factors which will make the traits have weights which have been determined as desirable.
5. Making the real weights conform to a desired pattern must be done by a central agency after analyzing the ratings turned in, and this is a process requiring a technician trained in statistics.
6. Any system of weights determined arbitrarily in advance of an analysis of the ratings turned in will not be the same as the true weights and will be misleading.

Before leaving the weighting problem, I should like to point out that everything I have said applies equally to the weighting of factors in job evaluation systems. Here again the arbitrary weights assigned the various factors are not necessarily the true weights of the factors. Here again the true weights must be established by statistical analysis of the variance of the ratings on the different factors. There are other applications, too, of these statistical concepts of weighting in industry. For example, in establishing bonus standards it may be desired to combine a measure of quantity of production with one of quality, weighting each in accordance with some arbitrary system. Again, the variability of the quality and quantity measures must be studied in order to establish the true weights.

TRAINING RATERS

A merit rating program must include specific plans and procedures for training the raters. In my opinion, lack of training of raters is the most usual source of weakness in rating programs. I am not nearly so concerned about the type of rating form to use as I am about the training of raters in use of the form adopted. The feeling is all too prevalent that the way to obtain better ratings is to get a better rating form. It is not surprising that this feeling is common, for if a tool doesn't work it is natural to look for a deficiency in the tool rather than for a fault in the user of the tool. Nevertheless, I believe that if all raters were properly trained, almost any rating form would give reasonably good results, providing it was chosen in the first place to conform to the objectives of the rating program.

That more and better training of raters is needed is not solely my opinion. An opinion study of some 1,800 Army officers on rating showed that 84 per cent of them favored more and better training as a means of improving ratings. In my own company, Owens-Illinois Glass, 95 per cent of the personnel directors said that better training of raters would greatly improve ratings. Yet these same personnel directors indicated that little rater training is going on in their plants, as is shown by the following data:

1. Only 16 per cent have a rater training conference before each rating period.

2. Fifty-one per cent say a personnel department representative *never* sits down with the rater to help him make out his ratings; 27 per cent say this happens *infrequently;* 17 per cent say this happens *sometimes;* and only 5 per cent say this happens *frequently.*

Apparently our raters are getting neither group nor individual training in sufficient amounts. Perhaps Owens-Illinois is unique in this respect but I doubt it. It is interesting to note that there is considerable clamor in our company for a change in the merit rating form, even though it is extremely doubtful that our form has ever been given a fair chance to prove its worth. We shall be obliged to change the form, too, I think, because sentiment against it has crystallized to such an extent that systematic training introduced at this late date would probably not break down the resistance.

The foregoing emphasizes that systematic rater training should be an integral part of any merit rating system. It should be carefully planned, with safeguards taken to insure that it be carried out. Furthermore, it should be introduced concurrently with the introduction of the merit rating system and not after bad rating habits have been formed—or, what is worse, after resistance to the procedure has developed.

There is experimental evidence to show that training increases the validity of ratings. Studies have been reported where training has reduced the "halo effect"—i.e., the tendency for raters to rate an individual at about the same level on all traits. Our company has also found in experiments that the relationship between ratings and length of service can be radically changed by a single dramatic demonstration taking but a few minutes to perform. But such experiments merely demonstrate that changes in ratings can be brought about by training. They do not necessarily prove that the changes actually result in ratings that are a more accurate reflection of the ratee's real competence. We are indebted to the Army for studies that bear directly on this latter point.

A controlled experiment was made involving 603 Army officers who rated a total of 2,401 men. On each of the men rated there was developed a measure of competence independent of the rater's evaluations. The total group of raters was divided into two groups matched on the basis of ability to rate. Each group rated the men selected as raters. Then one group was given training consisting of a two-hour period of instruction on the basic principles of accurate rating, the meaning of the rating scale traits and the numerical points on the scales, how to use the rating form, a practical problem in rating, and concluding with a test on what they had been taught. The other group was given no training. Finally, both groups rerated their men. The two sets of ratings made by each group were then studied in relation to the independent measure of each ratee's competence. The results led to the following conclusions:

1. Training resulted in small but consistent increases in the validity of the ratings—i.e., the accuracy with which they reflected true competence.

2. Training decreased the average of the rating scores—a desirable change, since there was a marked tendency for men to be rated too high.

In addition to these conclusions which stemmed directly from the data, it was thought that the effects of training might have been even greater if:

1. More time had been devoted to it.
2. More practice and less lecture had been given.
3. The instructional staff had been of higher caliber.
4. Raters had not already been experienced raters—possibly already trained in bad practices.

A second experiment by the Army sought an answer to the question whether the inclusion of training materials as a part of the rating form would increase the validity of ratings. A special rating form including training material was developed and ratings made with this form were compared with those made by use of a form identical in every way but minus the extra training material. The result was that the training material increased the validities appreciably at all levels of officers but was especially effective on ratings of the higher-grade officers. A by-product of this study also showed that *training is no substitute for better knowing of the men to be rated.* This latter finding merely emphasizes what has already been said about the importance of choosing raters who are familiar with the work of the ratees. Training is not a panacea for all ills of the rating procedure, but there is ample evidence that we need more training and that it will bear fruit.

The rater training program must be designed to accomplish two purposes: (1) Raters must be "sold" on the value and importance of merit ratings; and (2) raters must be taught how to do a good job of making accurate ratings. Selling raters on the value and importance of merit ratings sets the stage for the success of the methods training and, indeed, the success of the whole rating procedure. This should begin early in the development of the procedure, for unless raters *want* merit ratings there is little chance they will ever make good ratings. They will go through the motions of rating, but that is about all it will amount to.

Selling raters on merit ratings should follow a carefully mapped out campaign. Hit-and-miss methods will not do the trick. The development of the campaign is a project on which your sales promotion department should be able to give valuable assistance. This is fundamentally a selling job, so why not consult the experts? I am not an expert, so I shall not try to outline a program for you—anyway, it should be developed to fit your particular problems. I should like, however, to mention a few points that I think bear attention:

1. Start selling merit ratings at the top levels of supervision and work down. Unless top management and top supervisors believe in and actively support the merit rating program, there is a poor chance of being able to sell the lower levels of supervision who comprise the majority of raters.

Get these top men to give their endorsement to the procedure in every possible way—through speeches, letters, editorials in plant papers, etc.

2. Bring the raters into the development of the rating procedure from its earliest stages. Let them make it *their* procedure by giving them a part in its development. This can be done by several means. Have a committee of supervisors work with others who are developing the procedure. In supervisory conferences, discuss the aims and objectives of merit ratings, their uses, etc. Use an opinion survey to get every supervisor to think about the problem and to elicit his suggestions.

3. Send delegations of raters to other companies to investigate their rating plans and report back to a meeting of all supervisors.

4. Don't be too impatient to get the program started; give plenty of time to the selling job. The desire for action is a real virtue in the executive, but don't move in on this until the groundwork has been properly laid.

5. Selling raters is a continuous process; it is not a one-shot proposition. Raters must be sold and then *kept* sold by periodic reapplications of the treatment.

Training raters in the techniques of making accurate ratings is essentially a job of improving the rater's ability to make accurate judgments. Regardless of the rating scale employed, judgment still enters heavily into the rating process. Good rating scales are designed to minimize errors of judgment, but they do not rule them out. Of course, judgment enters into any measurement problem, but in making physical measurements accuracy is more nearly assured. If you offer a foot rule, a voltmeter, and a thermometer to a group of men and ask them to measure the length of a line they will all choose the foot rule and measure the line with great accuracy. There is common agreement about the meaning of length which causes them to select the proper scale, and there is common agreement on the meaning of the points on the scale so they all arrive at about the same result. The only judgment really involved is in where the end of the line falls with respect to two points very close together on the scale. This analysis of physical measurement gives us clues for training raters. There must be brought about common understanding of the trait to be measured and common understanding of the meaning of the points on the scale which is used to measure this trait. In addition, the rater must understand the sources of error that lie within himself and know how to guard against them.

It is often assumed that common understanding of the meaning of a trait is brought about by defining the trait carefully. An interesting finding from research on ratings in our company bears on this. We have found that many raters cannot even distinguish sheer ability to do the job from personality despite elaborate definitions of these characteristics. And to make matters worse, these raters were rating people working on routine production jobs where personality was not a component of successful performance.

It is often assumed, too, that the meaning of the points on a trait scale will be clear to raters if they are defined carefully. Again an interesting and curious finding from our research bears on this. We had raters put 20 of their workers in rank order from 1 to 20. Then they were asked to run down the list starting with the best and choose the person they considered most nearly just an average run-of-the-mill worker. In 14 out of a total of 19 groups rated, the raters chose for the average worker the persons ranked either best, second best, or third best. In only two groups did a rater go as low as seventh best for the average worker. Apparently, "average" to these raters meant someone outstandingly good and defining the meaning of "average" did not clarify the point for them.

What should be included in the training program? In setting up your training program, proceed as you would in any other training program—analyze the job to find out what the rater has to do, then develop procedures for teaching him to do these things well. Most training programs should include the following:

1. Clarification of the aims and purposes of merit rating.
2. Instruction on the meaning of the characteristics or traits to be evaluated.
3. Instruction on the meaning of the points on the scale used.
4. Instruction on the avoidance of common pitfalls in rating, such as:
   a. Lack of objectivity—basing ratings on supposition, guesswork, emotional bias.
   b. Rating one trait in the light of ratings on other traits.
   c. Rating on the basis of general impressions.
   d. Rating on the basis of a single dramatic incident.
   e. Restricting the spread of ratings.
5. Supervised practice and discussion of practice ratings made.
6. Instruction in how to use and interpret the ratings.
7. Periodic refresher training.

Where the rating system includes a post-rating interview with the person rated, the training program should include instruction and practice in conducting this interview. The post-rating interview can be a powerful force for good if conducted properly. If it is not conducted well, it can be just as potent a troublemaker. There is nothing especially unique about conducting this interview; it should merely conform to the principles of good interviewing. However, good interviewers are *made*, not *born*, so raters should be given instruction in interviewing. This instruction should include training in the principles of good interviewing combined with liberal doses of demonstration and practice in conducting this particular type of interview.

There is still one more phase of the training program that deserves more attention than it usually gets. This is the training or educating—or "selling," if you wish to call it that—of the persons to be rated. If these persons are organized into a union, attention must be given to selling their organization as well as the members individually. An educational program should be designed especially for this purpose and vigorously carried out. In general, the same principles mentioned for developing a program for selling raters will apply here, too.

USING MERIT RATING RESULTS

Merit ratings filled out, filed, and forgotten do not justify the time, effort, and money expended on them. The justification of ratings lies only in the uses to which they are put, and their uses are many. However, I do not want to develop a list of those uses here; you are probably familiar with most of them anyway. What is more important are certain problems involved in using merit ratings which have a considerable bearing on how effective their use will be. It is to some of these problems that I should like to direct attention.

Merit ratings are sometimes made the basis upon which administrative actions affecting the worker *can* or *must* be taken. Here are some examples: Sometimes a rating at a certain level must be obtained before the person can receive a raise in pay. In the Army, a promotion in rank cannot be obtained unless the officer's merit rating average is at a certain level. Under some systems, persons who get low ratings must be discharged. In industry, the most usual case is for the merit rating to be tied in with salary increases. The theory is that salary increases should be made on the basis of merit, and making a certain merit rating a requirement will insure that salary increases will not be made on other bases. The theory is good, but it doesn't work that way in practice. People will still be given salary increases for reasons that have nothing to do with merit. People will still be promoted whether they merit it or not. People will still be kept on the payroll even if they do not merit being retained.

As soon as you attach direct consequences to the merit rating, you do something to the ratings. Raters will see to it that the merit ratings do not prevent them from taking action they feel desirable. An example drawn from my own experience in the Army is not atypical. In order to be promoted in the Army an officer must, as I have indicated, have a certain average rating. The result was that most all officers were rated at or above this critical level. Commanding officers were generally unwilling to hold a man back. In addition, it was difficult to get rid of a low-rated officer. He could not be fired, and when it was attempted to transfer him a low rating militated against his acceptance by a new unit. Accordingly, the thing to do was to rate the man high so you could palm him off on someone else.

It is my belief that merit ratings should not be tied directly to salary changes or any other administrative action made consequent upon them. Take them into consideration, yes, but do not make them a specific requirement.

Another problem in using merit ratings is the failure to recognize the inexactness of the rating. We are accustomed to think of measurements as being highly exact. We can measure length, width, and thickness with great exactness. But the measurement of human traits and capacities is a long way from achieving this accuracy. Every measurement of this type has a considerable probable error, as the statistician would say. This means that if a person's rating is entered in the record as 7, the chances are that his true rating may lie anywhere between 7 plus some amount and 7 minus some amount. Thus there is always a zone of uncertainty surrounding any person's rating. This zone, or probable error, can be calculated by qualified research men; it depends on the reliability of the ratings.

Failure to recognize the inexactness of ratings and to allow for the zone of uncertainty can lead to unwarranted interpretations of ratings. Here are some examples taken from an actual study of industrial ratings: Person A, who has a rating of 350, is considered significantly better than person B, who has a rating of 340. Actually, they do not differ significantly at all because the probable errors of these ratings were such that a difference of 60 points was necessary to give assurance that the two persons were actually different in the traits measured. Or take the case of the person who was rated 270 at the last rating period and 300 this time. It *might* be said that this person had made definite improvement, when actually his improvement was not significant when the zone of uncertainty was taken into account. Thus in using ratings safeguards should be taken that they will not be invested with more accuracy than they deserve.

Another problem in using merit ratings arises from the practice of reporting results to the employee in terms of numerical scores. We can dispose of this rather quickly in view of what has just been said. Employees are even more accustomed than executives to take a score at its face value—a rating of 100 to a worker is exactly that, no more and no less. He has never heard of probable error or zones of uncertainty, so he draws false conclusions in comparing his rating with those of his fellows or his previous ratings. It is folly to attempt to teach him how to allow for the inexactness of the ratings, so the answer is, don't give him numerical ratings. Give him his rating in terms of a descriptive scale such as good, average, fair, poor.

There is one other problem involved in the use of merit ratings that I should like to discuss. This arises from the failure to consider the group to which the person belongs when comparing his rating with those of other people. It is entirely possible, and in fact quite likely, that certain groups will average higher in their ratings. This may be because the members of these groups are intrinsically better. On the other hand, it may be due to some artifact which has been reflected in the ratings—e.g., differences in rating standards, differences in the applicability of the scales, etc. It may or may not be possible to determine the real reason for these differences and make reasonable allowances for them. At any rate, the fact that they exist must affect the way we interpret and use the ratings.

Group differences that are not uncommonly found are the following:

1. Departmental groups often differ substantially in their average ratings. One study showed that the average ratings in three departments—engineering, maintenance, and plant protection—were 409, 356, and 266, respectively. Here only intradepartment comparisons would be warranted.
2. Job groups often differ, too, in their average ratings. In the study mentioned above, the averages for 51 jobs ranged from 290 for Janitor to 385 for Tinner. It would appear that a person's rating should be evaluated in terms of others on the same job.
3. Different age groups may be found to have different average ratings. One study showed that average ratings increased from age 18 to 33 and then dropped off. It was concluded that a rating of 330 would be definitely below average for a man 30 to 35 years but well above average for a man 55 to 60 years.
4. Groups with different lengths of service are likely to differ in their average ratings. We have found that within job groups, at least, as length of service increases so do average ratings. Another study reports that, taking the plant at large, there is a decrease in average rating with length of service.

The implication of this for the use of ratings is that such factors have a bearing on the interpretation and use of your ratings. These group relationships need to be studied in your own situation and account of them taken in using the ratings. Lest there be misunderstanding, the data cited here on this problem are not to be taken as having general application. These relationships will vary from company to company.

"Forced-choice" Merit Rating

In the War of 1812 the Army gave us our oldest example of merit rating. In the first World War, the Army gave us the man-to-man rating method, which, though little used in that form, provided considerable impetus to the development of merit ratings generally. In World War II the Army came up with the newest idea in merit rating, one which I feel will have far-reaching significance.

This new method was designed to cure several of the ills prevalent in most rating techniques: First it was designed to minimize the effect of the raters' biases. Second, errors resulting from the raters' differing interpretations of trait names were to be minimized. Third, errors resulting from raters making different interpretations of the points on a trait scale were to be minimized.

It was believed that bias could be largely removed if a rating technique could be set up in such a way that the rater, when making his rating, could not tell how the final rating was going to turn out. That is, the direction and extent of the rating should be disguised so that the rater would be forced to give an actual description of the man's performance rather than to rely on biases or any other preconceived notions of what the person's final rating should be.

It was believed that errors resulting from interpretations of trait names and points on the trait scales could be pared to the bone by not using trait scales. Instead, descriptions of behavior commonly used in describing performance on the job should be used.

Let us see what kind of merit rating procedure resulted from these ideas. A number of groups of four statements descriptive of supervisors were set up, like the following:

1. Avoids responsibility
2. Inspires pride in the organization
3. Lacks sense of humor
4. Offers suggestions

The rater was then asked to choose from each group of four statements the one that was most descriptive of the person to be rated and the one that was least descriptive.

Now two of the statements are favorable to the person and two of them unfavorable. The two favorable statements look equally attractive to the rater and the two unfavorable look equally unattractive. At least they would if they had been paired on the basis of research. The important point is that only one of the favorable statements counts for the person and only one of the unfavorable ones counts against him. But the rater does not know which these are because the scoring key is not revealed to him. So he is forced to decide solely on the basis of how *he* describes the man. If he is biased, he cannot mark the one that will reflect his bias because he does not know which one that is. He does not have to wrestle with trait names or the problem of how many points to give because he is merely asked to choose which of four rather dissimilar statements best or least describes the person.

The trick, of course, is to set up these groups of four statements, and much research must go over the dam before this is achieved. I shall not attempt to go into this in detail but shall merely sketch the steps involved. They are the following:

1. Gather actual words and phrases used in describing supervisors.
2. Cull them for observability and universality.
3. Scale them for their degree of attractiveness or unattractiveness.
4. Determine how well each discriminates between good and poor supervisors.
5. Determine the score that each gets in adding up the total score.
6. Verify the scoring system set up by check experiments.

The important thing to note is that each of these steps is based on experimental research rather than on armchair theorizing. Each step, too, involves technical problems requiring the best of research men.

The efficiency of this type of rating scale was compared with the results obtained with two different trait rating scales, a ranking system, and a system involving a combination of trait scales and a performance check list. The results showed that this new type yielded more accurate ratings than any of the others.

What are the prospects for using this type of rating scale in industry? My feeling is that it is a coming thing, but it has not yet arrived. There are several reasons for my attitude. In the first place, this rating scale will work only when the method of scoring the rater's evaluations is kept secret, and I am not at all sure that industry is ready to do this.[1] It would certainly take a real job of selling to convince the rater and labor unions that this was either wise or necessary. In the second place, the research necessary to develop the rating scale will prove a barrier for many companies, especially if they are small. Perhaps a general scale that will apply to supervisors wherever you find them will eventually be developed, but at the present time it is believed that each organization must have one tailor-made to its own measure.

13. Establishing a Graphic-Rating Scale*

Lee Stockford and H. W. Bissell

BY NOW, enough has been written in the form of textbook chapters and formal articles on the subject of merit rating to allow one to make two broad and important generalizations:

1. That the performance of employees in industry is constantly being rated or appraised by their supervisors and others, whether or not these judgments are recorded on a specially constructed scale.
2. That more often than not formal appraisals or ratings are to be preferred over informal appraisals, providing all the conditions and restrictions of scale construction, timing, policy control, training, etc., have been observed.

The purpose of this article is not to restate the fundamental principles underlying the whole rating procedure, but to present the results of a series of controlled statistical studies which were conducted as part of a program to revise the rating procedure at the Lockheed Aircraft Corporation, particularly as it affects the review of hourly-rated employees.

For many years, in accordance with its union contract, Lockheed has conducted reviews of its hourly-paid employees every 16 weeks, primarily for the purpose of appraising the value of their work in connection with the merit pay increase program. Several years ago, in order to make the 16-week reviews more "objective," supervisors were required

---

[1] Editor's note: Since this article first appeared many companies have adopted "forced choice" programs.

* From "Factors Involved in Establishing a Merit-Rating Scale," *Personnel*, Vol. 26, 1949, pp. 94–116.

to record the progress of their employees every four weeks on what was termed the "Progress Report." These progress reports were scored and averaged, and the results of the last four progress reports were recorded on the 16-week review sheets as numerical scores for each trait rated. The idea was to avoid a last-minute "halo" effect at the time merit raises were considered.

This system of grading four-week progress reports soon became so burdensome and routine in nature that the results were hardly worth the effort. The progress reports were therefore eliminated; and, at the time of the regular 16-week review, the supervisor's opinion of the employee was expressed in terms of numbers in a box on the review form originally intended to carry a summary of four detailed progress reports (see Exhibit A). This system was in effect when the present study was begun to improve the Lockheed hourly rating program.

PURPOSE AND SCOPE OF THE STUDY

The purpose of this study was to determine the degree to which certain weaknesses inherent in the ratings obtained on the existing merit-rating scale could be reduced or overcome by designing a new scale and by training supervisors in the principles and techniques of rating.

The scope of the study included an analysis of basic reference literature in the field of industrial psychology; a review of previous research studies on merit rating which were conducted at Lockheed; the construction of a type of scale different from the scale then in use; an *experimental* study of ratings submitted on the new scale in comparison with those submitted on the old scale; and a series of follow-up studies on the new scale to validate its use in *practical* situations in order to determine the degree to which the gains observed in the original experiment were preserved.

RESULTS

Since this report covers the essential findings of four relatively independent studies, the results will be presented in four parts.

Part I will be a summary of the principal findings of the background studies.

Part II will cover the approach to the construction of the descriptive rating scale.

Part III will contain a discussion of original research study.

Part IV will present the follow-up statistical analysis of ratings submitted on the new scale.

Part I
Principal Findings of Background Studies

In the development of the current Lockheed Management Selection and Placement Plan, 54 separate items were subjected to a fairly rigorous analysis. Of these 54 items, one was merit rating. Several studies were conducted to determine the value of merit rating as a measure of the performance of the individual supervisors.

The rating scale used for the review of supervisory personnel was similar in form (but not in traits) to that used for the review of non-supervisory personnel. The subordinate was rated on an evaluational scale in which his "worth" was appraised in terms of "Poor," "Below Average," "Average," "Above Average," and "Excellent," and the evaluation was expressed directly in terms of a numerical equivalent (ranging from 0 to 100) for this subjective appraisal.

In this study there were 485 supervisors in 30 departments working in a broad but homogenous type of work—airframe structure and final assembly. These supervisors were rated by the department heads for whom they worked. Three types of analyses of the ratings were made, the results of which are summarized in the following paragraphs.

1. *Leniency-Severity.*   The differences in leniency between raters were so great that all the supervisors working for the four most severe raters were given ratings the scores of which were lower than the scores for the poorest ratings given by the two most lenient raters. The mean deviation of the mean ratings given by the 30 raters was 12 points.

2. *Differences between "known" and "unknown" ratings.*   Up to the time that the experimental studies were conducted, the supervisors were never shown the results of the ratings. The department heads merely filled in the merit-rating scales, and sent them directly to the Personnel Records Department to be filed in the personnel folders of the men. At this time, it was decided that the department head should have a private interview with each man that he rated and explain the results of the ratings to him. At the close of the interview the rater and the subordinate were each to sign the review sheet to indicate that the interview had been conducted. Then, the rating scale was to be sent to the Personnel Records Department.

Two weeks after a regular periodic review (one that occurred at the official review period and in conjunction with which there were no interviews), the 30 department heads were asked to re-rate their subordinate supervisors, and, following these ratings, to explain them to their subordinates on an individual basis. The mean score for all 485 ratings in the regular review where the results of the ratings were "unknown" by those who were rated was 60 ($S.D. = 21$); in the experimental ratings made two weeks later, in conjunction with which the interviews were held, the mean rating was 84 ($S.D. = 14$). The difference of 24 points between the means for these two sets of ratings was significant beyond all reasonable doubt (Critical ratio $= 20.0$). This would indicate that the general level of leniency is significantly raised when the results of the ratings are known by the subordinate.

3. *Correlational Analysis.*   Three correlational analyses were made to determine the reliability and validity of the ratings.

EXHIBIT A

The Original Rating Form

LOCKHEED AIRCRAFT CORPORATION

EMPLOYEE PERIODIC REVIEW

DEPT	PLANT	S		NAME				REV. GROUP	½ PT	OCCUPATION	SENIORITY DATE			EMPLOYEE NO.
			PRESENT RATE	WAS EFFECTIVE MO. DAY YEAR	SENT TO DEPT. MO. DAY YEAR	TO BECOME EFFECTIVE MO. DAY YEAR	THIS REPORT MUST REACH PLANT PERSONNEL BEFORE				MO. DAY YEAR			

DESCRIBE BRIEFLY THE SPECIFIC
WORK THIS EMPLOYEE IS NOW DOING

REMARKS AND REASON FOR THE RECOM-
MENDED RATE OR OCCUPATION CHANGE.

S U M M A R Y 16 W E E K P E R I O D	GRADE	WT.	SCORE
QUALITY		X 5	
QUANTITY		X 5	
KNOWLEDGE		X 1	
DEPENDABILITY		X 2	
COOPERATION		X 2	
TOTAL			

LEADERSHIP CHARACTERISTICS   DOUBTFUL ☐   POSSIBLE ☐   POSITIVE ☐

DEPARTMENTAL RECOMMENDATION

INCREASE IN RATE	☐ YES ☐ NO	HR.	DEPT HEAD
NEW CODE	NEW RATE	HR.	
NEW OCCUPATION			EXECUTIVE
RECORDED BY			PERSONNEL
	DATE		

APPROVING SIGNATURES

DATE

PROGRESS REPORTS WERE RATED BY: 1   ,2

16 WEEK PERIOD GRADED BY _____   DATE

FORM 3411-5

PERSONNEL COPY

To obtain the coefficient of reliability, two sets of ratings were made with a time lapse of 10 days between each set. The range of reliability coefficients was from $r = +.40$ to $r = +.92$. The mean coefficient of reliability was $M_r = +.70$.

To obtain the validity of the ratings, the scores were correlated with (a) an objective measure of work performed by the mechanics under each supervisor; (b) the length of time the department heads knew each of the subordinate supervisors; and (c) the social stimulus value of the personality of the supervisors who were being rated. The results of these studies are presented in the following table.

TABLE 1

MEAN COEFFICIENT OF CORRELATION BETWEEN
SCORES ON RATING SCALES AND EACH OF THREE OTHER FACTORS

NATURE OF INTERRELATIONSHIP	MEAN COEFF. CORR.
Scores on rating scales vs. measurable output	$r = +.22$
Scores on rating scales vs. social stimulus value of personality	$r = +.59$
Scores on rating scales vs. length of acquaintanceship	$r = +.65$

From these data it is quite obvious that the ratings submitted on the scale are providing a measure of something other than actual production.

The results of the foregoing studies permit the following statements:

a) There are differences between supervisors, not only in the leniency with which they rate their subordinates, but also in the reliability with which they rate their subordinates.

b) Supervisors are more lenient in evaluating the worth of subordinates when they must confront the subordinate with the results of the ratings than they are when the results are withheld from the subordinate.

c) The score on the rating scale which has been designed to measure performance reflects personal-social relationships between supervisor and subordinate better than it reflects the actual productivity of the subordinate in question.

As a result of this study, the review sheet for the rating of the salaried employees was radically changed to conform more closely with typical graphic or descriptive type of rating scale. A restudy of ratings provided the following improvements:

a) Differences between "signed" and "unsigned" ratings were reduced from 24 to only 7 points.

b) Differences in leniency and severity were reduced significantly. In the first study, the mean deviation between raters was 12; here the mean deviation in leniency and severity is only 4.

Before the correlational analysis to determine the reliability and validity of the new ratings could be conducted, the decision was made to study and to revise the scale used in the review of hourly-paid employees.

Part II
Construction of the Descriptive Rating Scale
for the Review of Hourly-Paid Personnel

In order to construct a scale that would be acceptable by those who would have to use it, the supervisors themselves were asked to participate in the study.

One hundred and thirty-eight supervisors (selected at random) were asked to submit a list of 15 traits or characteristics on which hourly-paid people could be rated. They were asked to place a "3" before each of the five items they considered to be of most importance, a "2" before each of the five items they considered to be next in importance, and a "1" before each of the least important items. The supervisors were also asked to define the terms and to give descriptions of desirable, neutral and undesirable behavior under each of these traits.

When the lists of traits were returned to the Personnel Department, they were divided into three groups: (1) those submitted by supervisors in office-clerical functions; (2) those submitted by supervisors in direct functions; and (3) those submitted by supervisors in engineering functions. The items submitted by each group were then subjected to statistical analysis to determine the relative importance or popularity of each.

On the basis of all opinions studied in the preliminary investigation, eight traits were found to be of sufficient importance (popularity) to warrant further research. These were *Adaptability, Cooperation, Dependability, Initiative, Job Knowledge, Judgment, Quality, Quantity.* The trait *Initiative*, although ranking high in the opinion of most supervisors, was dropped from the list because the definitions submitted for this term overlapped too much with the definitions submitted for *Dependability*. The trait *Dependability* was the better of the two, as it was subject to more reliable ratings. The trait *Morale* (willingness and attitude) was substituted in the place of *Initiative*.

The final list included *Adaptability, Cooperation, Dependability, Job Knowledge, Judgment, Morale, Quality, Quantity.* These traits were then defined, and four degrees of behavior were established for each trait. The definitions for several of the traits were adapted from a scale used by the company several years ago. The definitions of the remaining traits were adapted from the definitions submitted by supervision. The scale was constructed along the line of a typical graphic scale without numbers and with no reference to qualitative terms such as "average," "excellent," "poor," etc. All ratings were to be made, then, in terms that "describe" behavior rather than in numerical equivalents for terms that "evaluate" supposed worth.

The reason for removing numbers and qualitative terms from the scale was twofold: first, to control one of the causes of differences between raters in leniency and severity; and, second, to increase reliability of the judgment on which the actual rating was predicated.

That individual differences in leniency could be reduced was supported by several demonstrations, the most significant of which was a survey of more than 100 supervisors and 100 college upper-division and graduate students. In this study the people were asked to rate (on a hundred-point scale) the value they would assign to each of several phrases which could be used as a basis for a rating scale. The results showed that the ranges and standard deviations of the values for those phrases which contained evaluational words ("average," "excellent," and "poor," etc.) were significantly greater than were the ranges and standard deviations of the values for those phrases which were devoid of any subjective words. It was felt, then, that language and its scaling in rating employees was among the most important problems with which to cope. Further studies on this phase of the problem are now in progress.

In reference to reliability it was believed that by making the language of the scale more objective, the supervisor's judgment or opinion would be less affected by changes in his mood or feeling tones than might otherwise be the case.

Part III
Original Research Study

The purpose of this phase of the study was to analyze ratings submitted on both the old evaluational scale and the experimental descriptive scale. The scope of the analyses included an investigation of (1) individual differences in *leniency* and *severity;* (2) *reliability* of rating; (3) a limited measure of *validity* of the ratings; and, finally, (4) a study of *factors* involved in rating.

At the time of the regular review period in September, 1947, 56 supervisors from five different operating units in the company were asked to participate in the study. These supervisors were asked to rate their subordinates on the regular company scale then in use, and also on the experimental scale. The following table shows the name of each of the operating units, the number of supervisors participating in this study, and the number of hourly employees who were rated.

TABLE 2

AREAS AND NUMBER OF PERSONNEL INCLUDED IN STUDY

OPERATING UNITS	NUMBER OF SUPERVISORS	NUMBER OF EMPLOYEES RATED
Inspection	3	57
Manufacturing	18	408
Office Manager	9	132
Engineering	24	276
Lockheed Aircraft Service, Inc.	2	42
TOTAL—Five Units	56	915

Upon completion of the ratings, the scales were sent to the Personnel Records Department for scoring and analysis. The results of this study are presented as follows:

1. *Individual Differences in Leniency and Severity.* There were several major aspects in which the ratings on the two scales differed:

   a) The shape of the distribution curves of the ratings on the company scale was bi-modal whereas the distributions of the scores on the experimental scale approximated the normal curve of distribution. (Chart 1.)
   b) The ratings on the regular company scale were skewed more to the higher end of the scale than were the ratings on the experimental curve. In fact, on the company scale, the curve did not close at the upper end of the base line. (Chart 1.)
   c) There was less difference between supervisors in the range or the portion of the scale they used when rating on the descriptive scale than when rating on the evaluation scale. (Chart 1.)
   d) A study of the individual mean ratings for each of the raters revealed several points worth noting. (See Table 3.)

(1) On both scales the mean of the 56 ratings was slightly higher than was the mean of all 915 ratings. Later studies showed this to be caused by the fact that there is a slight negative correlation ($-.20$) between leniency and the number of cases a supervisor must rate.

Since the mean rating submitted by each supervisor was treated as a single item regardless of the number of subordinates he rated, and since there is a slight tendency for supervisors to be more lenient when rating a small group than when rating a large group, it is not surprising that on the evaluational scale the mean of the 56 mean ratings was 112.5 compared to a mean of 109 for 915 ratings, or that the mean of the 56 means on the experimental descriptive scale was 64.7 and the mean of the 915 individual ratings was 64.0.

TABLE 3

RANGE, MEANS AND STANDARD DEVIATIONS OF RATINGS OBTAINED FROM SUPERVISORS ON BOTH SCALES

RANGE, MEANS AND STANDARD DEVIATIONS	COMPANY SCALE	EXPERIMENTAL SCALE
Mean of All Ratings........................	109.1	64.0
S.D. of All Ratings.........................	18.0	10.1
Range of Means for 56 Supervisors		
Minimum—Maximum.......................	81–35	56–72
Mean of Means............................	112.5	64.7
S.D. of Means.............................	14.2	4.9

(2) The standard deviation of the means for the 56 supervisors when using the company scale was 14.2 or about three times as great as the standard deviation of the means when the supervisors were rating on the experimental scale ($S.D. = 4.9$).

(3) Whereas three of the supervisors when rating on the company scale had means that deviated more than the 18 points above 109 (the mean of all 915 ratings), and two supervisors had means more than 18 points below

CHART 1

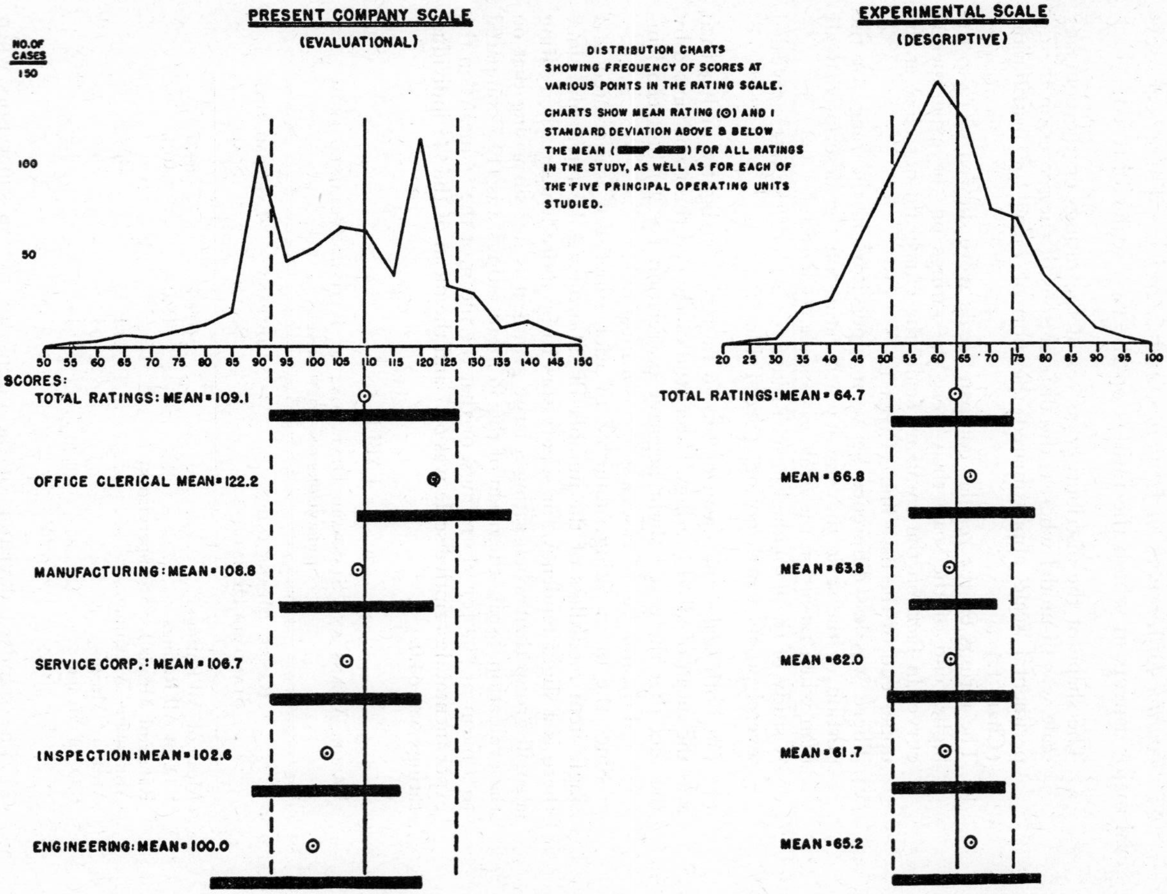
PRESENT COMPANY SCALE
(EVALUATIONAL)
NO. OF CASES
150
100
50
50 55 60 65 70 75 80 85 90 95 100 105 110 115 120 125 130 135 140 145 150
SCORES:
TOTAL RATINGS: MEAN = 109.1
OFFICE CLERICAL MEAN = 122.2
MANUFACTURING: MEAN = 108.8
SERVICE CORP.: MEAN = 106.7
INSPECTION: MEAN = 102.6
ENGINEERING: MEAN = 100.0
DISTRIBUTION CHARTS
SHOWING FREQUENCY OF SCORES AT
VARIOUS POINTS IN THE RATING SCALE.
CHARTS SHOW MEAN RATING (⊙) AND 1
STANDARD DEVIATION ABOVE & BELOW
THE MEAN (▬▬) FOR ALL RATINGS
IN THE STUDY, AS WELL AS FOR EACH OF
THE FIVE PRINCIPAL OPERATING UNITS
STUDIED.
EXPERIMENTAL SCALE
(DESCRIPTIVE)
20 25 30 35 40 45 50 55 60 65 70 75 80 85 90 95 100
TOTAL RATINGS: MEAN = 64.7
MEAN = 66.8
MEAN = 63.8
MEAN = 62.0
MEAN = 61.7
MEAN = 65.2

109, none of the supervisors had means when rating on the experimental scale which deviated more than 8 points from 64 (the mean of all 915 ratings on the experimental scale). That is, when using the experimental scale the mean of the ratings given by each of the supervisors was within one standard deviation of the mean of all 915 individual ratings.

2. *Reliability.* Ten days after the original ratings were submitted to the Personnel Department, the 56 supervisors were asked to re-rate their employees. Coefficients of reliability or consistency were then obtained for each rater on each scale as well as for the various traits on the scale.

    a) The coefficient of reliability for each of the raters was higher for the experimental scale than for the company scale. The mean coefficient of reliability for the entire group of supervisors was $r = +.77$ on the experimental scale, and $r = +.55$ on the company scale.

    b) Certain items in the new scale were more reliable than others. The most reliable item was *Dependability* ($r = +.78$); the least reliable item was *Cooperation* ($r = +.49$).

3. *Validity.* The only measure of validity to be obtained in the study was based upon the ability of two or more equally qualified supervisors to agree with each other when independently rating the same group of employees. Because of the difficulties in obtaining a sufficiently large number of cases on whom this study could be conducted, the results are held in doubt and shall not be reported in full. However, mention shall be made of several significant findings:

    a) The coefficient of correlation between the ratings submitted by two raters on the same group of men is lower than the coefficient of reliability.

    b) The raters were better able to agree with each other when rating people on an objective scale, than the same raters were able to agree with themselves when rating the same people on a subjective scale.

    c) *Quality* of work was the trait on which the supervisors were best able to agree with each other (coefficient of agreement $r = +.70$). *Cooperation* was the trait on which they were least able to agree with each other (coefficient of agreement $r = +.04$).

4. *Basic Factors in the Scale.* In order to determine the statistical factors which were involved, the rating on each trait was correlated with the rating on each of the other traits. From this inter-correlational analysis of the ratings, it was apparent that these were three general clusters of traits to which supervisors were reacting:

    a) Technical Proficiency (Quality and Quantity)
    b) Mental Proficiency (Judgment, Adaptability and Job Knowledge)
    c) Social Proficiency (Morale and Cooperation)

This should certainly not be taken to indicate that these are the only three clusters or factors to which supervisors react, since this depends in part upon the nature and the number of the traits included in the scale.

Since the type of and the number of factors which appear in ratings is dependent in part upon the number and the nature of the traits which make up the scale, the question was raised as to the degree to which other aspects of the scale might influence the *factors* to be obtained. In answer to the question, a further investigation was conducted. In this analysis the principle of *proximity* was studied by determining the mean coefficients of correlation between ratings given to adjacent traits ($r_{12} + r_{23} + r_{34} + r_{45}$, etc.), between ratings given to alternate traits ($r_{13} + r_{24} + r_{35} + r_{46}$, etc.), and between ratings given to every third trait ($r_{14} + r_{25} + r_{36} + r_{47}$, etc.).

The results of the study showed that the average inter-correlation for adjacent traits was +.66. As the distance between the various traits was increased, the size of the inter-correlations decreased to a point where the

TABLE 4

MEAN INTER-CORRELATION OF TRAITS BY RELATIVE POSITION ON SCALE,
SHOWING INFLUENCE OF PROXIMITY

	MEAN COEFFICIENT OF CORRELATION	
PROXIMITY OF TRAITS	Traits on Original Experimental Scale	Traits on Scrambled Scale
Adjacent Traits	$M_r = +.66$	$M_r = +.65$
Alternate Traits	$M_r = +.60$	$M_r = +.58$
Traits Separated by Two Intervening Traits	$M_r = +.59$	$M_r = +.58$
Traits Separated by Three Intervening Traits	$M_r = +.51$	$M_r = +.55$
Traits Separated by Four Intervening Traits	$M_r = +.51$	$M_r = +.52$
Traits Separated by Five or More Intervening Traits	$M_r = +.46$	$M_r = +.48$

mean inter-correlations between ratings on traits separated by five or more intervening traits was +.46. This presented some good evidence to support the speculation that it is likely that the nature of the factors to be obtained from a statistical analysis of ratings is partially determined by the proximity of the items.

To verify this speculation a new scale was prepared. It consisted of the same traits appearing in a very different or "scrambled" order so that traits adjacent to each other in the first scale were not adjacent to each other in the "scrambled" scale.

Following the same procedure it was found that the mean coefficient of correlations of ratings given to traits adjacent to each other was +.65; and the mean coefficient of correlation of the ratings separated by five or more intervening traits was +.48. A summary of these mean coefficients of correlation is presented in Table 4.

SUMMARY

From the results of the experimental study, the following major points deserve summarization.

a) Differences between supervisors in the leniency or severity with which they rate their subordinates are significantly less when ratings are made on a *descriptive* scale than when they are made on an *evaluational* scale.

b) When rating on a *descriptive* scale, the supervisor's judgment is significantly more reliable than it is when the rating is made on an *evaluational* scale.

Also, the reliability of ratings on traits such as *Dependability* ($M_r = +.78$) and *Quality* of work ($M_r = +.70$) is greater than the reliability of ratings on the more "subjective" traits such as *Morale* ($M_r = +.50$) and *Cooperation* ($M_r = +.49$).

c) Validity of ratings is a subject that needs much more study. However, the pertinent though limited finding in this aspect of the original experimental study is that the coefficient of validity of *descriptive* ratings is significantly higher than is the coefficient of reliability of *evaluational* ratings.

d) Any further study of statistical *factors* in ratings should be conducted with due regard for the number of and kind of traits in the scale, and for the principle of proximity of these various traits.

Part IV
Follow-Up Statistical Analysis of Ratings Submitted on the Descriptive Scale

PURPOSE

On the basis of the findings presented in Part III, a final draft for a rating scale was prepared. This scale contained the five traits on which the most reliable ratings were obtained (Exhibit B).

To validate the experimental findings, a follow-up study was conducted on the ratings submitted by 107 supervisors on 2,185 hourly-paid subordinates. The specific purpose of this study was to determine: (1) the degree to which the gains observed in the experiment were to be retained when the new scale was put to practical use, and (2) the degree to which ratings are influenced by certain traits or characteristics of the rater.

APPROACH

This study was restricted to a statistical analysis of ratings of subordinates submitted by 107 supervisors during the second regular review period in which the new scale was used (December, 1948). None of these supervisors knew in advance of the study that an analysis of their ratings was to be made, nor was there any general announcement that a study would be conducted at that time. It is believed that the withholding of this information permitted the obtaining of ratings under the most natural conditions possible at the time.

EXHIBIT B

The Revised Rating Form

LOCKHEED AIRCRAFT CORPORATION
EMPLOYEE PERIODIC REVIEW

DEPT.	PLANT	S	NAME		M/ F	OCCUPATION	SENIORITY DATE MO. DAY YEAR	▼	EMPLOYEE NO.

| | | PRESENT RATE | WAS EFFECTIVE MO. DAY YEAR | SENT TO DEPT. MO. DAY YEAR | TO BECOME EFFECTIVE MO. DAY YEAR | THIS REPORT MUST REACH PERSONNEL BEFORE | MO. DAY YEAR | |

Describe briefly the specific work this employee is now doing and state the approximate length of time he has been on this work

Approximately how long have you known this employee?_____

The following factors are to be rated. The factors are listed alphabetically, therefore their position as listed in no way reflects the respective value of the individual factors.

ADAPTABILITY
Versatility; Adjustment to Job or Changed Conditions; Ease with which New Duties are Learned

| Is slow to learn; has trouble adjusting himself to changed conditions, needs constant instruction. | Learns fairly well; is a routine worker and needs detailed instruction for a new job. | Learns well with minimum amount of instruction; adjusts himself well in a short time. | Meets changed conditions with little effort; has outstanding ability to pick up new jobs. |

DEPENDABILITY
Your Confidence in Employee's Ability to Accept Responsibility

| Does top grade work with minimum of supervision; outstanding ability to follow through | Willing to accept responsibility, requires very little follow-up. | Usually follows instructions; needs some follow-up | Refuses to or not able to carry much responsibility; needs constant follow-up. |

JOB KNOWLEDGE
Technical Knowledge of Job and Related Work

| Has excellent knowledge of his job and related work; is very well-informed. | Seldom needs help; has good knowledge of his job and related work; is well-informed. | Knows his job fairly well; has little knowledge of related work. | Has limited knowledge of his job; knows nothing of related work. |

QUALITY
Accuracy in Work; Freedom from Errors

| Makes practically no mistakes; highest accuracy. | Seldom makes errors; is accurate; does high-grade work. | Makes some errors but does passable work. | Makes mistakes frequently. |

QUANTITY
Output - Speed

| Output below standard definitely slow | Output meets standard is satisfactory | Does more work than expected; is fast; exceeds standard. | Exceptionally fast, unusual output |

COMMENTS

Rated by _____

Dept. head _____ Date _____

Executive _____ Date _____

| Will changes in rate or occupation be recommended at this time? | Yes ☐ No ☐ |
| If answer is "Yes" be sure to attach a completed Change of Status notice to this form. | |

Personnel Dept. _____ Date _____

FORM NO. 3411-8

SCOPE OF THE STUDY

It is apparent from a review of literature and from the data presented so far that three of the most important problems in merit rating are *reliability, individual differences in leniency,* and the influence of bias or *"halo."*

The results of the study will show:

1. The reliability with which raters expressed their judgment of the performance of their subordinates;
2. The differences between raters in *leniency;*
3. The influence of bias or *"halo";*
4. The interrelationship of *reliability, leniency* and *"halo,"* and the degree to which these three aspects of rating are influenced by such factors as:

    a) The level of mental ability of the rater;
    b) Special training in the function of rating;
    c) Amount of experience as a rater;
    d) The age level of the supervisor;
    e) Certain components in the Kuder Interest Preference record;
    f) Certain characteristics of the ratings themselves.

The analyses were conducted on the ratings submitted by 77 of the original group of 107 supervisors. These 77 supervisors rated 1,928 subordinates. The size of the groups rated by each supervisor ranged from 18 to 56 subordinates with a mean of 25 subordinates per supervisor. The ratings from the remaining 30 supervisors were excluded from the study because of the small number of subordinates assigned to each supervisor. For these supervisors, the groups ranged in size from 4 to 15 with an average number of eight subordinates.

TRAINING IN THE RATING FUNCTION

Before presenting the results of the follow-up study, it is essential that certain points regarding the 77 supervisors be made clear. These people were all in the lowest level of full-time salaried personnel responsible for the direct supervision of hourly-paid employees. The supervisors did not comprise one homogeneous group in all respects. There was at least one known factor on the basis of which the subjects could be divided into two separate groups. This was the factor of specialized training in the function of rating.

The specialized training consisted of approximately six hours of instruction on the philosophy and principles of rating drawn from the sources listed earlier in the report; participation in the selection of items to be used in the scale; participation as experimental subjects in the original research studies; and the benefit of follow-up interviews in which their performance as raters was explained to them in detail. This training was restricted to 32 of the 77 supervisors in the study.

The remaining 45 supervisors received only the two-hour general orientation or explanatory session given to all members of all levels of supervision throughout the entire company. This orientation session was for the purpose of acquainting all members of supervision with the fact that there would be a change in the rating scale, the reasons for the change, and a statement of the changes in the merit review procedure required as a result of installing the new scale.

The following table shows a list of the factors which were held in control: that is, those known, measured traits in which there were no significant differences in either means or ranges between the "trained" and the "untrained" classes of supervisors.

TABLE 5

MEAN AND RANGE OF SCORES FOR TRAITS ON WHICH THERE WERE NO DIFFERENCES BETWEEN SUPERVISORS IN "TRAINED" AND "UNTRAINED" GROUPS

TRAIT	TOTAL GROUP (N = 77)		TRAINED GROUP (N = 32)		UNTRAINED GROUP (N = 45)	
	Mean	Range	Mean	Range	Mean	Range
Mental Maturity (Calif. Test M.M.)	IQ—123	91 to 153	123	94 to 147	123	91 to 153
Persuasive Compon. (Kuder Pref. Record)	63 %ile	1 to 99	65 %ile	1 to 99	62 %ile	1 to 99
Social Service Comp. (Kuder Pref. Record)	54 %ile	1 to 99	52 %ile	1 to 90	55 %ile	1 to 99
Admin-Supervisory Int. (Out of Kuder Items)	68 %ile	5 to 99	70 %ile	10 to 99	65 %ile	1 to 99
Age (Chronological)	38 Yrs.	26 Yrs. to 55 Yrs.	37 Yrs.	27 Yrs. to 53 Yrs.	39 Yrs.	26 Yrs. to 55 Yrs.
Supervisory Experience (Number of Years)	5 Yrs.	6 Mos. to 10 Yrs.	5 Yrs.	1 Yr. to 10 Yrs.	5 Yrs.	6 Mos. to 10 Yrs.
Training (Formal Academic)	H.S.— 2 Yrs. Adv.	9th Grade thru 4 Yrs. Col.	H.S.— 2 Yrs. Adv.	10 Grade thru 4 Yrs. Col.	H.S.— 2 Yrs. Adv.	9th Grade thru 4 Yrs. Col.

RELIABILITY

The coefficients of reliability for the 77 supervisors ranged from $r = +.13$ to $r = +95$; and the mean coefficient of reliability was $r = +.80$. Yoder gives $r = +.75$ as the lowest acceptable coefficient of reliability for rating scales. Of the 77 supervisors, 55, or approximately 70 per cent of the group submitted ratings the reliability of which equaled or exceeded this point.

These results compare favorably with the results obtained in the experimental study. In the original study, for a comparable group of supervisors, the mean coefficient of reliability was $r = +.77$ for the experimental "descriptive" scale, and a coefficient of reliability of $r = +.55$ for the old "evaluational" scale. The results indicate that the gains observed in the experiment were retained when the "descriptive" scale was put to practical use.

LENIENCY

Leniency was measured in terms of the mean score on the rating scale given by each of the supervisors to their respective subordinates. A frequency distribution was made of these means. The mean of the means was 66.0, and the standard deviation of the means (S.D.) was 6.7. In the original experimental study the mean of the means was 64.7 and the standard deviation was 4.9. The difference between the two sets of figures is not statistically significant.

"HALO"

For this study "halo" or bias is approximated through the medium of length of personal acquaintance between the respective supervisors and each of the subordinates they rated. Although not a perfect measure of bias, there are two good reasons for using this measure for the criterion of "halo."

1. It is highly reliable.

2. A previous investigation on over 400 cases showed a coefficient of $r = +.64$ between length of acquaintance and acceptability of personality. This last measure was obtained by reconstructing items typical of those used in personality inventories so that they could be used in a "buddy" rating scale rather than in a self-inventory. A coefficient of correlation of this magnitude ($r = +.64$) justifies the generalization that the longer one has known another the more acceptable becomes the other's personality.

A coefficient of correlation was obtained between the length of time each of the 77 raters knew each of the subordinates he rated and the scores on the rating scales. These coefficients ranged from $r = -.07$ to $r = +.76$ with a mean coefficient of $r = +.42$.

This indicates that, generally speaking, "halo," as measured, exerts a low positive but significant influence upon the degree to which the supervisor rates the output of the subordinate. However, the principles of individual differences operate to a very strong degree (as seen by the range of coefficients of correlation: $r = -.07$ to $r = +.76$).

It is interesting to note that when using an evaluational type of scale, the mean coefficient of correlation between length of acquaintance and the score on the rating scale was $r = +.65$; on the descriptive scale this coefficient of correlation was only $r = +.42$.

INFLUENCE OF VARIOUS FACTORS ON RELIABILITY

As previously reported, the mean coefficient of reliability for the entire group of 77 supervisors was $r = +.80$. Additional studies indicated that the reliability of merit ratings is modified by various factors. The factors considered in this report are those presented in Table 5, in addition to the special training. The degree to which each of these factors is related to the reliability of the ratings for the total group of supervisors as well as for those in the "trained" class and for those in the "untrained" class was determined.

It was found that the mean coefficient of reliability for the entire group is $r = +.80$, the mean for the "trained" class is $r = +.85$, and the mean for the "untrained" class is $r = +.76$. Before training, the mean coefficient of reliability for the "trained" group was $r = +.77$, or virtually the same as the mean reliability of the present "untrained" class. This difference in the coefficients of reliability ($r = +.85$ and $r = +.77$ or $r = +.76$) is significant, and, so far as can be determined, is attributable almost wholly to training alone.

The standard deviation of the rating scores bears a positive relationship to the reliability of the ratings ($r = +.42$ in the total group). Reliability is less dependent upon the standard deviation of the ratings among those who were trained ($r = +.24$) than it is for those in the untrained class ($r = +.66$).

For the total group, the mental level of the raters bears a low but positive relationship to the reliability of his ratings (r I.Q. vs. Coeffi-

TABLE 6

RELATIONSHIP OF I.Q. TO MEAN RELIABILITY IN THE "TRAINED" AND "UNTRAINED" CLASSES

	MEAN RELIABILITY	
I. Q. GROUPING	TRAINED	UNTRAINED
I.Q. = 125 or greater	$M_r = +.88$	$M_r = +.79$
I.Q. = 124 or less	$M_r = +.79$	$M_r = +.74$

cient of Reliability $= +.33$). Among those in the "trained" class the correlation between I.Q. and reliability of ratings is $r = +.52$; whereas among those in the "untrained" class, this coefficient of correlation is $r = +.20$. This would indicate that the I.Q. level of raters in itself bears little relationship to the reliability of ratings, but that it is the brighter supervisors who make the greatest improvement when subjected to training. This last contention is supported by the data presented in Table 6.

From these data it is to be seen that the mean coefficient of reliability is the same for the more intelligent supervisors in the "untrained" group as it is for the "trained" supervisors in the less intelligent group ($M_r = +.79$). Also, that training the more intelligent supervisors results in a mean coefficient of reliability in rating of $+.88$, which is greater than the sum of the independent gains in reliability attributable to *intelligence* and *training* alone.

It must be remembered that the supervisors in this study constitute a generally superior group from the standpoint of mental maturity. Whether these same relationships between I.Q. and reliability would be obtained in a comparable study of supervisors drawn from a different level of mental maturity or from a more extended range of I.Q. scores is a matter to be left untouched by this study.

The items of Administrative-Supervisory Interest, Chronological Age, Persuasive Interest and Years of Experience as a Supervisor bore no relationship to reliability of ratings among those in either the "trained" or "untrained" class of supervisors.

Leniency of ratings, the size of the group rated, amount of formal academic training, and the influence of "halo" all yield significant but low negative correlations with reliability among those who were in the "untrained" class. Among those in the "trained" class, the influence of these items on reliability of the ratings was reduced to coefficients of negligible size. To a small but definite degree, then, it was found among raters in the "untrained" class that:

1. The more lenient the rater, the lower was the reliability of the ratings;
2. The larger the number of people rated, the lower the reliability of the ratings;
3. The more formal academic training, the lower the reliability of the rater; and,
4. The more the individual ratings are influenced by "halo," the lower the reliability of the ratings.

INFLUENCE OF VARIOUS FACTORS ON LENIENCY

As in the case of reliability, it was found that several of the factors in the study were directly related to the leniency with which the supervisors rated their subordinates. Of the various items studied in relation to leniency, only those bearing a significant relationship will be discussed in detail. Whereas the "trained" class of supervisors rated their subordinates with a degree of reliability that was significantly greater than the reliability with which the "untrained" supervisors rated their subordinates, it is interesting to note that there was no significant difference between the two groups of supervisors in the leniency with which they rated their employees.

Only two of the factors studied yielded significant correlations with leniency. These were the Persuasive Component of the Kuder Preference Record and the California Test of Mental Maturity. In each case the coefficient of correlation was $r = -.43$. It is of interest to note that the coefficient of correlation between the Persuasive Component and the I.Q. obtained from the test of Mental Maturity was $r = -.07$. This would indicate that:

1. The more intense the persuasive interest and the higher the I.Q., the less lenient will be the rater in rating his subordinates; and,
2. Whatever relationship either of these factors has with leniency, it is (within this group) relatively free from the influence of the other factor.

INFLUENCE OF VARIOUS FACTORS ON "HALO"

"Halo," the third of the basic problems in merit rating, is not a unitary problem to be treated by itself; but, as in the case of reliability and leniency, a phenomenon related to other factors. Of the various items studied in relation to "halo," five yield correlations of sufficient magnitude or significance to warrant specific mention. These are *"training" in rating, mental maturity, reliability of ratings, supervisory-administrative interest and persuasive interest.*

Whereas within the entire group of 77 supervisors the mean coefficient of correlation between length of personal acquaintance and score on the rating scale is $r = -.42$; for those supervisors in the "untrained" class this mean r is $-.48$, and for those in the "trained" class, this mean

TABLE 7

MEAN COEFFICIENT OF CORRELATION BETWEEN EACH OF SEVERAL CHARACTERISTICS OF THE RATERS AND OF THE RATINGS AND THE FACTOR OF "HALO" FOR ALL SUPERVISORS AND FOR THOSE IN THE "TRAINED" AND "UNTRAINED" GROUPS

RELATIONSHIP OF "HALO" WITH OTHER FACTORS	COEFFICIENT OF "HALO"		
	Total Group	Trained	Untrained
Mean Coefficient of "Halo........$r = -.42$		$r = -.32$	$r = -.48$
Range of Coeff. of "Halo"........$r = +.07$		$r = +.07$	$r = +.06$
to $r = -.76$		to $r = -.71$	to $r = -.76$
I.Q. of Rater vs. "Halo"..........$r = -.46$		$r = -.68$	$r = -.30$
Reliability of Ratings vs. "Halo"....................$r = -.31$		$r = -.21$	$r = -.38$
S.D. of Ratings vs. "Halo"........$r = -.20$		$r = -.17$	$r = -.24$
Supervisory-Administrative Interest vs. "Halo"..............$r = -.25$		$r = -.30$	$r = -.16$
Age of Rater vs. "Halo"..........$r = +.07$		$r = +.04$	$r = +.09$
Persuasive Interest vs. "Halo"....................$r = -.25$		$r = -.35$	$r = -.12$
Social Service Interest vs. "Halo"....................$r = -.17$		$r = -.15$	$r = -.19$
Size of Group Rated vs. "Halo"....................$r = +.08$		$r = +.06$	$r = +.11$
Leniency vs. "Halo"..............$r = -.17$		$r = -.26$	$r = -.11$
Academic Training vs. "Halo".....$r = -.10$		$r = -.08$	$r = -.14$
Supervisory Experience vs. "Halo"....................$r = +.14$		$r = +.09$	$r = +.21$

r is only $-.32$ (see Table 7). This would support the assumption that special training in rating reduces the influence of bias on ratings.

The correlation between mental maturity and "halo" for the total group is $r = -.46$. For the "trained" class this correlation is $r = -.68$; and for the "untrained" class it is $r = -.30$. These results indicate that, generally speaking, the ratings submitted by brighter supervisors are less colored by bias than are the ratings submitted by those supervisors who are less intelligent. In addition, training serves to intensify this difference between the more intelligent and less intelligent supervisors. This point can be shown in another manner (Table 8).

The mean coefficient of correlation between length of acquaintance and scores on the rating scale is shown for each group. These data reveal that (1) the ratings submitted by the less intelligent "untrained" supervisors are most colored by bias (coefficient of "halo" is $r = +.55$); (2) the ratings submitted by the more intelligent "trained" supervisors are those that are least colored by bias (coefficient of "halo" is $r = +.28$); and that (3) intelligence may be more important than "training" in reducing bias as seen by a comparison of the mean coefficient of "halo" for the more intelligent "untrained" supervisors ($r = +.35$) and the mean coefficient of "halo" for the less intelligent "trained" supervisors ($r = +.41$).

In the case of the Supervisory-Administrative and Persuasive Interest components, the relationship with "halo" were low negative correlations (Supervisory-Administrative Interest vs. "halo" $r = -.30$; and Persuasive Interest vs. "halo" $r = -.35$).

TABLE 8

RELATIONSHIP OF I.Q. TO "HALO" IN
"TRAINED" AND "UNTRAINED" CLASSES

	MEAN CORRELATIONS	
I.Q. SCORES	Trained	Untrained
I.Q. = 125 or higher	$M_r = +.28$	$M_r = +.35$
I.Q. = 124 or lower	$M_r = +.41$	$M_r = +.55$

This would indicate that the more intense the levels of these interests within the supervisor, the less the ratings he submitted would be colored by bias. The relationship of reliability to "halo" was covered in the discussion of reliability of ratings, where it was shown that a negative correlation existed between these two variables.

Summary and Conclusion

As stated in the introduction to this article, the general purpose of the study was to determine the degree to which certain weaknesses inherent in the ratings submitted on an existing scale could be reduced or overcome by designing a new scale and by training supervisors in the principles and techniques of rating. To obtain the information required for the study, several problems were investigated:

1. To determine the degree to which reliability, leniency and bias existed in the former merit-rating system;
2. To determine the influence of the format of the rating scale, special training in rating and certain characteristics of the supervisors upon reliability, leniency and bias.
3. To modify the rating procedure and to conduct several follow-up studies in order to determine the net gains once the new procedure had been put to practical use.

The specific isolated studies conducted during these investigations revealed certain facts which are of sufficient interest and importance to warrant special mention:

1. The type of scale to be used has a marked influence on the value of merit ratings. Ratings on "objective" or *descriptive* scales are more reliable, less influenced by bias, and show less deviation between raters in leniency and severity than is characteristic of ratings on "subjective" or *evaluational* scales.
2. Special training given to supervisors in the principles and techniques of rating raises the reliability of, and reduces the influence of bias on, the merit ratings that they give their subordinates.
3. The higher the level of mental maturity of the rater, the more reliable, less lenient, and less biased will be the ratings he gives his subordinates.
4. Certain components of the interest inventory provide measures that related to a reduction of leniency and of the influence of bias in rating.
5. Within the scope of this specific study, the data revealed that the scores on merit-rating scales measure primarily the personal-social relationships between supervisor and subordinate rather than the output of the subordinate in question.

From this study, two points at least can be concluded. *First*, the study represents a good illustration of an accepted "fact" in industrial relations that work will be performed more efficiently if people with the suitable characteristics are selected to do the job, if they are given the proper tools with which to work, and if they are trained to use these tools. *Second*, that further assertions regarding the use and value of merit-rating scales should be based upon tested and demonstrable fact and not upon speculation and assumption.

14. Using Critical Incidents to Measure Job Proficiency Factors*

Wayne K. Kirchner and Marvin D. Dunnette

WHILE NEARLY EVERY newspaper, magazine, or professional journal is bemoaning the current shortage of engineers and offering sage advice as to what should be done about it, there is another manpower problem, less publicized but nonetheless crucial—the shortage of salesmen. Large and small companies alike are "beating the bushes" hoping to flush reasonably competent males to handle their selling jobs. It has been estimated that over 400,000 new salesmen are needed in 1957 alone. As matters stand now, the basic question in hiring a salesman is not *can he sell* but *will he try.*

* From "Identifying the Critical Factors in Successful Salesmanship," *Personnel*, Vol. 34, 1957, pp. 54–59.

To increase the flow of applicants, recruiting programs have been stepped up by many companies and emphasis has been placed on making selling a more prestigeful job. Both these approaches have produced results. Generally speaking, however, not enough emphasis has been placed on the most important question of all: *What are the critical factors in successful selling?* If these can be identified, certainly the selection and placement of applicants, as well as the utilization of the current sales force, can be greatly improved.

Determining the "critical" factors is a tough job, however. There is no shortage of *opinions* about what constitutes salesmanship, but *facts* are harder to come by. The reason is that it is difficult to define in any objective form the actual behavior that characterizes the successful salesman. Such indicators as volume of sales, number of calls made, or number of orders taken certainly provide some measures of the over-all effectiveness of a salesman, but they do not tell *why* he is or is not successful. Nor do they yield any clues, in most cases, as to why one salesman is better than another. Here again there is no dearth of personal opinions— "he looks like a good boy," or "he's not too sharp"—but these are of little help in actually defining the elements that go to make up "good" or "poor" sales behavior.

A real need exists, therefore, for measures of sales effectiveness based on the actual behavior of salesmen on the job. With such data, the training of new sales people, the appraisal of selling performance, and the selection of candidates can be undertaken with greater accuracy and assurance.

While many approaches are available for studying behavior on the job, the technique of critical incidents seems ideally suited to our purposes. Originally developed by Flanagan,[1] this method has been used by many firms to obtain information about behavior in various kinds of jobs. The major purpose of this article is to describe certain critical incidents in selling behavior that actually occurred among salesmen in one company and to show how such incidents may be categorized into meaningful factors or functions in effective selling.

THE CRITICAL INCIDENTS APPROACH

The rationale of this technique is simple enough. Critical incidents are just what the name implies—occurrences that have proved to be the key to effective performance on the job. They involve not routine activities but rather those essentials in job performance which make the difference between success and failure. In applying the technique, critical incidents are recorded in the form of stories or anecdotes about how a person handles certain situations, and from these data a composite picture of job behavior is built up.

[1] John C. Flanagan, "A New Approach to Evaluating Personnel," *Personnel*, Vol. 26, 1949, pp. 35–42.

The study reported here was carried out in the Minnesota Mining and Manufacturing Company which employs over 1,000 salesmen. Critical incident forms were printed and sent to 85 sales managers in four separate product divisions (see Exhibit 1). Each manager was asked to report as many critical incidents as possible illustrating both effective and noneffective behavior among his own group of salesmen. It was felt that sales managers would be acquainted with many such incidents because of their day-to-day contact with the problems of their salesmen, and this belief was amply confirmed. A total of 135 incidents was reported, of which 96 could be classified as "usable." Of these 96, 61 were instances of effective performance while 35 concerned noneffective performance. Each incident was reviewed and summarized.

To illustrate the type of information contained in these reports, five of the incidents reported are given below in summary form:

1. A salesman received a complaint from a customer about the quality of a particular type of tape. He failed to look into the matter or write up a formal complaint. The defective tape was returned to the jobber and no credit was issued to the jobber or to the retailer involved. While the account was not lost, the customer was dissatisfied for a long time.
2. A large customer complained about our tape and decided to try out a competitor's tape. The complaint was justified and a substitution run was recommended. The salesman told the customer about this new run and said it would come in the next order. He did not tie this down with the jobber, however, and the jobber shipped more of the old run when the customer's order came through. As a result, the customer felt that the salesman could not be trusted and withdrew his business.
3. A salesman driving down the street saw a truck containing equipment for which company products might used. He followed the truck to find the delivery point, made a call on this account, which was a new one, and obtained an order.
4. A jobber account had been lost. The salesman made it a point to contact the account once a month for over a year, explaining company policy and showing that our products would be easier to sell. After a year, the jobber returned to the company.
5. A large plant working on a defense project suddenly discovered that they were out of belts of a certain length which had to be made to order. The salesman borrowed utility rolls of the correct width and grit from a jobber, took them to a woodworking plant which made endless belts, and had enough belts made to keep the defense project going.

CRITICAL FACTORS IN SELLING

Since many of the incidents reported were overlapping, they could be grouped into broad and more meaningful categories. For example, a number of incidents concerned failures or successes in following up various types of requests, orders, and leads; hence it was a fairly simple matter to group these under the general head of "Following-up." Similar groupings were made for other related incidents, and this procedure yielded the following categories of critical functions or factors in selling:

1. Following-up:
   a. Complaints.
   b. Requests.
   c. Orders.
   d. Leads.
2. Planning ahead.
3. Communicating all necessary information to sales managers.
4. Communicating truthful information to managers and customers.
5. Carrying out promises.
6. Persisting on tough accounts.
7. Pointing out uses for other company products besides the salesman's own line.
8. Using new sales techniques and methods.
9. Preventing price-cutting by dealers and customer.
10. Initiating new selling ideas.
11. Knowing customer requirements.
12. Defending company policies.
13. Calling on all accounts.
14. Helping customers with equipment and displays.
15. Showing non-passive attitude.

These 15 factors derive from the actual job behavior of salesmen. A good salesman had to handle all or most of them well in order to succeed, and failure on any one count could lead to failure on the entire job.

As might be expected, however, these factors were not of equal weight in terms of the number of incidents reported for each category. The factor most often cited was that of "Following-up." Another was persistence on the part of the salesman. It seems that good salesmen do not give up easily; they tend to keep after tough accounts. In addition, they plan their activities well, as indicated by the number of incidents related to planning or the lack of it.

All 15 factors, however, seemed to characterize the behavior of the best salesmen in the company. Different items might be added to the list from studies made at other companies, of course, but these 15 seem to be the core of effective selling behavior.

The practical uses of critical incident data are evident. With information of this kind at hand, it becomes possible to pinpoint areas of strength or weakness in selling behavior. Checklists, appraisals by supervisors, self-appraisal, and similar methods can be used to compare the actual behavior of salesmen with the "model" and to institute improvements where needed.

One example of these methods is the sales behavior rating sheet derived from critical incidents, shown in Exhibit 2. Each item on the questionnaire represents a summary of a particular incident or group of incidents reported by sales managers. This questionnaire is now being

EXHIBIT 1

Critical Incident Record Form (Type I)*

Think back over a period of time (six months or so) long enough for you to have observed the activities of all your salesmen. Focus your attention on any one thing that one of your salesmen may have done which made you think of him as an outstandingly *good* or *very effective* salesman. In other words, think of a *critical incident* which has added materially to the overall success of your sales group. *Please do not record any names of persons involved in the following incident.*

What were the general circumstanced leading up to this incident?

Tell exactly what your salesman did that was so *effective* at that time.

How did this particular incident contribute to the overall effectiveness of your sales group?

When did this incident happen?

How long has this salesman been on his present territory?

How long has this salesman been with 3M? (*the company*)

---

* Type II is designed for incidents involving ineffective performance and is similar in form.

used in further research to establish criteria of sales effectiveness that will aid in validating tests of applicants for sales positions.

Another possibility is the use of the questionnaire in setting up criteria of sales effectiveness focused on the company's actual job requirements. Here, obviously, is a major advantage of the critical incident method. It is "tailor-made." Whatever the company, its needs can be served most directly by data based on the performance of its own employees.

Inasmuch as this kind of information gives clues to the type of person needed on sales jobs, it is also valuable, of course, in the actual selection of sales candidates.

EXHIBIT 2

A Behavior Rating Sheet
Derived From Critical Selling Incidents

Name of person being described _____

Below are listed several statements about selling behavior. Consider each statement in terms of the person named above. Would you agree or disagree with the statement if you heard it used to describe that person? How strongly would you agree or disagree?

For each statement, please check the category which most accurately reflects your agreement or disagreement. Remember to base each answer on how well or how poorly the statement describes the person named above.

Thanks a great deal for your help.

1. Allows too much credit to doubtful customers.
    ____Strongly Agree ____Agree ____Undecided ____Disagree ____Strongly Disagree

2. Gossips about customer's confidential information.
    ____Strongly Agree ____Agree ____Undecided ____Disagree ____Strongly Disagree

3. Writes poor sales reports.
    ____Strongly Agree ____Agree ____Undecided ____Disagree ____Strongly Disagree

4. Assists fellow salesmen with displays, etc. when needed.
    ____Strongly Disagree ____Disagree ____Undecided ____Agree ____Strongly Agree

5. Apt to be late in passing along price changes to customers.
    ____Strongly Disagree ____Disagree ____Undecided ____Agree ____Strongly Agree

6. Shows lackadaisical attitude.
    ____Strongly Disagree ____Disagree ____Undecided ____Agree ____Strongly Agree

7. Follows up quickly on requests from customers.
    ____Strongly Disagree ____Disagree ____Undecided ____Agree ____Strongly Agree

* * *

21. Promises too much to customers.
    ____Strongly Agree ____Agree ____Undecided ____Disagree ____Strongly Disagree

22. Is familiar with competitive products and sales methods.
    ____Strongly Disagree ____Disagree ____Undecided ____Agree ____Strongly Agree

15. Some New Insights into Performance Appraisal*

Kenneth E. Richards

HARDLY A MONTH goes by without the appearance somewhere of an article on performance appraisal, a subject of controversy for over 40 years. The article, moreover, will fall into one of two distinct categories. Its title will be either something on the order of "How to Establish a Performance Appraisal Program" or else a variant of "An Agonizing Reappraisal of Appraisal."

When a topic keeps the center of the stage as long as this, it is evident that the heart of the problem has not yet been reached—let alone the solution!

In the past, most of the discussion about performance appraisal centered on the difficulties inherent in the rating process itself—the "halo effect" and the unwillingness or inability of raters to use the extremes of the rating scale. It was to counteract these weaknesses that such methods as group appraisal and forced-choice rating were devised. Similarly, the "critical incident" technique was developed to provide more "objective" ratings than were forthcoming from the use of conventional rating scales.

More recently, however, attention has been focused less on the difficulties of the rating procedure than on the problems presented by the way people react to being appraised. Among such problems, for example, are these:

1. Low grades make people angry.
2. Criticism arouses defensiveness and resentment. Hence, far from stimulating the employee to improve, it tends to reinforce his present behavior.
3. There is a steady widening of differences between people who must work together.

In short, the more modern approach to performance appraisal views it as essentially a problem in communications—the establishment of a constructive relationship between the rater and the employee. This approach, which we use at United Air Lines, sees performance appraisal as a supervisory tool, a means of helping the employee maintain satisfactory performance on his *present* job. Hence, our program is based on the idea that an appraisal system should provide opportunities for

* From *Personnel*, Vol. 37, 1960, pp. 28–38.

talking with, and counseling, the employee, thereby creating mutual understanding and better supervisory-employee relations.

But before an appraisal program can actually operate in this manner, we need to know more than we do about what really goes on between the participants in an appraisal interview. At United Air Lines, we have explored this problem through a projective device designed to tap attitudes and feelings at a deeper, unconscious level.[1]

We adopted this method because we believe that until the unconscious feelings about appraisal have been uncovered, it is not possible to develop a program that will be effective in terms of the goals defined above.

The device we used, called the PEP Situation Survey, after our Personnel Evaluation Program, consists of four pictures about performance appraisal. It follows the pattern of such familiar projective tests as the Rorschach and the TAT. Each picture appears on a separate sheet of paper, with space to write a story about it.

This article will discuss what we learned from administering the PEP Situation Survey to 47 supervisors and managers from various UAL departments. At the outset, the participants were given the following instructions:

We'd like to get your reactions to these pictures about the Personnel Evaluation Program. You are to write a brief story about each picture, describing the thoughts and feelings that are involved.
If you wish, you may give the people in the pictures a name and a job classification. Tell what each person in the picture is thinking, feeling, and saying. In concluding your stories, tell the outcome or results of the meeting.

(Participants were allotted about five minutes to write each story.)

ANTICIPATING THE APPRAISAL INTERVIEW

The first picture (Figure 1) was designed to find out what supervisors imagined their subordinates were thinking as they came in for their annual PEP review. It elicited three kinds of stories:

1. This particular employee's work throughout the past year has been generally satisfactory. He looks forward to the interview with confidence, knowing full well that his supervisor is eager to help him by counseling him about his career with the company.
2. "I wonder if he's noticed that I tried to improve the factors I was rated low in last year. I wish I'd had more opportunities to meet with him. How can he possibly evaluate me when our contacts are so limited?"
3. "I wonder where I'm going to be downgraded. I have plenty of material to refute anything my supervisor will say. I doubt if he is qualified to evaluate certain aspects of my work. He never knows about some of the better things I do because I don't tell him, while I do tell him about the problems—perhaps too freely."

---

[1] The term "unconscious" is viewed differently by different schools of psychology. For our purposes, the best definition is the one given in Collier's *Encyclopedia*, Vol. XIX, p. 16: "We will call a process 'unconscious' when we have to assume that it was active *at a certain time* although *at that time* we knew nothing about it."

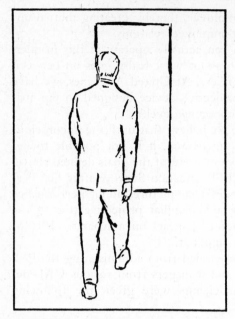

FIGURE 1

INSTRUCTION: In this picture the employee is about to enter his supervisor's office for his annual PEP review. Write a story describing his thoughts and feelings.

The most salient feature of these stories is the direct correlation they show between the feelings expressed by the employee and the quality of his relations with his supervisor. The employee in the first story, who shows no anxiety, knows his supervisor wants to help him. The second employee, who is anxious about the conference, regrets the lack of contact with his supervisor. The third, who is defensive, already has unsatisfactory relations with his supervisor, and the relations are likely to become worse.

The three categories *non-anxious, anxious,* and *defensive* can be applied to the feelings expressed in all 47 stories written about Figure 1. As Table 1 indicates, most of the stories show the employee feeling anxious or defensive about the forthcoming interview.[2] These feelings correlate with another element of the stories—mention of plans for improvement. The table shows that only two out of the 24 anxious employees and none of the defensive ones are planning to improve their job performance. Comments like "I know I've been doing a good job, but does my boss know it?" reveal that what these employees want is not suggestions for improvement but reassurance that everything is all right. On the other hand, more than half the non-anxious employees plan to do better in the coming year.

These findings suggest that a relaxed atmosphere, characterized by mutual understanding, is effective in motivating the employee to improve

---

[2] Table 1 is reproduced through the courtesy of the *Journal of Business,* Graduate School of Business of the University of Chicago, Chicago, Ill. It appeared in an article by the author entitled "A New Concept of Performance Appraisal," July, 1959, pp. 229–43. It is discussed there in greater detail.

TABLE 1

CORRELATION BETWEEN REACTIONS TO APPRAISAL AND PLANS TO IMPROVE

REACTION	Number	PLANS TO IMPROVE Yes	No
Non-Anxious Feelings:			
Glad, pleased, hopeful..................	4	3	1
Confident...........................	7	2	5
Looking forward to meeting.............	4	3	1
Reflective..........................	1	1	—
Sub-total........................	16	9	7
Anxious Feelings:			
Apprehensive, insecure, anxious.........13		—	13
Uncertain..........................10		2	8
Hurt.............................. 1		—	1
Sub-total........................24		2	22
Defensive Feelings...................... 7		—	7
Grand total................. 47		11	36

his performance, whereas a threatening atmosphere is not. Of course, it does not follow that even in a threatening situation employees may not be highly interested in bettering their positions in terms of higher status and pay. Several stories mention this kind of intention to improve.

WHAT HAPPENS IN THE INTERVIEW?

The second picture (Figure 2) provided information about the interaction between the supervisor and the employee during the review meet-

FIGURE 2

INSTRUCTION: In this picture the employee feels he is doing a good job. The supervisor thinks so too, but he would like to see improvement in a few areas. Tell what each person is thinking, feeling, and saying and describe the outcome of the meeting.

ing. The stories written about this picture show that the supervisors are concerned about their own ability to tell the employee his weak points in such a way as not to have an adverse effect on his attitude and future performance. About half the supervisors—23 of the 47—think they must emphasize the employee's weak points in order to help him. This is revealed by such comments in the stories as the three that follow:

1. Asking the employee what he would like to talk about gives the supervisor an opportunity to discuss frankly the areas that need further strengthening.

2. "If I can get my thoughts across, then John should be able to improve."

3. *Supervisor:* "I think you're doing a fine job, but I have listed the items on which you could improve." *Employee:* "Yes, I see you have." As the interview ends, both parties feel it was highly unsatisfactory.

But, as Table 2 shows, only one of these 23 supervisors envisions the employee as planning to improve. Only three of the 47 supervisors choose to emphasize the employee's *good* points; the interviews they describe, however, do result in plans to improve. Of the 13 stories in which the

TABLE 2

Supervisor's Behavior in Review Meeting and
Employee's Reactions and Plans to Improve

	Supervisor's Behavior				
Employee's Reactions	Supervisor establishes climate for exchanging ideas or is eager to mention employee's good points.	Supervisor emphasizes strong points; makes suggestions or guides employee into discussing improvement.	Supervisor mentions strong points in order to bring up weak points.	Supervisor feels he must emphasize the employee's weak points to help him; establishes formal atmosphere.	Total
Defensive or not accepting......	0	0	3	18	21
Friendly, at ease...	1	6	3	3	13
Pleased.........	2	7	2 (with good points)	0	11
Not indicated....	0	0	0	2	2
Total.....	3	13	8	23	47
Plans to improve.	3	10	3	1	17

supervisor makes suggestions and guides the employee into discussing improvement, ten show plans to improve. In eight stories the supervisor uses the "sandwich" method, interlarding compliments with references to weak points; in only three of these does the method bring success. More often, the pictured employee senses that the supervisor is trying to manipulate him, as the following story illustrates:

Supervisor: "I'll start with some of his good points. Perhaps I can get him to bring up the weak ones. If not, I'll mention them."

Employee: "The supervisor is trying for something. I don't like his paternalistic attitude. If he has something on his mind, let him say it and leave psychology out of it." The conference represented a battle of wits.

The stories about Figure 2 do not merely tell which techniques are the most effective. The fact that only 36 per cent of the respondents chose to give their stories a happy ending suggests that supervisors are for the most part pessimistic about their ability to motivate and develop their employees.

But, as Table 2 shows, the more "permissive" the approach, the greater the likelihood of improvement in the employee's performance

—or, stated another way, the "employee-centered" approach is more effective than the "production-centered" approach. The supervisor who emphasizes the employee's weak points may thus be able to satisfy some of his own personal needs, but "laying it on the line" is likely to raise defensiveness and inhibit improvement on the part of the employee.

MORE SUPPORT FOR "PERMISSIVENESS"

The last two pictures (Figures 3 and 4) were designed to give further insights into the differences in behavior that produce success and

FIGURE 3

INSTRUCTION: The PEP review meeting is over and both the supervisor and the employee look pleased with the results. The supervisor is pleased because he is sure the employee is going to improve. The employee does improve! Tell what went on during the meeting and how the employee improved.

FIGURE 4

INSTRUCTION: The situation is the same as in the last picture—except that the employee does not improve! Tell what went on during the meeting and what kind of improvement the supervisor had expected.

failure in motivating improvement. The two pictures, and the situations they represent, are identical, but in Figure 3 the employee improves after the meeting, and in Figure 4 he does not.

A comparison of supervisors' behavior in the stories written about these two pictures (Table 3) confirms the greater effectiveness of the permissive approach. The stories about Figure 3 show the supervisor complimenting the employee, listening to him, and letting him discover his weaknesses for himself—evidently feeling safe in doing so—whereas the stories about Figure 4 show the supervisor emphasizing the negative side of the employee's work, speaking very frankly, using threats, and doing all the talking.

In writing about the successful interview, some participants pictured the supervisor as an older, wiser man, or one with some other special attributes, thus revealing their feeling that extraordinary powers are needed to gain the employee's confidence and get him to follow instructions. A few "success" stories showed the supervisor winning the employee's cooperation by dangling the possibility of promotion in front of him. Of course, supervisors who actually use this technique have trouble in finding something to say to an employee they don't consider

TABLE 3

SUPERVISOR'S BEHAVIOR IN SUCCESSFUL AND UNSUCCESSFUL INTERVIEWS

DESCRIPTION	FIGURE 3 Review Meeting Resulting in Improvement	FIGURE 4 Review Meeting Resulting in No Improvement
GROUP 1: Supervisor recognizes the employee's good performance, compliments him; establishes a relaxed atmosphere for listening, exchanging ideas, and letting the employee discover his own weaknesses.	25	0
GROUP 2: Supervisor has special attributes or methods that enable him to instill confidence in the employee and get his cooperation.	10	1
GROUP 3: Supervisor promises or implies promotion or suggests that the employee has potential.	8	2
GROUP 4: Supervisor lists the employee's weaknesses or places major emphasis on them.	2	9
GROUP 5: Supervisor is not effective in communicating ideas, does all the talking, or overgeneralizes.	1	19
GROUP 6: Supervisor is blunt and critical in reporting weaknesses or frankly warns of loss of job or opportunity for promotion.	0	15

(Only 46 of the 47 stories could be tabulated.)

promotable and are therefore likely to suggest that he shouldn't be evaluated every year—even though it is this kind of employee who may be most in need of guidance.

In general, then, the stories written by our 47 supervisors and managers reveal considerable anxiety and apprehension in the supervisory-employee relationship. Most of the imaginary employees are anxious for reassurance that their work is being favorably noticed. It is mostly the few who are not anxious who make plans to improve their performance. The anxious employees are so engrossed in protecting their feelings or defending themselves that they have little energy left for growth and development.

The pictured supervisors have mixed feelings. In most of the stories, the supervisor is in a dilemma—he knows that it is important to discuss the employee's weak points in such a way as not to affect his performance, but he does not seem to know how to do this. Only 4 per cent of the supervisors who felt that they had to tell the employee to do better actually secured plans for improvement.

If even the stories about successful appraisal situations manifest so much anxiety, it is no wonder that supervisors and managers frequently offer arguments for minimizing the use of performance appraisal or doing away with it entirely.

IS THERE A WAY OUT?

One of the most common rationalizations runs this way: "We do not need an annual performance review because we should be talking with our employees more than once a year, anyway." This argument is, of course, theoretically sound, but the supervisors who propound it are seldom the ones who provide year-round performance counseling for their men.

This was well brought out in R. H. Finn's report on a series of discussions about performance appraisal that was held at the Plantation Pipe Line Company.[3] The supervisors, while agreeing that it was desirable to evaluate and discuss job performance with each employee, did not believe a formal program was necessary. The employees, on the other hand, wanted a formal program because they doubted whether their supervisors would voluntarily provide them with the opportunity to "talk things over." Ironically enough, the supervisors invariably said they wanted and needed periodic private discussions with their own bosses. Apparently, it's only when they are confronted with the responsibility of discussing their evaluations with their subordinates that supervisors find reasons for doing away with performance appraisal altogether.

It has also been said that supervisors resist making appraisals because they dislike "feeling like God." No such feeling was evident, however, in the stories written by the UAL supervisors. On the contrary, as has been seen, most of them reveal feelings of inadequacy. The argument about feeling like God seems to be simply a rationalization of the desire to avoid a particularly distasteful responsibility. After all, supervisors do not demur that they feel like God when they are called upon to promote one person rather than another, or to uproot a man and his family by transferring him hundreds or thousands of miles away. These are recognized and accepted responsibilities of management. Why, then, the special qualms about appraisal?

APPRAISAL GOES HAND-IN-HAND WITH AUTHORITY

No doubt the process of having to explain their judgments to their subordinates does make supervisors uneasily aware that they have indeed been "acting like God"—but though this makes appraisal more

---

[3] R. H. Finn, "Is Your Appraisal Program Really Necessary?" *Personnel*, Vol. 37, 1960, pp. 16–25.

difficult, it is no argument for dispensing with it. One way or another, managers cannot escape making judgments about their subordinates— and so long as management entails the power and the privilege of making decisions affecting other people, the responsibility of advising those affected must go with it.

Another argument against performance appraisal that has been gaining favor lately holds that appraisal is not the supervisor's responsibility at all —if the employee is to grow, he must know and criticize *himself*. There is truth in this also, but it is, after all, the supervisor's opinion that determines the employee's work assignments and his progress in the company. The employee knows what he thinks of himself—his problem is, "What does the boss think?" If there is to be mutual understanding, the supervisor must take the initiative in reconciling his evaluation of the employee's performance with the employee's self-evaluation.

Since, as our study shows, there seems to be a general awareness that permissiveness is likely to stimulate plans for improvement, whereas the supervisor who "lays it on the line" most commonly encounters resentment and defensiveness, we may well ask, why aren't supervisors more permissive? Why do they feel it necessary to threaten the employee with separation or hint that he will not be promoted if he does not improve?

One possible explanation is that permissiveness is somehow incompatible with the supervisor's concept of his own role. He may think his role demands only that he give orders and enforce rules and regulations. This self-definition precludes permissiveness by making him increasingly insensitive to the impact his methods have on his subordinates.

Another explanation may lie in the concept of the supervisor's role held by his company's higher-level management. His superiors' attitudes provide a "climate" that conditions his behavior. If they see permissiveness as weakness, the supervisor is not likely to employ it.

WHAT PERFORMANCE APPRAISAL CAN—AND CANNOT—DO

Supervisors' views of appraisal and appraisal methods, then, are often distorted by their own anxieties and self-perceptions and by pressures from above. Similarly, top management's opinions frequently stem from a false perspective. While business leaders generally agree on the need for formal appraisal, many of them are disappointed in its actual workings.[4] They see its value seriously diminished by its three kinds of limitations—limitations that, from another point of view, are inherent in appraisal but are not particularly relevant:

1. Its inaccuracy as a measuring device. As has already been noted, the newer approach sees this limitation as largely a result of difficulties in communications and interpersonal relations.

2. Its inadequacy as an administrative tool. According to the newer ap-

---

[4] For a fuller discussion of this point, see "A New Concept of Performance Appraisal," *loc. cit.*

proach, performance appraisal cannot and should not be used for determining wage increases, promotions, and the like. Moreover, management's purposes in applying appraisal are often mutually contradictory: a report that was written to help an employee improve his job performance is not likely to give the sort of information that would be needed to justify a salary increase.

3. Its failure to provide universally accepted standards of judgment. How, for example, can a mere procedure for evaluating performance make two supervisors—one aggressive and gregarious, the other quiet and reserved—see any one employee in the same light?

The fact of the matter is, performance appraisals are likely to be neither more nor less than a reflection of the relationship existing between the people involved—in other words, the supervisor-subordinate relationship. But that's surely important enough! The successful operation of the company hinges upon successful supervisory-employee relationships at every level, from the bottom to the top. From vice presidents on down, every employee has a supervisor—and for that matter, the president himself can be said to participate in a supervisory-employee relationship with the chairman of the board or with the board of directors. Any device for improving this relationship throughout the organization cannot help but have a profound effect on it.

PERFORMANCE APPRAISAL AS A SUPERVISORY TOOL

At United Air Lines, therefore, we regard performance appraisal as a *supervisory* tool—not a management tool. We take the view that the major activity of all employees is the work they perform from day to day. They are not always being considered for salary increases or for promotion to another job. Important as these events are, they take place only once or twice a year or even less frequently. Hence, we believe that assisting the employee to maintain satisfactory performance on his *present* job is a worthwhile objective in itself and have other programs for administering salaries and appraising potential.

In our program, the supervisor prepares a narrative report from which all grades and scores have been eliminated. We train him to write this report in such a way as to stimulate, rather than inhibit, discussion. When a report has been completed, the supervisor reviews it with his superior —a procedure that helps to insure accuracy and completeness and also serves the purpose of preparing the supervisor for his interview with the employee who is being appraised.

This approach gives the supervisor considerable freedom—and also calls for the exercise of considerable judgment on his part. For example, if he feels that a comment he might write about a particular phase of the employee's work is likely to cause resentment or raise the employee's defenses, he can decide not to mention it on the evaluation report. On the other hand—and this is important—if the employee is doing something that simply cannot be tolerated any longer, the supervisor must include it in his report and discuss it with the employee.

Of course, some supervisors see this whole arrangement as an "out" and put down only the favorable aspects of the employee's performance. Then, when a problem crops up that should have been discussed with the employee earlier, difficulties may arise. But this disadvantage is not peculiar to our system—there are some supervisors who cannot face issues regardless of the form or system in use. Even when we used grades, many employees who had received satisfactory reports came up with problems that should have been faced previously. One cannot *force* a supervisor to face an uncomfortable situation with any system. One can only continue to work with him and use every situation such as this as a training opportunity to develop mutual understanding between supervisors and higher-level managers.

Teachers and practitioners of counseling have often maintained that written reports should not be used in a performance appraisal program. But this view overlooks the fact that the supervisor is in a different situation from that of the professional counselor. Because of his own stake in the work unit the supervisor cannot always wait for the employee to bring up a problem and work it through. The professional counselor, on the other hand, while he wants to help the individual, is not personally involved in the job situation and can afford to wait.

Basically, I suppose, our program might be described as "non-directive." But all labels are misleading—certainly, we have found that there are times when our supervisors can be very direct when working with employees. In fact, as I have mentioned, there are times when the supervisor *must* be very direct.

For the most part, we do try to teach supervisors to be better listeners, to be sensitive to the impact their own leadership and suggestions are having on the employee and to learn to reflect the employee's comments in such a way as to serve as a mirror through which the employee can see himself as others see him. In this way, the employee can obtain insights about himself—a more effective way, as this study indicates, of bringing about change. Once the employee begins to find out things about himself he does not like, he has taken the essential first step along the road to improvement, because he himself is the only person who can bring about real and lasting change in his behavior.

Section Three

TRAINING EMPLOYEES AND MANAGERS

Introduction

THE TRAINING OF employees and managers represents one of the most extensive personnel activities in modern organizations. This section describes some representative contributions of psychologists to principles and developments in this area.

We must point out that a recent trend in training has been to broaden its scope in industry. Companies are becoming more concerned with developing the individual in more ways than in his immediate job behavior. Thus, many companies offer employees courses ranging from public speaking and blueprint reading to psychology and mathematics. Or executives may participate in programs to improve their reading speed or to become "more sensitive" to interpersonal relations. In one company, some managers are sent back to college for a year of "liberal arts," which, it is hoped, may broaden their approach to complex decisions and policy-making problems. The precise value of many of these programs is not yet known, but many of these developments and ideas are exciting and present a challenge to educators and researchers in this field.

We must not lose sight of the fact that much training activity is still concerned with specific job skills. Studies of learning from basic psychology should be of help in determining the optimum conditions of training. The first article in this section by McGehee, "Learning Theory and Training," presents some of the issues and problems in applying such principles in the industrial training environment.

The training department must make day-to-day decisions of the proper procedures and methods to use in relation to the skills in question. Traditional approaches may not always be the best ones and are being questioned more and more. This is where research comes in. The next three articles illustrate specific research on the relative effectiveness of different training approaches.

One sometimes forgets that motivation and attitudes are important factors influencing learning. Since the function of training is to change behavior, traditional lecture methods may not always be effective. In "Lecture versus Group Decision in Changing Behavior," Levine and Butler show this in training supervisors to improve their merit ratings.

The article by Adams, "The Comparative Effectiveness of Electric and Manual Typewriters in the Acquisition of Typing Skill," illustrates an evaluation of a highly specific training problem. The study illustrates how the important question of "transfer of training" can be evaluated. The article also presents a typical leaning curve for this kind of motor skill learning.

The important learning variable of "knowledge of results" is well known; without some kind of "feedback" of performance, the learner cannot improve very much. Yet, in industry, this principle is too often ignored. This is especially true of on-the-job training where the worker is often "turned loose." He may actually learn poor working habits and methods. Even when knowledge of results is provided, there is still the question of the *kind* of "feedback" that would be most effective. Thus, the worker may know he is producing defective items, but he may not know how to develop the skill to operate his machine more effectively. Mosel's article, "How to Feed Back Performance Results to Trainees," summarizes much of the research on these questions and applies the results to specific training problems. Many of these studies demonstrate that experience is not necessarily the best teacher and that systematic training procedures may benefit even experienced operators.

How does one develop a curriculum for a complex training program? Glickman and Vallance in "Curriculum Assessment with Critical Incidents," describe how to evaluate and improve the *content* of training programs using a novel approach, which should have wider application in industry.

The article by Skinner, "Teaching Machines," is a basic reference in the rapidly developing field of "automated teaching." Since this article was written, many industrial and other organizations have begun to use variations of "teaching machines," and there is little doubt this trend will continue. Skinner's approach is not the only one, but all effective devices have in common the advantages of providing: (1) immediate knowledge of results, (2) reinforcement for a correct response, (3) new material presented as fast as each individual trainee's progress will permit, and (4) a learning situation in which the trainee is actively practicing his responses rather than passively reading a text or listening to a lecture. Skinner's article describes these issues as well as the basic philosophy and technology of "teaching machines."

Two primary management skills involve "interpersonal relations" and "administrative decision making." The next two articles describe specific training methods in each of these areas. The article by Maier and Zerfoss discusses "Multiple Role Playing: A Technique for Training Supervisors," and illustrates a method used in "human relations" training. Dill's article, "Management Games for Training Decision Makers," illustrates the use of "management games" which allow a simulation of "real life" industrial problems. With the assistance of high-speed computers, management trainees make decisions and get feedback of the consequences of these decisions.

The final article, by Harris and Fleishman, shows how a supervisory training program was evaluated. Their article, "Human Relations Training and the Stability of Leadership Patterns," shows that sometimes the effects of such courses may depend on the individual and the situation in which he finds himself. This latter statement is reinforced in an article by Fleishman in the section on leadership. However, it would be well to emphasize here that the role of the immediate supervisor in training should not be overlooked. The supervisor is really "training" his men every day in the types of feedback he supplies to them and in the kinds of behavior he rewards on the job.

16. Learning Theory and Training*

William McGehee

THERE IS NO way to make this subject light. So I am going to start by defining the various concepts in my topic so that we (or at least I) will be reasonably certain about what I am trying to write.

First let us look at the term "theory." This is generally an anathema to the practical man. Yet in spite of its rather disreputable status among the "doers," these same characters make use of theory at least in a crude form. So let us examine the nature of theory.

A theory according to George Kelly is "a way of binding together a multitude of facts so that one may comprehend them all at once."[1] Kelly maintains that a theory, even if it is not highly scientific, can be useful since it can give meaning to our activities and provide a basis for an active approach to life. So even the theory that "13" is an unlucky number can lighten the life of a bookie. Likewise the theory that role playing, or case study, or visual aids, or the incident method is an answer to a training director's prayer is extremely comforting in his everyday life even if the theory is not highly scientific.

When a theory enables us to make reasonably precise predictions, one may call it scientific. The nearer theories come to precision of predictions, the more useful they are for controlling the phenomena with which they deal. To quote Kelly again, "Theories are the thinking of men who seek freedom amid swirling events. The theories concern prior assumptions about certain realms of these events. To the extent that the events may, from these prior assumptions, be construed, predicted, and their relative courses charted, men may exercise control and gain freedom for themselves in the process."[2]

Learning theory, then, is simply a way of binding together the facts known about the process we call "learning." Learning, itself, is a construct—an abstraction. No one of you has ever seen "learning." You have seen people in the process of learning, you have seen people who behave in a particular way as a result of learning, and some of you (in fact, I guess the majority of you) have "learned" at some time in your

---

* From "Are We Using What We Know about Training?—Learning Theory and Training," *Personnel Psychology*, Vol. 11, 1958, pp. 1–12.

[1] George A. Kelly, *The Psychology of Personal Constructs* (New York: W. W. Norton & Co., 1955), Vol. I, p. 18.

[2] *Ibid.*, p. 22.

life. In other words we infer that learning has taken place if an individual behaves, reacts, responds as a result of experience in a manner different from the way he formerly behaved. Changes in behavior which result from learning, by definition, exclude those changes which result from maturation or from physiological induced changes arising from fatigue, illness, intoxication and similar pleasant and unpleasant organic experiences. So when we talk about learning theory we are trying to derive from the facts known about the changes in behavior resulting from experience, generalizations which enable us to make predictions concerning changing behavior by experience. The more accurately these generalizations describe the processes by which experience changes behavior, the more useful will learning theory be in controlling the processes.

The central process in industrial training is learning. I am certain that the traditional man from Mars would not deduct this if he listened to training directors talking shop at conventions or weeping in each other's martinis about the lack of top management support for training activities. Very simply, industrial training consists in the organized experiences used to develop or modify knowledges, skills and attitudes of people involved in the production of goods and services.

What training directors are trying to do is to expose people in their companies to those types of experiences which will develop most effectively, or modify, knowledge, skills, and attitudes. Whether we are willing to admit it or not, the experience to which we expose our employees are those which we believe and/or can convince management to believe, will expedite the learning process. In other words, on the basis of "our prior assumptions about a certain realm of events," we establish vestibule training or send a reluctant member of middle management to the Harvard Advanced Management Course. Some of us in doing these things also have some theory as to how experience modifies behavior.

THE PROFESSIONALS AND LEARNING THEORY

Now let us take a look at what the professionals in learning theory have to offer. These are the gents who are not concerned with top management support. They do not have to deal with foremen who have been "learning" men a long time before training directors became epidemic in industry. Certainly they have their problems with the "butcher, the baker, and the candlestick maker" even as you or I, but the pressures are different and their goals are different. So I think we should understand a few things about these professionals before we try to see how their efforts at learning theory are applicable to industrial training.

First, these men are trying to develop "scientific" theories, i.e., generalizations, which closely approximate the phenomena under consideration. Consequently, they have had to adhere to procedures in their experiments which hold all variables constant except the experimental variable. This has resulted in too many reported studies which appear to the man, who is trying to train weavers or mill wrights, as almost puerile. Yet it is only by the careful addition of this bit of knowledge gained from studying the maze learning behavior of the white rats or of that bit from pursuit meter responses of college sophomores, that precise knowledge concerning learning is developed. This, of course, has led to a difficulty in applying these bits of knowledge to everyday problems of training. An experiment which demonstrates conclusively that white rats tend to repeat "rewarded" responses in learning on an elevated maze does not lead easily to the generalization that Rosie the Riveter responds in a similar manner as that of a lower order mammal. So the research, on which many theories of learning are based (since they deal with rats, chimpanzees, pre-school children, and college students) are not easily assimilated into the mores of the individual who must plan a training program to cut learning time for a group of operators assembling electrical relays or sewing seams on towels.

Second, the language used by learning theorists is esoteric and often (what is worse) mathematical. Again this is a penalty of their trade. Not only must generalizations be discovered but they must be stated also in unequivocal terms. Much of the English language is vague and pluralistic. Common words have multiple meanings and each hearer interprets in his own way. For example, Hull states "reaction-evocation potentiality is the product of a function of the habit strength multiplied by a function of the strength of the drive."[3] This can mean different things to different listeners. However, if the same principle can be expressed (as Hull does state it) $_sE_r = f(_sH_r) \times f(D)$ and these symbols are substituted for mathematically, everyone understands precisely what Hull means. Or do they? Actually where common everyday concepts are used, considerable misinterpretations arise. Thorndike, for example, reviewed the old Hedonistic controversy with his law of effect by using the everyday terms like "satisfaction" and "annoyance." It is unfortunate that the necessity for exactness in terminology has obscured (except to the initiated) the general principles of learning postulated by leading theorists like Hull and Tolman.

Finally, these searchers after fundamental truths are human, even as you and I. They bring to their search for underlying principles their own predispositions and they become enmeshed in their own theories. Accordingly not only do they interpret the results of their experiments in terms of their theoretical orientation, they also design experiments which serve to test their theories in terms of their theoretical orientation. Again the hypothetical man from Mars provided he was a non-connectionist, non-reinforcement theorist, and non-Gestalter, could find

---

[3] Clark L. Hall, *Principles of Behavior* (New York: D. Appleton-Century Company, 1943), p. 242.

definite evidence to support each of these theories in the famous study of the learning of simians reported by Kohler. The dispute among theorists concerning the learning process has increased the confusion of the layman without an appreciable gain in controlling the process.

GENERALIZATIONS CONCERNING LEARNING FOR INDUSTRIAL TRAINING

It is not possible, even if I could, in this article to present the subtleties of the major modern learning theories including among others Thorndike's connectionism, Hull's reinforcement theory, Lewin's topological psychology or Tolman's sign Gestalt theory. Rather on the basis of what these investigators and many others have learned about learning, I am going to try to make a few simple declarative statements about learning and then try to indicate their implications for industrial training. In trying to write these sentences I must acknowledge my indebtedness to certain individuals who have tried to synthesize the major concepts from various learning theories including J. F. Dashiell,[4] D. K. Adams,[5] T. R. McConnell,[6] Ernest Hilgard,[7] and Lee Cronbach.[8] They, however, should not be made to accept any criticism for my synthesis of their syntheses.

From this attempt to synthesize, the following generalizations concerning the learning process have evolved. They may be considered a statement of "what happens" when an individual learns. They can serve as guide posts for ordering experiences planned to modify behavior i.e., train the individual. I shall leave it to you to judge how nearly they describe learning. Later I want to cite their implications for industrial training. These statements are:

> The learner has a goal or goals, i.e., he wants something.
> The learner makes a response, i.e., he does something to attain what he wants.
> The responses, which he makes initially and continues to make in trying to attain what he wants, are limited by:
> The sum total of his past responses and his abilities.
> His interpretation of the goal situation.
> The feed back from his responses, i.e., the consequences of his response.
> The learner, having achieved his goal (or goal substitute), can make responses which prior to his goal seeking he could not make. He has learned.

---

[4] J. F. Dashiell, "A Survey and Synthesis of Learning Theories," *Psychological Bulletin,* 1932, pp. 261–75.

[5] D. K. Adams, "A Restatement of the Problem of Learning," *British Journal of Psychology,* Vol. 22, 1931, pp. 150–78.

[6] T. R. McConnell, "Reconciliation of Learning Theories," *National Society for Studies in Education,* 41st Yearbook, Part II, pp. 243–86.

[7] Ernest R. Hilgard, *Theories of Learning* (New York: Appleton-Century-Crofts, Inc., 1948).

[8] Lee Cronbach, *Educational Psychology* (New York: Harcourt, Brace & Co., Inc., 1952), p. 617.

IMPLICATIONS OF GENERALIZATIONS FOR INDUSTRIAL TRAINING

You at this point might easily say "so what." If this is an accurate description of learning, what are its implications for training in industry. As I have indicated, a theory gives the theorist a way to think about his phenomena. It can give him suggestions for predicting and for controlling the phenomena with which he is concerned. Now let us see what thinking about learning as outlined in my declarative sentences leads to in planning and directing industrial training activities.

First, I have postulated that if learning occurs the learner has a goal i.e., he wants something. Now goals can be many kinds—they can be short ranged or long ranged; they can be clearly thought out and verbalized or vague and subverbal. The question I raise here is just how much thought is given in planning any training program to the goals of the individuals who are to be trained. If you are planning training for a production worker, are his goals your goals? I imagine quite different outcomes of training would result if the employee accepted as his goal the production of the maximum units of a given quality in a given time (industry's goal) rather than accepting work group goals of producing enough to keep the foreman off his neck and the time study man from cutting his rate. What also of the training programs designed to improve the human relations behavior of foremen when the foreman's goal is to please a superior whose only concern is costs and units produced.

A recent study[9] gives a clear example of modifying goals which resulted in a significant change in the performance of a group of four operators. These four operators were rewinding bobbins from a spinning frame. In this salvage operation they produced waste at a ratio of 2.50 per week above standard. Methods were used with these operators to change their goal from rewinding so many bobbins a day to rewinding so many bobbins in such a way as to minimize waste. Within a 15 week period of training, these operators learned to handle bobbins in such a way that the waste was reduced to .87 of standard. This reduction with slight variation has persisted for over two years in this operation.[10] This represents a considerable savings in material in two years by careful attention to the goals of four operators. There was no decrease in amount of production during this period.

My second postulate is that the learner makes a response, i.e., he does something to attain his goal or goals. In learning rote verbal material or

[9] W. McGehee and D. H. Livingstone, "Training Reduces Material Waste," *Personnel Psychology*, Vol. 5, 1952, pp. 115–23. [Editor's note: The reader needs to know that the jobs of the operators, loopers, and setters, to which McGehee refers, are in a textile mill (Fieldcrest Mills).]

[10] W. McGehee and D. H. Livingstone, "Persistence of the Effects of Training Employees to Reduce Waste," *Personnel Psychology*, Vol. 7, 1954, pp. 33–39.

motor skills, we call this "practice"; perhaps in learning facts and developing attitudes and sentiments, we call this "experience."

One of the immediate consequences of accepting this postulate concerning learning is to acknowledge that effective industrial training must make provision for the learner to make a response. Training programs which emphasize elaborate visual aids, demonstrations, clever lectures, and similar devices for inducing learning at the price of learner activity become immediately suspect as to their effectiveness.

The second problem this postulate creates is the question as to whether all responses, "practice or experience," are equally valuable in the goal seeking activity of the learner. Fortunately, the learning theorists have gotten a reasonably clear answer to this question and the answer is "No." Certain valid statements can be made concerning the conditions necessary for effective practice and experience. The following are a few of these statements:

1. The more nearly responses made in a learning situation are those which an individual must make in "playing for keeps" the more quickly he'll learn to play for keeps effectively. For example, if both speed and accuracy are required to perform a task, the learner should be urged to make responses characterized by both speed and accuracy.

2. The order in which various responses are made in learning a task will facilitate or retard effective completion of the task at some subsequent time. If two responses to the similar situations are practiced before either response is firmly established, the situation may call out either one of these responses—one adequate and the other inadequate.

3. Immediate knowledge of the results of a response tends to correct the response most effectively. This was demonstrated in World War I by English's experiment in training rifle shooting and again in several situations in World War II in training radar operators, teaching code, and training director finders.[11] Lindahl's study in industry on cutting discs substantiates the same conclusion.[12] In spite of these results, very few industrial training programs provide for this feature of immediate knowledge of result.

4. Spacing of practice is extremely important. Again laboratory studies, while differing in details as to the application of this principle, have shown generally that spacing practice sessions results in more efficient learning. We have been able to demonstrate the value of spaced practice in learning several repetitive operations such as spinning and sewing machine operation. The major industrial ob-

---

[11] Dael Wolfe, "Training," in S. S. Stevens, *Handbook of Experimental Psychology* (New York: John Wiley & Sons, Inc., 1951), pp. 1,267–86.

[12] L. C. Lindahl, "Movement Analysis as an Industrial Training Method," *Journal of Applied Psychology*, Vol. 29, 1945, pp. 420–36.

jection to spaced practice is that the learner is at work for 8 hours a day and should be kept busy. Ingenious trainers, in spite of the 8-hour day, still can arrange for spaced practice. In this connection, I have wondered about the intensive training sessions which characterize many training programs for supervisors and managers. Could spacing these sessions result in more effective learning?

I could cite other points which have emerged from the investigations of the nature of practice and its effectiveness. You are as familiar with them as I am. What I want to stress again is that if we accept "responses" as integral part of learning, we immediately start asking questions about the necessary conditions for these responses to result in the most effective learning.

I would like to repeat my third postulate here since it is more involved verbally than either of the other two: What I have said is that the responses made by a learner in a goal situation are limited both initially and as he continues in the goal situation. I then stated there exists three general classes of limitations. Let us expand about the first limitation. I have said a learner cannot make a response to a goal situation which is not already in his repertoire of responses or is beyond his abilities.

Let me illustrate this by one example in foreman training since I believe the point is overlooked frequently in training designed to modify behavior of supervisors. Many of us, I expect, have sponsored so called "appreciation" courses in time study for foremen. We hope with these courses to secure the wholehearted support of our supervisors in our methods and standard work. We are disappointed if the same buck passing and lack of appreciation of the value of time study continues in our foremen group after completion of the course. Now time study is a relatively complex discipline. Telling people about time study does not equip them with knowledge and skills required to answer employee questions about rates or to discuss intelligently, with time study engineers, proposed rates. Lacking the knowledge and skill required, the foreman is put in an impossible position. He cannot make the responses required because they are not in the sum total of his past responses and abilities.

In designing a course in time study for our supervisors, we give full consideration to the limitation. We designed and exposed a group of our foremen to a course in time study which gave them competence in, rather than appreciation of, time study. We compared their improvement in: (1) knowledge of time study (2) handling of time study activities in their department both before and after the course with a matched group of foremen who did not take the course. The trained group showed 26.3% gain in knowledge compared to no change by the untrained group. What is even more important, the trained group showed 42.1% improvement in handling of time study in their department versus a 9% (non-significant) gain for the untrained group. I must add that in both groups each foreman had had at least 10 years experience with time study in his department. Each foreman had had at least one "appreciation" course in time study and several had had two or three such courses.[13]

The second limitation to responses are imposed by the learner's interpretation of the goal situation. We found that loopers who were urged to work "carefully" failed to develop speed. We found that battery hands who were allowed to fill batteries using only two bobbins rarely "pick up" a more effective method of handling 4 or 5 bobbins. They saw the situation as fill the batteries with 2 bobbins not fill the battery efficiently. Further, in human relations training, we may find the interpretation of the course as a method of manipulating people more easily, not as instruction in how to perceive people differently. The supervisor then learns certain superficial skills but fails to experience basic changes in attitudes toward human relations problems. Operators who interpret methods improvements as threats to job security react in a different manner to those who interpret methods improvements as aids to company and employee progress. Finally, in training in a rather complex job called setting, we found learners develop skills more rapidly when they were urged to visualize the pattern in terms of several strands of yarn rather than reacting to each square on the pattern as an individual strand.

A third limitation placed on responses is the feed-back the learner gets from making the responses. This is clearly illustrated in a skill like playing the piano or driving a golf ball or fly casting. Both visual, auditory, and kinesthetic cues "tell" the performer when the response feels right or wrong. The feed-back which tells the learner that the response is not goal directed encourages him to try some other response; while the response which "feels" good tends to be used again and again.

This limitation points up one practical consideration in industrial training, i.e., the importance of the instructor in the learning situation. It is the instructor who can analyze the adequacy of responses and serve as an effective "feed-back" device for correction of responses. If there is one thing that is known about industrial training, it is that organized training is more effective than unorganized training. I suspect the reason is that organized training provides a more effective feed-back.

My fourth declarative sentence really says that the individual has learned. In other words, he is capable of making responses which he could not make prior to wanting something and responding. It does, however, point up the fact that the process called learning produces responses which can be classified both as adequate and inadequate. Erroneous information, poor skills, and undesirable attitudes are just as

[13] W. McGehee and J. E. Gardner, "Supervisory Training and Attitude Change," *Personnel Psychology*, Vol. 8, 1955, pp. 449–60.

much a product of learning as are correct information, effective skills and desirable attitudes. From a practical standpoint, this means that we must continually evaluate the results of placing employees in learning situations. We need to know what facilitates and what retards practice. Many techniques used in modern training such as visual aids in training devices have "face validity," i.e., they look good. Actually such aids to training may not facilitate and may even retard learning. It is entirely possible, for example, that the case study method of training executives may increase the elegance with which a problem is approached but have absolutely no effect upon the quality of the solution.

LEARNING THEORY AND INDUSTRIAL TRAINING

These, then, are some aspects of learning theory in relationship to industrial training as I see them. One more sentence or two. A fully adequate theory of learning will not emerge from the animal laboratories and the classroom. These theories must hold also in the factory and the office. Likewise, learning experience in the factory and office should give cues for laboratory investigations. I would plead therefore for more and more interchange between the learning theorist and the industrial trainer. This cohabitation will aid in giving both "freedom from the swirling events" surrounding the problems of learning and training.

17. Lecture versus Group Decision in Changing Behavior*

Jacob Levine and John Butler

IN THIS STUDY, group decision is compared with formal lecture as a method of producing changes in behavior. Both methods are then compared with one in which no attempt is made to bring about any change. Thus, the experiment was designed to answer two questions: (1) Is the acquisition of knowledge enough to lead a group of individuals to change a socially undesirable behavior pattern? (2) Is group decision a more effective method of producing a change in behavior than is the formal lecture?

THE EXPERIMENT

The subjects consisted of 29 supervisors of 395 workers in a large manufacturing plant. The workers were on an hourly rate. These fac-

* From *Journal of Applied Psychology*, Vol. 36, 1952, pp. 29–33.

tory workers represented a wide variety of jobs and skills, ranging from unskilled manual labor to the most highly skilled machinist and tool-makers. All of these jobs were classified into nine different grades on the basis of skill and training required.

Within each job grade three different hourly wage rates prevailed. The particular rate paid to any worker was determined in large part by the quality of his performance on the job. Performance was evalu-ated by one of the 29 foremen who supervised the work of these 395 men. Every 6 months each worker was rated by his foreman on estab-lished rating scales for 5 factors: (1) Accuracy; (2) Effective use of working time; (3) Output; (4) Application of job knowledge; and (5) Cooperation. The sum of the scores on each of these five scales com-prised a worker's total performance rating and determined what wage rate he would get.

Unfortunately, the results of this rating system were not equal to ex-pectations. The foremen, in executing their ratings, tended to overrate those working in the higher job grades and to underrate those in the lower grades. This positive and negative "halo effect" resulted in the workers in the lower grades of jobs receiving the lowest of their re-spective wage rates while the more highly skilled workers consistently received the highest of their respective wage rates. Evidently the fore-men were not rating performance of the individual worker but the grade of the job as well.

The problem was set up to determine the most effective method of getting these supervisors to change the basis for the ratings so that a more equitable rating system would prevail. Our objective was to help these supervisors see that their task in rating each worker was to con-sider only how well he did his job and not how difficult the job was. He was to understand that he was to rate the man and not the job. The task of the present experiment was to determine which was the more effective method of achieving this change in behavior of the 29 rating supervisors, group decision or the formal lecture.

EXPERIMENTAL PROCEDURE

The 29 supervisors were randomly divided into three groups of 9, 9, and 11. It may be pointed out that all supervisors were experienced raters and had been rating employees for a number of years. The first group, Group A, consisting of 9 supervisors of 120 workers, served as a control group, and received no special instructions prior to rating. The second group, Group B, consisted of 9 supervisors of 123 men and served as the discussion group. The third group, Group C, consisted of 11 super-visors of 152 men, and served as the lecture group.

Several days prior to rating, the members of Group B were gathered together around a table with the discussion leader. The leader did not sit at the head of the table nor did he lead the discussion. He introduced the problem by showing a graph of the previous rating and raised the question why it was that the high skilled workers were consistently rated higher in performance than the low skilled. From that point on, the leader merely acted as moderator and avoided injecting himself into the discussion. All decisions and opinions were made solely by the group members. The discussion lasted one hour and a half. The group expressed a number of ideas and arrived at several conclusions. They finally reached one decision acceptable to the group: The way to avoid the inequalities in rating was to disregard the difficulty of the jobs and rate only the man doing the job. Consideration was to be given only to how well a worker was doing his job. All 9 members agreed on this decision.

Group C, the lecture group, gathered in a formal lecture room and all sat facing the leader. They were given a detailed lecture on the technique and theory of employee performance rating. Some background material on wage administration and job evaluation was also included. The lecture carefully pointed out the errors of their previous ratings and interpreted the reasons for their occurrence. He illustrated his lecture with graphs and figures. He finally explained what each rater was supposed to do: that he was to rate individual performance and not difficulty of the job. After the lecture, questions were encouraged and asked by the raters; complete answers were given. The total session lasted about one hour and a half.

EXPERIMENTAL RESULTS

The relationships between mean ratings for pre- and post-training are shown graphically in Figures 1, 2, and 3. For Group A, the two curves are seen to be essentially the same. All pretraining curves slope downward from high to low ratings more or less similarly. In the post-training

FIGURE 1

Average Rating of Raters with No Training Sessions (Group A)

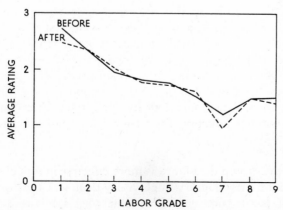

FIGURE 2

AVERAGE RATING OF RATERS AND AFTER GROUP DECISION SESSION (GROUP B)

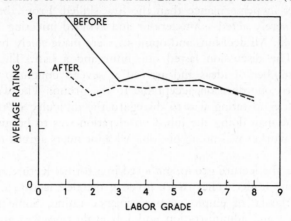

FIGURE 3

AVERAGE RATING OF RATERS BEFORE AND AFTER LECTURE SESSION (GROUP C)

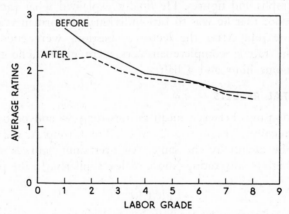

curves it is only the Group B, which shows a flattening or equalization of mean ratings for the 9 labor grades. It is interesting to note that of the three groups, Group B had shown the greatest difference between high and low labor grades prior to training. The post-training ratings of Group C, the lecture group, show a consistent lowering all along the curve from the previous ratings. This reduction might be the result of an increased conservatism in rating by these raters as a consequence of the lecture, without affecting their basically prejudiced ratings.

DISCUSSION

It is clear that group decision was more effective in reducing the preju-diced ratings of these factory supervisors than was the formal lecture. This in itself is a significant finding. But what seems to be even more striking is the fact that the lecture method had practically no influence upon the discrepancies in rating. It is generally assumed that once an individual or a group of individuals learn that they have been behaving in a socially undesirable way, they will immediately take steps to change, particularly if is clear to these individuals that it is their responsibility to eliminate such errors. Our findings do not support such a notion. The acquisition of knowledge does not automatically lead to action.

The findings also indicate that once a group arrives at a decision to act, the members, even though they may act as individuals, take on that decision and act in accordance with it. The force of this group decision was evidently sufficient to overcome the resistance to change in habitual ways of thinking and acting. How these group forces were able to operate upon the individual the present study does not reveal. Further research is necessary to determine whether or not group decision leads to a "freezing of decision to act" whereas the lecture method does not.

SUMMARY

A formal lecture method was compared with group decision in inducing 29 supervisors of 395 factory workers to overcome their biased performance ratings. The results showed that only the group of supervisors involved in group decision improved in their ratings. The lecture group did not change and persisted in overrating the more highly skilled workers and underrating the less skilled. The conclusion was drawn that group decision is more effective than the formal lecture in overcoming resistance to change in behavior.

18. The Comparative Effectiveness of Electric and Manual Typewriters in the Acquisition of Typing Skill*

Henry L. Adams

THE CAPABILITIES of electric typewriters in speed and ease of operation exceed those of manual typewriters. For this reason, many business education authorities believe that typing students will reach a higher pro-

* From "The Comparative Effectiveness of Electric and Manual Typewriters in the Acquisition of Typing Skill in a Navy Radioman School," *Journal of Applied Psychology*, Vol. 41, 1957, pp. 227-30.

ficiency level in less time when electrics are used for training and will experience little difficulty in transferring from electric to manual machines. Winger[1] reviews and summarizes a number of classroom comparisons of the two kinds of typewriters, all of which are in agreement with these beliefs. However, in an Air Force study[2] it was found that using electric typewriters was not advantageous in teaching beginning typists.

Although many of the reports favoring electric typewriters are based on subjective opinion rather than controlled experimentation with significance tests of the results, the possible advantages of the electric typewriter as a teaching device justify experimental comparisons. The Navy has a critical need for efficient manpower utilization. Typing skill is a performance requirement for many Navy ratings. Improvement in typing instruction might reduce the total training time in a number of Navy schools. On the other hand, where it is found that electric typewriters are not superior teaching devices, the Navy can effect a large, justifiable monetary saving by continuing to use manual typewriters.

The present study was requested by the Service School Command, Naval Training Center, San Diego, California. This Command considers the typing instruction problem to be especially critical in its Radioman (RM) School. Therefore, it was decided to limit this study to investigating the acquisition of the typing skills required of radiomen rather than conventional typing skills. Radiomen use typewriters for Morse code reception, and trainees are taught typing during the first four weeks of their course. Since effective code-taking speed cannot exceed typing speed, code-speed acquisition may be retarded by lack of typing skill.

Accordingly, this experiment was designed to investigate two specific hypotheses:

1. Radioman trainees will achieve more proficiency in typing mixed groups of letters and digits (cipher groups) when they are trained on electric typewriters than when they are trained on manual typewriters.

2. The typing skill acquired on electric typewriters will be rapidly transferred to manual typewriters.

PROCEDURES

With 20 electric typewriters of the same make available, it was possible to train 20 experimental Ss [subjects] at one time. Therefore the control group was also limited to 20 Ss at a time.

From Class 8, which entered the Radioman School on 17 October 1955, the 40 students with the least typing skill, as determined by a 2-min. plain language

---

[1] F. Winger, "What We Know About Electrics," *Business Educational World*, June, 1954.

[2] "The Electric Typewriter as an Aid in the Training of Beginning Typists" (Francis E. Warren Air Force Base, Wyo.: Office of Training Analysis and Development).

pretest, were selected. These 40 students were stratified into two categories: those without previous typing experience and those with previous typing experience. Within these strata, students were randomly divided into an experimental group (to be trained on electric typewriters) and a control group (to be trained on manual typewriters). Of the 20 students in each group, 10 were typists and 10 were nontypists. Separate rooms were used for training the electric and manual typewriter groups. Both kinds of typewriters had standard keyboards.

The assignment procedures—and subsequent training procedures—were replicated with 40 students from Class 10, which entered school on 14 November 1955. One typist was hospitalized during the course of the experiment, leaving a total of 39 Ss in the experimental group and 40 Ss in the control group.

The experimental and control group means were equivalent for age (18.21 vs. 18.28), years of education (11.79 vs. 11.75), general ability as determined by scores on the Navy general classification and arithmetic tests (113.74 vs. 111.55), and code aptitude as determined by scores on the radio code aptitude test used by the Navy (65.44 vs. 66.18).

Each typing class was taught by one instructor who remained with the class for the entire four weeks of typing instruction. For Class 10, the Class 8 electric and manual typing instructors were switched. These two instructors were requested to follow their customary teaching methods throughout the eight weeks of the experiment.

The Radioman School completes its typing instruction in the first four 5-day weeks of the 16-week course. There are eight 45-min. class periods each day. For the first two weeks, typing class periods alternate with "rectype" class periods (during which instruction in code reception is given). During the third and fourth weeks one of the previous typing periods is used for instruction in radio procedures. Thus beginning students receive four periods of typing instruction per day for the first two weeks and three periods of typing instruction per day for the third and fourth weeks.

The Ss received three weeks of basic typing instruction on their respective machines (Part I of the experiment). In the fourth week the experimental Ss were taught to use manual typewriters while the control Ss continued practice on the manual typewriters (Part II of the experiment). Since radiomen aboard ship normally receive code on manual typewriters, it was considered important to obtain information regarding progress in typing proficiency during the period of transfer from electric typewriters to manual typewriters.

From the 36-character alphabet (26 letters and 10 digits), 250 characters were selected by the use of a table of random numbers. These 250 characters were divided into fifty 5-character mixed groups of letters and digits for use as 2-min. tests. Five different arrangements of these 50 mixed groups were made. Three other arrangements of the same 50 mixed groups constituted the 150-group "final examination" (a 6-min. test with 15-sec. rest intervals every 2 min.). These tests are considered to be equivalent, with the different arrangements eliminating practice effects.

From the last day of the first week of training until the last day of the third week, Ss were given one of the 2-min. tests at the close of the final typing period each day. There were 10 of these test administrations. The 6-min. Part I final examination was administered at the close of the final typing period on the last day of the third week.

During the fourth week (when the group trained on electric typewriters learned to use manual typewriters and the group trained on manual typewriters continued practice on manual typewriters), a 2-min. test was given at the close of every typing class up to the last class. There were also 10 of these test administrations. The 6-min. Part II final examination was given at the close of the final typing class.

For all the above tests a combination speed and accuracy score was obtained: the number of "words" typed per minute (with five strokes, including the space, counted as a word) minus the number of errors per minute.

The general aim of the experimental procedures was to control unnecessary between-groups variation in instructional procedures, content, and other factors affecting learning so that differences in proficiency between the groups would be due to differences in the training devices and/or necessarily confounded procedures.

TABLE 1

MEAN SCORES OF THE ELECTRIC TYPEWRITER Ss
AND MANUAL TYPEWRITER Ss ON THE SERIES OF
TYPING PROFICIENCY TESTS

TEST	MEAN SCORE OF ELECTRIC TYPEWRITER Ss	MEAN SCORE OF MANUAL TYPEWRITER Ss
PART I		
1	7.13	7.85
2	9.95	10.08
3	10.78	10.53
4	11.55	10.45
5	12.48	11.90
6	12.73	12.30
7	14.03	13.58
8	14.93	13.90
9	15.43	14.78
10	15.60	14.60
Final Exam	16.05	14.98
PART II		
11	11.79	15.20
12	13.36	16.05
13	13.64	16.00
14	14.67	16.80
15	14.82	17.23
16	14.72	16.35
17	16.28	17.63
18	16.18	18.10
19	17.10	18.55
20	17.38	18.68
Final Exam	16.90	18.55

Note—Scores on all tests were the number of 5-stroke "words"
typed per minute minus the number of errors per minute.

RESULTS AND DISCUSSION

As previously stated, there were ten 2-min. tests and a 6-min. final test given during Part I of the experiment and ten 2-min. tests and a 6-min. final test given during Part II of the experiment. As estimates of the reliability of these tests at three different points in training, test-retest correlation coefficients were obtained. The correlation between scores for all *S*s on Test 3 and Test 4 was .79. For scores of all *S*s on the second and third 2-min. sections of the Part I final examination, the correlation was .84, and for scores on the second and third 2-min. sections of the Part II final examination, the correlation was .81. The four test-retest coefficients for the electric and manual experienced and non-experienced categories at each of these three points in training were examined and judged sufficiently homogenous to permit combining them into the above over-all coefficients.

Means of the scores on all tests for the two groups of *S*s are presented in Table 1. These means are depicted graphically in Figure 1.

As Figure 1 indicates, while the electric typewriter group showed a

FIGURE 1

PERFORMANCE CURVES OF THE ELECTRIC AND MANUAL GROUPS

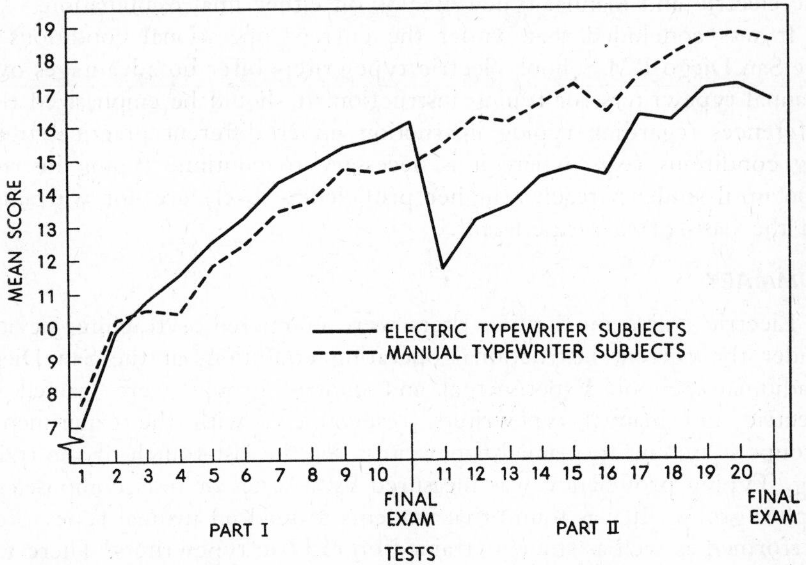

substantial decrement in performance on the first test after changing to manual typewriters (Test 11), there was considerable positive transfer of training from the initial test (Test 1). For measuring transfer, only the scores for the 20 electric nontypists and the 20 manual nontypists are appropriate. Using the Gagne, Foster, and Crowley formula,[3]

$$\frac{\text{Experimental Group Mean on Test 11} - \text{Control Group Mean on Test 1}}{\text{Control Group Mean on Test 11} - \text{Control Group Mean on Test 1}} \times 100,$$

[3] R. M. Gagne, H. Foster, and M. E. Crowley, "The Measurement of Transfer of Training," *Psychological Bulletin*, Vol. 45, 1948, pp. 97–130.

with the applicable nontypist means, the per cent transfer was

$$\frac{10.05 - 5.75}{13.20 - 5.75} \times 100,$$

which equals 58%.

Differences between scores on the Part I final examination and on the Part II final examination were tested by analysis of variance techniques. For the analyses, Ss' scores were partitioned by typewriter, experience, class and instructor—class and instructor being necessarily confounded. This confounding is unimportant for the purposes of the study, however, since only the typewriter comparison is of primary interest. To obtain an equal number of cases in each category after losing one S through hospitalization, a S from each of the other seven categories, with the same rank on the test immediately preceding the hospitalization, was discarded, leaving nine Ss in each of the eight categories. The results of this analysis showed that there were no practical differences between the electric and manual typewriter Ss on either final examination.

It was concluded that, under the current operational conditions at the San Diego RM School, electric typewriters offer no advantages over manual typewriters for typing instruction. It should be emphasized that inferences regarding typing instruction under different practical training conditions (e.g., where it is necessary to continue typing instruction until students reach a higher proficiency level) are not warranted on the basis of this experiment.

SUMMARY

Electric and manual typewriters were compared as teaching devices under the current instructional operating conditions at the San Diego Radioman School. Experimental and control groups were trained on electric and manual typewriters, respectively, with the experimental groups switching to manual typewriters for the last fourth of the training. Typing proficiency was measured by a series of tests composed of cipher groups. It was found that students trained on manual typewriters performed as well as students trained on electric typewriters. There was considerable positive transfer of training from electric to manual typewriters but direct practice on manual typewriters was preferable.

19. How to Feed Back Performance Results to Trainees*

James N. Mosel

REDUCED TO SIMPLEST terms, the process of personnel training consists of an "input" phase (the showing, telling, and explaining) and an "output" phase (the trainee's attempt to reproduce what is taught). The input is the instruction that goes into the trainee. The output is his response.

But there is still a third phase which is necessary if training is to be successful—the "feedback" phase. The trainee not only must attempt to make the responses which the trainer teaches, but he must also know how well he has succeeded in doing this. There must be a feedback from the output phase of the trainee's behavior into the input phase of the instruction. As training progresses the instruction must come more and more to incorporate information concerning the adequacy of the trainee's performance.

Feeding back to employees the results of their work embodies what psychologists call the "principle of knowledge of performance." This principle is one of the most thoroughly validated principles of learning. It is also one of the most neglected in industrial training. It may be stated as follows: *As knowledge of performance increases, learning increases both in rate and level.* A few studies will illustrate the kind of result we can expect.

In a government agency, calculating machine operators increased their performance by 60% as a result of seeing their output recorded in relation to the output of others.

In a Pittsburgh public utility, furnace stokers had no indication of how well they were doing. Gauges were installed to show the efficiency of the individual boilers and the data from these gauges were plotted to show individual improvement in the technique of firing the boilers. The result was an annual saving of $333,000 in coal.

In training operators to cut tungsten discs with a foot operated abrasive wheel, trainers developed a recording device which showed the learner his cutting patterns and thereby brought out the specific errors

---

* From *Journal of American Society of Training Directors*, Feb., 1958. Paper read before the Employee Training Institute at the Annual Conference of Public Personnel Administration of the Civil Service Assembly, Oct. 9, 1956, Washington, D.C.

he was making in his cutting cycles. This technique was found to improve both the quality and quantity of work at various stages of training and also to decrease the use of abrasive wheels. After 11 weeks of training with this device, new employees reached the level of production of workers who had been on the job for 20 weeks.

In a wartime study, men were being trained to track aircraft with a tracking apparatus. Two groups of equal tracking ability, as determined by previous performance, were studied. One group was provided with knowledge of results in the form of a buzzer which the trainer sounded whenever a trainee was off the tracking point by more than two miles. The other group received no such information, and were given only the customary practice on the tracking apparatus. After only 68 minutes of practice, the group trained with the electric buzzer was found to be off target only 32% of the time, while the group trained without the buzzer were off about 58% of the time.

Almost without exception, where knowledge of performance is given to one group of trainees and the same knowledge is withheld or reduced in the case of another group, the former group learns more rapidly and reaches a higher level of proficiency.

But the ways in which this principle works, and the conditions under which it works are many and complex. Consequently, it does little good merely to say, "Give your trainees knowledge of how well they are doing in training." As a matter of fact, as we shall see later, there are certain conditions under which giving knowledge of performance produces no effect. Rather, we need to know something about how to give the knowledge of performance, who should give the information, how much information and what kind should be given, and the conditions under which it should be given.

There is little to be gained by trying to develop gimmicks or packaged techniques for feeding back to employees the results of their performance. Instead, specific procedures must be designed to fit the individual training situation. The intention of this report is to present certain reasonably well validated principles from which the training official can tailor-make his own techniques.

HOW DOES IT WORK?

Feeding back knowledge of performance affects the trainee's learning in two ways. First, it gives the trainee information on what response he should learn. Research on human learning shows that very frequently the learner takes a long time to learn simply because he spends time in learning the wrong or irrelevant things which must then be unlearned.

To learn efficiently, he must be able to discriminate quickly those responses which he is to acquire. For instance, very often in supervisory training we tell the trainee that he must "create a non-threatening climate" in dealing with his subordinates. But "creating a non-threatening climate" represents a tremendous range of possible supervisor responses and the trainee is bound to be unsure, as to which ones are non-threatening. He needs an opportunity to react to situations, make what he considers "non-threatening" responses, and then learn how well his behavior came close to the mark. Without feedback he may well understand and accept the principles of non-threatening behavior, but he will never learn actually to produce such behavior.

A second reason why knowledge of performance aids learning is that it affects motivation to keep learning. One of the basic requirements for motivation is that the trainee set goals for himself. But once goals are set, they will serve as incentives to performance only as long as the person experiences some sense of progress toward those goals.

One of the findings of research on human learning is that normal people tend to abandon a goal if they cannot move toward it. To do otherwise leads to frustration and tension. It is unnatural for a person to persist after a goal which he is unable to achieve. Consequently the sense of movement toward a goal is an absolute requisite for motivation to learn. Knowledge of performance enables the trainee to set effective goals and to experience the sense of movement toward them. There are some interesting experiments on learning in which people gave up their attempts at skill mastery even though they were making good progress, simply because they could not experience their progress. They felt all the frustration and loss of interest that ordinarily characterized a person who was failing to learn.

The experimental studies on this point suggest that *the incentive effect of knowledge of performance is likely to be more important in the later stages of practice than in the earlier.* In the earlier stages there is a certain initial enthusiasm which carries the trainee forward. Later, when the going is tougher, this initial drive must be replaced by a sense of progress which only knowledge of performance can give.

There is also a caution suggested by the same research. It seems that increasing knowledge of performance does not *always* increase motivation. There is probably little effect when the trainee is already performing at a high level of proficiency; and if he is doing poorly, increased knowledge of this fact may actually decrease his motivation. So we must go carefully in supplying knowledge of performance when the trainee's performance is at the extremes of the proficiency range.

WHAT INFORMATION TO GIVE?

Feeding back knowledge of performance will be effective only if we give the trainee information which will help him learn. Not all information about his performance does this. It goes without saying, of course, that the information we feed back must be relevant to the trainee's learning task. It must really be useful to him in achieving the training goals we impose on him.

But beyond this, *the information we give him must be unique or non-*

redundant. By this I mean that it must be information which he does not already possess about his performance. The trainee always has some information of his own about his performance. In feedback we must add to this knowledge. The consequences of over-looking this point are nicely illustrated in a case of military training. In teaching aerial gunners to track aircraft, a special training device was used which made the view in the gunsight turn red when the trainee was on target. This device was found to improve the trainee's ability at fixing the target's range but not at tracking the target. The reason was that the trainees were receiving all the knowledge they needed about tracking just from looking into the gunsight. The red filter added no new information. In this case the knowledge of performance so ingeniously provided by the trainers failed to improve tracking skill because it was redundant.

In this connection we must realize that the trainee almost always has *some* knowledge of performance, whether we give it to him or not. If it is not provided for him, the trainee will attempt to develop his own. And in so doing, is very likely to rely upon incorrect or irrelevant sources of information. Furthermore, research shows, if the trainee cannot discover such sources, he will *create* his own information. That is, he will set up his own standards about right and wrong performance, standards against which he can judge himself in some way. It is almost inevitable that in so doing he will adopt standards which do not correspond to those of the trainer. Under these conditions the trainee will indeed make progress toward his own self-developed standards, but his progress will not be the kind which the trainer intends.

Very frequently, what the training official perceives as a failure to learn is in reality learning of a different kind. The trainee learns all right, he just doesn't learn what we want him to learn. Thus we see that the trainee naturally seeks knowledge of performance, and that if it is not forthcoming, he will invent his own, which in turn usually leads to learning the wrong performance.

One of the commonest sources of such self-developed standards is other trainees. In the absence of external, trainer-provided standards, the training group will originate its own "myths" about what is a good performance and how to judge when you are producing it. These myths are psychologically very similar to rumors; they exist and flourish in the absence of adequate external information, and they are accepted by trainees because they want to accept them, because they have a need to know how well they are doing.

As to the content of feedback, it is extremely important that such information be positive as well as negative. That is, the information must tell him what to do, as well as what not to do. Negative information alone helps learning by telling the trainee what responses he should avoid, but this does not always make clear just what the correct response is. We see this principle violated in other areas of employee relations. Safety posters, for instance, which merely admonish the employee "to be careful" or to avoid accidents are usually worthless because they do not tell the employee what he needs to know in order to be careful or avoid accidents.

It is important, then, in critiquing a trainee's performance that the nature of the correct response be clearly communicated. This means that frequently the trainee must see a demonstration of the correct response, possibly from the trainer or from audio-visual aids. Ordinarily such displays are used only in the early stages of training for the purpose of giving an initial picture of what the correct performance looks like. This is a good practice. But often it is not realized that such devices should also be repeated later as a means for enabling the trainee to compare his performance with the correct one. *Such displays should be inserted as soon as possible after the employee's own performance in order that a comparison can be made.*

In general, then, whenever the trainee is not making the desired response, simply giving negative information will do very little toward installing the correct performance. Under these circumstances we must give positive information, and to do this we must include in our feedback a demonstration of the correct performance.

Furthermore, if feedback indicates only that the trainee is not making the correct performance, his motivation may decline. As we have already noted, people usually abandon goals when they do not experience progress toward them. To provide this experience of progress, the trainee must make some successful performances. And here again, demonstrations of the correct response are necessary—to be combined perhaps with guidance to insure the trainee's successful reproduction of what he has seen.

In cases where the trainee hits upon the correct performance and thus actually experiences the correct response, positive information to this effect should always be given. In this instance, the purpose of positive information is not so much to show the trainee what the correct performance is like, but to let him know that he has made it. In this way he learns the "feel" of doing it right so that in the future he is able to provide himself with sound knowledge of his own performance. Thus by teaching the trainee to recognize a correct performance in his own behavior, we prepare him to continue his self-teaching long after he has left the training situation. In this way he can train himself, and training official's efforts are supplemented by the trainee's own private efforts. But unless this happens, the trainee's performance is likely to deteriorate after leaving the training situation, simply because he cannot critique himself.

Finally, the information we supply the trainee should be specific. Experimental results in the field of learning give us a statement of this principle: *The more specific the knowledge of performance, the more rapid the improvement and the higher the level of performance.* Other things being equal, the more exactly the trainee knows how he has performed, the more he is able to make the appropriate improvements.

Research also shows, however, that there is an *optimum* specificity of information, and that knowledge of performance beyond this optimum will not improve performance or may even lead to its deterioration. This optimum represents the trainee's capacity to absorb and use the information we give him. When the knowledge we give exceeds this capacity, the trainee becomes confused. To protect himself against this confusion, he is likely to disregard the information we give him. The optimum amount of specificity of knowledge of performance is known to be related to the stage of training.

In the early stages of training, the trainee's ability to use feedback is limited so that a little information goes a long way. The trainee's progress is, in fact, dependent upon his ability to utilize the knowledge of performance we give him. *This means that effective training must not only provide the trainee with knowledge of his performance, but it must also teach him how to use it to improve his learning.* He must be shown how to relate the feedback to his own performance.

HOW TO GIVE KNOWLEDGE OF PERFORMANCE?

Once the content of the feedback information is determined, the question arises as to the most effective way of supplying the information. The time relations between the trainee's performance and provision of the feedback are an important factor. Again, experimental studies of learning have given us a generalization of this point: *The longer the delay in giving knowledge of performance, the less effect the information has.* This has been widely verified in a number of training investigations.

An illustration comes from the military problem of training men to receive telegraphic code. In the traditional method, a long series of code signals are presented by earphones and the trainee's reading of these was scored at the end of each training session. Thus, there was feedback but it was delayed until the end of the training period. A new method was developed, called the "code-voice" method, in which the presentation of each code-letter signal over the earphones was followed three seconds later by the name of the letter. This enabled the trainee to know immediately whether he had made a mistake. It was found that the voice-code method with its immediate knowledge of results was markedly superior to the conventional procedure.

Now we come to what is perhaps the most cardinal consideration in providing trainees with knowledge of performance; namely *that the information we feed back is always a carrier of social values and meanings for the trainee's concept of himself.* Our information is never completely impersonal and objective; it always constitutes "praise" or "reproof." It always contains implications for the trainee's ego and for the kind of mental picture which he has of himself. All of us hold a mental image of the kind of person we consider ourselves to be and of the kind we wish to become. Psychologists call this perception of ourselves the "self-concept."

Knowledge of performance always contains implications for the trainee's self-concept. If the information is consistent with this self-concept, or if it enhances it, the information will be accepted and used to improve performance. If the information we give is inconsistent with the self-concept, if it denies the kinds of things the trainee perceives himself to be, the information will be rejected or discounted. Stated in this way, we see that the question of how to give knowledge of performance is much broader than the simple question of which is more effective, praise or reproof. The real issue is whether the feedback affirms or denies the kind of person which the trainee wishes to be.

Psychologically, "praise" consists of giving a person experiences or evidence which indicate that he is the kind of person he wishes to become. Similarly, "reproof" consists of giving a person experiences which disaffirm that he is the kind of person he seeks to become.

Only when praise and reproof act in this way are they really praise and reproof; and only then do they have an effect on training. As popularly used by many trainers, however, "praise" means any kind of compliment, and reproof means any kind of criticism. But now we see that just any kind of compliment—or "praise," if you will,—will not improve training. If the compliment merely affirms something which the trainee is *not* trying to be or become, it will not aid his learning. Furthermore, if it affirms something that he wishes not to become, it may even hinder learning. To tell a trainee, for instance, that his performance shows he has good mathematical ability will not motivate him to learn until he wishes to perceive himself as a capable mathematician. And to tell a person who likes to think of himself as a mathematician that he is a very capable garbage collector is not praise at all.

Our feedback will be effective only if it affirms to the trainee the kinds of things he is trying to assert himself. If this happens, the trainee will eagerly accept and use the information, because it "fits" into his customary way of viewing himself.

If, on the other hand, the feedback disaffirms or denies to the trainee the kinds of things he is attempting to assert about himself, the feedback becomes a form of psychological threat and will be resisted. The reason for the resistance is that we just naturally tend to defend ourselves against events which force us to experience ourselves in terms that we do not value. If the feedback gives this experience, we will defend ourselves by resisting the information.

There are several kinds of resistive reactions which trainees will make when faced with feedback which is threatening to their self-concept. One of the most common is *rigidity*—the trainee's behavior becomes fixed and unchanging. The result is that the trainee's incorrect responses become more deeply ingrained. Under these circumstances feedback will actually impede the process of training. On the other hand, research has shown that in the absence of threat, the person's behavior becomes more flexible and susceptible to change. The trainee becomes capable of accepting the feedback and using it to modify his performance in the desired direction.

We see then that feedback, indeed the entire training situation, must avoid arousing a threat to the trainee's self-concept. It must be permissive and accepting so that the trainee's behavior will remain open to change. Unfortunately, however, the training situation is often a threatening affair. Sometimes the very fact that an employee is sent to training threateningly suggests that he is in need of training because he is not such a "hot" employee.

Another resistive reaction to threatening feedback is for the trainee to accept the information but distort its meaning so that he escapes its threatening implications. The trainee is essentially protecting himself against the threatening information by misinterpreting its meaning. He may even interpret critical feedback as a sign that he is doing the right thing, rather than the wrong. He simply does not get the meaning to knowledge of performance which we wish to communicate. When this happens, knowledge of performance is of little value because the trainee resists making the necessary application.

Now, if the threatening information we give is so clear that the trainee finds it impossible to change its meaning, he can still resist simply by rejecting the information. He can do this in many ways. He may say it is inaccurate, unfair, or "asking too much." But in one way or another, he will discount or minimize it, and thus protect himself against its unwanted implications.

When we stop to think about it, we realize that whether our feedback re-enforces or denies the trainee's self-concept is to a large degree determined by the *manner* in which the knowledge is given to him, rather than by the actual content of the information. It is the "how" rather than the "what." And to employ the proper method requires that we know something about how trainees view themselves. We must see things from their view-point, in terms of what they are trying to accomplish in training, and understand a little about what kind of employees they consider themselves to be.

With these considerations in mind, we can now understand the experimental results which have been obtained in studies of human learning. In general, the evidence shows that praise tends to be slightly more effective than most reproof. More specifically, research suggests the following ranking in decreasing order of effectiveness:

1. public praise.
2. private praise.
3. private reproof.
4. public reproof.

However, reproof is sometimes helpful and sometimes detrimental. It appears that mild reproof can be rather effective in aiding learning. The reason being that such reproof is mild enough to avoid being threatening, and yet strong enough to motivate the trainee to keep improving. He tries to improve because improvement is seen as a feasible way to escape from the mild threat. Strong reproof, however, seems to be injurious to learning. It is threatening to the point that the trainee gives up; he ceases trying to improve because he cannot see how further effort will relieve him of the threat. In place of improvement, he adopts other reactions to escape the threat. Instead of learning what we want, he learns to protect himself against threat. He learns to do the things we have described above. This is especially likely if the training situation itself is threatening, for then the trainee learns that accepting and using our feedback is pointless (even though in itself it is non-threatening) because the total situation continues to be threatening.

Finally, it should be pointed out that the trainee's view of himself is different at different stages of training, and consequently, the implications of knowledge of performance for his view of himself will vary accordingly. In the early stages of training, the trainee may respond to a negative feedback by saying to himself, "I'm just a beginner, so it's natural for me to make mistakes." Later on when he is a more advanced learner, he may respond to the same information by saying, "Even old hands slip up occasionally." But note that in both instances the nature of the reaction is the same: the trainee is accepting the information by adjusting it so that it fits his view of himself.

20. Curriculum Assessment with Critical Incidents*

Albert S. Glickman and T. R. Vallance

BY AND LARGE, even in industry, adequacy of training programs has been assessed by subjective judgment rather than by research methods.[1] As Flanagan[2] has remarked, there is need to supplement the usual collection in conference of "leaders" or "experts" by systematic collection and analysis of factual data.

* From *Journal of Applied Psychology*, Vol. 42, No. 5, 1958, pp. 329–35.

[1] W. R. Mahler and W. H. Monroe, "How Industry Determines the Need for and Effectiveness of Training," *USA Personnel Research Section Report*, No. 929, 1952.

[2] J. C. Flanagan, "Research Techniques for Developing Educational Objectives," *Educational Record*, Vol. 28, 1947, pp. 139–48; J. C. Flanagan, "The Critical Requirements Approach to Educational Objectives," *School and Society*, Vol. 71, 1950, pp. 321–24.

This investigation explores the use of "critical incidents"[3] for assessing the relevance of various aspects of a training program to the job performance requirements of its graduates. Specifically, it involves the relevance of subject matter taught in the Navy's Officer Candidate School (OCS) to the duty requirements of new officers aboard destroyer-type ships.

The 17-week OCS training aims to prepare the new ensign to profit from experience and rapidly achieve a satisfactory level of job performance. It is not intended to produce specialists. Rather, the purpose is to provide junior officers with the familiarity in subject matter areas containing technical problems needed to develop an understanding of a variety of technical functions, and to develop ability to supervise technicians.

The critical incident procedure, as adapted here, takes cognizance of the supervisory nature of the junior officer's duties and at the same time permits the use of duty performance behaviors of sufficient specificity to indicate OCS curriculum elements most and least relevant to significant shipboard duties. Also, by concentrating upon observed actual performances on duty, the procedure makes it possible to identify duty areas which are not covered by instruction, thus contributing to a further definition of what the objectives and content of training should be.

The essential questions to which this research is addressed are these: "What are the things which happen frequently to ensigns, or which their superiors think they ought to be able to handle soon after reporting aboard?" and then, "Are these the things to which attention and emphasis are also given by OCS instruction?"

Our legitimate concern is exclusively with the performance requirements (and relevant training) reflected in the content of incidents, whether they be found in reports of "effective" or "ineffective" incidents. This research does not tell us how much OCS training contributes to causing effective or ineffective incidents.

Determining the Gross Relevance of OCS Curriculum to Duty Incidents

BASIC DATA

An earlier study[4] had accumulated incidents involving destroyer officers from all training sources. Of those, 1,073 incidents reported on general line ensigns constituted our pool of basic data. This sample of incidents is used here to provide a description and operational definition of the critically significant elements of the duties of new officers aboard

---

[3] J. C. Flanagan, "Research Techniques for Developing Educational Objectives," *op. cit.*; J. C. Flanagan, "The Critical Requirements Approach to Educational Objectives," *op. cit.*; J. C. Flanagan, "The Critical Incident Technique," *Psychological Bulletin*, Vol. 51, 1954, pp. 327–58.

[4] T. R. Vallance, A. S. Glickman, and J. M. Vasilas, "Critical Incidents in Junior Officer Duties Aboard Destroyer-Type Vessels," *USN Bureau of Naval Personnel Research Technical Bulletin*, No. 54–4, 1954.

destroyers. Incidents were typed on IBM cards to facilitate handling and analysis.

ANALYSIS OF THE INCIDENT POOL WITH REFERENCE TO CURRICULUM AREAS

The incident cards were submitted to subject matter specialists, OCS officer-instructors, who carried out a review sequence that ultimately required that each incident be identified with a lesson in the lesson-plan of one of the seven sections of the curriculum: (1) Seamanship, (2) Orientation and Military Justice, (3) Navigation, (4) Operations, (5) Naval Weapons and Fire Control, (6) Engineering and Damage Control, and (7) Military. Category 8, labelled "Other," was established for those incidents which reflected motivation and interest in the job rather than the possession of specific skills or knowledges.

The instructional set for sorting effective incidents concerned the curricular locus of skills, knowledges and attitudes shown in each incident. For the ineffective incidents the emphasis was on the skills, knowledges and attitudes which, if learned, could have prevented the ensign from getting involved in the incident.

Within each subject matter category, incidents were classified in two ways: "Taught"—the relevant skills, knowledges and attitudes are currently the subject of specific lessons of instruction; and "Not Taught"—pertains to material not covered, but which logically belongs in one of the school sections and probably would be taught were time and facilities available. All "Other" incidents were, of course, of the "not taught" variety.

No assumption can be made that individual incidents, or even incidents of a given sort, are equally significant from the operational standpoint. Yet, if a large number of the critical incidents reported fall into a given subject matter area, it is difficult to escape the conclusion that there is much important activity aboard ship to which that area of instruction is relevant. Likewise, if the number of incidents in certain instructional areas is small, unless it is found that the incidents are individually of vital significance, it would seem that the learnings in such areas are not heavily drawn upon in the performance of a new officer's duties.

It appears from Table 1 that it is from his background in the courses Orientation and Military Justice, Seamanship, and Operations, that on reporting to a destroyer the new ensign might expect to draw most frequently, while being less likely to be called upon to make use of what he learned in Navigation, Engineering and Damage Control, and Naval Weapons and Fire Control.[5]

---

[5] Some incidents were considered relevant to more than one lesson. However, in Table 1, no incident was counted more than once, since when an incident was identified with more than one lesson, these lessons were always in the same curriculum section. The judges could not classify 17 of the original 1073 incidents.

TABLE 1

RESULTS OF SORTING CRITICAL INCIDENTS BY SUBJECT MATTER AREAS

	EFFECTIVE		INEFFECTIVE		SUMMARY	
	N	%[a]	N	%[a]	N	%[a]
1. Seamanship						
Taught	52	4.8	106	9.9	158	14.7
Not-Taught	12	1.1	40	3.7	52	4.8
Total	64	6.0	146	13.6	210	19.6
% Taught[b]	81.3		72.6		75.2	
2. Orientation and Military Justice						
Taught	125	11.6	240	22.4	365	34.0
Not-Taught	46	4.3	88	8.2	134	12.5
Total	171	15.9	328	30.6	499	46.5
% Taught[b]	73.1		73.2		73.1	
3. Navigation						
Taught	5	0.5	4	0.4	9	0.8
Not-Taught	0	0.0	1	0.1	1	0.1
Total	5	0.5	5	0.5	10	0.9
% Taught[b]	100.0		80.0		90.0	
4. Operations						
Taught	19	1.8	66	6.2	85	7.9
Not-Taught	22	2.1	57	5.3	79	7.4
Total	41	3.8	123	11.5	164	15.3
% Taught[b]	46.3		53.7		51.8	
5. Weapons						
Taught	7	0.7	8	0.7	15	1.4
Not-Taught	11	1.0	28	2.6	39	3.6
Total	18	1.7	36	3.4	54	5.0
% Taught[b]	38.9		22.2		27.8	
6. Engineering						
Taught	16	1.5	14	1.3	30	2.8
Not-Taught	4	0.4	18	1.7	22	2.1
Total	20	1.9	32	3.0	52	4.8
% Taught[b]	80.0		43.8		57.7	
7. Military						
Taught	0	0.0	2	0.2	2	0.2
Not-Taught	2	0.2	0	0.0	2	0.2
Total	2	0.2	2	0.2	4	0.4
% Taught[b]	0.0		100.0		50.0	
8. Other						
Taught	0	0.0	0	0.0	0	0.0
Not-Taught	26	2.4	37	3.4	63	5.9
Total	26	2.4	37	3.4	63	5.9
% Taught[b]	0.0		0.0		0.0	
Total						
Taught	224	20.9	440	41.0	664	61.9
Not-Taught	123	11.5	269	25.1	392	36.5
Total	347	32.3	709	66.1	1056	98.4[c]
% Taught	64.6		62.1		62.9	

[a] Percentages in these columns are based on the original total number; $N/1073$ rounded to nearest tenth.

[b] Percentages in these rows represent the number of "taught" incidents in relation to the total number of incidents within respective subject categories (i.e., "taught"/"total").

[c] Seventeen incidents (1.6%) were incapable of being judged with confidence and are not included in this summary.

Can the fact that 62.9% of the classifiable incidents are said by instructor-judges to be taught at OCS be considered to reflect a "good" state of affairs? Since the limits imposed by time and facilities have not been considered and since there is no standard of what "percentage taught" can be considered good, this question cannot be answered in an absolute sense. However, we might say that the higher the "percentage taught" the better.

Thus, it might be presumed that of the six academic courses, Seamanship and Orientation and Military Justice most completely cover their respective areas, and that the Naval Weapons course least adequately treats of the kinds of situations that destroyer officers report as critical.[6] However, there are instances where 50 or more incidents are considered relevant to one hour of instruction, leading one to discount the direct interpretation of "percentage taught" as a sufficient criterion of the adequacy of subject matter coverage.

References to the number of incidents assigned to specific hours of instruction, along with further examination of the contents of sessions by subject matter experts, would seem to provide a more meaningful employment of data such as these for purposes of curriculum analysis.

Developing an Index of Incident-Behavior "Importance for Early Usefulness"

RATIONALE

The main objective of the next phase was to obtain expert judgments regarding the significant aspects of duty for which training should prepare the new ensign.

To place the notion of importance clearly in the framework of training, it was reasoned that to the extent that preduty training provides the trainee with skills, knowledge, or attitudes required of him in the first few months of duty, or a sound background on which experience will develop them, that training is successful. To the extent that it concentrates on that which the trainee will not be called upon to use until after he has had a year or more of duty, or has been sent to other schools to acquire or reacquire them, initial training is being misdirected. From this standpoint, the immediacy of the opportunity or requirement to handle any given situation would be an index of its "importance." It is in this sense that "importance," standing for "importance for early usefulness," is used in this article.

---

[6] If the "percentage taught" figures for effective and ineffective incidents for the six academic courses (all except Military) are arranged in rank order, the correlation between ranks for "effectives" and "ineffectives" is .79, suggesting that, whether relevant effective or ineffective incidents are used, the relative coverage by courses is much the same. Table 1 also reveals that overall the "percentage taught" is not much different for effective and ineffective incidents (64.6% vs. 62.1%).

Procedure

A questionnaire, the Junior Officer Training Requirements Checklist (JOTRC), was prepared in 10 forms containing an aggregate of 985 items.[7] The final format evolved from four preliminary try-out versions.

Each form listed approximately 100 incidents and was divided into two parts. Part I contained effective incidents and Part II ineffective incidents for Forms 1, 3, 5, 7, and 9. For Forms 2, 4, 6, 8, and 10, the order was reversed. About one hour was needed to fill out a form. The incidents related to all OCS instructional areas, and included those judged earlier to be among the "not taught" as well as those included in the curriculum.

The specific questions were:

1. For the situations involving effective incidents: "How soon after reporting aboard would you expect the new officer to be able to do this?"

2. For the situations involving ineffective incidents: "How soon after reporting aboard would you expect the new officer to be able to handle this situation satisfactorily?"

The questions specified the writing of the number of months (directly after being commissioned), ranging from 0 (for judgments that the reserve officer should be able to perform well immediately on reporting aboard) to 12. "X" was to be used if the respondent would not expect the new officer to be able to handle the given type of situation satisfactorily until after he had been aboard for more than a year. "N" was to be used if the reporter felt unable to make a judgment because of wording or interpretation of the incident items.[8]

Two copies of the checklist were sent to each of 170 destroyer-type ships, one for the commanding officer (CO) and one for his executive officer (XO). Each of the 10 forms was sent to 30 to 50 officers. A total of 301 JOTRCs were returned in time to be analyzed.

For each of the 985 incidents, the estimates obtained from COs and XOs were tallied and a median value was found. We call these medians TESP ("time expectancy for satisfactory performance") values.

Analyses of Results

RELIABILITY OF TESP VALUES

Using Form 8 of the JOTRC, a reliability estimate for the CO-XO TESPs was obtained. The 44 questionnaires returned (out of 50) were divided in two groups of 22 each. For each item two TESPs were obtained.[9] Correlation of the two sets of TESPs over the 95 items gave a coefficient of .93.

---

[7] This number is smaller than that involved in the two instructor sorts because of deletion of incidents: (*a*) of clear duplication; (*b*) which might be misinterpreted by the judges because the situations represented contraventions of Navy policy (e.g., a number of incidents originally submitted as "effectives," turned out to be violations of regulations).

[8] The results to be presented must be interpreted in terms of the *status quo* at the time of this investigation. To the extent that the operational, training, or personnel factors in the Navy change conditions, the values obtained might be altered.

[9] In all computational work the "X" response, meaning "more than 12 months," was assigned a value of 13; the lower the value, the greater the relevance of the incident to the OCS curriculum.

DISTRIBUTION OF TESP VALUES

The distribution of TESPs for the 985 JOTRC items was divided into incidents of "effective" (E) and "ineffective" (I) performance.

There was a distinct difference in TESPs assigned to E and I performances (median values of 6.0 and 2.5 months, respectively). The officers responsible for operating these ships were most immediately concerned with keeping the novice (and themselves) out of trouble, and were content to wait longer for a quality of performance exceeding what is normally considered satisfactory. Overall the TESPs tended to pile up at the bottom (more "important") end of the scale (Table 2).

TABLE 2

FREQUENCY DISTRIBUTION OF INCIDENTS BY CURRICULUM AREA, SUBCATEGORIZED AS "TAUGHT" AND "NOT TAUGHT," WITH MEAN OF TESP VALUES FOR THE INCIDENTS IN EACH SUBCATEGORY INDICATED

	TAUGHT			NOT TAUGHT			TOTAL		
CURRICULUM AREA	No. of Incidents	% of Incidents[a]	Mean TESP	No. of Incidents	% of Incidents[a]	Mean TESP	No. of Incidents	% of Incidents[a]	Mean TESP
1. Seamanship	143	16.3	4.34	46	5.2	4.28	189	21.5	4.32
2. Orientation and Military Justice	300	34.2	2.73	99	11.3	2.92	399	45.4	2.78
3. Navigation	8	0.9	5.13	1	0.1	2.00	9	1.0	4.78
4. Operations	77	8.8	4.48	67	7.6	5.00	144	16.4	4.72
5. Naval Weapons	12	1.4	7.30	38	4.3	6.26	50	5.7	6.51
6. Engineering and Damage Control	26	3.0	5.46	18	2.1	5.50	44	5.0	5.48
7. Military	2	0.2	1.00	2	0.2	7.00	4	0.5	4.00
8. Other	—	—	—	39	4.4	4.32	39	4.4	4.32
Summary	568	64.7	3.62	310	35.3	4.33	878	100.0	3.87

[a] Percentages based on 878 incidents; $N/878$. Eliminated, because more than 10% of respondents omitted an answer or indicated that they could not clearly interpret the incident, were 91 of the original 985 items. Not included because they could not be judged with confidence as to area of relevance were 16 incidents.

These estimates seem to bear out assertions that destroyer duty requires of an officer rapid learning and assumption of responsibility involving manifold skills and knowledges, even allowing for the fact that all ensigns are not expected to become competent in all of the 985 incident situations.[10] The fact that the COs and XOs expected the ensigns to be able to handle a sizable majority of the situations after only a few months on board seems to lend corroboration to the notion that the over-all adequacy of the curriculum is, in general, proportionate to the coverage given to these situations, even allowing for differences in TESPs of different incidents. In other words, if the relevant skills, knowledges, and attitudes are "taught," the curriculum conforms to

---

[10] As indicated in the questionnaire instructions, the respondent is required to "Suppose [with respect to each incident] that his [the ensign's] responsibilities as an officer will give him the opportunity to handle the situation as shown."

CO-XO judgments. If these are not taught, COs and XOs say, in effect, they ought to be.

TESP VALUES OF INCIDENTS ASSIGNED TO SUBJECT MATTER AREAS

The next analyses deal with the relative "importance" of incidents assigned to different subject matter areas and the relation between the number of incidents found to be relevant to a given area and the TESP values assigned to those incidents.

In order to provide a basis of interpretation least vitiated by ambiguity, the following analyses were restricted to 878 of the original 985 incidents included in the 10 JOTRC forms. Those 91 items, which more than 10% of respondents did not answer or indicated that they could not clearly interpret, were deleted. Sixteen items, which the OCS experts had not been able to assign with confidence to relevant subject matter areas, were also removed. The numbers of incidents "taught" and "not taught" in the six academic courses and in military training were counted, and the mean TESP was calculated for each of these categories and subcategories, as well as the "Others," as shown in Table 2. Among the academic courses there is a close correspondence between the number of incidents said to be relevant to a given course by OCS instructors and the mean TESPs derived independently from the judgments of "importance for early usefulness" by the COs and XOs. The three academic courses which embrace the largest number of incidents are also, in the same order, the courses which are the most "important" as indicated by the mean TESP values. Of the six, only the courses in Navigation and Naval Weapons, the former with a small number of cases, are out of order with respect to these two quantities. Again it would appear that there is substantial parallelism between number and TESP value of incidents when sorted into OCS curriculum areas.

Some indication of the curricular validity of OCS academic offerings is shown by the fact that the mean TESP for material "taught" is lower (more important) than for material "not taught." However the caution introduced earlier, because of the large proportion of incidents said to be related to the material taught in a relatively small number of sessions, still applies.

We have gone one step further and pursued the analysis of the 568 incidents said to be "taught" in the sample of 878 incidents. We determined the mean TESP for the incidents assigned to each instructional session to which one or more incidents were judged to be relevant. A distribution of these 157 sessions against mean TESPs of incidents assigned to each session made it apparent that the lessons covering the largest number of relevant incidents also tend to be considered more "important for early usefulness" aboard ship. Using 28 lessons for which somewhat more reliable mean TESPs are available (based on 10 or more incidents) we again established a fair correspondence between "number" and "importance" of incidents in a given category. The correlation for these 28 lessons was .65.[11]

An inspection was made of the content of these 28 lessons. It supports the view that of all his background, his skills in human relations will be those which a new officer will be most immediately and most frequently called upon to demonstrate. It appears that the first thing a junior officer has to learn is how to manage his relations with contemporaries and seniors. Leadership and management of subordinate personnel show up as next most "important" skills. Demands upon his technical skills and knowledges are not made until later.

Discussion

It has been pointed out that the general purpose of OCS training is to develop officers with general familiarity in subject matter areas containing technical problems and with ability to supervise technicians, not technical specialists. It would appear that officers responsible for operating destroyers are in general agreement with that emphasis. They are perhaps inclined to give greater emphasis to the requirement that he be able to take up quickly, and carry on satisfactorily, responsibilities requiring "know-how" in dealing with people rather than technical skill. Critical incidents involving such skills are also, by far, the kind most frequently reported about ensigns.

Other uses of the results are available. For example, we have concentrated comment on the curriculum areas or lessons most frequently the subject matter of relevant incidents and to which most "importance" is attributed. We have not spoken much of the lessons involving relevance with none of our pool of incidents or those of low "importance." Obviously, these would be examined first in terms of their contribution to the training program and for the possibility of using the time given them for instruction on some of the incident-behaviors which were highly concentrated in a few sessions of the program studied (e.g., leadership).

Summary

This research sought to identify those aspects of the Navy OCS curriculum which were most and least relevant to duties of newly commissioned ensigns aboard destroyers; thus to provide information useful in improvement of training.

More than 1,000 critical incidents of effective and ineffective performance by destroyer ensigns were available from earlier research. These were sorted according to the OCS curriculum area to which each was most relevant. The "relevant" incidents assigned to each area were

---

[11] The sign of the coefficient has been reversed here, to account for the fact that the more "important" items have lower TESP's, and thus permit direct reading and interpretation.

then classified as: (*a*) "Taught"—currently the subject of specific lessons of OCS instruction, and (*b*) "Not Taught"—pertains to a subject matter area in the curriculum, but not covered due to time or facility limitations.

A Junior Officer Training Requirements Checklist was sent to 340 commanding and executive officers of destroyer-type vessels, and was completed by more than 300 of them. The checklist was prepared in 10 forms, each containing approximately 100 incidents. Each form was sent to 30 to 50 officers, with instructions to make a judgment for each incident as to: "How soon [in number of months] after his reporting abroad [directly after being commissioned], under normal conditions, would you expect the new [reserve] officer to be able to handle the situation to your satisfaction?" From their answers an index of "time expectancy for satisfactory performance" was determined for each incident with high reliability. It was assumed that the sooner the ensign is expected to handle a situation satisfactorily, the more "important" it is that the relevant material be learned at OCS.

The findings indicate that the new ensign most frequently and most immediately will be called upon to draw on background relevant to human relations, leadership, and personnel administration skills; technical skills are expected to be developed later.

Suggestions are made for utilization of the current findings.

Naturally, if any considerable changes in the curriculum were to be made, follow-up studies should be conducted to see if the desired changes in on-the-job performance came about.

The case in point here has been the Navy's Officer Candidate School. However, the applicability of the methodology to other training and educational settings is apparent.

21. Teaching Machines*

B. F. Skinner

THERE ARE MORE people in the world than ever before, and a far greater part of them want an education. The demand cannot be met simply by building more schools and training more teachers. Education must become more efficient. To this end curricula must be revised and simplified, and textbooks and classroom techniques improved. In any other field

---

* From *Science*, Vol. 128, No. 3330, 1958, pp. 969–77.

a demand for increased production would have led at once to the invention of labor-saving capital equipment. Education has reached this stage very late, possibly through a misconception of its task. Thanks to the advent of television, however, the so-called audio-visual aids are being reexamined. Film projectors, television sets, phonographs, and tape recorders are finding their way into American schools and colleges.

Audio-visual aids supplement and may even supplant lectures, demonstrations, and textbooks. In doing so they serve one function of the teacher: they present material to the student and, when successful, make it so clear and interesting that the student learns. There is another function to which they contribute little or nothing. It is best seen in the productive interchange between teacher and student in the small classroom or tutorial situation. Much of that interchange has already been sacrificed in American education in order to teach large numbers of students. There is a real danger that it will be wholly obscured if use of equipment designed simply to *present* material becomes widespread. The student is becoming more and more a mere passive receiver of instruction.

PRESSEY'S TEACHING MACHINES

There is another kind of capital equipment which will encourage the student to take an active role in the instructional process. The possibility was recognized in the 1920's, when Sidney L. Pressey designed several machines for the automatic testing of intelligence and information. A recent model of one of these is shown in Figure 1. In using the device the student refers to a numbered item in a multiple-choice test. He presses the button corresponding to his first choice of answer. If he is right, the device moves on to the next item; if he is wrong, the error is tallied, and he must continue to make choices until he is right.[1] Such machines, Pressey pointed out,[2] could not only test and score, they could *teach.* When an examination is corrected and returned after a delay of many hours or days, the student's behavior is not appreciably modified. The immediate report supplied by a self-scoring device, however, can have an important instructional effect. Pressey also pointed out that such machines would increase efficiency in another way. Even in a small classroom the teacher usually knows that he is moving too slowly for some students and too fast for others. Those who could go faster are penalized, and those who should go slower are poorly taught and unnecessarily punished by criticism and failure. Machine instruction would permit each student to proceed at his own rate.

The "industrial revolution in education" which Pressey envisioned

---

[1] The Navy's "Self-Rater" is a large version of Pressey's machine. The items are printed on code-punched plastic cards fed by the machine. The time required to answer is taken into account in scoring.

[2] S. L. Pressey, *School and Society*, Vol. 23, 1926, p. 586.

FIGURE 1

Pressey's self-testing machine. The device directs the student to a particular item in a multiple-choice test. The student presses the key corresponding to his choice of answer. If his choice is correct, the device advances to the next item. Errors are totaled.

stubbornly refused to come about. In 1932 he expressed his disappointment[3] "The problems of invention are relatively simple," he wrote. "With a little money and engineering resource, a great deal could easily be done. The writer has found from bitter experience that one person alone can accomplish relatively little and he is regretfully dropping further work on these problems. But he hopes that enough may have been done to stimulate other workers, that this fascinating field may be developed."

Pressey's machines succumbed in part to cultural inertia; the world of education was not ready for them. But they also had limitations which probably contributed to their failure. Pressey was working against a background of psychological theory which had not come to grips with the learning process. The study of human learning was dominated by the "memory drum" and similar devices originally designed to study forgetting. Rate of learning was observed, but little was done to change it. Why the subject of such an experiment bothered to learn at all was of little interest. "Frequency" and "recency" theories of learning, and principles of "massed and spaced practice," concerned the conditions under which responses were remembered.

Pressey's machines were designed against this theoretical background.

---

[3] S. L. Pressey, *ibid.*, Vol. 36, 1932, p. 934.

As versions of the memory drum, they were primarily testing devices. They were to be used after some amount of learning had already taken place elsewhere. By confirming correct responses and by weakening responses which should not have been acquired, a self-testing machine does, indeed, teach; but it is not designed primarily for that purpose. Nevertheless, Pressey seems to have been the first to emphasize the importance of immediate feedback in education and to propose a system in which each student could move at his own pace. He saw the need for capital equipment in realizing these objectives. Above all he conceived of a machine which (in contrast with the audio-visual aids which were beginning to be developed) permitted the student to play an active role.

ANOTHER KIND OF MACHINE

The learning process is now much better understood. Much of what we know has come from studying the behavior of lower organisms, but the results hold surprisingly well for human subjects. The emphasis in this research has not been on proving or disproving theories but on discovering and controlling the variables of which learning is a function. This practical orientation has paid off, for a surprising degree of control has been achieved. By arranging appropriate "contingencies of reinforcement," specific forms of behavior can be set up and brought under the control of specific classes of stimuli. The resulting behavior can be maintained in strength for long periods of time. A technology based on this work has already been put to use in neurology, pharmacology, nutrition, psychophysics, psychiatry, and elsewhere.[4]

The analysis is also relevant to education. A student is "taught" in the sense that he is induced to engage in new forms of behavior and in specific forms upon specific occasions. It is not merely a matter of teaching him *what* to do; we are as much concerned with the probability that appropriate behavior will, indeed, appear at the proper time—an issue which would be classed traditionally under motivation. In education the behavior to be shaped and maintained is usually verbal, and it is to be brought under the control of both verbal and nonverbal stimuli. Fortunately, the special problems raised by verbal behavior can be submitted to a similar analysis.[5]

If our current knowledge of the acquisition and maintenance of verbal behavior is to be applied to education, some sort of teaching machine is needed. Contingencies of reinforcement which change the behavior of lower organisms often cannot be arranged by hand; rather elaborate apparatus is needed. The human organism requires even more subtle instrumentation. An appropriate teaching machine will have several im-

---

[4] B. F. Skinner, "The Experimental Analysis of Behavior," *American Scientist*, Vol. 45, 1957, p. 4.

[5] ———, *Verbal Behavior* (New York: Appleton-Century-Crofts, 1957).

portant features. The student must *compose* his response rather than select it from a set of alternatives, as in a multiple-choice self-rater. One
reason for this is that we want him to recall rather than recognize
—to make a response as well as see that it is right. Another reason is
that effective multiple-choice material must contain plausible wrong responses, which are out of place in the delicate process of "shaping" behavior because they strengthen unwanted forms. Although it is much
easier to build a machine to score multiple-choice answers than to evaluate a composed response, the technical advantage is outweighed by these
and other considerations.

A second requirement of a minimal teaching machine also distinguishes
it from earlier versions. In acquiring complex behavior the student must
pass through a carefully designed sequence of steps, often of considerable length. Each step must be so small that it can always be taken, yet
in taking it the student moves somewhat closer to fully competent behavior. The machine must make sure that these steps are taken in a
carefully prescribed order.

Several machines with the required characteristics have been built and
tested. Sets of separate presentations or "frames" of visual material are
stored on disks, cards, or tapes. One frame is presented at a time, adjacent
frames being out of sight. In one type of machine the student composes
a response by moving printed figures or letters.[6] His setting is compared
by the machine with a coded response. If the two correspond, the machine automatically presents the next frame. If they do not, the response
is cleared, and another must be composed. The student cannot proceed
to a second step until the first has been taken. A machine of this kind
is being tested in teaching spelling, arithmetic, and other subjects in the
lower grades.

For more advanced students—from junior high school, say, through
college—a machine which senses an arrangement of letters or figures
is unnecessarily rigid in specifying form of response. Fortunately, such
students may be asked to compare their responses with printed material
revealed by the machine. In the machine shown in Figure 2, material
is printed in 30 radial frames on a 12-inch disk. The student inserts
the disk and closes the machine. He cannot proceed until the machine
has been locked, and, once he has begun, the machine cannot be un-
locked. All but a corner of one frame is visible through a window.
The student writes his response on a paper strip exposed through a second opening. By lifting a lever on the front of the machine, he moves
what he has written under a transparent cover and uncovers the correct
response in the remaining corner of the frame. If the two responses correspond, he moves the lever horizontally. This movement punches a

---

[6] B. F. Skinner, "The Science of Learning and the Art of Teaching," *Harvard
Educational Review*, Vol. 24, 1954, p. 2.

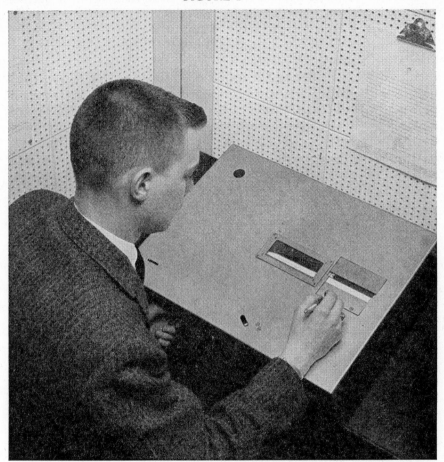

Student at work on a teaching machine. One frame of material is partly visible in the left-hand window. The student writes his response on a strip of paper exposed at the right. He then lifts a lever with his left hand, advancing his written response under a transparent cover and uncovering the correct response in the upper corner of the frame. If he is right, he moves the lever to the right, punching a hole alongside the response he has called right and altering the machine so that that frame will not appear again when he goes through the series a second time. A new frame appears when the lever is returned to its starting position.

hole in the paper opposite his response, recording the fact that he called it correct, and alters the machine so that the frame will not appear again when the student works around the disk a second time. Whether the response was correct or not, a second frame appears when the lever is returned to its starting position. The student proceeds in this way until he has responded to all frames. He then works around the disk a second time, but only those frames appear to which he has not correctly responded. When the disk revolves without stopping, the assignment is finished. (The student is asked to repeat each frame until a correct response is made to allow for the fact that, in telling him that a response is wrong, such a machine tells him what is right.)

The machine itself, of course, does not teach. It simply brings the student into contact with the person who composed the material it presents. It is a labor-saving device because it can bring one programmer into contact with an indefinite number of students. This may suggest mass production, but the effect upon each student is surprisingly like that of a private tutor. The comparison holds in several respects. (1) There is a constant interchange between program and student. Unlike lectures, textbooks, and the usual audio-visual aids, the machine induces sustained activity. The student is always alert and busy. (2) Like a good tutor, the machine insists that a given point be thoroughly understood, either frame by frame or set by set, before the student moves on. Lectures, textbooks, and their mechanized equivalents, on the other hand, proceed without making sure that the student understands and easily leave him behind. (3) Like a good tutor the machine presents just that material for which the student is ready. It asks him to take only that step which he is at the moment best equipped and most likely to take. (4) Like a skillful tutor the machine helps the student to come up with the right answer. It does this in part through the orderly construction of the program and in part with techniques of hinting, prompting, suggesting, and so on, derived from an analysis of verbal behavior.[7] (5) Lastly, of course, the machine, like the private tutor, reinforces the student for every correct response, using this immediate feedback not only to shape his behavior most efficiently but to maintain it in strength in a manner which the layman would describe as "holding the student's interest."

PROGRAMMING MATERIAL

The success of such a machine depends on the material used in it. The task of programming a given subject is at first sight rather formidable. Many helpful techniques can be derived from a general analysis of the relevant behavioral processes, verbal and nonverbal. Specific forms of behavior are to be evoked and, through differential reinforcement, brought under the control of specific stimuli.

There is not the place for a systematic review of available techniques, or of the kind of research which may be expected to discover others. However, the machines themselves cannot be adequately described without giving a few examples of programs. We may begin with a set of frames (see Table 1) designed to teach a third- or fourth-grade pupil to spell the word *manufacture*. The six frames are presented in the order shown, and the pupil moves sliders to expose letters in the open squares.

---

[7] B. F. Skinner, *Verbal Behavior, op. cit.*

TABLE 1

A Set of Frames Designed to Teach a Third- or Fourth-Grade
Pupil to Spell the Word "Manufacture"

1. **Manufacture** means to make or build. *Chair factories manufacture chairs.* Copy the word here:
   □□□□□□□□□□□

2. Part of the word is like part of the word **factory**. Both parts come from an old word meaning *make* or *build*.
   m a n u □□□□ u r e

3. Part of the word is like part of the word **manual**. Both parts come from an old word for *hand*. Many things used to be made by hand.
   □□□□ f a c t u r e

4. The same letter goes in both spaces:
   m □ n u f □ c t u r e

5. The same letter goes in both spaces:
   m a n □ f a c t □ r e

6. **Chair factories** □□□□□□□□□□□ **chairs.**

The word to be learned appears in bold face in frame 1, with an example and a simple definition. The pupil's first task is simply to copy it. When he does so correctly, frame 2 appears. He must now copy selectively: he must identify "fact" as the common part of "manufacture" and "factory." This helps him to spell the word and also to acquire a separable "atomic" verbal operant.[8] In frame 3 another root must be copied selectively from "manual." In frame 4 the pupil must for the first time insert letters without copying. Since he is asked to insert the same letter in two places, a wrong response will be doubly conspicuous, and the chance of failure is thereby minimized. The same principle governs frame 5. In frame 6 the pupil spells the word to complete the sentence used as an example in frame 1. Even a poor student is likely to do this correctly because he has just composed or completed the word five times, has made two important root-responses, and has learned that two letters occur in the word twice. He has probably learned to spell the word without having made a mistake.

Teaching spelling is mainly a process of shaping complex forms of behavior. In other subjects—for example, arithmetic—responses must be brought under the control of appropriate stimuli. Unfortunately the material which has been prepared for teaching arithmetic[9] does not lend itself to excerpting. The numbers 0 through 9 are generated in relation to objects, quantities, and scales. The operations of addition, subtraction, multiplication, and division are thoroughly developed before the number 10 is reached. In the course of this the pupil composes equations and expressions in a great variety of alternative forms. He completes not only $5 + 4 = \square$, but $\square + 4 = 9$, $5 \square 4 = 9$, and so on, aided in most

---

[8] *Ibid.*

[9] This material was prepared with the assistance of Susan R. Meyer.

cases by illustrative materials. No appeal is made to rote memorizing, even in the later acquisition of the tables. The student is expected to arrive at $9 \times 7 = 63$, not by memorizing it as he would memorize a line of poetry, but by putting into practice such principles as that nine times a number is the same as ten times the number minus the number (both of these being "obvious" or already well learned), that the digits in a multiple of nine add to nine, that in composing successive multiples of nine one counts backwards (*nine, eigh*teen, twenty-*seven*, thirty-*six*, and so on), that nine times a single digit is a number beginning with one less than the digit (nine times *six* is *fifty* something), and possibly even that the product of two numbers separated by only one number is equal to the square of the separating number minus one (the square of eight already being familiar from a special series of frames concerned with squares).

Programs of this sort run to great length. At five or six frames per word, four grades of spelling may require 20,000 or 25,000 frames, and three or four grades of arithmetic, as many again. If these figures seem large, it is only because we are thinking of the normal contact between teacher and pupil. Admittedly, a teacher cannot supervise 10,000 or 15,000 responses made by each pupil per year. But the pupil's time is not so limited. In any case, surprisingly little time is needed. Fifteen minutes per day on a machine should suffice for each of these programs, the machines being free for other students for the rest of each day. (It is probably because traditional methods are so inefficient that we have been led to suppose that education requires such a prodigious part of a young person's day.)

A simple technique used in programming material at the high-school or college level, by means of the machine shown in Figure 2, is exemplified in teaching a student to recite a poem. The first line is presented with several unimportant letters omitted. The student must read the line "meaningfully" and supply the missing letters. The second, third, and fourth frames present succeeding lines in the same way. In the fifth frame the first line reappears with other letters also missing. Since the student has recently read the line, he can complete it correctly. He does the same for the second, third, and fourth lines. Subsequent frames are increasingly incomplete, and eventually—say, after 20 or 24 frames—the student reproduces all four lines without external help, and quite possibly without having made a wrong response. The technique is similar to that used in teaching spelling: responses are first controlled by a text, but this is slowly reduced (colloquially, "vanished") until the responses can be emitted without a text, each member in a series of responses being now under the "intraverbal" control of other members.

"Vanishing" can be used in teaching other types of verbal behavior. When a student describes the geography of part of the world or the anatomy of part of the body, or names plants and animals from specimens or pictures, verbal responses are controlled by nonverbal stimuli. In setting up such behavior the student is first asked to report features of a fully labeled map, picture, or object, and the labels are then vanished. In teaching a map, for example, the machine asks the student to describe spatial relations among cities, countries, rivers, and so on, as shown on a fully labeled map. He is then asked to do the same with a map in which the names are incomplete or, possibly, lacking. Eventually he is asked to report the same relations with no map at all. If the material has been well programmed, he can do so correctly. Instruction is sometimes concerned not so much with imparting a new repertoire of verbal responses as with getting the student to describe something accurately in any available terms. The machine can "make sure the student understands" a graph, diagram, chart, or picture by asking him to identify and explain its features—correcting him, of course, whenever he is wrong.

In addition to charts, maps, graphs, models, and so on, the student may have access to auditory material. In learning to take dictation in a foreign language, for example, he selects a short passage on an indexing phonograph according to instructions given by the machine. He listens to the passage as often as necessary and then transcribes it. The machine then reveals the correct text. The student may listen to the passage again to discover the sources of any error. The indexing phonograph may also be used with the machine to teach other language skills, as well as telegraphic code, music, speech, parts of literary and dramatic appreciation, and other subjects.

A typical program combines many of these functions. The set of frames shown in Table 2 is designed to induce the student of high-school physics to talk intelligently, and to some extent technically, about the emission of light from an incandescent source. In using the machine the student will write a word or phrase to complete a given item and then uncover the corresponding word or phrase shown here in the column at the right. The reader who wishes to get the "feel" of the material should cover the right-hand column with a card, uncovering each line only after he has completed the corresponding item.

Several programming techniques are exemplified by the set of frames in Table 2. Technical terms are introduced slowly. For example, the familiar term "fine wire" in frame 2 is followed by a definition of the technical term "filament" in frame 4; "filament" is then asked for in the presence of the nonscientific synonym in frame 5 and without the synonym in frame 9. In the same way "glow," "give off light," and "send out light" in early frames are followed by a definition of "emit" with a synonym in frame 7. Various inflected forms of "emit" then follow, and "emit" itself is asked for with a synonym in frame 16. It is asked for without a synonym but in a helpful phrase in frame 30, and "emitted" and "emission" are asked for without help in frames 33 and 34. The relation between temperature and amount and color of light is developed

TABLE 2

PART OF A PROGRAM IN HIGH-SCHOOL PHYSICS

The machine presents one item at a time. The student completes the item and then uncovers the corresponding word or phrase shown at the right.

SENTENCE TO BE COMPLETED	WORD TO BE SUPPLIED
1. The important parts of a flashlight are the battery and the bulb. When we "turn on" a flashlight, we close a switch which connects the battery with the ———.	bulb
2. When we turn on a flashlight, an electric current flows through the fine wire in the ——— and causes it to grow hot.	bulb
3. When the hot wire glows brightly, we say that it gives off or sends out heat and ———.	light
4. The fine wire in the bulb is called a filament. The bulb "lights up" when the filament is heated by the passage of a (n) ——— current.	electric
5. When a weak battery produces little current, the fine wire, or ———, does not get very hot.	filament
6. A filament which is *less* hot sends out or gives off ——— light.	less
7. "Emit" means "send out." The amount of light sent out, or "emitted," by a filament depends on how ——— the filament is.	hot
8. The higher the temperature of the filament the ——— the light emitted by it.	brighter, stronger
9. If a flashlight battery is weak, the ——— in the bulb may still glow, but with only a dull red color.	filament
10. The light from a very hot filament is colored yellow or white. The light from a filament which is not very hot is colored ———.	red
11. A blacksmith or other metal worker sometimes makes sure that a bar of iron is heated to a "cherry red" before hammering it into shape. He uses the ——— of the light emitted by the bar to tell how hot it is.	color
12. Both the color and the amount of light depend on the ——— of the emitting filament or bar.	temperature
13. An object which emits light because it is hot is called "incandescent." A flashlight bulb is an incandescent source of ———.	light
14. A neon tube emits light but remains cool. It is, therefore, not an incandescent ——— of light.	source
15. A candle flame is hot. It is a(n) ——— source of light.	incandescent
16. The hot wick of a candle gives off small pieces or particles of carbon which burn in the flame. Before or while burning, the hot particles send out, or ———, light.	emit
17. A long candlewick produces a flame in which oxygen does not reach all the carbon particles. Without oxygen the particles cannot burn. Particles which do not burn rise above the flame as ———.	smoke
18. We can show that there are particles of carbon in a candle flame, even when it is not smoking, by holding a piece of metal in the flame. The metal cools some of the particles before they burn, and the unburned carbon ——— collect on the metal as soot.	particles
19. The particles of carbon in soot or smoke no longer emit light because they are ——— than when they were in the flame.	cooler, colder
20. The reddish part of a candle flame has the same color as the filament in a flashlight with a weak battery. We might guess that the yellow or white parts of a candle flame are ——— than the reddish part.	hotter
21. "Putting out" an incandescent electric light means turning off the current so that the filament grows too ——— to emit light.	cold, cool
22. Setting fire to the wick of an oil lamp is called ——— the lamp.	lighting
23. The sun is our principal ——— of light, as well as of heat.	source
24. The sun is not only very bright but very hot. It is a powerful ——— source of light.	incandescent

TABLE 2 (*Continued*)

SENTENCE TO BE COMPLETED	WORD TO BE SUPPLIED
25. Light is a form of energy. In "emitting light" an object changes, or "converts," one form of ———— into another.	energy
26. The electrical energy supplied by the battery in a flashlight is converted to ———— and ————.	heat, light; light, heat
27. If we leave a flashlight on, all the energy stored in the battery will finally be changed or ———— into heat and light.	converted
28. The light from a candle flame comes from the ———— released by chemical changes as the candle burns.	energy
29. A nearly "dead" battery may make a flashlight bulb warm to the touch, but the filament may still not be hot enough to emit light—in other words, the filament will not be ———— at that temperature.	incandescent
30. Objects, such as a filament, carbon particles, or iron bars, become incandescent when heated to about 800 degrees Celsius. At that temperature they begin to ———— ————.	emit light
31. When raised to any temperature above 800 degrees Celsius, an object such as an iron bar will emit light. Although the bar may melt or vaporize, its particles will be ———— no matter how hot they get.	incandescent
32. About 800 degrees Celsius is the lower limit of the temperature at which particles emit light. There is no upper limit of the ———— at which emission of light occurs.	temperature
33. Sunlight is ———— by very hot gases near the surface of the sun.	emitted
34. Complex changes similar to an atomic explosion generate the great heat which explains the ———— of light by the sun.	emission
35. Below about ———— degrees Celsius an object is not an incandescent source of light.	800

in several frames before a formal statement using the word "temperature" is asked for in frame 12. "Incandescent" is defined and used in frame 13, is used again in frame 14, and is asked for in frame 15, the student receiving a thematic prompt from the recurring phrase "incandescent source of light." A formal prompt is supplied by "candle." In frame 25 the new response "energy" is easily evoked by the words "form of . . ." because the expression "form of energy" is used earlier in the frame. "Energy" appears again in the next two frames and is finally asked for, without aid, in frame 28. Frames 30 through 35 discuss the limiting temperatures of incandescent objects, while reviewing several kinds of sources. The figure 800 is used in three frames. Two intervening frames then permit some time to pass before the response "800" is asked for.

Unwanted responses are eliminated with special techniques. If, for example, the second sentence in frame 24 were simply "It is a(n) ———— source of light," the two "very's" would frequently lead the student to fill the blank with "strong" or a synonym thereof. This is prevented by inserting the word "powerful" to make a synonym redundant. Similarly, in frame 3 the words "heat and" preempt the response "heat," which would otherwise correctly fill the blank.

The net effect of such material is more than the acquisition of facts and terms. Beginning with a largely unverbalized acquaintance with flash-

FIGURE 3

Self-instruction room in Sever Hall at Harvard. Ten booths contain teaching machines, some equipped with indexing phonographs.

lights, candles, and so on, the student is induced to talk about familiar events, together with a few new facts, with a fairly technical vocabulary. He applies the same terms to facts which he may never before have seen to be similar. The emission of light from an incandescent source takes shape as a topic or field of inquiry. An understanding of the subject emerges which is often quite surprising in view of the fragmentation required in item building.

It is not easy to construct such a program. Where a confusing or elliptical passage in a textbook is forgivable because it can be clarified by the teacher, machine material must be self-contained and wholly adequate. There are other reasons why textbooks, lecture outlines, and film scripts are of little help in preparing a program. They are usually not logical or developmental arrangements of material but stratagems which the authors have found successful under existing classroom conditions. The examples they give are more often chosen to hold the student's interest than to clarify terms and principles. In composing material for the machine, the programmer may go directly to the point.

A first step is to define the field. A second is to collect technical terms, facts, laws, principles, and cases. These must then be arranged in a plausible developmental order—linear if possible, branching if necessary. A mechanical arrangement, such as a card filing system, helps. The material is distributed among the frames of a program to achieve an arbitrary density. In the final composition of an item, techniques for strengthening asked-for responses and for transferring control from one variable to another are chosen from a list according to a given schedule in order to prevent the establishment of irrelevant verbal tendencies appropriate to a single technique. When one set of frames has been composed, its terms and facts are seeded mechanically among succeeding sets, where they will again be referred to in composing later items to make sure that the earlier repertoire remains active. Thus, the technical terms, facts, and examples in Table 2 have been distributed for reuse in succeeding sets on reflection, absorption, and transmission, where they are incorporated into items dealing mainly with other matters. Sets of frames for explicit review can, of course, be constructed. Further research will presumably discover other, possibly more effective, techniques. Meanwhile, it must be admitted that a considerable measure of art is needed in composing a successful program.

Whether good programming is to remain an art or to become a scientific technology, it is reassuring to know that there is a final authority—the student. An unexpected advantage of machine instruction has proved to be the feedback to the *programmer*. In the elementary school machine, provision is made for discovering which frames commonly yield wrong responses, and in the high-school and college machine the paper strips bearing written answers are available for analysis. A trial run of the first version of a program quickly reveals frames which need to be altered, or sequences which need to be lengthened. One or two revisions in the light of a few dozen responses work a great improvement. No comparable feedback is available to the lecturer, textbook writer, or maker of films. Although one text or film may seem to be better than another, it is usually impossible to say, for example, that a given sentence on a given page or a particular sequence in a film is causing trouble.

Difficult as programming is, it has its compensations. It is a salutary thing to try to guarantee a right response at every step in the presentation of a subject matter. The programmer will usually find that he has been accustomed to leave much to the student—that he has frequently omitted essential steps and neglected to invoke relevant points. The responses made to his material may reveal surprising ambiguities. Unless he is lucky, he may find that he still has something to learn about his subject. He will almost certainly find that he needs to learn a great deal more about the behavioral changes he is trying to induce in the student. This effect of the machine in confronting the programmer with the full scope of his task may in itself produce a considerable improvement in education.

Composing a set of frames can be an exciting exercise in the analysis of knowledge. The enterprise has obvious bearings on scientific methodology. There are hopeful signs that the epistemological implications will induce experts to help in composing programs. The expert may be interested for another reason. We can scarcely ask a topflight mathematician to write a primer in second-grade arithmetic if it is to be used by the average teacher in the average classroom. But a carefully controlled machine presentation and the resulting immediacy of contact between programmer and student offer a very different prospect, which may be enough to induce those who know most about the subject to give some thought to the nature of arithmetical behavior and to the various forms in which such behavior should be set up and tested.

CAN MATERIAL BE TOO EASY?

The traditional teacher may view these programs with concern. He may be particularly alarmed by the effort to maximize success and minimize failure. He has found that students do not pay attention unless they are worried about the consequences of their work. The customary procedure has been to maintain the necessary anxiety by inducing errors. In recitation, the student who obviously knows the answer is not too often asked; a test item which is correctly answered by everyone is discarded as nondiscriminating; problems at the end of a section in a textbook in mathematics generally include one or two very difficult items; and so on. (The teacher-turned-programmer may be surprised to find this attitude affecting the construction of items. For example, he may find it difficult to allow an item to stand which "gives the point away." Yet if we can solve the motivational problem with other means, what is more effective than giving a point away?) Making sure that the student knows he doesn't know is a technique concerned with motivation, not with the learning process. Machines solve the problem of motivation in other ways. There is no evidence that what is easily learned is more readily forgotten. If this should prove to be the case, retention may be guaranteed by subsequent material constructed for an equally painless review.

The standard defense of "hard" material is that we want to teach more than subject matter. The student is to be challenged and taught to "think." The argument is sometimes little more than a rationalization for a confusing presentation, but it is doubtless true that lectures and texts are often inadequate and misleading by design. But to what end? What sort of "thinking" does the student learn in struggling through difficult material? It is true that those who learn under difficult conditions are better students, but are they better because they have surmounted difficulties or do they surmount them because they are better? In the guise of teaching thinking we set difficult and confusing situations and claim credit for the students who deal with them successfully.

The trouble with deliberately making education difficult in order to teach thinking is (1) that we must remain content with the students thus selected, even though we know that they are only a small part of the potential supply of thinkers, and (2) that we must continue to sacrifice the teaching of subject matter by renouncing effective but "easier" methods. A more sensible program is to analyze the behavior called "thinking" and produce it according to specifications. A program specifically concerned with such behavior could be composed of material already available in logic, mathematics, scientific method, and psychology. Much would doubtless be added in completing an effective program. The machine has already yielded important relevant by-products. Immediate feedback encourages a more careful reading of programmed material than is the case in studying a text, where the consequences of attention or inattention are so long deferred that they have little effect on reading skills. The behavior involved in observing or attending to detail—as in inspecting charts and models or listening closely to recorded speech—is efficiently shaped by the contingencies arranged by the machine. And when an immediate result is in the balance, a student will be more likely to learn how to marshal relevant material, to concentrate on specific features of a presentation, to reject irrelevant materials, to refuse the easy but wrong solution, and to tolerate indecision, all of which are involved in effective thinking.

Part of the objection to easy material is that the student will come to depend on the machine and will be less able than ever to cope with the inefficient presentations of lectures, textbooks, films, and "real life." This is indeed a problem. All good teachers must "wean" their students, and the machine is no exception. The better the teacher, the more explicit must the weaning process be. The final stages of a program must be so designed that the student no longer requires the helpful conditions arranged by the machine. This can be done in many ways—among others by using the machine to discuss material which has been studied in other forms. These are questions which can be adequately answered only by further research.

No large-scale "evaluation" of machine teaching has yet been attempted. We have so far been concerned mainly with practical problems in the design and use of machines, and with testing and revising sample programs. The machine shown in Figure 2 was built and tested with a grant from the Fund for the Advancement of Education. Material has been prepared and tested with the collaboration of Lloyd E. Homme, Susan R. Meyer, and James G. Holland.[10] The self-instruction room

---

[10] Dr. Homme prepared sets of frames for teaching part of college physics (kinematics), and Mrs. Meyer has prepared and informally tested material in remedial reading and vocabulary building at the junior high school level. Others who have contributed to the development of teaching machines should be mentioned. Nathan H. Azrin cooperated with me in testing a version of a machine to teach arithmetic. C. B. Ferster and Stanley M. Sapon used a simple "machine" to teach German (see "An Application of Recent Developments in Psychology to the Teaching of

shown in Figure 3 was set up under this grant. It contains ten machines and was recently used to teach part of a course in human behavior to Harvard and Radcliffe undergraduates. Nearly 200 students completed 48 disks (about 1400 frames) prepared with the collaboration of Holland. The factual core of the course was covered, corresponding to about 200 pages of the text.[11] The median time required to finish 48 disks was 14½ hours. The students were not examined on the material but were responsible for the text which overlapped it. Their reactions to the material and to self-instruction in general have been studied through interviews and questionnaires. Both the machines and the material are now being modified in the light of this experience, and a more explicit evaluation will then be made.

Meanwhile, it can be said that the expected advantages of machine instruction were generously confirmed. Unsuspected possibilities were revealed which are now undergoing further exploration. Although it is less convenient to report to a self-instruction room than to pick up a textbook in one's room or elsewhere, most students felt that they had much to gain in studying by machine. Most of them worked for an hour or more with little effort, although they often felt tired afterwards, and they reported that they learned much more in less time and with less effort than in conventional ways. No attempt was made to point out the relevance of the material to crucial issues, personal or otherwise, but the students remained interested. (Indeed, one change in the reinforcing contingencies suggested by the experiment is intended to *reduce* the motivational level.) An important advantage proved to be that the student always knew where he stood, without waiting for an hour test or final examination.

SOME QUESTIONS

Several questions are commonly asked when teaching machines are discussed. Cannot the results of laboratory research on learning be used in education without machines? Of course they can. They should lead to improvements in textbooks, films, and other teaching materials. Moreover, the teacher who really understands the conditions under which learning takes place will be more effective, not only in teaching subject

---

German," *Harvard Educational Review*, Vol. 1, 1958, p. 28). Douglas Porter, of the Graduate School of Education at Harvard, has made an independent schoolroom test of machine instruction in spelling (see "Teaching Machines," *Harvard Graduate School of Educational Association Bulletin*, Vol. 1, 1958, p. 3). Devra Cooper has experimented with the teaching of English composition for freshmen at the University of Kentucky. Thomas F. Gilbert, of the University of Georgia, has compared standard and machine instruction in an introductory course in psychology, and with the collaboration of J. E. Jewett has prepared material in algebra. The U.S. Naval Training Devices Center has recently contracted with the University of Pennsylvania for a study of programs relating to the machine instruction of servicemen, under the direction of Eugene H. Galanter.

[11] B. F. Skinner, *Science and Human Behavior* (New York: Macmillan, 1953).

matter but in managing the class. Nevertheless, some sort of device is necessary to arrange the subtle contingencies of reinforcement required for optimal learning if each student is to have individual attention. In nonverbal skills this is usually obvious; texts and instructor can guide the learner but they cannot arrange the final contingencies which set up skilled behavior. It is true that the verbal skills at issue here are especially dependent upon social reinforcement, but it must not be forgotten that the machine simply mediates an *essentially verbal* relation. In shaping and maintaining verbal knowledge we are not committed to the contingencies arranged through immediate personal contact.

Machines may still seem unnecessarily complex compared with other mediators such as workbooks or self-scoring test forms. Unfortunately, these alternatives are not acceptable. When material is adequately programmed, adjacent steps are often so similar that one frame reveals the response to another. Only some sort of mechanical presentation will make successive frames independent of each other. Moreover, in self-instruction an automatic record of the student's behavior is especially desirable, and for many purposes it should be foolproof. Simplified versions of the present machines have been found useful—for example, in the work of Ferster and Sapon, of Porter, and of Gilbert[12]—but the mechanical and economic problems are so easily solved that a machine with greater capabilities is fully warranted.

Will machines replace teachers? On the contrary, they are capital equipment to be used by teachers to save time and labor. In assigning certain mechanizable functions to machines, the teacher emerges in his proper role as an indispensable human being. He may teach more students than heretofore—this is probably inevitable if the world-wide demand for education is to be satisfied—but he will do so in fewer hours and with fewer burdensome chores. In return for his greater productivity he can ask society to improve his economic condition.

The role of the teacher may well be changed, for machine instruction will affect several traditional practices. Students may continue to be grouped in "grades" or "classes," but it will be possible for each to proceed at his own level, advancing as rapidly as he can. The other kind of "grade" will also change its meaning. In traditional practice a *C* means that a student has a smattering of a whole course. But if machine instruction assures mastery at every stage, a grade will be useful only in showing *how far* a student has gone. *C* might mean that he is halfway through a course. Given enough time he will be able to get an *A*; and since *A* is no longer a motivating device, this is fair enough. The quick student will meanwhile have picked up *A's* in other subjects.

Differences in ability raise other questions. A program designed for the slowest student in the school system will probably not seriously

---

[12] Refer to footnote 10.

delay the fast student, who will be free to progress at his own speed. (He may profit from the full coverage by filling in unsuspected gaps in his repertoire.) If this does not prove to be the case, programs can be constructed at two or more levels, and students can be shifted from one to the other as performances dictate. If there are also differences in "types of thinking," the extra time available for machine instruction may be used to present a subject in ways appropriate to many types. Each student will presumably retain and use those ways which he finds most useful. The kind of individual difference which arises simply because a student has missed part of an essential sequence (compare the child who has no "mathematical ability" because he was out with the measles when fractions were first taken up) will simply be eliminated.

OTHER USES

Self-instruction by machine has many special advantages apart from educational institutions. Home study is an obvious case. In industrial and military training it is often inconvenient to schedule students in groups, and individual instruction by machine should be a feasible alternative. Programs can also be constructed in subjects for which teachers are not available—for example, when new kinds of equipment must be explained to operators and repairmen, or where a sweeping change in method finds teachers unprepared.[13] Education sometimes fails because students have handicaps which make a normal relationship with a teacher difficult or impossible. (Many blind children are treated today as feeble-minded because no one has had the time or patience to make contact with them. Deaf-mutes, spastics, and others suffer similar handicaps.) A teaching machine can be adapted to special kinds of communication—as, for example, Braille—and, above all, it has infinite patience.

CONCLUSION

An analysis of education within the framework of a science of behavior has broad implications. Our schools, in particular our "progressive" schools, are often held responsible for many current problems—including juvenile delinquency and the threat of a more powerful foreign technology. One remedy frequently suggested is a return to older techniques, especially to a greater "discipline" in schools. Presumably this is to be obtained with some form of punishment, to be administered either with certain classical instruments of physical injury—the dried bullock's tail of the Greek teacher or the cane of the English schoolmaster—or as disapproval or failure, the frequency of which is to be increased by "raising standards." This is probably not a feasible solution. Not only education but Western culture as a whole is moving away from aversive

---

[13] K. Menger, "New Approach to Teaching Intermediate Mathematics," *Science*, Vol. 127, 1958, p. 1,320.

practices. We cannot prepare young people for one kind of life in institutions organized on quite different principles. The discipline of the birch rod may facilitate learning, but we must remember that it also breeds followers of dictators and revolutionists.

In the light of our present knowledge a school system must be called a failure if it cannot induce students to learn except by threatening them for not learning. That this has always been the standard pattern simply emphasizes the importance of modern techniques. John Dewey was speaking for his culture and his time when he attacked aversive educational practices and appealed to teachers to turn to positive and humane methods. What he threw out should have been thrown out. Unfortunately he had too little to put in its place. Progressive education has been a temporizing measure which can now be effectively supplemented. Aversive practices can not only be replaced, they can be replaced with far more powerful techniques. The possibilities should be thoroughly explored if we are to build an educational system which will meet the present demand without sacrificing democratic principles.

22. Multiple Role Playing: A Technique for Training Supervisors*

Norman R. F. Maier and Lester F. Zerfoss

HUMAN RELATIONS skills are difficult to learn merely through reading or by hearing lectures. To be effective, training in the skills must be accompanied by attitude and feeling changes. A supervisor who does not respect his employees will have difficulty in practicing effective methods because his approaches will not hide his basic attitude. It is because skills and attitudes are so interdependent in personnel work that training methods must incorporate both.

One of the important approaches in the improvement of supervisors is that of increasing their employees' participation in the solving of some of the day-to-day job problems. Many employees are distrustful of changes in the job, and there frequently is a feeling that the supervisor plays favorites and discriminates against others. Techniques of selling employees on changes that affect them, and the usual procedures designed

* From "MRP: A Technique for Training Large Groups of Supervisors and Its Potential Use in Social Research," *Human Relations*, Vol. 5, 1952, pp. 177–86.

to develop fair practices, usually fail to solve these attitudinal problems.[1] It is exactly in these areas that employee participation seems to be most valuable and for which the group decision method[2] (in which the supervisor shares his problem with his group) has been developed.

However, there is a great deal of resistance on the part of supervisors to sharing work problems with their groups because they feel they are giving up something in the process.[3] In order to overcome this resistance, new types of training methods are needed. These new methods require that supervisors learn through participation because they, like rank and file employees, also shy away from changes that effect them.

Discussion meetings[4] and role-playing procedures[5] are two of the best participation training methods. However, their nature is such as to limit their uses to training in small groups. In training large groups it has been necessary to confine one's procedures to lectures, visual aids, movies, and demonstrations. None of these approaches permits active participation and practice. An audience participation technique, recently developed by Donald Phillips,[6] has received a high degree of acceptance in industry. It is one of the first methods to permit small group discussions within the general framework of an audience situation. The procedure, often referred to as "Phillips 66," accomplishes general participation by dividing the audience into committees of six, each of which holds a discussion for six minutes on some specific question previously put to them. The major limitation of the Phillips 66 method is that the subject-matter to be used for discussion is limited in scope, and it can only be adapted to certain types of situations.

Recently, we have tested a procedure at The Detroit Edison Company which combines the role-playing approach with Phillips 66, and which

---

[1] L. Coch and J. R. P. French Jr., "Overcoming Resistance to Change," *Human Relations*, Vol. 1, No. 2, 1948, pp. 512–32; K. Lewin, "Group Decision and Social Change," in T. M. Newcomb and E. L. Hartley (eds.), *Readings in Social Psychology* (New York: Henry Holt and Co., 1947), pp. 330–44.

[2] L. P. Bradford and R. Lippitt, "Building a Democratic Work Group," *Personnel*, Vol. 22, 1945, pp. 2–13; K. Lewin, *op. cit.*; K. Lewin, R. Lippitt, and R. K. White, "Patterns of Aggressive Behavior in Experimentally Created Social Climates," *Journal of Social Psychology*, Vol. 11, 1939, pp. 271–99; N. R. F. Maier, "A Human Relations Program for Supervision," *Industrial and Labor Relations Review*, Vol. 1, 1948, pp. 443–64.

[3] N. R. F. Maier, "Improving Supervision through Training," in A. Kornhauser (ed.), *Psychology of Labor Management Relations* (Champaign, Ill.: Industrial Relations Research Assn., 1949), pp. 27–42.

[4] L. Coch and J. R. P. French, Jr., *op. cit.*; N. R. F. Maier, "A Human Relations Program for Supervision," *op. cit.*; N. R. F. Maier, "Improving Supervision through Training," *op. cit.*

[5] A. Bavelas, "Role-Playing and Management Training," *Sociatry*, Vol. 1, 1947, pp. 183–91; L. P. Bradford and R. Lippitt, "Building a Democratic Work Group," *op. cit.*; R. Lippitt, L. P. Bradford, and K. D. Benne, "Sociodramatic Clarification of Leader and Group Roles," *Sociatry*, Vol. 1, 1947, pp. 82–91.

[6] J. D. Phillips, "Report on Discussion 66," *Adult Education Journal*, Vol. 7, 1948, pp. 181–82.

may be described as Multiple Role Playing (MRP). This method permits role-playing to be carried out in such a manner that all members of a large audience can participate. The purpose of the technique is to give each member of an audience a first-hand experience in the group decision method. It permits the training of supervisors in skills of leading discussions and at the same time gives them an experience of the way things appear to employees, by finding themselves placed in the employee's position. Training supervisors to use group decision requires that they develop: (1) confidence in the way employees behave when given an opportunity to solve job problems, and (2) skill in putting a problem to the group. The MRP method serves in both of these capacities. The experiences obtained in these group discussions give the participants an opportunity to discover that the way employees behave depends greatly upon the kind of situation the supervisor creates. Thus, both the attitude of the supervisor and his skill in leading the discussion directly determine the outcome of the conference. Participants who function as employees see the errors that the supervisor makes and discover how their own reactions are influenced by the situation he creates. Participants who serve as supervisors can discover how conflicts in groups become resolved and find ways to help the process along. All can experience some of the emotional loadings that attach themselves to matters of prestige and fair play. The few participants who function as observers can discover how lifelike a role-playing process might become, and they can observe how the discussion process leads to attitude changes. As an observer, a person can have a disinterested attitude and objectively evaluate the process.

In repeating this method, different persons can function as observers, supervisors, and employees and thus gain a variety of experiences from these exchanges in function.

In order to make the group decision experience a success with untrained leaders, it is important that the problem be so structured that the leader is likely to do a good job and that the group will readily participate in the discussion. To accomplish good discussion leadership, the problem used for our demonstration was one for which the supervisor is unlikely to have a ready-made solution. In having no preferred solution himself, he is inclined to act permissively, and thus encourage free and frank discussion instead of imposing or selling his own views. To produce a lively discussion, the problem that is used must be one which creates a conflict in attitudes. In order to solve the problem these attitudes have to become reconciled.

The work situation described in this article is based on an actual case in industry and raises the type of problem that a crew can solve more satisfactorily than a supervisor. As such, it readily lends itself to a group decision rather than an autocratic decision which is imposed on the crew by the supervisor. In the real life situation the foreman had a new truck to distribute. He realized that his decision would not meet with approval since each man would feel he had a claim. He therefore put the problem to the crew. The crew solved the problem in such a way that there was a general exchange of trucks, so that each man got a different truck and at the same time the poorest truck was discarded. Everyone was satisfied with the solution.

In setting up this problem for role-playing, we have given each participant a personal attitude, so that a typical set of life-like conflicts would be created. This is the usual procedure in role-playing. The deviation from the usual procedure is that the same roles are simultaneously played by many groups, each without the guidance of a trainer. This absence of specific guidance during the role-playing process makes standardization more essential and requires the use of clear-cut problems. However, we find that these limitations are not serious.

SETTING UP THE ROLE-PLAYING PROCEDURE

1. The first step in the procedure is for the trainer or the person in charge of the meeting to request the audience to divide itself into groups of six, with three persons in one row turning around to meet with three persons directly behind them. Assistants can be an aid to help persons in odd seats join others in making up these groups. By arranging the seating rows in multiples of three, the task of organizing the groups is simplified. (In our situation the seats themselves could be turned around and thus made for more comfort.)

Since the number of persons required in a group is six, there may be a remainder of from 1 to 5 persons. Each of those extra persons is asked to join one of the discussion groups and serve as an observer.

2. When the audience has been divided into groups, the trainer announces that each group will receive a set of instructions. The persons who pass out the material will hand these instructions to one member of each group. This member will play the part of Walt Marshall, the foreman of a crew of repairmen. The other five members of the group will be repairmen who report to Walt Marshall. The foreman is to keep this material until instructed further. In the meantime he may look over the top page, labelled "Walt Marshall—Foreman of the Repair Crew."

3. The trainer then asks the crew members of all groups to give their attention while he reads them their instructions.

General Instructions for Crew:

You are repairmen for a large company and drive to various locations in the city to do your work. Each of you drives a small truck, and you take pride in keeping it looking good. You have a possessive feeling about your trucks and like to keep them in good running order. Naturally, you like to have new trucks, too, because a new truck gives you a feeling of pride.

Here are some facts about the trucks and the men in the crew who report to Walt Marshall, the supervisor of repairs:

George—17 years with the company, has a 2-year-old Ford truck.

Bill—11 years with the company, has a 5-year-old Dodge truck.

John—10 years with the company, has a 4-year-old Ford truck.

Charlie—5 years with the company, has a 3-year-old Ford truck.

Hank—3 years with the company, has a 5-year-old Chevrolet truck.

Most of you do all of your driving in the city, but John and Charlie cover the jobs in the suburbs.

In acting your part in role-playing, accept the facts as given as well as assume the attitude supplied in your specific role. From this point on let your feelings develop in accordance with the events that transpire in the role-playing process. When facts or events arise which are not covered by the roles, make up things which are consistent with the way it might be in a real life situation.

The names of the five men, years of service, age, and make of truck should then be placed on an easel-chart or black board, so that ready reference to them can be made.

4. The foreman is then asked to pass out the material he has been given, which consists of six sets of instructions, one for each person in the group. He should keep the top set for himself and pass out one set of instructions, beginning on his left, to each of his five crewmen. The sequence of the instructions should be George, Bill, John, Charlie, and Hank so that the seating order corresponds to the order of seniority as listed on the easel.

The content of the specific instructions for each member of the group is as follows:

Walt Marshall—Foreman of Repair Crew

You are the foreman of a crew of repairmen, each of whom drives a small service truck to and from his various jobs. Every so often you get a new truck to exchange for an old one, and you have the problem of deciding to which of your men you should give the new truck. Often there are hard feelings because each man seems to feel he is entitled to the new truck; so you have a tough time being fair. As a matter of fact, it usually turns out that whatever you decide, most of the men consider wrong. You now have to face the issue again because a new truck has just been allocated to you for distribution. The new truck is a Chevrolet.

Here are some brief facts about your situation:

George—17 years with the company, has a 2-year-old Ford truck.

Bill—11 years with the company, has a 5-year-old Dodge truck.

John—10 years with the company, has a 4-year-old Ford truck.

Charlie—5 years with the company, has a 3-year-old Ford truck.

Hank—3 years with the company, has a 5-year-old Chevrolet truck.

All of the men do city driving, making fairly short trips, except for John and Charlie who cover the suburbs.

In order to handle this problem you have decided to put the decision up to the men themselves. You will tell them about the new truck and will put the problem in terms of what would be the most fair way to distribute the truck. Avoid taking a position yourself because you want to do what the men think is most fair.

George: *When a new Chevrolet truck becomes available, you think you should get it because you have most seniority and don't like your present truck. Your own car is a Chevrolet, and you prefer a Chevrolet truck such as you drove before you got the Ford.*

Bill: *You feel you deserve a new truck. Your present truck is old, and since the senior man has a fairly new truck, you should get the next one. You have taken excellent care of your present Dodge and have kept it looking like new. A man deserves to be rewarded if he treats a company truck like his own.*

John: *You have to do more driving than most of the other men because you work in the suburbs. You have a fairly old truck and feel you should have a new one because you do so much driving.*

Charlie: *The heater in your present truck is inadequate. Since Hank backed into the door of your truck, it has never been repaired to fit right. The door lets in too much cold air, and you attribute your frequent colds to this. You want a warm truck since you have a good deal of driving to do. As long as it has good tires, brakes, and is comfortable you don't care about its make.*

Hank: *You have the poorest truck in the crew. It is five years old, and before you got it, it had been in a bad wreck. It has never been good, and you've put up with it for three years. It's about time you got a good truck to drive, and you feel the next one should be yours. You have a good accident record. The only accident you had was when you sprung the door of Charlie's truck when he opened it as you backed out of the garage. You hope the new truck is a Ford since you prefer to drive one.*

Members are asked to study their roles until they have a feeling for them. It is perhaps necessary to caution them not to show their roles to each other, but to put them aside when they have finished with them.

5. When everyone is ready, the trainer gives the signal for the foreman to take the responsibility of starting their meetings. Each foreman should assume that he has called his men together and that he is seated with them to discuss a problem.

6. Less than half an hour is adequate for most groups to solve the problem. (If the leader and his assistants observe the groups they can pretty well judge when most of the groups have reached a solution.) Before interrupting the discussion, it is desirable to announce from the

floor that three more minutes will be allowed the groups to settle on some arrangement.

7. At the end of the three-minute period, the members are asked to break off their discussions and join in the analysis of the results.

ANALYZING THE RESULTS

The extent of the analysis need not be confined to the points discussed below, but the analysis should cover the following points:

1. Determination of the number of groups arriving at a solution. (In obtaining this figure, only the foreman should vote.)

2. Determination of the number of men who are satisfied with the solution. (In this case only the repairmen of crews which reached a solution should raise their hands.) This figure is important because it indicates the degree of satisfaction obtained from the procedure. The chairman may ask how this degree of acceptance compares with what would have been obtained if the foreman had supplied the solution.

3. Determination of number of crews which discarded Hank's truck. (In this case only the foremen should raise their hands.) The proportion of the number of times that Hank's truck was discarded to the number of groups becomes a measure of the quality of the solution. The fear that men might fail to discard the poorest truck would constitute one of the reasons why a foreman might hesitate to put such a problem to them. If the proportion of crews discarding the poorest truck is very large, it indicates that the danger of not having the poorest truck discarded is more imagined than real.

4. Determination of the number of crews in which the new truck went to various members of the crew. (In this case only the foremen should vote on the five alternatives.) This analysis brings out the variety of solutions obtained and shows that the same problem with the same roles produces different solutions. Under such circumstances it becomes clear that a company could not work out a policy that would be satisfying to all crews.

This analysis might also be followed by questions such as, "In how many cases did George use his seniority and make a strong demand for the new truck?" "How often did he get it when he was that kind of a George?" "How often did George get the new truck when he did not throw his seniority around?" Such questions frequently reveal that George is more likely to get the new truck when he is a reasonable person and considerate of men with less service than when he is demanding.

5. Determination of the number of crews in which:

a) All men obtained a different truck.

b) Four men obtained a different truck.

c) Three men obtained a different truck.

d) Two men obtained a different truck.

e) No exchange in old trucks were made and only the man receiving the new truck benefited.

(Only the foreman should vote on these alternatives.) This analysis gives an idea of the extent to which all men were given consideration. If time is taken to analyze these data, it might be found that the foreman's conduct of the meeting determined the number of men who benefited by the addition of a new truck to the crew.

Following the analysis of the crews, the persons serving as observers should be asked to give their evaluations of the discussion meetings they observed. Their report may include: (a) the way foreman put the problem, (b) the extent to which he hampered the discussion, (c) the extent to which he imposed his own ideas, and (d) evaluation of things he did which helped things along. These reports not only involve the observers in the procedure, but add supplementary material on the different approaches various foremen may have used.

SOME SAMPLE RESULTS

We have tested the case in three audiences. In one of these, 17 groups were formed and in 14 of these, all persons were satisfied with the solution they had reached. A total of 5 individuals out of 102 were dissatisfied with the solutions of their groups. In the second group tested, 6 groups were used and 2 persons (in two different groups) out of 42 were dissatisfied. In the third audience, 19 out of 21 groups had time to reach a decision and only one person in each of two groups was dissatisfied. If we combine our groups, we find that 42 out of 44 groups reached a decision and only 9 out of 220 repairmen (4.1 per cent) were dissatisfied.

In each of three tests of the method, all persons participating readily agreed that anything approaching the degree of satisfaction shown could not have been obtained if supervisors had supplied the solution.

In 41 out of the 42 groups, Hank's truck (the poorest one) was eliminated. This result clearly shows that the group decisions were in accordance with the interests of good management. Thus, the fear that group decisions might lead to poor-quality decisions was not supported.

The new truck went to George, the senior man, in 20 of the 42 groups. In 16 cases out of 28 he got it when he did not insist on it because of his seniority, and in 4 cases out of 10 he got it by defending his rank. Thus George gained most when he acted least in his own selfish interests.

A great variety of solutions developed in these groups. The new truck went to each of the individuals in one group or another; the frequency being in the order of George, John, Hank, Bill and Charlie. In most instances there was a general exchange of trucks. All men got a different truck in 4 groups; 4 men got a different truck in 10 groups; 3 men in 16 groups; 2 in 8 groups; and only 1 got a different truck (the new one) in 4 groups.

From descriptions of the discussion process, there seemed to be a trend in which the general exchange of trucks was greatest when the leader was permissive. The first part of the discussion develops a conflict of interests, and if the leader is permissive at this stage, the idea of exchanging trucks develops. Many men who played the part of the supervisor were surprised at this development because most of them went into the discussion with the idea of getting the new truck assigned to some particular individual and getting the rest of the group to agree on who was most needy. It is this emphasis on the leader's part which prevents the general exchange which usually develops out of the free discussion. Thus, the idea that all can profit when the crew gets a new truck emerges as a new idea, and it is a group product.

GENERAL EVALUATION

The technique of MRP has some distinct advantages over ordinary role-playing. When many groups of persons engage in role-playing at the same time, the process is facilitated since all of them enter into it without the embarrassment that comes from feeling that they are being observed. Thus groups which have never experienced role-playing quickly get the spirit of the procedure and go into the process in a natural and interested manner. The feeling that the situation is unreal and artificial, which non-participants frequently report, is eliminated because all become involved. Because this method reduces self-consciousness, it is particularly helpful for initiating role-playing techniques in supervisory training.

A second value that emerges is the fact that real live data are obtained from the subsequent analysis. A single role-playing case raises questions which have to do with the fact that a certain individual determined the outcome and so the result may not be typical. In being able to draw upon various groups, one is able to make comparisons and generalizations which could not be made without a rich background of experience. The idea that solutions are tailored to fit a particular group of personalities is clearly brought home by the fact that solutions vary even when the problem and the roles are identical.

Thus we find that in the process of attempting to induce into a large group some of the benefits of small group discussion and role-playing, we not only succeeded in achieving some of these advantages, but captured some entirely new ones.

The MRP method can be used for all types of role-playing which are so effective for attitude change and the development of skills. One must however structure the roles so as to conform to the purpose of the training and the experience of the participants. Thus, if one wishes to emphasize (*a*) leadership skills in putting a problem to a group, (*b*) discussion leading skills, (c) sensitivity to the feelings of others, (d) ways for dealing with hostile persons, (e) skills to up-grade the quality of decisions, and (f) methods to cause a group to feel responsible for reaching decisions acceptable to all, one must design role-playing situations which will highlight these performance areas.

USES OF MRP IN SOCIAL RESEARCH

MRP also can be used as a tool to evaluate various kinds of leadership approaches, as well as to measure the effect of different kinds of participants on the outcome of a discussion. For example, the leaders of half of the groups may receive instructions which differ from those supplied by the other half. These differences may be as follows:

a) Encourage disagreement in your group vs. discourage disagreement in your group;

b) Suggest possible solutions to your group vs. be careful not to suggest any solutions yourself;

c) Try to sell a particular solution that seems fair to you vs. be careful not to show any preference for any solution suggested; and,

d) Have your group explore a variety of solutions before selling on any one idea vs. hurry the group along so that leisurely exploration of many ideas is discouraged.

The effect of different kinds of participants can be tested by making the roles slightly different for two sets of groups. For example, (a) George can be asked to insist on getting the truck in one set and asked to help out Hank's case in the other; (b) one set of groups might be so instructed that they form two cliques, whereas the other set of groups are not so instructed; and (c) one set of groups may have one member who is asked to play the part of a conciliatory individual, whereas in the other set of groups the same individual may be requested to play the part of a belligerent person.

By comparing the outcomes of two sets of groups with similarly instructed leaders and the differences obtained with differently instructed leaders working with similarly instructed groups, one can demonstrate the importance of the injected differences.

The use of the observer can also be expanded by having one or two such persons in each group. (The purpose of two observers is to see to what extent different persons vary in what they see in the same situation. With experience these differences rapidly decline.)

The observers' reports are of particular value in pointing up how each person's remarks has an effect on the behavior of others. Their comments would tend to sensitize participants to important details in the discussion process, and the reports of skilled observers would become a valuable training aid to participants. The use of observers would be of special value in the training of individuals who meet repeatedly in conferences.

23. Management Games for Training Decision Makers*

William R. Dill

MANAGEMENT GAMES are a recent innovation in business school teaching and research programs. The excitement and confusion that they have generated is evident in recent articles in *Business Week*,[1] and a symposium held at the University of Kansas in December, 1958.[2] It already seems apparent that when the dust settles, gaming will bring the same kind of basic changes to our methods for training managers that the "case method" and renewed emphasis on fundamental subjects like economics, statistics and the behavioral sciences have brought.

THE CONCEPT OF "GAMING"

Gaming is not a new concept. Management games are close cousins to the "war games" that military groups pioneered many years ago. Businesses and business schools cannot even claim credit for the first games that involved the use of electronic computers to simulate the actions of the environment. Here the Air Force had a head start in setting up elaborate man-machine simulations of the military environment to design logistics organizations and to train personnel for air defense work.[3]

The concept of a management decision game is simple. One or more teams, each representing a "firm," make a series of decisions governing their firms' operations during the next period of play. Then a "model" of how the industry or the economy operates is used to figure out for each team the outcomes of their decisions. If the "model" is simple, calculations can be made by a human referee; otherwise, they are made by computer. The teams get partial or complete information about the

_____

* From "A New Environment for Training Decision Makers—The Carnegie Management Game" (Unpublished report, Carnegie Institute of Technology, Graduate School of Industrial Administration, 1960).

[1] "The Gentle Art of Simulation," *Business Week*, Nov. 29, 1958; "In Business Education, the Game's the Thing," *Business Week*, July 25, 1959.

[2] *Proceedings of the First National Symposium on Management Games* (Lawrence, Kans.: University of Kansas, Bureau of Business Research, Dec., 1958).

[3] R. M. Bauner, "Laboratory Evaluation of Supply and Procurement Procedures," Rand Paper R-323, July, 1958; S. Enke, "On the Economic Management of Large Organizations," *Journal of Business*, Oct., 1958.

results of their decisions and then make new decisions for the next period. A period of play in the different games that are now available represents anything from a week to a year of "real time" in the life of the industry. The process is diagrammed in Figure 1.

The early business games were relatively simple in structure. The first was developed by the American Management Association for their executive training seminars.[4] Similar games were devised by James R. Jackson at UCLA,[5] Truman Hunter at IBM, and Albert Schrieber at the University of Washington.[6] Andlinger of McKinsey and Company has

FIGURE 1

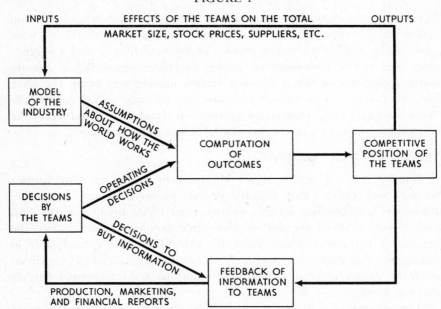

published a simpler game that does not require a computer.[7] All these games ask teams of four or five players to make about a dozen decisions every "quarter" about price; gross production rates; and overall expenditures for things like research, sales promotion, and plant investment. Players have 15–30 minutes to make each set of decisions, and they need wait only a few minutes before they know the results. In one day of play, teams can simulate several years of actual business operations.

[4] L. A. Appley, "Executive Decision-Making: A New Strategy," *Think*, Dec., 1957; J. McDonald and F. Ricciardi, "The Business Decision Game," *Fortune*, March, 1958.

[5] J. R. Jackson, "Learning from Experience in Business Decision Games," *California Management Review*, Winter, 1959.

[6] A. N. Schrieber, "Gaming—A New Way to Teach Business Decision Making," *University of Washington Business Review*, April, 1958.

[7] G. R. Andlinger, "Business Games—Play One!" *Harvard Business Review*, March–April, 1958.

These games are labeled as general management training devices because the teams must make decisions concerning all three basic management functions—production, marketing, and finance. The total number of decisions they must make and the amounts of information they have about what goes on within each functional area, however, are very small.

Emphasis in these simple games is placed on making good judgments under time pressure, more than on the analysis of complex problem situations. It does not take many moves or large amounts of skill to deduce effective strategies for playing the simple games because the models of the environment from which outcomes are computed are relatively simple. Players have found the games challenging, and they claim to have gained some insight into the problems of general management. They are not likely to see the relation between these and the problems of specialized areas of production or finance, though, because the latter are not built into the early games with sufficient detail.

Even the simplest games have proved challenging and exciting to play—in part because of their novelty appeal, but to a large extent because they give players a chance to experiment with different kinds of decisions and to get first hand feedback about their results. It is easier in a game than in a discussion of "case problems" to give students or managers an indication of the cumulative influence of their decisions on company performance.

The limits of simple games, though, are readily apparent. Managing a company involves more than making a small number of general policy decisions under time pressure. An executive has hundreds of decisions he can make in a month or a quarter; his skill, to a large extent, lies in knowing which ones he should make.

An effective manager must be able to abstract information from a complex environment under time pressure. He must decide which problems are worth attention, and he must continually evaluate how well his organization is doing. He is expected to develop alternative courses of action and to make decisions that will benefit the organization under conditions where it is hard to predict what the outcome of a decision will be. He has to translate his general decisions into programs of action that specialized units of the organization can—and will—carry through.

THE CARNEGIE MANAGEMENT GAME

The Carnegie management game has been developed to mirror more realistically the problems of running a company. We have deliberately made our game slower to play in order to make it more complex and more challenging for players.

For example, in earlier games, if players choose a specific production level, they get that much output. To get a desired level of output, players in the Carnegie game must do more than request it. They have to worry about maintenance, overtime policies, hiring policies, raw materials purchasing, and other variables that affect the extent to which scheduled production and actual output coincide. Instead of making a dozen decisions every "quarter," players in the Carnegie game have to record between 100 and 300 decisions for every "month" of simulated time. To make these decisions, they get on a regular basis or through special purchase several hundred pieces of information about their own performance and about their relations with competitors, suppliers, customers, and financial institutions.

The easiest way to describe the Carnegie game is to present it as it appears to the players. Three teams of players form the "industry" in the Carnegie game. Each set of decisions covers a month of operating time. Each team can market up to three products at one time in four regional markets.

Each team has one factory, located in the Central Region. At the factory, there is a raw materials warehouse and a warehouse for finished goods. Factory facilities can be used interchangeably to produce different mixes of product. In each of the four marketing regions, a team leases a district warehouse for finished goods, from which deliveries are made to the wholesalers and retailers who are the customers in the game.

All products which the teams can make can be manufactured from a basic set of seven raw materials which must be ordered from suppliers one to three months before they are delivered to the factory. Raw material prices fluctuate, and discounts are available for prompt payment of bills to suppliers.

The players schedule production; but to get what they schedule, they must make sensible decisions about raw materials, maintenance, changes in plant capacity, overtime, hiring, and firing. Finished goods can be consigned to any of the five warehouses; and within cost and time constraints on transshipments, can be moved from one warehouse to another. Inventory run-outs at a warehouse carry penalties for future sales.

Products are not available for delivery to customers until the month following their manufacture. Sales in any one month depend on the total market for detergents; on consumers' reactions to product characteristics such as "sudsiness"; and on the teams' decisions about advertising, price, and outlays for sales promotion. Consumer behavior may not be the same in the four market regions.

By spending money for product research, teams can generate new products. Not all new products will be worth marketing, though, and laboratory reports on their characteristics will be only partially reliable. A team must buy market surveys to get better, but still not perfect, estimates of consumer reactions to new products. A team must also spend for market research to get information about what consumers think of their current products and to get estimates of competitors' prices and expenditures by product and region for advertising and sales promotion.

The teams can expand production facilities and the central warehouses by building new facilities, but new construction takes six months to complete. Additional space in the district warehouses can be leased as needed. Expenditures for maintenance must be large enough to cover repair and renovation of existing facilities.

To finance their operations, players will start the game with a reserve of cash and government bonds. If they need additional funds, they can defer the payment of bills and negotiate bank loans in the short run (30–60 days). By making application four to six months in advance, they can obtain funds by issuing debentures or common stock. Funds from outside sources are available only if the company's financial position satisfies a number of realistic constraints.

Teams must plan and budget carefully to survive. For some sequences of action, plans must be made 12 to 15 months ahead to achieve desired results. In addition to the regular obligations for raw materials, production, marketing, and research, the teams must deal with such other financial variables as depreciation, income taxes, dividends, and investments in new construction.

The information that players receive and the decisions they must make are summarized in Figure 2.

The game is mutually being played at the rate of one or two moves a week with graduate student teams during the regular school year. Because we believe that organizing to make decisions and to plan for effective long-run performance is an important element in the game, we are using teams of seven to ten players to represent each company. A great deal of emphasis is put on discussing results with the teams. They review their moves with faculty members during class sessions of courses like Marketing or Business Policy that can contribute to playing the game. Periodically, players must report on their performance and their plans to a faculty board of directors. Faculty reactions to the reports are one of the factors that determine the going price for each company's stock.

The complexity of the Carnegie game makes it slow and expensive to play. Making a set of decisions takes two to three hours, not fifteen minutes; and teams need to play 30 or 50 moves in order to experience the long-run consequences of their decisions. The computation of results for each move ties up an IBM 650 computer (with a RAMAC memory unit) for about 45 minutes. Faculty guidance and supervision takes a great deal of time.

THE REASONS FOR COMPLEXITY

Why, then, is the Carnegie game so complex? We believe, first of all, that complexity is an essential ingredient in training good "problem solvers"—men who can succeed as innovators and managers in a diverse and rapidly changing industrial environment.

FIGURE 2

INFORMATION RECEIVED AND DECISIONS MADE IN THE CARNEGIE GAME

INFORMATION

AT START OF GAME	MONTHLY	AS REQUESTED OR REQUIRED
Historical data on operations.	Balance sheet.	Statement of construction obligations.
Constraints on policy and operations.	Income statements.	Statement on loans and securities.
Instructions for organizations and play.	Statement of inventory position.	Availability of financing.
Hints about strategy.	Status of plant and equipment.	Inventory losses.
	Receipts and disbursements.	Product preference tests.
	Financial commitments.	New product descriptions.
	Report on money market.	Market survey data.
	Cost of raw materials.	
QUARTERLY	Cost of goods sold.	
	Raw materials usage and inventory.	
Balance sheets, income statements for competitors.	Warehouse stocks and shipments.	
	Finished product inventories.	
	Work force and equipment down time data.	
	Deliveries to customers.	

DECISIONS

MONTHLY	AS DESIRED
Advertising, distributions expenditures.	Applications for financing.
Price levels.	Market and product research expenditures.
Sales forecasts.	New construction.
Raw material orders.	
Payment of current obligations.	
Amount of production.	
Allocation of products to regions.	
Number of workers.	
Overtime authorized.	
Maintenance expenditures.	

Simpler games tend to fall in two categories: those which are challenging because in time it is possible to develop something close to an optimal strategy for playing the game and those which are challenging because they involve making a small number of critical, risky decisions under time pressure. Through its complexity, the Carnegie game gives players more information than they can easily use in making decisions and presents them with important problems of codifying and evaluating information to interpret the environment and understand the results of their decisions. The players learn, if they have not already learned, that different indices of performance (like profit and rate of growth) do not always correlate. They find that decisions faced in any one month are closely related to events in past and future months.

A spokesman for one of the early games says that his game teaches mainly that the world is complicated, and that company decisions are interdependent. We accomplish this, but by challenging players with a complex set of problems and by spending lots of time discussing the results, we hope to help them learn ways to beat complexity by systematic analysis. There is no simple analytic method that will guarantee success in the game, but there are many ways that players can profitably apply basic problem-solving concepts to help arrive at a good strategy. The basic ideas of marginal analysis from economics, for example, can furnish a framework for evaluating the effects of advertising expenditures or price changes, but the complexity of the market and the inherent limits to the reliability of market information soon force the players to recognize the dangers of over-reliance on simple economic models. Similarly, players who understand statistical sampling theory can use this knowledge to estimate how much they need to spend on market research to get information with a given degree of precision from competitors. Those who do not know elementary concepts of statistical sampling, can learn them in the context of the game.

A second reason for building a complex game is that it permits an organization with differentiated roles. We believe that there are very few executives who are concerned only with overall company decisions, to the exclusion of detailed problems in production, finance, or marketing. Even in large companies, the top vice-presidents are generally vice-presidents over a function or a group of functions. The executive, in our view, must be both generalist and specialist; and some of his most difficult moments come when he must compromise his ideas as a specialist to satisfy the requirements of other functions in the organization.

In the Carnegie game, players have the dual role of specialist and generalist. Each of the three major functional areas of the game—production, marketing, or finance—present problems as complex as those presented by the simpler general management games. Yet, in the Carnegie game, there is a genuine interdependence among functions at several levels that makes the effective coordination of production, financial, and marketing operations vital to success in the game.

A third reason for complexity is to provide players with organizational as well as analytical experience. One shortcoming of the simpler games is that they are played by small, homogeneous teams. Efforts to use larger teams or to impose hierarchical patterns of organization seldom work out because the task does not warrant such steps. In the Carnegie game, we believe we have an environment that can keep teams of seven to ten men busy planning, deciding on moves, and evaluating earlier performance. With teams of this size, whose members have differentiated functions to perform, we can expect (and by control of external conditions, can help induce) some of the symptoms of bureaucracy and some of the problems of rank and status that men have to deal with in real organizations.

By complexity, then, we hope to achieve a game which fits with Carnegie's emphasis on the importance of systematic analysis and problem-solving strategies in the mastery of managerial problems. We hope to make players aware of the problems of overall coordination at the top management level in business, but we also hope to fit them for the role they will play for most of their careers—the role of the functional specialist in interaction with other specialists at his own level on problems that involve conflict and compromise. We hope, finally, to provide experience in interpersonal interaction that involves not only the kinds of relations we find in small face-to-face groups, but in formalized organizational situations.

Complexity, we might also argue, is necessary if the game is to be realistic. We have placed considerable value on making our game like the detergent industry, but it would obscure the issue to say that this was a major objective. A truly realistic game might take a lifetime to play. The kind of realism we have tried to achieve is a realism in the behavioral demands that we make on players, not a realism in the model we use to represent the world. The job of the players is to diagnose the model that we have used and to develop effective strategies for working against it and their competitors. If the model requires the kinds of approaches to diagnosis and decision making that the players will use in later life, it does not really matter whether the model is a mirror image of a real industry.

We do not insist, for example, in teaching mathematics to engineers that all the practice problems be drawn from engineering. They can be phrased in other terms so long as the basic methods of solution are taught and practiced.

THE VALUE OF DEVELOPING GAMES

We are only beginning to assess the potential of management games in general, and of the Carnegie game, in particular. An important dividend of gaming—and one not often mentioned—is its effect on the men who develop it. It has taken a year and a half to get the Carnegie game ready for trial runs. As a first step, those of us who worked on the game had to agree on its basic structure. In doing this, we raised fundamental questions about what we were trying to teach and about the nature of the industry we had decided to simulate. It is one thing to say that the sale of detergents in a given month depends on advertising expenditures, on price, and on product characteristics; it is quite another to specify *how* sales depends on these variables in a way that makes sense both to an experienced soap salesman and to an electronic computer. Hundreds of questions of this kind had to be answered.

The final computer program which governs the play of the game contains about 20,000 separate instructions and several thousand "words" of data.

We have gained almost as much in the process of developing the game as we will in playing it. The men who planned the game had a variety of special interests in fields like marketing, finance, production, organization theory, and information processing. Simply to design the game and to carry through the designs to an operating computer program and a set of instructions for players, we have faced basic questions of how to educate our students, how a real industry operates from month to month in a complex environment, and how we simulate industrial operations on the computer. Our efforts to answer these questions will not only help us design better decision games, but will also help us do a better job with many other aspects of our task of training managers.

THE CARNEGIE GAME AS A WAY OF LEARNING HOW TO MANAGE

The educational benefits for ourselves of developing a management game seem obvious. What, though, are the benefits of playing a game like the Carnegie game? Some of these have already been suggested, but it will be worthwhile to summarize them here.

Games are an important innovation in management training because they are the only means, short of real on-the-job experience, of putting trainees—whether students or executives—up against an environment which responds definitely and consistently to all the different strategies that the trainees may try and of forcing trainees to make and "live with" sequences of decisions over time. Even at current levels, the computational capacities of the electronic computer make it a better and more reliable source of estimates about how the world will react to certain kinds of decisions than discussion leaders who have only limited, second-hand information about the effects that decisions will create.

Games are also effective for teaching men to deal with a changing world. Case problems, drawn from actual company experiences, tend to focus on the world as it was; games, with careful development, can present the world as it *may be* five, ten, or twenty years ahead, when the men who are now trainees become managers.

Simple games are useful as "ice-breakers"—as ways of raising questions for exploration and discussion in other parts of a training program. Complex games, like the Carnegie game, though, seem to have real promise for posing trainees with problems like those that managers face. Players must be able to separate the important from the trivial in the large masses of information that they receive, that they can buy, or that they can produce for themselves. They must decide which of the decisions that they might make are worth making. They must plan and coordinate because decisions cannot be taken in isolation. To make better decisions, they can apply many of the concepts and tools they learn in courses or in their work experience; but analytic prowess alone will not guarantee good results.

We already have some evidence from trial runs that these effects are achieved in the Carnegie game and that in addition, organizing as a team to play the game is a challenging experience for participants.

To be successful as a means for learning how to manage, though, any game requires large amounts of time for the discussion and analysis of results. In playing the Carnegie game with graduate students and executives, we are not only making teams report to boards of directors; we are also working with them on various aspects of their performance in other kinds of courses. The game is meant to supplement, not to replace other sorts of training.

Enthusiasm for games as *the* method for teaching management should be tempered by these observations:

1) Playing games will not produce the "complete manager." No games yet conceived really incorporate the problems that managers have in interacting with subordinates in the organization to explain, introduce, and implement decisions. In fact, one real danger of the game for naive players is that they will become accustomed to getting all the information they need from a computer. In industry, though, they will need also to know how to get information and ideas from workers, clerks, engineers, salesmen, and the like. Organizational and labor problems can be built into the game; but so far only in a way which de-emphasizes the importance of skillful person-to-person dealings with other individuals and groups outside the top management group.

2) Particularly if we succeed at making games realistic, we may accentuate the problem that some bright young men already have when they go into industry. Now instead of "thinking" they know how to run a company, they may really "believe" from their experience with a game that they can run a company better than its present managers. A manager is judged in the final analysis, not by the amount he knows about performing well in his previous environment, but by his ability to adapt to new environmental demands.

3) It is not appropriate to try to create games simply on the principle of duplicating existing or anticipated conditions in industry. Our job is to train men to learn and develop in the face of constantly changing problems, not to train them to solve some particular set of problems that have been important or typical in the past. Games are only effective if they prepare men to look ahead and to continue learning from their experiences. We cannot hope to anticipate accurately many of the problems they are going to be called on to solve.

The Carnegie game is being used initially with graduate students and executives as a "laboratory" assignment which supplements the regular courses. It presents an opportunity for students to integrate, to apply, and to evaluate the things they have learned in more traditional ways.

If early experiences are borne out, it also feeds back on courses such as economics, production, or administration by stimulating players to seek knowledge and strategies which they can use in the game.

USES OF THE CARNEGIE GAME IN RESEARCH

In addition to helping to educate business school faculty members and young men who want to become managers, we hope that the Carnegie game, and others like it, will become valuable settings for research. At the most obvious level, we need research that will tell us more precisely what we are accomplishing when we use the game as part of our educational programs. Our confidence in the educational value of the simpler management games rests more heavily than it should on the testimony of men who have played them. Players enjoy the experience, and they are sure that they learned a great deal from it. But, when pressed, as one industrial training expert has reported, players have a hard time saying what they learned.

We need comparative analysis of the educational effects of the Carnegie game, of simpler and more specialized games, and of alternative patterns of teaching (such as the "case method" or "role playing").

In addition to doing research *on* the Carnegie game, though, it is important that we do research *with* it. Two of the many research possibilities are of immediate interest to managers. The first is the possibility that something like the Carnegie game, which lies midway between the simplicity of the behavioral science laboratory and the complexity of the real world, can serve as a bridge between the two. Concerning leadership, for example, we have many findings that stem from psychological and sociological experiments involving small groups and simple tasks assignments. The applicability of such findings to real life situations may be explored at an intermediate level among groups of seven to ten people playing the Carnegie game.

Conversely, much of the businessman's "folklore" about leadership can be evaluated more effectively in the game environment than in real life because, in the game, it is possible to eliminate or to control the effects of many extraneous variables. To the extent that the Carnegie game provides a realistic simulation of industrial conditions, we can plan and carry through experiments that will compare the gains and costs associated with different policies for action or with different styles of organization.

More basically, the Carnegie game will permit the exploration of fundamental questions in organization theory and in the theory of the firm. Field research that involves observation of on-going organizational processes and decisions is expensive to conduct; and in the field situation, experimental controls are difficult to impose. We plan to use the Carnegie game partly as a substitute for field studies and partly as a preparation for doing field research more effectively. Among the questions we plan to explore are these:

1) What effects do time constraints, initial job assignments, and restrictions on communication among players have on the speed with which teams organize, on the kinds of organization that they develop, and on the amount of long-range planning and budgeting that they do?

2) Under conditions where players do not have time to reconsider all possible decisions every month, how do they decide which problems deserve attention? How does the choice of problems that a team will work on affect its performance against competition?

3) By varying the number and size of firms in an industry, what changes do we observe in competitive patterns (decisions on price, advertising, product research, etc.)

4) In what ways does a team's pattern of organization affect its short and long run performance? Does a team which is allowed to develop its own organization structure, for example, perform better or worse against competition than a team whose organization has been imposed by the Board of Directors?

24. Human Relations Training and the Stability of Leadership Patterns*

Edwin F. Harris and Edwin A. Fleishman

RECENT YEARS have seen the development of an increasing number of supervisory training programs among industrial organizations. These programs deal in large measure with the area broadly defined as "human relations." Essentially, these training courses must be viewed as attempts to modify or "improve" the behavior of supervisors in dealing with their groups in their everyday working relationships.

Until recently, however, little evidence was available concerning the actual outcomes of such training. What few evaluations had been made were often quite limited, dealing for example with trainees' or supervisors' impressions of the value of the training or with indices of supervisory attitudes immediately before and after the training course. In a recent study by Fleishman,[1] an attempt was made to obtain a more

* From *Journal of Applied Psychology*, Vol. 39, No. 1, 1955, pp. 20–25. The study was carried out with the cooperation of the International Harvester Company.

[1] E. A. Fleishman, "Leadership Climate, Human Relations Training, and Supervisory Behavior," *Personnel Psychology*, Vol. 6, 1953, pp. 205–22. (Editor's note: See Section V, pp. 315–28).

meaningful evaluation of a human relations training program for foremen in a large industrial organization. Supervisory training was evaluated in terms of descriptions of the foreman's leadership *behavior*
as well as his own leadership attitudes. Moreover, evaluations were made
back in the actual plant situation sometime after the foremen had returned from training.

The present paper represents an extension of this previous research and
describes a further study of some additional effects of such training in
the same motor truck manufacturing plant.

PURPOSE

The problem. The previous study compared matched groups of
foremen in the plant situation. One group had not been sent to training,
whereas the remaining three groups had different amounts of time elapse
since training. In general, the results showed that in terms of the measures used, the effects of the training were minimal and certainly did not
last when evaluated back in the plant. Except for the most recently
trained group (which differed in an unexpected direction), over-all differences between the trained and untrained foremen in leadership attitudes
and behavior were not significant. In the present study it was possible to
employ a "longitudinal" methodology in that measures of leadership attitudes and behavior were obtained on the same groups of foremen before
and after the training period. The purpose here was to compare the results of this analysis with that obtained from the "cross-sectional" approach used by Fleishman.[2]

A second problem investigated was the effect of a "refresher" human
relations training course on the behavior and attitudes of foremen who
had received the original and more extensive training course some time
before.

Both of the above evaluations were made with a view to a third problem. The concern here was with the stability of leadership behavior patterns over a period of time for those foremen who had received human
relations training as compared with those foremen who had not received
such training. Aside from the training implications, data on the stability
of leadership patterns in complex organizations would be of considerable interest in themselves. Although the problem appears to be a crucial one, little evidence on this is currently available. However, such
data would have direct bearing on the extent to which one can generalize from observations of leadership behavior made at one point in time
to later behavior of the same individual in the same general situation. Or
in other terms, within a given organizational framework, to what extent
can we predict future behavior of the leader from knowledge of present or past leadership behavior?

[2] *Ibid.*

PROCEDURE

The research instruments.   The Supervisory Behavior Description[3] and the Leadership Opinion Questionnaire,[4] whose development has been described in detail previously, were the primary instruments used in the study. Briefly, the Supervisory Behavior Description contains 48 items which describe how supervisors operate in their leadership role. The questionnaire is scored on two reliable and factorially independent dimensions called "Consideration" and "Initiating Structure."

A high score on the Consideration dimension characterizes supervisory behavior indicative of friendship, mutual trust, respect, a certain warmth between the supervisor and his men, and consideration of their feelings. A low score on this dimension indicates the supervisor to be more authoritarian and impersonal in his relations with group members. This dimension comes closest to reflecting the "human relations" aspect of group leadership.

The Initiating Structure dimension reflects the extent to which the supervisor defines or facilitates group interactions toward *goal attainment*. A high score on this dimension characterizes supervisors who play a more active role in directing group activities through planning, communicating, scheduling, criticizing, trying out new ideas, etc. The questionnaire is typically filled out by group members who mark for each item how frequently their own supervisor does what each item describes.

The Leadership Opinion Questionnaire contains 40 parallel items and is filled out by the supervisor himself. It is scored along the same two dimensions and reflects the supervisor's own attitudes about how work groups should be led.

Leadership patterns before and after training.   In this phase of the study, only the Supervisory Behavior Description questionnaire was involved. At least three workers drawn randomly from the work groups under each of 98 different foremen filled out the questionnaire describing the behavior of their own foremen. Similar data had already been collected on these foremen eleven months previous to this administration. Of the 98 foremen, 39 had since been sent to the company's Central School which administers the Supervisory training Program for foremen from all its diverse plants.[5] The remaining 59 had received no such training during this same period. No selective factors could be found which determined the order in which foremen were sent to this training, and the two groups may be considered comparable.

RESULTS

Table 1 presents a comparison of the two groups in terms of each of the two leadership dimensions.

It is clear from Table 1 that no significant differences existed in mean scores made by either group before and after the training period. The

---

[3] E. A. Fleishman, "The Description of Supervisory Behavior," *Journal of Applied Psychology*, Vol. 37, 1953, pp. 1–6.

[4] E. A. Fleishman, "The Measurement of Leadership Attitudes in Industry," *Journal of Applied Psychology*, Vol. 37, 1953, pp. 153–58.

[5] The program involves eight hours a day for two weeks of intensive training. Group discussion, lecture methods, visual aids, and a variety of techniques are employed. For a description of the program and its workings, see C. L. Walker, Jr., "Education and Training at International Harvester," *Harvard Business Review*, Vol. 27, 1949, pp. 542–58.

TABLE 1

COMPARISON OF SUPERVISORY BEHAVIOR DESCRIPTION SCORES FOR FOREMEN WITH
AND WITHOUT INTERVENING CENTRAL SCHOOL TRAINING

GROUP	LEADERSHIP DIMENSION	BEFORE TRAINING		AFTER TRAINING		
		MEAN	SD	MEAN	SD	r
With intervening training (N = 39)	Consideration	70.6	13.8	72.1	13.0	.27
	Initiating Structure	43.2	6.4	40.8	7.3	.22
Without intervening training (N = 59)	Consideration	73.8	15.0	74.4	12.6	.58
	Initiating Structure	41.5	7.1	39.6	6.1	.46

mean scores for each group on each leadership dimension were not significantly different before training (indicating adequate matching), and were not significant after the training period. Moreover, no significant charges in mean scores occurred within either group during the 11-month interval, whether or not they had or had not been sent to training.

Perhaps the most striking results in Table 1 bear on the test-retest coefficients for the trained group as compared with the group without training during the same period. The correlations between administrations for the trained group do not reach the 5% level of confidence, whereas those for the group without intervening training are significant beyond the 1% level. This trend occurs in the case of both the "Consideration" and "Initiating Structure" dimensions. Thus, the data would seem to indicate that the intervention of training in some way affects the stability of leadership patterns. Although the group means are not statistically significant before and after training, there is apparently a differential effect of such training on the behavior of different foremen within the trained group. This suggestive finding will be pursued later.

With regard to the stability of leadership patterns for the foremen without intervening training, some stability was demonstrated ($r = .58$ for Consideration and .46 for Initiating Structure). However, these correlations should not be interpreted as reflecting the upper limit of the stability of leadership behavior over this particular time interval. Undoubtedly, some of the variance is attributable to, among other things, the use of different workers to describe the same foremen in each of the two administrations. Some idea of the effects of using different workers can be gained from estimates of interrater agreement in describing the same foremen.

Table 2 presents the coefficients of interrater agreement estimated by the method described by Horst.[6] This was done separately for the trained and untrained groups of foremen.

[6] P. Horst, "A Generalized Expression for the Reliability of Measure," *Psychometrika*, Vol. 14, 1944, pp. 21–24.

TABLE 2

INTERRATER AGREEMENT AMONG WORKERS DESCRIBING
THE SAME FOREMEN ON THE SUPERVISORY
BEHAVIOR DESCRIPTION

| | COEFFICIENT OF AGREEMENT | |
LEADERSHIP DIMENSION	For Foremen without Intervening Training	For Foremen with Intervening Training
Consideration	.55	.57
Initiating Structure	.50	.48

These coefficients, although indicative of significant agreement among respondents, are low enough to support the idea that the use of different samples had the effect of lowering the "test-retest" coefficients. Furthermore, one would not expect the "test-retest" coefficients obtained to be any higher than the interrater agreement. Table 2 also indicates that the interrater agreement coefficients for workers who described trained foremen are comparable to those who described the untrained foremen. Hence, there is nothing in these results to minimize the importance of the finding that the stability of leadership patterns is lower for the trained foremen than for the untrained foremen.

The Effects of a Refresher Training Course

In addition to sending foremen to the company's Central School, this particular plant subsequently organized a refresher leadership course for the foremen who had already attended the original and more extensive centralized program. This refresher course was organized in conjunction with a local college. Since the purpose of this program was to "reinforce" the material presented in the Central School, the courses were organized around the same subject matter, although in somewhat shorter form. The refresher course lasted one week and used the lecture-discussion approach, with classes averaging around 25 foremen. It was decided to see if attending the refresher course resulted in any measurable change in leadership behavior or attitudes back in the plant. Although over-all results from the original course appeared to be minimal, the additional course might still have produced some effects. This seemed possible, especially in view of the apparent differential effects found in the stability analysis described above and from the fact that this "refresher" training was given closer to the actual work situation.

PROCEDURE

Two groups of 31 foremen were selected, each of whom had been to the Central School in Chicago. Measures of the leadership attitudes and behavior of each of the foremen had already been obtained. After these measures were obtained, one of the groups (experimental) attended the refresher training course, while the other group (control) did not. Information about attitudes and behavior after this course was obtained from a readministration of the same questionnaires. The average time since attending the second course was 3.2 months (standard deviation, 1.6 months).

The groups were matched on the mean scores achieved in the initial administration of the Supervisory Behavior Description (filled out by workers) and the Leadership Opinion Questionnaire (filled out by the foremen), as well as on the variables of age, education, years as a supervisor, seniority, number of men supervised, and months since attending the Central School. Differences between these groups were also checked in terms of the leadership of the foremen's own bosses. This was done since Fleishman[7] had found previously that the "leadership climate" under which the foremen themselves operate is a potent variable related to the foreman's own leadership attitudes and behavior. Since any change in foreman behavior or attitudes might possibly be a function of a corresponding change in their bosses' behavior or expectations, it was important that this be checked in both the pre- and post-training administrations. Suffice it to say here that no differences were found between the two groups at either administration for these "climate" variables.[8]

RESULTS

Table 3 summarizes the mean behavior attitude scores obtained before and after the refresher training for the experimental (trained) and control (untrained) groups.

TABLE 3

COMPARISON OF BEHAVIOR AND ATTITUDE SCORES OF FOREMEN WITH (EXPERIMENTAL GROUP, $N = 31$) AND WITHOUT (CONTROL GROUP, $N = 31$) REFRESHER TRAINING

QUESTIONNAIRE	LEADERSHIP DIMENSION	GROUP	BEFORE REFRESHER TRAINING		AFTER REFRESHER TRAINING	
			Mean	SD	Mean	SD
Supervisory Behavior Description	Consideration	Exp.	70.9	12.7	73.0	12.7
		Con.	72.6	15.4	75.5	13.2
	Initiating Structure	Exp.	42.8	6.3	40.7	7.3
		Con.	40.3	7.8	37.5	6.3
Leadership Opinion Questionnaire	Consideration	Exp.	54.1	6.6	54.3	7.1
		Con.	56.0	8.1	54.9	6.8
	Initiating Structure	Exp.	52.9	6.1	53.5	7.0
		Con.	52.6	9.1	50.9	8.5

It can be seen from Table 3 that no striking differences appear in the data obtained from the experimental group relative to that obtained from

---

[7] E. A. Fleishman, "Leadership Climate, Human Relations Training, and Supervisory Behavior," *op. cit.*

[8] For a discussion of the measures used to evaluate "leadership climate," see E. A. Fleishman, "The Description of Supervisory Behavior," *op. cit.*; E. A. Fleishman, "The Measurement of Leadership Attitudes in Industry," *op. cit.*

the control group. The data in this table were evaluated in several ways. The first evaluation compared the mean behavior and attitude scores made by the control and experimental groups after training. In this comparison, none of the differences on either leadership dimension were significant at the 5% level of confidence. A second method of evaluation analyzed the data to see if there were significant *changes* within the refresher group relative to that of the control group. In this analysis, one statistically significant change was noted. This, however, was a significant drop in the mean "structure" behavior score for those foremen comprising the *control* rather than the experimental group. None of the other critical ratios approached statistical significance.

A third and more rigorous method of analysis employed a statistical regression technique. In this method, the mean, sigmas, and correlation between the first and second administration for the *control* group are used to establish a regression equation which predicts the second score on the basis of the first score. This equation is then used to predict the second score for each of the members of the *experimental* group, given their first score. This provides the best prediction of the second score if the intervening training has had no effect. The differences between the predicted and obtained scores are summed algebraically and treated for significance. A significant difference implies that the introduction of training has resulted in a significant change in the scores of the experimental group.[9] The results of this analysis in the present instance showed none of the differences to be statistically significant.

The results of these evaluations of the refresher course may be viewed as largely negative in terms of changes in mean behavior and attitude scores resulting from training. However, one other set of results qualifies a completely negative conclusion. This is the correlation between scores made by the foremen after the course with scores they made before training. Table 4 summarizes these.

We find in Table 4 that those foremen who have had the refresher training showed considerably less pre- and postscore agreement than did those foremen who had not attended. This is true for both the foreman's leadership attitudes *and* behavior along both the Consideration and Initiating Structure dimensions. Confidence in these results is increased when we recall that our estimates of behavior and attitudes were derived independently (from reports of workers and foremen, respectively). Thus, these results indicate greater stability of leadership patterns for those foremen who did *not* have this intervening refresher training.

This result confirms the earlier results obtained when we compared the stability of leadership patterns for foremen who had been to the

---

[9] This method does not assume that the initial scores of each group are the same and makes allowances for this, and thus obviates the necessity of having perfectly matched groups. See C. C. Peters and W. Van Voorhis, *Statistical Procedures and Their Mathematical Bases* (New York: McGraw-Hill Book Co., Inc., 1940).

TABLE 4
COEFFICIENTS OF LEADERSHIP STABILITY

QUESTIONNAIRE	LEADERSHIP DIMENSION	FOREMEN WITHOUT INTER-VENING REFRESHER TRAINING ($N = 31$)	FOREMEN WITH INTER-VENING REFRESHER TRAINING ($N = 31$)
Supervisory Behavior Description	Consideration	.56	.42
	Initiating Structure	.53	.25
Leadership Opinion Questionnaire	Consideration	.80	.54
	Initiating Structure	.74	.49

original Central School with foremen who had not had this training. These stability coefficients were .58 (for Consideration behavior) and .46 (for Initiating Structure behavior) for the untrained group. For the group with intervening training, these shrink to .27 and .22 for Consideration and Initiating Structure, respectively. Again, as in the case of the refresher course, the lowest agreement between scores was in the group which had the intervening program.

SUMMARY AND CONCLUSIONS

A supervisory training program was evaluated in terms of changes in the leadership behavior and attitudes of the trainees back in the work situation. Scores made on questionnaires administered before training were compared with scores obtained after training for an experimental group (with intervening training) and a control group (without intervening training). The questionnaires employed were the Supervisory Behavior Description (worker descriptions of foreman behavior) and the Leadership Opinion Questionnaire (foreman's own leadership attitudes). Each questionnaire yields a score on two reliable and factorially independent dimensions called Consideration and Initiating Structure. The same general methodology was used to evaluate an original supervisory training course and also a refresher training course.

The results generally confirm previous findings in the same plant[10] that *in terms of mean scores* before and after training, the effects of such training appear minimal when evaluated back in the plant. This was true, in the present instance, for both the original and refresher training courses.

However, other findings in the present study must qualify any com-

---

[10] E. A. Fleishman, "Leadership Climate, Human Relations Training, and Supervisory Behavior," *op. cit.*

pletely negative conclusion regarding the effectiveness of the training. These findings bear on the stability of leadership patterns for individual foremen. It was found, for example, that relatively consistent patterns of leadership behavior and attitudes existed over time for foremen who had not been sent to training. This was indicated by test-retest correlations between questionnaire administrations for the control groups. However, for foremen who had intervening training, a much lower coefficient of agreement was found between questionnaire administrations. This was found for the intervening refresher course as well as for the original course, and was found for leadership behavior as well as attitudes.

These results are consistent with the previous finding in the training situation itself that wide individual differences exist among foremen in the leadership attitudes they hold after training.[11] Moreover, large individual shifts in scores occur in both directions. From the point of view of training evaluation research, one cannot assume that insignificant changes in group means among trained foremen are indicative of *no* training effects. The problem appears more complicated than that. It raises the possibility of differential effects according to the individual and the situation in which he finds himself. Future training research might well be directed toward finding the personal and situational variables which interact with the effects of such training.

---

[11] *Ibid.*

Section Four

MOTIVATION, ATTITUDES, AND MORALE

Introduction

WHY DO PEOPLE act as they do? Why does one group of workers restrict their production while others produce at high levels? What do people want out of their jobs? What are their needs? What goals do they seek to satisfy these needs? Why do some join unions? What factors make for satisfying work relationships and job satisfaction? How are the incentives provided in industry related to the motivations of organization members? What is "high morale" and how can we recognize it?

In this section we examine some principles and research bearing on these questions. The first article by McGregor, "The Human Side of Enterprise," introduces us to the central role of motivation in the social-industrial milieu and questions many of the assumptions reflected in traditional organizational structures and managerial policies. The article provides a framework for describing the complexities of human motivation. The organizing principle is the "need heirarchy" and McGregor shows how this principle relates to the motivation of human effort in organizations.

Too often management has taken an oversimplified view of employee motivation, placing the emphasis on economic motives. McGregor's article certainly illustrates how oversimplified the "economic man" assumptions are. Nevertheless, pay certainly *is* an incentive widely used in industry. The next article, by Rothe, takes a closer look at various financial incentive plans tried by industry. In "Does Higher Pay Bring Higher Productivity?" he reviews the research evidence on financial incentives and evaluates them in terms of motivational principles.

Next, Ross and Zander describe some research on "Need Satisfactions and Employee Turnover." This study focuses on employee needs for affiliation, recognition, autonomy, achievement, and fair evaluation and examines their relation to organizational stability.

The most effective incentives are those which are intrinsic in the job itself. However, traditional industrial engineering principles may work against this. Some of these principles are work specialization, repetitiveness, assignment of work loads, and assembly line pacing. There is increasing evidence that some of these principles have been carried too far and may not be as "efficient" as they seem when one considers the social and psychological "costs" involved. In "Job Design and Productivity," Davis reviews these issues and describes some research aimed at providing job designs which maximize worker satisfactions while still achieving organizational goals.

The Davis article illustrates an attempt to develop intrinsic satisfactions through the design of the job itself. Another approach has been to increase employee participation in decisions (e.g., setting production goals, changing work methods) which, heretofore, had been imposed on him by management, time-study engineers, or other "specialists." The article, "Employee Participation in a Program of Industrial Change," by French, Ross, Kirby, Nelson, and Smyth takes us through a specific industrial case of this kind and describes its results.

Often it is extremely useful to be able to quantify attitudes. This allows us to compare the attitudes of different individuals, to detect changes in attitudes, and to relate attitudes to other conditions. One approach to the measurement of attitudes toward the job is described by Brayfield and Rothe in "An Index of Job Satisfaction." They take us step by step through these procedures and show how the dependability of such an instrument can be evaluated.

The final two papers deal with the concept of "morale." Everyone has some idea about what this term means, but there are differences of opinion about it. "Morale" is certainly not just another term for job satisfaction. Yet, the concept relates to job attitudes as well as to aspects of motivation. The paper by Guion, "Some Definitions of Morale," reviews the confusion surrounding this term and then presents a useful working definition which contains five "attributes" of morale. Stagner's article, "Motivational Aspects of Industrial Morale," defines morale in terms of an individual-group relationship and suggests an approach to improving morale.

25. The Human Side of Enterprise*

Douglas M. McGregor

It has become trite to say that the most significant developments of the next quarter century will take place not in the physical but in the social sciences, that industry—the economic organ of society—has the fundamental know-how to utilize physical science and technology for the material benefit of mankind, and that we must now learn how to utilize the social sciences to make our human organizations truly effective.

Many people agree in principle with such statements; but so far they represent a pious hope—and little else. Consider with me, if you will, something of what may be involved when we attempt to transform the hope into reality.

I.

Let me begin with an analogy. A quarter century ago basic conceptions of the nature of matter and energy had changed profoundly from what they had been since Newton's time. The physical scientists were persuaded that under proper conditions new and hitherto unimagined sources of energy could be made available to mankind.

We know what has happened since then. First came the bomb. Then, during the past decade, have come many other attempts to exploit these scientific discoveries—some successful, some not.

The point of my analogy, however, is that the application of theory in this field is a slow and costly matter. We expect it always to be thus. No one is impatient with the scientist because he cannot tell industry how to build a simple, cheap, all-purpose source of atomic energy today. That it will take at least another decade and the investment of billions of dollars to achieve results which are economically competitive with present sources of power is understood and accepted.

It is transparently pretentious to suggest any *direct* similarity between the developments in the physical sciences leading to the harnessing of atomic energy and potential developments in the social sciences. Nevertheless, the analogy is not as absurd as it might appear to be at first glance.

* From "Adventure in Thought and Action," *Proceedings of the Fifth Anniversary Convocation of the School of Industrial Management, Massachusetts Institute of Technology* (Cambridge, Mass.: Massachusetts Institute of Technology, June, 1957).

To a lesser degree, and in a much more tentative fashion, we are in a position in the social sciences today like that of the physical sciences with respect to atomic energy in the thirties. We know that past conceptions of the nature of man are inadequate and in many ways incorrect. We are becoming quite certain that, under proper conditions, unimagined resources of creative human energy could become available within the organizational setting.

We cannot tell industrial management how to apply this new knowledge in simple, economic ways. We know it will require years of exploration, much costly development research, and a substantial amount of creative imagination on the part of management to discover how to apply this growing knowledge to the organization of human effort in industry.

May I ask that you keep this analogy in mind—overdrawn and pretentious though it may be—as a framework for what I have to say.

MANAGEMENT'S TASK: CONVENTIONAL VIEW

The conventional conception of management's task in harnessing human energy to organizational requirements can be stated broadly in terms of three propositions. In order to avoid the complications introduced by a label, I shall call this set of propositions "Theory X":

1. Management is responsible for organizing the elements of productive enterprise—money, materials, equipment, people—in the interest of economic ends.

2. With respect to people, this is a process of directing their efforts, motivating them, controlling their actions, modifying their behavior to fit the needs of the organization.

3. Without this active intervention by management, people would be passive—even resistant—to organizational needs. They must therefore be persuaded, rewarded, punished, controlled—their activities must be directed. This is management's task—in managing subordinate managers or workers. We often sum it up by saying that management consists of getting things done through other people.

Behind this conventional theory there are several additional beliefs—less explicit, but widespread:

4. The average man is by nature indolent—he works as little as possible.

5. He lacks ambition, dislikes responsibility, prefers to be led.

6. He is inherently self-centered, indifferent to organizational needs.

7. He is by nature resistant to change.

8. He is gullible, not very bright, the ready dupe of the charlatan and the demagogue.

The human side of economic enterprise today is fashioned from propositions and beliefs such as these. Conventional organization structures, managerial policies, practices, and programs reflect these assumptions.

In accomplishing its task—with these assumptions as guides—management has conceived of a range of possibilities between two extremes.

THE HARD OR THE SOFT APPROACH?

At one extreme, management can be "hard" or "strong." The methods for directing behavior involve coercion and threat (usually disguised), close supervision, tight controls over behavior. At the other extreme, management can be "soft" or "weak." The methods for directing behavior involve being permissive, satisfying people's demands, achieving harmony. Then they will be tractable, accept direction.

This range has been fairly completely explored during the past half century, and management has learned some things from the exploration. There are difficulties in the "hard" approach. Force breeds counterforces: restriction of output, antagonism, militant unionism, subtle but effective sabotage of management objectives. This approach is especially difficult during times of full employment.

There are also difficulties in the "soft" approach. It leads frequently to the abdication of management—to harmony, perhaps, but to indifferent performance. People take advantage of the soft approach. They continually expect more, but they give less and less.

Currently, the popular theme is "firm but fair." This is an attempt to gain the advantages of both the hard and the soft approaches. It is reminiscent of Teddy Roosevelt's "speak softly and carry a big stick."

IS THE CONVENTIONAL VIEW CORRECT?

The findings which are beginning to emerge from the social sciences challenge this whole set of beliefs about man and human nature and about the task of management. The evidence is far from conclusive, certainly, but it is suggestive. It comes from the laboratory, the clinic, the schoolroom, the home, and even to a limited extent from industry itself.

The social scientist does not deny that human behavior in industrial organization today is approximately what management perceives it to be. He has, in fact, observed it and studied it fairly extensively. But he is pretty sure that this behavior is *not* a consequence of man's inherent nature. It is a consequence rather of the nature of industrial organizations, of management philosophy, policy, and practice. The conventional approach of Theory X is based on mistaken notions of what is cause and what is effect.

"Well," you ask, "what then is the *true* nature of man? What evidence leads the social scientist to deny what is obvious?" And, if I am not mistaken, you are also thinking, "Tell me—simply, and without a lot of scientific verbiage—what you think you know that is so unusual. Give me —without a lot of intellectual claptrap and theoretical nonsense—some practical ideas which will enable me to improve the situation in my organization. And remember, I'm faced with increasing costs and narrowing profit margins. I want proof that such ideas won't result simply in new and costly human relations frills. I want practical results, and I want them now."

If these are your wishes, you are going to be disappointed. Such requests can no more be met by the social scientist today than could comparable ones with respect to atomic energy be met by the physicist fifteen years ago. I can, however, indicate a few of the reasons for asserting that conventional assumptions about the human side of enterprise are inadequate. And I can suggest—tentatively—some of the propositions that will comprise a more adequate theory of the management of people. The magnitude of the task that confronts us will then, I think, be apparent.

II.

Perhaps the best way to indicate why the conventional approach of management is inadequate is to consider the subject of motivation. In discussing this subject I will draw heavily on the work of my colleague, Abraham Maslow of Brandeis University. His is the most fruitful approach I know. Naturally, what I have to say will be over-generalized and will ignore important qualifications. In the time at our disposal, this is inevitable.

PHYSIOLOGICAL AND SAFETY NEEDS

Man is a wanting animal—as soon as one of his needs is satisfied, another appears in its place. This process is unending. It continues from birth to death.

Man's needs are organized in a series of levels—a hierarchy of importance. At the lowest level, but preeminent in importance when they are thwarted, are his physiological needs. Man lives by bread alone, when there is no bread. Unless the circumstances are unusual, his needs for love, for status, for recognition are inoperative when his stomach has been empty for a while. But when he eats regularly and adequately, hunger ceases to be an important need. The sated man has hunger only in the sense that a full bottle has emptiness. The same is true of the other physiological needs of man—for rest, exercise, shelter, protection from the elements.

A satisfied need is not a motivator of behavior! This is a fact of profound significance. It is a fact which is regularly ignored in the conventional approach to the management of people. I shall return to it later. For the moment, one example will make my point. Consider your own need for air. Except as you are deprived of it, it has no appreciable motivating effect upon your behavior.

When the physiological needs are reasonably satisfied, needs at the next higher level begin to dominate man's behavior—to motivate him.

These are called safety needs. They are needs for protection against danger, threat, deprivation. Some people mistakenly refer to these as needs for security. However, unless man is in a dependent relationship where he fears arbitrary deprivation, he does not demand security. The need is for the "fairest possible break." When he is confident of this, he is more than willing to take risks. But when he feels threatened or dependent, his greatest need is for guarantees, for protection, for security.

The fact needs little emphasis that since every industrial employee is in a dependent relationship, safety needs may assume considerable importance. Arbitrary management actions, behavior which arouses uncertainty with respect to continued employment or which reflects favoritism or discrimination, unpredictable administration of policy—these can be powerful motivators of the safety needs in the employment relationship *at every level* from worker to vice president.

SOCIAL NEEDS

When man's physiological needs are satisfied and he is no longer fearful about his physical welfare, his social needs become important motivators of his behavior—for belonging, for association, for acceptance by his fellows, for giving and receiving friendship and love.

Management knows today of the existence of these needs, but it often assumes quite wrongly that they represent a threat to the organization. Many studies have demonstrated that the tightly knit, cohesive work group may, under proper conditions, be far more effective than an equal number of separate individuals in achieving organizational goals.

Yet management, fearing group hostility to its own objectives, often goes to considerable lengths to control and direct human efforts in ways that are inimical to the natural "groupiness" of human beings. When man's social needs—and perhaps his safety needs, too—are thus thwarted, he behaves in ways which tend to defeat organizational objectives. He becomes resistant, antagonistic, uncooperative. But this behavior is a consequence, not a cause.

EGO NEEDS

Above the social needs—in the sense that they do not become motivators until lower needs are reasonably satisfied—are the needs of greatest significance to management and to man himself. They are the egoistic needs, and they are of two kinds:

1. Those needs that relate to one's self-esteem—needs for self-confidence, for independence, for achievement, for competence, for knowledge.

2. Those needs that relate to one's reputation—needs for status, for recognition, for appreciation, for the deserved respect of one's fellows.

Unlike the lower needs, these are rarely satisfied; man seeks indefinitely for more satisfaction of these needs once they have become important to him. But they do not appear in any significant way until physiological, safety, and social needs are all reasonably satisfied.

The typical industrial organization offers few opportunities for the satisfaction of these egoistic needs to people at lower levels in the hierarchy. The conventional methods of organizing work, particularly in mass production industries, give little heed to these aspects of human motivation. If the practices of scientific management were deliberately calculated to thwart these needs—which, of course, they are not—they could hardly accomplish this purpose better than they do.

SELF-FULFILLMENT NEEDS

Finally—a capstone, as it were, on the hierarchy of man's needs—there are what we may call the needs for self-fulfillment. These are the needs for realizing one's own potentialities, for continued self-development, for being creative in the broadest sense of that term.

It is clear that the conditions of modern life give only limited opportunity for these relatively weak needs to obtain expression. The deprivation most people experience with respect to other lower-level needs diverts their energies into the struggle to satisfy *those* needs, and the needs for self-fulfillment remain dormant.

III.

Now, briefly, a few general comments about motivation:

We recognize readily enough that a man suffering from a severe dietary deficiency is sick. The deprivation of physiological needs has behavioral consequences. The same is true—although less well recognized—of deprivation of higher-level needs. The man whose needs for safety, association, independence, or status are thwarted is sick just as surely as is he who has rickets. And his sickness will have behavioral consequences. We will be mistaken if we attribute his resultant passivity, his hostility, his refusal to accept responsibility to his inherent "human nature." These forms of behavior are *symptoms* of illness—of deprivation of his social and egoistic needs.

The man whose lower-level needs are satisfied is not motivated to satisfy those needs any longer. For practical purposes they exist no longer. (Remember my point about your need for air.) Management often asks, "Why aren't people more productive? We pay good wages, provide good working conditions, have excellent fringe benefits and steady employment. Yet people do not seem to be willing to put forth more than minimum effort."

The fact that management has provided for these physiological and safety needs has shifted the motivational emphasis to the social and perhaps to the egoistic needs. Unless there are opportunities *at work* to satisfy these higher-level needs, people will be deprived; and their behavior will reflect this deprivation. Under such conditions, if management continues to focus its attention on physiological needs, its efforts are bound to be ineffective.

People *will* make insistent demands for more money under these conditions. It becomes more important than ever to buy the material goods and services which can provide limited satisfaction of the thwarted needs. Although money has only limited value in satisfying many higher-level needs, it can become the focus of interest if it is the *only* means available.

THE CARROT AND STICK APPROACH

The carrot and stick theory of motivation (like Newtonian physical theory) works reasonably well under certain circumstances. The *means* for satisfying man's physiological and (within limits) his safety needs can be provided or withheld by management. Employment itself is such a means, and so are wages, working conditions, and benefits. By these means the individual can be controlled so long as he is struggling for subsistence. Man lives for bread alone when there is no bread.

But the carrot and stick theory does not work at all once man has reached an adequate subsistence level and is motivated primarily by higher needs. Management cannot provide a man with self-respect, or with the respect of his fellows, or with the satisfaction of needs for self-fulfillment. It can create conditions such that he is encouraged and enabled to seek such satisfactions *for himself,* or it can thwart him by failing to create those conditions.

But this creation of conditions is not "control." It is not a good device for directing behavior. And so management finds itself in an odd position. The high standard of living created by our modern technological know-how provides quite adequately for the satisfaction of physiological and safety needs. The only significant exception is where management practices have not created confidence in a "fair break"—and thus where safety needs are thwarted. But by making possible the satisfaction of low-level needs, management has deprived itself of the ability to use as motivators the devices on which conventional theory has taught it to rely—rewards, promises, incentives, or threats and other coercive devices.

NEITHER HARD NOR SOFT

The philosophy of management by direction and control—*regardless of whether it is hard or soft*—is inadequate to motivate because the human needs on which this approach relies are today unimportant motivators of behavior. Direction and control are essentially useless in motivating people whose important needs are social and egoistic. Both the hard and the soft approach fail today because they are simply irrelevant to the situation.

People, deprived of opportunities to satisfy at work the needs which are now important to them, behave exactly as we might predict—which indolence, passivity, resistance to change, lack of responsibility, willingness to follow the demagogue, unreasonable demands for economic benefits. It would seem that we are caught in a web of our own weaving.

In summary, then, of these comments about motivation:

Management by direction and control—whether implemented with the hard, the soft, or the firm but fair approach—fails under today's conditions to provide effective motivation of human effort toward organizational objectives. It fails because direction and control are useless methods of motivating people whose physiological and safety needs are reasonably satisfied and whose social, egoistic, and self-fulfillment needs are predominant.

IV.

For these and many other reasons, we require a different theory of the task of managing people based on more adequate assumptions about human nature and human motivation. I am going to be so bold as to suggest the broad dimensions of such a theory. Call it "Theory Y," if you will.

1. Management is responsible for organizing the elements of productive enterprise—money, materials, equipment, people—in the interest of economic ends.

2. People are *not* by nature passive or resistant to organizational needs. They have become so as a result of experience in organizations.

3. The motivation, the potential for development, the capacity for assuming responsibility, the readiness to direct behavior toward organizational goals are all present in people. Management does not put them there. It is a responsibility of management to make it possible for people to recognize and develop these human characteristics for themselves.

4. The essential task of management is to arrange organizational conditions and methods of operation so that people can achieve their own goals *best* by directing *their own* efforts toward organizational objectives.

This is a process primarily of creating opportunities, releasing potential, removing obstacles, encouraging growth, providing guidance. It is what Peter Drucker has called "management by objectives" in contrast to "management by control."

And I hasten to add that it does *not* involve the abdication of management, the absence of leadership, the lowering of standards, or the other characteristics usually associated with the "soft" approach under Theory X. Much on the contrary. It is no more possible to create an organization today which will be a fully effective application of this theory than it was to build an atomic power plant in 1945. There are many formidable obstacles to overcome.

SOME DIFFICULTIES

The conditions imposed by conventional organization theory and by the approach of scientific management for the past half century have tied men to limited jobs which do not utilize their capabilities, have discouraged the acceptance of responsibility, have encouraged passivity, have eliminated meaning from work. Man's habits, attitudes, expectations—his whole conception of membership in an industrial organization—have been conditioned by his experience under these circumstances. Change in the direction of Theory Y will be slow, and it will require extensive modification of the attitudes of management and workers alike.

People today are accustomed to being directed, manipulated, controlled in industrial organizations and to finding satisfaction for their social, egoistic, and self-fulfillment needs away from the job. This is true of much of management as well as of workers. Genuine "industrial citizenship"—to borrow again a term from Drucker—is a remote and unrealistic idea, the meaning of which has not even been considered by most members of industrial organizations.

Another way of saying this is that Theory X places exclusive reliance upon external control of human behavior, while Theory Y relies heavily on self-control and self-direction. It is worth noting that this difference is the difference between treating people as children and treating them as mature adults. After generations of the former, we cannot expect to shift to the latter overnight.

V.

Before we are overwhelmed by the obstacles, let us remember that the application of theory is always slow. Progress is usually achieved in small steps.

Consider with me a few innovative ideas which are entirely consistent with Theory Y and which are today being applied with some success.

DECENTRALIZATION AND DELEGATION

These are ways of freeing people from the too-close control of conventional organization, giving them a degree of freedom to direct their own activities, to assume responsibility, and, importantly, to satisfy their egoistic needs. In this connection, the flat organization of Sears, Roebuck and Company provides an interesting example. It forces "management by objectives" since it enlarges the number of people reporting to a manager until he cannot direct and control them in the conventional manner.

JOB ENLARGEMENT

This concept, pioneered by I.B.M. and Detroit Edison, is quite consistent with Theory Y. It encourages the acceptance of responsibility at the bottom of the organization; it provides opportunities for satisfying social and egoistic needs. In fact, the reorganization of work at the factory level offers one of the more challenging opportunities for innovation consistent with Theory Y. The studies by A. T. M. Wilson and his associates of British coal mining and Indian textile manufacture have added appreciably to our understanding of work organization. Moreover, the economic and psychological results achieved by this work have been substantial.

PARTICIPATION AND CONSULTATIVE MANAGEMENT

Under proper conditions these results provide encouragement to people to direct their creative energies toward organizational objectives, give them some voice in decisions that affect them, provide significant opportunities for the satisfaction of social and egoistic needs. I need only mention the Scanlon Plan as the outstanding embodiment of these ideas in practice.

The not infrequent failure of such ideas as these to work as well as expected is often attributable to the fact that a management has "bought the idea" but applied it within the framework of Theory X and its assumptions.

Delegation is not an effective way of exercising management by control. Participation becomes a farce when it is applied as a sales gimmick or a device for kidding people into thinking they are important. Only the management that has confidence in human capacities and is itself directed toward organizational objectives rather than toward the preservation of personal power can grasp the implications of this emerging theory. Such management will find and apply successfully other innovative ideas as we move slowly toward the full implementation of a theory like Y.

PERFORMANCE APPRAISAL

Before I stop, let me mention one other practical application of Theory Y which—while still highly tentative—may well have important consequences. This has to do with performance appraisal within the ranks of management. Even a cursory examination of conventional programs of performance appraisal will reveal how completely consistent they are with Theory X. In fact, most such programs tend to treat the individual as though he were a product under inspection on the assembly line.

Take the typical plan: substitute "product" for "subordinate being appraised," substitute "inspector" for "superior making the appraisal," substitute "rework" for "training or development," and, except for the attributes being judged, the human appraisal process will be virtually indistinguishable from the product inspection process.

A few companies—among them General Mills, Ansul Chemical, and General Electric—have been experimenting with approaches which involve the individual in setting "targets" or objectives *for himself* and in a *self*-evaluation of performance semi-annually or annually. Of course, the superior plays an important leadership role in this process—one, in fact, which demands substantially more competence than the conventional approach. The role is, however, considerably more congenial to many managers than the role of "judge" or "inspector" which is forced upon them by conventional performance. Above all, the individual is encouraged to take a greater responsibility for planning and appraising his own contribution to organizational objectives; and the accompanying effects on egoistic and self-fulfillment needs are substantial. This approach to performance appraisal represents one more innovative idea being explored by a few managements who are moving toward the implementation of Theory Y.

VI.

And now I am back where I began. I share the belief that we could realize substantial improvements in the effectiveness of industrial organizations during the next decade or two. Moreover, I believe the social sciences can contribute much to such developments. We are only beginning to grasp the implications of the growing body of knowledge in these fields. But if this conviction is to become a reality instead of a pious hope, we will need to view the process much as we view the process of releasing the energy of the atom for constructive human ends— as a slow, costly, sometimes discouraging approach toward a goal which would seem to many to be quite unrealistic.

The ingenuity and the perseverance of industrial management in the pursuit of economic ends have changed many scientific and technological dreams into commonplace realities. It is now becoming clear that the application of these same talents to the human side of enterprise will not only enhance substantially these materialistic achievements but will bring us one step closer to "the good society." Shall we get on with the job?

26. Does Higher Pay Bring Higher Productivity?*

Harold F. Rothe

IN PRACTICALLY all companies today, the preferred method of inducing employees to work faster, or better, or both, is to offer them more money. The particular inducement used may take any one of a variety

---

* From *Personnel*, Vol. 37, 1960, pp. 20–38.

of forms—group or individual incentive systems, merit increases, length-of-service increases, bonuses, commissions, profit-sharing plans, to name but a few. But whatever incentive is offered, its underlying rationale is the belief that workers are spurred to greater efforts by the prospect of higher earnings.

In actual fact, there is remarkably little experimental evidence to support this view. This is not to say, of course, that money is not an effective motivator *per se*. Any company paying substandard wages eventually learns that, though people may not work for money alone, they are seldom particularly receptive to the idea of working for less than they can earn in a similar job elsewhere. But this is hardly the point at issue. The question to be resolved is not so much whether people work primarily for money, or even whether they work better for more money. What we really want to know is which financial inducements can be relied upon to increase productivity and which cannot. Or, to put the question another way, how can money be used to motivate employees to produce more?

Actually, "motivate" is hardly the right word to use in this connection. Expressed in its simplest psychological terms, a "motive" is an inner urge toward something—food, drink, recognition, security, and the like. The external object that satisfies the need—a hot dog, a milk shake, a pat on the back, insurance—is an "incentive." Thus, money, strictly speaking, is an incentive, and our question would be more properly phrased: How can money be used to incentivate employees to produce more? Rather than fall back on this barbarism, however, let us continue to say "motivate," remembering that when we offer people something over and above their base wages or salaries, it is their incentives, not their motives, that are being changed.

SOME CLASSIC STUDIES

Before coming to grips with our main question, it may be pertinent to review here some research findings about the effectiveness of money as a reward. One study, for example, that compared college freshmen of equal ability but varying economic status found that the students who needed money received better grades than those who were financially secure. The researchers concluded that the hope of winning scholarships stimulated the needy students to work harder.

In another study, conducted in a school for the unemployed in England, four girls who were paid by the day stitched on canvas for two months to establish a production standard. After a six months' interval, they returned to stitch for five weeks under a wage incentive system. Though they had presumably lost some skill in the meantime, the girls exceeded their old standard from the first week onward.

Still another study found that children learned to read better when rewards of candy, toys, or money were held out to them. Though candy was the most effective incentive, money could be, and always was, exchanged for candy, and so it too was effective.

While all these studies apparently showed that money motivated people, none of them can be considered in any way definitive. They are too academic and cover too short a time span and too few persons. As a group, however, they do suggest that money can be an effective incentive to produce more.

On the other hand, an English factory study similar to the ones described above showed that this is not necessarily so. Here, a group of young girls was employed threading needles for older girls to use. The girls threaded an average of 96 dozen needles a day and were paid on a day rate. When a piece-rate system was installed, their average dropped to 75 dozen needles. Then a new system was introduced: When the girls reached a daily standard of 100 dozen, they were allowed to go home. Production immediately jumped; the girls reached their quota on an average of two-and-one-half hours early each day.

The explanation in this case was simple: Money had no incentive value in this situation because the girls' parents were taking all their earnings. The chance to get out of work early, on the other hand, had a real appeal to them and hence was a real incentive.

The evidence offered by industrial engineers, though taken from more pertinent situations than these classic studies, is equally inconclusive and even more likely to involve oversimplification. In his book, *Lincoln's Incentive System*, J. F. Lincoln tells how his plant's productivity increased over the years after the introduction of an incentive system and a profit-sharing bonus. Concluding that piecework is the only proper way of paying for production, he advises management to study the job in question, set the best method of doing it, establish a price for the job, and stick to it regardless of what happens to earnings.

Unfortunately, this kind of study does not really demonstrate the effect of any one variable like money. It merely shows that over a period of years productivity, pay, and sales went up, prices went down, and so forth. With so many variables to take into account, it is impossible to determine what effect a particular one might have had, especially over an extended period of time.

MAYBE IT'S NOT THE MONEY

The Hawthorne studies covered a shorter period and were more limited in scope than most industrial engineering studies. There it was found that small groups of employees increased their production under varying working conditions and pay systems. An incentive system brought about greater productivity—or was accompanied by greater productivity—than a time system, and when one group was later put back on a day rate, its production fell off. There were indications, however, that the increased production under the incentive system was a result not of the system itself but of the reduction in the size of the work group from a whole department to only four or five employees.

This explanation receives some support from an English study that found small work groups producing about 6 per cent more than large work groups, regardless of the pay system. If we subtract this figure from the 15–30 per cent productivity increase at the Hawthorne plant, we are left with 9–24 per cent to be accounted for by other factors, including the pay system. The Hawthorne researchers noted that the effects of different wage systems were completely entwined with other variables in the situation and agreed that there was therefore no real evidence that the productivity increases were due to wages alone.

A similar experiment in an English candy factory, carried out around the same time as the Hawthorne studies, pointed up another factor modifying the effects of wage incentives. The ten girls studied rotated on five operations. For nine weeks, each girl was paid a straight day rate, and production was roughly constant; for the next 15 weeks, a competitive bonus system was used, and production increased 46 per cent; for the final 12 weeks, an individual piece rate was in effect, and production increased another 30 per cent. Interestingly enough, however, the production rate on one of the five operations—unwrapping poorly wrapped pieces of candy—showed no change throughout the entire study, simply because the girls disliked this particular task. Here again, more money was not necessarily an infallible spur to greater productivity.

Still another factor that can reinforce or counteract the effect of wage incentives cropped up in a study conducted in the boot and shoe industry. Out of 454 comparisons made in 43 English factories, 430 found piece workers producing at a higher rate than day workers. In fact, piece workers produced about twice as much as day workers. Pitting these averages against American figures, however, the researchers discovered that not only did American workers in both categories far outproduce their English counterparts, but American day workers came much closer to the production rates of the English piece workers. It seems likely that the substantial increase in productivity that accompanied the incentive systems in England was as much a function of the way the work had been reorganized before the incentive systems were installed as of the incentives themselves. (Incidentally, the work was as well organized for the average American day worker as for the average English piece worker.)

To summarize thus far, the evidence from empirical studies indicates that while financial incentives do seem to result in greater productivity, their precise influence is impossible to determine. Productivity is clearly affected also by such factors as the size of the work group, the inherent nature of the task, the organization of the work, the nature of the incentive system itself, and perhaps the length of time involved. There are undoubtedly still others, such as union-management attitudes and collective bargaining agreements, whose effect has not yet been fully analyzed.

EVIDENCE FROM SURVEYS

The conclusions drawn from these empirical and quasi-experimental studies of incentive systems are supported by the findings of various surveys. Thus, in 1948, the Dartnell Corporation surveyed 117 companies with incentive systems. The respondents agreed that their systems had resulted in lower unit costs, higher productivity, higher morale, and lower absenteeism. (Needless to say, these were merely the opinions of the participating companies, and there is no way of knowing how far they were actually based on objective data.)

Another survey, of 514 incentive plans, which was carried out in 1953, found that production had increased about 38.99 per cent, labor costs had decreased about 11.58 per cent, and take-home pay had increased about 11.76 per cent. Like the industrial studies, however, this survey could not measure the exact contribution of the wage incentive itself.

Though our discussion thus far has centered on formal wage incentive systems, principally because these have been so extensively studied, there are, of course, other supplements to base pay that might be mentioned here. Profit-sharing plans, for example, are often regarded in this country as a kind of incentive system. In other countries, however, they are not considered to be incentives, and no evidence has yet been adduced that entitles us to conclude that profit sharing results in greater productivity. In fact, a worldwide survey carried out by the Australian Government in 1947 found that profit sharing had no effect on output and efficiency. Though companies with profit-sharing plans may be happy with them, their main benefit seems to be that they induce employees to stay with the company, not necessarily to work harder.

Industrial research, then, throws little light on the question: Does more money spur employees to greater effort—and if so, what kind of inducement constitutes the most effective means of increasing productivity? To answer this question, and to formulate a set of basic principles as a guide for action, we must employ an entirely different approach. We must begin by asking ourselves: When an employer offers some financial inducement to his employees in the hope of raising their productivity, what actually is he trying to do?

Analysis of this question will quickly show that, in effect, the employer is trying to change the employees' behavior. He is trying to *teach them a new habit*—the habit of producing at a faster rate, or perhaps at a higher level of quality. The effectiveness of the inducements he offers will depend, therefore, on how far they fulfill the requirements that must be met if learning is to take place.

What are these requirements—the basic conditions of the learning process? The following simple formulation should be adequate for our purposes here, as well as acceptable to the various schools of psychological thought, regardless of their differences on more specific points:

Learning proceeds better—faster, more accurately, and so forth—when

1. The learner is motivated—when he has a need for something.
2. There is an incentive appropriate to the motive. For the traditional rat in the maze, food is an effective incentive only if he is hungry; drink, only if he is thirsty. Similarly, for the Engilsh girls threading needles, money was an ineffective incentive, but time off was highly effective.
3. The learner intends to learn. The teacher should gratify his intention by keeping him informed of his progress. There must be an awareness of the relationship between the activity and its motive and incentive.
4. The learner understands what he is supposed to be learning—a principle that we implicitly recognize by instituting indoctrination programs.
5. The reward immediately and invariably follows the successful completion of the task, while failure is equally certain not to be rewarded.

In summary, then, the learning process requires that there be (1) a *motive*, even if it is only the intent to learn; (2) *understanding* of what is to be learned; and (3) an *incentive* that is *appropriate* to the motive, recognized as being *related* to the action, and *certain* of being applied *immediately* as soon as the correct action has been successfully completed.

The accompanying table represents an attempt to apply these criteria to various types of financial incentives. (Two criteria—motivation and understanding—have been omitted as being applicable to all types.) Though the table clearly shows which incentives meet the necessary criteria and which do not, some explanatory notes on each type of incentive may be helpful.

1. Merit increases. These are usually given at a predetermined review date and thus are not associated with any particularly good piece of work. In fact, the employee seldom perceives any relation between his work and the increase, except that someone may tell him that he has done a good job over the past year. In the case of an employee's talking his boss into a raise, the performance record is even less relevant. The employee is being rewarded for his persuasiveness, not his performance. He need not even have intended to do well in his job, though he no doubt intended to get a raise.

Then, too, merit increases are usually determined by the supervisor's opinions of the employee's performance, which may not be objectively sound. (A recent study using the "critical incident" technique found that supervisors forgot even important actions by their subordinates within one or two weeks.) Since merit ratings may, and generally do, bear little relationship to actual performance, there is little or no reason to expect the raises to have any influence on output. As a matter of fact, employees may come to expect a periodic raise and become bitter if they

TABLE 1

How Various Types of Financial Incentives
Meet Conditions Required for Increasing Productivity

Type of Incentive	Conditions Required for Increasing Productivity			
	Appropriate to Intent	Related to Some Behavior	Immediate upon Behavior	Certain upon Behavior
Merit increases........	Possibly	Possibly	Possibly	Possibly
Negotiated increases...	Possibly	No	No	No
General increases......	No	No	No	No
Productivity increases..	Possibly	Possibly	No	No
Cost-of-living increases.	No	No	No	No
Length-of-service increases..........	No	No	No	No
Profit-sharing plans.....	Possibly	Possibly	No	No
Bonuses and commissions........	Yes	Yes	Possibly	Yes
Individual incentive plans..............	Yes	Yes	Yes	Yes
Group incentive plans...	Yes	Yes	Yes	Yes

don't get it, or don't get it on time, or don't get as much as they expected.

As they are usually administered, then, merit increases do not meet the four criteria of an effective incentive. They can work, though—if they are given soon after an outstanding accomplishment, if the employee is told the reason for the increase, and if, on the other hand, his undesirable actions are immediately pointed out to him as grounds for the withholding of a raise.

2. Negotiated increases. It would be unrealistic to expect an increase in production to follow a negotiated wage increase, which does not recognize either the group's or the individual's productivity and whose timing is determined by quite another set of factors. There is no certainty under this system, either: negotiations during a period of rising employee productivity do not necessarily result in an increase, whereas negotiations during a period of low productivity sometimes do result in an increase. The behavior that is really being rewarded here is skill or power in negotiating, but not productivity. Moreover, sharp labor-management conflict in the course of negotiations is likely to result in an immediate lowering of productivity.

Individually negotiated increases usually take the form of a contract such as salesmen have and include some sort of bonus or commission. For this reason, they ought really to be considered as individual incentive systems and hence will not concern us here.

3. General increases. General increases, whether or not they are won by negotiation, have the same defects as negotiated increases: they bear no relation to what the employees are doing or to their intent, since the poor producer is rewarded as well as the good producer; and, of course,

they are neither immediate nor certain upon good performance. The only possible source of increased productivity under this system is a slight temporary feeling of gratitude on the part of the employees.

4. Productivity increases. Despite their name, productivity increases are, most commonly, negotiated general increases with no necessary relation to the contributions of the beneficiaries. A company might raise its productivity through better tooling or better design, thereby achieving lower costs regardless of the actions of its labor force. These gains would then be passed on to employees who might have had nothing at all to do with the increase in output. This kind of increase thus has no relation to employees' intentions or behavior, it is not applied immediately upon their performing some desirable action, and it is not certain.

5. Cost-of-living increases. Though they seem at first glance to be ethically "right," cost-of-living increases are basically inequitable and, unless accompanied by greater productivity, inflationary. In any event, as the table shows, they are totally ineffective in assuring productivity. Actually, they are nothing but negotiated general increases.

In passing, it may be said that the increases we have been examining may, of course, have a strong and direct effect on the company's productivity—by forcing the employer to develop better products or methods, or buy better tools and equipment, in order to offset the cost of the increase. Needless to say, this is not the direct effect he is seeking, and should not be equated with an actual increase in the productivity of the employees.)

6. Length-of-service increases. Though often valuable in reducing labor turnover, these increases bear no more than a coincidental relation either to productivity or to the intent to produce more. They do have immediacy and certainty, but the achievement they reward—ten years of service, for instance—is altogether irrelevant to productivity.

7. Profit sharing. Since profit-sharing plans bear some relationship to the productivity of individual employees, if only remotely, it can be presumed that employees will want to produce more in order to share in greater profits. Under most plans, however, the rewards are granted only once a year and thus lack immediacy. They also lack certainty, though the employees often have some idea whether or not things are going well for the company.

These plans could be more effective if the connection between performance and reward were made clearer by a more frequent distribution of the profits—perhaps quarterly instead of annual. One defect, however, would still remain: the individual employee's performance does not determine his share of the pie.

8. Bonuses and commissions. These two forms of compensation are sufficiently alike to be treated together. For our purpose, the term "bonus" means extra payment for extra results, such as a salesman might get, rather than, say, a Christmas bonus, which is usually a form of

profit sharing. Bonuses and commissions need not be related to profits, but they *are* related to some activity, and are, obviously, appropriate to the intent to make more money by producing more. In general, the reward is sure to follow the results, and it comes soon after. These forms of compensation meet, or can easily be made to meet, the four requirements of an effective incentive.

9. Individual and group incentive plans. Incentive plans score on all four criteria: the incentive is directly related to performance and to the intent to earn more by producing more; the rewards are certain, and they come quickly.

To make group incentives wholly satisfactory on the first two criteria, the size of the group may need adjusting. As was noted earlier, small groups are usually more productive than large groups. In small groups the individual's contribution is more apparent, and there is more room for his intent to produce to come into play. Industrial engineers usually equate the group with an operational unit, which may actually be quite large. To achieve the optimum operation of an incentive plan they might do well to make the group as small as timekeeping and other control activities will permit.

27. Need Satisfactions and Employee Turnover*

Ian C. Ross and Alvin F. Zander

THIS STUDY WAS undertaken in order to determine whether the satisfaction of certain psychological needs by an employment situation has a demonstrable relationship to labor turnover. We were primarily interested in needs which could be satisfied by the social dimensions of the work situation. Of course, all organizations satisfy some of the needs of their members otherwise the membership could not exist because persons would not belong to it. Even the few organizations with involuntary memberships, such as prisons, meet some needs, if only the physical requirements of inmate members. We found it helpful to distinguish between two kinds of need satisfactions that organizations give their members. One kind of need satisfaction is provided by means of money payments. These payments permit the member to obtain need satisfaction by purchasing goods and services that will meet at least some of his

* From *Personnel Psychology*, Vol. 10, 1957, pp. 327–38.

needs. The other kind of need satisfaction an organization provides its members results from the intrinsic process of participating in the social system of the organization. For purposes of this study we have distinguished five personal needs that can be gratified on the job. These needs are for affiliation, achievement, autonomy, recognition, and fair evaluation. We undertook to find out whether the satisfaction of these needs is important to the members. Our measure of importance was whether the people who are more dissatisfied with regard to these needs are more likely to leave. We used a limited number of needs which we expected to be important and which might be useful in an operational attempt to increase the intrinsic satisfaction of the job situation.

Our objective was to determine to what degree satisfaction of the five personal needs affects the cohesiveness of the industrial organization with which we are concerned. Cohesiveness is the resultant of all the forces acting on all members in the direction of their remaining in the organization. Our major hypothesis was developed by assuming that if satisfaction of these needs is important, those members who are not satisfied will relinquish their membership, which in this industrial case means resigning from their jobs. Thus, we can state our principal operational hypothesis: People who resign will be less satisfied than those who stay with regard to the five needs of affiliation, achievement, autonomy, recognition, and fair evaluation.

DESIGN

The design of this study was determined in part by the necessity to handle carefully two important methodological problems while meeting the objectives just described. First, it was necessary to keep the effects of personal satisfactions on the job independent of the effects of earnings and of the needs which can be met by money. To some extent people may be expected to put up with a lack of satisfaction of personal needs in order to obtain money. Also, people who are more financially independent may be willing to experience very little deprivation of personal needs.

The second problem to which our study design was oriented is that of causality in time. In order for our hypothesis to be tested in a meaningful way, it was necessary to obtain measures of dissatisfaction that preceded the act of resignation in time. Measurements taken after the decision to resign has been made are likely to be complicated by the necessity to justify the resignation, by the resigned worker's attempting to be sure that he will be able to re-enter the organization at some time in the future, and by the release of tension which the announcement of intention to resign probably brings.

The design of the study will be described in six steps. As each step is discussed, its relevance to the major design problems is made explicit.

The first step was the administration of a questionnaire to 2,680 female skilled workers in 48 sections of a large company. These sections were located in a number of cities. Since we wanted to measure needs and satisfaction before resignations took place (and thus before the people resigning were identified), a large number of questionnaires was necessary in order that the small percentage resigning within a reasonable period after measurement would constitute a statistically useful number of cases.

The second step consisted in gathering personal data on these employees from supervisors' reports.

The third step was to place each employee in one of six categories depending upon certain personal characteristics. These categories, in general, describe types of domestic situations which influence the likelihood that a woman will need to have a job. These categories are used to help separate the effects of money from on-the-job satisfactions in a manner to be described shortly. We shall refer to the categories as types of employees.

The fourth step was the identification of those employees who resigned during the four-month period following administration of the questionnaires. There were 169 resignations among the 2,680 people who completed questionnaires.

As the fifth step, two control cases who did not resign were selected to match each resigned employee. The controls were selected by picking the person of the same type, in the same section, who had next higher seniority with the company and the person with next lower seniority. This method of control provided us with people of comparable experience having the same work, supervision, and employee benefits in addition to similar financial circumstances.

The sixth and final step of the design was the comparison of the extent to which the need satisfaction of the control persons was equal to or different from that of those who resigned. According to our general hypothesis, those who resigned should have felt greater dissatisfaction of their personal needs and should have experienced more interference with satisfactions derived from off-the-job sources. Comparisons were made between each resigned employee and the matched control persons. The major hypothesis states that the mean difference is not zero but is of such sign that greater dissatisfaction is evidenced by the resigned people.

The classifications of types of employee were intended to hold constant, for purposes of control, personal characteristics which are economically important and which have a bearing upon the continued employment of women workers. The six types are: single tentatives, married tentatives, objectives, mothers, careerists, and permanents. In general, both single and married *tentatives* have events ahead of them which will raise questions about their continued employment. These events are, of course, marriage and motherhood. The *objectives* are people whose terminations are expected when foreseen events take place. A common event is the return of husbands from military service. *Mothers* are a separate class because they have returned to work after an event which often terminates a woman's participation in the labor force. The return of these mothers may indicate responsibilities which are a reason for them to continue working. *Careerists* are those whom the supervisors consider especially motivated to succeed in the industry with which we are concerned. *Permanents* are those who have been employed for a relatively long time and who, for many reasons, are likely to remain employed until they reach retirement age.

These types were so defined that they are not all mutually exclusive. For example, a person may be a mother as well as a careerist. We, therefore, had to decide on an order of priority by which individuals would be placed in only one type. The basic principle used was that a person would be placed in that type which is deemed a stronger predictor of length of service with the organization.

Operational criteria for each type were set up in terms of the personal data given by supervisors. The careerists were selected first. Thus, anyone who might meet the criteria for careerist, permanent, and mother was classified as a careerist. From those who were not careerists, we next selected the permanents. Then we selected the objectives, mothers and tentatives in that order. The two classes of tentatives are mutually exclusive so that no ordering decision had to be made between them.

The measurement of satisfaction for the needs of recognition, achievement, and autonomy required a pair of questions for each need. One question measured the strength of the need, and the other the extent to which the need was met by the employment situation. Respondents were asked to indicate their feelings about each question by marking a point on a graphic rating scale. For example, the following pair of items was used to measure the need for recognition and the degree of recognition obtained:

How important is it to you that you know how well you are doing?
How fully are you informed about the quality of your work?

The first question is directed to the strength of the need and the second to the extent that the need was met. For scoring purposes the marks on the accompanying scale were counted as having the values 0 through 9.

The amount of dissatisfaction was computed by subtracting the degree of satisfaction from the strength of the indicated need. This procedure was based on the assumption that it is not how much need satisfaction one receives that is important, but rather the extent to which needs are met or not met. For example, let us compare two workers, A and B, who indicate that their need for recognition is 5 and 8, respectively. Let us assume that they report satisfaction in this area of 4 and 6. In spite of the fact that worker B is receiving greater satisfaction, we consider him less satisfied. His dissatisfaction is 2, i.e., 8 minus 6. Since worker A has only one unit of dissatisfaction (5 minus 4), his needs are met to a greater extent, and by our hypothesis worker A is more likely to remain with the organization.

The method of using the difference gives some protection against differing interpretations among respondents in regard to the scaled values. To the extent that the same relationship is perceived between the two scales (strength of need and satisfaction) by various subjects, the differences in the level of need or satisfaction implied by the words have no effect.

The need for affiliation was measured by a series of paired questions of a similar type. We asked how important it was for the person to know and to be known by the management and the extent to which they were known. We also asked questions about co-workers. The need to be evaluated by fair standards was handled with a single question about fairness of the company's expectations.

The questionnaire also included items on the degree to which the job prevented gratification of needs in family life and social life, as well as questions about anxiety, quality of supervision received, and the necessity of having a job.

RESULTS

The results were evaluated by computing, for each resigned employee and each person selected as a control, the extent to which her needs were not met. These scores were computed by subtraction of the degree of each satisfaction received from the amount of the corresponding need expressed. Then from the dissatisfaction scores of the resigned employee were subtracted the mean dissatisfaction scores of the two persons with whom the resigned worker had been matched. These differences between the dissatisfactions of the resigned person and the matched people who remained were the main statistics with which we worked. The standard errors of these differences were computed and evaluated for the 169 sets of resigned workers and comparable employees who remained. Since the hypothesis is that the needs of resigned workers will be satisfied to a lesser degree, the differences are confirmatory of the hypothesis only in one direction of divergence from zero. In the significance tests applied, the probability values quoted are for the one-tailed test.

It is in the area of *recognition* that we find the largest and most significant difference in degree of dissatisfaction between the 169 persons who resigned and their controls. This is evident in the accompanying table. Most of this difference is associated with responses to a question about the extent to which a respondent is informed about the quality of her work. If we take the entire scale of response as having ten units, those who resigned were on the average .64 of a unit more dissatisfied than were the comparable persons who stayed. This difference is significantly different from zero in the predicted direction well beyond the one per cent level of significance.

In this study the need for *achievement* was interpreted as feeling that one is doing something important when one is working. The resigned employees had .23 of a unit greater dissatisfaction in this respect and the difference is significant at the five per cent level.

Autonomy was understood to be the extent to which a person is on his own when he works. There was substantially no difference between the resigned workers and the matching continuing workers in regard to the strength of the need for autonomy. There was a substantial difference in the autonomy which they indicated they experienced. Those who resigned reported .53 of a unit greater dissatisfaction in the autonomy area at the 2.5 per cent level.

The results for these three needs are summarized in Table 1.

TABLE 1

DIFFERENCES IN SATISFACTIONS BETWEEN RESIGNED WORKERS AND MATCHED CONTINUING WORKERS

MEASUREMENT	MEAN DIFFERENCE BETWEEN* RESIGNED WORKERS AND MATCHED CONTINUING WORKERS	p
Strength of need for recognition.................................	.08	ns
Degree of recognition received.................................	−.56	.0025
Dissatisfaction with recognition.............................	.64	.0025
Strength of need for achievement..............................	.15	ns
Degree of achievement received................................	−.08	ns
Dissatisfaction with achievement.............................	.23	.05
Strength of need for autonomy.................................	.09	ns
Degree of autonomy received..................................	−.44	.025
Dissatisfaction with autonomy................................	.53	.025
N = 169		

* The negative difference (−) means that the scores of the resigned workers were lower.

It is worth noting that the strength of the needs for recognition, achievement, and autonomy were essentially the same for those who resigned and the matched continuing workers. Both groups also rated their ability to do the work equally. These findings suggest that the resigned and matched continuing workers are approximately the same kind of people but that they receive differentially satisfying experiences in the course of their employment.

In our questions on the *affiliation* need we found that those who stayed wanted to know management better and also reported a greater acquaintance with management. Consequently, their dissatisfaction in the affiliation area was essentially equal to that of the resigned group. Surprisingly, we found that there was no difference in the compared groups' evaluation of the suitability of co-workers for friends.

One question was asked about the standards used in the *evaluation* of workers. The resigned workers rated the fairness of the expectations held by the company as .32 of a unit lower than did the controls. This difference is significant at the 5 per cent level. In another section of the questionnaire we asked the respondents to rate their own performance and the company's expectations with regard to five specific items of skill. There was no difference whatsoever in the ratings of own best performance of the two matched groups. However, the resigned workers rated the company's expectations .20 of a unit higher, and on three out of the five items, the resigned workers reported significantly higher expectations for their performance. Taken together, these responses seem to indicate that those who resigned thought that more was expected of them. We cannot say whether they considered these expectations unreasonable, but they did not accept them to the same extent as did the workers who remained. Also, the workers who remained did not consider the expectations so difficult as did the ones who resigned.

ANXIETY

In addition to our main interest in the effects of need satisfaction on turnover, we had a secondary interest in anxiety as a possible result of dissatisfaction that would increase the likelihood of resigning. Anxiety, in the sense we used it, is typified by feelings of uneasiness which lead to rejection of the perceived sources of the anxiety. It was our desire to find out whether deprivations of the on-the-job satisfactions studied here were associated with anxiety. We also wished to find out if anxiety increased the likelihood that a person would resign.

Only a small part of the questionnaire could be devoted to evaluation of anxiety; thus measurement depends on the responses to eight questions. Two of these questions inquired about the value and representativeness of the quality control checks used by management to measure performance of the respondents. The other six inquired about the frequency of feeling uneasy in specified social situations that occur on the job. Two of these eight anxiety items are significantly related to resigning. Those who left felt that work observations are inferior measures of ability, and they reported more frequent uneasiness when their supervisors stand close behind them. These two items have low but significant correlations with dissatisfactions of the need for autonomy and for fair evaluation. However, the anxiety differences are fully accounted for in a statistical sense by the correlation of these two items with lack of need satisfaction. When expected anxiety was computed for those who resigned from the relationship of the dissatisfactions to anxiety, it was found to be almost identical with the reported anxiety. We conclude that those who resigned are more anxious than those who remain but that little if any additional dynamic effect on turnover is induced by the anxiety itself.

JOB INTERFERENCE WITH OTHER SATISFACTION SOURCES

Three questions about the interference of employment with sources of satisfaction in home or community showed significant differences between the responses of the resigned workers and those of matched people who remained. These questions indicated that those who resigned felt that they were kept from doing things at home, that their jobs were interfering with their social life, and were preventing participation in clubs and similar activities. These differences are all about one-half of a unit on a ten-unit scale and are significantly different from zero at the 3 per cent level, or better.

Since the resigned employees reported greater dissatisfaction on the job and more interference with family and social life, the possibility was suggested that the dissatisfaction on the job might be due to the outside difficulties. However, when correlations were computed between the various interference responses and the on-the-job lack of need satisfaction, most of the correlation coefficients turned out to be quite small. The largest of these coefficients was $r = .22$. While this correlation is significantly greater than zero at the 5 per cent level, it hardly leads us to believe that workers will say very often that they are dissatisfied on grounds of personal needs when actually the job interferes with home life, or vice versa. We have concluded, therefore, that on-the-job deprivations and off-the-job interferences are independent social forces upon workers toward resigning.

OTHER ITEMS

The responses of the resigned workers on several other questions were not different from those made by persons who stayed with the company. These concerned the quality of supervision, the adequacy of on-the-job training, and the necessity for having a job. The discriminating ability of this last question was to some extent reduced by the control on personal characteristics. The people whose responses were compared are in the same life circumstances because they were matched in respect to their job motivation and thus have essentially similar needs for continued employment. It is also interesting to note that those who resigned did not rate their ability to do the job significantly lower than those who stayed.

We also asked workers whether they feel that the community has respect for workers in this industry and how well the employee's family and friends understand their work. None of these items was found to be significantly related to leaving.

SUMMARY

In this study we establish the fact that the degree of satisfaction of certain personal needs supplied by a person's place of employment has a significant direct relationship to his continuing to work for that company. These personal needs are for recognition, for autonomy, for a feeling of doing work that is important, and for evaluation by fair standards. In addition, knowing important people in the organization is related to continued employment. There are some indications that anxiety develops in those employees who state that their needs for autonomy and fair evaluation are not satisfied.

In addition to the degree of need satisfaction provided by the job, we examined the degree to which the employment situation limits satisfactions which the worker can receive from his family and from his community. We found that the extent to which the job interferes with family and community satisfactions is related to turnover as strongly as the failure to receive need satisfactions on the job. But interference with off-the-job sources of satisfaction is not related to experiencing dissatisfaction on the job. We interpret these results to mean that there are two essentially different kinds of reasons for leaving the employing organization. Some people resign for reasons of both kinds: the job itself does not satisfy needs, and it also keeps them from receiving satisfactions from other sources.

28. Job Design and Productivity*

Louis E. Davis

IT HAS LONG been taken for granted that specialization is the organizing principle of modern industry and the mainspring of its phenomenal productivity. However unfortunate some of the by-products of specialization, they have been accepted by and large as necessary evils. Better to put up with them, it seemed, than to attempt remedies which might impair efficiency and thus jeopardize the material gains of industrialization.

But are these actually the alternatives today? In the light of recent research and experiment, it appears to be high time to re-examine the issue. Has specialization perhaps been carried too far—to the point where productivity is *adversely* affected? Are fatigue, tension, low morale, absenteeism, turnover, and other causes of inefficiency actually the result

* From "Job Design and Productivity: A New Approach," *Personnel*, Vol. 33, 1957, pp. 418–30. The author wishes to express his appreciation to Dr. Ralph R. Canter for his collaboration in developing the concepts and supervising the experiments reported in this paper.

268 STUDIES IN PERSONNEL AND INDUSTRIAL PSYCHOLOGY

of over-specialization? Can increases in productivity be achieved by *reversing* the principle of specialization?

Specialization and Job Design

The approach to these questions has always been blocked by the assumption—accepted implicitly by management, engineers, and social scientists alike—that *the content of each job in an organization is fixed by the requirements of the production process and the organization structure* and therefore cannot be altered without jeopardizing economic efficiency.

It is this assumption which has persistently biased the judgment of both experts and laymen and ruled out the possibility of an objective approach to the problems created by specialization. Engineers and industrial managers have designed jobs on the basis of this assumption, and their concepts and methods of job design, reinforced by the economists', have set the pattern of industrial organization.

In its classical form, then, job design incorporates the principles of specialization, repetitiveness, reduction of skill content, and mimimum impact of the worker on the production process. The basic criteria for job design are minimizing immediate cost and maximizing immediate productivity.

Social philosophers, it is true, have long deplored the dehumanizing effects of this type of job design—monotony, the lack of mental stimulus, rigid adherence to job specifications and standards of output, and, not least, a hierarchical social order in which subordinates depend upon their superiors for the satisfaction of basic needs and aspirations. Whether the worker subjected to such a life experience could ever become a responsible citizen in a free democratic society seemed open to question.

Although the social scientists, beginning with Mayo, were the first to put to the test some of the basic assumptions of industrial society, they too took for granted the critical assumption that job content is fixed by technology, and hence focused their investigations for the most part on other aspects of the work situation, leaving job content to be prescribed by the engineer.

More to the point, therefore, are the criticisms being made today of the concept of job design itself.[1]

Drucker has argued, for example, that the use of the worker as a single-purpose machine tool is poor engineering and a waste of human resources. As he states the case:

---

[1] See for example, J. C. Worthy, "Organization, Structure and Employee Morale," *American Sociological Review,* Vol. 15, No. 2, April, 1950, p. 169; C. R. Walker and R. H. Guest, *The Man on the Assembly Line* (Cambridge, Mass.: Harvard University Press, 1952); F. L. Richardson and C. R. Walker, *Human Relations in an Expanding Company* (New Haven, Conn.: Yale University Press, 1948); R. H. Guest, "Men and Machines: An Assembly-Line Worker Looks at His Job," *Personnel,* Vol. 21, 1955, p. 496.

The principle of specialization is productive and efficient. But it is very dubious, indeed, whether we yet know how to apply it except to machinery. There is first the question of whether "specialization" as it is understood and practiced today is a socially and individually satisfying way of using human energy and production—a major question of the social order of industrial society.[2]

Or as Walker, even more boldly, has suggested:

We are only at the threshold of a scientific understanding of man's relation to work and especially his relation to the new technological environments within which much of the work of the modern world is being performed.[3]

It may well be, then, that society has bowed too soon to the expert in accepting the principle of specialization as inviolate. Once the critical assumption of fixed job elements is put to the test, it may prove to be invalid and the traditional concepts of job design may have to be reformed.

It is from this point of view that current trends in job design will be analyzed in this article and the outlines of a new approach to the problem presented.

CURRENT APPROACHES TO JOB DESIGN

Job design[4] is a phase in production planning which follows the planning and design of product, process, and equipment. It specifies the content of each job and determines the distribution of work within the organization.

This simple definition of job design does not take into consideration the many choices open to the job designer in specifying the content of a particular job. Generally speaking, however, the job design process can be divided into three phases:

1. The specification of individual tasks.
2. The specification of the method of performing each task.
3. The combination of individual tasks into specific jobs to be assigned to individuals.

The first and third determine the content of a job while the second indicates how the job is to be performed. It is possible, therefore, to distinguish between the design of *job content*—content design—and the design of job methods—*methods design*. There is a large body of knowledge about methods design—it is the subject of a specialized

---

[2] P. F. Drucker, *The New Society* (New York: Harper & Bros., 1950), p. 171.

[3] C. R. Walker, "Work Methods, Working Conditions and Morale," in A. Kornhaumer *et al.* (ed.), *Industrial Conflict* (New York: McGraw-Hill, 1954), p. 358.

[4] This and other technical terms used hereafter are defined in the Appendix to this article.

branch of industrial engineering, called methods engineering[5]—but relatively little information about content design.

According to a recent survey,[6] however, it is the prevailing practice in designing the content of industrial jobs to rely upon the criterion of minimizing immediate costs, as indicated by minimum unit operation time. To satisfy the minimum-cost criterion, the following rules are generally applied:[7]

In specifying the content of individual tasks:

1. Specialize skills.
2. Minimize skill requirements.
3. Minimize learning time.
4. Equalize workloads and make it possible to assign full workloads.
5. Provide for the workers' satisfaction (no specific criteria for job satisfaction are known to be in use, however).
6. Conform to the layout of equipment or facilities or, where they exist, to union restrictions on work assignments.

In combining individual tasks into specific jobs:

1. Limit the number and variety of tasks in a job.
2. Make the job as repetitive as possible.
3. Minimize training time.

In contrast with this *process-centered approach*, another concept of job design has been developed in recent years—the *worker-centered approach* which emphasizes the participation of the worker in certain areas of decision making as a way of giving meaning to the work situation.

Representative of this approach are the group planning method and job enlargement. In group planning,[8] a team of workers participates in deciding the content of the various jobs to be performed by members of the team. In job enlargement,[9] the job is specified in such a manner that the worker performs a longer sequence or a greater variety of operations and may be responsible as well for testing the quality of his work, setting up and maintaining his equipment, and controlling his own production rate.

---

[5] L. E. Davis, "Work Methods Design and Work Simplification," *Progress in Food Research*, Academic Press, Vol. 4, 1953, p. 37.

[6] L. E. Davis *et al.*, "Current Job Design Criteria," *Journal of Industrial Engineering*, Vol. 6, No. 2, 1955, p. 5.

[7] See for example, H. G. Thuesen and M. R. Lohman, "Job Design, Parts I and II," *Oil and Gas Journal*, Vol. 41, No. 35–36; H. B. Maynard *et al.*, *Methods-Time Measurement* (New York: McGraw-Hill, 1948).

[8] E. A. Woodhead, "Jobs Break-Down Under Group Study Plan," *Electrical World*, Vol. 120, No. 4, 1943.

[9] C. R. Walker, "The Problem of the Repetitive Job," *Harvard Business Review*, Vol. 28, No. 3, 1950; E. J. Tangerman, "Every Man His Own Inspector, Every Foreman His Own Boss at Graflex," *American Machinist*, Vol. 7, No. 3, 1953, p. 7; J. D. Elliott, "Increasing Office Productivity Through Job Enlargement," *AMA Office Management Series*, No. 114, 1954, p. 3.

There is a third approach which combines the process-centered and worker-centered approaches. In job rotation, for example, the operator is assigned a series of jobs to be performed in rotated order.[10] This method is often used to counteract the unfavorable effects of process-centered job designs in circumstances where the basic job specifications cannot be altered for one reason or another.

SOME CRITICISMS

These new approaches to job design—the outgrowth of social science research and experiment in industry—may be welcomed on the whole as a step in the right direction.[11] By calling attention to the critical role of the worker himself in the modern industrial system, they have challenged some of the basic premises of traditional job design.

A strong word of caution is in order, however. Most, if not all, social science research in industry, as was pointed out earlier, has been based on the assumption that the contents of a job are technically inviolate. If this assumption is invalid, as it may well be, the research findings cannot be accepted without question.

Given this basic limitation, it is not surprising that most of the recent experiments in job design have been haphazard—a kind of trial-and-error attempt to remedy the defects of completely "engineered" job specifications. As yet, there has been relatively little systematic analysis, under controlled conditions, of the actual relationship between job content and other variables. (long-term cost, productivity, motivation, and so on). Hence, in the absence of adequate theories of job design and experimental evidence to back them up, the doctrine of minimum costs still holds the field.

There are, however, three pioneering studies of job design to which this criticism does not apply. Since these investigations focused on actual job content and were carried out under controlled conditions, they may serve as models for future research in this area.

The first of these is the study made by Walker and Guest of the Institute of Human Relations at Yale University,[12] one of the first systematic investigations into the consequences of job specialization. Using

---

[10] A. Wood and M. L. Okum, "Job Rotation Plus That Works," *American Machinist*, Vol. 96, No. 9, 1946.

[11] They have been greeted with enthusiasm in many quarters. See for example, "Broadening the Job," *Time*, Vol. 63, April 12, 1954, p. 100; D. R. Wright, "Job Enlargement," *Wall Street Journal*, March 11, 1954, p. 1; D. Wharton, "Removing Monotony from Factory Jobs," *American Mercury*, October, 1954, p. 91; J. K. Lagemann, "Job Enlargement Boosts Production," *Nation's Business*, Vol. 42, No. 12, 1954, p. 34.

[12] C. R. Walker and R. H. Guest, *The Man on the Assembly Line* (Cambridge, Mass.: Harvard University Press, 1952); Walker and Guest, "The Man on the Assembly Line," *Harvard Business Review*, Vol. 30, No. 3, 1952, p. 71; Guest, "Men and Machines," *Personnel*, May, 1955.

depth interviews to explore workers' experiences on automobile assembly line jobs, the investigators analyzed the effects of mass production technology on job satisfaction and human relations.

JOB DESIGN ON THE ASSEMBLY LINE

The characteristic principles of mass production technology are defined in the study as follows:

1. Standardization.
2. Interchangeability of parts.
3. Orderly progression of the product through the plant in a series of planned operations at specific work stations.
4. Mechanical delivery of parts to work stations and mechanical removal of assemblies.
5. Breakdown of operations into their simple constituent motions.

The study focuses on the consequences of these principles as translated by the engineer into specific job designs—that is, the resulting gains and costs, both social and economic, for workers and for the company. Looking first at the gains, it is evident that the "engineered" job has yielded high levels of output per man-hour at low cost, providing profits for the company and a relatively low-priced product for the public.

In examining the social costs, however, some disturbing facts come to light. These can be summed up in the one overwhelming fact that the workers despise their jobs. This dissatisfaction does not seem to arise from the circumstances usually considered important by management such as pay, security, working conditions, pension plan, and supervision—the workers regarded these as satisfactory on the whole—but from certain features of job design:

1. *The anonymity of the individual worker* (what has been referred to previously as the principle of "minimum impact of the worker on the production process"). This is a consequence of designing *out* of the job virtually everything that might be of personal value or meaning to the worker. Specifically:
   a. The worker has no control over his work pace.
   b. His job is highly repetitive, having been broken down into the simplest motions possible.
   c. There is little or no need for skill because of the simple movements required.
   d. Methods and tools are completely specified and the worker has no control over them or any changes made in them.
   e. Because he never works on more than a small fraction of the product, the worker does not see the final results of his work, has no identity with the product, and cannot estimate the quality of his contribution to it.
   f. Since the job requires only surface attention, the worker does not become really absorbed in his work.
   g. The geographic arrangement of the production line severely limits social interactions. Men on the line work as individuals rather than as a work group, and the lack of group awareness seems to reinforce the feeling of anonymity.

2. *The depersonalization of the job,* as evidenced in the lack of job progression vertically. Since tasks have been simplified, skill differences between jobs are practically eliminated. Very few workers in the study had experienced any substantial change in job classification during a period of 12 to 15 years.

The manager and the engineer, of course, may feel that these social costs are more than justified by the gains for the company and the consumer. This, however, is not the point. Granting that low unit cost production—or minimum total economic cost, which amounts to the same thing—is the fundamental requirement for progress and well-being in an industrial society, the main question is this: Is the method of job design chosen by the engineer the *optimum* one for achieving minimum total economic cost *which includes social costs by definition?*

The question implies, of course, that the engineer's criteria for measuring the effectiveness of job design are inadequate, and this inference is strongly supported by the evidence of this study. As Walker and Guest point out, turnover was high; the quality of performance was far from optimum; and labor-management relations were in a constant state of tension.

AN EXPERIMENT IN REDESIGNING JOBS

The second study to be examined,[13] one of the first controlled experiments on job design in an industrial plant, was aimed at investigating how productivity could be improved by altering job content. The experiment was designed to test the hypothesis that higher economic productivity could be achieved by:

1. Increasing the number of tasks in a job.
2. Combining tasks that (a) have similar technological content and skill demands; (b) are sequentially related in the technical process; (c) include final activities in the process or sub-process; (d) increase worker responsibility by enlarging the area of decision-making concerning the job; and (e) increase the opportunity for the worker to perceive how his contribution is related to the completion of the work process.

Two major criteria were chosen for analyzing the effectiveness of these modifications in job design: quantity of production per man-hour, and quality of work. Certain measures of attitude and satisfaction were also used.

The experimental setting was a manufacturing department of a unionized company on the West Coast. The department had been the subject of detailed engineering study for some years and its activities were organized according to the latest engineering practices. A similar department in the same company was used as a control group to permit moni-

---

[13] A. R. N. Marks, "An Investigation of Modifications of Job Design in an Industrial Situation and Their Effects on Some Measures of Economic Productivity," Ph.D. dissertation, University of California, 1954. This study was under the direction of Dr. R. R. Canter and the author.

TABLE 1
Experimental Conditions for the Modification of Job Designs

Type of Job Design	Purpose	Criteria	Locations	Number of Workers	Total Number of Days Assigned	Number of Days Each Worker Assigned	Production Method
Line Job Design	Obtain reference base of job design where separate tasks are performed on rotated basis.	Quantity, quality, some measures of attitude and satisfaction.	Main department	29	26	26	Workers rotate among nine stations on belt conveyor, performing minute specified operations at pace of conveyor.
Group Job Design	Eliminate conveyor packing. Other conditions same as above.	Quantity, quality.	Adjacent room	29	14	2	Workers rotate among nine individual stations using batch method.
Individual Job Design No. 1	Give workers experience on experimental job design.	Quantity, quality.	Adjacent room	29	16	2	Workers perform all nine operations at own stations, plus inspection and getting own supplies.
Individual Job Design No. 2	Obtain measure of experimental job design.	Quantity, quality, some measures of attitude and satisfaction.	Main department	21	27	6	Same as Individual Job Design No. 1.

toring of plantwide changes which might affect employee attitudes and performance.

At the start of the experiment, the product—a hospital appliance—was being made on an assembly line at which 29 of the department's 35 members worked, the rest of the workers being engaged in supplying the line and inspecting the product. The 29 line workers were unskilled women with an average of four-and-a-half years' experience on the line (the range was from one to seven years approximately).

Each job on the line consisted in performing one of nine operations (these had similar skill requirements and technological content) as well as inspection in the form of rejecting defective parts. The operations were spaced at stations along the conveyor line, and the women rotated between hard and easy stations every two hours. Since the conveyor line set the pace, the workers were not responsible for the rate of output, and job rotation in effect eliminated any individual responsibility for the quality of output.

The experiment was divided into four phases (the details are given in Table 1):

1. *Line Job Design.* The original assembly line job, used as a reference base.
2. *Group Job Design.* In this modification, the conveyor is eliminated and the workers set their own pace. Otherwise, the operations are the same as above.
3. *Individual Job Design No. 1.* Workers perform all nine operations at their own stations, control the sequence of assembly, procure supplies, and inspect their own product.
4. *Individual Job Design No. 2.* Job content is the same as in (3) but workers are located in the main production area.

The changes in productivity resulting from the modifications in job design may be seen in Figure 1. In Group Job Design which eliminated conveyor pacing, productivity fell markedly below the Line Job Design average, indicating how conveyor pacing maintained output. The introduction of Individual Job Design, however, raised productivity above the Group Job Design average.

Although productivity under Individual Job Design did not reach the Line Job Design norm of 100, the level actually achieved is nonetheless impressive in view of the fact that the workers had only six days' experience on Individual Job Design No. 2 (only two days' experience on Individual Job Design No. 1), whereas they had an average of over four years' experience on Line Job Design. Moreover, the daily averages shown in Figure 1 do not reflect the trend resulting from consecutive days of experience with the modified job designs since workers were assigned to the experimental designs on an overlapping basis. The data given in Figure 2, however, showing the average output of the whole group for *each successive day* of the trial period, indicate that the trend was consistently upward and that, on the sixth day, the group achieved an average productivity *higher* than that reached under Line Job Design.

An examination of the dispersion of points about the averages in Figure 1 reveals an even more significant result. The narrow dispersion about

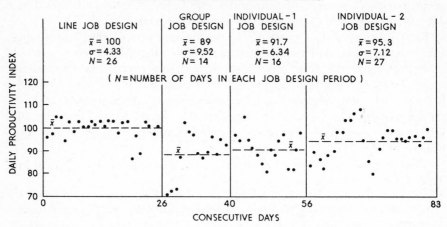

FIGURE 1

AVERAGE DAILY PRODUCTIVITY INDEXES

the average for Line Job Design reflects the fixed work pace imposed by the line—workers could not deviate from this pace unless there were absences on the line. On the other hand, when the workers set their own pace, individual differences came into play, as indicated by the wide

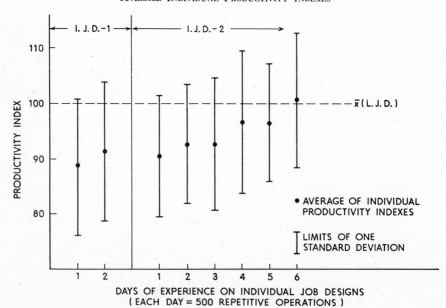

FIGURE 2

AVERAGE INDIVIDUAL PRODUCTIVITY INDEXES

dispersion about the average for the three experimental designs, and some individual performances were as much as 30 to 40 per cent higher than the Line Job Design average.

The superiority of the experimental job designs is demonstrated further in the quality data shown in Figure 3. (The number of kinked as-

FIGURE 3

PERCENTAGE OF KINKED ASSEMBLIES IN CONSECUTIVE LOTS

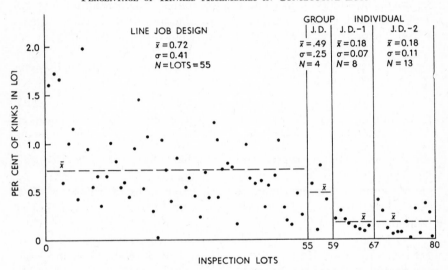

INSPECTION LOTS

semblies produced gave a direct measure of workmanship since the quality of parts and sub-assemblies was not involved.) Beginning with a high level of quality under Line Job Design, quality levels rose with the removal of conveyor pacing. Under Individual Job Design, when responsibility for quality was placed in the hands of the workers, quality levels rose still higher, kinked assemblies dropping to one-fourth of the original value.

It was concluded that Individual Job Design, besides bringing about improvements in productivity and quality, had:

1. Increased the flexibility of the production process.
2. Permitted identification of individual deficiencies in productivity and quality.
3. Reduced the service functions of the department such as materials delivery and inspection.
4. Developed a more favorable attitude toward individual responsibility and effort—after experience with Individual Job Design, workers disliked the lack of personal responsibility characteristic of Line Job Design.

The third piece of research, a study carried out in an Indian textile mill, highlights the importance of the organizational component in job design.[14]

---

[14] A. K. Rice, "Productivity and Social Organization in an Indian Weaving Shed," *Human Relations,* Vol. 6, No. 4, 1954, p. 297.

AN INDIAN TEXTILE MILL

The research problem was posed by the fact that the mill's production was unsatisfactory although new equipment had recently been installed and work loads assigned on the basis of an intensive study by engineers.

In reviewing job designs, it was found that existing worker-machine assignments produced organizational groupings and interaction patterns which mitigated against continuity of production. In one room containing 240 looms, for example, 12 activities were organized as follows:

A weaver tended approximately .... 30 looms
A battery filler .... 50 looms
A smash-hand .... 70 looms
A gater, cloth carrier, jobber, and assistant jobber .... each 112 looms
A bobbin carrier, feeler-motion fitter, oiler, sweeper, and humidification-fitter .... each 224 looms.

Since these activities were highly interdependent, the utmost coordination was required to keep production going.

Each weaver came into contact with five-eighths of a battery filler, three-eighths of a smash-hand, one-quarter of a gater, and one-eighth of a bobbin carrier.

After a study of travel and communication patterns, the work groups were reorganized so that all of the workers who were interdependent became part of the same work group. Each group was then made responsible for the operation and maintenance of a specific bank of looms—a geographic rather than a functional division of the weaving room which produced regular interaction among individuals whose jobs were interrelated. As a result of these changes, efficiency rose from an average of 80 per cent to an average of 95 per cent after 60 working days, and the mean per cent of damage dropped from 32 per cent to 20 per cent. In those parts of the weaving shed where job design remained unchanged, efficiency dropped to 70 per cent, finally rising again to 80, and damage continued at 32 per cent.

SOME BASIC QUESTIONS

The results of these investigations underscore the criticism made earlier of the usual approaches to job design. Relying as it does on extremely narrow criteria, traditional job design has often failed to yield the gains in efficiency which have been anticipated. On the other hand, it has produced a host of *unanticipated* and disturbing secondary effects —monotony, dissatisfaction, resistance, and even obstruction. These failures have often been laid to the "contrariness" of human nature, but this is merely another way of saying that, given the current state of knowledge, the effects of job design are unpredictable.

Yet when jobs have been manipulated or redesigned in order to enlarge job content or personal responsibility, even within a given state of technology, *reduced costs have been reported as well as gains in productivity and morale.* These results could not have been achieved on the basis of the classical theory of job fractionalization.

In short, the traditional concepts and methods of job design have obviously failed to provide satisfactory answers to two fundamental questions:

1. What criteria should guide the design of jobs?

2. What criteria should be used to evaluate the effectiveness of job designs?

If adequate criteria for job design are to be developed, research and experiment toward this end must be based on the following conditions:

1. A recognition of the limitations of the traditional minimum-cost criterion.

2. A new approach to job design which encompasses not only the technical requirements of production but the organizational requirements, the social elements in the work situation (the individual's relationship with fellow workers and with management), and the interaction between the human and the technological imperatives of the job.

3. The formulation of explicit theories of job design which will permit prediction. This requires systematic analysis of how specific changes in job content affect productivity, morale, and other variables.

4. Validation of these theories by experimental evidence gathered under controlled conditions so that causal factors can be identified and general principles established.

A NEW APPROACH

Since many of the flaws in job design can be traced to the inadequacies of the minimum-cost criterion, what is needed is a criterion of *total economic cost* which takes account of the multi-dimensional character of job design and includes relevant long term changes for economic, engineering, organizational, social, psychological, and physiological costs.

To determine how such costs are to be measured poses, of course, some formidable research problems. Among the variables that would have to be measured are the following:

Labor turnover and absenteeism.
Learning time.
Flexibility of work skills.
Quality deficiencies and production bottlenecks associated with job performance.
Grievances and interpersonal conflicts arising out of job and process requirements.
Organizational rigidities.

Service requirements such as supervision and inspection, engineering, maintenance, and personnel services.
Other overhead costs.

These considerations dictate a new approach to job design—the *job-centered approach*—which goes beyond the process-centered and worker-centered approaches. The job-centered approach operates on the premise that a job cannot be adequately designed without taking into account all three of the basic variables—process, worker, and organization—as well as the variables arising from their interaction, and that changing any of these in isolation may affect economic productivity—that is, total economic-cost—adversely.[15]

It is hoped that this approach will point the way for future research and lay the basis for a more satisfactory theory of job design.

THE OUTLOOK FOR RESEARCH

Research and experiment must reflect the multi-dimensional character of job design. While job content remains the focus of research, other variables should be included in experimental designs, and certainly the range of data required is such as to call for a problem-centered, research-team approach by engineers, psychologists, sociologists, anthropologists. economists, and others.

Job design research can be expected to pay off in a number of areas: For management, in re-examining organizational designs, reward systems, control devices, communications, and the administration of the personnel function; for the engineering sciences, in improving design theories and methods in every area—product, process, equipment, plant layout, control systems, and so on; and for the social sciences, in re-evaluating human relations, programs, leadership methods, personnel techniques, communication networks, and organizational design at all levels.

The need for more effective job design, though urgently felt at present, will become even more acute as our economy moves into the era of automation. The introduction of automatic equipment makes rigorous demands on job design theory and methods in determining what processes should be automated, how automation systems should be designed, and how the human links in the control system should be related.

Even where automation is not applicable—and only a small number of jobs relative to the total will actually be transformed by automation—the design of non-automated jobs, either in automated plants or elsewhere, will be a critical factor in maintaining operations and meeting competition.

Hence—despite the popular illusion that automation will solve most

---

[15] L. E. Davis and R. R. Canter, "Job Design," *Journal of Industrial Engineering*, Vol. 6, No. 1, 1955, p. 3. See also, L. R. Sayles, "Human Relations and the Organization of Work," *Michigan Business Review*, November, 1954, p. 21; R. H. Guest, "A Neglected Factor in Labor Turnover," *Occupational Psychology*, October, 1955.

of our problems by making the machines do the work—job design will remain a central problem for industry not only in the area of production and clerical jobs but, in view of the requirements of functional organization, at supervisory and managerial levels as well.

Appendix

DEFINITIONS OF TERMS

1. *Job:* The structure of tasks assigned to an individual together with the work methods and the setting. The *content* of a job comprises the following:
   a. *Work Content:* The assigned series of tasks which arise from the requirements of the technical process or the equipment used or from traditionally established needs.
   b. *Methods Content:* The specification of the ways in which the work activities are to be performed, including tools, equipment, and location. It is often referred to as methods design.
   c. *Organization Content:* The organizational setting in which the assigned tasks are to be carried out—for example, the location of the job in a work group, hierarchical relations, and so on.
   d. *Personal Content:* The factors in the job that affect personal behavior, growth, motivations, etc.

2. *Job Design:* The process of specifying the content of a job (work, methods, organizational, and personal content) in terms of a job definition or a job description.

3. *Total Economic Cost:* The total cost of producing a unit of product or service. In addition to the immediate charges for labor, materials, overhead, and so on, it includes the relevant long-term charges for economic, engineering, organizational, social, psychological, and physiological costs.

4. *Economic Productivity:* Productivity measured on the basis of total economic cost—that is, direct productivity modified by the addition of appropriate overhead or hidden charges stemming from absenteeism, labor turnover, quality failures, inflexibility, and so on.

5. *Minimum Cost:* The cost of producing a unit of product or service which includes only the immediate charges for direct labor, materials, and overhead.

29. Employee Participation in a Program of Industrial Change*

John R. P. French, Jr., Ian C. Ross, S. Kirby, J. R. Nelson, and P. Smyth

SEVERAL YEARS ago the management of a well-known men's apparel manufacturing company decided to modernize its production methods. In the past, programs to improve work methods had often provoked so much

---
* From *Personnel*, Vol. 35, 1958, pp. 16–29.

trouble in management-employee relations that the savings hoped for were largely offset by the costs of conflict. On the other hand, several small changes had been successfully introduced by having the employees participate in their design.[1] However, the modernization program to be reported here differed from these earlier innovations in that it entailed much more extensive change than anything that had been attempted with employee participation in the past. Furthermore, the general lines along which the methods changes were to take place had already been developed by the company's engineering consultants.

Management was aware that the attitudes and feelings of the workers toward the change were a matter of prime concern. It therefore decided to encourage their participation in the change process as much as possible within the limitations of the situation. This article describes how management went about doing this and presents some tangible evidence of the success with which the extended series of changes was carried out. Since few instances of successful plant-wide modifications have been reported in the literature, this account may be helpful to companies contemplating similar far-reaching changes in their present operations.

The changes were scheduled to take place in three of the company's plants, each producing similar garments. These plants are located close enough to each other to be effectively run by one management team. In these plants about 75 per cent of the production workers are women, highly skilled at their jobs. Two of the plants employ about 150 workers each and the third employs about 500. Wages are based on "production units," i.e., the worker is paid according to the number of units produced. While each worker does one small operation in the assembly of the product, there is sufficient work in process at each step for her to be seldom immediately dependent upon the productivity of the preceding operator to keep her pace.

The workers in these plants are represented by a strong, progressive labor union. Important issues of industrial relations are negotiated at the head office of the company, but all ordinary operating problems are usually settled by local management and local union representatives. In general, labor-management relations have been very good, and the fixing of working conditions and specific rates at the local level has proved to be satisfactory.

However, the workers had always manifested great resistance to any change in production methods. The decision to revise them was taken by management as part of its duty to keep the plants modern, progressive, and efficiently run. With rising labor costs, the introduction of labor-saving processes had become mandatory; otherwise, the company would

---

[1] For the story of these earlier changes, see L. Coch and J. R. P. French, Jr., "Overcoming Resistance to Change," *Human Relations*, Vol. 1, No. 4, 1948, pp. 512–32. Reprinted in D. Cartwright and A. Zander (eds.), *Group Dynamics: Research and Theory* (Evanston, Ill.: Row Peterson, 1953).

not be able to maintain its competitive position. Its competitors had already begun to change their manufacturing methods, and were introducing a continuous-flow form of production in place of the older batch process.

AIMS OF THE PROGRAM

The re-engineering program had these objectives: (1) to reduce the in-process inventory and to shorten the length of time it took to complete a particular garment; (2) to attain more flexible control of production; (3) to reduce manufacturing costs by introducing semi-automatic flow procedures; and (4) to improve the quality of the garments by better care of the material during manufacture.

The major innovation involved the transport of each batch of garments from station to station. Heretofore, each operator had obtained her work from a centrally located rack, returning the batch to the same rack when her job was done. The proposed change provided for more rapid movement of material, along with substantially less handling. Much lifting of the batches of heavy goods was to be eliminated. In several instances, two operations were to be integrated in a short production line. In addition, various work aids were to be introduced for folding, trimming, holding, and directing material. The sequence of operations was also to be rearranged. These changes would have the effect of altering the work of some operators to a considerable extent; others would be affected only by the new system of transporting the material along the assembly line.

In this type of factory, minor changes in methods of performing a job occur quite frequently. Now the differences between minor changes in work methods and major production changes, such as the re-engineering of an entire assembly line, are differences of degree rather than kind. In handling ordinary minor changes the management had firmly adhered to three principles, based partly on a recognition of the psychological factors involved and partly on legal considerations, inasmuch as these principles had gradually been incorporated into the pattern of labor-management relations over the years. The principles in question were: (1) Earning opportunities on the job should not be deliberately reduced for the purpose of adjusting rates which experience had shown to be too generous. In other words, management would carefully avoid actions that appeared to be any kind of disguised rate-cutting. (2) The worker should always be informed of an impending change in the job as soon as it was definitely decided upon. (3) If a change required relearning on the part of the worker, the cost of relearning should be borne wholly or partially by management.

In the case of relatively major changes, it was management's belief that the workers should participate in the definition of the change to the maximum possible extent. Of course, this does not mean that management was prepared to abdicate its responsibility for the growth, development, and operation of the organization. Management alone decided to make the changes in question here and—as has been said—their general nature was determined by management with the help of its engineering consultants.

What is to be gained from employee participation in a program of this kind? Above and beyond the general positive effects on morale and labor-management relations, two highly practical benefits may be noted. First, the technical program develops more rapidly. Any problems encountered by the workers are early brought to management's attention so that adjustments can be made with a minimum of delay. The workers' suggestions can be incorporated into the new procedure before a scheme of payments is fixed. Through participation, it is possible to head off any misunderstandings that might arise. This helps to avoid any deliberate obstruction of the new system by the workers.

The second advantage of having the employees participate is that the new method becomes the brain child of the workers themselves. Its success gives them a feeling of pride and accomplishment. Their very desire not to fail at their own project exerts a major influence on its success.

Participation is also a form of communication. When a man's job has been changed, some of his skill becomes obsolete and it is easy for him to view management as frustrating him, and as unjustly and even hostilely cutting his earning opportunities. If management's reasons for the change are not hostile but are actually for the good of all concerned, the worker's participation in planning for the innovation is an appropriate way of explaining it to him and letting him know the real reasons for it.

One form of participation is interactive discussion between management and the workers. This type of discussion gives management the opportunity to communicate and to be challenged at the same time. Of course, where communication is only one way and the workers merely listen politely, no participation takes place at all. A minimum requirement of participative discussion is that the workers should ask questions and that management should answer them in a straightforward and honest way. Furthermore, the workers must feel free to raise important issues —questions that are perhaps impolite and that recognize the possibility of conflict between management and the workers. Discussions are not participative if the workers have no real opportunity to speak up. It should be added that "opportunity" in this sense is not merely a matter of providing adequate meeting time coupled with a polite request for questions. Management must deem it proper for the workers to ask hard questions at such meetings—and the workers must have the assurance that no reprisals will be taken against frank discussion. (In passing, it may be suggested that participation may perhaps be more readily obtained from workers in unionized shops because the employees feel that they have the union to fall back on.)

Admittedly, interactive discussion is a minimal form of participation. Naturally, it is better to have the workers actually share in designing the change, if this is possible. When, as in this case, the nature of the problem calls for skilled engineering, employee participation must necessarily take a more limited form.

Nevertheless, the main benefit of participation can be achieved even when there are practical limits as to how far the employees can actually contribute to the change. The goal is to have the workers feel that they are truly part of the company, that in some sense it is their enterprise as well, and that they are as dependent upon and responsible for its success as management is. But unless management really believes that the workers have such a place in the organization, it is extremely difficult, if not impossible, to communicate this message to them. Management must begin by considering the workers to be an integral part of the enterprise. This is a basic condition—without it, participation cannot be attained.

HOW THE CHANGE WAS INTRODUCED

At the outset, the precise changes to be introduced in the re-engineering of the production lines were not known; these were to be worked out experimentally within the plants. The methods proposed were as yet unproved; nevertheless, they offered great promise, and it was decided to develop them in the two smaller plants first. This strategy was based on various considerations—some technical, others having to do with employee morale. On the technical side, simpler and more standardized items were produced in the smaller plants. Since these two plants accounted for a smaller proportion of the firm's total output than the large plant, less risk was involved should serious production delays be encountered during the changeover. It was also felt that there was more personal communication between management and workers in the smaller plants. Furthermore, since the large plant had intra-union difficulties, the small plants were considered less sensitive places in which to try out the rather fundamental changes contemplated.

GROUP MEETINGS

The program was introduced to the workers by a series of meetings. Each group of operators performing the same operation in the same plant met with the local plant management. In the course of the program, approximately 80 such meetings were held, the number of workers attending varying from one to eight. When there were only a few workers on a particular operation, they were accompanied to the meeting by the shop steward.

At the first meeting, the proposed change in methods was announced and its general objectives were stated. Emphasis was placed on the need for the change and the importance of the program to both the company and the workers. The relationship of the company's success to steady employment was pointed out. No technical details were presented at this time, but the workers were assured that while the new methods were being developed their incomes would continue at the average level of the preceding six weeks. They were also told that when the new system was working well enough, new rates would be established and that a subsidy fund was being set up to help maintain their incomes until their skills were fully re-adapted. Frank discussion of these matters by all participants was encouraged.

Immediately after the initial meeting, things began to happen on the production floor. Machines were moved; new devices and small carts appeared. Experts gave demonstrations and instructions to individual workers in the new procedures. Engineers and supervisors watched, asked questions, and answered them. This gradual and outwardly tentative introduction of the changes was a deliberate policy. Only a few workers at a time were given revised tasks. Usually, it took several weeks before the whole garment was being made by the new methods.

Problems were solved as they arose. Many informal discussions of the new methods took place between engineers, supervisors, and workers. As the new methods were mastered, additional changes were made, sometimes at the suggestion of management, but often at the prompting of the workers themselves.

After the new system had been in effect long enough to be stable and was operating with some smoothness, another series of small group meetings was called to discuss revised wage rates. Separate meetings were held for each group of workers who were doing the same job in the same plant and who would experience the same changes in rates and the same revision of work procedures. After the workers were thanked for their help in developing the new system, they were given an explanation of how a time study had been applied to their jobs, along with the time allotted for each part of their operation. Time studies had been carried out on both the old and new systems, and this means of arriving at standards of time and pay was fully explained. While this technical discussion may have been beyond the understanding of many employees, its primary purpose was to show that management was not trying to hide anything, and that a rational method had been used to determine the new rates.

THE SUBSIDY PROGRAM

At these meetings, management also said that the new rates would go into effect shortly and that the subsidy program promised at the first meeting would now start. The initial subsidy ranged from 10 per cent for those jobs which involved only minor changes to 65 per cent for those with the greatest changes. These amounts were decreased by 5 per cent each week until the subsidy ended.

In addition to protecting earnings during the readjustment period, the subsidy was also an indication of management's opinion as to how fast workers should recover a normal level of productivity after the disturbing effect of the change. The gradual reduction of the subsidy and its eventual termination was intended to provide a financial incentive for the workers to regain their normal production as soon as possible.

Many operators expressed satisfaction with the new rates. Some quickly did enough work in one day to attain their expected earnings. Others had obviously been holding back their production until the new rates were announced; when they saw that their earning opportunities had been protected and preserved, they, too, quickly recovered their former level of productivity. Although there were some expressions of dissatisfaction with the new scale, discussion of this was postponed until after the subsidy program had been given a chance to operate.

The workers also raised a great many complaints at these meetings, not all of which had anything to do with the new system. There were complaints about equipment, inaccurate cutting of parts, and other mechanical difficulties which are regularly experienced in factories. Management listened carefully and promised to investigate. This pledge was kept and the difficulties were subsequently remedied. (In a sense, these complaints were a favorable measure of the extent to which management was able to create a participative atmosphere. The workers did complain; they accused management of many shortcomings, and management on its part accepted the complaints as matters that merited its attention.)

The meetings at which the new rates were announced were the last such get-togethers for most operators. However, management continued to hold individual consultations on the production floor and to listen attentively to complaints. Problems and difficulties presented by the new methods were talked over and ironed out. A senior operator was given the job of interviewing other operators to find out what problems they have having and how they felt about the change. Through this channel management became aware of some technical problems that had not been raised at the meetings or during those times when its representatives were available on the production floor. By taking the initiative in establishing communication with the workers involved, management was able to solve these problems also.

After the new system had been developed and refined in the smaller plants, and the workers there were well on the way to reaching their former level of productivity, the change was finally introduced into the third and largest plant. The same methods of introducing the change were used here, but by now, of course, management was able to point to many examples of proven success with the new methods in the smaller plants. Development work in the third plant was limited to conditions arising from the manufacture of the many special items produced there.

The whole change was carried out much more rapidly than in the other plants because the best procedures had already been worked out and most of the rates had been set.

REACTIONS TO THE NEW SYSTEM

After the rates were announced, there were two instances where a few workers tried to prove them unfair by deliberately restricting production. But most of the workers responded well to the innovations, gradually raising their output to satisfactory levels. In the two cases of deliberate restriction of production, a satisfactory recovery of output has not yet been achieved. These involved two machine operations performed by groups of four and six women respectively. One operator in each group made a satisfactory recovery. It is worth noting that each was the only one in her group who had thought the rate was fair when it was proposed. Though these two women were able to resist considerable group pressure on them to hold down their production, their successful examples were insufficient to win over their co-workers to their point of view. Management finally had to make adjustments on these rates so that its policy of maintaining earning opportunities might not appear to have been contradicted. The benefits of these adjustments have also accrued to the two productive operators, but at this writing the others are still limping along, still convinced that the new system has drastically cut down their earning power.

These two very similar instances were about the only ones in which the new method was not accepted. While they were only a small flaw in an otherwise resounding success, they emphasize the importance of the proper initial presentation of a program of change, and show how firmly people cling to their original reactions to it.

There were, of course, noteworthy examples of a happier kind. Thus, the job of an older worker with almost 10 years' experience under the old system was completely changed, and for a long time her attitude was one of discouragement and hopelessness. However, thanks to the correct engineering of the rate for her new job, coupled with continuous attention and encouragement from her supervisor, and a substantial relearning pay adjustment, her job improvement was constant. A year later, her earnings were higher than ever before and she was able to look back on her period of hopelessness with equanimity.

In any such change as this, the engineering problems are so complicated that it is impossible to present a uniform picture of future experience to the workers. Some will meet genuine difficulties, others will find difficulties where none exist; some will be better off, and some but not all of these will know that things are better. The success of the whole operation depends upon the distribution of these partly psychological assessments. If management has been honest, has done its computations fairly, and spoken openly, there should be enough successes to carry the operation to a good conclusion. Otherwise, difficulties and negative re-actions will be so widespread that the entire project can result in failure.

At this point, it may be pertinent to present some rather more tangible evidence of the success with which these plant changes were introduced. This evidence takes the form of "before and after" records of produc-tivity, turnover, and grievances in the three plants in question.

PRODUCTIVITY AND TURNOVER

Of these three indices, productivity is, of course, the most direct meas-ure of the degree of adjustment to change. In calculating productivity, workers producing the same item in the same plant were considered to have experienced the same change process. Since, in the two smaller plants, there were changes in the production of one item apiece, while two items were re-engineered in the larger plant, this gave us four groups, large enough to be statistically stable, whose productivity before and after the change could be compared.

The average productivity of these four groups for two six-week pe-riods, one immediately before the change was introduced, and the other one year later, is shown in Table 1. (It should be added that only those

TABLE 1

AVERAGE PRODUCTION BEFORE AND AFTER RE-ENGINEERING

WORKER GROUP		AVERAGE PRODUCTION IN STANDARD UNITS	
Plant	Item	Base Period	One Year Later*
1	A	79	76
2	B	67	75
3	A	79	80
3	B	69	75

* The base periods differ for the several groups, being the six weeks just prior to the start of the change. In each case, the one year later is the same six week period of the next year.

workers who were still in the same plant and working on the same item are included in these figures. However, the average of all workers em-ployed in the latter period is only slightly below that shown for workers who were employed both before and after the change.)

As will be seen, a year after the changes had been made, the general level of productivity had increased by about 10 per cent on Item B and stayed essentially the same on Item A. There was also a substantial gain of about 10 per cent less direct-labor costs on each item because of the engineering improvements.

While to some extent the changes involved the substitution of capital equipment for direct labor, the capital costs were modest in relation to the savings in labor costs.

It should be stressed that, thanks to a market for additional production, the workers were able to maintain their incomes even though direct-labor costs were being substantially reduced. New jobs were rated so that the workers could earn as much as before; and the change was introduced in such a way that the workers' motivation to produce was not disturbed.

Besides providing information about the final recovery of earnings, production statistics may also be used to chart the pattern with which that recovery took place. As had been expected, when the new methods were introduced there was an immediate and drastic decline in production. The program of subsidies was designed to maintain the workers' incomes as long as their production did not drop to an unreasonably low level, and modest progress was made each week. The expectations upon which the subsidy program was based are generally justified by the production curves shown in Figure 1.

As the figure shows, in three cases there was an initial drop and then a general upward trend toward the previous level of output. The trends are generally upward; the slight drops can be attributed to the normal fluctuation associated with different fabrics and other usual sources of variations in output. In the fourth case—Item A in Plant 1—production was more erratic in its progress toward recovery. This may be attributed to the fact that the new methods were first developed on this operation and there were a number of special difficulties to be overcome. It is interesting to note that the fluctuations were least for Item A in Plant 3, the last operation to be changed. This would seem to indicate that the methods for introducing change had become routine and that their acceptance was less of a problem here.

The production records shown in Figure 1 are for all employees of moderate experience regardless of whether or not they worked in the base period before the changes were made. This accounts for the difference in the "one year later" results between Figure 1 and Table 1.

The second check on the success of the re-engineering process is provided by turnover statistics. It may be assumed that if the new methods were unsatisfactory to the employees, more than the normal number would leave in the period immediately following the changes, either because of dissatisfaction with their new earnings or because they felt frustrated in other ways. *No such increase in turnover occurred.* In fact, the turnover rate continued to decline right through the period of change. Table 2 shows the turnover rate by plants in terms of the ratio of resignations for 12 months to the average number on the payroll during the year.

It may be added that absenteeism also decreased during the period of the change. Since absenteeism and turnover are both generally regarded as indicators of frustration and dissatisfaction and neither increased during the period of the change, it may be assumed that the change was introduced without serious effects on morale.

TABLE 2

TURNOVER RATES BY YEAR

YEAR	PLANT 1	PLANT 2	PLANT 3
1952	*	*	.703
1953	*	*	.623
1954	.618	.398	.320
1955	.545	.291	.282
1956	.380	.243	.248

* Data not available.

Note—The changes were begun late in 1954 and were completed in the first part of 1956.

THE GRIEVANCE RECORD

One remedy open to employees who are dissatisfied with their earnings is to file a rate grievance. Complaints about rates are, of course, sometimes due to causes other than dissatisfaction over money; but probably more than the usual number of rate grievances can be expected after any change in which a great many new rates are set.

Because of constant changes in styles and fabrics, as well as various minor alterations in the specifications of the garments being produced, the company has always had a fair number of rate grievances. However, after the change these increased quite substantially over the totals recorded for previous years. As can be seen from Table 3, there was an

TABLE 3

NUMBER OF GRIEVANCES BY PLANT, TYPE, AND YEAR

PLANT	TYPE	1953	1954	1955	1956	1957 (5 mos.)
1	Rate	1	0	1	8	3
	Non-rate	0	0	0	3	0
2	Rate	1	0	4	21	3
	Non-rate	1	0	4	5	2
3	Rate	4	9	8	21	7
	Non-rate	24	31	16	14	11
	Total	31	40	33	72	26
All	Rate	6	9	13	50	13
	Non-rate	25	31	20	22	13

Note—The changes were begun late in 1954 and were completed in the first part of 1956.

increase in all plants after the new method had been in operation for some time.

Though, on the face of it, the 50 rate grievances recorded in 1956 would seem to indicate considerable dissatisfaction with earnings after

FIGURE 1

Productivity after the Change

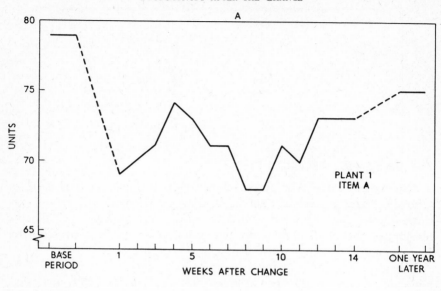

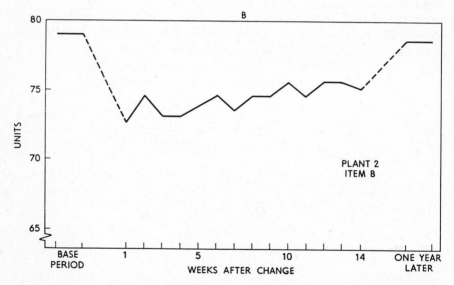

the change, it must be remembered that approximately 1,300 rate changes were made. Compared with this total, the number of grievances may well be small. Nevertheless, it seems large when set against the usual number of complaints. However, many of these grievances were actually about long-standing issues which were again brought to the fore during the installation of the new system. Unfortunately, the record does not show how many separate issues lay behind the new grievances since, in

FIGURE 1 (Continued)

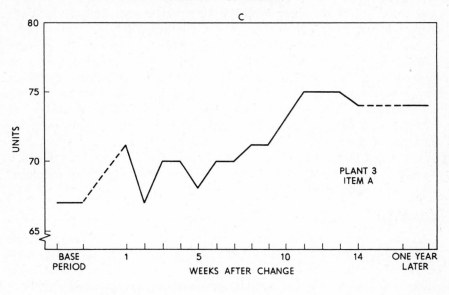

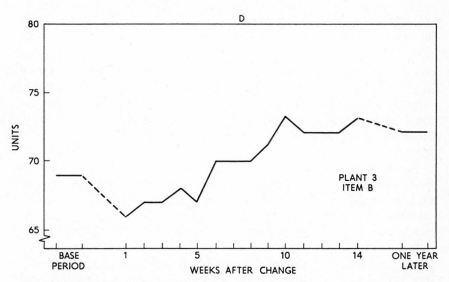

resolving them, one decision generally settled many complaints. Also, the number of grievances includes complaints about the same issues that arose in more than one plant. Without going into an extended analysis of the precise nature of the grievances, it is impossible even to estimate the number of separate issues involved. It is best, therefore, to consider their significance not in terms of the number of grievances filed but rather according to the manner in which they were settled.

Disposing of the grievances called for intensive joint work between the company and union engineers. Most of the rates checked by the union were left at the same level set by management. In the few cases where management's figures were not confirmed by the union study, principles were agreed upon which increased the rates by 8 per cent. This amount was considered small since most of the increased rates were on special styles of garments and were connected with controversies that had arisen in principle before the re-engineering project began. In only two instances were the new rates adjusted on regular products.

In management's opinion, the number of grievances was not excessive in view of the number of new rates that had been set and the kind of issues raised in the majority of the complaints. The negotiations which settled most of the grievances were amicable and an acknowledgment of management's honest intentions.

SUMMARY

The radical change in production methods described here brought about results that were highly gratifying to management. The cost of production was reduced; a better product was turned out; production time was shortened; and productive capacity was expanded without heavy overhead charges. Since the plants were highly engineered before the changes were effected, these gains cannot be attributed to any lack of efficiency earlier. These were substantial accomplishments which taken by themselves certainly justified the program. However, the achievements in the company's labor-management relations were also highly gratifying. To management the minimal nature of the difficulties met with during the change was at least as noteworthy as the economic gains. Indeed, the company's heads believe that the economic success could not have been obtained without the accomplishments in labor-management relations.

In addition to a sound beginning in production engineering, management attributes the program's success to the policies which it followed with its employees. These might be summarized as an honest attempt to maximize the participation of the workers in the change. Management considered the workers as part of the enterprise, with an interest in its success, and with the right to expect fair treatment. Hence management's plans were disclosed as early as possible before unfounded rumors got started, the workers' ideas were given attention, and their problems with new methods were investigated. In addition, their earning opportunities were protected and any economic loss brought about by the new methods was properly compensated for. Moreover, management was careful not to inspire resistance to the change by any action which appeared to be provocative.

Throughout the whole process, management did not lose sight of its right to make the changes it contemplated, but it was equally aware of what the changes meant to the employees. Basically, management laid down a policy of fairness and openness and stuck to it. The results continue to be highly satisfactory.

30. An Index of Job Satisfaction*

Arthur H. Brayfield and Harold F. Rothe

INCREASINGLY, BUSINESS and industrial concerns are studying the job satisfaction and morale of their employees. It has been recognized that the effectiveness of selection, training, and supervisory programs should be gauged in part by their effect on employees' satisfaction with their work and that specific personnel techniques and procedures should be validated against a job satisfaction criterion. Unfortunately, adequate indices of job satisfaction are difficult to obtain. This report describes the construction and validation of a quantitative index of job satisfaction which has been used as a criterion measure in subsequent personnel studies to be reported elsewhere.

CONSTRUCTION

A careful survey of the literature reveals that attempts to identify and estimate job satisfaction have preceded precise definition. Employee satisfaction and morale are often equated but seldom defined.[1] Hull and Kolstad aptly summarize the state of affairs: "Although the term 'employee morale' is widely used, it remains a more or less undefined concept whose meaning, usually, is simply taken for granted. Such definitions as have been offered are of little help to the psychologist in the construction of items designed to measure morale. Thus it was (is) necessary to proceed on the basis of subjective judgment."[2]

As a working approach for this study it was assumed that job satisfaction could be inferred from the individual's attitude toward his work. This approach dictated the methodology—attitude scaling.

An attitude scale elicits an expression of feeling toward an object. It may be used directly with an individual to obtain such an expression. It permits quantification of the expression of feeling. These characteristics suggest the utility of attitude scaling methodology in developing an index of job satisfaction.

---

* From *Journal of Applied Psychology*, Vol. 35, No. 5, 1951, pp. 307–11.

[1] A. Kornhauser, "Psychological Studies of Employee Morale," *Journal of Consulting Psychology*, Vol. 4, 1944, pp. 127–43.

[2] R. L. Hull and A. Kolstad, "Morale on the Job," in G. Watson (ed.), *Civilian Morale* (New York: Reynal and Hitchcock, 1942), p. 350.

The following requirements were formulated as desirable attributes of an attitude scale designed to provide a useful index of job satisfaction:

1. It should give an index to "over-all" job satisfaction rather than to specific aspects of the job situation.
2. It should be applicable to a wide variety of jobs.
3. It should be sensitive to variations in attitude.
4. The items should be of such a nature (interesting, realistic, and varied) that the scale would evoke cooperation from both management and employees.
5. It should yield a reliable index.
6. It should yield a valid index.
7. It should be brief and easily scored.

At the time this study was undertaken the two most widely known and used attitude scaling techniques were those of Thurstone[3] and Likert.[4] Initially the choice between them was made on the basis of a practical consideration. Since it would have been extremely difficult to obtain employed persons as subjects for the item analysis required by the Likert technique, the Thurstone method was chosen. The latter method requires a number of judges to sort items. On the basis of other studies it was assumed that employed persons were not necessarily required as judges but that almost any mature person could make a judgment regarding the "value" of a statement on an attitude continuum regardless of his own job situation.[5]

The construction of this scale was made a class project in Personnel Psychology[6] for members of an Army Specialized Training Program in personnel psychology at the University of Minnesota in the summer and fall of 1943. Seventy-seven men cooperated. Their average age was around 30 years. The majority had had at least several years occupational experience ranging from unskilled labor to professional occupations. The number of judges appears adequate.[7]

The class was given instructions similar to those outlined by Thurstone for the construction of items. Approximately 1,000 statements were turned in by the class and an additional 75 by the investigators.

---

[3] L. L. Thurstone and E. J. Chave, *The Measurement of Attitude* (Chicago: University of Chicago Press, 1929).

[4] R. Likert, *A Technique for the Measurement of Attitudes,* Archives of Psychology, No. 140 (New York: Columbia University, 1932).

[5] E. B. Hinckley, "The Influence of Individual Opinion on Construction of an Attitude Scale," *Journal of Social Psychology,* Vol. 3, 1932, pp. 283–96; R. Pintner and G. Forlano, "The Influence of Attitude upon Scaling of Attitude Items," *Journal of Social Psychology,* Vol. 8, 1937, pp. 39–45.

[6] Class time was made available for this project through the cooperation of Dr. H. P. Longstaff.

[7] G. H. Nystrom, "The Measurement of Filipino Attitudes toward America by Use of the Thurstone Technique," *Journal of Social Psychology,* Vol. 4, 1933, pp. 249–52; R. S. Uhrbrock, "Attitudes of 4,430 Employees," *Journal of Social Psychology,* Vol. 5, 1934, pp. 368–77.

This collection was edited and the resulting 246 statements were mimeographed, sorted into sets, and distributed to the ASTP men for judging. Each judge sorted the statements under supervision according to the instructions suggested by Thurstone. After tabulating the results the scale and the Q values for each statement were determined graphically. Careful checks were made for accuracy.

Four specific criteria determined the inclusion or exclusion of items for the preliminary scale. First, it was desired to have items covering the entire range of the attitude continuum at approximately .5 step intervals although the statements at the ends of the continuum were eliminated as being too extreme to be practical. Second, the Q value, which is based on the degree of uniformity in the sorting of statements, was used as an objective measure of ambiguity in accordance with Thurstone's recommendations. Consequently no item was selected which had a Q value of 2.00 or above. Third, from a purely subjective appraisal by the investigators, items were judged as to specificity. Items referring to specific aspects of a job were eliminated since an "over-all" attitudinal factor was desired; thus items regarding pay, working conditions, etc., were eliminated even though it might be argued that they reflect a general attitude. Finally, acceptability to employees and management as judged by the investigators and management representatives was a criterion. For example, the item "I am tempted to use illness as an excuse to stay home from this job" was typical of those rejected because they seemed to reflect unfavorably upon the individual.

Next a preliminary scale containing eighteen selected statements was administered to 10 employed female office workers and a rank order correlation was computed for the odd versus even items paired according to Thurstone's directions. The resulting rho was .31 which was converted to an estimated product moment r and boosted by the Spearman-Brown formula to .48.

This finding indicated a shift in method. Since Likert had found that his method of scoring attitude scales gave a higher reliability than Thurstone's, his scoring technique was adopted and a second experimental scale was developed.[8]

As a result of experience with the preliminary administration, additional comments of management, and to replace two "neutral" items 9 new items were substituted. The resulting blank contained 18 items with Thurstone scale values ranging from 1.2 to 10.0 with approximately .5 step intervals. The items were not arranged in order of magnitude of scale values. The Likert scoring system consisting of five categories of agreement-disagreement was applied to each item. From the Thurstone scale value it was known in what direction to apply the new scoring

---

[8] R. Likert, S. Roslow, and G. Murphy, "A Simple and Reliable Method of Scoring the Thurstone Scales," *Journal of Social Psychology*, Vol. 5, 1934, pp. 228–38.

method so that a low total score would represent the dissatisfied end of the scale and a high total score the satisfied end. The items were selected so that the satisfied end of the scale was indicated by *Strongly Agree* and *Agree* for one-half the items and by *Strongly Disagree* and *Disagree* for the other half. The neutral response was *Undecided*. The Likert scoring weights for each item ranged from 1 to 5 and the range of possible total scores now became 18 to 90 with the undecided or neutral point at 54.

FIGURE 1

REVISED JOB SATISFACTION BLANK

JOB QUESTIONNAIRE

Some jobs are more interesting and satisfying than others. We want to know how people feel about different jobs. This blank contains eighteen statements about jobs. You are to cross out the phrase below each statement which best describes how you feel about your present job. There are no right or wrong answers. We should like your honest opinion on each one of the statements. Work out the sample item numbered (0).

0. There are some conditions concerning my job that could be improved.
   STRONGLY AGREE   AGREE   UNDECIDED   DISAGREE   STRONGLY DISAGREE
1. My job is like a hobby to me.
   STRONGLY AGREE   AGREE   UNDECIDED   DISAGREE   STRONGLY DISAGREE
2. My job is usually interesting enough to keep me from getting bored.
   STRONGLY AGREE   AGREE   UNDECIDED   DISAGREE   STRONGLY DISAGREE
3. It seems that my friends are more interested in their jobs.
   STRONGLY AGREE   AGREE   UNDECIDED   DISAGREE   STRONGLY DISAGREE
4. I consider my job rather unpleasant.
   STRONGLY AGREE   AGREE   UNDECIDED   DISAGREE   STRONGLY DISAGREE
5. I enjoy my work more than my leisure time.
   STRONGLY AGREE   AGREE   UNDECIDED   DISAGREE   STRONGLY DISAGREE
6. I am often bored with my job.
   STRONGLY AGREE   AGREE   UNDECIDED   DISAGREE   STRONGLY DISAGREE
7. I feel fairly well satisfied with my present job.
   STRONGLY AGREE   AGREE   UNDECIDED   DISAGREE   STRONGLY DISAGREE
8. Most of the time I have to force myself to go to work.
   STRONGLY AGREE   AGREE   UNDECIDED   DISAGREE   STRONGLY DISAGREE
9. I am satisfied with my job for the time being.
   STRONGLY AGREE   AGREE   UNDECIDED   DISAGREE   STRONGLY DISAGREE
10. I feel that my job is no more interesting than others I could get.
    STRONGLY AGREE   AGREE   UNDECIDED   DISAGREE   STRONGLY DISAGREE
11. I definitely dislike my work.
    STRONGLY AGREE   AGREE   UNDECIDED   DISAGREE   STRONGLY DISAGREE
12. I feel that I am happier in my work than most other people.
    STRONGLY AGREE   AGREE   UNDECIDED   DISAGREE   STRONGLY DISAGREE
13. Most days I am enthusiastic about my work.
    STRONGLY AGREE   AGREE   UNDECIDED   DISAGREE   STRONGLY DISAGREE
14. Each day of work seems like it will never end.
    STRONGLY AGREE   AGREE   UNDECIDED   DISAGREE   STRONGLY DISAGREE
15. I like my job better than the average worker does.
    STRONGLY AGREE   AGREE   UNDECIDED   DISAGREE   STRONGLY DISAGREE
16. My job is pretty uninteresting.
    STRONGLY AGREE   AGREE   UNDECIDED   DISAGREE   STRONGLY DISAGREE
17. I find real enjoyment in my work.
    STRONGLY AGREE   AGREE   UNDECIDED   DISAGREE   STRONGLY DISAGREE
18. I am disappointed that I ever took this job.
    STRONGLY AGREE   AGREE   UNDECIDED   DISAGREE   STRONGLY DISAGREE

The new scale was administered to 8 additional employed female office workers and a rank order correlation computed for the odd versus even items. The resulting rho of .61 was converted to an estimated product-moment r and boosted by the Spearman-Brown formula to .77. This was believed to be satisfactory for further experimentation and the revised scale was then printed (see Figure 1).

RELIABILITY

The revised scale was administered subsequently as part of a larger study to 231 employed female office employees in positions including entry, typing and stenographic, low and high skill level machine clerical, and accounting jobs. The blanks were signed along with other test materials. One of the investigators personally administered the tests to employees in small groups. Typically, the subjects were young, unmarried girls without dependents. The average girl in the sample had completed 12 years of schooling. She had been on her present job for more than one year and had been employed by the company for one and three-fourths years. The range of job satisfaction scores for this sample was 35–87. The mean score was 63.8 with an S.D. of 9.4.

The odd-even product moment reliability coefficient computed for this sample was .77 which was corrected by the Spearman-Brown formula to .87.

VALIDITY

The nature of the individual items is partial, although not crucial, evidence for the validity of the scale. This is an appeal to "face" validity.

Additional evidence of a like nature is furnished by the method of constructing the scale. In developing the scale an attitude variable was specified. This was job satisfaction which was to be inferred from verbal reactions to a job expressed along a favorable-unfavorable continuum. The statements used in this scale uniformly had small Q values which indicates a marked consistency among the judges. With the attitude variable specified, 77 adult judges were consistent in saying, "This statement expresses a feeling of satisfaction or dissatisfaction with a job and should be placed at such and such a point along such a feeling continuum."

A more rigorous requirement for validation is to use an outside criterion. An attempt was made to provide such a criterion. The job satisfaction blank was administered to 91 adult night school students in classes in Personnel Psychology at the University of Minnesota[9] during 1945 and 1946. Responses were anonymous. The group included 49 males and 42 females. The age range was from 22 to 54 with a median of 35 years. Practically the entire membership was engaged in either

---

[9] These subjects were made available through the cooperation of Dr. H. P. Longstaff.

clerical, semi-professional and professional, or managerial and supervisory occupations. The range of job satisfaction scores for this sample was 29–89. The mean score was 70.4 with an S.D. of 13.2.

The common denominator for the members of this sample was their enrollment in an evening class in Personnel Psychology. *Enrollment in the class was considered to be an overt expression of their interest in personnel work.* Some indication of the strength of this interest is afforded by their continued attendance in a night class (after a full day's work) for a full semester at the end of which time the blank was administered.

Given this circumstance, the following assumption may be made: Those persons in the class employed in occupations *appropriate* to their expressed interest should, on the average, be more satisfied with their jobs than those members of the class employed in occupations *inappropriate* to their expressed interest in personnel work.

This assumption seemed reasonable to the investigators and provided a test of the validity of the job satisfaction blank.

The 91 persons accordingly were divided into two groups (Personnel and Non-Personnel) with respect to their employment in a position identified by pay-roll title as a personnel function. Four occupationally unidentified persons were placed arbitrarily in the Non-Personnel group. In all, 40 persons comprised the Personnel group; 51 the Non-Personnel. A comparison was then made between the mean scores for the two groups on the job satisfaction blank. The mean for the Personnel group was 76.9 with an S.D. of 8.6 as compared to a mean of 65.4 with an S.D. of 14.02 for the Non-Personnel group. This difference of 11.5 points is significant at the 1% level; the difference between the variances also is significant at the 1% level. Since Fisher and Behren's *d*-test is appropriate when significant differences are found both between two means and their respective variances, it was applied and the difference between the means was found to be significant at the 5% level.[10] Sukhatme's tables give only the 5% level values.

If the original assumption as to the differential significance of membership in one or the other of the two groups is accepted, these data furnish evidence for the validity of the job satisfaction blank.

COMPARISON WITH THE HOPPOCK BLANK

Perhaps the most systematic attempt to develop an index of job satisfaction was the one made by Hoppock in the early 1930's.[11] Originally Hoppock tried out a series of simple attitude scales as part of an interviewing study of 40 employed adults. These scales were revised to consist of four items each with seven responses at step intervals. Values of

---

[10] P. V. Sukhatme, "On Fisher and Behren's Test of Significance for the Difference in Means of Two Normal Samples," *Sankhya: The Indian Journal of Statistics*, Vol. 4, 1938, pp. 39–48.

[11] R. Hoppock, *Job Satisfaction* (New York: Harper and Brothers, 1935).

1 to 7 were assigned arbitrarily to the responses in each item, the smaller numbers being assigned to the responses indicating dissatisfaction. The range of possible total scores was 4 to 28. This system of scoring correlated .997 for 301 cases with a system of scale values assigned on the basis of z-scores. The corrected split-half reliability coefficient for the scale for the same 301 cases was reported to be .93. The scale evidently has been assumed to have "face" validity.

The night school classes completed both blanks. The product-moment correlation between scores on the Hoppock blank (Form 11) and on the Brayfield-Rothe blank was .92. Although the two blanks were developed by different methods and contain items which over-lap only slightly they give results which are highly correlated.

A comparison was made between the means of the Personnel and Non-Personnel groups on the Hoppock blank. The mean for the Personnel group was 22.2 with an S.D. of 2.6; the mean for the Non-Personnel group was 19.2 with an S.D. of 4.0. The difference between the means is significant at the 1% level; the variances do not differ significantly.

SUMMARY

An attitude scale which purports to be an index of job satisfaction was constructed by a combination of Thurstone and Likert scaling methods. A reliability coefficient of .87 was obtained for one large group. Evidence for the high validity of the blank rests upon the nature of the items, the method of construction, and its differentiating power when applied to two groups which could reasonably be assumed to differ in job satisfaction. Scores on this blank were highly correlated with scores on the Hoppock blank in the sample studied.

31. Some Definitions of Morale*

Robert M. Guion

THE PURPOSE OF this article is to discuss various definitions of the term "morale." There is some confusion in how the term "morale" is used, so it seems useful to review this problem and to clarify some of the meanings attached to this concept, leaving aside related terms such as "job satisfaction," and "job attitudes."

* From "Industrial Morale (A Symposium) 1. The Problem of Terminology," *Personnel Psychology*, Vol. 11, 1958, pp. 59–61. This symposium was presented at the 1957 Chicago Meetings of the Midwestern Psychological Association.

Smith[1] in his recent text, leaves out the word "morale" but has used the term "job satisfaction," another term of many meanings. He seems to mean something much more personal and dynamic than is usually meant when this term is used. Many readers will feel that his discussion under this heading is really a discussion of morale, but one which avoids the definitional limb that those who write about "morale" find themselves on. Blum,[2] however, insists that the concepts of morale and of job satisfaction are different and that the terms must not be used interchangeably. The Brayfield and Crockett survey[3] made no mention of either; they held that the term "attitude" better provided, in their words, "the general and ambiguous connotation that is required to describe measurement in this field." Some people avoid the term, as though it were possible to hide in a corner and wait for it to go away. Such confusion of concept makes communication collapse, and argument inevitable. We will have to make realistic attempts to bring some kind of conceptual order to this chaos if meaningful and coordinated research is to be stimulated.

Students in a seminar on morale have been collecting definitions for me. As we go through a few of these, I'm sure you'll recognize an old friend or two:

1. *Morale is the absence of conflict.* I don't know that anyone has ever seriously proposed this as a fundamental concept, but it is certainly implied in much management action and conversation. It seems rather negative; at best, it reflects behavior usually associated with the ostrich.

2. *Morale is a feeling of happiness.* Again, this is a rather empty sort of definition; a person might be quite euphoric while at work in spite of his job, not because of it. If so, he could hardly be described as one having "high morale." Yet, at its own naive level, this notion may have some real utility.

3. *Morale is good personal adjustment.* About all that this definition has to offer is a weak attempt to refine the happiness concept as something more than mere euphoria. It would hardly be worth separate mention were it not for the contention appearing in one source[4] that adjustment is an adequate concept for describing individuals, and that therefore the term "morale" may be reserved for groups. I believe that, for the general domain of concepts to which the word has been linked, we need a concept that is more job related than adjustment as such. This does not deny that personal adjustment is a worthy concept!

4. *Morale is ego-involvement in one's job.* This is an intriguing concept; it led me to the opinion, reported in an unfortunate press release

---

[1] N. R. F. Maier, *Psychology in Industry* (2d ed., Boston: Houghton-Mifflin, 1955).

[2] M. L. Blum, *Industrial Psychology and Its Social Foundations* (New York: Harpers, 1956).

[3] A. H. Brayfield and W. H. Crockett, "Employee Attitudes and Employee Performance," *Psychological Bulletin*, Vol. 52, 1955, pp. 396–424.

[4] N. R. F. Maier, *op. cit.*

as fact, that such things as absence of conflict, happiness, or "good" adjustment might be antithetic to morale. There is something to be said for the attitudinal frame of reference in which a man perceives his job to be so important to himself, to his company, and to society that his superiors' "blunders" are not to be tolerated. Operationally and conceptually, this definition is difficult; it raises many questions. For example, when is a man to be considered ego-involved in his job as opposed to being involved in the job *as a symbol* of some other involvement? Certainly, this concept is a useful one—for more study.

5. *Morale is the extent of "we-feeling" or cohesiveness of the group.* In part, this definition disturbs me because it seems to ignore the individual; in part, it disturbs me as a gross oversimplification. Certainly it is an exact reversal of the concept of morale as a highly generalized attribute of individuals. It is, of course, extremely meaningful as a basis for useful work.

6. *Morale is a collection of job-related attitudes.* Here morale is defined neither as an attribute of the group nor of the individual, as such. Mainly, it is defined in terms of the environment in which individuals and groups are at work: attitudes toward supervision, attitudes toward physical conditions, attitudes toward financial rewards, attitudes toward product, and the like. This, which those who have made distinctions, believe should be called "job satisfaction," seems to be a surface concept —although not a superficial one, in the sense of being unimportant—and as such may tend to be somewhat unstable.

7. *Morale is the personal acceptance of the goals of the group.* Among those who have seriously thought about it, this hybrid definition is probably the one most widely accepted. It considers morale an attribute of the individual, but it is an attribute which exists *only with reference to a group* of which he is a member. It seems to me that the essential implication of such a definition is that morale is a function of the amount of personal need satisfaction the individual can get from the activities and aspirations of a group with which he identifies. I have one quarrel with this concept: I perceive no justification for restricting the term to only those satisfactions which are defined by the group. There are, potentially, at least, other sources of satisfaction—other needs which are predominantly social, but which are at least partly satisfied in the job situation. There are jobs, in fact, in which there is no immediate group affiliation; under this definition, holders of such jobs could not be said to "have" any morale at all, either high or low. To use this concept of morale on such jobs requires the formulation of abstractions of possible group identifications; such abstract groups will be highly subjective.

8. Since I have been finding fault with these definitions, I must present a final definition—one which pleases me, although I hasten to point out that it will not please everyone. *Morale is the extent to which an individual's needs are satisfied and the extent to which the individual per-*

ceives that satisfaction as stemming from his total job situation. I believe that this definition includes the most useful parts of each of the other concepts. High morale, under this concept, would be reflected by little aggressive or frustration-instigated conflict, by a reasonably euphoric work force, by fairly well-adjusted employees who can become quite ego-involved in their work, by many favorable attitudes, and by the cohesiveness which comes from finding personal need satisfactions within a group.

This definition contains five attributes which are, I believe, essential to an adequate concept of morale: (a) it recognizes the dynamic complexity of morale. It is the kind of complexity which can use—which, in fact, calls for—the factor analytic approach to definition. It tells us that morale is not a single dimension but that it has many components or factors. It asks only that the factors be defined in terms of human needs, rather than in terms of environmental sources of satisfaction of those needs. (b) It considers morale as basically an attribute of the individual. Groups too can be described in terms of morale, but such a description takes as its point of departure the perceived satisfactions of the individuals within the group. It seems to me that the morale of a group is at least partly based upon what I choose to call the morale of the individuals in it. This, I think, is something more than the usual concept of job satisfaction. (c) It recognizes that morale exists with reference to the job, not merely as a generalized trait existing in much the same form regardless of the job situation. (d) It recognizes the role of the motivational processes in morale. It implies that an individual may have many needs, and that these can be satisfied, either objectively or within the perceptions of the individuals, by the job at which a man makes his living. (e) It can apply to employees at any job level or in any job classification: street sweepers or college professors, traveling salesmen or lighthouse operators, authors, and even industrial psychologists.

32. Motivational Aspects of Industrial Morale*

Ross Stagner

MY DEFINITION OF morale falls into the category which is "almost acceptable" to Dr. Guion, as he has outlined it in the preceding paper.

* From "Industrial Morale (A Symposium) 2. Motivational Aspects of Industrial Morale," *Personnel Psychology*, Vol. 11, 1958, pp. 64–70.

Morale, I think, must always be defined in terms of an individual-group relationship; it is an index of the extent to which the individual perceives a probability of satisfying his own motives through coopera-tion with the group. Obviously, then, there is no such phenomenon as morale *in general;* the state of an individual's morale must be gauged relative to some specific group, such as his company, his informal work group, or his union.

Morale, to me, is not a meaningful term if the individual is seeking individual goals through individualistic action. At least from the sub-jective or *phenomenal* view, if he does not perceive himself as a mem-ber of a group, the term morale simply is not relevant. Of course, he may be *objectively* a member of a group, as when he is an employee of a company; and so from an external point of view, we may speak of his morale as a part of the employing organization. In this case, if he is acting in a purely individualistic fashion, we must conclude that his mo-rale is low. Nevertheless, as Brayfield and Crockett[1] have recently em-phasized, his productivity may be high. Morale and efficiency have a complex, not a linear relation.

High morale exists when the individual perceives himself as a member of a group, and perceives a high probability of achieving both individual and group goals through a course of action. He consciously seeks to achieve the goals of the group because these are important to him— they have become individual goals—or because they provide a *pathway* to his own personal goals which are not related to the group.

When we attempt to apply motivational analysis to the problem so de-fined, we find that there are three separate phases to be examined: (a) the individual's private goals; (b) the group goals; and (c) the perceived relationship between these sets of goals.

An extended treatment of individual goals would be out of place here. Let me say only that I consider the lists of common motives so widely used to be both inaccurate and misleading. Motivation is prop-erly a *state of energy-mobilization* oriented toward some perceived or imagined goal-object or goal-situation. Thus an individual may have an infinity of motives, and his motives are constantly subject to change as the incidence of deprivation and satiation make some goals *more* or *less* attractive. It is useful to classify goals into categories and to ob-serve that, in a specific individual's life-history, he has shown a tendency to mobilize more energy in behalf of income, or power, or prestige; this gives us something better than chance prediction as to his future motiva-tions. But, as is obvious in industrial situations, the same goal—e.g., more money—may serve security, prestige or power needs.

The differences between individuals, and especially between classes

[1] A. H. Brayfield and W. H. Crockett, "Employee Attitudes and Employee Performance," *Psychological Bulletin,* Vol. 52, 1955, pp. 396–424.

of individuals, e.g., executives, workers, and union officials, arise from other than internal motivational tensions. As I have pointed out elsewhere,[2] one major determinant is the perceived probability of success. Executives have a history of successful achievement, which makes them willing to take chances, since they are optimistic as to the outcome. Workers more often perceive their probabilities of success as low when they take a chance; hence we say they are "security-oriented."

A second consideration which is important with reference to the concept of individual goals is that these goals are often group-determined. The executive sets many facets of corporate policy in terms of group norms; the group here may be composed of his associates in the company, or of industrialists in general. The worker is influenced by informal work groups, by his family group, and by the union. The union leader is influenced by his members and by other union executives. Hence the difference between individual and group goals may seem to get blurred even before we have started using the two terms. However, I think we can say that, in the instances I have cited, the individual seeks the goal for purely personal satisfaction; he has merely accepted the *group definition* of what is good for him. Goodwin Watson used to define Utopia as a place in which a person was paid for doing work which he would have enjoyed doing even if unpaid. By contrast, George Orwell, in *1984*, depicted a society in which the individual was so manipulated that he wanted to do that which society compelled him to do. These two situations get alarmingly close to one another in some writings. Perhaps we can establish a criterion for differentiation by saying that in Utopia, the person is the independent variable; in *1984*, society is the independent variable.

A further clarification of the relationship I want to emphasize may be achieved by a more precise analysis of the concept of *group goal*. This is a slippery concept, because it tends to become associated with the old group-mind fallacy. Obviously, I will maintain that *only* individuals mobilize energy on behalf of goals. In a phenomenal frame of reference, however, we know that groups *seem* to have goals and *seem* to work (more or less vigorously) to attain them. I suggest that the resolution of this paradox derives from perception. If members of a group perceive it as a unit, and perceive it as striving for a goal, this gives us a phenomenological basis for treating group goals as real.

This definition differs, I realize, in some respects from tradition. I am proposing, essentially, that a decision at the top does not estalish a group goal unless the members accept it. The goal chosen by the leader becomes a group goal *when* the members perceive it as the goal of their group and perceive the group as making efforts to attain it. Notice that

---

[2] Ross Stagner, *Psychology of Industrial Conflict* (New York: John Wiley & Sons, 1956).

I am still not stating that any specific member is making efforts to accomplish this purpose.

We come now to the question of morale. Morale, as I see it, derives from the person's perception of himself as a component of this group-unit, and perception of his goals as being identical to or contiguous with the group-goals as defined. Let me illustrate this latter relationship by diagramming some of the principal possibilities:

1. The achievement of the group goal and the individual goal is a single process (see Figure 1). E.g., the worker turns out a product which meets company specifications at low cost, and he is proud of his work. The union leader wins a contract which protects his members and also protects him. Morale is at a maximum when the group goal and the individual goal are seen as identical.

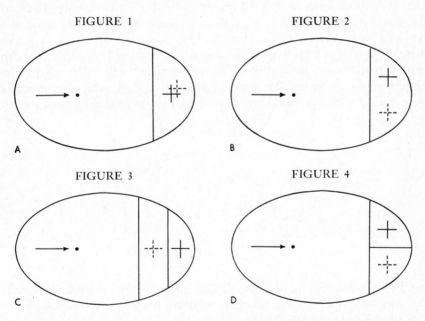

FIGURE 1 FIGURE 2

A B

FIGURE 3 FIGURE 4

C D

2. The two goals are closely associated (see Figure 2). E.g., a group of workers raise their team output and receive bonus payments. The union leader wins a contract which brings a pay raise to his members and more prestige for himself.

3. The attainment of the group goal is a necessary precondition of the individual goal (see Figure 3). E.g., a corporation executive helps expand sales, expects more pay and status. The union leader tries to organize more workers, and expects a rise in prestige and status.

4. Group and individual goals are perceived as separable and as attainable independently (see Figure 4). In this case a worker may produce at a high rate, and ignore the informal group goal of security. His morale as a group member is low, even though his output is high. The

union leader accepts a job as foreman, fails to pursue the union goal of strong organization. His morale as a union member is low.

Obviously, each of these examples is oversimplified, since there may be several individual goals and even varying group goals involved; especially, the person may be a member of overlapping groups and hence subject to conflicting group goals. These latter will be effective accordingly as the person perceives them to be compatible with his own goals.

Let me consider for just a moment the question of how this analysis relates to studies of job satisfaction. Instead of speaking of a single personal goal, we should more accurately conceive of the individual as seeking numerous rewards in the industrial situation. The situation may be one in which some of these goals are barred from achievement by company policy or by the nature of the situation (see Figure 5). Job satisfaction in such cases will be determined by the relative importance *as perceived by the employee* of the satisfactions achieved and those not achieved or perceived as unattainable. Questionnaires often try to get at these employee perceptions. If his over-all evaluation is negative, we can predict that his morale in relation to the company will suffer; that is, he cannot attain an acceptable level of individual goal achievement while cooperating with the company. However, this may or may not raise his

FIGURE 5

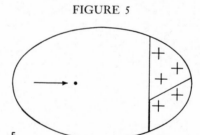

morale as a member of the union. Our dual allegiance studies[3] indicate that, on the average, those workers who are hostile to the company are also dissatisfied with the union.

These last examples suggest that wherever the individual perceives a substantial separation of group goals and individual goals, morale will suffer. This is true even though the person may outwardly seem to conform to the group policy. He still feels attracted to his individual goals, and some of his energy will be directed to them, not to the group goal.

The task of the person who wishes to raise morale within an organization, therefore, is to create situations in which group and individual goals coincide to the maximum extent possible. Work and social role assignments which separate these two are asking for trouble. The classical

---

[3] Ross Stagner *et al.*, "Dual Allegiance to Union and Management (A Symposium)," *Personnel Psychology*, Vol. 7, pp. 41–80.

instance in this connection is that of the executive who believes—and behaves as if—workers desire only money. This attitude encourages attempts on the part of the workers to get more money without cooperating in the goal-seeking activity of the company. They want more pay without doing more for the company—a fine example of the motivation the executive has attributed to them. But when the work-situation is made intrinsically satisfying, this conflict does not arise.

The union leader, who knows he is dealing with a political institution and recognizes the importance of getting "a little something for everybody" in a settlement has, by and large, done a better job of morale-engineering than the corporation executives. The unions have been fairly ingenious in devising ways by which individuals obtain feelings of satisfaction of a personal nature through group action. Management, by and large, has neglected this approach. As far as I can see, this is not a necessary consequence of any psychological law. I do think, however, that it represents the major challenge to managerial skill and wisdom at the present time.

Section Five

LEADERSHIP AND SUPERVISION

Introduction

LEADERSHIP once was thought of as a personality trait that some people "had" and others didn't. However, research indicated that no dependable traits could be isolated which consistently identified effective leaders or which differentiated leaders from non-leaders in all situations. It takes only a little reflection to realize this when one considers the diversity of people in history, politics, religion, athletics, as well as in industry, who would be considered "effective leaders." A more fruitful approach is to think of leadership in terms of "activities which influence others." By this definition leadership cannot be separated from the activities of groups. The leader is effective only to the extent that his group is influenced by his behavior to move toward certain shared goals. By this definition people in supervisory positions may or may not be leaders. Conversely, other individuals in the group not officially designated as supervisors may turn out to be leaders. We can evaluate leadership only in terms of its effects on the behavior of individuals in the group.

There still remains the question of identifying those patterns of leader behavior which are effective with certain kinds of groups. In this section we will focus on leadership patterns and practices in industrial settings. We will examine what these patterns are, the situational forces that influence them, and their relation to group effectiveness.

It is immediately apparent that two basic problems in this area are (1) the identification of meaningful leadership patterns and (2) the development of methods to measure these patterns. The Ohio State University Leadership Studies made these problems major research objectives. Focusing on the kinds of behavior engaged in by people in leadership roles, these investigators developed over 1,800 items (e.g., He calls the group together to talk things over; He knows about it when something goes wrong) descriptive of what supervisors do in their leadership roles. These items were then classified into ten broad categories of leader behavior (e.g., initiation, domination, evaluation, com-

311

munication). Questionnaires were developed by means of which leader behavior could be described and scored on these ten dimensions. Each supervisor was described in terms of how frequently (e.g., always, often, . . . never) he did what each item stated. Repeated use of these questionnaires in a variety of leader-group situations (foreman-worker, executive-subordinate, school principal-teacher, university department head-professor, aircraft commander-crew, submarine officer-crew) showed that these ten categories overlapped with one another and that the items could be grouped into two more basic dimensions of leader behavior. These were labeled *Consideration* and *Initiating Structure*.

We have already met these dimensions in the Harris and Fleishman article on human relations training in Section III. Briefly "Consideration" includes behavior indicating mutual trust, respect, and a certain warmth and rapport between the supervisor and his group. This does not mean that this dimension reflects a superficial "pat on the back," "first name calling" kind of human relations behavior. The meaning of this dimension goes more deeply into respect for the individual and includes such behavior as allowing subordinates more participation in decision making, engaging in more reciprocal two-way communication with subordinates, explaining actions which affect them, etc. "Initiating Structure" includes behavior in which the supervisor organizes and defines the role he expects each member to assume, plans ahead, establishes ways of getting things done, and pushes for production. The important point is that these two dimensions are uncorrelated; that is, supervisors may be high on Consideration and still be either high or low on the Structure dimension. Thus, they are more usefully considered as separate dimensions and not as opposite poles of the same dimension.

The first article by Fleishman, "Leadership Climate, Human Relations Training, and Supervisory Behavior," describes how measures of these patterns were developed and used in a complex industrial setting. The article focuses on some situational variables that influence the particular leadership patterns used by supervisors. It is shown that the organizational value system, particularly the "leadership climate," influences the supervisor's leader behavior, and may even negate the intended effects of management training.

As a follow-up to this study, it was later found that management in this plant actually rated as "most proficient" those foremen who turned out (on independent measurement) to be low in Consideration and high in Structure. In other words, the supervisor was rewarded in the plant for behavior patterns different from that intended by the training. It was also found that foremen with these patterns most often had work groups with higher grievance rates, accidents, turnover, and absences. It appeared, then, that management was responding more to a "stereotype" of effective leadership and was not focusing on leadership acts which actually "influenced group members toward shared goals."

Still later results in this same plant indicated that the foremen who are higher in Consideration, could also be higher in Structure with no increase in grievances, turnover, etc. Our evidence to date on these patterns suggests that supervisors who emphasize one pattern at the expense of the other are apt to be less effective, but that some balance between them is needed to satisfy organizational as well as individual needs. Supervisors who are low in both patterns are not even seen as "leaders" by their groups—they are frequently bypassed by their own work groups.

The article by Pelz explores another organizational variable related to the supervisor's behavior. In "Influence: A Key to Effective Leadership in the First-Line Supervisor," he deals with the problem of "power" and "authority" and shows how these condition whether certain supervisory acts turn out to be effective acts or not.

In the article "Patterns in Management," Likert summarizes some management concepts and reviews many of the recent findings of the University of Michigan's Institute for Social Research. Likert uses the terms "employee centered" and "production centered" supervision, but it will be recognized that these seem similar to our Consideration and Structure patterns just described. The studies described focus on the complex relations between supervisory behavior, morale, and productivity. It is important to note Likert's conclusion that "those employee-centered supervisors who get the best results tend to recognize that getting production is also one of their major responsibilities." This, of course, fits our previous discussion regarding the proper balance of Consideration and Structure.

The next three studies focus on specific supervisory attitudes and practices. The important role of participation in motivating employees at all levels has been made in several sections of this book, including this section. Solem's study examines a critical point often raised about this. Suppose the group arrives at decisions contrary to the supervisor's opinion? Is the whole matter of delegation full of hypocrisy? Is the supervisor merely manipulating his subordinates to make them *think* they are participating, when really he is going to make the final decision? Part of the answer is that the supervisor has to define the areas in which he reserves the right to decide. But, there is still the question of his attitude toward delegation in areas in which group participation is practiced. In "An Evaluation of Two Attitudinal Approaches to Delegation," Solem reviews this problem and shows the influence of the supervisor's attitude on the success of the delegation procedure.

The two related articles by Maier and Danielson deal with some practical supervisory decision-making situations involving people. In the first article, "Supervisory Problems in Decision Making," they examine a problem of "safety violation" and illustrate the forces at work and the steps involved in taking effective action. The study shows that the usual approach (the "judicial approach") may not be the most effective. In "An Evaluation of Two Approaches to Discipline in Industry," they compare the "judicial approach" with a "human relations" approach in handling a common disciplinary problem.

The final article in this section deals with the leadership dilemma often faced by the manager in industry. Since the effective supervisor, apparently, must keep a balance between Consideration and Structure (or between satisfying employee and organizational needs), how is he to know which leadership pattern to emphasize at particular times. Tannenbaum & Schmidt in "How to Choose a Leadership Pattern," attempt to resolve this dilemma as they describe the factors involved and the forces in the manager, his subordinates, and in the situation which must be considered.

33. Leadership Climate, Human Relations Training, and Supervisory Behavior*

Edwin A. Fleishman

INDUSTRIAL ORGANIZATIONS are becoming more deeply concerned with the interpersonal relations of their members. They seem increasingly anxious to reduce conflict and to promote harmonious working relationships. They are searching for policies and programs which can be used to promote greater satisfaction. Evidence of this can be seen in recent business and industrial literature which has given considerable emphasis to problems of human relations. Other evidence can be seen in the increasing number of leadership training programs which have been instituted in various industries. These industries want their supervisors to understand and be able to use certain techniques which will develop and sustain mutually satisfying human relations in the industrial situation. Implicit in these programs is the assumption that such relationships will result in increased organizational effectiveness.

The crucial role of leadership in this complex area of human relations has long been recognized but significant research in this area is a fairly recent development. The present paper represents a summary of research that was undertaken to throw at least some light on certain complex factors which might affect the leadership role of the foreman in industry.

PURPOSE OF THE STUDY

The study consisted of two major phases. The first phase was concerned with the development of dependable research instruments for measuring different aspects of leadership behavior, attitudes, and expectations. The present paper will discuss this developmental work only briefly. More detailed descriptions of this work have been presented elsewhere.[1]

* From *Personnel Psychology*, Vol. 6, 1955, pp. 205–22. This paper represents a summary of research carried out with the cooperation of the International Harvester Company.

[1] E. A. Fleishman, *Leadership Climate and Supervisory Behavior* (Columbus, Ohio: Personnel Research Board, Ohio State University, 1951); E. A. Fleishman, "The Description of Supervisory Behavior," *Journal of Applied Psychology*, Vol. 37, 1953, pp. 1–6; E. A. Fleishman, "The Measurement of Leadership Attitudes in Industry," *Journal of Applied Psychology*, Vol. 37, 1953, pp. 153–58.

The second phase, with which this paper is primarily concerned, consisted in using these instruments to investigate some specific industrial leadership problems. An investigation was made of the relationship between how the foreman leads his group and the attitudes and behavior of those above him in the organization. The study also investigated the extent to which certain leadership attitudes and behavior were maintained by foremen over periods of time elapsed since leadership training, when foremen returned to different kinds of supervisors in the industrial situation.

FIRST PHASE—DEVELOPING MEASURES OF LEADERSHIP BEHAVIOR AND ATTITUDES

One hundred foremen, representing 17 company plants, participated in this phase of the research. They filled out three questionnaires. On a Leadership Opinion Questionnaire containing 110 items, they described their own *attitudes* about how to lead their work groups. Next, they filled out a 136 item Supervisory Behavior Description questionnaire[2] in which they described their own supervisor's leadership *behavior*. In a third 110 item questionnaire they described how they felt their own supervisor *expected* them to lead their work groups.

In each questionnaire, the foremen checked one of five frequency alternatives which followed each item (e.g., always, often, occasionally, seldom, never). In the case of the Supervisory Behavior Description, the foreman indicated for each item how frequently his own supervisor did what the item described. Examples of items in this questionnaire are:

He plans each day's activities in detail.

He insists that everything be done his way.

He helps his men with their personal problems.

A similar procedure was used with the other two questionnaires. Thus, on the Leadership Opinion Questionnaire, the foremen were asked to indicate how frequently they felt they should do what each item described. Examples of such items are:

Speak in a manner not to be questioned.

Follow to the letter standard procedures handed down to you.

Treat people in the work group as your equals.

Extensive statistical analysis was then made of the scores and answers given by these foremen on the questionnaires. Response distributions among the five choices for each item, tetrachoric correlations of the items with total scores on the questionnaires, and factor analysis data

---

[2] The Supervisory Behavior Description developed in this study is based on earlier work by J. K. Hemphill, *Leader Behavior Description* (Columbus, Ohio: Personnel Research Board, Ohio State University, 1950) and subsequent work reported by A. W. Halpin and B. J. Winer, "Studies in Aircrew Composition III: The Leadership Behavior of the Airplane Commander," *Technical Report No. 3* (HRRL contract) (Columbus, Ohio: Personnel Research Board, Ohio State University, 1952).

were utilized. On the basis of these analyses revised forms were developed which were shortened considerably and contained only items found most applicable to the industrial situation.

Items on each revised questionnaire were scored into one or the other of two leadership "dimensions" identified by factor analysis procedures. One dimension, called "Consideration," reflected the extent to which the leader was established rapport, two way communication, mutual respect, and consideration of the feelings of those under him. It comes closest to the "human relations" aspects of group leadership. The other dimension, called "Initiating Structure," contained items reflecting the extent to which the supervisor defines or facilitates group interactions toward *goal attainment*. He does this by planning, scheduling, criticizing, initiating ideas, organizing the work, etc. It was found in subsequent analyses of these revised forms, that these two behavior (or attitude) patterns were quite *independent* of each other and that they possessed adequate reliabilities.[3]

SECOND PHASE—THE MAIN STUDY IN A SINGLE PLANT

Samples. Various forms of these revised questionnaires were used in a research design within one of the Company's plants. Four groups of foremen, totaling 122 foremen in a motor truck plant, constituted the primary sample in the study. One group of 32 foremen had not received leadership training at the Company's Central School.[4] The three remaining groups of foremen had received training 2 to 10 (30 foremen), 11 to 19 (31 foremen), and 20 to 39 (29 foremen) months previous to the study. No biasing factors which determined the order in which foremen were sent to training could be found. Differences between the four groups of foremen in average age, years with the company, years as a supervisor, education, and number of men supervised, were not statistically significant.

All 122 foremen, 60 supervisors above these foremen, and 394 workers drawn randomly from the foremen's work groups filled out the questionnaires.

The Information Obtained. Each *foreman* in the study filled out the following three generally parallel questionnaires:

1. A 40-item *Foreman's Leadership Opinion Questionnaire:* A description of how the foreman thinks he should lead his own work group.

2. A 48-item *Supervisory Behavior Description:* A description of the

---

[3] E. A. Fleishman, *Leadership Climate and Supervisory Behavior, op. cit.;* E. A. Fleishman, "The Description of Supervisory Behavior," *op. cit.;* E. A. Fleishman, "The Measurement of Leadership Attitudes in Industry," *op. cit.*

[4] The School has been in operation several years. Each plant has a regular quota of foremen which it sends to the School every two weeks. The course involves eight hours a day for two weeks. A summary of the purpose, scope, and workings of the School has been published by C. L. Walker, Jr., "Education and Training at International Harvester," *Harvard Business Review,* Vol. 27, 1949, pp. 542–58.

leadership behavior toward the foreman of the foreman's own boss.

3. A 40-item questionnaire entitled, *"What Your Boss Expects of You": A* description of how the foreman feels his own boss wants him to lead the work group.

Representatives of each foreman's *work group* filled out the following two questionnaires:

1. A 48-item *Foreman Behavior Description:* A description of the leadership behavior of the foreman with his work group.

2. A 40-item questionnaire entitled, *"How You Expect an Ideal Foreman to Act":* A description of worker expectations regarding leadership behavior.

Each foreman's boss filled out the following two questionnaires:

1. A 40-item *Leadership Opinion Questionnaire:* A description of how the boss thinks he should lead the foremen under him.

2. A 40-item questionnaire entitled, *"What You Expect of Your Foremen":* A description of how the boss wants his foremen to lead their workers.

All these forms were variations of the questionnaires revised on the basis of the pilot study. Each questionnaire yielded a score for "Consideration" and a score for "Initiating Structure."

Background data such as age, education, years with the company, years as a supervisor, and number of men supervised also were collected for each foreman.

How the Data Were Analysed. The foreman's description of his own boss' behavior, the foreman's perception of what his boss expected of him, what the boss said he expected, and the boss' own leadership attitudes about leading foremen were considered aspects of "leadership climate" under which different foremen operate. We then examined the behavior and attitudes of foremen who operated under different kinds of bosses ("leadership climates") in the industrial situation. This was done by dividing the foremen groups (as close to the median score on the "climate" measures as possible) into those operating under "climates" high and low on either "Consideration" or "Initiating Structure." Also, by comparing the four groups of foremen (with different amounts of time elapsed since training) we could get some indication of how the attitudes and behavior of these foremen had changed when they returned from training to different kinds of "leadership climates" in the work situation.

Some evaluation also was made of changes occurring *during* the training course. This was done by administering the attitude questionnaires immediately before and immediately after training. A comparison was then made of the leadership attitudes held immediately after training and attitudes held in the actual industrial environment by foremen who had been trained some time before.

RESULTS AND DISCUSSION

Background Factors Related to the Foreman's Leadership Attitudes and Behavior. No significant relationships were found between personal data items and scores on the questionnaires measuring the attitudes and behavior of the foremen. Age, education, years with the company, years as a supervisor, and number of men supervised did not seem to make a difference in how the foremen behaved leadershipwise with their workers. These data do not support the popular stereotype of the dominating, driving old-line foremen as typical of older foremen. For example, age and years as a supervisor seem to have no relationship with how "considerate" the foreman is or how much he pushes for production, plans, criticizes, etc.

The data of this study do tend to emphasize again that the nature of leadership depends more on certain factors in the particular situation than on these background characteristics of the leader.

The Foreman's Leadership Attitudes and Behavior as Related to the Kind of Boss He Works Under. What did seem to make a difference in how different foremen led their work groups, was the kind of boss under whom the foremen themselves had to operate. Those foremen who operated under a supervisor who was "considerate" toward them, tended to express more "considerate" attitudes toward their own workers. Moreover, these same foremen were described by their own work groups as *behaving* more "considerately" toward the workers. For example, the foremen operating under supervisors high in "consideration" received a mean score of 76.5 on "consideration" when described by their workers, while foremen under supervisors low in "consideration" received a mean score of 70.6 (difference significant beyond the .01 level).

The same "chain-reaction" effect was observed when we examined the "initiating structure" attitudes of different foremen. Those foremen who were under bosses who planned a great deal, stressed deadlines, assigned people to particular tasks, etc., tended themselves to score higher in their "structuring" attitudes. Although differences in "structuring" *behavior* between groups of foremen operating under "climates" high and low in "structuring" were not statistically significant, the trends were in the same direction.

Changes in the Attitudes and Behavior of the Foremen Produced by the Leadership Training Course. By giving our attitude questionnaires to foremen the first day and again the last day of training we could get some indication of changes produced during the training course. The results of this before and after evaluation indicated a general increase in "consideration" attitudes (significant beyond the .05 level) and a decrease in "initiating structure" attitudes (significant beyond the .01

level) during the course. The correlations between "consideration" and "initiating structure" before and after training presented a check on whether some functional relationship was "learned" between the two dimensions during training. In each case the correlations did not differ significantly from zero. This presents further evidence of the independence of these leadership patterns and indicates that the decrease in "initiating structure" was *not necessarily* a function of the increase in "consideration." The increase in "consideration" and decrease in "structure" are fairly independent phenomena. Figure 1 shows this shift graphically.

The objectives of the training, however, are to produce a *lasting* change in the trainee's behavior. A comparison of this before and after evaluation with what happened in the actual plant situation revealed an obvious discrepancy. Figure 2 presents the results of this "back-in-the-plant" evaluation. Differences in the leadership behavior as well as differences in leadership attitudes for the four groups of foremen (at different stages since training) are presented.

Although the effects of the training generally appear minimal, back in the plant the *behavior* of the most recently trained group of foremen was significantly lower in "consideration" ($P < .01$) than that of the untrained group of foremen. In the case of "consideration" *attitudes* this initial drop does not reach statistical significance although the trend is in the same direction. Moreover, there appeared to be a trend in the direction of increased "initiating structure" attitudes and behavior in certain of the trained groups at the plant. Confidence in these results is increased when we observe the close correspondence between the attitudes expressed by the foremen and our independent reports of their behavior made by their workers (especially in the case of the "structure" curves and the initial drop in "consideration").

Since "leadership climate" was found related to the attitudes and behavior of the foremen, a check was made to see if our four primary groups of foremen (trained at different times) were matched on the "climate" measures. This analysis showed that the four groups did not differ significantly with respect to our measures of "leadership climate" under which they operated. Hence, this drop in "consideration" and rise in "structuring" in the overall comparison of the trained and untrained groups is not attributable to differences between *these* groups in overall "leadership climate."

These results seem puzzling because in the course the "human relations" approach is stressed. It may be that being sent to supervisory training made the foremen more aware of their leadership role. Perhaps they really felt more "membership character" (as "one of the boys") in the work groups before training, and being selected for training made them feel "separate" from their work groups. Although "human relations" are stressed in the course, the foreman is certainly made more

FIGURE 1

Distributions* of Foreman's Leadership Opinion Questionnaire
Scores before and after Training $(N = 46)$

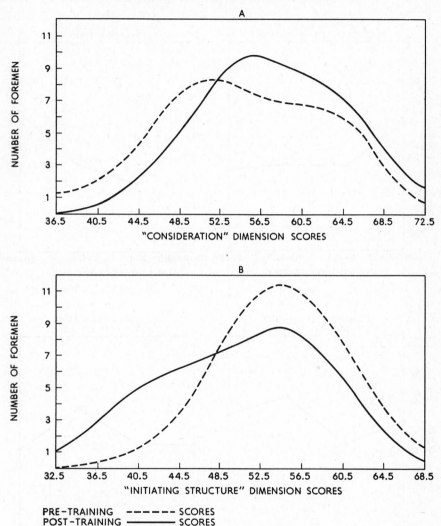

PRE-TRAINING ------ SCORES
POST-TRAINING ———— SCORES

*The distributions have been smoothed arithmetically by the method suggested by J. P. Guilford, *Psychometric Methods* (New York; McGraw-Hill, 1936).

aware of his part as a member of management. The human relations aspect may persist only briefly, whereas what he actually takes back to the plant is a tendency to assume more of a leadership role; that is, do more "structuring" and behave less "considerately."

The discrepancy between our results at the School and at the plant points up the danger of evaluating training outcomes immediately after training. The classroom atmosphere is quite different from that in the

FIGURE 2

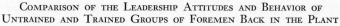

Comparison of the Leadership Attitudes and Behavior of
Untrained and Trained Groups of Foremen Back in the Plant

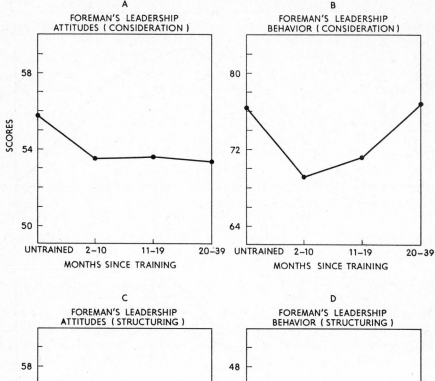

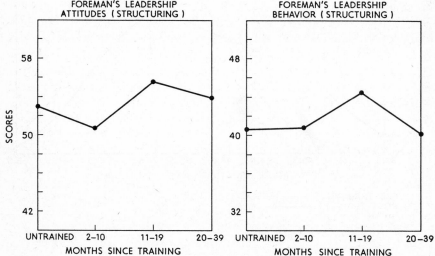

actual work situation. Our results suggest that the foreman may learn different attitudes for each situation. The attitude that is "right" in the training situation may be very different from the one that "pays off" in the industrial environment.

The Interaction of the Training Effects with the Industrial Environment. The kind of supervisor ("leadership climate") under whom the foreman operated seemed more related to the attitudes and behavior of the foremen in the plant than did the fact that they had or had not received the leadership training course. In the untrained group and at each stage since training, the behavior and attitudes of the foremen were generally related to the "leadership climate" under which they operated. Figure 3 presents some of these results.

It can be seen in Figure 3 that the attitude and behavior curves of the foremen operating under "climates" high in "consideration" and high in "structuring" are generally above the curves of foremen under "climates" low on each of these leadership patterns.

An implication of these results seems to be that if the old way of doing things in the plant situation is still the shortest path to approval by the boss, then this is what the foreman really learns. Existing behavior patterns are part of, and are moulded by, the culture of the work situation. In order effectively to produce changes in the foreman's behavior some changes in his "back-home-in-the-plant" environment would also seem to be necessary. The training course alone cannot do it.

Comparison of the Degree of "Conflict" among Trained and Untrained Foremen. Further evidence along these lines is furnished by the degree of conflict within trained foremen who return to different kinds of bosses. A "conflict index" was computed between "what the foremen thought they *should* do" and what they were reported as "actually *doing*" in the plant situation. This index was derived from the absolute discrepancy between scores on the Foreman's Leadership Opinion Questionnaire and the Foreman Behavior Description. It was found that whenever our differences were statistically significant these were in favor of more "conflict" within trained foremen when they returned to supervisors higher in "structuring" and lower in "consideration." As indicated previously, the foremen apparently learned to do *less* "structuring" and to show more "consideration" in the training course.

Comparison of the "Leadership Adequacy" of Trained and Untrained Foremen. It will be recalled that the workers filled out the Foreman Behavior Description and a questionnaire entitled, "How You Expect an Ideal Foreman to Act." The absolute discrepancy between scores on these questionnaires present measures of "leadership adequacy" for each foreman with respect to his own work group's expectations. The lower the discrepancy, the higher the "adequacy" from the group's point of view. Our results showed that with respect to "consideration" behavior there was no significant improvement in "leadership adequacy" for the trained foremen who returned to "climates" low in "consideration," but there was significant improvement among foremen who returned to "climates" higher in "consideration." The foremen who returned to supervisors high in "consideration" seemed now to conform more closely to their group's leadership ideal, but no such change occurred in the case of foremen who returned to supervisors lower in "considera-

FIGURE 3

COMPARISON OF THE LEADERSHIP ATTITUDES AND BEHAVIOR OF FOREMEN
OPERATING UNDER DIFFERENT "LEADERSHIP CLIMATES" BACK IN THE PLANT

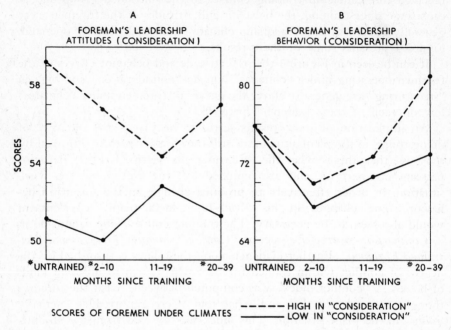

SCORES OF FOREMEN UNDER CLIMATES   – – – – HIGH IN "CONSIDERATION"
——— LOW IN "CONSIDERATION"

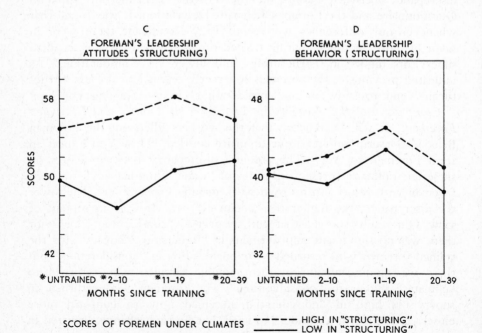

SCORES OF FOREMEN UNDER CLIMATES   – – – – HIGH IN "STRUCTURING"
——— LOW IN "STRUCTURING"

* INDICATES DIFFERENCE BETWEEN THE CURVES
STATISTICALLY SIGNIFICANT AT THESE POINTS

tion." These results present still further evidence of the interaction of the training effects with the "back in the plant" environment. Differences in "leadership adequacy" along the "initiating structure" dimension, however, were generally not significant.

Comparison of the Leadership Attitudes of the Foremen, Their Workers, and Their Own Supervisors. It was possible to compare the leadership attitudes about how work groups should be led at four clear-cut levels in the plant. The results of this comparison showed no significant differences between the attitudes of the foremen and their supervisors, but highly significant differences between the attitudes of the foremen and their workers. The workers preferred more "consideration" and less "structuring." It also appeared that the higher up people were in the plant heirarchy, the less "consideration" they felt the workers should get. Moreover, the higher the level, the more "structuring" the people felt should be initiated with the work groups. The tendency was for the foreman's attitudes to fall somewhere between what the workers expect and what people higher up in the organization expect.

IMPLICATIONS OF THE RESULTS FOR LEADERSHIP TRAINING IN INDUSTRY

Final evaluation of such training must depend on some kind of intensive criterion study relating supervisory behavior to group effectiveness. This criterion study would be aimed at finding out what kinds of leadership behavior make for higher productivity and/or morale. On the basis of this kind of study recommendations about "What to teach?" could be made. The present research made little attempt to investigate this problem. Some limited evidence was obtained which showed some relationship between labor grievance rates and certain kinds of leadership attitudes and behavior. For example, based on a very small sample of 23 departments, correlations as high as .53 were found between grievance rates in these departments and scores made by supervisors on these questionnaires. The trend was for high grievance departments to be those whose supervisors were lower in "consideration" and tended to do more "structuring."

These results are regarded as merely suggestive and certainly no substitute for a well-controlled criterion study.* Ideally such a criterion study would take into consideration the situational nature of leadership. For example, comparative studies of effective leadership in production, maintenance, and administrative departments could be made. It is possible that different combinations of "consideration" and "initiating struc-

---

* Editor's note: This study subsequently was carried out and is described in E. A. Fleishman, E. F. Harris, and H. E. Burtt, *Leadership and Supervision in Industry* (Columbus Ohio: Ohio State University, Bureau of Educational Research, 1955). We have summarized some of these findings in the introduction to this section.

ture" may be found desirable for different kinds of departments. This might suggest setting up separate leadership training courses for supervisors in these different kinds of departments. An important contribution of the present study in this regard was the development of instruments to measure relatively independent dimensions of leadership which in a later study could be related to criteria of group effectiveness. If important relationships with external criteria are found some interesting implications would be pointed up. For example, a combination of such things as group characteristics, needs and expectations, leadership attitudes, behaviors, and perceptions, pressures from supervisors, etc., might yield more successful predictions where ordinary testing procedures have failed in the field of leadership. With larger samples and adequate criteria it may be possible to predict group effectiveness given measures of several aspects of the social situation.

The present study presents evidence of what changes occurred in the attitudes and behavior of foremen after training. There is no implication, however, as to whether these changes are desirable or undesirable. Pending the availability of more ultimate criteria, training can be evaluated with respect to the major objectives set for such courses. The objectives of this particular course was to make the foremen more "human relations" oriented. This corresponds to a desired increase on the "consideration" dimension of the instruments used in this study. Although training objectives with regard to the "initiating structure" dimension were not defined, changes along this dimension were also investigated.

In terms of changes in "consideration" attitudes, this course met this objective partially. When the leadership attitude scales were administered immediately before and immediately after training, there was an average increase in "consideration" scores during the course. "Initiating structure" attitudes showed a general decrease for the foremen during the course. A limitation of this pre-post training evaluation was the fact that it was not feasible to use a control group in this phase of the study and these same men could not be followed back to their plants.

The training, however, did not produce any kind of permanent change in either the attitudes or behavior of the trained foremen. Evaluation of the training back in the actual work situation yielded results quite different from the pre-post training evaluation. In fact, there were trends in the direction of more "structuring" and less "consideration" in those foremen who returned to the industrial environment. Further study is needed to determine how to make the intended effects of such courses more permanent. Indications from this study are that the back home "leadership climate" is an important variable related to the behavior and attitudes of foremen in the work situation. Although the effects of training were minimal among foremen working under either of the kinds of "leadership climates" investigated, those foremen who operated under bosses higher in "consideration" tended themselves to be more "considerate" with their workers. This was also generally true of the foreman's "structuring" attitudes and behavior under "climates" higher in "structuring." Further evidence along this line was furnished by the comparison of the attitudes of the foremen in the plant with those of their bosses and workers. No significant differences were found between the attitudes of the foremen and their bosses, but there were highly significant differences between the attitudes of the foremen and their workers. In addition, there was greater conflict between the attitudes and actual behavior of the trained foremen who returned to "climates" at variance with what the foremen learned in training than among those who returned to "climates" consistent with what they learned. It was also found that the behavior of foremen who returned to "climates" consistent with what was taught in training conformed more closely to the leadership expectations of their work groups. No such improvement was found among foremen who returned to "climates" at variance with the training course.

These results suggest that leadership training cannot be considered in isolation from the social environment in which the foremen must actually function. In this sense leadership training must be viewed as an attempt at *social change* which involves the reorganization of a complex perceptual field. It is difficult to produce in an individual a behavior-change that violates the culture in which this behavior is imbedded. When foremen are trained and sent back to the factory it is unrealistic to expect much change when so many factors in the social situation remain constant. The implication seems to be that certain aspects of the foreman's environment may have to be reorganized if training is to be effective in modifying his behavior. It would appear, then, that more intensive training of supervisors above the level of foreman in the organization might be more effective in making the training effects more permanent among the foremen. If he could return to an environment where the boss behaved in a way consistent with what the foreman was taught in the training course, where these new modes of behavior were now the shortest path to approval, we might expect a more permanent effect of such training.

On the basis of the data of this study some re-examination of course *content* might be made. For example, what is in such courses that might account for the increase in "structuring" and the decrease in "consideration" when the foremen get back to the plant? Do such courses make the foreman too aware of his role as a member of management and how does he interpret this when he goes back? Does the foreman tend to lose his "membership character" in the work group after he has returned from training? In terms of the "human relations" objective, is there anything in the course content or in the attitudes fostered there which defeats this purpose? Research in training *methods* is another possibility.

Would a more therapeutic or individualistic approach produce greater or more permanent effects? At least it would seem that something more than classroom training is probably needed if real changes in the attitudes or behavior of supervisors is to be expected.

Similar evaluations of the training in the plant situation need to be made in other plants and in other industries. This drop in "consideration" and the trend in increased "structuring" may not occur in other industrial situations. It may be, for example, that the overall "leadership climate" in this plant was lower in "consideration" than the overall "climate" in some other plant. This study afforded no opportunity for comparing this plant on the whole with some other plant.

In general, interest in the course among foremen is very high. Enthusiasm at the verbal level is almost universal. A frequent comment made by the foremen during the course was, "I certainly wish my own boss would get this course." Favorable comments about the course also are expressed by people at all levels in the organization. The writer sat through the course and was very favorably impressed with the teaching methods and the participation of the foremen. Before any reorganization of the course, criterion research revealing what to teach, and further research on how to make the effects of what is taught more permanent should be undertaken.

34. Influence: A Key to Effective Leadership in the First-Line Supervisor*

Donald C. Pelz

THE SPOTLIGHT these days is very much on the first-line supervisor. The reasons are obvious—and good ones. The first-line supervisor is the most direct link between employees and management. On him hangs much of the responsibility for seeing that employees understand and support the goals adopted by management. And in turn he is responsible for seeing that the employees' difficulties and complaints get transmitted up the line and that these problems get solved. Much management attention has therefore been concentrated on this link. Are your employees unhappy or unproductive? The popular panacea is: Put your first-line supervisors through another training course.

But what is this flood of training supposed to accomplish? How is the

* From *Personnel*, Vol. 29, 1952, pp. 209–17.

effective supervisor supposed to act? Everyone has his opinion on this score, and numerous studies have been conducted, but there still is no clear-cut answer based on scientific evidence. This problem has therefore occupied a central position in several studies conducted at the University of Michigan's Survey Research Center as part of its Human Relations Program.

Since the start of the program, we have been forced more and more to a major realization: that the question we started with—what are the methods for effective supervision?—may not have any one answer! This doesn't mean that there are no rules for supervision. Rather, it means that before we can give an answer we must know what kind of an organization it is that we are dealing with and *what kind of relations the individual supervisor and his group have to the organization*. To talk of "good supervision" or "poor supervision" as if the supervisor and his group existed in a social vacuum may be meaningless.

To put it in technical terms, the surrounding organization and the way the group fits into the organization may "condition" the way in which the behavior of the supervisor affects his employees. It is likely that a great many organizational factors can act as "conditioners" of supervisory leadership. The focus of this article is on just one of these organizational factors: what we can call the supervisor's *power* or, more accurately, his *influence within the department*. How much weight does the supervisor swing? Is he simply a work leader who passes on instructions from higher-ups? Or is he an influential person whose opinions are respected and sought by his superiors? Our findings to date show that the low-influence supervisor may have to behave rather differently toward employees from the high-influence supervisor, if maximum employee morale is to be achieved.

THE DRAMA OF RESEARCH

But we are jumping ahead of the story. The idea just expressed has emerged only after long and tedious searching. Discovery of scientific truth is a little like discovering the culprit in a detective novel. You are faced at first with a meaningless jumble of tangled facts. Only after a long search, full of ventures up blind alleys, do you finally piece together a systematic explanation in which many facts fit together and reinforce each other. Instead of looking for "whodunit," of course, you are looking for "whatduzit"—what are the factors, the conditions, the elements in the situation that produce the tangle of facts which you have observed?

One of your difficulties is that very likely you will have not one culprit but many, and all will be at work affecting the data you are trying to explain. Another major difficulty is that your culprits may be so many "undercover agents"; unless you suspect they are there, and go out to find them, you may never know that they exist. That was the case with our crucial factor of supervisory "power or influence," which was uncovered only rather late in the specific investigation reported here.

THE SETTING OF THE INVESTIGATION

This particular search had its beginning in 1948, and the results to be described were not achieved until three years later. As part of the Human Relations Program, we were invited by the Detroit Edison Company to undertake a study of its employees' attitudes. The company employes well over 10,000 people and provides Detroit and the surrounding areas with electric power and other utilities. Its employees perform a wide range of functions, such as constructing and operating power plants, building and maintaining power lines, reading meters, collecting money, conducting electrical research, and many other office and manual jobs. Some 8,000 nonsupervisory employees filled in a paper-and-pencil questionnaire; all supervisory and managerial personnel in the company were given a personal interview.

The Detroit Edison Company has encouraged and supported several scientific studies of this and other material. One of these studies was the problem tackled by the author: What attitudes and behavior in the first-line supervisor lead to greater employee satisfaction? We were especially interested in employee satisfaction regarding the supervisor himself, but we were also interested in satisfaction regarding the job, fellow-employees, and the company in general.

We were concerned with a number of supervisory behaviors. For example, to what extent should the supervisor involve his employees in the decision-making process, if employee satisfaction and job performance are to be of the highest? This area is part of what is often referred to as "democratic supervision."

Another part of the same concept is what might be called the supervisor's "equalitarian philosphy." Should the supervisor remain dignified and aloof? Or should he mingle freely with his employees as a social equal? These behaviors are indicative of the "social distance" between the supervisor and his group. What degree of social distance has the best effect on employee attitudes?

A third problem, somewhat similar to these, is the matter of "identification" with management or with employees. In the case of conflicts between what management wants and what the employees want, does the supervisor go to bat for management or does he go to bat for the employees? These and many other aspects of supervisory behavior toward employees and toward superiors were explored in personal interviews, and quantitative measures of them were obtained.

INSTALLMENT NO. I: LOOKING INTO EFFECTIVE SUPERVISION

The first installment of our detective story was begun with no expectation that other installments would follow. It was intended to answer questions, not to raise them. It was designed, specifically, to answer the following single question: What are the characteristics of effective supervisors—effective, that is, in terms of high employee satisfaction? The method selected in an attempt to find the answer was a simple one. A criterion of effective leadership was chosen in terms of the work group's "over-all satisfaction" (you might, loosely, call it "group morale"). A measure of over-all satisfaction was obtained by combining seven satisfaction items answered by each employee, and group averages were then computed. Forty high-satisfaction and 30 low-satisfaction groups were pulled out, and their supervisors were compared. We inspected differences between these two sets of supervisors in terms of 50 items of information obtained from interviews with them, expecting to find a number of items which distinguished between the two sets of supervisors. The items on which they differed might therefore be said to account in part for the high or low satisfaction within their groups.

The tantalizing fact was that only 6 out of the 50 items showed differences large enough to be trustworthy—technically, large enough to be "statistically significant at the 5 per cent level of confidence." This was hardly more than we should expect solely from chance. Firm conclusions cannot be based on so insubstantial a foundation.

What was wrong? What psychological or sociological culprits were concealing the clear-cut facts we had hoped to find?

INSTALLMENT NO. 2: A NEW STRATEGY

If you take a close look at the method used in the first analysis, you find a hidden assumption there. Implicitly, we were assuming that a certain leadership practice will produce high employee satisfaction in *all* groups. But sober and common-sense reflection shows that this assumption is not necessarily true. For example, self-reliant employees will probably enjoy a supervisor who thrusts responsibility upon them; dependent employees will probably dislike a supervisor who does this. These two reactions will simply cancel each other out if all employees are thrown together, as was the case in the first analysis.

In Installment No. 2 of our detective story, then, a different strategy was used. Here different types of employees and different types of situations were studied separately rather than being thrown together. We tried to anticipate what types of employees or situations would react in different ways to the same supervision. For example, men and women were studied separately; those performing white-collar or office work were treated apart from those doing blue-collar or manual work; those in small work groups (10 employees or under) were studied separately from those in large work groups, and so on.

This approach paid off. The relationships between supervisory behaviors and employee attitudes emerged much more clearly. Trustworthy or statistically significant results were now approximately seven times as numerous as chance alone would yield. But now many of the relationships seemed contradictory!

For example, there was the supervisory measure of "taking sides with employees in cases of employee-management conflicts." In small work-groups, employees thought more highly of the leader who took their side in cases of conflicts with management. But, in large white-collar work groups, employees were significantly *less* satisfied with such a supervisor; they preferred the supervisor who sided with management. Other supervisory measures showed similar contradictory results.

Why? What was there about the large work group situation that produced some relationships apparently opposite to those found in small work groups?

AN "UNDERCOVER AGENT" UNCOVERED

It seemed likely that some factors which we had not attempted to measure up to now were producing these puzzling results. A number of candidates for this "undercover agent" role were suggested. One of the most promising was the idea of the first-line supervisor's *power or influence within the department*. While new to this particular study, such a factor had been hinted at in one of the previous studies conducted under the Human Relations Program. In the home office of a large insurance company, it was possible to locate a number of "high-producing" work groups and a number of "low-producing" groups. The supervisors of these groups were compared on a number of items (in a manner similar to that used in our own first analysis). For example, what practice did the supervisor follow in recommending promotions for his employees?

It was found that the supervisors of high-producing work groups in the insurance company played one of two roles in the promotion process. Either they made recommendations which generally went through, or they made no recommendations at all. In contrast, the supervisors of low-producing work groups often recommended promotions, but these generally did not go through. To recommend promotions was not, as such, related to high employee productivity. A more basic factor seemed to be operating—the supervisor's power within the department. The high-producing supervisors were more realistic about their power; they entered the promotion process only when they could influence the outcome.

Could such a factor of power or influence within the department be partly responsible for the contradictory effects obtained in our second analysis? It seemed a worth-while avenue to explore.

The whole area of the first-line supervisor's power or influence seems to be a critical one. One effect of the centralization of business, of piling up supervisory layer on top of supervisory layer, is inevitably to take away power or control from the lower levels of supervision. And one of the arguments given in favor of decentralization is that in relatively small organizations the immediate supervisors (and all other supervisors) have more control over the destiny of their respective groups.

But it was one thing to suspect activity on the part of this undercover agent called "power" or "influence," and another thing actually to locate and measure it. We searched through the supervisory data hoping to find items that would yield a measure of the supervisor's influence within the department. Three items seemed to do this: the amount of *voice he felt he had in his superior's decisions*, the amount of *autonomy* he had with respect to his superior (as indicated by the nonfrequency of contact with the superior), and his *salary* (a general indication of his status, level of responsibility, etc.). These three items were combined into a single measure which we called "influence."

A THEORY OF INFLUENCE

Kurt Lewin was fond of saying that "nothing is so practical as a good theory." A theory is like the detective's "reconstruction of the crime." It forces the researcher to piece the facts together to see if they jibe with each other, to find out if there are missing parts, and to determine where to look for the crucial facts that may solve the mystery. A good theory, like a useful reconstruction, is not a complete picture. It leaves out a great many facts, but it highlights the essential ones. The particular theory of influence that seemed to fit the present situation looked like this:

1. Employees (and for that matter the members of any group) will think well of the leader who helps them to satisfy their needs, to achieve their goals.

2. If a supervisor (or any group leader) has considerable influence within his organization, then when he behaves so as to help employees toward their goals, he will achieve concrete benefits for them. Consequently, their satisfaction regarding him will increase. Not his good intentions, but his actual accomplishments, are what pay dividends in employee satisfaction.

3. We must also recognize that the supervisor's power can be used to harm as well as to help employees. Sometimes the supervisor is mainly a disciplinarian, a checker-up, a pusher whose chief function is to see that employees hew to the line. If a supervisor behaves mainly in this way, and if he has considerable influence, then he can be a substantial restraint on employees, and they are likely to be dissatisfied with him or even fearful of him.

4. On the other hand, if the supervisor has *little* power or influence, then neither his helpful behavior nor his restraining behavior will have much concrete effect on the employees. He cannot help them to get what they are after or restrain them substantially. Neither

behavior will have any marked effect on their satisfaction. In fact, the more helpful he tries to be, the more we might expect to find some increase in *dis*satisfaction, because employees' hopes will have been aroused, only to be disappointed.

These four points lead us to expect something like the picture of relationships between supervisory behavior and employee satisfaction shown in Figure 1. If such a picture should emerge, we could say that the supervisor's influence "conditions" his leadership. That is, his amount of influence (high or low) determines whether his supervisory behavior will cause employee satisfaction to rise (the solid line) or to fall (the dotted line).

INSTALLMENT NO. 3: HOW INFLUENCE "CONDITIONS" LEADERSHIP BEHAVIOR

For the third analysis of our study, to determine how the supervisor's influence "conditions" the effects of his leadership behavior, two kinds of supervisory behavior were selected: the degree to which he "takes sides with employees or with management" and the degree of his "social closeness" to employees. In general, it seems likely that the supervisor

FIGURE 1

Theoretical Effect of Supervisor's Behavior on Employee Satisfaction

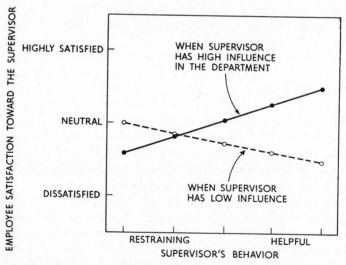

who sides with employees and is socially close to them will behave more in the "helpful" direction. And, in general, it seems likely that the supervisor who sides with management and who is socially distant from employees will behave more in the "restraining" direction.

We then computed statistical measures to find out how these supervisory behaviors seemed to affect various employee attitudes. A "positive" measure of relationship would indicate that employee satisfaction was higher under those supervisors who tended to take the employees' side and who were socially close to employees. A "negative" relationship would indicate the reverse: Employees were more dissatisfied under supervisors showing these behaviors.[1]

The results were, in general, pretty much in line with the theory. Data never fit a theory completely; there are too many other factors at work. But note the striking correspondence between the theoretical diagram shown in Figure 1 and some of the actual results shown in Figure 2.

FIGURE 2

RELATIONSHIP OF SUPERVISOR'S "TAKING SIDES" TO EMPLOYEE SATISFACTION

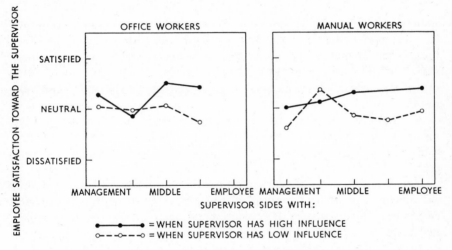

Figure 2 shows that under influential supervisors (solid line) an increase in "siding with employees" is accompanied by a general rise in employee satisfaction. But under noninfluential supervisors (dotted line) the same behavior produces no rise but a slight drop in employee satisfaction.

This diagram shows only one aspect of the results. The complete picture is given in Figure 3. For the group of high-influence supervisors, we obtained 28 measures of relationship between the supervisory behavior and various employee attitudes in different types of situations. For

---

[1] A technical note: The strength of these positive or negative relationships was measured with product moment correlations. Several employee attitudes were used, the main one being an index of employees' satisfaction with the way the supervisor himself was doing his job. The relationships were measured separately under influential and under noninfluential supervisors for each of seven different types of employees or work situations. That is, separate analyses were performed for white-collar *vs.* blue-collar occupations, men *vs.* women, small groups *vs.* large groups, and groups covered by a union contract *vs.* groups not so covered. Several statistical controls were used which need not be described here.

FIGURE 3

ALL RELATIONSHIPS BETWEEN SUPERVISORY BEHAVIORS
AND EMPLOYEE SATISFACTIONS

```
+ =POSITIVE RELATIONSHIPS ( r = +.06 OR GREATER )
0 =ZERO RELATIONSHIPS     ( r = ±.05 OR LESS )
− =NEGATIVE RELATIONSHIPS ( r = −.06 OR GREATER )
```

```
HIGH-INFLUENCE SUPERVISORS   +++++++++++++++++++000 ——————
LOW-INFLUENCE SUPERVISORS    ++++++++00000000 ———————————
```

the low-influence supervisors, we obtained a parallel set of 28 measures. According to the theory, we should obtain generally positive relationships under high-influence supervisors but zero or negative relationships under low-influence supervisors.

Under high-influence supervisors, in 19 times out of 28 we find that "siding with employees" and "social closeness" are accompanied by some rise in employee satisfaction. (Seven of the positive correlations are large enough to be "statistically significant," a result which is 11 times better than chance.) But, under low-influence supervisors, these supervisory behaviors are accompanied by a rise in satisfaction only 8 times out of 28; a loss in satisfaction (negative effect) is the more common result.

All the measures of relationship were modest in size. But the positive results under influential supervisors were sufficiently uniform that the total set may be regarded as highly trustworthy (or "statistically significant").

It seems fairly clear, then, that a supervisor's influence or power within the department does "condition" the way his supervisory behavior affects employee attitudes. It is plausible to conclude that *the supervisory behaviors of "siding with employees" and "social closeness to employees" will tend to raise employee satisfaction only if the supervisor has enough influence to make these behaviors pay off in terms of actual benefits for employees.*

LIGHT ON MYSTERY OF INSTALLMENT NO. 2

The contradictory effects which we discovered in the second analysis can be solved in part by these new findings, although—as always with social data—an explanation in terms of any single factor is never complete. Further analysis of the data showed that in this company's *small* groups the supervisors who sided with employees also tended to be the ones who had high influence and could get results when they attempted to do something. On the other hand, in this company's *large* work groups the supervisors who took the employees' side were generally the ones without influence; they could not follow up their helpful attempts with concrete gains for employees; as a result, employees were less satisfied than if their supervisors had maintained a neutral position. Facts such as these helped to clear up the mystery of our previous findings.

We do not know at the present time whether these facts about work-group size and supervisor's influence are true of other companies. We must be careful not to claim a general principle here before studying more companies.

IMPLICATIONS FOR ADMINISTRATORS

According to these findings, if an influential supervisor attempts to help employees achieve their goals, his efforts will tend to succeed. Concrete results will be achieved, and therefore employee satisfaction will rise. But—according to the data—if a noninfluential supervisor tries to get the same results, his efforts may often fail. Employee expectations will be frustrated, and consequently their satisfactions will not rise and may even fall.

Such findings have several implications:

1. It may not be possible to give supervisors a universal set of rules on how to behave so as to maximize their employees' satisfaction. What each man should do or should not try to do will depend, among other things, on how much weight he carries within the organization. In general, the supervisor should probably not attempt to do more for his employees than he can reasonably hope to accomplish.

2. The same principle applies to the current emphasis on the training of first-line supervisors. If the supervisors lack the authority or the influence to put the training into practice, in a way that produces concrete changes, then perhaps we may question whether the training should be given at all. Training courses should urge the supervisor to introduce changes only in matters where he has considerable authority or where he has the real support of supervision at higher levels. Otherwise the result may only be frustration for himself and his group.[2]

3. Even further, it may in some cases be necessary to *increase* the amount of influence given to first-level supervisors—by increasing their voice in higher decisions, by delegating more autonomy to them. These are substantial changes, not to be suggested lightly. But it may be that many training courses cannot improve the effectiveness of supervisory leadership unless management is willing to give a larger share of influence to this supervisory level.

4. At the same time, it becomes essential to examine the effects of giving supervisors a larger voice, as many writers on administration are advising. How is this increased power to be used? It is a potential source of threat to employees as well as a benefit. Perhaps it should not be undertaken unless steps are taken simultaneously to make sure the increased power is used in helpful ways rather than in restraining and hindering ways.

---

[2] This same conclusion about training is illustrated in an article by Monroe Berkowitz called "Education of Foremen Can Be Dangerous," in the March, 1952, issue of *Personnel*.

5. And, finally, from the long-range standpoint of the science of management, it becomes clearer that "group leadership" and "organization" are not distinct concepts but are inseparably intertwined. The organization "conditions" the effects of leadership, and probably the reverse is true. An organization cannot be understood simply by breaking it up into small groups and studying them in isolation. Nor can we understand the way a leader relates to his group unless we also study how they both relate to the rest of the organization.

35. Patterns in Management*

Rensis Likert

THE TIME HAS come to examine the findings that are now emerging from research on organization and leadership and to ask what are the implications of these findings for the development and training of those who will occupy positions of executive leadership in the next decade or two.

In trying to look into the future, it will be useful to consider historical trends as well as to examine the general pattern that is emerging from research findings. Two important trends have resulted in significant improvement in industrial performance and are exercising a major influence on current management practices. It will be of value to examine these trends, the character of their contribution, and the problems which they are creating.

"SCIENTIFIC MANAGEMENT"

The first of the two trends to be examined began almost a century ago. This was the earlier of the two and is the one which has had by far the greater influence upon both management practices and industrial productivity. I refer to the whole movement in which Frederick W. Taylor and his colleagues provided pioneering leadership. In discussing this trend, for purposes of brevity, I shall use the term "scientific management" to refer to this whole movement and related developments.

Generally speaking, the very great improvements in productivity brought about by scientific management have resulted from the elimination of waste. Functionalization, work simplification, motion study, analysis of work flow, standardization, and so on, have all resulted in

---

* From "Developing Patterns in Management," General Management Series No. 178, American Management Association, Inc., 1955.

simpler work cycles with the elimination of much waste motion and effort. They have also reduced the amount of learning required. Similarly, the establishment of clear-cut and specific goals and the creation of well-defined channels of communication, decision making, and control have contributed to better productivity. But associated with these gains have been some serious problems and adverse effects.

The setting of production goals through the use of time standards often has been accompanied by a higher level of expected productivity and increased pressure on the workers to produce more. Workers resented and resisted this, and the "speed-up" was and still is a major source of conflict and bitterness. Moreover, workers and supervisors often resented an industrial engineer's providing evidence that they had been stupid when he showed that a much simpler and easier way of doing the work was possible. Another aspect of this method of managing which caused resentment was the view that workers could contribute nothing of value to the organization of their jobs and to the methods of work to be used. As Henry Ford expressed it, "All that we ask of the men is that they do the work which is set before them."[1]

These and similar adverse effects of scientific management were recognized more and more clearly during the second, third, and fourth decades of this century. The "speed-up" and "efficiency engineering" were the source of much hostility on the part of workers and supervisors. The resentments and hostilities manifested themselves in a variety of ways. They resulted in widespread restriction of output, even under incentive pay, and in a demand for protection through unions which led to the Wagner Act.

HUMAN RELATIONS TREND

The second trend which I wish to examine started at the end of the First World War when a few business leaders and social scientists began to appreciate the consequences of these and similar problems which accompanied the use of the scientific management approach. More general recognition of these problems, however, was brought about dramatically by the famous Western Electric studies. In the midtwenties the National Research Council arranged with the Massachusetts Institute of Technology for Vannevar Bush and Joseph Barker to study the effect of different amounts of illumination, ventilation, and rest periods upon the production of industrial workers. They conducted this research in the Hawthorne plant of the Western Electric Company. After a few years of experimentation it became clear that morale and motivation factors were so important that they were completely obscuring the effect of the illumination, ventilation, and fatigue factors being

---

[1] H. Pord and S. Crowther, *Today and Tomorrow* (New York: Doubleday, 1926).

studied. Bush then withdrew, suggesting that the morale factors were important and should be studied by social scientists, whereupon Elton Mayo and his colleagues undertook the research which resulted in their famous reports.[2]

These studies showed conclusively and quantitatively that workers were responding to scientific management methods by restricting production to levels which the workers felt were appropriate. Moreover, incentive methods of payment, either individual or group, did not prevent this restriction. These studies also showed that the workers had developed an "informal organization" which differed from the "formal" or organization-chart organization. Through this informal organization, workers exercised an important influence upon the behavior of themselves and their colleagues, often effectively countermanding the orders given officially through the formal organization. The Western Electric studies also showed that when the hostilities, resentments, suspicions, and fears of workers were replaced by favorable attitudes, a substantial increase in production occurred. The results showed that unfavorable attitudes exert an appreciable restraining influence upon productivity.

Mathewson,[3] Houser,[4] and others in a modest number of studies during the thirties showed that conditions existing in the Western Electric Company were relatively widespread. Morale and motivational factors were found to influence production. Restriction of output was common, and "informal organizations" were found to exist in most of the companies studied.

EMERGING PATTERN

During the past decade this second trend, which might be called the human relations trend, has gained greater impetus. The volume of research is still small but growing. The findings are consistent with the earlier studies and have important implications for the future trend of management theories and practices.

Some of the relevant parts of the pattern of results emerging from this more recent research can be shown by presenting a few findings from studies conducted by the Institute for Social Research. Since 1947 we have been conducting a series of related studies[5] seeking to find what kinds of organizational structure and what principles and methods of

---

[2] E. Mayo, *The Human Problems of an Industrial Civilization,* Harvard Business School, Division of Research, 1946 (first printing by the Macmillan Co., 1933); F. J. Roethlisberger and W. J. Dickson, *Management and the Worker* (Cambridge: Harvard University Press, 1939).

[3] S. B. Mathewson, *Restriction of Output among Unorganized Workers* (New York: The Viking Press, 1931).

[4] J. D. Houser, *What People Want from Business* (New York: McGraw-Hill Book Co., Inc., 1938).

[5] Generous support from the Office of Naval Research, the Rockefeller Foundation, and the companies and agencies involved have made this research possible.

leadership and management result in the highest productivity, least absence, lowest turnover, and the greatest job satisfaction.[6] Studies have been conducted or are under way in a wide variety of organizations. These include one or more companies in such industries as the following: public utilities, insurance, automotive, railroad, electric appliances, heavy machinery, textiles, and petroleum.[7] Studies also have been made in government agencies.[8]

In general, the design of the studies has been to measure and examine the kinds of leadership and related variables being used by the best units in the organization in contrast to those being used by the poorest. In essence, these studies are providing management with a mirror by measuring and reporting what is working best in industry today.

Briefly stated, some of the findings which are relevant for this discussion follow.

Orientation of Supervision. When foremen are asked what they have found to be the best pattern of supervision to get results, a substantial proportion, usually a majority, will place primary emphasis on getting out production. By this they mean placing primary emphasis on seeing that workers are using the proper methods, are sticking to their work, and are getting a satisfactory volume of work done. Other supervisors, whom we have called employee-centered, report that they get the best results when they place primary emphasis on the human problems of their workers. The employee-centered supervisor endeavors to build a team of

---

[6] "A Program of Research on the Fundamental Problems of Organizing Human Behavior" (Ann Arbor: Institute for Social Research, University of Michigan, 1946).

[7] L. Coch and J. French, "Overcoming Resistance to Change," *Human Relations*, Vol. 1, 1948, pp. 512–32; R. Kahn and D. Katz, "Leadership Practices in Relation to Productivity and Morale," a chapter in D. Cartwright and A. Zander (eds.), *Group Dynamics Research and Theory* (Evanston: Row, Peterson and Company, 1953); D. Katz and R. Kahn, "Human Organization and Worker Motivation," a chapter *Industrial Productivity*, Industrial Relations Research Association, 1952; D. Katz and R. Kahn, "Some Recent Findings in Human Relations Research," a chapter in E. Swanson, T. Newcomb, and E. Hartley (eds), *Readings in Social Psychology* (New York: Henry Holt and Co., 1952); D. Katz, N. Maccoby, G. Gurin, and L. Floor, *Productivity, Supervision and Morale among Railroad Workers* (Ann Arbor: University of Michigan Press, 1951); D. Katz, N. Maccoby, and N. Morse, *Productivity, Supervision and Morale in an Office Situation, Part 1* (Ann Arbor: University of Michigan Press, 1950); F. Mann and H. Baumgartel, *Absences and Employee Attitudes in an Electric Power Company*, Institute for Social Research, 1953; F. Mann and H. Baumgartel, *The Supervisor's Concern with Costs in an Electric Power Company*, Institute for Social Research, 1953; F. Mann and J. Dent, *Appraisals of Supervisors and Attitudes of Their Employees in an Electric Power Company*, Institute for Social Research, 1954; N. Morse, *Satisfactions in the White-Collar Job* (Ann Arbor: University of Michigan Press, 1953); S. Seashore, *Group Cohesiveness in the Industrial Work Group* (Ann Arbor: University of Michigan Press, 1955).

[8] E. Jacobson and S. E. Seashore, "Communication Practices in Complex Organizations," *The Journal of Social Issues*, Vol. VII, No. 3, 1951; D. Marvick, *Career Perspectives in a Bureaucratic Setting* (Ann Arbor: Institute of Public Administration, University of Michigan Press, 1954).

people who cooperate and work well together. He tries to place people together who are congenial. He not only trains people to do their present job well but tends to train them for the next higher job. He is interested in helping them with their problems on the job and off the job. He is friendly and supportive, rather than punitive and threatening.

Higher levels of management, in discussing how they want their foremen to supervise, tend to place more emphasis on the production-centered approach as the best way to get results than do foremen.[9] Workers, on the other hand, tend to place less.

But which orientation yields the best results? A variety of studies in widely different industries show that supervisors who are getting the best production, the best motivation, and the highest levels of worker satisfaction are employee-centered appreciably more often than production-centered.[10] This is shown in Exhibit 1.

EXHIBIT 1

"EMPLOYEE-CENTERED" SUPERVISORS ARE HIGHER PRODUCERS
THAN "PRODUCTION-CENTERED" SUPERVISORS . . .

NUMBER OF FIRST-LINE SUPERVISORS

	PRODUCTION-CENTERED	EMPLOYEE-CENTERED
HIGH SECTIONS	1	6
LOW SECTIONS	7	3
HIGH DIVISIONS	3	7
LOW DIVISIONS	7	4

There is an important point to be added to this finding: Those employee-centered supervisors who get the best results tend to recognize that getting production is also one of their major responsibilities.

Closeness of Supervision. Related to orientation of supervision is closeness of supervision. Close supervision tends to be associated with lower productivity and more general supervision with higher productivity. This relationship, shown in Exhibit 2, holds for workers and supervisors.[11]

Low productivity, no doubt, at times leads to closer supervision, but it is clear also that it causes low productivity. In one of the companies involved in this research program it has been found that switching managers of high- and low-production divisions results in the high-produc-

---

[9] E. A. Fleishman, "Leadership Climate, Human Relations Training, and Supervisory Behavior," *Personnel Psychology*, Vol. 6, No. 3, 1953.

[10] D. Katz, N. Maccoby, and N. Morse, *Productivity, Supervision and Morale in an Office Situation, Part I, op. cit.*

[11] *Ibid.*

EXHIBIT 2

LOW-PRODUCTION SECTION HEADS ARE MORE CLOSELY
SUPERVISED THAN ARE HIGH-PRODUCTION HEADS . . .

NUMBER OF FIRST-LINE SUPERVISORS

	UNDER CLOSE SUPERVISION	UNDER GENERAL SUPERVISION
HIGH SECTIONS	1	9
LOW SECTIONS	8	4
HIGH DIVISIONS	4	11
LOW DIVISIONS	11	5

tion managers' raising the productivity of the low-production divisions faster than the former high-production divisions slip under the low-production managers. Supervisors, as they are shifted from job to job, tend to carry with them and to maintain their habitual attitudes toward the supervisory process and toward their subordinates.

Closeness of supervision is also related to the attitudes of workers toward their supervisors. Workers under foremen who supervise closely have a less favorable attitude toward their boss than do workers who are under foremen who supervise more generally.

EXPERIMENT DESCRIBED

These results which have just been presented on closeness of supervision and on employee-centered supervision were among those found early in the series of studies conducted by the Institute. They led to an experiment which I should like to describe briefly.

As we have seen, the research findings indicate that close supervision results in lower productivity, less favorable attitudes, and less satisfaction on the part of the workers; while more general supervision achieves higher productivity, more favorable attitudes, and greater employee satisfaction. These results suggest that it should be possible to increase productivity in a particular situation by shifting the pattern of the supervision so as to make it more general. To test this we conducted an experiment involving 500 clerical employees.[12]

Very briefly, the experiment was as follows: Four parallel divisions were used, each organized the same as the others, each using the same technology and doing exactly the same kind of work with employees of comparable aptitude. In two divisions, the decision levels were pushed down, and more general supervision of the clerks and their supervisors was introduced. In addition, the managers, assistant managers, supervisors, and assistant supervisors of these two divisions were trained in group

[12] N. Morse, E. Reimer, and A. Tannenbaum, "Regulation and Control in Hierarchical Organizations," *The Journal of Social Issues*, Vol. VII, No. 3, 1951.

methods of leadership.[13] The experimental changes in these two divisions will be called Program I.

In order to provide an effective experimental control on the changes in supervision which were introduced in Program I, the supervision in the other two divisions was modified so as to increase the closeness of supervision and move the decision levels upward. This will be called Program II. These changes were accomplished by a further extension of the scientific management approach. One of the major changes made was to have the jobs timed by the methods department and standard times computed. This showed that these divisions were overstaffed by about 30 per cent. The general manager then ordered the managers of these

EXHIBIT 3

CHANGE IN PRODUCTIVITY

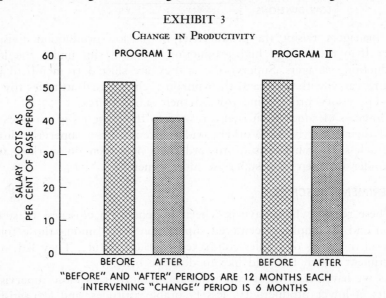

"BEFORE" AND "AFTER" PERIODS ARE 12 MONTHS EACH
INTERVENING "CHANGE" PERIOD IS 6 MONTHS

two divisions to cut staff by 25 per cent. This was to be done by transfers and by not replacing persons who left; no one, however, was to be dismissed.

Productivity in all four of the divisions depended upon the number of clerks involved. The work was something like a billing operation; there was just so much of it, but it had to be processed as it came along. Consequently, the only way in which productivity could be increased was to change the size of the work group. The four divisions were assigned to the experimental programs on a random basis, but in such a manner that a high- and low-productivity division was assigned to each program.

The experiment at the clerical level lasted for one year. Several months were devoted to planning prior to the experimental year, and

---

[13] Methods developed by the National Training Laboratory in Group Development were drawn upon heavily in this training.

there was a training period of approximately six months just prior to the experimental year. Productivity was measured continuously and computed weekly throughout the period. Employee and supervisory attitudes and related variables were measured just before and after the experimental year.

Productivity Reflected in Salary Costs. Exhibit 3 shows the changes in salary costs which reflect the changes in productivity that occurred. As will be observed, Program II, where there was an increase in the closeness of supervision, increased productivity by about 25 per cent. This, it will be recalled, was a result of direct orders from the general manager to reduce staff by that amount.

EXHIBIT 4

EMPLOYEES' FEELING OF RESPONSIBILITY TO SEE THAT WORK GETS DONE

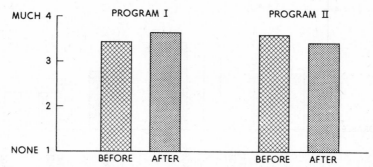

Exhibit 3 shows, furthermore, that a significant increase in productivity was achieved in Program I, where supervision was modified so as to be less close. The increase in productivity in Program I was not so great as in Program II but, nevertheless, was a little more than 20 per cent. One division in Program I increased its productivity by about the same amount as each of the two divisions in Program II. The other division in Program I, which historically had been the poorest of all of the divisions, did not do so well.

Productivity and Workers' Responsibility. Although both programs were alike in increasing productivity, they were significantly different in the other changes which occurred. The productivity increases in Program II, where decision levels were moved up, were accompanied by shifts in an adverse direction in attitudes, interest, and involvement in the work and related matters. The opposite was true in Program I. Exhibit 4, for example, shows that when more general supervision is provided, as in Program I, the employees' feeling of responsibility to see that the work gets done is increased. In Program II, however, this responsibility decreased. In Program I, when the supervisor was away, the employees kept on working. When the supervisor was absent in Program II, the work tended to stop.

Effect of Employee Attitudes. Exhibit 5 shows how the programs changed in regard to the workers' attitudes toward their superiors. In Program I all the shifts were favorable; in Program II all the shifts were unfavorable. One significant aspect of these changes in Program II was that the girls felt that their superiors were relying more on rank and authority to get the work done. In general, the shifts were greatest, both favorable in Program I and unfavorable in Program II, for those relationships which other studies have shown to be the most important in influencing behavior in the working situation. A number of other meas-

EXHIBIT 5

SATISFACTION WITH SUPERIORS AS REPRESENTATIVES

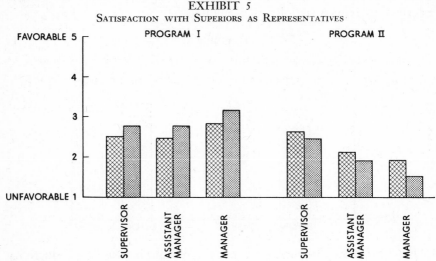

ures of attitudes toward superiors all showed similar shifts: favorable in Program I and unfavorable in Program II.

FUNDAMENTAL CONCLUSION

This very brief description of this experiment, I hope, has made clear the pattern of results. Both experimental changes increased productivity substantially. In Program I this increase in productivity was accompanied by shifts in a favorable direction in attitudes, interests, and perceptions. The girls became more interested and involved in their work, they accepted more responsibility for getting the work done, their attitudes toward the company and their superiors became more favorable, and they accepted direction more willingly. In Program II, however, all these attitudes and related variables shifted in an unfavorable direction. All the hostilities, resentments, and unfavorable reactions which have been observed again and again to accompany extensive use of the scientific management approach manifested themselves.

This experiment with clerical workers is important because it shows that increases in productivity can be obtained with either favorable or unfavorable shifts in attitudes, perceptions, and similar variables. Further application of classical methods of scientific management substantially increased productivity, but it was accompanied by adverse attitudinal reactions upon the part of the workers involved. With the other approach used in the experiment, a substantial increase in productivity was also obtained, but here it was accompanied by shifts in attitudes and similar variables in a favorable direction. A fundamental conclusion from this experiment and other similar research is that direct pressure from one's superior for production tends to be resented, while group pressure from one's colleagues is not.[14]

EXHIBIT 6

THE RELATION OF PRODUCTIVITY AND MORALE
TO SUPERVISOR'S PRESSURE FOR PRODUCTION

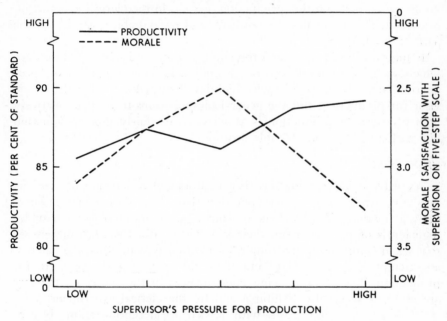

PRESSURE FOR PRODUCTION

Keeping in mind these results, let us look at another chart. The solid line in Exhibit 6 shows the relation between the amount of pressure a worker feels from his foreman for production and the productivity of the worker. Productivity is measured, and shown in the chart, as a percentage of standard; i.e., jobs are timed, standards are set, and production is then expressed as a percentage of standard. As will be observed, the chart shows that greater pressure from the supervisor is associated with higher production. The differences in production from low pressure to high pressure are not great, but they are large enough to be important in any highly competitive industry.

[14] L. Coch and J. French, *op. cit.*

The broken line in Exhibit 6 shows the relationship between amount of pressure the worker feels from his supervisor and his attitude toward his supervisor. In interpreting this curve, it is important to keep in mind that a worker's attitude toward his supervisor has a major influence upon all his other attitudes toward his work and his work situation, as well as his motivations toward his work. Little interest in production on the part of the supervisor, a laissez-faire point of view, is associated both with low production and with a less favorable attitude toward the supervisor. Workers who experience an average amount of pressure from their supervisors express the most favorable attitude toward them, while those workers who report feeling the greatest pressure from their supervisors have the least favorable attitude of all workers toward their supervisors. Direct pressure for production, here as in the clerical experiment, is associated with hostility, resentment, and unfavorable attitudes on the part of workers.

Exhibit 6 is based on several thousand workers and shows relationships which we have found also in other studies. In some situations the production curve drops slightly with high levels of pressure from the supervisor for production. But the general picture seems to be that relatively high pressure for production is associated with fairly good production but with relatively unfavorable attitudes.

HIGH COST

Available evidence indicates that a substantial proportion of workers generally are working under conditions like those shown in Exhibit 6. Only a fraction of all workers, of course, are working at present under high levels of pressure from their supervisors. But the probabilities are that when competition gets tough for a company, and costs must be cut, an attempt will be made to cut them by increasing the pressure for production. The accompanying consequences of this increased pressure are clear, as shown by Exhibit 6 and by the clerical experiment.

A similar situation exists with regard to decentralization. Decentralization is generally viewed as one way of pushing decisions down and providing more general supervision. But, when the decentralization involves basing the compensation of the man in charge of the decentralized unit largely on the earnings shown by this unit, increased pressure on subordinates often occurs. Substantial earnings over the short run can occur from supervising subordinates more closely and putting more pressure on them to increase production and earnings. But the adverse effects both on subordinates and on workers can be predicted. If current reports are correct, the staffs of some decentralized units are genuinely unhappy over the pressure which they are experiencing. Trained engineers as well as non-supervisory employees are leaving, even for jobs that pay less.

Thus, though the scientific management approach has clearly demonstrated its capacity to get high production, this productivity is obtained at a serious cost. People will produce at relatively high levels when the techniques of production are efficient, the pressures for production are great, the controls and inspections are relatively tight, and the economic rewards and penalties are sufficiently large. But such production is accompanied by attitudes which tend to result in high scrap loss, lowered safety, higher absence and turnover, increased grievances and work stoppages, and the like. It also is accompanied by communication blocks and restrictions. All these developments tend to affect adversely the operation of any organization. Restricted communications, for example, tend to result in decisions based on misinformation or a lack of information.

INITIATIVE AND PARTICIPATION

In considering the strengths and weaknesses of the scientific management approach and how to deal with them, I believe that there is an important long-range trend to keep in mind. Supervisors and managers report in interviews that people are less willing to accept pressure and close supervision than was the case a decade or two ago. For example, one supervisor said:

Girls want to and do express themselves more today than when I started to work. In the past, girls were more cringing and pliable, but not now. We get a great many girls who have had no restraints at home, and we have to do the teaching.

The trend in America generally, in our schools, in our homes, and in our communities is toward giving the individual greater freedom and initiative. There are fewer direct, unexplained orders in schools and homes, and youngsters are participating increasingly in decisions which affect them. These fundamental changes in American society create expectations among employees as to how they should be treated. These expectations profoundly affect employee attitudes, since attitudes depend upon the extent to which our experiences meet our expectations. If experience falls short of expectations, unfavorable attitudes occur. When our experience is better than our expectations, we tend to have favorable attitudes. This means, of course, that if expectations in America are changing in a particular direction, experience must change in the same direction or the attitudinal response of people to their experiences will be correspondingly influenced.

In my opinion, the cultural changes occurring in the United States will, in the next few decades, make people expect even greater opportunities for initiative and participation than is now the case.

POSSIBLE ADVANTAGES

There are important advantages to be gained if the resources of the scientific management approach and the human relations approach can be combined. These are illustrated schematically in Exhibit 7, which shows the relation between morale and production.

On the basis of a study I did in 1937,[15] I believed that morale and productivity were positively related; that the higher the morale, the higher the production. Substantial research findings since then have shown that this relationship is much too simple. In our different studies we have found a wide variety of relationships. Some units have low morale and low production; they would fall in Area A on the chart. Other units have fairly good morale and low production; these fall in Area B. Still others have fairly good production but low morale; these

EXHIBIT 7

SCHEMATIC RELATIONSHIP BETWEEN MORALE AND PRODUCTIVITY

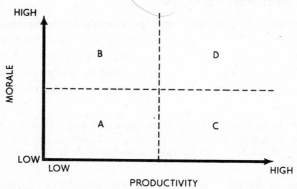

fall in Area C. Finally, other units have both high morale and high production and fall in Area D on the chart.

Units with low morale and low production (Area A) tend to have supervision which is laissez faire in character and in which the leadership function has been abandoned to all intents and purposes. Units which fall in Area B and have fairly good morale but poor production tend to have supervisors who try to keep people "happy." These supervisors are often found in companies in which human relations training programs have been introduced and emphasized.

Some supervisors in these companies interpret the training to mean that the company management wants them to keep employees happy; therefore, they work hard to do so. The morale of these workers is essentially complacent in character. The result is a nice "country club" atmosphere. Employees like it, and absence and turnover are low; but, since little production is felt to be expected, the workers produce relatively little.

Into Area C, of course, fall those units which have technically compe-

---

[15] R. Likert and J. Willits, *Morale and Agency Management* (Hartford: Life Insurance Agency Management Association, 1940).

tent supervision that is pressing for production. Area D includes those units which have a kind of supervision which results in high production with high morale, high satisfactions, and high motivation. Here the nature of the morale can be characterized as "the will to achieve."

INTEGRATED APPROACH

Most of us would agree, I believe, that the kind of supervision which we desire is that which is represented by Area D. It is my further belief that this kind of supervision represents an integration of the scientific management and human relations approach which has not yet been fully achieved and about which we know relatively little.

What will be required for the resources of these two approaches to be integrated fully and effectively? I am not sure that I know the answer to this question, but I should like to suggest a way of coping with it which I believe has real promise. Fundamentally, what I wish to propose is that the major resources of human relations research be focused upon what experience and research have shown to be the major weakness in the scientific management approach.

The tremendous contribution which scientific management and related management theories have made to increasing production and to improved organizational performance provides adequate evidence as to the great power of the basic concepts involved. These concepts include emphasis on such processes as the following:

1. The elimination of waste and inefficiency through functionalization, work simplification, and related processes.
2. The establishment of specific work goals.
3. The measurement of work accomplished and the continual examination of the extent to which the specified goals are being achieved.
4. Coordinated and clear-cut channels of control, communication, and decision making.

IMPORTANCE OF MOTIVATION

The critical weaknesses in the scientific management approach, of course, are the resentments, hostilities, and adverse motivational and attitudinal reactions which it tends to evoke. In my judgment, these hostilities and unfavorable attitudes stem from powerful motives which the scientific management approach has ignored in its over-all conceptualization and in the day-to-day operating procedures which it has developed. Although the scientific management approach has ignored these powerful motives, it has not been able to avoid the substantial impact of their influence in daily operations.

The fundamental cause, therefore, of the adverse motivational reactions produced by the scientific management approach is the inadequate motivational assumption upon which it is based. It assumes, as classical management and economic theories do generally, that all persons are simple economic men.[16] More specifically, the underlying motivational assumption upon which scientific management is based is that it is only necessary to buy a man's time and he will then do willingly and effectively everything which he is ordered to do. Management textbooks emphasize authority and control as the foundation of administration. They either take for granted the power to control or hold that "the relationship of employer and employee in an enterprise is a contractual obligation entailing the right to command and the duty to obey."[17]

The critical weakness of the scientific management approach occurs at precisely the point where the human relations research approach has its greatest strength: motivation. The great power of human relations research findings is in the understanding and insight which they provide as to:

1. The character and magnitude of the powerful motivational forces which control human behavior in working situations.
2. The manner in which these forces can be used so that they reinforce rather than conflict with one another.

MODIFIED THEORY CALLED FOR

The fundamental problem, therefore, is to develop an organizational and management theory, and related supervisory and managerial practices for operating under this theory, which will make use of the tremendous resources of the scientific management concepts while fully utilizing in a positive and reinforcing manner the great power of all the major motivational forces which influence human behavior in working situations. To develop this organizational and management theory will be slow, complex, and difficult work. The motives upon which this modified theory should be based include:

1. All the economic motives.
2. All the ego motives including the desires for status, recognition, approval, sense of importance and personal worth, etc.
3. The desire for security.
4. The desire for new experiences.

Human relations research is yielding concepts which appear to be important tools in deriving a modified theory of management. For example, the research findings have clearly demonstrated that there is no set of specific supervisory practices which is the right or best way to supervise. A way of supervising which may yield the best results in one specific situation may produce poor results in a different situation.[18] The behavior

---

[16] The gross inadequacy of this assumption with regard to the behavior of people as consumers has been amply demonstrated. See, e.g., Katona, *Psychological Analysis of Economic Behavior* (New York: McGraw-Hill, 1951), or Klein, Katona, Lansing, and Morgan, *Contributions of Survey Methods to Economics* (New York: Columbia University Press, 1954).

[17] J. D. Millett, *Management in the Public Service* (New York: McGraw-Hill, 1954); C. O'Donnell, "The Source of Managerial Authority," *Political Science Quarterly*, Vol. 67, 1952, p. 573.

of the superior is not the only variable which determines the subordinate's response. The subordinate's response is also determined by what he has learned to expect. Consequently, the response of the subordinate to the behavior of the supervisor will be influenced by the "culture" of the plant or organization and the expectations of the subordinate. To help superiors meet the problems created by this major finding, human relations research is providing evidence as to general principles which can serve as guides to the most appropriate way to supervise in a given situation. Moreover, it is also providing rapid and efficient methods of measuring what the culture and expectations are in any given plant or unit.

CURRENT THINKING AND PRACTICE

The modified theory of management and the supervisory and managerial practices which can be derived, theoretically, when adequate motivational assumptions are used differ in important respects from the theory and practices commonly employed today. For example, with regard to methods of supervision, the current pattern of thinking and practic is in terms of a man-to-man pattern; each superior deals with each subordinate on a man-to-man basis. From a theoretical point of view, however, supervising each work group primarily as a group rather than relying on the man-to-man pattern should result in an appreciable improvement in performance. It is significant that there is an important and increasing body of research findings which indicate that group methods of supervision result in higher productivity, greater job satisfaction, and greater motivation than are obtained with the man-to-man pattern.

In discussing this particular derivation with a director of industrial relations a few months ago, I was impressed by his comment that top management in many of our most successful corporations implicitly recognize the value and power of group methods of supervision themselves and are using it in the top levels of their corporations. Apparently, these company officers recognize the value of group methods of supervision and use these methods personally. They have not generalized these methods, however, as standard operating procedures and extended them and related practices throughout the organization.

The available research findings, nevertheless, indicate that high group loyalty has an important influence upon performance at all levels in the organization. The data show that high group loyalty coupled with high production goals in the work group results in high productivity, accompanied by high job satisfaction and a feeling of working under little pressure. The data also show that in the work groups with high

---

[18] D. Pelz, "Influence: A Key to Effective Leadership in the First Line Supervisor," *Personnel*, Vol. 29, 1952. (Editor's Note: See the preceding article in this Section.)

group loyalty there is better communication between supervisors and men and each has a better understanding of the other's points of view.

FURTHER DERIVATIONS

Much more could be said about group methods of supervision and recent research findings bearing upon the importance of group loyalty. I hope, however, that this illustrates the kind of theoretical derivation of managerial practices that can be made, based upon more adequate motivational assumptions. Similar derivations can be made as to the manner in which selection, training, work simplification, functionalization, job evaluation, communication, compensation, decentralization, union-management relations, and so on, can and should be carried out so as to achieve the best all-around performance. In each case, the derivations that will be made are likely to point to procedures which will differ significantly from the practices now generally accepted.

Obviously, managerial and supervisory practices which are derived theoretically are bound to show some operational "bugs" or inadequacies when tested in operating situations. It is essential, therefore, to test and improve these derived practices in pilot or small-scale operations just as is done with any new process in chemistry or engineering. In these pilot projects it will be essential to have the full cooperation and participation of all those unions which represent the workers involved.

THE IMPLICATIONS

What are the implications of these developments for management and executive training? First, the proposed pilot projects offer a unique opportunity for training. Learning by doing has always been an effective training process. Consequently, I believe that one of the best ways to develop those persons who will become executives in the coming decades will be to have them play a major part now in conducting pilot projects.[19] These pilot projects would be devoted to testing and refining the improved supervisory and managerial practices which can be derived theoretically from available research findings.

A second major implication to be drawn is that important changes are occurring in the management and organizational theory and in the supervisory processes now being used by American industry. Managers and supervisors are in the process of developing and refining new theory and principles and improved practices. But, unfortunately, this is being done the hard and costly way, the trial-and-error way. Every research project dealing with supervision and leadership shows how the

---

[19] R. Likert and R. Lippitt, "The Utilization of Social Sciences," a chapter in L. Festinger and D. Katz (eds.), *Research Methods in the Behavioral Sciences* (New York: Dryden Press, 1953), pp. 581–646; *Training in Human Relations*, report of a seminar conducted by the Foundation for Research on Human Behavior, Ann Arbor, 1955.

most able supervisors and managers are struggling in company after company with trial-and-error methods to discover how to improve their supervision.

It is possible to wait for this trial-and-error process gradually to evolve and to make clear what the new organization and management theory and processes will be. It would be faster and much more efficient to use the power of systematic research and experimentation to accelerate their discovery and refinement.

In my judgment, those companies which support and cooperate in research to discover improved processes of management and to train their personnel will have a distinct advantage over companies which do not. Those which support research will discover at an earlier date the principles and practices which the successful companies of the future will be using and in which their own developing executives and managers should be trained. They will not experience the tragedy and cost of obsolete management.

36. An Evaluation of Two Attitudinal Approaches to Delegation*

Allen R. Solem

CURRENT PROBLEM-SOLVING procedures in business and industry indicate that there are many different points of view concerning the supervisory function of delegation. Although there appear to be relatively few problems in delegating the *execution* of decisions, there is a wide range of opinion concerning the degree to which it is advisable to share the decision-making function itself. Since not all decisions are properly subject to delegation the differences can be attributed in part at least to the types of problems involved. A more important factor, however, seems to be the superior's frame of reference toward his job and his subordinates. Some superiors prefer to decide things on their own with little or no prior consultation; others tend to seek the advice of staff experts or peers before deciding and still others frequently use consultative procedures for obtaining the views of subordinates as a basis for their decisions. Despite these variations in procedure a common factor in most approaches is that the superior must retain the authority

---

* From *Journal of Applied Psychology*, Vol. 42, 1958, pp. 36–39.

to modify or reject ideas or decisions which do not meet with his approval.

In contrast to this frame of reference is the attitude of placing final responsibility for certain decisions and for the end results in one's subordinates.[1] Such an attitude would imply that the superior reserves the right to decide what are the decisions he must make himself and what are those to be delegated. However, once the responsibility for making a decision or developing a solution has been placed in one's subordinates, the assumption is that the superior will accept and support the action regardless of whether he personally agrees with it or not. This means that subordinates are held accountable for results, not for developing solutions designed to obtain the approval of the superior.

The difference between these two views of delegation raises a number of relevant questions to problem-solving in management, including: (a) What influence, if any, does the delegation approach that is used have on solution quality? (b) Is there any difference between the two approaches as to the acceptance of the decisions by those who must carry them out? (c) What implications are there in the two procedures for the development of problem-solving and managerial abilities of subordinates? (d) To what extent do the differences between the two approaches reflect attitude differences as contrasted to such attributes as knowledge and skill? (e) What guides, if any, do the differences between these views of delegation indicate for management training and research?

Method

Subjects. The Ss were 456 supervisors attending a foremen's conference. They represented several levels of management and many different industries.

Role-playing problems. Two different management problems were used. Both problems have appeared in other previous publications[2] and are merely summarized here. One problem (referred to later as the New Truck Problem) concerns the allocation of a new truck among the five members of a crew of repairmen, all of whom want the truck. This creates an attitude conflict among the members which must be resolved before a solution can be reached. The other problem (designated as the Change of Work Procedure Problem) involves a crew of three men on a routine assembly operation who rotate positions periodically in order to prevent boredom. Meanwhile a methods study has revealed that if each man were to remain on the position

---

[1] K. Lewin, "Group Decision and Social Change," in T. M. Newcomb and E. I. Hartley (eds.), *Readings in Social Psychology* (New York: Henry Holt, 1947); N. R. F. Maier, "A Human Relations Program for Supervision," Industrial and Labor Relations Review, Vol. 1, No. 3, 1948, pp. 443–64; N. R. F. Maier, *Psychology in Industry* (2d ed., Boston: Houghton Mifflin, 1955); N. R. F. Maier, A. R. Solem, and A. Maier, *Supervisory and Executive Development; A Manual for Role Playing* (New York: Wiley, 1957).

[2] N. R. F. Maier, *Principles of Human Relations; Applications to Management* (New York: Wiley, 1952); N. R. F. Maier, *Psychology in Industry, op. cit.;* N. R. F. Maier, A. R. Solem, and A. Maier, *Supervisory and Executive Development; A Manual for Role Playing, op. cit.*

for which he is best suited there will be a considerable saving in time per unit. However, the men fear boredom and mistrust the management motives underlying the alteration in job procedure. Thus the problem typifies the forces involved in resistance to change.

Role-playing procedure. Multiple Role Playing[3] was used as the experimental procedure. Two separate experimental sessions were held (one for each problem) and the Ss in the two sessions were different so that practice effects were minimized.

PROBLEM 1

New truck problem. Following a lecture on the subject of attitudes, the Ss were formed into laboratory groups of approximately 40 individuals. These groups then met in separate rooms under the leadership of trained experimenters. When each group had assembled the Ss were informed that they were to participate in a discussion of a management problem involving a foreman and his crew of 5 repairmen, and since they were going to be these men in the discussion, the S's were asked to form into groups of six. A brief discussion was held as to the nature of role-playing procedures. Following this was a presentation of certain essential background information on the problem. The experimenter then gave one person at random in each group of six a set of roles (this person was thus designated as the leader of his group) with the instruction to retain the leader role (including the problem) and distribute the remaining five roles among the members in his crew. The sets of roles were the same for all crews; however, the individual member roles were different. Half of the leaders were given a written attitude instruction toward deciding what would be the fairest solution to the problem of allocating the new truck and then discussing the solution with their crews. The remaining half of the leaders were given a written attitude instruction toward presenting the problem to the crew for discussion and accepting whatever solution was developed. After 25 minutes of interaction, all discussions were ended and the experimenter then proceeded with the collection of the data and a general discussion of the results.

Data collection procedure. Data on the following aspects of the solutions were obtained from all groups, one group at a time.

1. Who got the new truck?
2. What disposition was made of that person's old truck [until all trucks had been accounted for]?
3. Are there any other aspects of the solution not already covered?
4. Is the leader satisfied or dissatisfied?
5. Which crew members are dissatisfied?

PROBLEM 2

Change of work procedure. The sequence of steps in the experimental procedure was the same as for the first problem. However, the experimental period was preceded with a lecture on frustration principles. In the laboratory session itself, the Ss were asked to form groups of four persons, as called for by the problem. Also the questions used in the collection of the data were different and consisted of the following:

1. What is the solution in your group [asked of the leader]?
2. Which of your crew members, if any, showed stubborn, hostile, or uncooperative reactions so as to create a problem in the discussion?

---

[3] Editor's Note: See Section III, Article 22.

3. What will happen to production if the solution you have settled on is put into effect [asked of all participants with separate tabulations for "increase," "decrease," and "stay about the same"]?
4. Are you [the leader] satisfied or dissatisfied with the solution?
5. Which crew members [if any] are dissatisfied?

Results

The results are shown in Table 1. The data which are unique to each problem are shown in Columns 2 through 7 and those which are common to both problems have been combined in Columns 8, 9, and 10.

TABLE 1

SOLUTIONS TO PROBLEMS DEVELOPED BY SUPERVISORS UNDER CONDITIONS OF LIMITED DELEGATION (LD) AND FULL DELEGATION (FD)

$(N = 456)$

| | NEW TRUCK PROBLEM | | CHANGE OF WORK PROCEDURE PROBLEM | | | BOTH PROBLEMS COMBINED | | |
	No. of Groups	Assign- ment of New Truck to Senior Man	Solutions Giving Varying Majori- ties Different Trucks (5, 4, & 3)	No. of Groups	Problem Persons	Estimating Production Increase	Satisfied Leaders	Dis- satisfied Group Members	Condi- tional Solutions
LD groups	19	10.5	21.1	20	20.0	71.2	84.6	19.7	23.1
FD groups	27	48.2	55.5	25	10.7	92.0	98:1	8.1	40.4
χ^2 (computed from fre- quencies)		7.18	5.48		2.30	13.42	6.60	10.08	3.02
Level of sig- nificance		(.01–.001)	(.01–.02)		(.10–.20)	(.001–.0001)	(.01–.02)	(.01–.001)	(.05–.10)

Under limited delegation (LD) the senior man had about one chance in ten of getting the new truck. However, under full delegation (FD) the new truck was assigned to the senior man in nearly half of the solutions. Thus it seems that the values in seniority as a basis for assigning the new truck tended to mean different things under the two delegation conditions.

When one crew member receives the new truck, then his previous one must be assigned to a different crew member or be disposed of. This means that several exchanges of vehicles may occur. Since such exchanges are voluntary they will occur when both parties feel they will gain in some way. The number of exchanges therefore may be taken as a measure of solution quality. Viewed in this light, the fact that three or more of the five crew members received different trucks about 2½ times as often under FD as under LD suggests that the superiors were less likely to see the possibility of rewarding several individuals than were the subordinates. A similar tendency is indicated with respect to the conditional solutions in Column 10. These are solutions which contain unique features or extras designed to satisfy particular needs of subordinates, and such solutions tended to occur more frequently under the FD condition. Further, an inspection of the raw data reveals an interesting qualitative difference in that the conditions developed under LD tend to be in the nature of concessions exacted from the superior, and under FD the conditions are in the nature of constructive improvements to the solution.

In Column 7 a somewhat different measure of solution quality is indicated for the Change of Work Procedure problem. These data represent the views of superiors and subordinates as to whether the adoption of the new solution will result in an increase in production vs. a decrease or no change. While it seems probable that feeling judgments of acceptance as well as intellectual evaluations of solution quality are both represented, the difference in proportion of those predicting a production increase to occur is significantly in favor of the FD condition.

In the Change of Work Procedure problem all superiors were provided with a ready-made solution to the problem for presentation to the subordinates. Given this limitation on the freedom of all superiors it is of some interest to note the greater tendency for subordinates under LD to be hostile, obstructive, or otherwise create a problem for the leader than was true under FD. In other words the superiors using the LD procedure apparently had a less pleasant experience in conducting their discussions than was true of those using the FD approach, yet were unable to improve things appreciably once the discussions got under way. Further evidence of a related nature is indicated in Columns 8 and 9 which shows that there were significantly fewer satisfied leaders under the LD condition and a significantly greater proportion of dissatisfied subordinates than under FD.

Discussion

The results indicate that a superior who reserves to himself the authority to make final decisions may not always expect as satisfactory results as when full responsibility for solving certain problems is delegated to one's subordinates. Regardless of how perceptive and fairminded the superior may try to be, it appears that he may often tend to misjudge the importance of group values and to overlook various opportunities for rewarding his subordinate group members. Further, the indications are that the LD approach as compared to FD is more likely to generate hostility and dissatisfaction among subordinates and result in a less satisfactory problem-solving experience for the superior himself.

In part at least, the differences in results appear to arise from the fact that the LD procedure causes the superior to take an initial position as to what is the proper solution so that, in reality, he is presenting a solution to the group, not a problem. To the degree that the solution is at variance with the needs and ideas of the subordinates, it becomes a focal point for the expression of dissatisfaction and criticism. A problem on the other hand tends to stimulate ideas and constructive thinking towards various alternative solutions. Hence, by presenting his own views as a solution the superior tends to place himself in the position of defending a given set of views rather than aiding his subordinates in the development of new ideas for solving the problem. Although logic may indicate the desirability of altering a decision in the light of important new information, this is not likely to occur when a superior feels that such action may be interpreted as a sign of weakness or indecision.

From this it appears that an important contribution of the full delegation attitude of the superior is that it influences subordinates toward constructive solution of a problem on its own merits. In so doing, it helps to avoid any tendencies toward merely giving lip service to a superior's solution, of arguing with him, or of doing as directed with reduced motivation.

The results from this one experiment yield only partial answers to some of the questions raised earlier in this report and even these answers must be viewed with reservations. For one thing the previous supervisory experiences of the subjects may have caused them to react differently to the experimental situation from other nonsupervisory employees in industry. In addition, the delegation conditions tested may not be representative of more than a very limited segment of managerial situations. Further studies for the exploration of these and other related issues are now in progress.

Summary

This experiment was concerned with the study of attitudinal influences on the delegation process. Management personnel were formed into groups of four and six members for the purpose of solving two different but typical industrial problems. In each group one member was selected at random to role play the part of the superior and the other members took the part of his subordinates. In half of the groups the superior was given an attitude cue toward arriving at a decision and then discussing things with his subordinates, thus limiting the delegation of problem solving. The remaining superiors were given an attitude cue toward presenting the problem to their subordinates for their solution, and accepting whatever decision was made, this being termed full delegation. In terms of solution quality, acceptance and satisfaction of superiors and subordinates, the full delegation procedure consistently yielded the more satisfactory results; five of seven differences being significant beyond the 2% level of confidence. The results are interpreted to mean that attitudes of supervision toward the delegation process may be an important factor in the solution of certain management problems.

37. Supervisory Problems in Decision Making*

Lee E. Danielson and Norman R. F. Maier

FREQUENTLY MEMBERS of management, especially at the first level, complain about the number of decisions that they are required to make and their lack of success in dealing with making decisions concerning human relations problems. Higher managements' discontent with the decisions made and the consequences of these decisions has caused many companies to institute some type of human relations training. Other companies have instituted similar courses because of their interest in developing their lower levels of management more fully. Regardless of the motivation, thousands of dollars are spent trying to improve supervisory decisions. One of the techniques of decision making that gained widespread recognition and use during World War II was the J. R. T. method of the T. W. I.[1] Basically this was the application of the "scientific method" to the industrial setting. The similarity is illustrated below.

J. R. T.	Scientific Method
Determine Objectives	State Problem
Get Facts (and Feelings)	Survey Literature
Weigh and Decide	Hypothesize and Select Hypothesis
Take Action	Test Hypothesis
Check Results	Check Results

Now let us apply such a technique to a situation where there is the possibility of a repairman violating a safety regulation. The regulation is known and the penalty for violation is a three-week layoff. How will the foreman proceed? One obvious path is a *judicial* one. The foreman accepts as his objective the establishment of the guilt or innocence of the worker and proceeds to gather facts and feelings to this end, then weigh and decide whether or not to lay off the worker, and to take the action deemed necessary. The pursuit of such a path frequently caused the foremen to lose sight of the more basic objective which lies beneath the original establishment of the rule and its accompanying penalty. Safety

---

* From *Journal of Applied Psychology*, Vol. 40, 1956, pp. 319–23.

[1] *The Training within Industry Report, 1940–1945: A Record of the Development of Management Techniques for Improvement of Supervision—Their Use and the Results* (Washington, D.C.: War Manpower Commission, Bureau of Training, Training within Industry Service, September, 1945), pp. 330 ff.

on the job is the objective of the worker, the foremen and the higher management. A foreman accepting this objective might collect entirely different facts and feelings, weigh and decide on the basis of these, and take very different actions. The purpose of this study is to determine what paths are followed and what are the consequences of such pursuits.

SUBJECTS

This study was conducted during a supervisory training course given in a large chemical company. The participants were first and second level supervisors, who met in 29 small groups of approximately 14 for training purposes. The total number of participants is 154 pairs of supervisors.

PROCEDURE

An ideal procedure for the investigation of the decision making process of supervisors would be to have trained observers follow the supervisors during their work day and thus observe, record and analyze how they handle problems in the "real" work situations. Time and personnel limitations make this impractical and great difficulty would be encountered when one would try to find comparability as to the problem solved. Multiple Role Playing[2] is a technique that approaches the "real" work situation, is practical, and permits replication of the problem. By dividing an audience into smaller groups, in this instance pairs of supervisors, the small groups can be presented with and attempt to solve the same problem simultaneously. While the problem is the same, this technique still permits each group to resolve the problem in terms of the participants in their particular group.

The Safety Belt Case[3] was used for the multiple role playing problem in this experiment. The particular situation is not one that would occur in a chemical plant, but the same basic objective exists (i.e., safer workers). The case involves an "ambiguous" situation in contrast to a "clearcut" one that was used by the authors in another investigation.[4] An "ambiguous" situation is defined as one in which there is uncertainty on the part of each participant as to what the other participant has seen or done. In the "clear-cut" situation, each participant knows what has been seen and done by the other participant. The ambiguous situation tends to increase the desire for facts and the degree of variability of outcomes.

Over a period of ten days, groups of approximately 14 supervisors each were subdivided into pairs. One person in each pair was assigned the

---

[2] N. R. F. Maier and L. F. Zerfoss, "MRP: A Technique for Training Large Groups of Supervisors, etc.," *Human Relations*, Vol. 5, No. 2, 1952.

[3] N. R. F. Maier, *Principles of Human Relations* (New York: John Wiley and Sons, 1952), pp. 106–7.

[4] N. R. F. Maier and L. E. Danielson, "An Evaluation of Two Approaches to Discipline in Industry," *Journal of Applied Psychology*, Vol. 40, No. 5, 1956.

role of Bill Smith, the repairman, and the other person was assigned the role of Jim Welch, the foreman. The Bill Smiths were requested to leave the room and the role of Jim Welch (see the Appendix to the article) was read to the remaining members of each pair. When it was ascertained that all the Jim Welches understood their role they were requested to leave the room and the Bill Smiths were asked to return to hear the reading of their role (Appendix B). When the Smiths were sufficiently briefed they were requested to stand on chairs in different parts of the room to simulate the location of the repairman working on top of a telephone pole. The Welches were then instructed to return and go directly to their respective Smiths.

The entry of the Jim Welches into the room designated their appearance on the scene and simultaneous role playing began at this point. The interaction continued until some decision was reached.

At the conclusion of the role playing, answers to the following questions were obtained:

1. Who talked the most?
2. Was the violation discussed?
3. Was the violation admitted?
4. Was the man laid off?
5. Will the man work more safely in the future?
6. Has the man's respect for the foreman increased?
7. Should the penalty have been invoked?

Each pair of participants was required to agree upon their answers to Questions 1–4: the Bill Smiths answered Questions 5–6; each training group (approximately 14 supervisors), through group discussion, answered Question 7.

Questions 1–5 deal with activities during the role playing; Questions 2–4 represent the logical sequence of events that might occur if the foreman attempted to establish the repairman's guilt or innocence and then penalize accordingly: Questions 5 and 6 are outcomes of the role playing, and Question 7 represents the rationale for courses of action decided upon during the role playing.

RESULTS

As a preface to the presentation of the results, the authors want to comment on the use of multiple role playing as an experimental technique in this situation. It is recognized that (1) the participants are not as emotionally involved as they might well be if this was an on-the-job situation, (2) consciously or unconsciously the participants might be trying to put their best foot forward to impress someone with their skill, and (3) the *expressed* future behavior of the repairmen might not be their *actual* future behavior. Despite these limitations the authors feel that the trends in results obtained with the use of this technique approximate those of the actual life situations and that the results are representative of what can be found in the actual situations. Controlled experiments with real life situations are difficult because the same case cannot be duplicated.

The logical sequence of situations that could occur if the supervisor pursued the judicial approach are represented by Questions 2, 3 and 4 (i.e., discussion, admission and layoff). Table 1 shows the percentage of cases responding in this manner and related these responses to expressed future behavior by the repairmen (i.e., Question 5, "Will the man work more safely in the future?"). The responses to Question 5 found in the last three columns can be used as a measure of the supervisor's success in

TABLE 1

RELATION OF ACTIONS DURING ROLE PLAYING TO FUTURE BEHAVIOR

		FUTURE BEHAVIOR (%)		
ACTION	OCCURRENCE	Safer Worker (69.3%)	Questionable (11%)	Not Safer Worker (19.5%)
Violation Discussed	Yes 75%	70	11	19
	No 25%	67	13	20
Violation Admitted	Yes 45%	70	9	21
	No 55%	67	14	19
Worker Laid-off	Yes 7%	50	0	50
	No 93%	71	11	18

attaining the underlying objective, safer workers. The first line of the second column shows that the violation was discussed by the majority of the foremen (75 per cent) and had approached the problem situation in the judicial manner. Discussion of the violation included supervisory approaches ranging from a general discussion of safety violations to a direct accusation. Line 3 of the second column shows that only in the minority of situations, (45 per cent) was the violation admitted, even though the role given the repairman indicates that a safety violation did occur. It is interesting to note that while 45 per cent of the repairmen admitted the violation, the responses to the "Laid-off" question indicate that only 7 per cent of the foremen said "yes."

Examination of the three columns describing "Future Behavior" show that there is a relationship between safer workers and a "no" answer to the "Laid-off" question. This relationship, based upon a chi-square analysis, is significant beyond the .01 level. The other two questions brought out no significant relationships. The over-all "Future Behavior" indicates that, as a result of this interaction between the foreman and the repairman, the majority of repairmen (69.5 per cent) expressed the opinion that they would be safer workers in the future. As gratifying as these results appear, it is important to determine why these supervisors succeeded, and it is equally important to determine why 19.5 per cent of the repairmen would not work more safely and why another 11 per cent of the repairmen gave the response "questionable."

The answers to Question 6 ("Has the man's respect for the foreman increased?") throw some light on a possible explanation for the success or failure of the foremen. Table 2 shows the relationship between the workers' respect for the foreman and their feelings about future safety precaution. It is apparent that an increase in respect is related to future safety and this relationship is significant beyond .01 level of confidence.

Once this relationship is established, one can determine if increased respect is related to who dominated the conversation, in responses to Question 1. This relationship was found not significant.

TABLE 2

RELATION OF RESPECT FOR FOREMAN AND FUTURE BEHAVIOR

RESPECT FOR FOREMAN	FUTURE BEHAVIOR (%)		
	Safer Worker	Questionable	Not Safer Worker
Increased (73%)	82	10	8
Questionable (6%)	51	33	11
Decreased (21%)	30	15	55

The responses to Question 7 ("Should the penalty have been revoked?") are based on group data and interestingly enough seven per cent of groups felt that the penalty should have been revoked and this is the same percentage of the instances in which the penalty was invoked.

The decision making process of the foremen can be understood more fully by an examination of Figure 1. Reading from left to right we move from the initial problem situation, through various situations, and ultimately end up with the degree of success resulting from these various situations. When the foreman enters the problem area, he *has to* make his first decision, "to discuss or not to discuss the possible violation" (Point A). A minority of the foremen (25 per cent) decide not to discuss the possible violation and 67 per cent of them are successful in gaining a safer worker. The foremen who follow this path to the objective have the fewest decisions to make and they are about as successful as the foremen who follow other paths. The primary emphasis of these foremen is on the problem "How can I encourage this worker to become safer, without putting him on the spot?" They are holding to their objective, and also considering the feelings in the situation.

On the other hand, the foremen who decide to discuss the violation (75 per cent of the cases) are following a judicial approach. Consciously or not, the foremen following this path are creating a situation in which they will be required to make at least one additional decision, each one of which can adversely affect his relationship with this worker and perhaps others. Despite this condition, three times as many foremen select this path, rather than the simpler one.

The foremen who discuss the violation reach Point B, where the worker is faced with a decision, whether or not to admit that he violated the safety practice. The foreman's actions to a great extent dictate the decision the worker will make. In 40 per cent of the cases the worker did not admit the violation and thus shortened the path to the

FIGURE 1

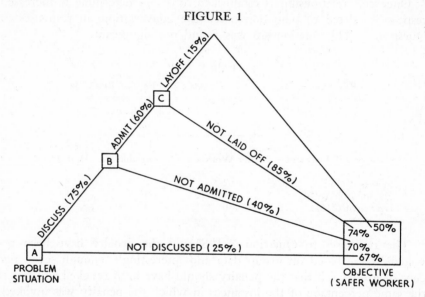

PROBLEM SITUATION

OBJECTIVE (SAFER WORKER)

objective. Of these cases, 70 per cent claimed that they would be safer workers. The violation was admitted in the other 60 per cent of the cases and as such the foreman's path was lengthened so that he reached Point C. He is now forced to make one more decision, whether or not to lay off the worker. The foremen who did not evoke the penalty (85 per cent) were successful in 74 per cent of these instances. Only 15 per cent of the foremen did carry out the penalty, and in only 50 per cent of these cases was the foreman successful in gaining the objective.

DISCUSSION

The results of this study do not afford a foolproof method of decision making in situations involving the possible violation of safety violations. As the title of the article implies, it does point up some of the problems involved. Assuming that the foremen are familiar with a technique similar to the J. R. T. method, let us outline how the results of this study might aid the foremen in increasing their effectiveness in decision making.

First, establish the objective. In the case of a violation of a safety regulation, the major objective should be increasing worker safety. If the foreman accepts the objective of establishing the worker's guilt or innocence and then taking appropriate action, he has limited the course of action available. He is assuming that such action will result in increased worker safety, which may not be the case, as the results of this study demonstrate. If the foreman accepts the objective of increasing worker safety, many courses of action are available, among them penalizing the offender if this is considered to be the "best" method of attaining the objective.

Second, collect the facts and feelings. The setting of the objective determines the facts and feelings that are assembled. Quite different answers are sought if one is trying to determine guilt or innocence, rather than an increase in worker safety.

The emotions in the situation are accentuated when a person is "on trial," whereas in a more positive or constructive atmosphere emotionality is minimized and greater opportunity for problem solving exists. The writers feel that one of the areas that made for success or failure in dealing with this problem was due to the degree of skill in the application of the human relations principles rather than to aspects of the principles themselves. It was a "fact" that the repairman was violating a safety regulation, but in the cases where the violation was discussed, the majority of repairmen did not feel free to admit this violation.

Third, weigh and decide what action should be taken. One of the most interesting aspects of this study is the lack of enforcement of regulation. Of the cases where the violation was discussed and admitted, only 15 per cent of the foremen laid off the worker. In another study which dealt with a disciplinary problem, the writers[5] found this same reluctance to enforce the penalty. The problem in that study involved a violation that was committed and both parties were aware of the violation. Still, the full lay-off was made in only 35 per cent of the cases and in over one-half of the instances some adjusted solution was decided upon. If other factors are going to be the determining ones in deciding upon what action is to be taken, it seems that there is little value in pursuing a judicial approach and encountering the additional problems that this method tends to create. Another point should be stressed in decision making and that is the influence of this decision on other workers. The foremen who did not lay off the workers who admitted the violation, may gain an increase in worker respect from this particular worker, but what effect will it have on other workers if the man tells others about the incident? Will he gain the reputation of "all you have to do is admit the violation and he'll let you off"? Will he be accused of showing favoritism? Will management be satisfied with a person who

---

[5] N. R. F. Maier and L. E. Danielson, "An Evaluation of Two Approaches to Discipline in Industry," *ibid*. (Editor's Note: See the article which follows.)

does not carry out their mandates? These are some of the possibilities that can result from the judicial approach without enforcement of the penalty. The experimental results indicated that when the repairman was laid off this action resulted in less success than any other action. Consequently, the value of the judicial approach is doubtful regardless of the final outcome.

Appendix*

A. Role of Jim Welch—Foreman: You are the Foreman of a repair crew of a utility company. You have 12 men who go on jobs and the men usually work alone or in pairs. As foreman you spend your time visiting the work locations of your men, checking on progress, giving such help, training and instruction as is needed. You are also responsible for the safety of your men and the company judges you partly on the safety record of your crew. At the present time there is a company safety drive. The slogan is, "No job is so important that it cannot be done safely." The company has passed a ruling that anyone found violating a safety practice will be laid off for 3 weeks.

You have just driven up to the place that Bill Smith is working. You stop your car some distance away (you cannot drive directly to the work location) and see Bill working on top of the pole. As you stop the car you have a distinct impression that Smith snapped his safety belt. Apparently he was working without using his belt and this is a safety practice violation.

Smith is an employee with 20 years of service. He has four children ranging in age from 5 to 12. He is a good workman, but is quite independent in his thinking. You wish to do what you can to correct this man and give him a better attitude toward safety. You have been supervisor of this crew for two years and don't know too much about Bill's past record. You have 10 years service with the company.

B. Role of Bill Smith—Repairman: You are a member of Jim Welch's repair crew in a utility company. You have been in the company for 20 years and for the past two years Jim has been your supervisor. You feel you know the job and consider your technical knowledge perhaps somewhat greater than Welch's who has worked in the company a total of 10 years. You believe Jim has done a fair job as foreman, but feel that he supervises too closely.

You usually work alone on repair jobs except for several visits a week from your supervisor. You are now working on top of a pole and haven't bothered to snap your saftey belt. You are a careful worker and use it when it is necessary, but find it uncomfortable and in the way and so frequently you don't bother to snap it.

Welch has just driven up so you hasten to snap your belt. There is an annual safety drive on and the company has threatened to lay men off for safety violations. You can't afford having time off. You have four children and living expenses use up all your earnings. You are quite sure Jim didn't see you snap your safety belt. He is walking toward your pole now.

* Reprinted with permission from N. R. F. Maier, *Principles of Human Relations* (New York: John Wiley and Sons, 1952), pp. 106–7.

38. An Evaluation of Two Approaches to Discipline in Industry*

Norman R. F. Maier and Lee E. Danielson

THE PROBLEM of disciplinary action in industry has long plagued supervision at all levels, especially at the first line. Although there are many approaches to the problem, they can be roughly classified into two main types: *judicial* and *human relations*. The *judicial* approach is characterized by an attempt to determine the *rightness or wrongness* of an employee's actions in a particular situation. If the worker was "wrong," the supervisor metes out the predetermined punishment. The emphasis is on the solution to the immediate problem rather than on the possible consequences of the decision. Getting the facts, screening out opinions, and finally weighing the evidence are important steps in the judicial approach.

The *human relations* approach is characterized by an emphasis on problem solving. The question of *rightness* or *wrongness* of behavior is subordinate to the question of "How can I encourage this worker to perform in a desirable manner?" As in most problem solving, the supervisor's behavior is characterized by flexibility and adaptiveness, with the result that a variety of solutions may be followed on different occasions in gaining the same objective.

The study reported uses a role-playing case to determine how supervisors behave in a situation involving a disciplinary problem. Multiple role playing[1] is used in order to permit a comparison of outcomes reached by different participants under identical test conditions.

Method

SUBJECTS

This study was conducted during the Foremen's Conference at the University of Michigan (April, 1954). Supervisors, representing a wide variety of industries and several levels of management, participated. The program was repeated on two successive days and data were obtained from over 500 individuals.

---

* From *Journal of Applied Psychology*, Vol. 40, 1956, pp. 319–23.
[1] Editor's Note: See Section III, Article 23.

PROCEDURE FOR ROLE PLAYING

After hearing a lecture on the topic of attitudes and how to deal more effectively with them, the audience was divided into 12 workshops averaging approximately 42 men, each being conducted by a trained conference leader. In dividing the audience into workshop groups, care was taken to see that two men from one company would not be in the same group.

When the workshops had convened in their separate rooms, each conference leader informed his group that they would participate in a case study called the "No Smoking" problem. Since this case involved three persons, the men were asked to form three-man groups so that many sets of persons could study the case independently. A little time was then spent to give the men a general idea of the role-playing approach to case studies. The conference leader then read some general instructions describing the job and the working conditions, and also mentioned the fact that the foreman had just laid off a worker for a period of three days for violating the company smoking rule. Separate instructions were supplied for the part each member of the group was to play. These were the foreman, the worker, and the union steward. The worker was not involved in the role playing, but was present only to observe so that he could later pass judgment on his satisfaction with the outcome. It was the steward's objective to get the foreman to reverse his decision, and it was the interview between the foreman and the steward that was role played. The situation described in the roles made it clear that a violation had occurred, that the worker knew he was violating a rule, and that there was a specific penalty. However, the worker felt he could not afford the layoff, and because the steward regarded the employee to be a conscientious worker who sneaks fewer smokes than others, he was willing to make an issue out of the incident. After 20 minutes of interaction, role playing was terminated and preparations for analysis and discussion were made.

PROCEDURE FOR OBTAINING DATA

Data on the following points were collected from one three-man team at a time:

1. The solution or decision reached.

2. The type of interaction between steward and foreman. Three classifications were described: (*a*) argument (each person presents his side of the case and appears unsympathetic with the other's side); (*b*) problem-solving discussion (each tries to understand the situation of the other and both proceed to work out a solution to the conflict in their situations); (*c*) intermediate type of interaction. Participants always reached agreement on the classification.

3. Satisfaction with the solution. Each participant reported his feeling about the decision.

4. Worker's response to three questions: (*a*) Were you satisfied with the steward's defense of you? (*b*) Will you vote for this steward at the next union election? (*c*) Will your work suffer because of the way your case was handled?

5. Steward's intention to file a grievance.

Results

The outcomes of the discussions have been grouped into three general classifications, as follows: (*a*) no decision, (*b*) full layoff, and (*c*) adjusted solutions. The "no decision" classification includes some incomplete discussions but most of them were deadlocks in which each refused to give in, but the foreman nevertheless was reluctant to carry out the penalty without the steward's support. The "full layoff" classification means that the foreman carried out the penalty as prescribed by the company rule. This was a three-day layoff, and since there was no question about the violation the "judicial" approach called for this solution. The "adjusted" classification includes all cases in which the foreman made some adjustment. Solutions in which an agreement is sought stem from the "human relations" approach. These ranged from reducing the penalty to overlooking the incident. Nearly half of the adjusted solutions were agreements to reduce the three-day layoff to a reprimand or warn-

TABLE 1

SATISFACTION WITH VARIOUS SOLUTIONS

	No Decision Reached	Full Layoff	Adjustment
INSTANCES IN 172 GROUPS	23 (13%)	60 (35%)	89 (52%)
Satisfaction with solution (%)			
Foreman	17	70	86
Steward	9	30	80
Worker	—*	15	71
Interaction (%)			
Argument	30	24	3
Intermediate	48	39	33
Problem solving	22	37	64
Worker's reaction (%)			
Satisfied with defense	61	52	93
Will vote for steward	74	47	91
Will reduce production	43	40	6
Steward will file grievance (%)	43	45	2

* Workers cannot express their satisfaction with the outcome because they are uncertain as to whether they will be laid off.

ing. In the case of adjusted solutions the steward usually agreed to support the no-smoking rule in the future.

The results are shown in Table 1. It is important to note that 52%, or better than half of the foremen, did not follow the letter of the rule, despite the fact that the rule was clear and had no provision for leniency. Included in this 52% are 9% decisions to consult higher management in order to get permission to make an exception or to let higher management make the decision, but the other 43% of the foremen took it upon themselves to follow the "human relations" approach. A little more than a third (35%) of the foremen had the courage, the confidence, or whatever trait is needed, to carry out the letter of the law and avoid the possible charge of discriminatory practice. Only 13% failed to settle the problem in the allotted time. The consequences of these three types of outcomes are apparent from the remainder of the table.

Satisfaction for foreman, steward, and worker increase together and is greatest for adjusted solutions and least for cases in which no decision is reached. For each person involved, the difference in satisfaction for full layoff and adjusted solutions is significant at better than the 1% level of confidence.

The type of solution reached also is related to the type of discussion that occurred. The problem-solving type of discussion was associated primarily with adjusted solutions, whereas argumentative approaches led to deadlocks and judicial solutions. A chi-square test for the relationship between type of meeting and type of outcome is significant at the 1% level of confidence.

The third set of comparisons, called worker reactions, shows the workers to be most often satisfied with their stewards when an adjustment results, and least often satisfied when given a full layoff. The percentages of workers who are satisfied with the steward, and percentages of those who will vote for him again when an adjustment results are each significantly different (at the 1% level of confidence) from the percentages obtained on these two items with the other two outcomes. The adjusted solution also resulted in only 6% of the workers saying that they would reduce production while 40 and 43%, respectively (both significant at the 1% level of confidence), indicated reduced production for "full layoffs" and "failure to reach a decision."

A comparison of the number of stewards who will file grievances may be used as a measure of the extent to which various solutions actually failed to lead to a final settlement of the dispute. Table 1 clearly shows that only when an adjustment is reached can there be any degree of confidence that the problem has been settled. Both of the other two outcomes led to more than 40% of the stewards saying that they intended to file grievances, and these frequencies are significantly different (at less than the 1% level of confidence) from the 2% figure obtained when an adjustment is reached.

A breakdown of the adjusted solutions that were lumped together in the last column of Table 1 include the following:

1. Reduced layoff (either two days or one).
2. Forgiven (no layoff and no reprimand stated, but a warning may be implied).
3. Warning and reprimand (it is made clear that the employee is at fault and that the next person violating the rule will be laid off; violation may be entered in personnel record).
4. Consulting higher management (to obtain permission to make an exception, to change the rule or make a special decision in the case).
5. Consulting workers (to determine what should be done in this case and be willing to abide by decision).
6. Other (refers to the few that cannot be classified in above categories).

Table 2 shows the satisfactions, the type of interaction, the worker's reaction, and the steward's follow-up for each of these adjusted solutions. Since the cases in some of the categories are rather small, the relationships obtained can merely be suggestive.

Discussion

In another investigation dealing with a disciplinary problem the writers[2] found foremen reluctant to enforce a safety rule as evidenced by the fact that only 7% of them laid off the man who violated the rule. The foreman gave two major reasons for not following the letter of the rule: (*a*) the penalty of a three-week layoff was too strict, and (*b*) the

TABLE 2

SATISFACTION WITH DIFFERENT ADJUSTMENTS

	REDUCED LAYOFF	FORGIVEN	WARNING REPRIMAND	CONSULT MANAGEMENT	CONSULT WORKERS	OTHER
INSTANCES IN 89 GROUPS	8	13	39	15	6	8
Satisfaction with solution (%)						
Foreman	87	85	90	67	100	100
Steward	75	100	79	60	100	75
Worker	62	100	74	40	83	63
Interaction (%)						
Argument	0	0	3	13	0	0
Intermediate	37	31	25	34	50	50
Problem solving	63	69	72	53	50	50
Worker's reaction (%)						
Satisfied with defense	75	100	95	93	100	87
Will vote for steward	62	100	95	93	100	75
Will reduce production	25	8	0	13	0	0
Steward will file grievance (%)	0	0	3	7	0	0

foremen used in the case were not sure that a violation had occurred. The fact that 45% of the workers admitted the violation indicates that the second reason given was more of an excuse than a reason for not applying the penalty.

In the present study the rule has been made less strict and the doubt as to whether a violation has occurred has been removed. Although the prescribed penalty is now applied in 35% of the instances, 52% of the foremen fail to follow the letter of the law and instead either reduce or omit the penalty. The other 13% are unable to resolve the problem in the time allowed. Regardless of how one feels about rules, the fact remains that the persons who are intrusted to apply them are not doing so to the extent that is ideally supposed. If a rule is used as a formula to treat everyone in the same way, it is not accomplishing this objective. If fair treatment is a sound management objective, it is reasonable to question whether fairness can be legislated in a company. Different foremen permit their own feelings and attitudes to determine how a violator

---

[2] L. E. Danielson and N. R. F. Maier, "Supervisory problems in decision making," *Personnel Psychology*, Vol. 10, 1957, pp. 169–80. (Editor's Note: See preceding article.)

will be treated, and they apparently accept this as a practical thing to do. Thus, human factors influence the methods of dealing with people as soon as the authority figure comes face to face with the person who is to be punished.

The present experimental data demonstrate not only that foremen are inclined to use what we have called the *human relations* approach, but that this approach is more likely to produce desirable results and satisfaction for all concerned than is the *judicial* approach, which is characterized by a consideration of the factual evidence and the determination of innocence or guilt.

What are the forces causing foremen to shy away from following company rules and avoiding the judicial approach? Group discussions in connection with problems of this kind reveal two kinds of reasons.

1. Foremen believe they can get better cooperation from their men if they treat them with consideration. Most foremen today believe that a layoff will not solve the problem if one uses case studies to present a particular situation. In general discussions, however, they will argue in favor of rules and the need for consistency.

2. Foremen are reluctant to risk a walkout. It is their belief that if a grievance results from disciplinary action, the company is likely to reverse the foreman's decision. In any case they do not cherish the emotional problems involved in grievance proceedings, and even if backed up by the company, they fear they lose out in the estimation of their superiors if they figure in the trouble that has been caused by grievance proceedings.

The first of these factors is emotional in nature in that there is a failure to accept the job of punishing a good employee. The second reason is more intellectual in nature and perhaps is a conclusion that has been reached through bitter experience. Foremen discover that they must learn to get along both with their superiors and with the union representatives. They have no final authority or power since the union has taken the big stick from them, and as a consequence they must use their wits. The judicial approach assumes that force is available and this is somewhat unrealistic in our present society. The human relations approach respects the feelings of people and these feelings become a factor in reaching decisions. In the present study the foreman had all the objective facts on his side and the steward had little more than "feelings" to support his position. The "feeling" side of the issue was strong enough to win adjusted solutions in 52% of the cases. That these adjusted solutions were not victories achieved by the steward through threat of a walkout is indicated by the fact that satisfaction with the outcome was highest for foremen when adjusted solutions were reached. No foreman experienced the adjusted solution as a defeat.

The experimental findings support the conclusion that rules and penalties can no longer be regarded as effective procedures for controlling behavior or maintaining discipline. This means that new ways of controlling behavior must be found. These must allow the foreman sufficient freedom to act so that he is not restrained by rules and can use his discretion. However, if the human factor is increased by moving away from judicial to the human relations approach, it means that foremen must be selected and trained to use human relations properly. In other words, foreman training is an essential part of a motivation program utilizing positive incentives.

Summary

In order to study the kinds of issues involved in a practical disciplinary problem, industrial supervisors were placed in a role-playing situation requiring that disciplinary action be taken. One person played the part of the supervisor, another the part of the union steward, and a third person identified himself with the worker who was to be disciplined. The background of the case made the violation of a no-smoking rule clear-cut so that a three-day layoff was in order. The steward intervened, however, and his function was to get the foreman to change his decision.

The results obtained are as follows:

1. A total of 89 (52%) foremen altered their decisions and reached adjusted solutions. They tended to follow the human relations approach.

2. A total of 60 (35%) foremen persisted in their decisions and were governed by the fact that the worker was guilty. They followed the judicial approach.

3. The remaining 23 foremen (13%) failed to settle the matter in the time allowed. They were reluctant to change their decisions and also hesitated to take a stand.

4. The human relations approach was more successful than the judicial approach in that (*a*) satisfaction for foremen, stewards, and workers was greater; (*b*) the interview was more of a problem-solving type discussion than an argument; (*c*) the worker was more inclined to be satisfied with the steward; (*d*) the worker was less inclined to reduce his future production; and (*e*) the steward was less inclined to file a grievance.

5. Adjusted solutions varied in nature, but more than half of them omitted the three-day penalty altogether.

It is concluded that rules hamper the supervisor and place him in the awkward position of either showing disrespect for higher management or a disregard for the feelings of his men. New ways in discipline must be sought and these require training in human relations. Rules can function only when power to enforce them exists. Even then they do not create positive motivation. In the absence of power, foremen must be allowed and trained to use human relations skills.

39. How to Choose a Leadership Pattern*

Robert Tannenbaum and Warren H. Schmidt

I put most problems into my group's hands and leave it to them to carry the ball from there. I serve merely as a catalyst, mirroring back the people's thoughts and feelings so that they can better understand them.

It's foolish to make decisions oneself on matters that affect people. I always talk things over with my subordinates, but I make it clear to them that I'm the one who has to have the final say.

Once I have decided on a course of action, I do my best to sell my ideas to my employees.

I'm being paid to lead. If I let a lot of other people make the decisions I should be making, then I'm not worth my salt.

I believe in getting things done. I can't waste time calling meetings. Someone has to call the shots around here, and I think it should be me.

EACH OF THESE statements represents a point of view about "good leadership." Considerable experience, factual data, and theoretical principles could be cited to support each statement, even though they seem to be inconsistent when placed together. Such contradictions point up the dilemma in which the modern manager frequently finds himself.

New Problem

The problem of how the modern manager can be "democratic" in his relations with subordinates and at the same time maintain the necessary authority and control in the organization for which he is responsible has come into focus increasingly in recent years.

Earlier in the century this problem was not so acutely felt. The successful executive was generally pictured as possessing intelligence, imagination, initiative, the capacity to make rapid (and generally wise) decisions, and the ability to inspire subordinates. People tended to think of the world as being divided into "leaders" and "followers."

NEW FOCUS

Gradually, however, from the social sciences emerged the concept of "group dynamics" with its focus on *members* of the group rather than solely on the leader. Research efforts of social scientists underscored the importance of employee involvement and participation in decision making. Evidence began to challenge the efficiency of highly direc-

---

* From *Harvard Business Review*, Vol. 36, 1958, pp. 95–101.

tive leadership, and increasing attention was paid to problems of motivation and human relations.

Through training laboratories in group development that sprang up across the country, many of the newer notions of leadership began to exert an impact. These training laboratories were carefully designed to give people a first-hand experience in full participation and decision making. The designated "leaders" deliberately attempted to reduce their own power and to make group members as responsible as possible for setting their own goals and methods within the laboratory experience.

It was perhaps inevitable that some of the people who attended the training laboratories regarded this kind of leadership as being truly "democratic" and went home with the determination to build fully participative decision making into their own organizations. Whenever their bosses made a decision without convening a staff meeting, they tended to perceive this as authoritarian behavior. The true symbol of democratic leadership to some was the meeting—and the less directed from the top, the more democratic it was.

Some of the more enthusiastic alumni of these training laboratories began to get the habit of categorizing leader behavior as "democratic" *or* "authoritarian." The boss who made too many decisions himself was thought of as an authoritarian, and his directive behavior was often attributed solely to his personality.

NEW NEED

The net result of the research findings and of the human relations training based upon them has been to call into question the stereotype of an effective leader. Consequently, the modern manager often finds himself in an uncomfortable state of mind.

Often he is not quite sure how to behave; there are times when he is torn between exerting "strong" leadership and "permissive" leadership. Sometimes new knowledge pushes him in one direction ("I should really get the group to help make this decision"), but at the same time his experience pushes him in another direction ("I really understand the problem better than the group and therefore I should make the decision"). He is not sure when a group decision is really appropriate or when holding a staff meeting serves merely as a device for avoiding his own decision-making responsibility.

The purpose of our article is to suggest a framework which managers may find useful in grappling with this dilemma. First we shall look at the different patterns of leadership behavior that the manager can choose from in relating himself to his subordinates. Then we shall turn to some of the questions suggested by this range of patterns. For instance, how important is it for a manager's subordinates to know what type of leadership he is using in a situation? What factors should he consider in deciding on a leadership pattern? What difference do his long-run objectives make as compared to his immediate objectives?

Range of Behavior

Exhibit I presents the continuum or range of possible leadership behavior available to a manager. Each type of action is related to the degree of authority used by the boss and to the amount of freedom available to his subordinates in reaching decisions. The actions seen on the extreme left characterize the manager who maintains a high degree of control while those seen on the extreme right characterize the manager

EXHIBIT 1

CONTINUUM OF LEADERSHIP BEHAVIOR

BOSS-CENTERED LEADERSHIP						SUBORDINATE-CENTERED LEADERSHIP
USE OF AUTHORITY BY THE MANAGER				AREA OF FREEDOM FOR SUBORDINATES		
MANAGER MAKES DECISION AND ANNOUNCES IT.	MANAGER "SELLS" DECISION.	MANAGER PRESENTS IDEAS AND INVITES QUESTIONS.	MANAGER PRESENTS TENTATIVE DECISION SUBJECT TO CHANGE.	MANAGER PRESENTS PROBLEM, GETS SUGGESTIONS, MAKES DECISION.	MANAGER DEFINES LIMITS; ASKS GROUP TO MAKE DECISION.	MANAGER PERMITS SUBORDINATES TO FUNCTION WITHIN LIMITS DEFINED BY SUPERIOR.

who releases a high degree of control. Neither extreme is absolute; authority and freedom are never without their limitations.

Now let us look more closely at each of the behavior points occurring along this continuum:

The manager makes the decision and announces it.   In this case the boss identifies a problem, considers alternative solutions, chooses one of them, and then reports this decision to his subordinates for implementation. He may or may not give consideration to what he believes his subordinates will think or feel about his decision; in any case, he provides no opportunity for them to participate directly in the decision-making process. Coercion may or may not be used or implied.

The manager "sells" his decision.   Here the manager, as before, takes responsibility for identifying the problem and arriving at a decision. However, rather than simply announcing it, he takes the additional step of persuading his subordinates to accept it. In doing so, he recognizes the possibility of some resistance among those who will be faced with the decision, and seeks to reduce this resistance by indicating, for example, what the employees have to gain from his decision.

The manager presents his ideas, invites questions.   Here the boss who has arrived at a decision and who seeks acceptance of his ideas provides an opportunity for his subordinates to get a fuller explanation of his thinking and his intentions. After presenting the ideas, he invites questions so that his associates can better understand what he is trying to accomplish. This "give and take" also enables the manager and the subordinates to explore more fully the implications of the decision.

The manager presents a tentative decision subject to change. This kind of behavior permits the subordinates to exert some influence on the decision. The initiative for identifying and diagnosing the problem remains with the boss. Before meeting with his staff, he has thought the problem through and arrived at a decision—but only a tentative one. Before finalizing it, he presents his proposed solution for the reaction of those who will be affected by it. He says in effect, "I'd like to hear what you have to say about this plan that I have developed. I'll appreciate your frank reactions, but will reserve for myself the final decision."

The manager presents the problem, gets suggestions, and then makes his decision. Up to this point the boss has come before the group with a solution of his own. Not so in this case. The subordinates now get the first chance to suggest solutions. The manager's initial role involves identifying the problem. He might, for example, say something of this sort: "We are faced with a number of complaints from newspapers and the general public on our service policy. What is wrong here? What ideas do you have for coming to grips with this problem?"

The function of the group becomes one of increasing the manager's repertory of possible solutions to the problem. The purpose is to capitalize on the knowledge and experience of those who are on the "firing line." From the expanded list of alternatives developed by the manager and his subordinates, the manager then selects the solution that he regards as most promising.[1]

The manager defines the limits and requests the group to make a decision. At this point the manager passes to the group (possibly including himself as a member) the right to make decisions. Before doing so, however, he defines the problem to be solved and the boundaries within which the decision must be made.

An example might be the handling of a parking problem at a plant. The boss decides that this is something that should be worked on by the people involved, so he calls them together and points up the existence of the problem. Then he tells them:

> "There is the open field just north of the main plant which has been designated for additional employee parking. We can build underground or surface multilevel facilities as long as the cost does not exceed $100,000. Within these limits we are free to work out whatever

---

[1] For a fuller explanation of this approach, see Leo Moore, "Too Much Management, Too Little Change," Harvard Business Review, January–February, 1956, p. 41.

solution makes sense to us. After we decide on a specific plan, the company will spend the available money in whatever way we indicate."

The manager permits the group to make decisions within prescribed limits.   This represents an extreme degree of group freedom only occasionally encountered in formal organizations, as, for instance, in many research groups. Here the team of managers or engineers undertakes the identification and diagnosis of the problem, develops alternative procedures for solving it, and decides on one or more of these alternative solutions. The only limits directly imposed on the group by the organization are those specified by the superior of the team's boss. If the boss participates in the decision-making process, he attempts to do so with no more authority than any other member of the group. He commits himself in advance to assist in implementing whatever decision the group makes.

Key Questions

As the continuum in Exhibit I demonstrates, there are a number of alternative ways in which a manager can relate himself to the group or individuals he is supervising. At the extreme left of the range, the emphasis is on the manager—on what *he* is interested in, how *he* sees things, how *he* feels about them. As we move toward the subordinate-centered end of the continuum, however, the focus is increasingly on the subordinates—on what *they* are interested in, how *they* look at things, how *they* feel about them.

When business leadership is regarded in this way, a number of questions arise. Let us take four of especial importance:

Can a boss ever relinquish his responsibility by delegating it to someone else?   Our view is that the manager must expect to be held responsible by his superior for the quality of the decisions made, even though operationally these decisions may have been made on a group basis. He should, therefore, be ready to accept whatever risk is involved whenever he delegates decision-making power to his subordinates. Delegation is not a way of "passing the buck." Also, it should be emphasized that the amount of freedom the boss gives to his subordinates cannot be greater than the freedom which he himself has been given by his own superior.

Should the manager participate with his subordinates once he has delegated responsibility to them?   The manager should carefully think over this question and decide on his role prior to involving the subordinate group. He should ask if his presence will inhibit or facilitate the problem-solving process. There may be some instances when he should leave the group to let it solve the problem for itself. Typically, however, the boss has useful ideas to contribute, and should function as an additional member of the group. In the latter instance, it is important that he indicate clearly to the group that he sees himself in a *member* role rather than in an authority role.

How important is it for the group to recognize what kind of leadership behavior the boss is using? It makes a great deal of difference. Many relationship problems between boss and subordinate occur because the boss fails to make clear how he plans to use his authority. If, for example, he actually intends to make a certain decision himself, but the subordinate group gets the impression that he has delegated this authority, considerable confusion and resentment are likely to follow. Problems may also occur when the boss uses a "democratic" façade to conceal the fact that he has already made a decision which he hopes the group will accept as its own. The attempt to "make them think it was their idea in the first place" is a risky one. We believe that it is highly important for the manager to be honest and clear in describing what authority he is keeping and what role he is asking his subordinates to assume in solving a particular problem.

Can you tell how "democratic" a manager is by the number of decisions his subordinates make? The sheer *number* of decisions is not an accurate index of the amount of freedom that a subordinate group enjoys. More important is the *significance* of the decisions which the boss entrusts to his subordinates. Obviously a decision on how to arranbe desks is of an entirely different order from a decision involving the introduction of new electronic data-processing equipment. Even though the widest possible limits are given in dealing with the first issue, the group will sense no particular degree of responsibility. For a boss to permit the group to decide equipment policy, even within rather narrow limits, would reflect a greater degree of confidence in them on his part.

Deciding How to Lead

Now let us turn from the types of leadership that are possible in a company situation to the question of what types are *practical* and *desirable*. What factors or forces should a manager consider in deciding how to manage? Three are of particular importance:

1. Forces in the manager.
2. Forces in the subordinates.
3. Forces in the situation.

We should like briefly to describe these elements and indicate how they might influence a manager's action in a decision-making situation.[2] The strength of each of them will, of course, vary from instance to instance, but the manager who is sensitive to them can better assess the problems which face him and determine which mode of leadership behavior is most appropriate for him.

_____
[2] See also Robert Tannenbaum and Fred Massarik, "Participation by Subordinates in the Managerial Decision-Making Process," *Canadian Journal of Economics and Political Science*, August, 1950, pp. 413–18.

FORCES IN THE MANAGER

The manager's behavior in any given instance will be influenced greatly by the many forces operating within his own personality. He will, of course, perceive his leadership problems in a unique way on the basis of his background, knowledge, and experience. Among the important internal forces affecting him will be the following:

(1) *His value system.* How strongly does he feel that individuals should have a share in making the decisions which affect them? Or, how convinced is he that the official who is paid to assume responsibility should personally carry the burden of decision making? The strength of his convictions on questions like these will tend to move the manager to one end or the other of the continuum shown in Exhibit 1. His behavior will also be influenced by the relative importance that he attaches to organizational efficiency, personal growth of subordinates, and company profits.[3]

(2) *His confidence in his subordinates.* Managers differ greatly in the amount of trust they have in other people generally, and this carries over to the particular employees they supervise at a given time. In viewing his particular group of subordinates, the manager is likely to consider their knowledge and competence with respect to the problem. A central question he might ask himself is: "Who is best qualified to deal with this problem?" Often he may, justifiably or not, have more confidence in his own capabilities than in those of his subordinates.

(3) *His own leadership inclinations.* There are some managers who seem to function more comfortably and naturally as highly directive leaders. Resolving problems and issuing orders come easily to them. Other managers seem to operate more comfortably in a team role, where they are continually sharing many of their functions with their subordinates.

(4) *His feelings of security in an uncertain situation.* The manager who releases control over the decision-making process thereby reduces the predictability of the outcome. Some managers have a greater need than others for predictability and stability in their environment. This "tolerance for ambiguity" is being viewed increasingly by psychologists as a key variable in a person's manner of dealing with problems.

The manager brings these and other highly personal variables to each situation he faces. If he can see them as forces which, consciously or unconsciously, influence his behavior, he can better understand what makes him prefer to act in a given way. And understanding this, he can often make himself more effective.

---

[3] See Chris Argyris, "Top Management Dilemma: Company Needs vs. Individual Development," *Personnel*, September, 1955, pp. 123–34.

FORCES IN THE SUBORDINATE

Before deciding how to lead a certain group, the manager will also want to consider a number of forces affecting his subordinates' behavior. He will want to remember that each employee, like himself, is influenced by many personality variables. In addition, each subordinate has a set of expectations about how the boss should act in relation to him (the phrase "expected behavior" is one we hear more and more often these days at discussions of leadership and teaching). The better the manager understands these factors, the more accurately he can determine what kind of behavior on his part will enable his subordinates to act most effectively.

Generally speaking, the manager can permit his subordinates greater freedom if the following essential conditions exist:

1. If the subordinates have relatively high needs for independence. (As we all know, people differ greatly in the amount of direction that they desire.)

2. If the subordinates have a readiness to assume responsibility for decision making. (Some see additional responsibility as a tribute to their ability; others see it as "passing the buck.")

3. If they have a relatively high tolerance for ambiguity. (Some employees prefer to have clear-cut directives given to them; others prefer a wider area of freedom.)

4. If they are interested in the problem and feel that it is important.

5. If they understand and identify with the goals of the organization.

6. If they have the necessary knowledge and experience to deal with the problem.

7. If they have learned to expect to share in decision making. (Persons who have come to expect strong leadership and are then suddenly confronted with the request to share more fully in decision making are often upset by this new experience. On the other hand, persons who have enjoyed a considerable amount of freedom resent the boss who begins to make all the decisions himself.)

The manager will probably tend to make fuller use of his own authority if the above conditions do *not* exist; at times there may be no realistic alternative to running a "one-man show."

The restrictive effect of many of the forces will, of course, be greatly modified by the general feeling of confidence which subordinates have in the boss. Where they have learned to respect and trust him, he is free to vary his behavior. He will feel certain that he will not be perceived as an authoritarian boss on those occasions when he makes decisions by himself. Similarly, he will not be seen as using staff meetings to avoid his decision-making responsibility. In a climate of mutual confidence and respect, people tend to feel less threatened by deviations from normal practice, which in turn makes possible a higher degree of flexibility in the whole relationship.

FORCES IN THE SITUATION

In addition to the forces which exist in the manager himself and in his subordinates, certain characteristics of the general situation will also affect the manager's behavior. Among the more critical environmental pressures that surround him are those which stem from the organization, the work group, the nature of the problem, and the pressures of time. Let us look briefly at each of these:

Type of Organization. Like individuals, organizations have values and traditions which inevitably influence the behavior of the people who work in them. The manager who is a newcomer to a company quickly discovers that certain kinds of behavior are approved while others are not. He also discovers that to deviate radically from what is generally accepted is likely to create problems for him.

These values and traditions are communicated in many ways—through job descriptions, policy pronouncements, and public statements by top executives. Some organizations, for example, hold to the notion that the desirable executive is one who is dynamic, imaginative, decisive, and persuasive. Other organizations put more emphasis upon the importance of the executive's ability to work effectively with people—his human relations skills. The fact that his superiors have a defined concept of what the good executive should be will very likely push the manager toward one end or the other of the behavioral range.

In addition to the above, the amount of employee participation is influenced by such variables as the size of the working units, their geographical distribution, and the degree of inter- and intra-organizational security required to attain company goals. For example, the wide geographical dispersion of an organization may preclude a practical system of participative decision making, even though this would otherwise be desirable. Similarly, the size of the working units or the need for keeping plans confidential may make it necessary for the boss to exercise more control than would otherwise be the case. Factors like these may limit considerably the manager's ability to function flexibly on the continuum.

Group Effectiveness. Before turning decision-making responsibility over to a subordinate group, the boss should consider how effectively its members work together as a unit.

One of the relevant factors here is the experience the group has had in working together. It can generally be expected that a group which has functioned for some time will have developed habits of cooperation and thus be able to tackle a problem more effectively than a new group. It can also be expected that a group of people with similar backgrounds and interests will work more quickly and easily than people with dissimilar backgrounds, because the communication problems are likely to be less complex.

The degree of confidence that the members have in their ability to solve problems as a group is also a key consideration. Finally, such group variables as cohesiveness, permissiveness, mutual acceptance, and commonality of purpose will exert subtle but powerful influence on the group's functioning.

The Problem Itself. The nature of the problem may determine what degree of authority should be delegated by the manager to his subordinates. Obviously he will ask himself whether they have the kind of knowledge which is needed. It is possible to do them a real disservice by assigning a problem that their experience does not equip them to handle.

Since the problems faced in large or growing industries increasingly require knowledge of specialists from many different fields, it might be inferred that the more complex a problem, the more anxious a manager will be to get some assistance in solving it. However, this is not always the case. There will be times when the very complexity of the problem calls for one person to work it out. For example, if the manager has most of the background and factual data relevant to a given issue, it may be easier for him to think it through himself than to take the time to fill in his staff on all the pertinent background information.

The key question to ask, of course, is: "Have I heard the ideas of everyone who has the necessary knowledge to make a significant contribution to the solution of this problem?"

The Pressure of Time. This is perhaps the most clearly felt pressure on the manager (in spite of the fact that it may sometimes be imagined). The more that he feels the need for an immediate decision, the more difficult it is to involve other people. In organizations which are in a constant state of "crisis" and "crash programing" one is likely to find managers personally using a high degree of authority with relatively little delegation to subordinates. When the time pressure is less intense, however, it becomes much more possible to bring subordinates in on the decision-making process.

These, then, are the principal forces that impinge on the manager in any given instance and that tend to determine his tactical behavior in relation to his subordinates. In each case his behavior ideally will be that which makes possible the most effective attainment of his immediate goal within the limits facing him.

Long-Run Strategy

As the manager works with his organization on the problems that come up day by day, his choice of a leadership pattern is usually limited. He must take account of the forces just described and, within the restrictions they impose on him, do the best that he can. But as he looks ahead months or even years, he can shift his thinking from tactics to large-scale strategy. No longer need he be fettered by all of the forces mentioned, for he can view many of them as variables over which he has some control. He can, for example, gain new insights or skills for himself, supply training for individual subordinates, and provide participative experiences for his employee group.

In trying to bring about a change in these variables, however, he is faced with a challenging question: At which point along the continuum *should* he act?

ATTAINING OBJECTIVES

The answer depends largely on what he wants to accomplish. Let us suppose that he is interested in the same objectives that most modern managers seek to attain when they can shift their attention from the pressure of immediate assignments:

1. To raise the level of employee motivation.
2. To increase the readiness of subordinates to accept change.
3. To improve the quality of all managerial decisions.
4. To develop teamwork and morale.
5. To further the individual development of employees.

In recent years the manager has been deluged with a flow of advice on how best to achieve these longer-run objectives. It is little wonder that he is often both bewildered and annoyed. However, there are some guidelines which he can usefully follow in making a decision.

Most research and much of the experience of recent years give a strong factual basis to the theory that a fairly high degree of subordinate-centered behavior is associated with the accomplishment of the five purposes mentioned.[4] This does not mean that a manager should always leave all decisions to his assistants. To provide the individual or the group with greater freedom than they are ready for at any given·time may very well tend to generate anxieties and therefore inhibit rather than facilitate the attainment of desired objectives. But this should not keep the manager from making a continuing effort to confront his subordinates with the challenge of freedom.

Conclusion

In summary, there are two implications in the basic thesis that we have been developing. The first is that the successful leader is one who is keenly aware of those forces which are most relevant to his behavior at any given time. He accurately understands himself, the individuals and group he is dealing with, and the company and broader social en-

---

[4] For example, see Warren H. Schmidt and Paul C. Buchanan, *Techniques that Produce Teamwork* (New London: Arthur C. Croft Publications, 1954); and Morris S. Viteles, *Motivation and Morale in Industry* (New York: W. W. Norton & Company, Inc., 1953).

vironment in which he operates. And certainly he is able to assess the present readiness for growth of his subordinates.

But this sensitivity or understanding is not enough, which brings us to the second implication. The successful leader is one who is able to behave appropriately in the light of these perceptions. If direction is in order, he is able to direct; if considerable participative freedom is called for, he is able to provide such freedom.

Thus, the successful manager of men can be primarily characterized neither as a strong leader nor as a permissive one. Rather, he is one who maintains a high batting average in accurately assessing the forces that determine what his most appropriate behavior at any given time should be and in actually being able to behave accordingly. Being both insightful and flexible, he is less likely to see the problems of leadership as a dilemma.

Section Six

COMMUNICATION AND ORGANIZATIONAL BEHAVIOR

Introduction

IN THIS SECTION we continue our examination of social-psychological aspects of behavior in organizations. For convenience we have linked the areas of communication and organization behavior, although these can scarcely be separated from much of our previous discussion of Leadership, Motivation, and Morale. All involve interpersonal relationships among individuals. However, in large organizations some problems take on additional emphasis and significance, and it is to these problems we now turn.

An important aspect of the behavior of individuals in organizations is the "communication" problem. This is the problem of the transmittal of information accurately and efficiently. More is involved here than factual information since feelings and attitudes are also communicated. As the organization becomes more complex, so do problems of communication.

In this section we examine the area of communication from several perspectives. First, there is the problem of *channels* of communication. This consists of the "network" of "channels" through which information flows. Some networks are more effective than others, and there are informal as well as formal communication channels. The first two articles deal with these aspects of communication. In "Studying Communication Patterns in Organizations," Davis explores this problem in the context of large organizations. He reviews previous research in this area and then describes a method for diagnosing and tracing the channels which are operating in a given organization. In "An Experimental Approach to Organizational Communication," Bavelas and Barrett approach the "network problem" from a different vantage point—from within the task-oriented group (department, team, etc.). Even small groups can differ in their communication patterns. What are these patterns and how do they affect group performance?

An understanding of communication channels and networks is important, but we can narrow our focus to an even more basic communication relationship—that between two individuals. Prominent examples of this are the student-teacher, child-parent, subordinate-supervisor, and union steward–plant manager relationship. One of the basic problems here is that different people have different "frames of reference" or attitudes, and a given communication may mean quite different things depending on this "frame of reference." It is not the objective nature of a communication which is important but the way in which it is experienced. Thus, a notice of a change in work methods carries certain meanings for the supervisor and quite a different set of meanings to the workers involved. In "Barriers and Gateways to Communication," Rogers takes a look at some of these "attitudinal" barriers and their consequences and offers some solutions to the problem. Next, Dearborn and Simon, in "Selective Perception: The Departmental Identifications of Executives," show us an industrial example of how one's "view of the world" influences what gets communicated to different individuals in the same organization.

We return now to the basic problem of transmitting information from one individual to another. The article by Leavitt and Mueller, "Some Effects of Feedback on Communication," discusses this problem. They describe some experiments on the important variable of "feedback" and its relation to different criteria of communication effectiveness. The implications of these studies to supervisor-subordinate communication are especially relevant.

Although the "interpersonal problems" may be the most critical ones, we should not overlook the "intelligibility" problem in communication. This is especially noticeable in written communication, although the same principles hold in oral communication. The simple fact is that the *readability* of management and employee communications does not always match the reading *ability* of the people for whom they are intended. The article by Carlucci and Crissy describes some research on "The Readability of Employee Handbooks," which illustrates this. The article discusses various criteria of readability as well as ways of evaluating and improving the readability of communications. The principles which are discussed apply as well to other industrial communications such as union contracts, company newsletters, notices of policy changes, inter-office memos, etc.

The final three articles take a broader view of human behavior in organizational settings. Leavitt first discusses "Recent Concepts in Administrative Behavior" and introduces some of the newer ideas in "organization theory." Most of these theories are in an early stage of development, but they also are stimulating research aimed at improving our understanding of organizational functioning. And they are suggesting alternative organizational structures which might better serve individual and organizational goals.

One of the challenges to traditional organization structures is the demand for flexibility in the face of technological change. Thus, the installation of a new data-processing payroll system or a new automated production process has a tremendous impact on the people involved, their interrelationships with the new system, and with each other. Jasinski's article "Adapting Organization to New Technology" describes some of these problems and illustrates some of the organizational changes which might need to be made to bring organizational patterns in line with technological efficiency.

The final article illustrates the increasing concern with methods of diagnosing "organizational effectiveness." There are also the prior questions of what criteria may be used to indicate the over-all state of the organization. Recent thinking suggests that traditional criteria have been too narrow in scope (e.g., profits during a given period) and need to be expanded to include such variables as development of the potentials of organization members, attitude of employees, and flexibility of the organization to meet new problems. Likert, in "Measuring Organizational Performance," reviews the research on these questions and provides some recommendations on the types of measurements psychologists can provide to assist in this task.

40. Studying Communication Patterns in Organizations*

Keith Davis

RECENTLY MUCH attention has been devoted to problems of communication in organizations, but methods of studying communication problems outside the laboratory have been fraught with all the usual difficulties of field research in social science. One area of particular difficulty has been the inability to record and "map" actual communication patterns in an organization. This paper reports a method of communication analysis which makes it possible to record and analyze communication patterns in terms of their variables, such as timing, media, subject matter, and organizational level.

A trial of the method in an operating business organization showed it to be effective in reporting patterns of communication accurately and in detail. This method of communication analysis is believed to be the first method providing by a simple questionnaire a large quantity of communication data for study. The method is called "ecco analysis."[1] By subjecting communication variables to measurement and tabulation, ecco analysis can do for communication problems what the development of attitude analysis did for morale problems two decades ago.

THE NEED FOR COMMUNICATION PATTERN ANALYSIS

Communication is a basic process of organization. It is the "nervous system" which makes organizations cohere and permits their members to cooperate and coordinate.[2] Laboratory research led Bavelas[3] to conclude that "communication is not a secondary or derived aspect of organization

---

* From "A Method of Studying Communication Patterns in Organizations," *Personnel Psychology*, Vol. 6, 1953, pp. 301–12.

[1] The term "ecco" is derived from "episodic communication channels in organization." The method reports data in the manner of a communication "echo."

[2] Charles H. Cooley, "The Significance of Communication," in Bernard Berelson and Morris Janowitz (eds.), *Reader in Public Opinion and Communication* (Glencoe, Ill.: The Free Press, 1950), p. 45.

[3] Alex Bavelas and Dermot Barrett, "An Experimental Approach to Organizational Communication," *Personnel*, Vol. 27, 1951, p. 368; Harold Leavitt, "Some Effects of Certain Communication Patterns on Group Performance," *Journal of Abnormal and Social Psychology*, Vol. 46, 1951, pp. 38–50.

—a 'helper' of the other and more basic functions. Rather it is the essence of organized activity and is the basic process out of which all other functions derive." Heise and Miller[4] in laboratory research have also concluded that communication patterns are a significant influence on organizational effectiveness.

The problem of moving communication research from the laboratory to the field of operations is difficult. Without a suitable framework and method of communication analysis, field research has often tended toward *techniques* of communicating rather than networks and other more basic variables.[5] Bavelas[6] makes the following comment about the jump from the laboratory to the field: "The job of mapping an existing net of communications even in a relatively small company is a complicated and difficult one. . . . The importance of bridging the gap between the simple, directly controlled experiment and the very complex, indirectly controlled social situation cannot be overestimated." Deutsch[7] says that, "If we can map the pathways by which information is communicated between different parts of an organization and by which it is applied to the behavior of the organization in relation to the outside world, we will have gone far toward understanding the organization."

EARLIER FIELD COMMUNICATION ANALYSIS

There are at least five ways to perform field study of communication patterns and networks, in addition to the experimental method which is probably in its pure form confined to the laboratory. Mayo and Roethlisberger,[8] who first emphasized the importance of communication problems in business organizations, used a "living-in" type of observation by which members of a small group were interviewed and observed for a period of years. In this manner the clinical observers got the "feel" of the group and were able to make subjective judgments about communication patterns.

A second method is "indirect analysis," which has been used by Helen

---

[4] George A. Heise and George A. Miller, "Problem Solving by Small Groups Using Various Communication Nets," *The Journal of Abnormal and Social Psychology*, Vol. 46, 1951, pp. 327–35.

[5] P. H. Cook, "An Examination of the Notion of Communication," *Occupational Psychology*, Vol. 25, 1951, p. 3.

[6] Alex Bavelas and Dermot Barrett, "An Experimental Approach to Organizational Communication," *op. cit.*, p. 371. (Editor's Note: See the next article.)

[7] Karl W. Deutsch, "On Communication Models in the Social Sciences," *The Public Opinion Quarterly*, Vol. 16, 1952, p. 367.

[8] Elton Mayo, *The Social Problems of an Industrial Civilization* (Boston: Harvard University, Graduate School of Business Administration, 1945); F. J. Roethlisberger and W. J. Dickson, *Management and the Worker* (Cambridge: Harvard University Press, 1939).

Baker,[9] E. W. Bakke,[10] C. L. Shartle,[11] Eugene Jacobson,[12] and others. For example, Shartle determined with what other executive each member of the organization spent the most time. The obvious assumption can be made that the member also communicated most with the executive with whom he spent the most time. Bakke determined whether respondents were satisfied with particular classes of information and types of media, which gave some idea of the channels of communication and the effectiveness of media.

A third method is "duty study" by which communications are studied as they pass any particular spot. This approach is similar to that used in a traffic survey in which the observer sits beside a particular road and records data about traffic as it passes before him. Duty study provides information about the flow of information, but it can show only in a general way the overall patterns of communication. For example, Moore,[13] in a study supervised by the author, determined that an Air Force squadron first sergeant spent 14% of his work day communicating by telephone.

A fourth method is "cross-section analysis," by which communications in process at any point in time are recorded and analyzed. In this approach a sample of communication is taken, from which generalizations can be drawn. For example, a group of interviewers might ring a bell as they enter an office and then immediately secure communication data from each person as of the moment the bell was rung. A random sample of communication can be secured by this method. Rubenstein[14] used this method to study communication in a research laboratory.

A fifth approach is to record and study communication sequences or chains, which is called "ecco analysis." The different nature of ecco analysis is apparent when it is compared with duty study. In transportation terms, duty study analyses the cars (units of information) as they pass a particular point in space at a particular time, but ecco analysis follows particular cars from the beginning of their journeys to the end. It focuses on a unit of information and follows it through time, space, and other dimensions.

---

[9] Helen Baker et al., *Transmitting Information through Management and Union Channels* (Princeton: Princeton University, 1949).

[10] E. W. Bakke, *Bonds of Organization* (New York: Harper and Brothers, 1950).

[11] C. L. Shartle, "Leadership and Executive Performance," *Personnel*, Vol. 25, 1949, pp. 370–80.

[12] Eugene Jacobson and Stanley E. Seashore, "Communication Practices in Complex Organizations," *The Journal of Social Issues*, Vol. VII, 1951, pp. 327–35.

[13] William W. Moore, *Time and Duty Study as a Method of Measuring Administrative Proficiency*, unpublished thesis, the University of Texas, 1950.

[14] Albert H. Rubenstein, "Research Communication," *Industrial Laboratories*, 1952.

THE FRAMEWORK AND METHOD OF ECCO ANALYSIS

There are probably many ways to secure communication sequence information. The following paragraphs will explain how one method was used to study communication patterns among the 67 management personnel of the Tex Tan Company,[15] a manufacturer of leather belts and billfolds sold in all 48 states. The basic approach was to get from each communication recipient data about how he first received that information. The same data were secured from each organizational member by questionnaire at the same time. The resulting jigsaw puzzle, when it was assembled, showed the pattern of how that information spread within the organization. For example, "A" and "B" said they got the information from "C," who said he got it from "D." The pattern is therefore "D" to "C" to "A" and "B." From this information a multitude of other variables were derived and compared with the pattern, such as whether the person was line or staff, what his function was, at what level he was, what his age was and what his seniority was. By a system of check marks on the questionnaire, other data were secured, such as when the communication took place, where it occurred, and the media used. The entire questionanire took less than two minutes for the person to complete *at the work place;* so there was negligible interference with production. The concept appears to be disarmingly simple; yet the results were relatively accurate and detailed.

In order to tabulate data mechanically, each person was given a code number which denoted whether he was management or operative, was line or staff, what his function, and his organizational level were. For example, 141116 meant respectively, management,[16] fourth level,[17] line,[18] belt factory[19] and Joe Smith. Each additional number or group of numbers could code one additional variable. Code numbers were also assigned to outside groups such as "my lodge brother." Code numbers and names were assembled into a list which each respondent had at his work place. When a person had to fill out a communication questionnaire, he looked on his list for the name of his communication initiator and wrote that person's code number in a box. The code was shorter, was less personal, avoided spelling problems, and discouraged looking over shoulders to see who told somebody (it is always possible to mis-read a number, but not a name). Use of the code also made the questionnaire information immediately ready for transfer to punch cards. All individual names were kept confidential by the surveyor, but the analytical data were available to management.

---

[15] Specific results of this study are being prepared for separate publication.

[16] Helen Baker *et al., op. cit.*

[17] P. H. Cook, *op. cit.*

[18] Helen Baker *et al., op. cit.*

[19] Helen Baker *et al., ibid.*

The actual survey procedure was as follows: the surveyor, with the assistance of company officials, selected the event or information which was to be the subject of the survey. A typist typed the question and time cut-off hour into a prepared stencil and copies were made. Each respondent's code was written on a questionniare and that questionnaire was personally delivered to him at his work place. The surveyor began collecting the questionnaires just as soon as he finished distributing them. Since each survey was carefully planned, it took little time. A survey of 67 persons was prepared, distributed, and collected in a morning; therefore many surveys were possible, and were conducted, in order to obtain general patterns of communication in the organization.

A key to the ecco method is proper selection and wording of the question asked, because the question directs each respondent's attention to the same unit of information. A sample question is: "By no later than noon today did you know the information in the box below, or ANY PART OF IT?" In the box were the words, "That John Doe is leaving Tex Tan soon to enter the insurance business in Yoakum." Respondents then designated which part of the information they knew, if any, and in what respects their information differed from that reported on the questionnaire. Each person gave the code number of the communication initiator who first gave him the information, and he also designated by a check mark the medium by which he received the communication.

KINDS OF DATA PROVIDED BY ECCO ANALYSIS

Ecco analysis has a dynamic quality because it portrays a sequence of communications about an event. It, for example, portrays the spread of a unit of information from its origin to all persons in the organization who knew it at the cut-off hour. This communication network can be superimposed on the organizational chart, or it may be otherwise charted in comparison to variables such as seniority, age, or physical proximity of regular work station.

The dynamics of flow are shown in almost any detail desired. Different types of relationships shown in the trial survey included: the proportion of communications between line and staff and within each, the proportion of communications between each organizational level, the direction of communications in relation to organizational level, the proportion of communications crossing functional lines, the types of communication in which line foremen showed most interest, the extent to which various media were used, the speed of the grapevine compared to formal communication, the extent to which the staff communicated by "paper work" instead of orally, work groups which were isolated from communication chains, work groups which receive information but tended not to re-communicate it, distortion of facts in communication chains and several other relationships. All this information was subject to comparison and correlation with other variables.

The following examples illustrate some of the information reported in the ecco surveys at Tex Tan Company. At all levels the staff both initiated and received communications more than the line, but the staff communicated orally more than on paper. Face-to-face communication was the predominant medium, and it spread information the fastest. Communications generally were blocked between the fourth and fifth organizational levels (there were six management levels). There were work groups at several levels which were generally isolated from communication networks. More than half of the communications crossed functional lines between production, sales, finance and office, and industrial relations. Communications tended to flow downward rather than upward, even when the information originated at lower levels. Grapevine patterns showed that only a few people tended to spread information; others acted as passive receivers only. The overall results clearly showed that the two major organizational variables, level and function, were major influences on communication patterns. Social factors were a third important influence.

SOME LIMITATIONS OF ECCO ANALYSIS

Since ecco data is secured from many individuals, it depends upon adequate rapport with respondents. The author found no difficulty in establishing rapport, except in the case of two or three individuals. Respondents can rather easily understand the basic objectives of the project, and the method is such that they do not have to be told the technical details. Since names are disclosed only to the surveyor, there is minimum hesitancy to report them. Furthermore, all data except *individual* sequence data can be secured without disclosing names to anyone, even the surveyor. In this variation, also used by the author, the code-number digits identifying each person are dropped leaving only a small-group identification.

Ecco analysis was judged to have adequate validity and reliability for business use. Results checked with information available from other sources. Furthermore, the method had certain built-in checks and balances. It encouraged accuracy and full disclosure because each respondent knew his response must fit the other pieces of the jig-saw framework. And in most cases the pieces did fit. Accuracy was further encouraged because the questionnaire asked for facts, rather than opinions. Since the full population was surveyed, problems of population sample did not arise, but there were problems of selecting representative types of information to be surveyed.

Another limitation is that individual communication sequences could not easily be secured in large organizations of 1,000 or more because the respondents would often not know their communicator's name. Large organizations would, therefore, have to be broken into smaller areas and studies made within each area in order to build a company pattern.

Ecco analysis is most suitable for showing how information is originally spread. Subsequent repetition of the same information to the same recipients might be more easily secured by duty study or cross-section analysis.

ADVANTAGES OF THE METHOD USED

A major value of ecco analysis is that research design permits an easy and simple questionnaire[20] instead of expensive interviewing, although interviewing could be used. Many of the criteria of effective survey method are met, such as low cost, short response period, simplicity, and adaptability.[21] The framework and method appear to be adaptable to various types of organizations and to both management and operative groups. As far as could be determined the method has negligible effect upon the phenomena being studied. It also gives minimum interference with organization activity. Each survey is a part of the whole, yet it is distinct in itself so that analysis can be made quickly available to those who will use it, such as the management of an organization.

Ecco analysis can be used to make comparisons between departments, branches or whole companies. For that purpose formulas were developed to portray data on a uniform basis for comparison. The first formula expresses the "receipt factor," which is simply the proportion of communications received by any unit. If seven out of 10 persons in a department were informed regarding a particular unit of information, the group receipt factor would be .7. If one person knew seven out of 10 units of information, his individual receipt factor would be .7. The formula is $\frac{R}{(PR)} = S$, where "R" is the number of receipt units, "(PR)" is the number of potential receipt units, and "S" is the receipt factor.

Another relationship is the "propensity to be communicated," which shows the extent to which a unit of information is communicated beyond its origin. This formula is the receipt factor adjusted for those units involved in the information's origin, which gives a more refined picture of information spread beyond its origin. For example, if four persons in a department of 10 persons saw an event happen in a meeting and seven persons now know the information, it has spread to only *three* of the six potential recipients. The "propensity to be communicated" in that case is .5, as expressed by the formula $\frac{R - O}{(PR) - O} = Y$, where "$O$" is the

---

[20] A copy of the questionnaire used will be mailed to those requesting it from the author.

[21] For a discussion of these criteria see Mildred Parten, *Surveys, Polls, and Samples* (New York: Harper and Brothers, 1950), especially Chapters 6 and 11.

number of persons involved in the communication origin and "*Y*" is the propensity to be communicated.

A third relationship is the "initiation factor," which is the proportion of initiation units compared to potential units. In a department of 10 persons, if seven act as initiators, the group initiation factor is .7. If one person has 10 opportunities to communicate and uses only seven of them, his initiation factor is .7. The formula is $\dfrac{I}{(PI)} = J$, where "*I*" is the number of initiation units, "*(PI)*" is the potential number of initiation units and "*J*" is the initiation factor.

A high initiation factor means that many people are spreading the information, but it does not indicate how many persons each initiator informs. If actual receipt units are divided by actual initiation units, the quotient is the average number of receipt units accomplished by each initiation unit. The formula is $R/I = M$, the "multiplier factor." If there are nine initiators within a group of 36 recipients, the multiplier factor is 4.0.

In 14 surveys of the management group at Tex Tan Company, the group receipt factor was .42, with a range of .08 to .81. In three surveys the group initiation factor ranged from .11 to .20 (average .15) and the multiplier factor ranged from 3.3 to 6.9 (average, 4.4). These relationships were computed for various departments, organizational levels, functional groups, and geographical groups. Additional formulas, not discussed herein, were also used; and additional relationships could have been analyzed from the wealth of data provided by ecco analysis.

USES OF ECCO ANALYSIS

Field application of ecco analysis showed that it provided concrete and useful information about communication patterns. Ecco analysis should be particularly useful to psychology, sociology, and business. In order to portray its application more concretely, let us explore how it can be used by business management. It should provide information which will help management of the individual firm, as well as management in general, to improve its planning, organizing, and controlling. Several specific applications are described briefly below.

1. A company can use ecco analysis to make a focused study of any communication problem area. Perhaps certain departments seem to be communication isolates, or the shop superintendent complains that rumors are destroying morale and efficiency. Ecco analysis would gather facts to help solve these problems.

2. Ecco studies can be made for purposes of interdepartmental or interplant comparisons. For a large company or a multi-plant company this is a special opportunity to learn more about its operations, because patterns in one unit can be compared with patterns in another to determine if one pattern is more consistently related to high management morale,

high turnover, low productivity, or other variables. This type of intra-company analysis would be similar to that used successfully by General Motors Corporation in attitude research.[22]

3. Ecco analysis can be used for either periodic or continuous audits of communication in a company. In a periodic audit, ecco surveys might be combined with the personnel audit or with an attitude survey. In a continuous audit, a departmental ecco survey might be made every week or two weeks in order to keep abreast of communication problems and to have current communication data available to top management when it needed such data for planning, organizing, and controlling.

4. In executive development, ecco surveys of management provide interesting case studies, and survey data can constitute the framework within which management training in communications is given. Even the process of making surveys will create management interest in its com-munication problems.

5. Ecco analysis should be especially useful for study of the informal organization and of "grapevine" chains of communication because it ap-pears to be the most effective method yet reported for recording grape-vine chains. Management needs a greater knowledge of the grapevine and more skill in using it.

6. A logical result of ecco studies over a period of time would be a search for generalities from which principles of communication will be drawn which can be used in business. Perhaps pattern "X" or "Y" can be shown to be generally effective for certain stated conditions. This de-velopment lies far in the background, but it is a potential, since labora-tory experiments by Bavelas (see below) and others have shown that communication patterns do affect such organizational factors as speed of work, accuracy of work, and worker morale.

41. An Experimental Approach to Organizational Communication*

Alex Bavelas and Dermot Barrett

COMMUNICATION AS a critical aspect of organization has been attracting more and more attention. If one may judge from articles and speeches,

---

[22] Chester E. Evans and La Verne N. Laseau, *My Job Contest* (Baltimore: Per-sonnel Psychology Monograph Number 1, 1950).

* From *Personnel*, Vol. 27, 1951, pp. 366–71.

much of the current thinking on communication centers around categories of problems which arise in day-to-day operations—"getting management's point of view to the workers," "stimulating communication up the line as well as down," "obtaining better communication with the union," "establishing more effective communication within management, and especially with the foremen." Knowing how such questions usually arise, it is not surprising that their discussion invariably resolves itself into considerations of *content* and *technique:* on the one hand, analyses of what management ought to be saying to the worker, the union, the foreman; on the other hand, descriptions of devices which can best say it—bulletin boards, letters, films, public address systems, meetings, etc. In its extreme form this approach becomes one of searching for a specific remedy for a specific ill. Helpful and practical as this may be, it is doubtful that such activity can lead to the discovery and understanding of the basic principles of effective organizational communication. Breakdowns and other difficulties at some point of a communication system are often only superficially related to the local conditions which appear to have produced them. They may, rather, be cumulative effects of properties of the entire communication system taken as a whole. But what are these properties, if, indeed, they exist?

Formal and Informal Systems

An organizational system of communication is usually created by the setting up of formal systems of responsibility and by explicit delegations of duties. These categories include statements, often implicitly, of the nature, content, and direction of the communication which is considered necessary for the performance of the group. Students of organization, however, have pointed out repeatedly that groups tend to depart from such formal statements and to create other channels of communication and dependence. In other words, informal organizational systems emerge. One may take the view that these changes are adaptations by the individuals involved in the direction of easier and more effective ways of working, or, perhaps, not working. It is no secret that informal groups are not always viewed by managers as favorable to the goals of the larger body. Also, it is by no means obvious that those informal groupings which evolve out of social and personality factors are likely to be more efficient (with respect to organizational tasks) than those set up formally by the managers. Altogether, if one considers how intimate the relations are between communication channels and control, it is not surprising that the managers of organizations would prefer explicit and orderly communication lines.

IS THERE "ONE BEST WAY"?

Unfortunately, there seems to be no organized body of knowledge out of which one can derive, for a given organization, an optimal communication system. Administrative thinking on this point commonly rests upon the assumption that the optimum system *can* be derived from a statement of the task to be performed. It is not difficult to show, however, that from a given set of specifications one may derive not a single communication pattern but a whole set of them, all logically adequate for the successful performance of the task in question. Which pattern from this set should be chosen? The choice, in practice, is usually made either in terms of a group of assumptions (often quite untenable) about human nature, or in terms of a personal bias on the part of the chooser. The seriousness of this situation is illustrated by the following example.

Let us assume that we have a group of five individuals who, in order

FIGURE 1

to solve a problem, must share as quickly as possible the information each person possesses. Let us also assume that there are reasons which prevent them from meeting around a table, and that they must share this information by writing notes. To avoid the confusion and waste of time of each person writing a message to each of the others, a supervisor decides to set up channels in which the notes must go. He strikes upon the pattern shown in Figure 1.

In this arrangement each individual can send to and receive messages from two others, one on his "left" and one on his "right." Experiments actually performed with this kind of situation show that the number of mistakes made by individuals working in such a "circle" pattern can be

FIGURE 2

reduced by fully 60 per cent by the simple measure of *removing one link*, thus making the pattern a "chain" as shown in Figure 2. The relevance of such a result to organization communication is obvious, simple though the example is. The sad truth, however, is that this phenomenon is not clearly derivable either from traditional "individual psychology" or from commonly held theories of group communication.

AN INTEGRAL PROCESS OF ORGANIZATION

Perhaps some headway can be made by approaching the general problem from a somewhat different direction. In the affairs of organizations, as well as in the affairs of men, chance always plays a part. However good a plan may be, however carefully prepared its execution, there is a point beyond which the probability of its success cannot be increased. With the firmest of intentions, agreements and promises may be impossible to carry out because of unforeseen events. Nevertheless, an organization whose functioning is too often interrupted by unforeseen events is looked upon with suspicion. Bad luck is an unhappy plea, and it may well be that the "unlucky" organization is more to be avoided than the simply incompetent one. On the other hand, few things about an organization are more admired and respected than the ability to "deliver" despite widely varying conditions and in the face of unusual difficulties.

In a very broad sense, it may be argued that the principal effort of organizational activities is the making of favorable conditions for the achievement of certain goals. In other words, an effort is made to increase, as much as the economics of the situation will permit, the probabilities of succeeding. This is the essence of the manager's job. The development of training and selection programs, the improvement of methods and the specification of techniques, the organization of research and development activities, the designation of responsibility and the delegation of duties— all these processes have one organizationally legitimate purpose: to increase the chances of organizational success. Upon this point rest almost all of the notions by which we are accustomed to evaluate organizations —in part or as a whole.

An organization is, in short, a social invention—a kind of "machine" for increasing certain sets of probabilities. (Which sets of probabilities are given to it to increase, which it chooses, how freely and by what means will not be discussed here. These problems, although they lie well within the scope of this subject, are outside the range of this paper. We will confine ourselves to a consideration of the process by which an accepted set of probabilities is optimized.) Probabilities of success are increased, however, only by taking relevant and appropriate actions. For the manager, these actions reduce in most instances to the gathering and evaluating of information in the form of reports, schedules, estimates, etc. It is entirely possible to view an organization as an elaborate system for gathering, evaluating, recombining, and disseminating information. It is not surprising, in these terms, that the effectiveness of an organization with respect to the achievement of its goals should be so closely related to its effectiveness in handling information. In an enterprise whose success hinges upon the coordination of the efforts of all its members, the managers depend completely upon the quality, the amount, and the rate at which relevant information reaches them. The rest of the organization, in turn, depends upon the efficiency with which the managers can deal with this information and reach conclusions, decisions, etc. This line of reasoning leads us to the belief that communication is not a secondary or derived aspect of organization—a "helper" of the other and presumably more basic functions. Rather it is the essence of organized activity and is the basic process out of which all other functions derive. The goals an organization selects, the methods it applies, the effectiveness with which it improves its own procedures—all of these hinge upon the quality and availability of the information in the system.

PATTERNS OF COMMUNICATION

About two years ago a series of studies was begun whose purpose was to isolate and study certain general properties of information handling systems. The first phase of this research program[1] is directed at a basic property of all communication systems, that of connection or "who can talk to whom."

This property of connection can be conveniently expressed by diagrams. The meaning of the picture in Figure 3 is obvious. Individuals A

FIGURE 3

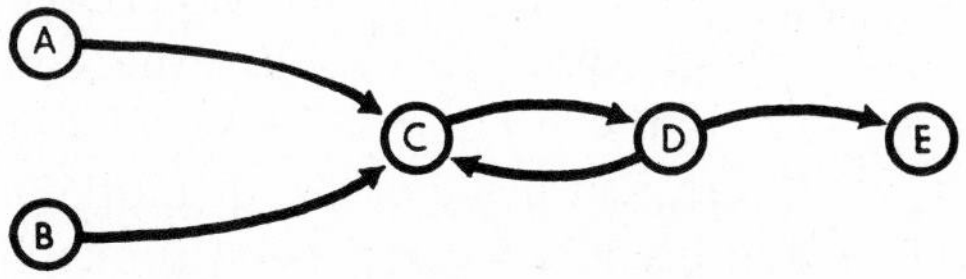

and B can send messages to C but they can receive messages from no one; C and D can exchange messages; E can receive messages from D, but he can send messages to no one. The pattern shown in Figure 3, however, is only one of the many that are possible. A group of others is shown in Figure 4. An examination of these patterns will show that they fall into two classes, separated by a very important difference. Any pair of individuals in each of the patterns d, e, and f can exchange messages either directly or indirectly over some route. No pair of individuals in each of the patterns a, b, and c can exchange messages. Patterns like a, b, and c obviously make any coordination of thought or action virtually impossible; we will be concerned from this point on only with patterns like d, e, and f.

Since the individuals in any connected pattern like d, e, and f can share ideas completely, should we expect that the effectiveness of individuals in performing group tasks or solving group problems would be the same in patterns d, e, and f except for differences in ability, knowledge, and personality? Should we expect differences in quality and speed of performance? Is it likely that the individuals working in one pattern

---

[1] These studies are supported jointly by the Rand Corporation and the Research Laboratory of Electronics at M.I.T.

FIGURE 4

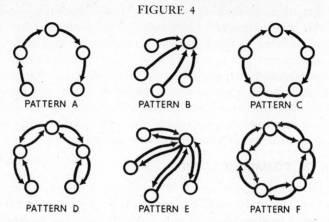

would show significantly better morale than the individuals working in a different pattern? Sidney Smith and Harold J. Leavitt conducted a series of experiments[2] which yielded very definite answers to these questions. An experimental design was used which made it possible to equate the difficulty of the tasks which the groups performed, and which permitted the cancelling of individual differences by randomizing the assignment of subjects to patterns. Also, the experiment was repeated with different groups enough times to establish the consistency of the results. A brief summary of the findings is given in Figure 5. The use of qualitative terms in Figure 5 in place of the quantitative measurements which were actually made blurs the comparison somewhat, but it gives a fair picture of the way these patterns performed. Since the original ex-

FIGURE 5

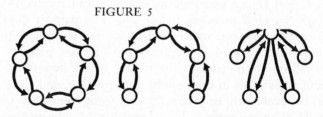

SPEED	SLOW	FAST	FAST
ACCURACY	POOR	GOOD	GOOD
ORGANIZATION	NO STABLE FORM OF ORGANIZATION	SLOWLY EMERGING BUT STABLE ORGANIZATION	ALMOST IMMEDIATE AND STABLE ORGANIZATION
EMERGENCE OF LEADER	NONE	MARKED	VERY PRONOUNCED
MORALE	VERY GOOD	POOR	VERY POOR

[2] Harold J. Leavitt reports these experiments in detail in the January, 1951, issue of the *Journal of Abnormal and Social Psychology*.

periments were done by Smith and Leavitt, this experiment has been repeated with no change in the findings.

The question very properly arises here as to whether these findings can be "explained" in the sense of being related to the connection properties of the patterns themselves. The answer to this question is a qualified yes. Without developing the mathematical analysis, which can be found in Leavitt's paper, the following statements can be made:

FIGURE 6

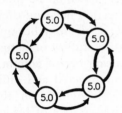 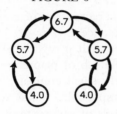 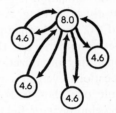

For any connected pattern, an *index of dispersion* can be calculated. Relative to this index, there can be calculated for *each position in each pattern* an *index of centrality*, and an *index of peripherality*. The data suggest strongly that the rapidity with which organization emerges and the stability it displays are related to the gradient of the indices of centrality in the pattern. In Figure 6 these indices are given for each position. It should be added at this point that in the patterns in which leadership emerged, the leader was invariably that person who occupied the position of highest centrality.

FIGURE 7

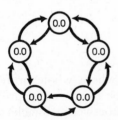 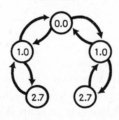 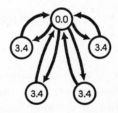

The index of peripherality appears to be related strongly to morale. In Figure 7 the indices of peripherality are given by position. Those individuals who occupied positions of low or zero peripherality showed in their actions as well as in self-ratings (made at the end of the experiments) that they were satisfied, in high spirits, and generally pleased with the work they had done. Those individuals who occupied positions of high peripherality invariably displayed either apathetic or destructive and uncooperative behavior during the group effort, and rated themselves as dissatisfied and critical of the group's operation.

A word of caution should be given concerning the slow, inaccurate, but happy "circle" pattern. Subsequent experiments by Sidney Smith indicate that this pattern possesses unusual abilities for adaptation to sudden and confusing changes of task—a quality lacking in the other two patterns.

A PROMISING FIELD FOR RESEARCH

Clearly, these experiments are only the beginning of a long story. The findings, although they promise much, settle nothing; but they do suggest that an experimental approach to certain aspects of organizational communication is possible and that, in all probability, it would be practically rewarding. As the characteristics of communication nets and their effects upon human performance *as they occur in the laboratory* become better understood, the need will grow for systematic studies of actual operating organizations. The job of mapping an existing net of communications even in a relatively small company is a complicated and difficult one, but it is not impossible. Some work is beginning on the development of field methods of observation. The importance of bridging the gap between the simple, directly controlled experiment and the very complex, indirectly controlled social situation cannot be overestimated.

42. Barriers and Gateways to Communication*

Carl R. Rogers

IT MAY SEEM curious that a person like myself, whose whole professional effort is devoted to psychotherapy, should be interested in problems of communication. What relationship is there between obstacles to communication and providing therapeutic help to individuals with emotional maladjustments?

Actually the relationship is very close indeed. The whole task of psychotherapy is the task of dealing with a failure in communication. The emotionally maladjusted person, the "neurotic," is in difficulty, first, because communication within himself has broken down and, secondly, because as a result of this his communication with others has been damaged. To put it another way, in the "neurotic" individual parts of himself which have been termed unconscious, or repressed, or denied to aware-

---

* Reprinted from Part I of the article, published in the *Harvard Business Review*, July–August, 1952.

ness, become blocked off so that they no longer communicate themselves to the conscious or managing part of himself; as long as this is true, there are distortions in the way he communicates himself to others, and so he suffers both within himself and in his interpersonal relations.

The task of psychotherapy is to help the person achieve, through a special relationship with a therapist, good communication within himself. Once this is achieved, he can communicate more freely and more effectively with others. We may say then that psychotherapy is good communication, within and between men. We may also turn that statement around and it will still be true. Good communication, free communication, within or between men, is always therapeutic.

It is, then, from a background of experience with communication in counseling and psychotherapy that I want to present two ideas: (1) I wish to state what I believe is one of the major factors in blocking or impeding communication, and then (2) I wish to present what in our experience has proved to be a very important way of improving or facilitating communication.

BARRIER: *THE TENDENCY TO EVALUATE*

I should like to propose, as a hypothesis for consideration, that the major barrier to mutual interpersonal communication is our very natural tendency to judge, to evaluate, to approve (or disapprove) the statement of the other person or the other group. Let me illustrate my meaning with some very simple examples. Suppose someone, commenting on this discussion, makes the statement, "I didn't like what that man said." What will you respond? Almost invariably your reply will be either approval or disapproval of the attitude expressed. Either you respond, "I didn't either; I thought it was terrible," or else you tend to reply, "Oh, I thought it was really good." In other words, your primary reaction is to evaluate it from *your* point of view, your own frame of reference.

Or take another example. Suppose I say with some feeling, "I think the Republicans are behaving in ways that show a lot of good sound sense these days." What is the response that arises in your mind? The overwhelming likelihood is that it will be evaluative. In other words, you will find yourself agreeing, or disagreeing, or making some judgment about me such as "He must be a conservative," or "He seems solid in his thinking." Or let us take an illustration from the international scene. Russia says vehemently, "The treaty with Japan is a war plot on the part of the United States." We rise as one person to say, "That's a lie!"

This last illustration brings in another element connected with my hypothesis. Although the tendency to make evaluations is common in almost all interchange of language, it is very much heightened in those situations where feelings and emotions are deeply involved. So the stronger our feelings, the more likely it is that there will be no mutual element in the communication. There will be just two ideas, two feelings, two judgments, missing each other in psychological space.

I am sure you recognize this from your own experience. When you have not been emotionally involved yourself and have listened to a heated discussion, you often go away thinking, "Well, they actually weren't talking about the same thing." And they were not. Each was making a judgment, an evaluation, from his own frame of reference. There was really nothing which could be called communication in any genuine sense. This tendency to react to any emotionally meaningful statement by forming an evaluation of it from our own point of view is, I repeat, the major barrier to interpersonal communication.

GATEWAY: LISTENING WITH UNDERSTANDING

Is there any way of solving this problem, of avoiding this barrier? I feel that we are making exciting progress toward this goal, and I should like to present it as simply as I can. Real communication occurs, and this evaluative tendency is avoided, when we listen with understanding. What does that mean? It means to see the expressed idea and attitude from the other person's point of view, to sense how it feels to him, to achieve his frame of reference in regard to the thing he is talking about.

Stated so briefly, this may sound absurdly simple, but it is not. It is an approach which we have found extremely potent in the field of psychotherapy. It is the most effective agent we know for altering the basic personality structure of an individual and for improving his relationships and his communications with others. If I can listen to what he can tell me, if I can understand how it seems to him, if I can see its personal meaning for him, if I can sense the emotional flavor which it has for him, then I will be releasing potent forces of change in him.

Again, if I can really understand how he hates his father, or hates the company, or hates Communists—if I can catch the flavor of his fear of insanity, or his fear of atom bombs, or of Russia—it will be of the greatest help to him in altering those hatreds and fears and in establishing realistic and harmonious relationships with the very people and situations toward which he has felt hatred and fear. We know from our research that such empathic understanding—understanding *with* a person, not *about* him—is such an effective approach that it can bring about major changes in personality.

Some of you may be feeling that you listen well to people and yet you have never seen such results. The chances are great indeed that your listening has not been of the type I have described. Fortunately, I can suggest a little laboratory experiment which you can try to test the quality of your understanding. The next time you get into an argument with your wife, or your friend, or with a small group of friends, just stop the discussion for a moment and, for an experiment, institute this rule: "Each person can speak up for himself only *after* he has first restated the ideas and feelings of the previous speaker accurately and to that speaker's satisfaction."

You see what this would mean. It would simply mean that before presenting your own point of view, it would be necessary for you to achieve the other speaker's frame of reference—to understand his thoughts and feelings so well that you could summarize them for him. Sounds simple, doesn't it? But if you try it, you will discover that it is one of the most difficult things you have ever tried to do. However, once you have been able to see the other's point of view, your own comments will have to be drastically revised. You will also find the emotion going out of the discussion, the differences being reduced, and those differences which remain being of a rational and understandable sort. . . .

If, then, this way of approach is an effective avenue to good communication and good relationships, as I am quite sure you will agree if you try the experiment I have mentioned, why is it not more widely tried and used? I will try to list the difficulties which keep it from being utilized.

Need for courage. In the first place it takes courage, a quality which is not too widespread. I am indebted to Dr. S. I. Hayakawa, the semanticist, for pointing out that to carry on psychotherapy in this fashion is to take a very real risk, and that courage is required. If you really understand another person in this way, if you are willing to enter his private world and see the way life appears to him, without any attempt to make evaluative judgments, you run the risk of being changed yourself. You might see it his way; you might find yourself influenced in your attitudes or your personality.

This risk of being changed is one of the most frightening prospects many of us can face. If I enter, as fully as I am able, into the private world of a neurotic or psychotic individual, isn't there a risk that I might become lost in that world? Most of us are afraid to take that risk. Or if we were listening to a Russian Communist . . . how many of us would dare to try to see the world from his point of view? The great majority of us could not *listen;* we would find ourselves compelled to *evaluate*, because listening would seem too dangerous. So the first requirement is courage, and we do not always have it.

Heightened emotions. But there is a second obstacle. It is just when emotions are strongest that it is most difficult to achieve the frame of reference of the other person or group. Yet it is then that the attitude is most needed if communication is to be established. We have not found this to be an insuperable obstacle in our experience in psychotherapy. A third party, who is able to lay aside his own feelings and evaluations, can assist greatly by listening with understanding to each person or group and clarifying the views and attitudes each holds.

We have found this effective in small groups in which contradictory or antagonistic attitudes exist. When the parties to a dispute realize that they are being understood, that someone sees how the situation seems to them, the statements grow less exaggerated and less defensive, and it is no longer necessary to maintain the attitude, "I am 100% right and you are 100% wrong." The influence of such an understanding catalyst in the group permits the members to come closer and closer to the objective truth involved in the relationship. In this way mutual communication is established, and some type of agreement becomes much more possible.

So we may say that though heightened emotions make it much more difficult to understand *with* an opponent, our experience makes it clear that a neutral, understanding, catalyst type of leader or therapist can overcome this obstacle in a small group.

Size of group. That last phrase, however, suggests another obstacle to utilizing the approach I have described. Thus far all our experience has been with small face-to-face groups—groups exhibiting industrial tensions, religious tensions, racial tensions, and therapy groups in which many personal tensions are present. In these small groups our experience, confirmed by a limited amount of research, shows that this basic approach leads to improved communication, to greater acceptance of others and by others, and to attitudes which are more positive and more problem-solving in nature. There is a decrease in defensiveness, in exaggerated statements, in evaluative and critical behavior.

But these findings are from small groups. What about trying to achieve understanding between larger groups that are geographically remote, or between face-to-face groups that are not speaking for themselves but simply as representatives of others, like the delegates at Kaesong? Frankly we do not know the answers to these questions. I believe the situation might be put this way: As social scientists we have a tentative test-tube solution of the problem of breakdown in communication. But to confirm the validity of this test-tube solution and to adapt it to the enormous problems of communication breakdown between classes, groups, and nations would involve additional funds, much more research, and creative thinking of a high order.

Yet with our present limited knowledge we can see some steps which might be taken even in large groups to increase the amount of listening *with* and decrease the amount of evaluation *about*. To be imaginative for a moment, let us suppose that a therapeutically oriented international group went to the Russian leaders and said, "We want to achieve a genuine understanding of your views and, even more important, of your attitudes and feelings toward the United States. We will summarize and resummarize these views and feelings if necessary, until you agree that our description represents the situation as it seems to you."

Then suppose they did the same thing with the leaders in our own country. If they then gave the widest possible distribution to these two views, with the feelings clearly described but not expressed in name-calling, might not the effect be very great? It would not guarantee the type of understanding I have been describing, but it would make it much more possible. We can understand the feelings of a person who hates us much more readily when his attitudes are accurately described to us by a neutral third party than we can when he is shaking his fist at us. . . .

SUMMARY

In closing, I should like to summarize this small-scale solution to the problem of barriers in communication, and to point out certain of its characteristics.

I have said that our research and experience to date would make it appear that breakdowns in communication, and the evaluative tendency which is the major barrier to communication, can be avoided. The solution is provided by creating a situation in which each of the different parties comes to understand the other from the *other's* point of view. This has been achieved, in practice, even when feelings run high, by the influence of a person who is willing to understand each point of view emphathically, and who thus acts as a catalyst to precipitate further understanding.

This procedure has important characteristics. It can be initiated by one party, without waiting for the other to be ready. It can even be initiated by a neutral third person, provided he can gain a minimum of cooperation from one of the parties.

This procedure can deal with the insincerities, the defensive exaggerations, the lies, the "false fronts" which characterize almost every failure in communication. These defensive distortions drop away with astonishing speed as people find that the only intent is to understand, not to judge.

This approach leads steadily and rapidly toward the discovery of the truth, toward a realistic appraisal of the objective barriers to communication. The dropping of some defensiveness by one party leads to further dropping of defensiveness by the other party, and truth is thus approached.

This procedure gradually achieves mutual communication. Mutual communication tends to be pointed toward solving a problem rather than toward attacking a person or group. It leads to a situation in which I see how the problem appears to you as well as to me, and you see how it appears to me as well as to you. Thus accurately and realistically defined, the problem is almost certain to yield to intelligent attack; or if it is in part insoluble, it will be comfortably accepted as such.

This then appears to be a test-tube solution to the breakdown of communication as it occurs in small groups. Can we take this small-scale answer, investigate it further, refine it, develop it, and apply it to the tragic and well-nigh fatal failures of communication which threathen the very existence of our modern world? It seems to me that this is a possibility and a challenge which we should explore.

43. Selective Perception: The Departmental Identifications of Executives*

DeWitt C. Dearborn and Herbert A. Simon

AN IMPORTANT proposition in organization theory asserts that each executive will perceive those aspects of the situation that relate specifically to the activities and goals of his department.[1] The proposition is frequently supported by anecdotes of executives and observers in organizations, but little evidence of a systematic kind is available to test it. It is the purpose of this note to supply some such evidence.

The proposition we are considering is not peculiarly organizational. It is simply an application to organizational phenomena of a generalization that is central to any explanation of selective perception: Presented with a complex stimulus, the subject perceives in it what he is "ready" to perceive; the more complex or ambiguous the stimulus, the more the perception is determined by what is already "in" the subject and the less by what is in the stimulus.[2]

Cognitive and motivational mechanisms mingle in the selective process, and it may be of some use to assess their relative contributions. We might suppose either: (1) selective attention to a part of a stimulus reflects a deliberate ignoring of the remainder as irrelevant to the subject's goals and motives, or (2) selective attention is a learned response stemming from some past history of reinforcement. In the latter case we might still be at some pains to determine the nature of the reinforcement, but by creating a situation from which any immediate motivation for selectivity is removed, we should be able to separate the second mechanism from the first. The situation in which we obtained our data meets this condition, and hence our data provide evidence for internalization of the selective processes.

---

* From "Selective Perception: A Note on the Departmental Identifications of Executives," *Sociometry*, Vol. 21, No. 2, June, 1958.

[1] H. A. Simon, *Administrative Behavior* (New York: Macmillan, 1947), ch. 5, 10.

[2] J. S. Bruner, "On Perceptual Readiness," *Psychological Review*, Vol. 64, 1957, pp. 132–33.

METHOD OF THE STUDY

A group of 23 executives, all employed by a single large manufacturing concern and enrolled in a company sponsored executive training program, was asked to read a standard case that is widely used in instruction in business policy in business schools. The case, Castengo Steel Company, described the organization and activities of a company of moderate size specializing in the manufacture of seamless steel tubes, as of the end of World War II. The case, which is about 10,000 words in length, contains a wealth of descriptive material about the company and its industry and the recent history of both (up to 1945), but little evaluation. It is deliberately written to hold closely to concrete facts and to leave as much as possible of the burden of interpretation to the reader.

When the executives appeared at a class session to discuss the case, but before they had discussed it, they were asked by the instructor to write a brief statement of what they considered to be the most important problem facing the Castengo Steel Company—the problem a new company president should deal with first. Prior to this session, the group had discussed other cases, being reminded from time to time by the instructor that they were to assume the role of the top executive of the company in considering its problems.

The executives were a relatively homogeneous group in terms of status, being drawn from perhaps three levels of the company organization. They were in the range usually called "middle management," representing such positions as superintendent of a department in a large factory, product manager responsible for profitability of one of the ten product groups manufactured by the company, and works physician for a large factory. In terms of departmental affiliation, they fell in four groups:

Sales (6): Five product managers or assistant product managers, and one field sales supervisor.

Production (5): Three department superintendents, one assistant factory manager, and one construction engineer.

Accounting (4): An assistant chief accountant, and three accounting supervisors—for a budget division and two factory departments.

Miscellaneous (8): Two members of the legal department, two in research and development, and one each from public relations, industrial relations, medical and purchasing.

THE DATA

Since the statements these executives wrote are relatively brief, they are reproduced in full in the appendix to the article. We tested our hypothesis by determining whether there was a significant relation between the "most important problem" mentioned and the departmental affiliation of the mentioner. In the cases of executives who mentioned more than one problem, we counted all those they mentioned. We compared (1) the executives who mentioned "sales," "marketing," or "distribution" with those who did not; (2) the executives who mentioned "clarifying the organization" or some equivalent with those who did not; (3) the executives who mentioned "human relations," "employee relations" or "teamwork" with those who did not. The findings are summarized in Table 1.

The difference between the percentages of sales executives (83%) and other executives (29%) who mentioned sales as the most important problem is significant at the 5 per cent level. Three of the five nonsales executives, moreover, who mentioned sales were in the accounting department, and all of these were in positions that involved analysis of product profitability. This accounting activity was, in fact, receiving considerable emphasis in the company at the time of the case discussion and the accounting executives had frequent and close contacts with the

TABLE 1

| | Total Number of Executives | Number Who Mentioned | | |
Department		Sales	"Clarify Organization"	Human Relations
Sales...................	6	5	1	0
Production............	5	1	4	0
Accounting...........	4	3	0	0
Miscellaneous.........	8	1	3	3
Totals..........	23	10	8	3

product managers in the sales department. If we combine sales and accounting executives, we find that 8 out of 10 of these mentioned sales as the most important problem; while only 2 of the remaining 13 executives did.

Organization problems (other than marketing organization) were mentioned by four out of five production executives, the two executives in research and development, and the factory physician, but by only one sales executive and no accounting executives. The difference between the percentage for production executives (80%) and other executives (22%) is also significant at the 5 per cent level. Examination of the Castengo case shows that the main issue discussed in the case that relates to manufacturing is the problem of poorly defined relations among the factory manager, the metallurgist, and the company president. The presence of the metallurgist in the situation may help to explain the sensitivity of the two research and development executives (both of whom were concerned with metallurgy) to this particular problem area.

It is easy to conjecture why the public relations, industrial relations, and medical executives should all have mentioned some aspect of human relations, and why one of the two legal department executives should have mentioned the board of directors.

CONCLUSION

We have presented data on the selective perceptions of industrial executives exposed to case material that support the hypothesis that each executive will perceive those aspects of a situation that relate specifically to the activities and goals of his department. Since the situation is one in which the executives were motivated to look at the problem from a company-wide rather than a departmental viewpoint, the data indicate further that the criteria of selection have become internalized. Finally, the method for obtaining data that we have used holds considerable promise as a projective device for eliciting the attitudes and perceptions of executives.

APPENDIX

EXECUTIVE	SALES

SALES

4. Apparent need for direct knowledge of their sales potential.
    Apparent need for exploitation of their technical potential to achieve a broader market and higher priced market.
    Apparent need for unit and operation cost data.
5. How to best organize the company so as to be able to take full advantage of the specialized market available.
6. Appointment of Production Manager familiar with business.
    Analysis of market conditions with regard to expansion in plastic market.
12. Develop a sales organization which would include market research.
20. Lack of organization to plan and cope with postwar manufacturing and sales problems.
25. The President's choice of executive officers.

PRODUCTION

1. Policy pertaining to distribution of product should be reviewed with more emphasis on new customers and concern for old.
15. Lack of clear-cut lines of responsibility.
16. Determine who the top executive was to be and have this information passed on to subordinate executives.
18. Review the organization.
    Why so many changes in some of the offices such as works manager.
24. Absence of policy—should be set forth by company head.

ACCOUNTING

7. Standards brought up to date and related to incentives. (Incentives evidently do not exist.)
9. Future of the company as to marketability of products—product specification—growth or containment or retirement (i.e., from product).
10. Distribution problems. Not necessarily their present problems in distribution, but those that undoubtedly will arise in the near future—plastics, larger companies, etc.

11.   Reorganization of the company to save its lost market for its product and to look for an additional market is the prime problem.

OTHER

3.   (Legal) Manufacture of one product which (a) competes against many larger manufacturers with greater facilities in competitive market, and (b) is perhaps due to lose to a related product much of its market.

14.   (Legal) Board of Directors.

8.   (Public relations) The handling of employee relations—particularly the company-union relationship.

17.   (Industrial relations) Can we get the various departments together to form a team in communications and cooperation.

19.   (Medical) 1. Reorganization of corporate structure
               2. Lines of authority and command
               3. Personnel relations.

21.   (Purchasing) We should start to think and organize for our peacetime economy.

22.   (Research and development) Overcentralized control by the president.

23.   (Research and development) No formal organization with duties defined.

44. Some Effects of Feedback on Communication*

Harold J. Leavitt and Ronald A. H. Mueller

THE EXPERIMENTS reported here are concerned with the transmission of information from person A to person or persons B. Our problem deals with only one of the many relevant variables, the variable of feedback. The question becomes: how is the transmission of information from A to B influenced by the return of information from B to A? It is apparently taken for granted in industry, in the lecture hall, and in radio that it is both possible and efficient to transmit information from A to B without simultaneous feedback from B to A. On the other hand, the information theories of the cyberneticists and, to some extent, trial and error concepts in learning theory suggest that for A to hit successfully

* From *Human Relations*, Vol. 4, 1951, pp. 401–10.

Readers familiar with the work of Professor Alex Bavelas will doubtless correctly recognize that many of the theoretical and experimental ideas in this research had their origins in his group. We are most grateful to Dr. Bavelas for both his direct and indirect help some target, B, requires that A be constantly informed of A's own progress. The servomechanism needs a sensory system that is capable of transmitting cues about the errors of its own motor system. The human being learning some motor skill apparently utilizes the same process. But when the human being (A) seeks to transmit information to another human being (B), A's own sensory system is hardly an adequate source of information *unless* B takes some action which will help A to keep informed of A's own progress. If A were trying to hit B with a brick, A's eyes combined with an inactive B would probably be adequate to permit A to hit his target after several trials. But if A seeks to hit B with information, he will probably be more successful if B helps to provide some cues which A's own sensory system cannot pick up directly. In other words, where communication between A and B is the goal, feedback, in the form of verbal or expressive language, should make for greater effectiveness.

If we take the human memory mechanism into account, we need not require that there be *contemporaneous* feedback between A and B. It may not even be necessary that there be any feedback from B_2 if feedback from a similar B_1 has already occurred. The practice sessions of the past may have provided enough feedback to permit one to hit his present target accurately. Language, for example, may be thought of as a tool originally learned with feedback, but currently useful in a multitude of situations without simultaneous feedback to help us at least to get within range of our targets. But if the material to be communicated is relatively new and relatively precise, previously learned language may not be enough. Accurate transmission may require some additional contemporaneous feedback.

In addition to this hypothesis that contemporaneous feedback should increase the accuracy of transmission of information from A to B, is the hypothesis that the completion of the AB circuit produces other effects on the AB relationship. Feedback from both A and B can increase the certainty of B that he is getting the intended information, and the certainty of A that he is getting it across. This increase in certainty, assuming motivated participants, should have some effect on feelings of frustration or achievement and, hence, on the feelings of hostility or security that pervade the relationship.

Our purpose, then, in these experiments is to try to test these hypotheses; to try to determine experimentally the effects of feedback (or the absence of feedback) on certain kinds of A to B communications.

Experiment I

WHAT ARE THE EFFECTS OF PROGRESSIVE LEVELS OF FEEDBACK?

We chose as our material-to-be-communicated in these experiments a series of geometric patterns. The patterns were all composed of six equal rectangular elements, but the relationships of the elements to one another differed from pattern to pattern (see Figure 1 *A* for sample pattern). *A*'s (the instructor's) job was to describe orally one of these abstract patterns to the members of his class as accurately as possible,

FIGURE 1

Sample Problems

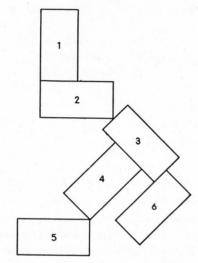

A. Sample of Problems Used in Experiment I

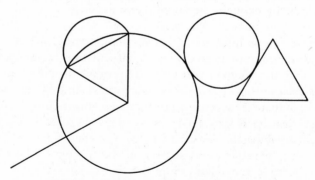

B. Sample of Problems Used in Experiment II

accuracy to be measured from the students' reproductions of the described (but unseen) patterns.

Two instructors were used, and four groups of students (total student $N = 80$), with each instructor describing four patterns to each student group. There were four conditions of feedback: 1. *Zero feedback* in which instructors sat behind a movable blackboard to describe the patterns. No questions or noises were permitted from the students. 2. The *visible audience* condition in which students and instructor could see one another but no speaking by students was allowed. 3. A *yes-no* condition in which the visible audience was permitted to say only yes or no in response to questions from the instructor. And 4. A *free feedback* situation in which students were permitted to ask questions, interrupt, etc.

It was possible to have each instructor use each condition of feedback in a different order. (See Table 1.)

TABLE 1

DESIGN OF EXPERIMENT I

Pattern No.	1	2	3	4		5	6	7	8
Class 1:	zero	V-A	Y-N	free		zero	V-A	Y-N	free
		(Instructor X)					(Instructor Y)		
Class 2:	V-A	Y-N	free	zero		V-A	Y-N	free	zero
		(Instructor Y)					(Instructor X)		
Class 3:	Y-N	free	zero	V-A		Y-N	free	zero	V-A
		(Instructor X)					(Instructor Y)		
Class 4:	free	zero	V-A	Y-N		free	zero	V-A	Y-N
		(Instructor Y)					(Instructor X)		

Besides reproducing the test patterns, students were asked to estimate their confidence in the correctness of their answers and, after the last pattern, to indicate the feedback condition they found most comfortable. We also timed the description of each pattern.

All students were given the same instructions at the beginning of the class period. They were told that the experiment was a test of their ability to understand instructions, and that they were to work as rapidly and as accurately as possible. Both instructors had had some previous experience in describing similar patterns, and both had participated in the construction of the test patterns.

Students' papers were scored for accuracy on a scale from 0 to 6. A particular rectangular element was scored correct if it bore the correct relationship to the preceding element. The first element was scored correct if it was correctly oriented on the page.

RESULTS:

1. Accuracy. The mean accuracy score for *all* patterns increased steadily from *zero* to *free feedback*. With *zero feedback* the mean was 4.7 out of a possible 6. The range of means for the eight different patterns given under this condition was 3.1 to 5.9. Under the *visible audience* condition the mean score was 5.3 with a range from 4.5 to 5.9. Under the *yes-no* condition the mean score was 5.5, the range 5.0 to 5.8. With *free feedback* the mean was 5.6 and the range 5.1 to 6.0.

2. Confidence Level. Students' estimates of their own accuracy correlated closely with actual accuracy. For all patterns the mean confidence levels were: *zero feedback*, 4.6; *visible audience*, 5.3; *yes-no*, 5.6; *free feedback*, 5.5. No effects of experience could be detected. There was a tendency to favor one instructor for the *free feedback* situation and the other for all others. These differences were slight and may indicate a differential skill on the part of the instructors in handling the different feedback conditions.

3. *Time.* The mean time required to give instructions under the four conditions were: *zero feedback*, 229 seconds; *visible audience*, 249 seconds; *yes-no*, 316 seconds; *free feedback*, 363 seconds. Any decrease in time with experience is once again obscured by differences in difficulty. No clear-cut differences between instructors were apparent.

4. *Other Observations.* Both instructors noticed some rather interesting behavior under certain conditions. When using *free feedback*, both found that on some occasions the students utilized their opportunities to speak by speaking aggressively and with hostility. There were comments like: "That's impossible"; "Are you purposely trying to foul us up?"; "You said left, it has to be right"; and so on. These comments even flowed on to students' papers, when they wrote beside their patterns such comments as: "The teacher made mistakes on this one, I didn't." These hostile reactions seemed to occur only when the *free feedback* condition *followed* other conditions. Both instructors noticed too that their *free feedback* experience stood them in good stead in the *zero feedback* situations. A student in the *free feedback* situation might say, "Oh, it looks like an L." In the next use of that pattern the instructors would find themselves saying, "It looks like an L."

COMMENTARY

Although these data indicate that *free feedback* does yield more accurate results than the other conditions, some new questions arise. Can it not be argued that the *free feedback* method is more effective simply because it requires more time? Would the time required decrease if *free feedback* were used continuously? Does the *free feedback* method always put the teacher on the spot? Will he be attacked for his errors or lack of knowledge? Though free feedback may be helpful at first, is it of any use after the student and the teacher have had an opportunity to straighten out their language difficulties? Can the teacher improve just as much after a series of experiences without feedback as after a series with feedback? Can we show continuous improvement in the course of several trials without feedback?

Experiment II

FEEDBACK vs. NO FEEDBACK

In an attempt to answer some of these questions we designed another series of experiments that seemed to permit the most efficient use of our limited supply of instructors and students. The purpose of these experiments was to compare the two extreme conditions, *free feedback* and *zero feedback,* over a longer series of trials.

METHOD

Using eight new geometric patterns, all made up of six elements (see Figure 1 *B*), we selected ten instructors and ten separate groups of students, the groups ranging in size from six to twenty-four. Five of the instructors were members of the English Department at the Institute, one taught German, one economics, and three psychology. Four of the classes were speech classes, six were general psychology. For *three* pairs of instructors the procedure was as follows:

Instructor *A* faced class *A* with four patterns in sequence and *zero feedback.* Then instructor *B* faced class *A* with four new patterns in sequence and *free feedback.* Instructor *A* then faced class *B* with his original four patterns and *free feedback.* Then instructor *B* faced class *B* with his original four patterns and *zero feedback.* For the other two pairs of instructors the procedure was reversed, instructor *A* beginning with free feedback.

We again asked for confidence levels, from both the students and instructors.

RESULTS:

1. Overall. The results of this experiment bear out the trend of the first. The mean student accuracy score for all *zero feedback* trials was 5.2 of a possible 6; the mean with *feedback* was 5.9. These means represent the students of ten instructors. The ranges for individual instructors were, with *zero feedback,* 3.8 to 5.8; with *free feedback,* 5.6 to 6.0. This difference between these means is significant at the 1% level.

In students' confidence in their results, the data again correlate closely with accuracy. The mean for *zero feedback* is 5.0 with a range from 3.5 to 5.7, while for *free feedback* the mean in 5.8 and the range 5.4 to 6.0. These differences are also significant.

In terms of time required to describe each pattern, *free feedback* remains a more time-consuming process. The average time for *zero feedback* is 166 seconds with a range from 60 to 273. For *free feedback* the average time is 284 seconds with a range of 193 to 423. These differences too are significant.

Finally in our measure of teacher confidence, means were 4.5 with *zero feedback* and 5.0 with *free feedback,* with respective ranges of 2.5 to 5.5 and 4.5 to 5.8. In all cases instructors were *less* confident than their students.

In every case individual instructors changed in the same direction as the means. Every instructor got better results with feedback than without, and every instructor took longer with feedback than without.

FIGURE 2

Accuracy

(Each Point Represents the Mean of 10 Groups)

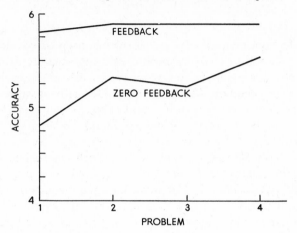

2. Effects of Experience. In Figure 2 are shown curves representing the changes in accuracy from pattern to pattern. Each instructor, you will recall, described four patterns in sequence under conditions of *zero feedback* and then *free feedback*.

From these accuracy curves one can see that *free feedback* starts at almost the maximum level and stays there. *Zero feedback* changes in the direction of greater accuracy from trial to trial.

As far as time (Figure 3) is concerned, the reverse is true. *Zero feedback* remains more or less constant, while *free feedback* time *declines progressively*.

FIGURE 3

Time

(Each Point Represents the Mean of 10 Groups)

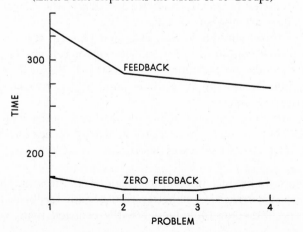

There is at least one other way of analyzing the data that provides some rather interesting results. Our experimental design supplied us with data for all combinations of (a) inexperienced (with these patterns) and experienced instructors, and (b) inexperienced and experienced classes, working (c) with and without feedback. The data broken down this way indicate that instructors' experience is the most significant factor present. Differences between experienced and inexperienced instructors are always greater than between experienced and inexperienced classes. This difference holds for *zero feedback* only, since with *free feedback* there are no perceptible differences among any of the different conditions.

3. Other Observations. One of our hypotheses in these experiments centered on the effects of feedback on the relationship between sender and receiver. We have no quantitative data that are relevant to this hypothesis, but we do have some observations that were astonishing in their consistency. These observations amounted to this. When an instructor faced a new class with *free feedback*, he got fairly rational feedback. That is, the students asked questions or asked for elaboration or repetition of a point. But when an instructor faced a class that had just been exposed to a *zero feedback* session, the instructor got an attack. The students asked lots of questions, but with barbs and implications about the instructor's (in)ability to do his job. The new instructor had innocently opened Pandora's box. This hostility did not last through more than one or two patterns, nor did it prevent the majority of students from expressing a preference for the *free feedback* method.

COMMENTARY

In a sense these experiments demonstrate the obvious. When a receiver *B* is free to ask questions he can get a better understanding of what the sender *A* is trying to communicate. Moreover, with *free feedback* both the sender and the receiver can feel, correctly, more confident that they have respectively sent and received accurately. *Free feedback* requires more time, but there is some evidence that this time differential decreases with increased understanding between the sender and the receiver. Apparently the use of continuing *free feedback* could lead directly back into *zero feedback*, for once the common areas of misunderstanding have been clarified, contemporaneous feedback will no longer be necessary.

Apparently it is possible to improve communication skill with minimal feedback. The fourth *zero feedback* pattern is almost always more accurately sent than the first. This improvement can perhaps be thought of as a kind of personal feedback in which the instructor's own words are utilized to help him to increase his own effectiveness in the future. Much of it is no doubt empathic, the instructor imagining himself in the receiver's place and correcting his sending as a consequence. Some of the improvement, however, may come from feedback which our experimental barriers failed to block out; feedback in the form of noises, sighs, shuffling of chairs. We do not know from these experiments whether or not an instructor using *zero feedback* could eventually reach the *free feedback* level of accuracy and confidence, but it is clear that under our experimental conditions he can improve over his own original *zero feedback* level.

Besides the findings about the direct effects of feedback, the data raise some questions about indirect effects. We observed in both experiments that *free feedback* after *zero feedback* is accompanied by hostility. This hostility was apparently an effect of the *zero feedback* experience. It lasts only through one or two *free feedback* trials. Why should this be so? We believe that the mechanism centers around the notion of "certainty." In our attempts to satisfy our needs we must be as certain as possible that we are successful. Uncertainty is frustrating. Without feedback uncertainty is prevalent.

In the same vein we noted that instructors' confidence is lower than students' confidence. We suggest that the instructor can be satisfied only by knowing that the receiver is getting the proper information. But the receiver can be satisfied by comparing his own work with the sender's directions. The receiver then has more information available against which to check his own progress toward his goal. Hence he can be more certain of his progress. But the sender is not sure of what the receiver is receiving. He can get *some* information with feedback, but almost none but his own empathy without feedback. Hence his certainty and confidence are low. These differential feelings of certainty, adequacy, and hostility seem to us to be the most significant differentials between our *free feedback* and *zero feedback* systems.

Summary and Conclusions

Since the scope of this research has been limited by the utilization of one kind of problem, one kind of sender-receiver situation, and a relatively short series of experiences, our conclusions must be severely circumscribed.

To summarize, we found that, within narrow limits: 1. a completion of the circuit between sender and receiver (feedback) increases the accuracy with which information is transmitted. 2. Feedback also increases receiver and sender confidence in what they have accomplished. 3. The cost of feedback is time. But the difference in time between *free feedback* and *zero feedback* appears to decrease. 4. A sender and a receiver can improve without what we have defined as feedback experience. 5. *Free feedback* experience improves subsequent *zero feedback* trials measurably. 6. Sender experience contributes more than receiver experience to improved accuracy of communication. 7. *Zero feedback* engenders some hostility in the receiver that becomes clearly percepti-

ble when the situation *changes* from *zero* to *free feedback*. This hostility is short-lived, lasting through only one or two *free feedback* trials.
8. *Zero feedback* engenders doubt in the sender.

These findings support the hypothesis that *free feedback* is an aid to accuracy in interpersonal communication. *Free feedback* seems to permit the participants to learn a mutual language, which language once learned may obviate the necessity for further feedback.

The findings also support the hypothesis that the presence or absence of feedback affects the sender-receiver relationship. *Zero feedback* is accompanied by low confidence and hostility; *free feedback* is accompanied by high confidence and amity.

45. The Readability of Employee Handbooks*

Cosimo Carlucci and William J. E. Crissy

"I DON'T KNOW what is expected of me," "I didn't get the word" are common complaints of the rank and file employee. The very bigness of today's modern business enterprise begets and nurtures communication problems. Many companies have come to grips with the problem of "getting the word around" by using various formal communication media. None of these shows more promise of lessening both the number and the intensity of communication problems than does the employee handbook. It is with the readability of such handbooks that the present paper is concerned.

Procedure

One of the writers, responsible for the basic research and analysis, wrote to the personnel director of each member company in the so-called "Billion Dollar Club"[1] requesting (a) copies of their employee handbooks, (b) data bearing upon the educational level of their employees, especially the median education of unskilled, non-supervisory employees. All except one company responded but for various reasons seven "members" were unable to participate in the study. In all, twenty-three

* From "How Readable are Employee Handbooks?" *Personnel Psychology*, Vol. 4, 1951, pp. 383–95.

[1] As defined by *Business Week*, i.e., companies with either gross assets or annual sales or both exceeding one billion dollars.

handbooks from seventeen corporations comprised the sample investigated.

Incidentally, the choice of this group of companies for this investigation seemed desirable on several counts—they are the "big business" of our economy and presumably would have need for formal communication media; each of them employs large numbers of workers so that solutions to problems of internal communication are vital; finally, they presumably have facilities more adequate for the best handling of these and related problems in contrast to smaller enterprises.

Readability means many different things to different people. An acceptable definition might be: an embracive quality of written material which involves the initiation of reading, its continuance once begun, and the understanding of what is read. These specific factors would seem to be important in readability thus conceived:

(1) *Reading Ease*—the simplicity of word and sentence structure.[2]
(2) *Human Interest*—the personal touch of what is said.[3]
(3) *Content*—the pertinence of what is said to the reader's needs and interests.
(4) *Attractiveness*—the eye-appeal of the printed medium.
(5) *Typography*—the perceptual aspects of the types used—fonts, leading, and pointage.

Results

The writers used the Flesch formula[4] for Reading Ease[5] to measure this quality. This involves, essentially, the computation of a "Reading Ease score" for a given piece of writing based upon word length and sentence length. It was found that most of the handbooks fell in the fairly difficult, difficult and very difficult categories. The mean Reading Ease score of 52.53 (Standard Deviation of 10.95) is categorized as fairly difficult which means that some high school education is required for understanding what is said.

In the case of eleven companies, the data furnished on educational level of their unskilled non-supervisory employees made possible a comparison between these data and the educational level required for understanding the handbook content according to the Flesch norms. These data are summarized in Table 1.

It can readily be seen that the handbooks of corporations 1, 2, 9, 13, 15,

---

[2] R. F. Flesch, *The Art of Readable Writing* (New York: Harper and Brothers, 1949).

[3] *Ibid.*

[4] Editor's Note: The actual formula is READING EASE = 206.835 − .846 (number of syllables per 100 words) − 1.015 (number of words per sentence).

[5] R. F. Flesch, *op. cit.*

TABLE 1

A Comparison between the Flesch Reading Ease Scores in Terms of Educational Level Required for Understanding and the Median Educational Level of Unskilled, Non-Supervisory Employees

Corporation	Flesch RE Scores	Educational Level	Median Education of Non-Supervisory Employees
1.	57	Some high school	5th Grade*
2.	55	Some high school	8th Grade*
4.	37	High school or some college	1 yr. High school*
8.	74	7th or 8th Grade	7th or 8th Grade*
9.	47	High school or some college	8th Grade*
10.	56	Some high school	4 yrs. High school†
12.	64	7th or 8th Grade	4 yrs. High school‡
13.	45	High school or some college	8th Grade*
14.	72	6th Grade	6th Grade*
15.	53	Some high school	8th Grade*
16.	25	College	4th Grade*

* Estimated educational level.
† Accurate data—65% of total employee force with 4 yrs. or more of high school.
‡ Accurate data—54% of non-managerial employees with 4 yrs. of high school.

and 16 are written "over the heads" of the unskilled non-supervisory employees. The messages of the handbooks fail to reach the employee group of greatest number and, perhaps, most in need of guidance and information. The greatest gap between the readability level and educational level occurs in corporation 16 where the estimate of educational level is 4th grade, and the readability level is that of college and above.

It is recognized, of course, that the estimates of educational level are at best approximate. However, within the limits of our data, we can see that six of the eleven corporations seem to be writing their handbooks at a level above the educational achievement of a sizable segment of employees. Such a finding suggests a need for revision downward of the difficulty level of language used in handbooks.

To demonstrate, concretely, hard-to-read versus easy-to-read handbook excerpts, samples are set forth below. Passage A, consisting of 100 words, 135 syllables, and 8.5 sentences received a Reading Ease score of 81.

A. Your supervisor will help all he can. So will the other folks on the ———.* They wish you the best of luck. They're looking forward to working with you for a long time to come. For they know that a steady job on the ———* is more than a job . . . it's an interesting and satisfying career. Knowledge of your company improves your chance to advance. It helps you do a better job; it makes your work easier. There are a number of free publications about the ———* that may interest you. If your supervisor hasn't an extra copy you can . . .

* Corporation name

Passage B consists of 100 words, 201 syllables, and 2.5 sentences. It received a Reading Ease score of 0.

> B. Employees will receive not less than the wage rate provided for the classification of work performed, taking into account temporary differentials for inexperienced employees in beginning job, the rate to become effective immediately upon the employee taking over the duties of the job on his own responsibility under normal supervision.
>
> An employee regularly employed in different classifications carrying different rates of pay will be paid the rate applicable to the classification in which he is working. An employee regularly employed in one classification will, if transferred to work carrying a higher rate, begin to receive such higher rate immediately upon transfer.

HUMAN INTEREST

As in the case of Reading Ease above the writers used the formula for Human Interest[6] developed by Flesch[7] to measure this quality. Essentially, this formula yields a Human Interest score based upon frequency of use of personal words and personal sentences. These data revealed that all except three of the handbooks score mildly interesting or better. The mean score of 32.74 (S.D. = 16.75) is interpretable as interesting which is descriptive of digests.

It is interesting to note that passage A, cited above as highly readable, received a human interest score of 50, highly interesting, while passage B, cited as difficult to read, received a score of 7, dull.

CONTENT

This quality was determined by checking the presence or absence of each of 25 topics adopted from a more extensive list by Powell and Schild published by the American Management Association.[8] Two raters did this independently and discrepancies between them were reconciled to yield a single measure. Figure 1 presents a facsimile of the form used. In Table 2 are set forth the number of topics covered by each handbook and the number of handbooks that cover each topic. The topics listed by number coincide with the numbers on the content analysis form in Figure 1. Notably absent was any significant contribution to the "other" category, 25, on the form. All items covered in the handbooks were categorized under the remaining specifically stated topic head-

---

[6] Editor's Note: The formula is HUMAN INTEREST = 3.635 (number of personal words per 100 words) + .314 (number of personal sentences per 100 sentences). Examples of personal words are: he, she, we, father, foreman—words with gender. Personal sentences are: questions, commands, exclamations, sentences addressed to the reader, spoken sentences quoted.

[7] R. F. Flesch, *op. cit.*

[8] American Management Association, *How to Prepare and Publish an Employee Manual* (New York, 1946).

TABLE 2

NUMBER OF TOPICS COVERED IN EACH HANDBOOK AND THE NUMBER
OF HANDBOOKS COVERING EACH TOPIC

HANDBOOK	NO. OF TOPICS COVERED	TOPIC	NO. OF HAND-BOOKS COVERING
1	16	1	15
2	17	2	10
3	18	3	21
4	1	4	13
5	14	5	18
6	16	6	10
7	17	7	15
8	14	8	12
9	10	9	10
10	18	10	15
11	6	11	17
12	17	12	6
13	17	13	12
14	14	14	19
15	12	15	6
16	11	16	15
17	17	17	4
18	16	18	17
19	12	19	15
20	19	20	5
21	3	21	17
22	2	22	10
23	16	23	10
		24	7
		25	0

$M = 13.3; \sigma = 5.3.$

ings. Thus the content analysis form as devised may be said to have "face validity" at least on a criterion of embraciveness in the topics covered.

FIGURE 1

Work Sheet for Handbook Content Analysis

Your name ——————— Title and number of book ——————— Date ———————
You are asked to study the list of topics set forth below and to be sure you understand each. Then read each handbook and determine which of the topics are covered therein. "Covered" means treated in some way—you are not asked to judge the adequacy of the treatment. Place a check alongside each topic.

—— 1. *Attendance* (or Absence), e.g., penalties for days off, jury duty policy, etc.
—— 2. *Permanence* (or Tenure), e.g., length of probationary period, guarantee of year round employment, etc.
—— 3. *Safety*, e.g., suggestions or rules concerned with protective goggles, special shoes, etc.
—— 4. *Health* (other than health insurance, hospitalization, etc.), e.g., annual company medical examinations, etc.
—— 5. *Health Insurance*, e.g., "Blue Cross," "Blue Shield," death benefits, etc.
—— 6. *Change of Personal Status*, e.g., employee's obligation to inform company of change of residence, marital status, etc.

—— 7. *Promotion* (or Advancement), e.g., statement of company's promotional policy, etc.
—— 8. *Athletic*, social, and recreational *Activities*, e.g., mention of bowling team, etc.
—— 9. *Security*, e.g., badges, mention of confidential "know how," etc.
——10. *Formal Training Facilities*, (both inside and outside the company).
——11. *Financial Benefits and Facilities*, e.g., pay roll savings plans, etc.
——12. *Cafeteria* or other dining facilities.
——13. *Grievances and Complaints* (including collective bargaining).
——14. *Company History*, e.g., story of its founding, evolution of the line of products, etc.
——15. *Company Policies*, e.g., "open door," the —— way of doing business, etc.
——16. *Employee Services* (other than noted under 4, 5, 11).
——17. *Hiring Policies and Practices*, e.g., descriptions of selection procedures.
——18. *Vacation and Holidays.*
——19. *Working Hours.*
——20. *Resignation and Termination of Employment.*
——21. *Wage and Salary* information, e.g., authorization and payment for overtime.
——22. *Suggestion System.*
——23. *Conduct on the Job*, e.g. prohibitions on drinking during working hours.
——24. *Company's Place in the Community.*
——25. *Other:* (specify) —————— ————— ————— .

Topics 12 (Cafeteria), 15 (Company Policies), 17 (Promotion), 20 (Resignation and Termination of Employment) and 24 (Company's Place in Community) did not appear more than seven times in the 23 handbooks. This is surprising in view of the patent importance of some of these topics to employees.

ATTRACTIVENESS

In order to assess this quality two judges, working independently, made two sets of paired-comparison judgments of the handbooks. The first aspect judged was external attractiveness, i.e., eye-appeal of the cover. The second aspect was internal attractiveness determined by an inspection of the inner pages of each handbook. The main finding here was the high correlation between judged external and internal attractiveness.

TYPOGRAPHY

Originally it was thought that the work of Paterson and Tinker[9] on the readability of type would facilitate an analysis of the typographical

---

[9] D. G. Paterson and M. A. Tinker, "Speed of Reading Nine-Point Type in Relation to Line Width and Leading," *Journal of Applied Psychology*, Vol. 33, 1949, pp. 81–82; D. G. Paterson and M. A. Tinker, "Eye Movement in Reading Optimal and non-Optimal Typography," *Journal of Applied Psychology*, Vol. 28, 1944, pp. 80–83; D. G. Paterson and M. A. Tinker, "Eye Movements in Reading Type in Op-

characteristics of the handbooks so that each one might be measured on this aspect of readability. Although these authors have done extensive work in this area, the data which they report are not in a form to enable this type of "scoring" to be done. The typographical data on the booklets used in this study are given in Table 3. On the basis of leading,

TABLE 3

Typographical Characteristics of 23 Employee Handbooks

Handbook Code No.	Points of Type	Leading	Pica Line Width	Type Font
1	10	2	21	Bodoni Book
2	11	2	24	Textype
3	10	2	24	Schoolbook
4	10	2	27	Bookman
5	10	2	23	Garamond Bold
6	10	2	23.5	Post Text # 5
7	10	2	22	Times Roman
8	10	2.5	17	Bodoni Book
9	10	2	18	Memphis Medium
10	10	4	16.5	Bodoni Book
11	10	Solid	24	Bodoni Book
12	10	1	12.5	Garamond
13	10	2	30	Garamond O. S.
14	10	2	22.5	Century Expanded
15	10	2	21	Century Expanded
16	10	Solid	24	Waverly
17	12	2	24	Brohman
18	12	2	23	Garamond O. S.
19	10	2	20	Bodoni Book
20	10	2	20.5	Bodoni
21	10	Solid	18	Century Expanded
22	8	Solid	18	De Vinne
23	10	4	20	Futura Medium

four books would be read more slowly than the others: 11, 16, 21 and 22. The type in these was set "solid," i.e., there was less than one point of leading between the characters. Booklet 11 would also be read more slowly because 8 point type is read more slowly than 11 point type and presumably more slowly than 10 point type. With regard to line width, all the handbooks fell within the recommended range of 14–30 pica. Paterson and Tinker's work on type fonts did not include very many of those used in these books so that the relative merits of the fonts here listed remained indeterminate.

timal Line Width," *Journal of Educational Psychology*, Vol. 34, 1943, pp. 547–51; D. G. Paterson and M. A. Tinker, "The Relative Readability of Newsprint," *Journal of Applied Psychology*, Vol. 30, 1946, pp. 454–59; M. A. Tinker and D. G. Paterson, "Differences among Newspaper Body Type in Readability," *Journalism Quarterly*, Vol. 20, 1943; M. A. Tinker and D. G. Paterson, "Eye-Movements in Reading Black Print on White Background, and Red Print on Dark Green Background," *The American Journal of Psychology*, Vol. 57, 1950, pp. 93–94.

INTERRELATIONSHIPS AMONG READABILITY FACTORS

Thus far, each readability factor has been considered singly. The writers correlated these separate factors to see what relationships existed among them. The intercorrelational matrix is set forth in Table 4.

TABLE 4

INTERCORRELATIONS OF READABILITY FACTORS

	HI	EA	IA	CONTENT
RE............78		−.35	.38	.31
HI............		.55	.61	.69
EA............			.67	.63
IA............				.66

The highest correlation obtained occurred between Reading Ease and Human Interest; the books which were easier to read tended to be more interesting as well. The correlation between the two qualities of attractiveness was also high, thus indicating the existence of a single, ratable attractiveness of a handbook.

Reliability

The writers were, of course, concerned about the reliability of the measures used. In the case of the two Flesch measures reliability has been elsewhere reported[11] as:

$$R.E. = .98$$
$$H.I. = .92$$

These are inter-rater coefficients with written samples held constant and corrected for a full range on each factor.

In the content analysis and in the determination of attractiveness there were two aspects to the reliability problem—intra-rater consistency and inter-rater consistency. The formula for the reliability coefficient in each of these instances was:

$$r_{11} = 1 - \frac{Ve}{Vc}$$

where:

Ve = variance within a rater or between two raters. ($Ve = 0$ when rater or raters' judgments are free from error)

Vc = variance if chance alone were operative; an upper bound to the total variance. (In each case in this study $Vc = .25$ since every judgment agreement involved a dichotomy.)

The content analysis used had an inter-rater reliability of .25. This, of course, puts a note of caution on using the form without very careful

---

[11] P. M. Hayes, J. J. Jenkins, and B. J. Walker, "Reliability of the Flesch Readability Formulae," *Journal of Applied Psychology*, Vol. 34, 1959, pp. 22–26.

checking among several raters. The content scores as finally used were carefully reconciled.

The two judged aspects of attractiveness had intra-rater reliability as follows:

	EA	IA
R_1	.54	.46
R_2	.71	.46

These coefficients are patently higher than the one found for content but are of a magnitude to warrant caution in accepting a judge's ratings of attractiveness.

The inter-rater reliability coefficients were: EA = .26, IA = .51. These, also, are too low to accept without reservation.

Summary

The writers investigated the readability of employee handbooks of the so-called "Billion Dollar Club." Included in readability were these factors: reading ease, human interest, attractiveness of external and internal layout, content and typography.

It was found that many of the handbooks included in the study were not comprehensible to the lowest levels of employees in the respective companies. It was also found that many of the handbooks studied lacked human interest. External and internal attractiveness were found to be correlated to an extent that a single attractiveness factor might be supposed. The handbooks, in general, covered far fewer topics than would be considered desirable in light of the American Management Association recommendations as reflected in the checklist used in this study. Finally, in view of Paterson and Tinker's research, there were evident typographical improvements that might be made in many of the handbooks, e.g., increase in type pointage and leading.

46. Recent Concepts in Administrative Behavior*

Harold J. Leavitt

MY PURPOSE here, which I can not possibly achieve, is to try to organize and summarize recent theoretical developments in administration and organization.

* From "Recent Concepts in Administration," *Personnel Psychology*, Vol. 13, 1960, pp. 287–94.

Let me start by saying that I shall use the terms "administration" and "organization" more or less interchangeably; assuming simply that we are all concerned with understanding and perhaps directing the behavior of ongoing groups of people.

We have enough perspective now on the rash of new developments in these areas so that it is feasible to set up some gross categories, and then to describe some examples of novel and stimulating activity within these categories.

My categories are four: The first is the jumping-off place in organizational thinking; i.e., the state of classical organizational theory. This category contains nothing notably new, but it is worth a quick look because it will help us spotlight what *is* new in the "new."

Second, we can look quickly at new descriptive approaches to organization. This category specifically includes the new March and Simon[1] book; Mason Haire's[2] use of biological analogies to organizational growth; a series of sociologically-based models like those of Whyte, Sayles, Selznick and others (which I shall not try to run through here); and the clinically-based work of Argyris.[3] Many of the sociological models and those of Argyris are not entirely descriptive; they have strong normative elements. These are not so much normative in an analytic sense, however, as in a value sense.

The next category covers analytic-normative studies. For the most part these have their origins in economics and mathematics, with close connection to game theory, and other quantitative and rigorous attacks on decision processes. I shall cite only one example of these, the work of Jacob Marschak.[4]

The fourth and final category is the action-influence category. The question here is not about theoretical developments that show promise of future influence but on currently influential ideas. Names cannot easily be attached to ideas in this realm, but I shall argue that the sophisticated practice of "human relations training" and the impact of "information technology" are the two currently vital and partially conflicting forces on the changing organizational scene.

The Jumping-off Place. Until relatively recently organization theory meant Taylor and Urwick and ideas like "span of control" and the "exception principle." It seems clear that the impact of these kinds of ideas on the thinking of managers and business school academicians (and

---

[1] J. G. March and H. A. Simon, *Organizations* (New York: John Wiley & Sons, 1959).

[2] M. Haire, "Biological Models and Empirical Histories of the Growth of Organizations," in M. Haire (ed.), *Modern Organization Theory* (New York: John Wiley & Sons, 1959).

[3] Chris Argyris, *Personality and Organization* (New York: Harper & Brothers, 1957).

[4] J. Marschak, "Efficient and Viable Organizational Forms," in M. Haire (ed.), *Modern Organization Theory* (New York: John Wiley & Sons, 1959).

they provide a pretty good cue about trends) has lessened. As Simon has pointed out, these early formalizations about administration suffered considerably from—among other things their hortatory qualities. In retrospect we can isolate at least three other major limitations:

a. They tended to treat only the physiological attributes of persons, ignoring the complexities of motivation and perception.

b. They began, usually, with the assumption of a known and fixed organizational task, which can then be differentiated into subparts. They thereby carry a static quality with no provision for organizational search for new tasks, or redefinition of present ones under pressure from a changing environment.

c. Traditional theory has focused almost exclusively on the individual as the unit of the enterprise, working implicitly toward a goal of functional specialization. Perhaps one reason these early theories missed the major phenomena of individual behavior is precisely because they failed to consider interaction among subparts of organizations.

Recent Descriptive Models. The freshest ideas about organization and administration belong in this category. There are many of them, semi-independent of one another. They have in common a concern about understanding organizational phenomena and about developing a more adequate underpinning for eventual applications in the real world.

The most important aspect of these descriptive models is that they are descriptive: i.e., impersonal efforts to comprehend, analyze, and predict organizational behavior. They either draw on empirical evidence or permit empirical tests of their propositions and hypotheses.

The March and Simon book is a good example. It is an effort to state a set of interrelated propositions that will account for variation in such diverse intra-organizational phenomena as, for example, intergroup conflict, innovative activities, and compensation.

It draws very heavily upon a dynamic model of individual motivation that includes variables like satisfaction level, search behavior, expected value of reward, and level of aspiration. It offers up some stimulating new concepts, too, differentiating "satisficing" from "optimizing" behavior and points out that the behavior of individuals and organizations is probably more accurately described by the first word than the second. Satisficing means searching for a satisfactory solution to a problem, rather than the optimal one—a process which is far more parsimonious of energy and other costs than optimizing, and a class of behavior which is also far more "sympatico" with dynamic personality theory than with classical economic theorizing.

Perhaps this is enough to give you a flavor of this view of organizational phenomena. It is descriptive-predictive; it is rigorous in that its propositions appear to be empirically testable; and it makes good use of what is known about individual and group behavior.

Let me turn now to another fresh look at organizations. Mason Haire has recently introduced some D'Arcy Thompson–type biological notions into organizational thinking. He cites the square-cube law; i.e., that as the mass of an object is cubed, its surface is only squared; then goes on to show how this surface-volume relationship becomes critical in relation to the biological size of organisms. The giant, in Jack the Giant Killer, were he proportioned like Jack but ten times as big, would include a mass so great as to break his own bones.

Haire's point is that as organisms grow they must change shape, and even create new organs to perform functions not required by another size and shape. He carries the analogy to organizations and then offers data to show similar, and predictable, change phenomena during organizational growth. Using historical data from small companies, he shows consistent relationships between, for example, numbers of people on the "surface" in the organization; i.e., who deal chiefly with the outside environment—receptionists, purchasing agents, salesmen, etc.—and numbers in the inside mass. The work is intriguing, suggestive, and a little worrisome.

Now to consider briefly the most clinically oriented of recent models of organization—the one offered up by Chris Argyris. Argyris' thesis, based largely on observational studies of worker-management relationships, is essentially that organizations are restrictive of individual psychological growth. Argyris argues that people grow from dependence toward independence, from an undifferentiated state to a differentiated one, etc., while some characteristics of large organizations press people back toward dependency, toward nondifferentiation, and toward other "unhealthy," "immature" conditions. Argyris offers prescriptions for cure, but not perfectly precise ones. He seems to offer at least a palliation in the form of organizational changes that will make for greater individual health; e.g., more freedom of decision-making for individual employees, etc.

Argyris' model does not belong entirely in the descriptive category. It lies rather in the limbo between description and prescription. It is concerned with individual mental "health" and the improvement thereof, and, whether intentionally or not, it has a hortatory quality—urging administrators to show greater concern for the mental health of their people.

In one sense Argyris' work seems to me an almost necessary outcome of the last decade's studies of human relations. It draws heavily upon human relations research, and measures almost entirely against criteria of individual and group "maturity." Very little emphasis is placed on other economic or social criteria of organizational effectiveness.

A Normative-Analytic Model.   The Marschak view is based less in psychology than the others I have described, and more in the mathematical economics from which he hails. But it is not psychological nonsense (as some ideas from economics seem to be); it is a good example of the way recent mathematico-economic developments can be focused on administrative processes.

Marschak makes an effort to construct a model of organizational behavior that does not contradict empirical data, and then to show an analytic method for deciding whether one organizational form is better than another.

Let me try to give you just a flavor of the Marschak model. Marschak treats an organization simply as "several persons" who "agree to follow a certain set of *rules* that are supposed to further certain *goals*." This set of rules (Marschak equates them with the sociologists' "roles") *is* the organizational form. Such rules are all concerned with communication: *action* rules about communication outside the organization; *internal communication* rules, which are rules about sending and receiving of messages between members (and which include communication with one's own memory); and *observation* rules which refer to the receipt of messages from outside the organization.

Marschak then specified a simplified problem in which the issue is centralization vs. decentralization; which is to say, whether we build in a rule for intercommunication between subunits or do not. By considering three functions—a payoff function, a probability function, and a factor of the cost of communication—he demonstrates that one can analytically determine (in his little example) the efficiencies of the two alternatives. He argues that such cognitive, analytic methods can be refined for use in real organizations. I would argue further that I see no *fundamental* reason why such methods cannot be integrated into real organizations, made up of real and complicated people.

Action-Influence Ideas. We can turn now from these efforts to describe or improve upon the behavior of complex organizations. The models we have sketched thus far exist mostly in universities, traveling in circles among academicians via academicians.

But it is appropriate also in this quick review to examine those ideas which are in fact currently having an impact on organizational practice —on the structure of organizations, on the relationships among members of organizations, and on the practices of administrators.

It might be said, first, that classical organization theories are having almost no noticeable *new* impact. Their old impact hangs on, of course; managers still talk about an authority-responsibility balance, about span of control, *et al*. But I have been unable to detect any recent changes in organizational behavior that appear to be consequent to extensions of old organization theory.

However, organizational practice is, I believe, changing under the serious and current influence of two kinds of phenomena, both of which are related to ideas we mentioned earlier. The two are "human relations" and "information technology."

By "human relations" I mean several fairly specific things: first, the techniques of human relations training; second, the related, business school-taught, business journal–promulgated, and consulting firm–carried-out techniques of "participative" management—techniques which include the use of committees, the encouragement of easy expression of feelings across status levels, etc.

These ideas are having effects, I believe, because they have been converted into technical mechanisms, and it is the technique that makes operational change possible.

These techniques are being adopted partially because they are novel, and we value the novel, but mostly because they offer promise for solving problems of social and self-esteem needs, and problems of interpersonal communication. These kinds of problems seem to have come necessarily to the fore in modern, complex organizations. They have come to the fore, I believe, mostly because some lower order problems have been resolved, and hence are less prominent; because, using Haire's analogy, the enlarged internal mass of most organizations has radically increased the need for better internal mechanisms for processing information.

Whatever the reasons, however, there is abundant evidence (numbers of consulting firms doing such work; the spread of "group dynamics" training activities into industry; the increasingly "human" views of executives about how to manage) that these ideas are changing industrial organizations, *especially at the middle levels* of the hierarchy.

Dr. Thomas Whisler and I[5] have elsewhere pointed out the practical conflict between this trend toward human relating middle management and the other major current trend in the technics of management—the intrusion of information technology. Information technology is a label for the amalgam of new mathematical techniques applicable to managerial problems, plus those that are growing up around the computer.

In any case, information technology is moving in on organizations. It is beginning in a very small way to cause quite agonizing reassessments of ideas about decentralization, about where creativity is needed, about what constitutes an executive job, and about the relative merits of human and organizational values. It seems to be leading in many cases to solutions to those same problems of efficient information processing that are very different to those offered by human relations techniques.

These two, the techniques of human relations and the techniques of information processing, are the sets of ideas currently finding most widespread application to the practice of management. Right now they seem to me to be causing a mild schizophrenia in organizations. It is my own opinion that the potential, short run power of information tech-

---

[5] H. J. Leavitt and T. L. Whisler, "Management in the 1980's," *Harvard Business Review,* Vol. XXXVI, 1958, pp. 41–48.

nology is, by far, the greater of the two powers; at least as long as the two technologies remain separate from one another. But it is already becoming clear, back at the theoretical level of describing organizations and building organizational models, that the two are inseparably intertwined. The computer is already a tool for psychological and organizational research. Human relaters are already going cognitive, studying with new vigor the processes of conscious thinking and problem solving; studies which will, I am confident, yield a general descriptive theory of organization and administration; a theory which will, in turn, bear practical fruit.

47. Adapting Organization to New Technology*

Frank J. Jasinski

GETTING A NEW machine or production process to live up to advance expectations is often a hard job. Few are the companies that have not had frustrating experiences at one time or another in achieving the improvements that were *supposed* to come from a new line of automatic presses, or a more modern extrusion process, or a promising change in the conveyer system.

Invariably the question comes up: What went wrong? Sometimes, of course, the trouble is simply that the estimates in cost savings or productivity increases were too optimistic. Sometimes the engineering is faulty. Sometimes the loss of a key supervisor, a strike, or a change in some other part of the plant is to blame. And sometimes the new technology is too hard on workers and supervisors, or threatens them in some way so that they resist it.

We are all familiar with such troubles. They are cited again and again. But there is another common type of difficulty—one that is rarely cited. It is a peculiarly *management* problem in that it both begins and ends with management, and no group *but* management can deal with it effectively.

Let me state this problem first in an abstract way; later we can go into detail and illustration. The idea is this: *a change in production or technology affects organizational relationships*. For example, a supervisor may find himself working with other supervisors and groups with whom

* From *Harvard Business Review*, Vol. 37, 1959, pp. 79–86.

he has had little contact before, or he may find himself reporting to different people, or different people reporting to him. *When management overlooks these social changes, it generally fails to realize the full potential of a change in technology*, however well thought out the innovation was from an engineering standpoint. The potential may then be achieved only after a difficult and costly period of readjustment. The duration of the readjustment period and the degree of technological potential finally attained depend, for the most part, upon management's awareness of the relationship between technology and organization and upon its ability to keep one in harmony with the other through changing times.

Management has established and maintains staffs of engineers who devote considerable time and effort to evaluating new plant sites, designing processes, and making meticulous plant layouts. In contrast, it makes only a nominal, if any, corresponding study of the organizational requirements of a new technological process. Rather, it usually tries to extend the existing organizational structure to the new process. And here is where much of the difficulty lies.

The Outmoded Vertical

Traditional business organization runs on a vertical line, relying almost solely on superior-subordinate relationships. Orders and instructions go down the line; reports and requests go up the line. But technology, including both integrated data processing and integrated machine production, has developed on what might be called a horizontal plane; that is, the machine cuts across superior-subordinate relationships, affecting the jobs of people in different areas, departments, and work groups. Superimposing a strictly vertical organization structure on a technology which emphasizes horizontal and diagonal relationships can and does cause obvious difficulties.

Typical of the kinds of relationships required by modern technology is the progressive fabricating and assembly line. Here the need to make the right decision or take the necessary action at the right time at the right place is immediate. Managers, in order to solve an immediate problem, have to deal horizontally with their peers and diagonally with people at different levels who are neither superiors nor subordinates. To follow established, formal routes would be too time-consuming, too costly, and too disruptive.

Necessary as these horizontal and diagonal relations may be to smooth functioning of the technology, or work flow, they are seldom defined or charted formally. Nonetheless, wherever or whenever modern technology does operate effectively, these relations exist, if only on a nonformal basis. In other words, certain individuals have developed their own techniques to work satisfactorily outside of (or in place of) the formal framework. They have usually done so after a period of trial and error and emerge as outstanding performers because they can deal effectively with equals, nonsubordinates, and nonsuperiors—undefined relationships which nevertheless are essential to the technology.

Certainly it is management's job not only to recognize these new kinds of relationships but also to take steps to enable them to function definitely and smoothly. A few managers have recognized the discrepancy between organization and technology, and have taken steps to integrate the two. They have achieved such integration in a variety of ways, which essentially may be classified as:

1. Changing the technology to conform with the existing organizational structure.
2. Changing the organization so as to define and formalize the relationships required by the technology.
3. Maintaining both the existing organization and the existing technology but introducing mechanisms to reduce or minimize the discrepancies between the two.

In appraising these steps we will want to look at the kinds of problems which arise when technology and organization are not integrated, and at specific examples of what can be and has been done to recognize and alleviate the basic causes of these problems.

Horizontal Relations

Let us start out by considering a technology which dramatizes the horizontal nature of the work flow—the automobile assembly line. I shall present the kinds of problems which can arise and the nonformal adjustments some members of management have made, as revealed by the Technology Project at Yale University.[1]

PRESSURE FOR SHORT CUTS

The automobile assembly line winds its way, almost uninterruptedly, for several miles through the plant. The conveyer carries each automobile "without a stop" through five departments, past the areas of 10 general foremen, through the sections of 50 or 60 foremen, and past the work stations of thousands of workers.

When the "body" starts out, it is a flat sheet of metal comprising the car floor; at the end of the conveyer the car, now complete, is driven off into the test area. In between there are innumerable feeder lines or tributaries which bring parts to the main conveyer to be attached to the gradually evolving body. The entire plant and the efforts of all the employees are geared to the task of getting the right part to the right place at the right time.

---

[1] For previous findings, see Charles R. Walker and Robert H. Guest, *The Man on the Assembly Line* (Cambridge: Harvard University Press, 1952); Charles R. Walker, Robert H. Guest, and Arthur N. Turner, *The Foreman on the Assembly Line* (Cambridge: Harvard University Press, 1956); also Walker and Guest, "The Man on the Assembly Line," *Harvard Business Review* May–June, 1952, p. 71; and Arthur N. Turner, "Management and the Assembly Line," *Harvard Business Review* September–October, 1955, p. 40.

There is, therefore, considerable interdependence both among production workers and between the production and nonproduction groups. The holes for a particular bit of chromium trim are drilled before the body is prepared for painting; the trim is attached a mile or so down the line. The piece of trim has to be on hand, brought there by a materials handler. And the tools of both driller and "attacher" have to operate at top efficiency—the responsibility of the maintenance man.

In other words, the foreman, to be effective, has to synchronize and coordinate the efforts of many individuals to achieve his production goals. He has to supervise the work of his direct subordinates; he has to make sure that parts are readily and continuously available; he has to ensure peak performance of all equipment in his area; he has to keep "tabs" on quality; and he has to track down and attempt to correct defective work done in previous sections which may be hampering his operators' work.

Yet, despite the importance of all these relations to smooth work flow, the organization does not define them formally. In fact, the formal relations are such that additional difficulties are introduced. For example:

1. Although the workers report to the foreman and he, in turn, to the general foreman, others who are essential to the work flow do not. The materials handler reports up a separate and distinct vertical plane. So do the maintenance man and the inspector.

2. Again, although production defects are within the line production organization, they may be caused by a foreman who reports to a different general foreman and sometimes even to a different superintendent.

Theoretically, the foreman can report any deficiency in services from supporting groups to his general foreman. This procedure is formally and clearly defined. Time on the assembly line, however, is crucial; cars pass a given work station at the rate of one every 1.5 minutes. Unless an error is corrected immediately, the consequences can be far-reaching. The foreman cannot afford to spend time hunting down the general foreman; he has to attend to the matters immediately and directly. To do so he has to deal with other foremen (on the horizontal plane) and also with materials handlers, maintenance men, inspectors, and other foremen's workers (on the diagonal plane).

READJUSTMENTS REQUIRED

In view of the importance of horizontal and diagonal relations to assembly-line technology, the whole concept of superior-subordinate relations is out of place—at least, in much of the plant during much of the time. The formal boxes and directional arrows on the organization chart cannot set the tone for everyday activities. Unless this is recognized, problems can arise.[2] As one perceptive foreman commented:

---

[2] Frank J. Jasinski, "Foreman Relationships Outside the Work Group," *Personnel*, September, 1956, pp. 130–36.

"When you deal with someone from another department, you have to show a smile."

Unfortunately, the Technology Project has revealed that many supervisors, accustomed to behaving according to the usual vertical channels, have not learned to relate effectively on a horizontal plane:

1. "In case I get stuff coming into my department that is wrong I usually let my general foreman know . . . and he goes over and gets it straightened out. I couldn't do that myself because, after all, I'm just another foreman."

2. "Actually, the job I'm doing now is that of a general foreman because I'm checking on these six foremen all the time. I've got the responsibility of letting them know that they're slipping up in one job or another, but I haven't got the authority to *tell* them to button up. Lots of times I have to go to my general foreman."

This lack of patterning and clarity in horizontal relationships frequently creates clashes between foremen. One worker provided this dramatic illustration:

The foremen go around sticking files into one another's heads in front of the men. Just today we thought we were going to see a fist fight between our foreman and another one. They were screaming like washerwomen at one another. Fine example—they hate one another.

Hardly the way to get a job done! Yet these difficulties do not derive from personality clashes. Repeated reports of similar incidents throughout this particular plant strongly indicate a basic shortcoming on the part of the organization to adjust to the incoming technology.

Interestingly enough, there are a number of foremen who *have* been able to establish and maintain satisfactory nonformal relations with other foremen and with staff and service groups. This means spending much time with persons other than their immediate subordinates. Indeed, contrary to the traditional emphasis on the importance of the vertical foreman-worker relationships, the demands of technology are such that good foremen actually have to interact *most* of the time in horizontal and diagonal relations. As a matter of fact, the foremen judged most effective by their superiors are the very ones who spend the least amount of time with their own workers.

At the time of our study, management was not aware of the relations required by the work flow—or, at least, it had not done much to formalize those relations. In fact, the individual foremen making the necessary adjustments sometimes had to do so in violation of official policy.

KEY TO SUCCESS

Horizontal and diagonal relationships, such as those described, exist in virtually all business and industrial organizations.[3] A classic example

---

[3] See William F. Whyte, *Money and Motivation* (New York, Harper & Brothers, 1955), pp. 53–66, and "Economic Incentives and Human Relations," *Harvard Business Review* March–April, 1952, p. 73.

involves a group of drill line operators in a factory who, even in the face of vigorous management disapproval, resisted the formal logics of an incentive system and continued to devise nonformal methods and relations for getting the work done.

There is no dearth of evidence to indicate that, whether or not the firm operates under the pressing immediacy of an automobile assembly line, the degree of production success depends in good measure upon the mutual adjustment or harmonious integration of the organizational structure and the technology. Where this integration is faulty, those individuals who are able to utilize satisfactorily the nonformal relations required are the successful ones. Where management has recognized the need for integration and has taken steps to achieve it, the efforts of individuals are made that much easier and more effective.

Having considered the kinds of conflict which can arise between the technology and the organization, let us now turn to examples of how some managers have effected a more satisfactory integration. As stated earlier, these methods are: changing the technology, changing the organization, and (less radically) introducing mechanisms to reduce discrepancies between organization and technology.

Changing the Technology

Ordinarily, managers consider technology to be inviolate. And frequently it is. After all, in making steel, for example, the metal has certain physical properties which require a certain timing and sequence of operations whether it is made in an American, Russian, or Indian mill. As a result, there are not many dramatic examples available of managers' making changes in the technology to adapt it to the existing organizational structure. The illustrations that are available, however, should serve to make the point. For instance, though it is not generally thought of in these terms, the shift from process to product layout in industry is a fairly widespread technique for effecting just such a change. Most of the integrated machine-processing units would fall into this category.

ONE-MAN SUPERVISION

Formerly, under the process layout, the manufactured item would go from the rough turning or lathe department to the mill and drill department, to the heat treat department, back to the grinding department, and so on until it finally went to the assembly department—with a different foreman in charge of each department. That is why there are so many meetings in such industrial organizations trying to pin down responsibility for schedule delays and errors in manufacturing.

It is true that, where volume warrants such a change, reorganizing the technology into a product layout brings about considerable savings in materials handling. This is usually the reason given for such a change. The product is no longer shunted between departments but goes uninterruptedly down a single line.

Yet the product layout conforms to the traditional organizational structure, and a number of managers have utilized it for that reason. With the product layout, one man, whether a foreman or superintendent, is responsible for the entire product. He has control over rough turning, mill and drill, heat treat, grinding, and even assembly. The operators who perform these diverse operations all report to him—in an established, clearly defined superior-subordinate relationship. Integration between organization and technology is thus achieved.

This kind of integration is possible only when the product can be made by the number of employees reporting to a specific foreman. When more workers are required, and two, three, or even more foremen are involved, closely knit integration becomes difficult.

As automatic equipment takes over more and more operations and as the actual number of employees is reduced, the number of products which can be manufactured in a product layout supervised by one foreman will increase. However, most industrial products, for one reason or another, still do not lend themselves to "one-foreman product layout" integration. In such instances, managers need to rely on one of the other methods to be discussed here.

Changing the Organization

The impact of recent technological innovations has forced many managers to take a second look at their organization, particularly with the advent of modern data-processing equipment. This equipment requires information in a certain form. Where managers have used it as more than simply a change in "hardware," the equipment has triggered sweeping revisions of data-processing departments. To prepare information efficiently for the processing equipment, managers have completely reorganized traditional departments. In this connection there are the telling, though perhaps exaggerated, stories of companies that revised their organizations in anticipation of delivery of data-processing equipment only to realize such great savings through the reorganization process itself that they canceled their orders for the equipment.

SUCCESSFUL SOLUTIONS

Charles R. Walker in his book, *Toward the Automatic Factory*,[4] describes one instance of conflict between the new technology and the existing formal organization and how that conflict was finally resolved:

A $40 million installation of a semiautomatic seamless tube mill failed to meet engineers' production estimates for nearly three years. There were a number of variables that were responsible for this delay, and most of them could be termed human factors.

Among these variables was the fact that the amount of production was pretty much regulated by the automatic machinery. An important variable

---

[4] New Haven, Yale University Press, 1957, pp. 126–42; see also Walker's "Life in the Automatic Factory," *Harvard Business Review* January–February, 1958, p. 111.

in the level of production was "downtime"—the length of time it took to make a repair or a mill changeover for a different size of product. As with most industrial organizations, those interruptions of production involved "nonproduction" personnel: crane operators, maintenance men, and repairmen. Most of these nonproduction men did not report to line management directly; they reported vertically along separate lines of authority. Further, while the men on the mill crew were paid for what they produced by an incentive plan, the crane operators and maintenance men were paid on day rates.

In other words, though the technology required the mill crew, the crane operators, and the maintenance men to work as a cohesive unit, management through its formal organization and its incentive plan treated them as separate entities, even to the extent of paying them differently. Productivity suffered as a result.

It was not until the workers convinced management (and the union, as a matter of fact) that the incentive plan should be extended to cover the entire work group—as required by the technology of the semiautomatic steel mill—that productivity increased. Following this and other changes, production not only met the engineer's original estimates of capacity but far exceeded them.

Had management recognized the new organizational structure required and made the necessary adjustments at the outset, then much of the three-year period of costly adjustment might have been avoided.

Undoubtedly, other managers have had similar experiences as one of the consequences of rapid technological innovation. Some may have recognized the nature of the problem and acted to alleviate it. Others may have simply let it ride. It is quite possible for a plant to function for quite some time with a conflict between its organization and the technology—but at less than optimal efficiency. It is also possible for such a plant to benefit from integration even after a lengthy period of such conflict.

A case in point is A. K. Rice's now famous Indian weaving-shed study:

Organization and technology had been firmly established for a long time. As in the steel mill, the weaving technology required a high degree of coordination between the weavers and a variety of service people—especially during a change of cloth, a break in the yarn, and the loading and unloading of the loom. But the representatives from the servicing units who worked with a particular weaver varied considerably from one group activity to the next. The groups lacked uniformity and continuity over time. There was confusion as to who reported to whom and who had authority over whom. This, and the lack of group continuity, resulted in inefficiencies as well as high damage in production.

Then changes in the organization were introduced so that it would conform more closely with the technological requirements. For example, small work groups were created, with internal leadership, which existed as a unit over time and so were better able to cope with technological requirements satisfactorily. As a result, efficiency jumped 10% and damage dropped 7%.[5]

---

[5] "Productivity and Social Organization in an Indian Weaving Shed," *Human Relations*, November, 1953, p. 297; see also a subsequent report, "The Experimental Reorganization of Non-Automatic Weaving in an Indian Mill," *Human Relations*, August, 1955, p. 199.

TEMPORARY MEASURES

Obviously, the dramatic and thorough revisions described above are not always feasible or practical in modern business and industry. But managers frequently have made smaller organizational changes that border on being mechanisms. They can be of a temporary or quasi-official nature, or permanently incorporated.

Such temporary measures include coordinators or project heads who provide an organizational short circuit for the duration of a crash program. Best known, perhaps, are the temporary realignments during World War II in invasion task forces. Just prior to and during the invasion one man headed all participating service units. Following the successful completion of the invasion, the task force regrouped into separate and independent units reporting along individual service lines.

In industry, similar groups or teams are temporarily formed to carry out a specified purpose. Many engineering research departments function on a project team basis permanently. Another kind of quasi-official organizational change is the use of an expediter, who, unlike the coordinator or project head, has no direct authority over the individuals with whom he relates.

Still another kind of organizational measure, widely used to cope with horizontal relations, is the meeting. This form enables representatives from the several departments to raise, discuss, and resolve problems requiring the joint efforts of two or more department heads attending the meeting. Here again, the traditional and time-consuming formal channel is bypassed. Usually interdepartmental or interdivisional meetings are held at a top-management level; their usefulness or necessity at lower levels has yet to be fully explored by many organizations.

Other managers have found it expedient to include functions which have been traditionally staff responsibilities under production personnel control. For instance, in an aircraft engine company on the East coast, management transferred its "tool trouble" groups from the master mechanic's department to production and created a new job classification (with quality control functions) under each production foreman.

In fact, considerable attention is currently being given by several large corporations to the question of how many of the service functions can be handed over to the foreman. This is an attempt, it would seem, to fall back on the well-established vertical, superior-subordinate relationships and thus avoid the nebulous and consequently difficult line-staff relationships. The limitations described previously in discussing the product-layout plan, however, would apply equally in this instance. The product must be one that requires no more individuals—machine operators and the transferred service personnel—than a foreman can adequately supervise or manage.

Introducing Mechanisms

Still other managers faced with a discrepancy between technology and organizational structure have attempted to solve the dilemma by changing neither technology nor organization but by introducing new mechanisms. In this case, we are not concerned with minor organizational moves such as have been described in the preceding section, but with procedures or routines.

A dramatic example taken from the restaurant industry of the introduction of a mechanism is provided by William F. Whyte.[6] The problem confronting him was a simple but vexing one:

Viewing the situation *in formal organizational terms*, the waitresses reported vertically to the hostess; the counterman reported along another vertical line of "command" to the kitchen supervisor. Although not explicit, there was some indication that the countermen considered themselves at a higher organizational level than the waitresses. But *technologically* the work flow was from the customer to the waitress to the counterman. This ran against the formal organization. Not only was the relationship between waitress and counterman formally undefined; it also went diagonally, from a lower to a higher level.

In the cases cited by Whyte, a few individuals were able to adjust to this nonformal relationship, but they emerged as exceptions to the usual conflict pattern. Unfortunately, management did not recognize and take advantage of this adjustment and formalize these effective nonformal relationships in order to extend them to others in the organization.

Recognizing the conflict, Whyte introduced a mechanism to reduce it:

As an experiment, one waitress wrote out her orders and placed them on a spindle. Her orders were always ready before those of other waitresses who had called theirs in at the same time. If she was not ready for a hot food order, the counterman would voluntarily place it in the warmer for her. Furthermore, he took a liking to her and made a bet with the bartender that she, like himself, was of Polish extraction—which she was not.[7]

Thus, an uncomplicated mechanism reduced the conflict between the technological work flow and the organizational setup without changing either.

OTHER ILLUSTRATIONS

The use of paper work as a mechanism to reduce possible conflict in formally undefined relationships is a commonplace in industry. Requests from production foremen, for example, go regularly to personnel, engineering, accounting, and other staff and service groups. Such requests cut across the formal organization both horizontally and diago-

---

[6] *Human Relations in the Restaurant Industry* (New York: McGraw-Hill Book Company, Inc., 1948), Chapter 6.

[7] *Ibid.,* p. 69.

nally. Conversely, reports may also cut across the organization through the "copy to . . ." technique while going up the line vertically.

Very often, the amount and type of paper work (copies of requests and reports) do not correspond to actual need. Many are destined to end up in the "circular file" simply because the paper work routes do not follow the lines required by the technology. (Machine accountants, aware of this discrepancy and pressed for tabulating time, occasionally run a check on the use made of various reports; they purposely delay circulation of a report for a few days or a week to see how many people will actually call for it. Thus they have been able, unofficially, to eliminate a number of outdated reports.)

The automobile assembly line provides additional illustrations of mechanisms employed by management to meet technologically required horizontal and diagonal relations:

An operator who hangs doors is in direct contact with the operator who puts them in proper sequence on the overhead conveyer. In the event of a misscheduled door, the line operator has a "squawk" box through which he can call for a substitute door. Here we have a horizontal relationship between two hourly operators, one in production and one in material control.

The worker who loads the overhead conveyer is guided in turn in his door scheduling by the "telautograph," which transmits information from an earlier point on the line from another hourly operator in the material control department. This operator notes the sequence of models and body types of cars passing his station on the line. The information is transmitted simultaneously to various schedulers in the plant who have to synchronize their operations with this sequence.

In the event of a mechanical or tool breakdown, time is especially important. When a line worker cannot perform his operation because of such a breakdown, he immediately signals for help through a whistle system: he uses one signal for a mechanical breakdown, another for an electrical one. The appropriate repairman (who is stationed nearby) comes over to repair the defect with a miniimum of delay. For a worker to stop the line until he finds his foreman to report the breakdown in the traditional vertical plane would be absurd.

Several managements have adopted programs to facilitate nonformal relations. These range from company-wide social affairs, such as picnics, banquets, or sports teams, to a systematic rotation program whereby individuals at supervisory and middle-management levels transfer periodically from one department to another. Ostensibly, the purpose of such a program is to "broaden" the experience of the individual; actually the more important by-product is that it establishes friendships horizontally and diagonally, and thus encourages and facilitates nonformal relations required by the work flow.

Although many of these and other mechanisms can be effective and may, indeed, be the only means to reduce a discrepancy between technology and organization, it still is worthwhile to make broader and more basic changes in either the technology or the organization.

Conclusion

Frequently, the traditional, formally defined vertical relations in business and industrial organization prove inadequate to cope with modern technology. New technologies require new organizational setups, and it is being found increasingly that industrial processes require horizontal and diagonal relations which are not patterned or clearly defined.

Such lack of clarity can impair the production process. The work flow can create difficulty where the vertical lines are strongly emphasized and where the flow violates those lines—as was the case in the restaurant example cited. But when the formal organization is permissive, non-formal relations in the horizontal and diagonal planes arise to cope with the technological process. We saw that the more successful assembly-line foremen learned to relate with other foremen and their workers. But these relationships were not usually recognized formally; they existed on an individual and nonformal basis.

Management can work toward an integration between technology and organization in several ways: (1) by changing the technology, (2) by changing the organization, and (3) by introducing mechanisms. All these methods have been used effectively to some degree, but the difficulty occurs in that management's attempts toward integration generally lack a systematic and purposeful approach. They may just happen over time, arise as temporary expedients, or emerge as a solution to a crisis situation. Many managers have yet to explore the deeper relation between technology and the organization.

The advent of electronic data processing and integrated machine processing has forced some managers to reorganize departments to meet technological needs. Many such revisions, however, are limited to a small portion of the organization, to the areas of greatest immediate pressure. Cannot more be done? The case studies cited, as well as the successful partial steps taken by businessmen and industrialists thus far, indicate a need for a systematic analysis of technology and organization. This analysis might include the following steps:

1. Examine the work flow of the technology to determine what relations are required.
2. Identify the points where the formal organization meets these requirements and where it does not.
3. Discover what nonformal relationships exist at present to meet the technologically required relations which are not encompassed by the formal organization.
4. Determine what formalization does exist to cope with relations falling beyond the traditional vertical planes.
5. Decide which of the nonformal relations might be profitably formalized.
6. Provide measures to facilitate the nonformal relations which are still required but which may best remain nonformal.

It will not be possible to formalize through new mechanisms or through technology and organization changes all of the nonformal relations required by the work flow. It should be possible, however, to remove or reduce the *major* points of variance between the technology and the organization. It makes sense for a company that has been farsighted enough to bring in a new technology to be equally farsighted in recognizing that established organizational patterns will not usually serve with the same effectiveness as they once did. If the new technology is to live up to production expectations, then management must see to it that organization relationships are carefully restudied and wisely redirected.

48. Measuring Organizational Performance*

Rensis Likert

DECENTRALIZATION and delegation are powerful concepts based on sound theory. But there is evidence that, as now utilized, they have a serious vulnerability which can be costly. This vulnerability arises from the measurements being used to evaluate and reward the performance of those given authority over decentralized operations.

This situation is becoming worse. While companies have during the past decade made greater use of work measurements and measurements of end results in evaluating managers, and also greater use of incentive pay in rewarding them, only a few managements have regularly used measurements that deal directly with the human assets of the organization—for example, measurements of loyalty, motivation, confidence, and trust. As a consequence, many companies today are encouraging managers of departments and divisions to dissipate valuable human assets of the organization. In fact, they are rewarding these managers well for doing so!

New Measures Needed

The advocates of decentralization recognize that measurements play a particularly important function. Ralph J. Cordiner, one of the most articulate spokesmen, has stated his views on the question as follows:

Like many other companies, General Electric has long felt a need for more exact measurements and standards of performance, not only to evaluate past results, but to provide a more accurate means for planning future activities and calculating business risks. The traditional measures of profits such as return

---

* From *Harvard Business Review*, Vol. 36, 1958, pp. 41–50.

on investment, turnover, and percentage of net earnings to sales provide useful information. But they are hopelessly inadequate as measures to guide the manager's effectiveness in planning for the future of the business—the area where his decisions have the most important effects.

When General Electric undertook the thorough decentralization . . . , the need for more realistic and balanced measurements became visibly more acute. For with the decentralization of operating responsibility and authority to more than a hundred local managerial teams, there was a need for common means of measuring these diverse business operations as to their short-range and long-range effectiveness. . . .

It was felt that, if a system of simple, common measurements could be devised, they would have these important values. . . .

1. Common measurements would provide all the managers of each component, and the individual contributors in the component, with means to measure and plan their own performance, so that their individual decisions could be made on the basis of knowledge and informed judgment.

2. Common measurements would provide each manager with a way of detecting deviations from establiished standards in time to do something about it—the feedback idea, in which current operations themselves provide a means of continuous adjustment of the operation.

3. Common measurements would provide a means of appraisal, selection, and compensation of men on the basis of objective performance rather than personality judgments, which is better for both the individual and the Company.

4. Common measurements would provide an important motivation for better performance, since they make clear on what basis the individual is to be measured and give him a way of measuring his own effectiveness.

5. Common measurements would simplify communications by providing common concepts and common language with which to think and talk about the business, especially in its quantitative aspects.

You will notice that all these points are directed at helping each decentralized manager and individual contributor measure and guide his own work, through self-discipline; they are not designed as a way for others to "second-guess" the manager of a component or the workers in his component. When measurements are designed primarily for the "boss" rather than for the man himself, they tend to lose their objectivity and frequently become instruments of deception.

An adequate system of common measurements, moreover, would have the additional advantage of providing the company's executives with a way of evaluating performance in some hundred different businesses without becoming involved in the operational details of each of them.[1]

TRADITIONAL THEORY

These specifications point to serious inadequacies in the measurements now being obtained. Virtually all companies regularly secure measurements which deal with such end results as production, sales, profits, and percentage of net earnings to sales. The accounting procedures of most companies also reflect fairly well the level of inventories, the investment in plant and equipment, and the condition of plant and equipment.

---

[1] Ralph J. Cordiner, *New Frontiers for Professional Managers* (New York: McGraw-Hill Book Company, Inc., 1956), pp. 95–98; this volume comprises the McKinsey Lectures, which Mr. Cordiner delivered in 1956 at the Graduate School of Business, Columbia University.

But much less attention is given to what might be called "intervening factors," which significantly influence the end results just mentioned. These factors include such qualities of the human organization that staffs the plant as its loyalty, skills, motivations, and capacity for effective interaction, communication, and decision making. At present there is not one company, to my knowledge, that regularly obtains measurements which adequately and accurately reflect the quality and capacity of its human organization. (But in two companies experimental programs are under way to develop measurements of this kind.)

There are two principal reasons for this situation: (1) The traditional theory of management, which dominates current concepts as to what should be measured, largely ignores motivational and other human behavior variables. (2) Until recently the social sciences were not developed enough to provide methods for measuring the quality of the human organization.

The traditional theory of management is based on scientific management, cost accounting and related developments, and general administrative concepts taken from military organizational theory. As a consequence, it calls for measurements that are concerned with such end result variables as profits and costs, or with such process variables as productivity.

Substantial research findings show, however, that the managers in business and government who are getting the best results are systematically deviating from this traditional theory in the operating procedures which they use.[2] The general pattern of these deviations is to give much more attention to motivation than the traditional theory calls for. High-producing managers are not neglecting such tools and resources provided by scientific management as cost accounting; quite to the contrary, they use them fully. But they use these quantitative tools in special ways—ways that achieve significantly higher motivation than is obtained by those managers who adhere strictly to the methods specified by the traditional theory of management.

MODIFIED THEORY

The exact principles and practices of high-producing managers have been integrated into a modified theory of management, which has been discussed elsewhere.[3] What I am interested in discussing here are the implications of this modified theory for control. Management needs to

---

[2] See, for example, R. Likert, "Motivational Dimensions of Administration," *America's Manpower Crisis* (Chicago: Public Administration Service, 1952), p. 89, and "Developing Patterns of Management," *General Management Series*, No. 178 (New York: American Management Association, 1955), pp. 32–51; and D. Katz and R. Kahn, "Human Organization and Worker Motivation," *Industrial Productivity*, edited by L. Reed Tripp (Madison: Industrial Relations Research Association, 1952), p. 146.

[3] R. Likert, "Developing Patterns of Management: II," *General Management Series*, No. 182 (New York: American Management Association, 1956), pp. 3–29.

make extensive changes in the measurements now being obtained. It should take into account such factors as the levels of confidence and trust, motivation, and loyalty, and the capacity of the organization to communicate fully, to interact effectively, and to achieve sound decisions.

It is important for all companies to obtain these new kinds of measurements to guide their operations, but it is especially important for companies making extensive use of decentralization to do so. The logic of decentralization and the underlying theory on which it is based point to the need for this. In the absence of the new measurements, as we shall see presently, many managers are enabled and may even be encouraged to behave in ways which violate the logic of decentralization and which run contrary to the best interests of their companies.

It is easy to see why. Managers, like all human beings, guide their behavior by the information available to them. The measurements which a company provides them as a basis for decision making are particularly important. They are used by top management not only to judge the performance of departmental and division heads but also, through promotions, bonus compensation, and similar devices, to reward them. If the measurements which companies use for these purposes ignore the quality of the human organization and deal primarily with earnings, production, costs, and similar end results, managers will be encouraged to make a favorable showing on those factors alone.

MANAGEMENT AND PRODUCTIVITY

Let us examine the evidence for these statements. A central concept of the modified theory is (1) that the pattern of interaction between the manager and those with whom he deals should always be such that the individuals involved will feel that the manager is dealing with them in a supportive rather than a threatening manner. A related concept is (2) that management will make full use of the potential capacities of its human resources only when each person in an organization is a member of a well-knit and effectively functioning work group with high interaction skills and performance goals.

A test of these concepts, and thereby of the modified theory, was made recently using attitudinal and motivational data collected in 1955 in a study done by the Institute for Social Research, University of Michigan:

Data are from a company that operates nationally. The company comprises 32 geographically separated units, varying in size from about 15 to over 50 employees, which perform essentially the same operations, and for which extensive productivity and cost figures are available continuously.

A single score was computed for the manager in charge of each of the 32 units. These scores, based on seven questions in the managers' questionnaire, measure the manager's attitude on the two concepts which represent the modified theory. These two concepts were found to be highly related, and consequently have been handled in the analysis as a single combined score—labeled, for convenient reference, *attitude toward men*. The results obtained are shown in Exhibit 1.

This study demonstrates clearly that those managers who, as revealed in their questionnaires, have a favorable *attitude toward men* score achieve significantly higher performance than those managers who have an unfavorable score. Managers who have a supportive attitude toward

EXHIBIT 1

RELATIONSHIP OF "ATTITUDE TOWARD MEN"
Score of Manager to Unit's Productivity

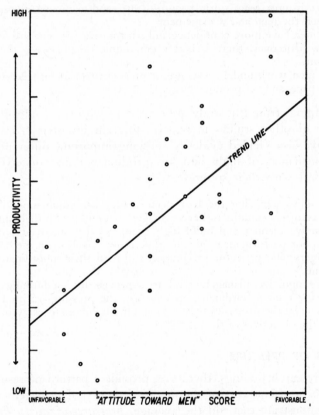

their men and endeavor to build them into well-knit teams obtain appreciably higher productivity than managers who have a threatening attitude and rely more on man-to-man patterns of supervision. (The correlation coefficient is 0.64.)

Information obtained from the nonsupervisory employees under these managers confirms the supervisory pattern reported by the managers. The material from the employees also confirms the character of the important intervening human variables contributing to the better productivity of the high-performance units. The men in those units in which the manager has an above-average *attitude toward men* score differ in their descriptions of their supervision and experience from the men in units whose managers are below average in their *attitude toward men* score. More specifically, the men in units whose managers had a favorable *attitude toward men* score are more likely than the men in the other units to indicate that:

1. The supervision of their unit is of a supportive character. This involves such supervisory behavior as being more interested in the men, friendlier, more willing to go to bat for them, and being less threatening, less punitive, less critical, and less strict (but still having high performance expectations).
2. There is more team spirit, group loyalty, and teamwork among the men and between the men and management.
3. The men have more confidence and trust in management and have higher motivation. Moreover, there is better communication between the men and management.
4. The men work under less sense of pressure, feel much freer to set their own work pace, and yet produce more.

The findings from this study are consistent with the results obtained in a number of other studies in widely different industries.[4] These other studies have also yielded evidence showing important differences in the way the managers of high- and low-producing units conceive of their job and deal with their subordinates:

1. The units achieving the best performance are much more likely than the poor performance units to have managers who deal with their subordinates in a supportive manner and build high group loyalty and teamwork.
2. The poor performance units are much more likely than the best units to have managers who press for production and treat their subordinates as "cogs in a machine."
3. The supportive managers tend to supervise by establishing goals and objectives for their subordinates; in contrast, the pressure-oriented managers tend to focus on the processes they want their employees to carry out in order to achieve the objectives of the manager.

DANGERS OF PRESSURE

These research findings, therefore, provide a pattern of results which confirms central concepts of the modified theory of management. These results demonstrate that, on the average, *pressure-oriented, threatening, punitive management yields lower productivity, higher costs, increased absence, and less employee satisfaction than supportive, employee-*

---

[4] R. Kahn, "The Prediction of Productivity," *Journal of Social Issues*, Vol. 12, No. 2, 1956, p. 41; D. Katz, N. Maccoby, G. Gurin, and L. G. Floor, "Productivity, Supervision and Morale among Railroad Workers," *SRC Monograph Series No. 5* (Ann Arbor: Institute for Social Research, 1951); D. Katz, N. Maccoby, and N. Morse, "Productivity, Supervision and Morale in an Office Situation," *SRC Monograph Series No. 2* (Ann Arbor: Institute for Social Research, 1950); and R. Likert, "Motivation: The Core of Management," *Personnel Series A155* (New York: American Management Association, 1953), pp. 3–21.

centered management which uses group methods of supervision coupled with high-performance expectations.

Since the supportive pattern of supervision tends to yield the best results, clearly this is the pattern which boards of directors and top company officials should foster in all situations including those that involve decentralization and delegation. Company officers believe, no doubt, that they are achieving this pattern of management in their operations. But, unfortunately, the performance measurements now being used by most top managements put pressures on lower levels of management to behave otherwise.

What often confuses the situation is that pressure-oriented, threatening supervision can achieve impressive *short-run* results, particularly when coupled with high technical competence. There is clear-cut evidence that for a period of at least one year supervision which increases the direct pressure for productivity can achieve significant increases in production. However, such increases are obtained only at a substantial and serious cost to the organization.

Testing Performance

To what extent can a manager make an impressive earnings record over a short-run period of one to three years by exploiting the company's investment in the human organization in his plant or department? To what extent will the quality of his organization suffer if he does so?

CONTRASTING PROGRAMS

On this further question, we also have some concrete evidence from an important study conducted by the Institute for Social Research in a large multidivision corporation:

The study covered 500 clerical employees in four parallel divisions. Each division was organized in the same way, used the same technology, did exactly the same kind of work, and had employees of comparable aptitudes.

Productivity in all four of the divisions depended on the number of clerks involved. The work was something like a billing operation; there was just so much of it, but it had to be processed as it came along. Consequently, the only way in which productivity could be increased under the existing organization was to change the size of the work group.

The four divisions were assigned to two experimental programs on a random basis. Each program was assigned at random a division that had been historically high in productivity and a division that had been below average in productivity. No attempt was made to place a division in that program which would best fit its habitual methods of supervision used by the manager, assistant managers, supervisors, and assistant supervisors.

The experiment at the clerical level lasted for one year. Beforehand, several months were devoted to planning, and there was also a training period of approximately six months. Productivity was measured continuously and computed weekly throughout the year. Employee and supervisory attitudes and related variables were measured just before and after the period.

Turning now to the heart of the study, in two divisions an attempt was made to change the supervision so that the decision levels were pushed *down*. More *general* supervision of the clerks and their supervisors was introduced. In addition, the managers, assistant managers, supervisors, and assistant supervisors of these two divisions were trained in group methods of leadership, which they endeavored to use as much as their skill would permit during the experimental year. (To this end we made liberal use of methods developed by the National Training Laboratory in Group Development.) For easy reference, the experimental changes in these two divisions will be labeled the "participative program."

In the other two divisions, by contrast, the program called for modifying the supervision so as to increase the closeness of supervision and move the decision levels *upward*. This will be labeled the "hierarchically controlled program." These changes were accomplished by a further extension of the scientific management approach. For example, one of the major changes made was to have the jobs timed by the methods department and to have standard times computed. This showed that these divisions were overstaffed by about 30%. The general manager then ordered the managers of these two divisions to cut staff by 25%. This was to be done by transfers without replacing the persons who left; no one was to be dismissed.

As a check on how effectively these policies were carried out, measurements were obtained for each division as to where decisions were made. One set of these measurements was obtained before the experimental year started, and the second set was obtained after the completion of the year. The attempts to change the level at which decisions were made were successful enough to develop measurable differences. In the hierarchically controlled program a significant shift upward occurred; by contrast, a significant shift downward occurred in the levels at which decisions were made in the participative program. Also, in the participative program there was an increase in the use of participation and in the extent to which employees were involved in decisions affecting them.

CHANGES IN PRODUCTIVITY

Exhibit 2 shows the changes in salary costs per unit of work, which reflect the changes in productivity that occurred in the divisions. As

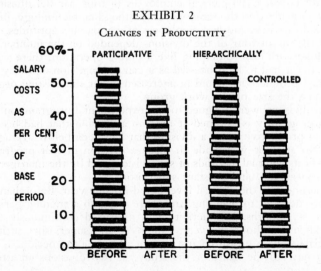

EXHIBIT 2

CHANGES IN PRODUCTIVITY

will be observed, the hierarchically controlled program increased productivity by about 25%. This was a result of the direct orders from the general manager to reduce staff by that amount. Direct pressure produced a substantial increase in production.

A significant increase in productivity of 20% was also achieved in the participative program, but this was not so great an increase as in the hierarchically controlled program. To bring about this improvement, the clerks themselves participated in the decision to reduce the size of the work group. (They were aware, of course, that productivity increases were sought by management in making these experiments.) Obviously, deciding to reduce the size of a work group by eliminating some of its members is probably one of the most difficult decisions for a work group to make. Yet the clerks made it. In fact, one division in the participative program increased its productivity by about the same amount as each of the two divisions in the hierarchically controlled program. The other participative division, which historically had been the poorest of all of the divisions, did not do so well and increased productivity by only about 15%.

CHANGES IN ATTITUDES

Although both programs had similar effects on productivity, they had significantly different results in other respects. The productivity increases in the hierarchically controlled program were accompanied by shifts in an *adverse* direction in such factors as loyalty, attitudes, interest, and involvement in the work. But just the opposite was true in the participative program.

For example, Exhibit 3 shows that when more general supervision and increased participation were provided, the employees' feeling of

EXHIBIT 3

EMPLOYEES' FEELING OF RESPONSIBILITY TO SEE THAT WORK GETS DONE

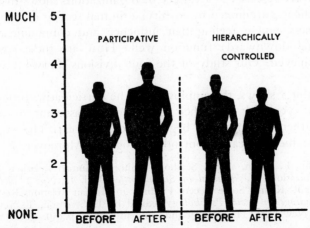

responsibility to see that the work got done increased. Again, when the supervisor was away, they kept on working. In the hierarchically controlled program, however, the feeling of responsibility decreased, and when the supervisor was absent, the work tended to stop.

Another measurement of the extent to which an employee feels involved in his work is his attitude toward workers who are high producers. The changes in attitudes toward the high producer by the employees in the two programs are shown in Exhibit 4. Here again there was a statistically significant shift in opposite directions. In the participative program the attitudes became more favorable, and there was less

EXHIBIT 4

EMPLOYEE ATTITUDES TOWARD HIGH PRODUCER

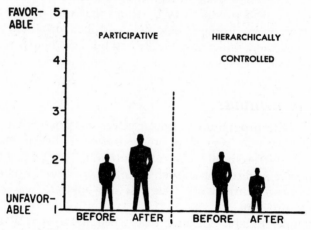

pressure to restrict production. In the hierarchically controlled program the opposite effect occurred.

In industrial organizations that are effective in achieving their objectives, extensive research in a variety of organizations shows that superiors and subordinates are linked by loyalty, a mutual feeling of understanding and closeness, and a feeling that influence and communication (both upward and downward) function well.[5] How are these attitudes and feelings achieved? Our study of the four divisions throws some light on the answer.

As Exhibit 5 shows, the employees in the participative program at the end of the year felt that their manager and assistant manager were "closer to them" than at the beginning of the year. The opposite was true in the hierarchically controlled program. Moreover, as Exhibit 6

[5] R. Kahn, F. Mann, and S. Seashore, Editors, "Human Relations Research in Large Organizations, II," *Journal of Social Issues*, Vol. 12, No. 2, 1956, p. 1; and D. Katz and R. Kahn, "Some Recent Findings in Human Relations Research in Industry," *Readings in Social Psychology*, edited by E. Swanson, T. Newcomb, and E. Hartley (New York: Henry Holt and Company, 1952), p. 650.

EXHIBIT 5

How Close Manager and Assistant Manager Were Felt to Be to Employees

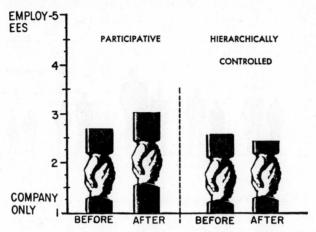

shows, employees in the participative program felt that their superiors were more likely to "pull" for them, or for the company *and* them, and not be solely interested in the company; while in the hierarchically controlled program, the opposite trend occurred.

EXHIBIT 6

Employee Opinions as to Extent to Which Superiors "Pulled" for Company Only or for Employees and Company

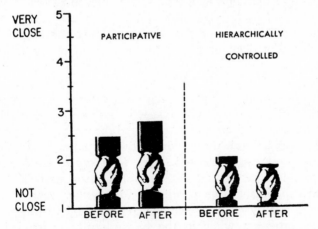

As might be expected from these trends, a marked shift in opposite directions showed up during the year in the employees' feeling of satisfaction with their superiors. Exhibit 7 shows the shifts in employees' feelings as to how well their superiors communicated upward and influenced management on matters which concerned them. Once again the participative program showed up better than the hierarchically

EXHIBIT 7

EMPLOYEES' SATISFACTION WITH SUPERIORS AS REPRESENTATIVES

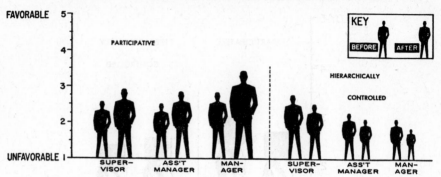

controlled program. One significant aspect of the changes in attitude in the hierarchically controlled program was that the employees felt that their superiors were relying more at the end of the year on rank and authority to get the work done than was the case at the beginning of the year. "Pulling rank" tends to become self-defeating in the long run because of the hostilities and counterpressures it evokes.

The deterioration under the hierarchically controlled program showed up in several other ways. For instance, turnover increased. Employees began to quit because of what they felt to be excessive pressure for production. As a consequence, the company felt it desirable to lessen the pressure. This happened toward the end of the experimental year.

Unfortunately, it was not possible to conduct the participative and hierarchically controlled programs for more than one year because of changes in the over-all operations of the company. However, the significant trends in opposite directions which occurred in these two programs are the trends which would be expected in the light of the studies cited earlier in the article. The attitudes which improved the most in the participative program and deteriorated the most in the hierarchically controlled program are those which these studies have consistently shown to be most closely related *in the long run* to employee motivation and productivity. This gives us every reason to believe that had the clerical experiment been continued for another year or two, productivity and quality of work would have continued to increase in the participative program, while in the hierarchically controlled program productivity and quality of work would have declined.

Implications for Policy

What are the implications of all this for management policy—particularly in the company that is decentralizing its operations or otherwise delegating a good deal of authority to various managers?

TREATMENT OF HUMAN ASSETS

To begin with, most executives will readily agree that it costs money to hire and train personnel. And, after personnel have been hired and trained, it takes additional time and money to build them into a loyal, well-knit, effectively functioning organization with well-established goals. Most businessmen will also agree with the research findings which show that the more supportive the supervision and the better the organization (in terms of loyalty, level of performance goals, communication, motivation, and so forth), the greater is its capacity for high-quality performance at low cost.

If we make these assumptions, we can come, I believe, to only one conclusion. As was demonstrated in the hierarchically controlled program of the experiment, putting pressure on a well-established organization to produce can yield substantial and immediate increases in productivity. *This increase is obtained, however, at a cost to the human assets of the organization.* In the company we studied, for example, the cost was clear: hostilities increased, there was greater reliance upon authority, loyalties declined, and motivations to produce decreased while motivations to restrict production increased. In other words, the quality of the human organization deteriorated as a functioning social system.

If the company had had an accounting procedure which showed the investment in the human organization, it would have shown that in the two divisions in the hierarchically controlled program the value of the human organization was less at the end of the experimental year than at the beginning. In other words, some of the increased productivity was achieved actually by liquidating part of the investment which the company had in the human organization in these divisions. The increase in productivity should have been charged with this cost.

On the other hand, had the company's accounting records reflected the value of the company's investment in the human organization in the two divisions in the participative program, they would have shown an opposite picture. During the year, the value of this investment increased. The management of the two divisions had been of such a character as to increase the productive capacity of the organization as a functioning social system: loyalties had increased, hostilities had decreased, communication was improved, decisions were better since they were based on more accurate and adequate information, and production goals and motivations to produce were increasing.

While a company's investment in its human organization is less tangible than the investment in plant and equipment, and therefore has not yet been given the kind of evaluation an accountant would give it, *it can be measured approximately with the methods now available.* These methods can enable management to size up present trends, analyze their relationships, and guide company operations accordingly.

QUANTITATIVE CONTROLS

Companies are very careful not to let managers of decentralized plants show spurious profits and earnings by juggling inventory or by failing to maintain plant and equipment. Their accounting procedures measure and report regularly on inventory and condition of plant and equipment. "Earnings" achieved by liquidating the assets represented in the human organization are just as spurious as though achieved by liquidating the investment in plant. Yet they are encouraged by compensation formulas that urge managers to press unduly for immediate production, cost reduction, and similar goals; by the present-day emphasis on measuring only the end results of the activities of the lower echelons or of decentralized operations; and by job evaluations focused on the immediate contribution to earnings and profits.

In the long run, of course, such measurements are valid. The executive who "milks the human franchise" today will not be in a position to show good profit-and-loss figures tomorrow. The catch is that, by the time the symptoms of trouble are clear, the human organization has deteriorated to a point where steps to correct it are difficult and costly. As a practical matter, moreover, there is often so much rotation in executive responsibilities, and so much change in the conditions of business, that short-run tests which will provide adequate measures of current performance, including trends in the human organization, are worth much more than long-run evaluations.

There is only one solution to this problem, and it does not yet lie in more precise accounting data. The solution is to obtain adequate periodic measurements of the character and the quality of the human organization. Judgment alone is notoriously inaccurate and tends to be most inaccurate in those situations which are unsatisfactory or deteriorating. Measurements and compensation formulas are needed which will penalize managers financially and otherwise when they permit the quality of the human organization under them to deteriorate, and reward them when they improve the quality of this organization.

Identically the same point can be made with regard to consumer attitudes, good will, and confidence in the company, in its products, and in its service. A manager of a decentralized operation can substantially increase current earnings by reducing the product quality with low-cost, shoddy output. However, the immediate earnings shown on the company books would be spurious and would actually represent a substantial liquidation of the investment made in developing consumer confidence and acceptance. Therefore, periodic measurements of consumer perceptions, attitudes, and acceptance should be made not only for the usual purposes, such as to provide direction in product development and to guide advertising and marketing, but also to protect the company's investment in consumer good will.

ADEQUATE APPRAISALS

It is not sufficient merely to measure morale and the attitudes of employees toward the organization, their supervision, and their work. Favorable attitudes and excellent morale do not necessarily assure high motivation, high performance, and an effective human organization. A good deal of research indicates that this relationship is much too simple. Favorable attitudes may be found, for example, in situations where there is complacency and general contentment but where production goals are low and there is little motivation to achieve high performance.

Similarly, measurements of behavior which reflect the past condition of the human organization, while useful, are also inadequate for current appraisals. Such measurements as absence, turnover, and scrap loss tend not only to be insensitive measurements but also to reflect changes in the human organization *after* they have become substantial. More sensitive and more current measurements than those are needed.

Progress in the social sciences in recent years enables any company which so desires to obtain measurements needed for adequate appraisals of the quality and performance capacity of its human organization. Instruments to measure many of the important variables are now available; for those variables for which measuring instruments are not now available, the basic methodology now exists to develop the necessary tools. The organization for which these measurements are obtained can be an entire corporation or any of its divisions.

The following illustrate the kinds of variables which are now being measured in some companies or for which satisfactory measuring instruments can be developed:

1. Extent of loyalty to and identification with the institution and its objectives.
2. Extent to which members of the organization at all hierarchical levels feel that the organization's goals are consistent with their own needs and goals, and that the achievement of the company's goals will help them achieve their own.
3. Extent to which the goals of units and of individuals are of a character to enable the organization to achieve its objectives.
4. Level of motivation among members of the organization with regard to such variables as:
   a. Performance, including both quality and quantity of work done;
   b. Concern for elimination of waste and reduction of costs;
   c. Concern for improving product;
   d. Concern for improving processes.
5. Degree of confidence and trust among members of the organization in each other and in the different hierarchical levels.
6. Amount and quality of teamwork in each unit of the organization and between units.
7. Extent to which people feel delegation is being effectively achieved.
8. Extent to which members feel that their ideas, information, knowledge

of processes, and experience are being used in the decision-making processes of the organization.

9. Level of competence and skill of different groups in the organization to interact effectively in solving problems and other tasks.
10. Efficiency and adequacy of the communication process upward, downward, sidewise.
11. Level of the leadership skills and abilities of supervisors and managers, including their basic philosophy of management and orientation toward the processes of leadership.
12. Aptitude scores of the members of the organization. If aptitude scores are obtained as people join the organization, then trends in these scores will show whether the current management is improving the basic quality of the personnel through its hiring practices or is letting quality deteriorate through unfavorable turnover.

JOB FOR EXPERTS

The measurement of these variables is a complex process and requires a high level of scientific competence. It cannot be done by an untrained person, no matter how intelligent he is. Nor can it be done simply by asking people questions that have not been pretested or by handing them a ready-made questionnaire. Few companies trust cost figures obtained by inexperienced personnel. It is equally dangerous to trust the untrained to obtain measurements of the state of a human organization.

Conclusion

Industry needs more adequate measures of organizational performance than it is now getting. Progress in the social sciences now makes these measurements possible. As a consequence, new resources are available to assist company presidents in their responsibility for the successful management of their companies.

The president's responsibility requires that he build an organization whose structure, goals, levels of loyalty, motivation, interaction skills, and competence are such that the organization achieves its objectives effectively. As tools to assist him and the other members of management, a president needs a constant flow of measurements reporting on the state of the organization and the performance being achieved. The measurements proposed here would provide a president with data which he needs to fill the current serious gap in the information coming to him and to his organization.

Section Seven

FATIGUE, MONOTONY, AND WORKING CONDITIONS

Introduction

THIS SECTION deals with an area that some writers have called "human efficiency." The term "efficiency" is typically expressed as the ratio of output to input. Thus a machine that requires 50 units of electric power to produce 25 units of work is more efficient than one which requires 100 units of electric power to produce the same 25 units. With human work it is usually easy to note the output side, but very difficult to measure input. The fact that employees in two departments are producing about the same, tells us nothing about their "efficiency," since those in one department may be expending more energy. This may be determined by physiological measures of metabolic functions such as heart and pulse rate, amount of oxygen consumed, blood pressure changes, etc. during work. There are many studies which show that different types of work and different methods of performing the same job require different amounts of energy. Similarly, different kinds of working conditions, (e.g., levels of noise, illumination, ventilation) will influence energy expenditure. Of course, it is very difficult to obtain such measures of energy input on the job. Furthermore, humans show psychological "costs" (e.g., feelings of tension, effort, and tiredness). The important thing is that these subjective feelings may be present with or without changes in the physiological measurements obtained. The overt physical effort of reading a novel and reading a text are much the same, but one is "hard work" while the other is not "work at all." And, as yet, there are no good procedures for evaluating such "psychological" costs.

A further complication is that actual output may have little relation to either physiological cost measurements or reported feelings of tiredness. Important factors here are those of motivation and attitude. If motivation is high, performance may continue to be high in the face of extraordinary physiological and psychological costs.

For these and other reasons, there has been a shift away from the traditional concept of "efficiency" to an emphasis on the behavioral, output side. The question here is "What factors are related to *work decrement* on the job, and how can we modify the conditions of work to minimize decrement and keep performance high?"

Even when everyone is highly motivated, it is clear that continuous activity or work, in certain tasks, leads to reduction in the ability to perform adequately. The term "fatigue" is frequently used to describe this phenomenon. There has been much controversy about the usefulness of this term, since there appears to be no single process which can be termed "fatigue." As stated above, feelings of tiredness, physiological indications (e.g., decreased sugar and increased lactic acid in the blood), and work decrement may or may not occur in the same individuals at the same time. The article by Fraser "Recent Experimental Work in the Study of Fatigue," outlines some of the problems in the study of fatigue, describes some recent advances in the identification and measurement of fatigue, and presents an up-to-date view of this complex problem.

Monotony, or boredom, is another on-the-job phenomenon, which may lead to performance deterioration. It is often difficult to distinguish between monotony and the feelings of tiredness associated with fatigue. Both are unpleasant and result from continuous work. However, monotony seems more a function of work which presents no challenge to the individual. In fact, many of the principles of motivation described earlier in Section Four (e.g., job enlargement) apply to the problem of reducing "monotony."

One of the important things about monotony is that it is, in large measure, dependent on the individual's perception of his job. This is demonstrated in Patricia Smith's article, entitled "The Prediction of Individual Differences in Susceptibility to Industrial Monotony." This article shows that some workers find one job boring, while other workers do not. But, what are some of the characteristics of people that make some of them more susceptible than others to monotony on a given job? Are they likely to be more intelligent, more ambitious, more extroverted, younger, etc? The article by Smith also presents considerable evidence on these questions.

The first article by Smith focused on the "experience" of monotony. There is the further question of the relation between these experiences and actual output on the job. Her second article examines "The Curve of Output as a Criterion of Boredom." She reviews the literature on this question, describes some definitive research on the problem, and suggests some job factors related to monotony and output.

A common procedure to reduce fatigue and monotony is the appropriate use of rest pauses. The most notable example is the "coffee break." There are, however, important questions of how, when, and if to introduce scheduled rest periods. The article by McGehee and Owen, "Authorized and Unauthorized Rest Pauses in Clerical Work," points up some of these issues and presents some important conclusions on the effects of rest pauses on employee feelings and productivity.

There is the further question of the effects of shift and night work on human functioning. Recent trends in our society have intensified, rather than reduced, the need to evaluate these effects. Examples of operations requiring round-the-clock work are the manning of national defense systems, the monitoring of automated factories, and the use of atomic reactors. In "Shift Work and Human Efficiency," Bloom describes some of the research on the sleep-wakefulness cycle and suggests how the scheduling of shift work might be improved.

The final three papers in this section deal with the effects of various environmental conditions on job proficiency. The important environmental factors which have been investigated include the effects of noise, lighting, temperature, ventilation, and more recently (see Section Nine), vibration, isolation, stress, and g-forces (positive, negative, and zero). Although we can be confident that extremes in these conditions affect human performance, we need to know the extent of these effects, the "critical levels" at which an increase in temperature, noise, etc. begin to affect performance, and we need to know if some skills are more affected than others. Of course, in the new military and space environments in which people will work, we need to know much about human tolerances and limitations under strange and extreme environmental changes. In many cases, entire "environmental systems" are being developed for man to take with him.

But what is known about the effects of environmental conditions likely to be found in industry? The article by Broadbent and Little investigates the "Effects of Noise Reduction in a Work Situation." This article also demonstrates the need for careful experimental design and the use of appropriate measurements in this area. The next article, by Tinker, presents a comprehensive review of the research evidence on "Illumination Standards for Effective and Comfortable Vision." He considers three primary aspects of lighting—color, intensity, and distribution. The final article in this section, "Music in a Complex Industrial Job," by McGehee and Gardner, investigates an environmental change currently fashionable in many companies.

49. Recent Experimental Work in the Study of Fatigue*

D. C. Fraser

THE SUBJECT of this paper, fatigue, is one of the major problems of human functioning. A good deal of rather sporadic research has been carried out on it, but it is perhaps only in the last five to ten years that intensive experimenting has made it possible to produce dependable and meaningful results.

Fatigue presents two basic difficulties to the experimenter—of definition and measurement. We are able to offer an answer to both, but we do not suggest that we have solved them completely, only that we have perhaps gone a little further than previous experimenters.

First, definition. The man in the street thinks he knows what he means by fatigue, but the experts are much less confident. Some people use the terms to indicate such things as weariness or boredom, subjective feelings in the individual. Others tend to restrict the term to more objective phenomena—to biochemical changes in tissue, deterioration in performance of some skilled task as the result of long periods of work, and so on. Many psychologists now tend to fight shy of the term altogether. This, I think, is a policy of despair.

However, as the result of systematic research, starting with the wartime studies of pilot error at the Applied Psychology Research Unit in Cambridge and using the well-known apparatus called the Cambridge Cockpit, it has been possible to show certain common features which develop as the individual becomes fatigued. This type of analysis has only proved applicable to studies of deterioration during the task itself. One of the biggest snags in the measurement of fatigue has been the difficulty of obtaining a good, objective test which is not part of the performance of the task under examination. It might seem likely that changes in threshold function, or differences in reaction time would provide a simple and reliable measure of fatigue, and indeed it would be very convenient if such changes did occur. But unfortunately a large amount of careful experimentation has shown that there appears to be virtually no change in isolated measures of function as the result of fatigue.

* From *Occupational Psychology*, Vol. 32, No. 4, Oct., 1958; this paper was originally read to the British Association for the Advancement of Science in Sept., 1955. It is a pleasure to express my thanks to Sir Frederic Bartlett for his critical reading of this paper.

The Cambridge Cockpit experiments have shown clearly that one of the first things to suffer as the individual becomes fatigued is "timing." By timing I mean the delicate, precise co-ordination of judgments and movements into a continuous smooth pattern. This is a fundamental characteristic of skilled activity, and is common to tasks such as hitting a golf-ball, driving a car, flying an aeroplane, performing a surgical operation, or even running down-stairs. All these call for a careful and precisely timed receptor-effector co-ordination. We define fatigue, therefore, as "a disorganisation of receptor-effector co-ordination, resulting from exposure to high speeds, loads, duration, anxiety, conflict, sleep-deprivation, or other form of stress condition."

Secondly, measurement. One of the most important techniques which we use was developed out of the research in vigilance which has been going on in Cambridge for about ten years. It would take some time to describe the technique fully, but what we do, in effect, is to obtain a series of judgments by a given subject of the time at which a slowly moving signal passes through the centre of a projected display; the significant signals (those to which the subject has to react) are interspersed randomly throughout a much longer series of neutral stimuli. We then calculate the variance of the subject's estimates about his own mean estimate. In measuring fatigue we make use of a measure known as Z-function. This is obtained by averaging the subject's second and third control scores (the first control score is often atypical), taking the natural logarithm of this average and subtracting it from the natural logarithm of the subject's experimental score. But for simplicity in presentation I shall just use the raw variances scores to indicate how we estimate the degree of fatigue.

Suppose we test an individual member of aircrew before flying, and we find that his variance score is 0.85, which is an average sort of value for a fresh subject. If we test him again immediately after a fifteen-hour trip, we shall very probably find that his variance score has risen to, say, 3.8. We therefore infer an increase in fatigue, that is, some degree of disorganisation of receptor-effector organisation. In this way, we have been able to show significant changes in performance before and after flying, between day and night flying, and between jet-engined and piston-engined aircraft, as fatigue inducers.

What does this rise in variance mean in practice? In determining how well an aircraft is being held on its course, we can calculate the average time dead on course, and the variance about this average. We might find no change in the average time on course, but an increase in the size and frequency of deviations from it with fatigue. In the case of critical incidents, such as landing in high-speed aircraft, an increased variability may well mean an increased likelihood of accident.

Another technique we have used is to fire a large number of signals in irregular order at an observer who is required to respond to all of them but does not know when one is coming. In such a case we have been able to show a very small but significant slowing-up of his reaction time as he becomes fatigued. We have also been able to show that an occasional signal is missed altogether. Such missed signals occur very seldom but the effect is quite reliable over a large number of signals. We have applied this technique to mine rescue work and to laboratory experiments on the effect of high temperatures.

A third technique which we have brought into play recently is the continuous recording and measurement of certain representative factors throughout the exercise of the skilled performance.

CRITERIA OF FATIGUE

It appears, then, that if we are looking for the effects of prolonged work in any field we need to adopt a rather sophisticated approach to the problem. A simple examination of average output, or before-after changes may prove very deceptive. Thus some of the earlier workers in this field sometimes found that performance on some isolated tests actually was improved after a long spell of hard flying. We need to know what sort of distinguishing features are most likely to give us a precise idea of what is happening as the individual becomes fatigued, and the research we have been doing has given us some of the answers to this.

In the first place, fatigue tends to affect high-grade performance long before there are signs of physiological exhaustion. The more complex the performance, the more delicate the discriminations, the greater the number of sources of information which have to be attended to, the more likely the performance is to suffer from fatigue. There is not necessarily a gross falling-off in performance, or extensive errors, or long patches of bad work. Rather we find at first the occasional slip, the momentary confusion of two similar signals, the slight pause in the smooth rhythm of skilled performance. The significance of this depends on the nature of the performance. If you are driving a car at a reasonable speed and the traffic is not heavy, such momentary lapses may be unimportant; but if you are driving at high speed and in heavy traffic the consequences may be disastrous. We ourselves are very concerned about these momentary lapses in attention and slight lengthening of reaction times, since the ever-increasing speed of aircraft means that they assume an importance out of all proportion to their size. It is not too much to say that the successful arrangement of instrumentation and flying schedules so as to avoid even this short-term fatigue effect may do much to save aircraft costing a quarter of a million pounds each, to say nothing of the priceless lives of some of the fittest and most highly skilled men in the country.

Secondly, it seems to be now well established that performance where knowledge of results of performance is small is likely to be most sensitive to fatigue. The importance of knowledge of results is, of course, well known to psychologists for its effectiveness in producing quick and stable learning. But it is also clear that the more complete, the more precise, the more immediate the information about the effects of each step in a continuous skilled performance, the more likely it is that the skill will withstand the effects of fatigue. Effective human engineering, in facilitating the provision of information about the effects of action through various forms of feedback, can do much to reduce impairment of performance as the result of fatigue.

The results obtained by using these varied techniques suggest that it is very misleading to consider fatigue as a single and simple phenomenon which builds up in the same way under different conditions and in different individuals. Already we can distinguish several types of fatigue occurring under different conditions, in different types of activity, and requiring different methods of study and measurement. With this point in mind, I shall now turn to a consideration of some of the practical findings of our research, considering particularly our experiments on aircrew fatigue since they are the most complete.

RESEARCH ON AIRCRAFT FATIGUE

In the first place we have been able to show considerable individual differences in what I can perhaps call 'fatigueability.' I think we have to be very cautious about the use of a term like this; but it does seem from our work on the Z-function technique, which I mentioned earlier, that an individual who makes a poor control score on this test is more likely to show a high fatigue effect after flying, or driving, or after a sleepless night. Taking this as a criterion, we have been able to show that the sample of R.A.F. aircrew we have tested is significantly less fatigueable than a more random sample of the ordinary population. We do not know whether this resistance to fatigue is achieved indirectly in the selection process (it is not tested for directly), or whether it is developed in the process of training, but it seems quite definite that the typical R.A.F. pilot or navigator is much above the average in this respect.

Secondly, applying our technique to flights of various lengths, we have been able to show that a short sortie of 4 to 6 hours in a piston-engined plane produces no appreciable fatigue effect, but measurable deterioration begins to set in after about 8 to 10 hours' flying. There is a good deal of support for this figure in the observations of experienced aircrew. This finding does not in the least imply that it is necessarily dangerous to fly for longer than 10 hours at a stretch, but it is the point at which we begin to get a measurable fatigue effect. We should need to do a good deal more research before we could definitely indicate the danger level for particular aircraft under particular conditions.

One interesting result is that two or three one-hour sorties in a jet-engined aircraft seem to produce as high a fatigue effect as ten hours or more in a piston-engined plane. This finding is rather tentative, since it is based on two different populations, but it does suggest that the high speed of the jet, and the tension involved in take-off, landing and conservation of the limited fuel supply take a greater toll of the crew than the more leisurely piston-engined craft. It is interesting, too, that many of the jet crews claim that they feel no marked subjective fatigue effects after the flights.

Another clear-cut result obtained in research with piston-engined aircraft is that a flight of, say, 15 hours' duration during the night gives a much higher fatigue effect than a flight of equivalent length during the day. This is probably due, amongst other things, to the disturbance of the normal diurnal rhythm involved.[1]

APPLICATIONS IN OTHER FIELDS

Although I have dealt so far largely with the aircrew research, some of the possible industrial applications will be obvious. Thus we have used two of the techniques in a study of mine rescue. The results of this investigation may throw some light on the occurrence of accidents, particularly at higher temperature conditions. We are studying also the most effective methods of presentation of information, and the effects of various lighting and heating conditions. The work described so far is reasonably well established. In this last part of the paper, however, I should like to mention one or two interim findings from work which is not complete. These findings are, I think, interesting but very tentative indeed.

One study in which we have collected some data is concerned with the relation of fatigue and time of day. A full study of this fascinating problem would require a huge sample of the population and careful statistical controls. We have not satisfied these requirements so far, but it is interesting that with the subjects tested we seem to be able to distinguish two rather opposite groups. One group tends to show a higher fatigue effect in the morning than in the evening, while the other group seems to fatigue more quickly in the evening than in the morning. This may be held to confirm the popular idea that some people jump brightly out of bed in the morning but start yawning ostentatiously by nine P.M.; while others are at their best in the evening but find life almost unbearable in the morning until they have had their eleven o'clock coffee. The afternoon appears to be relatively neutral.

At least one of our techniques appears to be quite sensitive to the effects of sleepless nights and to alcohol. In several cases where we have tested a subject who has been drinking we have found that he tends to fatigue more rapidly than normal; this seems to confirm the pharmacologist's unpopular doctrine that alcohol is not a stimulant. We hope

---

[1] (Editor's Note: See article 53, this section for a discussion of this problem.)

to do a more rigorous study of the effects of alcohol at a later date. This is one experiment where we anticipate no shortage of volunteers.

I do not want to convey the impression that results can be obtained in many of these intriguing but complex problems by penny-in-the-slot methods. The administration and scoring of the techniques is often a very complex and time-consuming task; the total time occupied in studying one problem may be two years. But as research instruments they appear to be of considerable potential value. We hope that it will prove possible in the future to study objectively many controversial questions in the field of fatigue, from the broad theoretical problem of how it builds up in the central nervous system down to practical questions such as the optimum number of hours of sleep for a given individual. It might even be possible to investigate the relation between depth of sleep and the amount of malted milk drunk the previous evening.

CONCLUSIONS

Summing up, we must conclude that:

a) Fatigue is capable of objective definition and measurement.

b) It must be differentiated from subjective feelings of weariness or boredom.

c) It appears to affect high-grade performance long before there are signs of physiological exhaustion.

d) It shows little or no effect on isolated measures of function; *e.g.*, visual acuity.

e) It appears most clearly in complex performance where knowledge of results is reduced or minimal.

f) It is shown typically by variability of performance, and bad timing or integration of different response patterns.

g) It is misleading to consider fatigue as a single and simple phenomenon which builds up in the same way under different conditions and in different individuals. Several types of fatigue can already be distinguished occurring under different conditions, in different types of activity, and requiring different methods of study and measurement. Individual differences in susceptibility to fatigue are also clearly evident.

50. The Prediction of Individual Differences in Susceptibility to Industrial Monotony*

Patricia Cain Smith

MOST MODERN industrial jobs are repetitive and alleged to be uncreative. Observers of the industrial scene have been greatly concerned about the consequent feelings of monotony and boredom by the workers. Superficially, it would seem that repetition in work would be a *cause* of boredom, that work which appeared repetitive to the observer would necessarily be accompanied by boredom, and work with apparent variety by absence of boredom. Industrial investigations established very early, however, that jobs with all the appearance of being repetitive were not always considered monotonous by the workers.[1] Investigations of clerical workers, school teachers, and professional workers, on the other hand, have repeatedly indicated that many persons find each of these more varied kinds of work boring. (For summaries of these studies, see Hoppock and Robinson[2] or Viteles.[3]

An observer of a job may classify it as repetitive solely on the basis of the observed frequency of repetition of the task. This type of classification does not take into account the perceptions of the worker. Repetition for the worker depends upon what he perceives in the task, and his perceptions are not subject to immediate scrutiny by an observer. For instance, if a worker perceives variety in the minute changes of detail or in the social situation around him, the job is for him one in which there is variety. Repetition as defined by externally observable frequency of occurrence cannot be stated as a valid *cause* of monotony. Repetition is

* From *Journal of Applied Psychology*, Vol. 39, No. 5, 1955, pp. 322–29. The writer is deeply indebted to Dr. T. A. Ryan for his guidance.

[1] P. S. Florence, *Economics of Fatigue and Unrest and the Efficiency of Labor in English and American Industry* (New York: Henry Holt, 1924); Chen-Nan Li, "A Summer in the Ford Works," *Personnel Journal*, Vol. 7, 1928, pp. 18–32; H. Münsterberg, *Psychology and Industrial Efficiency* (Cambridge: Houghton Mifflin, 1913), pp. 195–98; S. Wyatt, J. N. Langdon, and F. G. L. Stock, "Fatigue and Boredom in Repetitive Work" (London: Industrial Health Research Board, Report No. 77, 1937).

[2] R. Hoppock and H. A. Robinson, "Job Satisfaction Researches of 1950," *Occupations*, Vol. 29, 1951, pp. 572–78.

[3] M. S. Vitelis, *Motivation and Morale in Industry* (New York: W. W. Norton, 1953).

rather one characteristic of the task as perceived by the worker—one aspect of the experience of monotony.

These considerations enable us to define our terms, at least in a general way. For the purposes of this discussion, we shall use the terms monotony and boredom interchangeably to designate the experience which arises from the continued performance of an activity which is perceived as either uniform or repetitive, and which also induces a desire for change or variety. This definition, obviously, restricts monotony to the experience of the individual. It has frequently been suggested or assumed that there are individual differences in susceptibility to such experiences.[4] This study was undertaken to investigate factors in the individual which might predispose him to experiences of boredom.

PROCEDURE

The research was conducted in a small knitwear mill in northern Pennsylvania. Most operators in the plant, and all included in this study, were paid by piece rate. The active support of both the plant manager and the business agent of the union was a major factor in securing the confidence of the workers.

Although feelings of boredom are most directly assessed by verbal reports of the workers, we conducted a preliminary study in an attempt to obtain more objective supplementary criteria. As reported previously,[5] we found, however, that such indirect indicators of boredom as talking, frequency of rest pauses, average working speed, and the shape and variability of the output curve were both unreliable and invalid in this situation. Verbal report was the only available criterion.

Detailed interviews with a number of workers laid the groundwork for the main study, orienting the investigator and aiding the union and management in "selling" the workers on the desirability of the study. The subjects of the main study were 72 women workers, all engaged in light, repetitive work. We included only sewing-machine operators who had been on the job three months or more, and who remained continuously on the same task throughout each working day. The questionnaire form was used rather than interviews, both because it permitted contact with a larger number of workers and because any later application of the findings would be much more practical if information could be gathered in paper-and-pencil form. All questions were pretested and, when necessary, revised before administration to the main group. Questionnaires were unsigned.

Some criterion questions concerning the experience of monotony were adapted from the much-quoted studies of Wyatt, Langdon, and Stock[6]; others were suggested by the interviews. Included were such obvious items as "Do you often get bored with your work?," "Is your job too monotonous?," "Would you like to change from one type of work to another from time to

---

[4] O. Lipmann, "The Human Factor in Production," *Personnel Journal*, Vol. 7, 1928, pp. 94–95; H. Münsterberg *op. cit.*; S. Wyatt, J. N. Langdon, and F. G. L. Stock, *op. cit.*

[5] P. C. Smith, "The Curve of Output as a Criterion of Boredom," *Journal of Applied Psychology*, Vol. 37, 1953, pp. 69–74.

[6] S. Wyatt, J. N. Langdon, and F. G. L. Stock, *op. cit.*

time if the pay remained the same?," and some similar multiple-choice and completion items. The frequencies of choice of answers to each question were compared for the entire group, by the chi-square technique, and a weighted criterion score was devised on the basis of those items most closely agreeing with each other. Subjects were then separated into three approximately equal groups—the nonsusceptible, the susceptible, and an intermediate group of workers. This criterion seemed superior to the criteria used by most previous investigators, who relied either upon shape of the production curve or on answers to questions about preference for regularity in daily habits outside the work situation.[7] Table 1 shows the criterion questions.

TABLE 1

CRITERION QUESTIONS AND WEIGHTING OF EACH

QUESTION	ANSWER	WEIGHT
Do you often get bored with your work?	Yes	1
	?	0
	No	−1
Is your job too monotonous?	Yes	2
	?	0
	No	−2
Would you like to change from one type of work to another	Yes	1
from time to time, if the pay remained the same?	?	0
	No	−1
Would you like to be a forelady?		—
What time of day seems most boring to you?		
Choice of any hour from 7 A.M. to 3 P.M.		1
Choice of hour from 3 P.M. to 4 P.M.		0
Choice of any hour outside of working hours		0
How well do you like the work that you do?		
I think that it is extremely monotonous		1
I think that it is very monotonous		1
I think that it is pretty monotonous		1
I think that it is not very interesting		0
I think that it is pretty interesting		−1
I think that it is very interesting		−1
I think that it is fascinating		−1
Is there anything about the work which you particularly dislike?		
It is too monotonous		10
Other responses		0

The worker who does not suffer from monotony when doing repetitive work has been portrayed in the literature as an inferior, insensitive sort of person—placid, extraverted, happy,[8] unable to daydream,[9] uncreative,[10] and, above

---

[7] R. E. Dunford, "A Study of Monotony Types" (unpublished master's thesis, Ohio State University, 1925); S. Wyatt, J. N. Langdon, and F. G. L. Stock, *op. cit.*; H. Münsterberg, *op. cit.*; L. A. Thompson, Jr., "Measuring Susceptibility to Monotony," *Personnel Journal*, Vol. 8, 1929, pp. 172–97.

[8] R. N. McMurry, "Efficiency, Work-Satisfaction, and Neurotic Tendency, A Study of Bank Employees," *Personnel Journal*, Vol. 11, 1932, pp. 201–10; L. A. Thompson, Jr., *op. cit.*, S. Wyatt, J. N. Langdon, and F. G. L. Stock, *op. cit.*

[9] S. Wyatt, J. N. Langdon, and F. G. L. Stock, *ibid.*

[10] H. Wunderlich, "Die Einwerkung Einförmiger, Zwangslaüfiger Arbeit auf die Personlichkeitsstruktur," *Schr. Psychol. Berufseignung*, Vol. 31, 1925, pp. 49–50.

all, unintelligent.[11] Such portrayals in textbooks and in journals are distinguished more for their literary than for their scientific value. Nevertheless, they furnished us with a number of hypotheses concerning characteristics related to susceptibility to monotony. Further hypotheses were formulated during the preliminary interviewing and observational periods. Questions designed to test each of these hypotheses were included in the questionnaire, and answers to each question were compared for the three criterion groups. Significance of relationships was tested by the chi-square test.

All three criterion groups were included in every analysis. Where the response categories were "Yes, ?, No," the "?" response was, in most cases, chosen too infrequently to make the chi-square technique applicable. The interpretation of such responses is ambiguous, moreover, meaning for various respondents, "I don't know," "Sometimes one, sometimes the other," "I don't understand the question," "I don't wish to answer the question," or "The question does not apply to me." Usually these responses were omitted from the analysis. In a few cases, indicated in the tables, the "?" response was chosen sufficiently often to bring the predicted frequencies up to five. In these instances, as in all questions with multiple-response categories, the significance was first tested for all responses. Responses were then grouped into two categories for purposes of comparability. An additionnal p value is therefore reported in each case for a 3×2 chi-square table. Yates' correction for continuity was applied throughout.

Table 2 shows the questions, the most frequently choosen answers for each of the three groups, and the level of significance for each, for all those relationships found to be significant at the 5 per cent level or better and to differentiate between the extreme groups.

HYPOTHESES AND RESULTS

Hypothesis I. Younger workers are more susceptible to monotony than older ones. Age was compared with answers to the criterion questions. The results showed that workers under 20 were significantly more susceptible and those over 35 significantly less so, although no relationship obtained between 20 and 35. Three other kinds of personal history items were investigated—marital status, number of children, and number of years of experience at this or similar work—but trends in these proved to disappear when age was held constant. Age, then, is a correlate of susceptibility in this group.

Hypothesis II. Susceptible workers are more ambitious, either for themselves or for their children. No item in this list discriminated among the groups. Level of aspiration seemed not to be related to feelings of monotony in this sample.

Hypothesis III. The susceptible worker does not daydream. It has been suggested that the nonsusceptible worker does not feel the monot-

---

[11] I. Burnett, "An Experimental Investigation into Repetitive Work" (London: Industrial Fatigue Research Board, Report No. 30, 1925); W. W. Kornhauser, *op. cit.*; M. S. Viteles, "Selecting Cashiers and Predicting Length of Service," *Journal of Personnel Research*, Vol. 2, 1924, pp. 467–73; H. Wunderlich, *op. cit.*; S. Wyatt, "Experimental Study of a Repetitive Process," *British Journal of Psychology*, Vol. 3, 1927, pp. 192–209; S. Wyatt, J. A. Fraser, and F. G. L. Stock, "The Effects of Monotony in Work" (London: Industrial Fatigue Research Board, Report No. 56, 1929); S. Wyatt, J. N. Langdon, and F. G. L. Stock, *op. cit.*

TABLE 2

Summary of Items Significantly Related to Monotony Susceptibility

(Answers to questions and p values derived from the chi-square test of significance of relationships. All p's based on 3 × 2 tables unless otherwise indicated.)

Question	Answer	Answers Chosen Most Frequently by Monot. Susc.	Middle Group	Non-susc.	p
How old are you?	Under 20	X			
	20–24				.03*
	25–29				
	30–34				
	35 and over			X	
	Under 25	X			.02
	25 and over			X	
How long have you been doing the same work?	Less than 3 mo.			X	
	3–6 mo.	X			.05* **
	6 mo. and over			X	
Do you like to daydream at your work around the house?	Yes	X			
	?			X	.03*
	No				
	Yes	X			.02†
	?			X	
Do you especially like to have a definite schedule of home duties so that you can do them at the same time every day?	Yes			X	
	No	X			.03
If you had an evening to spend as you liked, what would you *usually* rather do? (CHECK AS MANY AS YOU LIKE)	Knit‡				
	Sew			X	.0003§
	Visit friends			X	.07§
	Go to the movies			X	.27§
	Listen to the radio			X	.06§
	Go down town	X			.36§
	Read		X		.08§
	Dance	X			.08§
	Drive around in the car		X		.19§
	Something else you would like to do very much. (If so, what?_____)			X¶	.0006§
	More than average number checked			X	
	Average number or fewer checked	X			.09
When you are working around the house, what job do you prefer? (CHECK AS MANY AS YOU LIKE)	Washing dishes			X	.11§
	Dusting			X	.08§
	Cleaning drawers			X	.02§
	Washing clothes			X	.01§
	Scrubbing floors			X	.006§
	Cooking			X	.35§
	Drying dishes			X	.32§
	Cleaning rugs			X	.32§
	Washing windows			X	.01§
	Ironing			X	.04§
	Making beds			X	.03§
	Mending			X	.01§
	Something else around the house which you like to do very much. If so, what? ( )			X¶	.13§
	More than average number checked			X	
	Average number or fewer checked	X			.02

* p based on more than two response categories.
** Trend disappeared when records of workers only between ages of 20 and 25 were analyzed.
† "No" was infrequently chosen and omitted from analysis.
‡ Item checked by only three workers.
§ Analyze with response checked vs. not checked.
¶ These were almost all quiet domestic activities.

TABLE 2—*Continued*

Question	Answer	Monot. Susc.	Middle Group	Non-susc.	p
Do you often quarrel with anyone in your home?	Yes	X			.002
	No			X	
Are you anxious to get away from home?	Yes	X			.005
	No			X	
Do you often quarrel with your mother?	Yes	X			.03
	No			X	
Do you often quarrel with your father?	Yes	X			.04
	No			X	
Have you had any other job, either in the mill or elsewhere, which you prefer to the one you have now?	Yes	X			
	No			X	.0002
Is there anything about the work which you particularly dislike? If so, what? ( )	Yes	X			
	No			X	.002
What part of the day do you enjoy more, the part of the day you spend in the mill?				X	.002
the part of the day you spend away from the mill?		X			
How good do you feel that your job is? Check the opinion which is most like yours. (CHECK ONLY ONE)					
a. I would not stay on my job for a minute if I could get something else. It is very unpleasant work.		X			
b. I would really prefer something else, but it is all right here.		X			
c. I like this job about as well as any job which pays the same.					.003*
d. I like this job better than most jobs I know about.			X		
e. I wouldn't take another job unless it paid a good deal more.			X		
f. I feel that it is the ideal job for me.			X		
Responses a, b, and c		X			.002
Responses d, e, and f			X		
Do you know of any job you would rather have than the one you have, even if the pay were the same?	Yes	X			
	No			X	.007
Is there anything that could be done to make your job more pleasant? If so, what? ( )	Yes	X			
	No			X	.008
Do you like it (the work) better or worse than when you started?	Better			X	
	Worse	X			.02

ony because he daydreams. This hypothesis was rejected by this study, the answers showing an insignificant tendency (8% level) in the other direction. The monotony-susceptible workers tended to daydream more, both in and out of the plant.

Hypothesis IV. The susceptible worker is likely to be extraverted. This suggestion is related to the preceding one, the extravert presumably needing more stimulation from his environment. However, none of the personality-questionnaire items, intended to measure introversion-extraversion, was related to the criterion in this study.

Hypothesis V. The susceptible worker will be more restless in his daily habits and in his leisure-time activities. Two kinds of questions were included to investigate this possibility.

First, questions concerning preference for definite schedules of home duties, walking the same way to school (or work) every day, of preferring to stay home during vacations, etc., had been used as *criterion* questions in several earlier studies.[12] The relationship of feelings of boredom at work to preference for variety in other situations had not been proved, and hence such questions scarcely seemed satisfactory as criteria. Preference for regularity might prove to be a general trait, however, so several such questions were included in the questionnaire. The results were in the direction of the hypothesis for eight of the ten questions, two being indeterminate. A total of all these items was related to the criterion at the 2% level.

Secondly, leisure-time preferences were investigated by two check lists of recreational and housework activities, constructed on the basis of the preliminary interviews. All but four of the 21 activities were checked more frequently by the nonsusceptible group, these 17 including all the housework items and all of the recreational activities which could be performed sitting down, with the exception of reading and driving around in the car, which were checked more frequently by the middle group. The susceptible group, in contrast, preferred dancing or going down town (which in this community meant window shopping). The total number of the items checked was related to the criterion at the 1% level. Since most of these activities were settled and routine, we must consider the hypothesis quite tenable that susceptible workers are more likely to be restless outside the plant than less susceptible workers.

These two groups of items proved not to be significantly related to each other when responses for workers in a restricted age range (20–35) were compared, although each group was still significantly related to the criterion. Differences in living arrangements and personal circumstances may make it possible for workers to develop preferences for irregularity in only limited portions of their lives, or preferences may actually be expressions of two separate traits.

Hypothesis VI. The susceptible worker will be less satisfied with his personal, home, and plant situation in aspects not directly concerned with uniformity or repetitiveness.

Questions concerning personal adjustment included a number from various personality questionnaires, designed to measure so-called neurotic tendencies. Most of these items showed no significant relationship to the criterion. The few differentiating items referred not to neuroticism in general, but to feelings of persistent depression and discouragement, and seemed to concern contentment more than tendency to show other

---

[12] H. Münsterberg, *op. cit.;* L. A. Thompson, Jr., *op. cit.*

neurotic symptoms. The distribution of obtained chi squares does not deviate from chance expectancy sufficiently to be sure that the relationships between these items and the criterion is not merely fortuitous. The consistency of kind of item, however, is encouraging. To a certain extent, then, the discontented persons in this group also found their work monotonous. This finding is probably related to the results concerning more frequent daydreaming in the susceptible group.

Questions concerning home life showed clear-cut relationships to the criterion. All but one of these items discriminated at better than the .05 level of significance, and the total of all at the .0002 level. Home adjustment is a close correlate of susceptibility in this sample.

General work adjustment, similarly, appeared to be closely related to complaints of monotony. Nine of the eleven questions concerning working conditions and work attitudes showed significant relationships at the 10% level or below, the median of the eleven being below the 1% level. For the total group, and also for the group with ages between 20 and 35, relationships among home, personal and work adjustment total scores were compared. All were statistically significant (p less than 5% level). (Extremely unfavorable comments concerning factory conditions and supervision occurred frequently in all criterion groups. Differences in frankness do not, therefore, account for the relationships found among the various kinds of dissatisfaction.) The overlapping was very great here; either feelings of monotony color all of the attitudes of the workers toward their families, personal lives, and work, or these feelings are a reflection of a general dissatisfaction.

Hypothesis VII. The monotony-susceptible workers are more intelligent than the others. Because of the correlation between intelligence and educational level in such groups, and because information concerning educational level could be readily obtained without sacrificing anonymity, educational background was compared with reported monotony for the entire group. Education ranged from fourth grade to two years of college. No significant relationship appeared with the criterion,[13] although there was a slight tendency toward higher educational levels in the nonsusceptible group.

Hypothesis VIII. Feelings of monotony are not merely a function of the task performed, but are related to other more general factors in the individual worker. This hypothesis, of course, underlies the others, and is clearly tenable in view of the number of personal correlates demonstrated in this sample.

----

[13] In an attempt to assess intelligence more directly, a group test was given to workers from the extreme categories. Turnover, transfer, and desire to retain anonymity reduced the groups to eight susceptible and 13 nonsusceptible workers, too few, of course, for drawing of broad generalizations. The median and mean, however, were *higher* for the nonsusceptible than for the susceptible groups, confirming the results obtained with education.

In summary, four kinds of items were to a significant degree negatively related to reports of monotony in this group:

1. Age, which was related to the other personal history items and to some extent to the adjustment or contentment score.

2. Preference for regularity in daily routine.

3. Lack of restlessness as expressed in preference for inactive leisure-time activities.

4. Satisfaction in personal, home, and factory life.

For the homogeneous age group (20–35), combined scores for these last three groups of items concerning preference for regularity, restlessness, and satisfaction proved to have no significant correlation with one another, when tested by the chi-square test (p's $= .52, .43,$ and $.19$). A combined weighted score of these factors clearly separated the criterion groups. Still better separation was achieved by the use of minimum cutting scores based on a pattern analysis.

DISCUSSION

Cross validation, with employees tested before employment, is obviously necessary in a study of this kind, despite the relative specificity of the predictions, to establish generality of relationships and direction of causation. Direct repetition of this study so far has been impossible. Confirmation of the results has, however, come from several sources.

First of all, the negative finding concerning intelligence has considerable support. One early study, that of Thompson,[14] found a slight inverse relationship between intelligence and susceptibility to uniformity. Even the classic study of Wyatt et al.[15] reported such small differences between the most and least bored groups that in only four of the ten comparisons were they statistically significant. Other studies[16] were based on turnover, rather than job satisfaction, and results might well be attributable to more able persons securing better jobs than less able. More recently, Heron[17] has reported results consistent with those of the present study, using male unskilled workers in England. His criterion of job adjustment (a special rating by supervisors) proved, when age and experience were partialled out, not to be predicted by "General Mental Ability." The relationship between intelligence and boredom is by no means established.

The positive findings concerning preferences, personality characteristics, and age have received support from several sources. Five studies have been completed by the writer, using women workers in garment

---

[14] L. A. Thompson, Jr., op. cit.

[15] S. Wyatt, J. N. Langdon, and F. G. L. Stock, op. cit.

[16] W. W. Kornhauser, "Some Business Applications of a Mental Alertness Test," *Journal of Personnel Research*, Vol. 2, 1922, pp. 103–21.

[17] A. Heron, "A Psychological Study of Vocational Adjustment," *Journal of Applied Psychology*, Vol. 36, 1952, pp. 385–87.

factories in various sections of the country, and comparing answers at the time of employment with later absences and with length of service. Results have been very consistent for age at time of employment, it being negatively related to absences and positively related to subsequent length of service up to the age of 45. Preference for regularity and lack of restlessness items predicted only absence rate, and only in the two studies in which the towns had populations of over 25,000. The satisfaction items predicted both absence and length of service in all situations, but to highly variable extents, possibly reflecting differences in the tendencies of applicants in various situations to fake such items. Even this degree of consistency is encouraging, however.

Other investigators have reported supporting evidence concerning the generality of the traits involved. Pierce,[18] using college students, showed a relationship between poor scores on a modification of the home adjustment items and flexibility as measured by Luchins' *Einstellung* test. Bews[19] similarly for college students showed a relationship of poor home adjustment scores to susceptibility to satiation in laboratory tasks. Heron's results are remarkably consistent.[20] In addition to the negative finding concerning intelligence, he reported a positive relationship between job maladjustment and "Emotional Instability" (which included "many Worries"), but *no* relationship with "Neurotic Extraversion" ("Hysteric Tendency"). A fourth factor, "Speed of Approach," not directly comparable to any in the present study, showed low predictive value.

The picture which emerges from these studies of the personality of the person who is satisfied doing repetitive work is one of contentment with the existing state of affairs, placidity, and perhaps rigidity. His satisfaction would seem to be more a matter of close contact with and acceptance of reality than of stupidity or insensitivity.

Since the preference for uniformity in work extends into daily habits outside the work situation, is related to lack of conflict or rebellion in the home, and is correlated with contentment both in the factory and out, feelings of monotony seem to be symptomatic of other discontent and restlessness rather than specific to any particular task.

SUMMARY AND CONCLUSIONS

Responses to questions concerning feelings of monotony and boredom on the job were compared, for a group of 72 women, with answers to other questions designed to test hypotheses derived primarily from accounts of previous writers concerning the personal characteristics as-

---

[18] I. R. Pierce, "A Study of Rigid Behavior and Its Relationship to Concrete and Abstract Thinking" (unpublished doctor's dissertation, Cornell University, 1950).

[19] B. Bews, "An Experimental Investigation of the Concept of Psychical Satiation" (unpublished master's thesis, Cornell University, 1951).

[20] A. Heron, *op. cit.*

sociated with susceptibility to monotony. Four hypotheses were not supported in this study: that the susceptible worker is more ambitious, tends not to daydream, is extraverted, and is more intelligent. Three remained tenable: that the susceptible worker is likely to be young, restless in his daily habits and leisure-time activities, and less satisfied with personal, home, and plant situations in aspects not directly concerned with uniformity or repetitiveness.

On the basis of this and confirming evidence, an eighth hypothesis was considered tenable: that feelings of monotony are not merely a function of the task performed, but are related to more general factors in the individual worker. It was suggested that satisfaction with repetitive work does not necessarily reflect insensitivity and stupidity, as the more romantic textbooks seem to imply.

51. The Curve of Output as a Criterion of Boredom*

Patricia Cain Smith

THE PURPOSE OF this study was to investigate the relationship between the experience of boredom and changes in rate of output or shape of production curves for industrial workers. The classic investigations of the British Industrial Fatigue Research Board[1] have satisfied the writers of our textbooks that the experience of monotony or boredom is characteristically accompanied by changes in the rate of output, and even that the nature of the worker's experience may be identified by examination of the shape of the curve of output. A re-examination of the work of the British investigators was made necessary by certain deviations from normally acceptable methods of scientific investigation, which will be discussed later in this paper.

* From *Journal of Applied Psychology*, Vol. 37, No. 2, 1953, pp. 69–74.

The writer is deeply indebted to Dr. T. A. Ryan for his guidance.

[1] H. M. Vernon, S. Wyatt, and A. D. Ogden, "On the Extent and Effects of Variety in Repetitive Work" (London: Industrial Fatigue Research Board, Report No. 26, 1924); S. Wyatt and J. A. Fraser, "Studies in Repetitive Work with Special Reference to Rest Pauses" (London: Industrial Fatigue Research Board, Report No. 32, 1925); S. Wyatt, J. A. Frazer, and F. G. L. Stock, "The Comparative Effects of Variety and Uniformity in Work" (London: Industrial Fatigue Research Board, Report No. 52, 1928); S. Wyatt, J. A. Frazer, and F. G. L. Stock, "The Effect of Monotony in Work" (London: Industrial Fatigue Research Board, Report No. 56, 1929); S. Wyatt, J. N. Langdon, and F. G. L. Stock, "Fatigue and Boredom in Repetitive Work" (London: Industrial Health Research Board, Report No. 77, 1937).

As early as 1941, Roethlisberger and Dickson failed to duplicate the English results. They stated: "With respect to the monotony hypothesis, no definite conclusion could be drawn. A curve resembling what is claimed to be a typical monotony curve was not encountered except in the case of Operator 1A. It was clearly understood, however, that monotony in work is primarily a state of mind and cannot be assessed on the basis of output alone."[2]

In 1946, Rothe undertook an investigation of the characteristics of production data, recognizing their importance as criteria in a wide variety of industrial investigations. He found that individual daily work curves "may take any of many different forms and do not assume any characteristic, predictable pattern."[3] Correlations of work curves for the same operators for different days varied widely, the median correlation being approximately .05. Rothe averaged work curves for each worker for one week, and obtained trend lines which were classified by inspection. Four of these curves were "mixed curves," two were "fatigue curves" and two were "monotony curves."

Rothe was interested in determining whether knowledge of the production curve for any individual or group for a specific work period would permit prediction of the characteristics of future work curves. Neither he nor Roethlisberger and Dickson attempted to relate the shape of the work curves which they obtained to the experience of the individual worker. Rothe's study, moreover, was performed using hourly-paid workers whose work flowed in a continuous and uninterrupted manner, so that his results could not be directly applied to the very different incentive conditions obtaining for piece-rate workers whose work is grouped into lots or bundles.

Since the existence of any convenient overt indicator of the psychological state of the worker would be of obvious practical importance, and would be highly useful for research purposes as well, the present investigation of the relationship between reported boredom and changes in the curve of output was undertaken. Also included in this investigation were such other proposed behavioral indices of boredom as talking, variability of production, and frequency of voluntary rest pauses.

This study was conducted in a small knit-wear mill in northern Pennsylvania. Most operators in the mill, and all operators studied in detail here, were paid by piece rate. Two operations were chosen for observation. Both were: (1) short enough so that variations in production would show up in the output curves; (2) long enough to permit timing of several operators at once; (3) performed in a uniform manner by several experienced operators; and (4) largely manual, so that the

---

[2] F. J. Roethlisberger and W. J. Dickson, *Management and the Worker* (Cambridge: Harvard University Press, 1941), p. 127.

[3] H. F. Rothe, "Output Rates among Butter Wrappers: I. Work Curves and Their Stability," *Journal of Applied Psychology*, Vol. 30, 1946, p. 209.

operator rather than the machine determined the rate of production. Eight women were engaged in each operation.

THE CRITERION

The subjective feelings of the workers were determined both by interview and by questionnaire. The British investigators used as a criterion of boredom the answers to a series of interview questions. It is not clear how the investigators avoided the influence of suggestion, since many of their questions inquire about the possibility of boredom and mention slowing of work at particular times of the day. A rather strange circularity in their reasoning is also evident. Their criterion of severity of boredom symptoms consisted of a total weighted score on a number of questions "based upon the various symptoms of boredom and discontent observed in previous investigations."[4] These questions included several involving changes in feelings and rate of working with the passage of time. (For example, "Do you think you work better in the morning or the afternoon? Why? When do you think you work best in the morning? Why? In what part of the morning does time seem to pass most quickly? Why? Do you feel bored at any time during the morning? When?" etc.) A report of boredom or slowing of work in the middle of the work spell was considered to be an indication of greater boredom than a report at other periods of time, and was, therefore, weighted more heavily. A total weighted score was thus compiled, and it was against this criterion that the investigators compared their classifications of production curves. It is not, then, startling, that those workers who thought that they slowed in the middle of the working period produced output curves with a sag in the middle, and that the investigators were therefore able to find fairly good agreement between boredom and shape of the output curves.

Such questions from the British list were therefore eliminated. The remainder were further modified so that they could be used in questionnaire form, and several others that seemed relevant were added. The business agent of the union called a special meeting of workers who were not to be part of the major study so that the preliminary form of the questionnaire could be tried out. After several revisions, the questionnaires were administered to seventy-five workers, including those observed in this study. At this point the help of the union was especially important in securing frankness and cooperation. The answers to the criterion questions were item-analyzed against total score, and a weighted criterion score devised.

In addition to the questionnaires, each of the workers was interviewed at least once. They responded quite freely, expressing their attitudes,

---

[4] S. Wyatt, J. N. Langdon, and F. G. L. Stock, "Fatigue and Boredom in Repetitive Work," *op. cit.*, p. 2.

favorable and unfavorable, toward various aspects of the factory situation, and of course, toward management personnel. On the basis of interview and questionnaire data, which agreed closely, the workers were classified according to the degree of their experience of monotony. These classifications were substantiated by gratuitous comments given from time to time during the observations.

PROCEDURE AND RESULTS

The first operation studied involved using a power sewing machine with a specialized folder attachment to hem the bottoms and the sleeves of men's cotton T-shirts. Work was counted in bundles of five dozen, one bundle being completed approximately every half-hour. All workers included in the study had been on the job over a year. Only a few of the operators reached standard. The spread between the guaranteed wage and standard was very large, however, so that almost all workers were receiving piece-rate earnings in addition to the guarantee. Workers, as might be expected, considered standards somewhat "tight, but not out of line" with others in the mill.

Attitudes toward management (and union) varied greatly within the group, several of the workers expressing very strong pro-management opinions and several speaking just as vociferously against company policies. A few questions concerning job satisfaction were included in the questionnaire. Results indicated that job satisfaction was at least fair for the 75 workers questioned. For example, on a scale running from 1 ("I would not stay on my job for a minute if I could get something else") to 6 ("I feel it is the ideal job for me"), the median choice was 3 ("I like this job about as well as any job which pays the same") and 70 per cent checked 3 or better. Furthermore, 90 per cent checked that now they liked their work better than when they started.

Operators were observed continuously for one week. The times were recorded for the beginning and completion of each bundle and the beginning and end of all delays, whether voluntary or caused by conditions beyond the operator's control. Nature of delays was noted, as well as the time of the occurrence of talking and singing.

Figure 1 shows the results of the observations concerning rate of output for one worker for the entire week. This operator had a very high boredom score, and reported on the interview that she was bored "from the first thing in the morning until the mill closes." The ordinates in the figure represent the number of garments sewed per minute, each block representing a bundle of five dozen; units on the base line are ten-minute periods through the working day, which is supposed to extend from 7 to 12 and from 1 to 4:30. It is not clear from the English reports how the investigators handled stoppages for voluntary rest pauses. Rothe[5] pro-rated his curves across the gaps caused by unscheduled pauses. We

---

[5] H. F. Rothe, "Output Rates among Butter Wrappers," *op. cit.*, p. 202.

FIGURE 1

Output Curve for One Week—Operator 7A: Hemming Operation

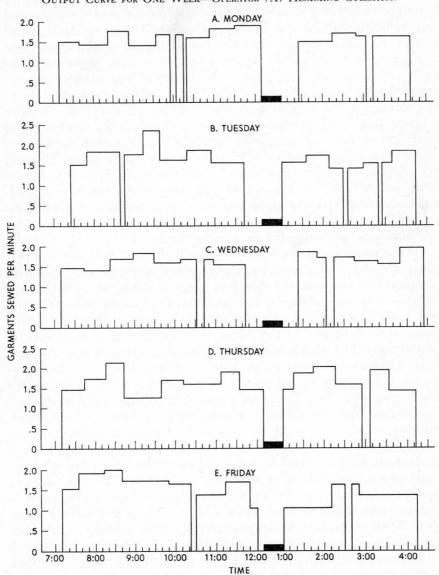

indicated voluntary stops by a drop to the base line, pro-rating the data to form a continuous line when the stoppage was beyond the control of the operator.

These charts illustrate the extreme inconsistency of the shapes of the curves from day to day. Curves for the other workers were equally dissimilar. Wyatt, Langdon, and Stock[6] reported that they kept detailed

---

[6] S. Wyatt, J. N. Langdon, and F. G. L. Stock, "Fatigue and Boredom in Repetitive Work," *op. cit.*

records of output "in some cases . . . over a period of two or three months" for 68 workers. Apparently these daily work curves were averaged to obtain a typical curve for each worker, and were classified according to shape, presumably by inspection. The curve classifications were then compared with their criterion of boredom, with fairly good agreement. Averaging daily figures from the present investigation resulted in a meaningless flat curve in all cases. The weekly averages were thus useless for criterion purposes. It was thought that the averaging process might be obscuring the characteristic shape of the daily curves. Two judges, therefore, attempted independently to classify the daily curves into four categories: (1) gradually ascending curves (the shape classically considered to indicate boredom without fatigue); (2) U-shaped curves (the mixed boredom-fatigue type which was supposed to occur most commonly on monotonous tasks); (3) gradually descending curves (supposed to indicate fatigue); and (4) miscellaneous curves which did not appear to belong in any of the standard classifications (including flat or straight curves).

In the entire group, there was no ascending curve. Judges agreed that there was one possibly U-shaped curve; unfortunately for the hypothesis, however, the operator reported that she was almost never bored, and was not bored that particular afternoon. Each judged approximately one-third of the curves as descending, but judges agreed on less than half of these. The remainder of the curves were considered unclassifiable by both judges. The relationships were not, of course, significantly different from chance when tested by the chi-squared test. It was not possible to utilize correlational techniques for comparing curves, as recommended by Rothe,[7] since these data were gathered in terms of equal work units rather than equal time units. It seemed apparent, however, that the individual work curves could not be reliably classified according to standard categories.

It was considered possible that social groupings were influencing the rates of working, thus accounting for the variability in shapes of work curves from day to day. During working hours workers on this operation formed two clearly defined social groups, with several isolated members. Visits to workers' homes and recreational areas established the fact that social groupings in the plant corresponded only to a minor extent with those formed after working hours. Two judges examined the work curves for each work period and attempted to group together curves of similar shape, disregarding traditional classification systems. Groupings by the judges did not agree to a significant extent. Moreover, the groupings of neither judge agreed with either work or recreational social groupings of the workers. None of these relationships was significantly different from chance when tested by the chi-squared test. Neither in the work nor in the recreational groups was there any evidence that work

---

[7] H. F. Rothe, "Output Rates among Butter Wrappers," *op. cit.*, p. 210.

curves of members resembled one another for the same period of work.

It seemed likely that another operation would yield more traditional results. One was chosen, therefore, in which there were two portions to the task, which could be observed and timed separately. The job was called taping. Two short stiffened pieces of cotton tape were sewed on the unhemmed bottom of the shirt. After the operator finished sewing the bundle, she cut the threads and folded the shirts. Again the operators were timed continuously for one week, and again no characteristic curves were found for cutting, for sewing, or for the two combined. Similarly, there seemed to be no relationship between any daily work curve and the reported feelings of the operator. Again, the only operator who produced either ascending or U-shaped curves reported that, despite the numerous disadvantages of her work and the company, she was certainly not bored. Thus the production curve criteria proved not only unreliable, in that observers could not agree upon classification of curves, but invalid as well.

One of the major difficulties in the use of production curves as criteria lies in the analysis of data. There are no satisfactory statistical measures available for the comparison of the shapes of curves. Interpretation of the results of correlational analyses is sometimes made difficult by the peculiarities of the distributions involved. Moreover, the correlation coefficient cannot allow for over-all similarities in the shapes of the curves, when the changes of slope are displaced slightly in time. The alternative method of visual inspection is subjective and, apparently, unreliable. Both methods show little agreement from day to day, so that even though it could be demonstrated that daily curves reflected the experience of the individual workers, it would be highly unlikely that any long-term relationships could be demonstrated. Their use in this kind of situation appeared to be impractical.

Other changes in behavior which have been related to boredom include frequency of talking, frequency of rest pauses, variability in rate of working, and average speed of working. It was possible to rank the workers within each group on each of these factors and on intensity of boredom symptoms, estimated from both questionnaire scores and interview responses. The rankings were compared and the relationships tested for significance by Kendall's non-parametric tau test.[8] No significant or even consistent relationship appeared between the boredom symptoms and the proposed indices. Reliability of the behavioral indices was estimated by comparing total rankings for each worker on Monday, Tuesday and Wednesday with the totals for Thursday and Friday. All of these relationships proved significant at the 5 per cent level or better by Kendall's tau test. Individual differences were, therefore, reasonably stable throughout the week.

---

[8] N. G. Kendall, *The Advanced Theory of Statistics* (London: Charles Griffin and Company, 1945), pp. 403–8.

DISCUSSION

Why were these results so different from those of the British Industrial Research Board? In the first place, comments of the workers showed that each had her own concept of the number of bundles that she should complete in a day. If she was behind schedule, she hurried toward the end of the day; if she was ahead, she slackened speed or stopped entirely. One operator, who had just completed all but one of her customary bundles for the day, commented, "You've seen how fast we can do them. Now do you want to see how slow?" Production figures reflected quite clearly what the workers considered to be the proper pace for them at that particular time, but not at all necessarily the way they felt about their work.

It has been the observation of the writer that such pacing of work occurs with much greater frequency in industrial situations than does spontaneous variation in rate. Even when there is no restriction due to fear of rate-cutting, it is normal for any worker to decide in advance how much he will produce, and earn, each day. Effort is unquestionably pegged, at least within narrow ranges, in most industrial situations.

A careful re-examination of the English studies suggests several differences in method which perhaps further account for the discrepancy between our results and theirs. The most serious has already been mentioned; they included in their criterion, items which were related to changes of rate of working, and weighted these items in the direction favorable to their hypothesis. The reader is not told, moreover, whether or not their curves were classified without knowledge of the accompanying verbal reports. Several other factors apparently operated to make the shape of their curves more consistent from day to day. Although they do not specify the kinds of jobs involved, one would infer from comparison of the various reports that at least six different operations were involved, with various hours of work and methods of payment. Such variations in jobs and conditions would tend to mask individual variability.

One last factor should be noted. There is no indication in any of their data of voluntary rest pauses, even for rest-room visits. If decreases in production due to such work stoppages were averaged into their curves, this procedure would account for the consistency of the curves from day to day, as well as for the preponderance of U-shaped curves, since rest-room and water fountain visits tend to be made at about the same time every day, and mostly in the middle of the work period.

SUMMARY

Continuous observation of two groups of eight women each, operating power sewing machines on light, uniform and repetitive work, led to the following conclusions:

1. There were fairly stable individual differences in speed of working, variability of production, frequency of rest pauses, and frequency of talking.

2. These differences showed no consistent relationship to the reports of the workers concerning their feelings of boredom or monotony.

3. No shape of work curve was found which would characterize the individual worker.

4. Work curves for individuals forming social groups showed no observable relationship with each other.

5. The approach of the closing hour had a noticeable effect on the production of many of the workers. The direction of the change in rate which appeared at the end of the day was determined by the concept of a day's work held by the worker.

6. Boredom is not necessarily accompanied by a depression in the curve of output, nor is a sag necessarily accompanied by feeling of boredom.

7. Output curves should be viewed with caution as indications of the subjective feelings of the worker.

There can be little quarrel with the claim of the British investigators that, other factors being equal, workers tend to slow down, talk, become restless and variable in their production when bored. In most industrial situations, however, one cannot assume that all other factors are equal, and many of these factors may heavily outweigh the influence of interest or boredom in producing changes in working behavior.

52. Authorized and Unauthorized Rest Pauses in Clerical Work*

William McGehee and Edwin B. Owen

HERSEY,[1] VERNON,[2] and others have demonstrated that workers employed in light and heavy industrial work manage to take rest pauses even when such rest pauses are not authorized by the employer. The

* From *Journal of Applied Psychology*, Vol. 24, 1940, pp. 605–14.

[1] R. B. Hersey, "Rest—Authorized and Unauthorized," *Journal of Personnel Research*, Vol. 4, 1925, pp. 37–45.

[2] H. M. Vernon, T. Bedford, and C. G. Warner, "Rest Pauses in Heavy and Moderately Heavy Industrial Work" (London: Industrial Fatigue Research Board, Report No. 41, 1927).

majority of investigators, as Viteles[3] points out in his excellent summary of the research on rest pauses, have indicated that authorized rest pauses increase both production and worker morale. However, it is generally assumed that authorized rest pauses are effective only when the time used for them is not added to the length of the day's work and the employee is not penalized in any way by the introduction of such pauses. In fact, Presgrave warns, "Do not make the worker earn his rest pauses, at least at the outset. If the operator is paid while resting, he will do much better while working."[4]

Much of the data on rest pauses has come from the study of light and heavy industrial workers. No direct evidence is available that similar conditions prevail in the case of clerical workers. The present investigation has as one of its purposes to determine the extent of unauthorized rest pauses among clerical workers and their relationship to production. A second purpose of the investigation is to determine the effect on the amount of unauthorized rest and on production of the introduction of authorized rest pauses when the amount of time used for the authorized rest is added to the length of the working day. The present investigators realize that, as Roethlisberger and Dickson[5] have shown, production depends on other things than the nature of rest periods. The results and conclusions coming from this study are stated with this acknowledged limitation.

The subjects in this study were sixteen female comptometer operators employed in the North Carolina office of the Agricultural Adjustment Administration. The median age of the group was 22.5 years with a quartile deviation of 1.5 years and a range of 18 to 39 years. Two of the operators had had no previous work experience before their present employment by the agency. All of the sixteen operators, however, were high school graduates and all but one of them had completed a twelve weeks' course in comptometer operation. The median experience of the group as comptometer operators was thirteen months with a quartile deviation of 7.5 months and a range of one month to 50 months.

These operators were all engaged in computing applications for crop loans. These applications were all very similar in nature and required similar amounts of work. A record of the number of applications worked by each operator each day was kept by the office manager. These records, with slight modifications as explained later, served as a basis for estimating production in this investigation.

The operators spent seven hours each day at work on the applications,

---

[3] M. S. Viteles, *Industrial Psychology* (New York: W. W. Norton & Co., 1932), pp. 470–82.

[4] R. Presgrave, "Frequent Rest Periods for Workers Prevent Fatigue and Increase Production," *Textile World*, Vol. 80, 1931, p. 1524.

[5] F. J. Roethlisberger and W. J. Dickson, *Management and the Worker* (Cambridge: Harvard University Press, 1939).

five days a week. They worked only four hours on Saturday. The only official rest pause in the day's work was a 45 minute intermission for lunch. The operators, however, were not forbidden to leave the room in which they all worked during working hours, although the practice was discouraged by the office manager.

All observations throughout the experiment of unauthorized rest pauses taken by the operators were made by the junior author. He was, during and sometime prior to the investigation, an employee of the agency and had his desk in the room in which the operators worked. His desk was located where he could easily see all the operators. He, therefore, was able to secure data on unauthorized rest pauses without any of the operators being aware of his mission. In order to facilitate the keeping of this record, he prepared, for each day of the experiment, a chart giving the names of the operators in code and dividing the working days into hour periods. On this chart, he marked down for each operator the time of day at which an unauthorized rest period began and the time at which it ended. From this record was computed the amount of time spent each day by each operator in unauthorized rest.

The criterion of unauthorized rest was taken as that of actual departure from the work room. The observer spent approximately two weeks prior to the period in which the data presented in this investigation were collected in perfecting his techniques of observation and in timing the duration of unauthorized rest pauses.

The authors believe that, due to the careful supervision of the operators, the criterion of unauthorized rest as stated in the preceding paragraph was adequate. In order to check this assumption, during the two weeks preceding the period of the actual experiment, the observer used a modified time sampling technique similar to that employed in the study of child behavior. He observed at ten minute intervals throughout an entire day the behavior of an operator and wrote down exactly what she was doing. Each subject in the study was observed in this manner for at least one day and records on five subjects were obtained for two days. The data thus gathered seem to indicate that the time spent in unauthorized rest pauses was consumed in actual absences from the work room.

At the end of the two weeks devoted to perfecting the experimental techniques, observations, in the manner previously described, were taken for a two week's period in which the only authorized rest was the 45 minute noon recess. At the end of this period, the office manager announced that the following Monday rest periods, one from 10:22 to to 10:30 A.M. and one from 2:23 to 2:30 P.M., would be inaugurated.[6] The manager explained that the time, 15 minutes, consumed by the rest

---

[6] Rest pauses were located at these times on the basis of a study of the time at which unauthorized rest was most frequently taken.

pauses would have to be added to the working day. He explained the purpose of the rest pauses as being an effort to improve working conditions and urged cooperation from the workers. He also told them that he had made arrangements with a nearby drug store for refreshments to be sent which the operators could purchase during these periods if they so desired. The time added to the working day extended the working time from 4:15 P.M. to 4:30 P.M. on Monday through Friday and from 12:30 to 12:38 on Saturday.

It was believed best to allow the operators time to adjust to this new system of authorized rest pauses; no records taken for the week subsequent to the introduction of rest pauses, therefore, are used in this investigation. It is entirely possible that a week was too short a time for adequate adjustment, but due to the fact that the operators were soon to be put on different types of calculations, it was impossible to allow a longer adjustment period.

After the week of adjustment, the observer, for the two subsequent weeks, kept records of the amount of unauthorized rest under conditions of authorized rest, *i.e.*, 8 minute rest period in the morning and 7 minute rest period in the afternoon with a 15 minute longer working day. The procedure of making observations during this period was identical with that used during the two week period of no authorized rest pauses. In subsequent discussion of the results, the period of no authorized rest pauses is designated as *the first period* and the period of authorized rest pauses as *the second period*.

Table 1 presents a comparison of the amount of time spent in un-

TABLE 1

A COMPARISON OF THE TIME IN UNAUTHORIZED REST UNDER
CONDITIONS OF UNAUTHORIZED AND OF
AUTHORIZED REST PAUSES
Time Given in Terms of Minutes Spent by Each Operator
per HourWorked in Unauthorized Rest*
(16 subjects)

Period	Mean	Standard Deviation	Critical Ratio
First................3.01		0.71	9.00
Second...............1.21		0.83	

* The r between unauthorized time spent in rest pauses in the first and second periods is .50.

authorized rest periods by the sixteen operators during the first and second periods of this investigation. The time spent by each operator in unauthorized rest has been reduced to the average number of minutes spent in unauthorized rest per hour worked. This seemed a preferable way to present the data rather than in terms of time per day, as in two days in each of the periods, the operators worked only four hours.

It is obvious from these data that less time is consumed in unauthorized rest by operators under conditions of authorized rest than under conditions of no authorized rest. It would seem, then, that it would be advantageous to introduce rest pauses under the conditions of this experiment if the sole purpose of such a policy were to reduce the amount of unauthorized rest.

One of the problems of this investigation is to determine the effect on production of the introduction of rest pauses under the conditions of adding the amount of time spent in such pauses to the working day. Records of production of the operators in terms of number of applications worked per day by each operator were secured from the office manager for both the first and second period of the investigation. The average number of applications computed per hour by each operator was calculated.

Although the applications were very similar, it was thought that some difference in those computed in the first period and second period might exist. Accordingly, a correction formula, based on the analysis of the applications worked, was derived and this formula was used to equate the relative difficulty of the applications worked in the different periods. The number of applications worked as reported in subsequent tables are the number worked in terms of the use of the correction formula. There is, of course, some source of error in making such a correction; however, the errors, if they do exist, are very small and would not influence the results of the investigation.

Table 2 presents a comparison of the production of the operators, after

TABLE 2

A COMPARISON OF THE PRODUCTION IN TERMS OF APPLICATIONS COMPUTED PER HOUR PER OPERATOR UNDER CONDITIONS OF UNAUTHORIZED AND OF AUTHORIZED REST PAUSES*
(16 subjects)

Period	Mean	Standard Deviation	Critical Ratio
First...........	20.38	7.34	5.92
Second..........	26.19	8.78	

* The r between production in the first and second period is .79.

the corrections were made as described in the preceding paragraph, for the first and second period of this investigation.

It is apparent from the data in Table 2 that the actual number of applications computed per hour under conditions of authorized rest pauses in this investigation is greater than that when no authorized pauses are allowed. The critical ratio is almost twice as large as that which is commonly accepted as indicative of statistical reliability.

It would seem, then, that rest pauses which are authorized, although the time consumed by them is added to the length of the day's work, result both in a decrease in the amount of unauthorized rest and an increase in the amount of production. In order to determine the reaction of the operators to the policy of authorized rests, a questionnaire was submitted to the group. This questionnaire was presented by the office manager at the end of the second period with the explanation that he desired the opinion of the operators regarding the policy of authorized rest pauses. The operators were instructed not to sign their names and that no attempt would be made to identify the respondents. The questionnaire is reproduced below with the number of operators giving each answer to each of the questions.

In general, the answers to the questionnaire indicate that the operators were not very favorably disposed toward the policy of authorized rest pauses as used in this investigation. Only six of the sixteen operators approved them while nine would prefer to return to the former system of unauthorized rest. The responses to questions five and six are not consistent with the general trend of the responses to the other questions. A possible explanation of this inconsistency is found in the complaints about the crowded condition of the rest room during the authorized

TABLE 3

Questionnaire Submitted to Operators and Summary of Answers
(Numerals Indicate Number of Operators Making Each Answer)

Please answer the following questions by checking (√) what you consider to be the correct answer. *Do not sign your name.*

1. Do you approve of the recently started system of a specific period for rest?

    Yes   6
    No   7
    Uncertain   3

2. Do you prefer scheduled rest periods to taking time out for rest at no specific time?

    Yes   6
    No   10
    Uncertain   0

3. Would you like to return to the former system of having no specific rest periods?

    Yes   9
    No   6
    Uncertain——(1 no answer)

4. Do you believe that specified rest periods are an undue interference with your personal freedom?

    Yes   2
    No   13
    Uncertain   1

5. Do you believe the specified rest periods are a good thing when the time taken out for them has to be added (due to government regulations) to the working day (*i.e.*, quitting at 4:15)?

    Yes   12
    No   4
    Uncertain   0

TABLE 3—*Continued*

6. Do you believe the specified rest periods would be more satisfactory if the time consumed by them was not added to the working day?

   Yes   5
   No   8
   Uncertain   3

7. How would you describe the efficiency of your work under the present system of
   fixed rest periods as compared with the former system of no fixed rest periods?

   More efficient   5
   Less efficient   1
   Of the same efficiency   10

8. How would you describe your degree of tiredness at the end of the day's work under
   the present system of fixed rest periods as compared with the previous system of no
   fixed rest periods?

   More tired   0
   Less tired   5
   No difference   11

9. Would you be in favor of lengthening the rest periods to 10 minutes each, with the
   time added on to the working day?

   Yes   2
   No   12
   Uncertain   2

10. Do you think the rest periods are sufficient to take care of all the necessary time out of
    the room?

    Yes   7
    No   8
    Uncertain   1

In a few words, describe as well as you can your personal reaction to the present system of fixed rest periods.
Give any unfavorable criticisms, favorable comments, or suggestions for improvement you may have:

7 mentioned crowded rest rooms as an objection.
3 approved of the present system.
6 gave no answer.

rest pauses. This explanation gains force in view of conversations held
with the operators by the junior author in which he found the principal
complaint was concerning the crowded rest room. It would seem, then,
that the unfavorable attitude of the operators toward authorized rests,
as defined in this study, was not directed so much against the addition
of 15 minutes to the working day as against certain conditions surrounding the rest periods.

The number of subjects in this experiment precludes any significant
results from correlational analysis of the data. It is interesting to note,
however, that there is a rank order difference correlation between production and amount of time spent in unauthorized rest of $-.54 \pm .13$
during the first period of this investigation. This correlation was reduced
to $-.34 \pm .16$ in the second period.

It was not possible, due to government regulations, to perform the
crucial experiment in this investigation, *i.e.*, a system of authorized rest
pauses, without increasing the length of the working day. In industrial
work, there is evidence that this would bring increased production.
There is some evidence that the same condition might prevail in the case
of clerical workers from an investigation made in the offices of the

T. V. A. Authority.[7] This study shows an increase of 3 per cent in the volume of work done by classifiers, a reduction of 50 per cent in filing errors, and an increased group morale with the introduction of rest pauses which decreased the actual working time 6 per cent.

The results of the present investigation, within the limits indicated in the description of the procedures used, seem to indicate that both unauthorized rest can be reduced and production can be increased by authorized rest pauses even when the worker is made to pay for his rest by a longer working day. They further indicate that conditions under which the authorized rest is taken must be made as free from sources of irritation as possible if the worker is to accept the policy without undue dissatisfaction. Finally, the results indicate that in clerical as well as in industrial work, employees secure rest pauses even if they are not specifically granted by the management.

53. Shift Work and Human Efficiency*

Wallace Bloom

SINCE THE END of World War II, the need for shift workers has been rapidly expanding, both in the services and in industry. Our national defense now requires constant operational manning of missile bases, air-warning nets, communication facilities, base-security systems, and the like. And in industry, and particularly the chemical, metallurgical, and atomic industries, modern technology poses the same necessity for round-the-clock, seven-day-a-week operations.

Finding the most effective way of scheduling and assigning shift work is a problem with a direct bearing, therefore, on both our national security and our continued economic progress. Thus far, however, the attempts to solve it seem to have given insufficient attention to one of its most important aspects—the effects of shift work upon the biological rhythm of workers.

By habitually observing socially determined schedules specifying the hours for work, play, meals, and sleep, man has developed a diurnal rhythm—that is, a regularly recurring day-night variation in the chemical constituents of the blood and in the activity of the liver, kidneys, and

---

[7] (ANOM.), "Rest Periods—Experiments Conducted at the Tennessee Valley Authority's office," *Management Review*, Vol. 27, 1938, p. 153.

* From "Shift Work and the Sleep-Wakefulness Cycle," *Personnel*, Vol. 38, 1961, pp. 24–31.

endocrine glands. It should be emphasized that this is not something with which we are born—it is induced by our observance of a particular pattern of sleep and activity. As our rhythm attains a degree of autonomy, it makes it easier for us to stay awake during certain hours of the day and harder for us to do so at other times.

Our diurnal rhythm also imposes a corresponding periodic character on our efficiency. This was shown as far back as 1906 in the tests of sensory activity, motor activity, and simple mental activity carried out by Marsh.[1] More recently, on the basis of a 20-year study of Munich industries, Lehman established a positive relation between efficiency and the amount of adrenaline in the blood.[2] And Kleitman, the recognized authority on sleep and wakefulness, has demonstrated that there is a marked inverse relation between reaction time and body temperature.[3] Reaction time is a good measure of alertness, while body temperature, which fluctuates through a range of about 2° F. each day, provides an accurate reflection of the rhythmic metabolic changes, for it reaches its low point between 2 and 5 A.M. and its high point in mid-afternoon. According to Kleitman's findings, we are most alert at the high point of our daily temperature curve and least alert at the low point.

But a particular temperature curve, like the rhythm of which it is an index, will eventually be altered if the day-night schedule that originally established it is replaced by a new one. As Kleitman points out:

If [a man] remains awake during the entire night, both temperature and performance fall below their drowsiness levels, reaching minima between 2:00 A.M. and 4:00 A.M., when it is hardest to keep awake. Then there begins an upswing which crosses the drowsiness level at the usual getting-up time. . . . The curve can be shifted, inverted, distorted, shortened, or lengthened, by following a new schedule of activities for a certain number of weeks.[4]

The fixity of any individual's temperature curve is thus a simple measure of the degree to which he has adapted to a particular time cycle. When he is suddenly subjected to a new 24-hour schedule—as happens when a worker is assigned to a new shift—we can expect that his temperature curve will change, with the high point moving toward his activity period. This assumption has been confirmed by studies of the physiological effects of long-distance flights. The results are of course the same whether the new time schedule is imposed by shift rotation or by geographical change.

---

[1] H. D. Marsh, *The Diurnal Course of Efficiency* ("Archives of Philosophy, Psychology, and Scientific Methods," No. VII) (New York: Columbia University Press, 1906), p. 95.

[2] G. Lehman, "Diurnal Rhythm in Relation to Working Capacity," *Acta Medica Scandanavica* (Suppl. 278), CXLV, pp. 108–9.

[3] N. Kleitman, *Sleep and Wakefulness* (Chicago: University of Chicago Press, 1939), p. 220.

[4] Kleitman, "The Sleep-Wakefulness Cycle of Submarine Personnel," *Human Factors in Undersea Warfare*, Navy Department, Washington, D.C., 1949, pp. 329–30.

WHEN THE RHYTHM IS DISRUPTED

Until the adjustment has been completed, the individual will suffer a discrepancy between his accustomed sleep-wakefulness cycle and the one required by his new environment. Strughold has called this discrepancy "incomplete time or cycle adaptation."[5]

The effect of this discrepancy on shift workers, and particularly on rotating-shift workers, should perhaps be spelled out here. As we have seen, efficiency is directly related to diurnal rhythm. The worker suffering incomplete time adaptation therefore undergoes not only some physical discomfort but a loss in efficiency, for his body and mind are most ready to perform well at hours when he is off duty, or at only a few of his on-duty hours. Thus shift rotation, which at first glance seems so eminently fair because it provides for the equal sharing of the inconvenience of night work, imposes a physiological hardship on all the workers every time the shifts are changed and may lead to a general decrease in efficiency.

How long incomplete time adaptation persists has not yet been determined, but it is known that a flight across the Atlantic, which occasions a gain or loss of five hours, generally requires an adjustment period of a week or more. A change to a work shift six hours earlier or later than one's previous shift, even if it is preceded by a 24-hour rest period, must therefore impose an incomplete-adaptation period of at least several days. At all events, it seems certain that rotating the shifts at whatever time interval is most convenient administratively does not result in optimal performance and that many companies rotate their shifts too frequently for the adaptive powers of the employees concerned.

Besides the length of the adaptation period, several questions about the adaptation process itself are worthy of further study. Does the adaptation proceed at a constant, gradual rate—say, one hour or two hours each day? Or is it irregular or even spasmodic—with no change occurring for the first several days and an abrupt change thereafter? Are there setbacks in the course of the adaptation—that is, reversions toward the original cycle? Research must provide the answers to these questions if management is to improve its shift scheduling to secure the highest possible degree of alertness on the part of the workers.

What we already know about the sleep-wakefulness cycle, however, affords a basis for several improvements upon current practice. The following suggestions will illustrate how the findings of physiological research might be applied by industry:

1. *Selection of Individuals for Rotating Shifts.* It has been established that people vary in their ability to modify their diurnal rhythms. Some

---

[5] H. Strughold, *The Physiological Day-Night Cycle in Global Flights*, U.S.A.F. School of Aviation Medicine, Randolph Field, Tex., 1952, p. 2.

can adjust to a six-hour change in about a week; others find the adaptation very difficult. Kleitman and a companion once experimented with living an artificial six-day week. After six weeks, Kleitman was still experiencing seven temperature cycles a week, while his partner had changed to six.

"Since an individual's curve of performance follows his body-temperature curve," he recommended, "considerations of efficiency in doing work, in addition to purely humanitarian reasons, demand that the services concerned employ for night duty, or other abnormal shifts, only individuals who are capable of shifting or inverting their body temperatures on short notice."[6]

The problem of adaptation is doubly severe under shift rotation, for the workers involved must adapt both to the rotation itself and to night work. Companies that use this system should therefore carry out tests of the candidates' adaptability to these changes. The tests could take the form of measuring their temperatures after an experimental six- or eight-hour change in shifts or a change to night hours. When the men have spent a week or ten days on the new shift, the adaptability of their temperature curves can then be determined.

2. *Special Training and Conditioning for Shift Work.* Training programs for shift workers should include sessions at which physicians explain the diurnal rhythm and what happens in shift changes and during night work. The workers should also be told how they can best arrange their time-off activities for easing the adjustment to the new hours and getting to sleep during daylight hours. During the training period, the company should institute a gradual transition to the time schedule on which they will be working—by shifting their schedule one hour each day, for instance.

3. *Fixed Shifts Instead of Rotating Shifts.* Companies now using rotating shifts should review their scheduling problem to determine whether fixed shifts can be substituted. If they do decide to switch, they should explain all the reasons for their decision to the men involved.

The advantages of such a change were demonstrated in 1956 by an overseas military communications center. Partly on the advice of this writer but primarily because of a personnel shortage, the center abandoned its rotating four-shift schedule in favor of a fixed schedule of three shifts—from midnight to 7:30 A.M., from 7:30 to 4:30 P.M. (including time for a noon meal), and from 4:30 to midnight. The results proved beneficial in a number of ways. Performance improved as the men became familiar with the variations in work load peculiar to their shift. They grew accustomed to eating at the same time every day, and they no longer had to look at a calendar to ascertain which hours and days they were scheduled to work.

---

[6] Kleitman, *Sleep and Wakefulness*, p. 267.

When some men were transferred and had to be replaced, the senior workers were given the option of changing their shifts. Most of them turned it down. The new men, though they did not like the system at first, soon adjusted to the schedule and fitted in well. Even those who had been accustomed to rotating shifts at their previous stations and were greatly upset by the new arrangement when they first arrived liked it better after a while.

The use of fixed shifts at this center also eased the manpower shortage: whereas 39 men had formerly been assigned to each shift to allow for rotation, the fixed shifts managed with from 33 to 39 men, according to the work load. The responsibility for setting the days-off schedule was given to the shift supervisors, and most men got two successive days off each week.

4. *Fewer Shift Rotations.* If rotating shifts prove unavoidable, the changes should be made infrequently. Rotating the assignments once a month rather than once a week (as many companies now do) would reduce the number of drastic physiological adjustments required of the workers from 52 to 12 a year. Since it takes air travelers at least a week to adjust to a six-hour change, we can expect that workers whose hours have been similarly altered are still suffering incomplete time adjustment on the third day of their new shift, when, in many companies, they once again have to change their working hours. The crews of transoceanic planes, Strughold recommended, should not be subjected to this change too often; and if they are regularly flying back and forth, they should be allowed to maintain the diurnal cycle of their home continent.

5. *Longer Rest Periods between Shift Changes.* Shift schedules should also be arranged to allow a maximum of time off between changes. With a reduction in the number of shift changes, it might be possible to allow workers as many as three days off.

6. *Shorter Time for the Graveyard Shift.* Since the early-morning shift (from midnight onwards, say) is the period when it is most difficult to keep alert, shortening it would probably improve efficiency, as well as reduce the stress on the workers. A company with a four-shift cycle could cut the graveyard shift down to five hours by simply adding 20 minutes to each of the other three shifts.

7. *More Attention to Personnel Problems.* Even with the aid of selection tests, no company can expect that it will assign to shift work only those employees who can make a healthy adjustment to it. Diagnostic interviews should therefore be held with shift workers who have accidents or show an above-average number of sick reports so that those with psychological difficulties can be weeded out.

These recommendations, derived as they are from the findings of physiological research, may perhaps seem somewhat unrelated to the practical requirements of a company that cannot confine its operations to a one-shift, five-day week. They are supported, however, by the findings of numerous studies of the effects of shift work, and particularly of shift rotation and night work, on the workers involved. Some of the more pertinent of these findings may be summarized.

In a survey of shift-work patterns among 50 large American companies in 1951, the National Industrial Conference Board found that fixed shifts were more usual than rotating shifts on a five-day operation with two or three shifts and that among companies with a rotating-shift system the rotation was generally on a weekly or fortnightly basis.[7] Some companies, the study found, added an extra (and versatile) man to each crew, so that it could work throughout the week while individual members still had regular days off. With seven men for every six jobs, say, there could be one man off each day, the extra man filling in for him; the latter, of course, would also get one day off a week.

RESEARCH ON SHIFT WORK

The effects of various shift-work patterns have been studied in a number of countries, and from several points of view. Among American studies, two should be mentioned here. The first was concerned with the effects on a group of women workers of a change from a single nine-hour shift to two alternating six-hour shifts. Under the new system, some of the women, who worked in the morning for one week and in the afternoon for the next, reported difficulty in adjusting their habits of eating and sleeping. The second study found that workers whose shifts were changed found it even harder to adjust to the change in mealtimes than to get enough sleep. Of the workers questioned, 62 per cent complained of this difficulty, and 35 per cent said the adjustment took them more than four days.

In Sweden, researchers found many instances of failure to adjust to changing shifts. The shift workers, they pointed out, were being forced to live in a different time sequence from that of their community and of the many people to whom they were intimately related. In a study of errors made in entering figures in the ledgers of a large Swedish gas works under a rotating three-shift system, it was found that a very high number of errors occurred around 3 A.M. (The night shift ran from 10 P.M. to 6 A.M.) The number of errors did not vary significantly either by season or by day of the week. Moreover, the same variation in errors appeared on the last night of the week as on the first, indicating that the plant's weekly rotation system was not allowing the workers enough time to change the general pattern of their diurnal rhythm.[8]

Reviewing the findings of German research, Pierach reported one study that found ulcers eight times more common among shift workers than among day workers and another that found them four times more

---

[7] See H. P. Northrup, *Shift Problems and Practices* ("Studies in Personnel Policy," No. 118). National Industrial Conference Board, Inc., New York.

[8] B. Bjerner *et al.*, "Diurnal Variation in Mental Performance," *British Journal of Industrial Medicine*, April, 1955, pp. 103–10. (Also reviewed in *National Safety News*, September, 1955, pp. 55–56.)

common.[9] Of the 170 shift workers covered by still another study he mentioned, half gave up shift work because of ulcers. Only about 50 per cent of night workers can change to day work in one week, Pierach maintained, also noting that the loss of man-days through illness was greater in a three-shift than in a two-shift activity. During World War II, some industries in Bavaria instituted a rotation system called the flying shift change, under which the crews worked for 12 hours and then had 24 hours off. This practice, however, had adverse effects on the workers' health.

A negative report on another scheduling system, the split shift, comes from a paper on the experience of the British munitions industries during the First World War. This system, under which a crew might work from 6 to 10 A.M. and then from 2 to 6 P.M., was very unpopular with workers, says the bulletin.

Finally, Japanese researchers have reported that officers engaged in coastal navigation lost sleep under a shift system and suffered chronic fatigue.

RESEARCH ON NIGHT WORK

Having to be awake during the usual hours for sleep poses a number of special problems, whether the workers involved are on a fixed night shift or are serving night duty on a rotating shift.

Perhaps the most obvious of these is the difficulty of getting enough sleep during the daytime. Of the workers questioned in a study by Maier, 42 per cent said that when they were on the night shift they did not sleep enough by day, and 75 per cent said they got less than eight hours' sleep a day.[10]

Of the night workers covered in a German study reviewed by Pierach, slightly less than half reported getting more than five hours' sleep a day. The workers also complained of sleepiness, headaches, and a loss of ability to concentrate. Errors and accidents were more frequent during night work than during day work, the same study found. Some other effects of night work have also been reported by Pierach. A study of nurses on a night shift found that they suffered loss of appetite (as demonstrated by weight) and digestive interruptions, and that there was too much acid in their small intestines. Doctors have recommended that an ulcer patient be removed from night shifts. And, of the night workers studied in one investigation, 25 per cent eventually gave up night work.

Similar data have been supplied by two studies of British industry. One cites as the main objection to night work the inability of workers to obtain adequate sleep by day. This problem may be attributable to

---

[9] See A. Pierach, "Biological Rhythm-Effects of Night Work and Shift Changes on the Health of Workers," *Acta Medica Scandanavica* (Suppl. 307), CLII.

[10] N. R. F. Maier, *Psychology in Industry*. (2d ed.; Boston: Houghton Mifflin Co., 1955), p. 450.

the disruption of the workers' ordinary habits, the paper suggests, or its causes may be social—noises and disturbances, or the responsibility of caring for one's children. The workers studied said they were often tempted to curtail their period of sleep in order to join the family midday meal or to obtain some recreation. The study of munitions industries mentioned above found that it was difficult for night workers to consume substantial food at an unfamiliar meal hour and that their digestion was likely to be upset.

Further word on the sleep problem has come from some investigators in the United States who point out that the night workers's sleep is likely to be disturbed by the presence of daylight and the extra noise and heat of the daytime. Their studies have convinced them that work should never be scheduled for the nighttime.

Since loss of sleep has been found to be so prevalent among night workers, its physiological effects deserve further mention.

In 1951, research psychologists at Tufts College conducted an experimental study of the effects of loss of sleep on subjective feelings.[11] As might be expected, of the 415 college undergraduates who participated, those who slept between eight and nine hours each day felt much better than those who slept only six hours. Subjects who went without sleep for long periods of time reported that feelings of sleepiness came in waves, reaching their peak between 3 and 6 A.M. The subjects also felt irritable and noted that their ability to carry out tasks requiring attention and effort had decreased. The 17 subjects who remained awake for 100 hours were restless as well, and complained of headaches. They did not recover until they had lived and slept normally for one week.

In a study of the effects of loss of sleep and rest on air crews, McFarland found that loss of sleep had marked effects on performance on mental tests requiring prolonged effort and continuous attention.[12] The most striking changes were loss of memory, hallucinations, heightened irritability, and wide fluctuations in emotional state.

The correlation between loss of sleep and loss of efficiency at tasks requiring continuous attention has been confirmed by other studies, though it is also known that short tasks may be performed with little diminution of efficiency over a considerable time. In general, the quality of work suffers more than the quantity.

THE NEED TO RESPECT RHYTHM

To sum up, then, most shift workers experience serious inconveniences of two kinds: disruption of their normal diurnal body rhythms and,

---

[11] Tufts College: Institute for Applied Experimental Psychology, *Handbook of Human Engineering Data*. Special Devices Center, Office of Naval Research, Port Washington, N.Y., Part VII, Chap. II, Sec. I, Data T. 1–6.

[12] R. A. McFarland, *Human Factors in Air Transportation* (New York: McGraw-Hill Book Co., Inc., 1953), p. 343.

largely as a result of this disruption, loss of sleep resulting in fatigue. The effects of fatigue are cumulative and, to make matters worse, frequently show no obvious sign, so that a man's performance may be severely impaired without his being aware of it.

The need to respect the normal diurnal rhythm has been forcefully expressed by Pierach: "No organ or organ system is exempt from the 24-hour rhythm in its function. . . . Rhythm heals; continued activities contrary to rhythm make one weak and sick."[13]

For centuries now, men have studied the ebb and flow of the oceans and have used the knowledge thus gained to schedule the comings and goings of ships with a high degree of exactitude. By comparison, we still have much to learn about the tides within the human body—and what little we do know is still not being used to schedule the activities of men to best advantage. It is to be hoped that with further research and experimentation we shall ultimately be able to design shift-work schedules that will insure maximum efficiency and a minimum of personal hardship.

54. Effects of Noise Reduction in a Work Situation*

D. E. Broadbent and E. A. J. Little

INTRODUCTION

THE PRESENT STATE of knowledge concerning effects of noise on man has been reviewed by Broadbent.[1] Roughly speaking, it is that results of laboratory experiments have now established that an effect of high intensity, meaningless, and continuous noise may appear on working efficiency in laboratory tasks which are long and require continuous attention. The effect of the noise is to increase the frequency of momentary lapses in efficiency rather than to produce decline in rate of work, gross failures of co-ordination, or similar inefficiency. Effects have never been shown with noises of less than 90 db (above the usual arbitrary level of .0002 dynes/sq. cm.). In view of the rather specific nature of the effect found in the laboratory, it remained a doubtful question

---

[13] Pierach, *op. cit.*, p. 159.

* From *Occupational Psychology*, Vol. 34, 1960, pp. 133–40.

The authors wish to thank the management and staff of Kodak Limited for permission to carry out the study and publish the results.

[1] D. E. Broadbent, "Effects of Noise on Behaviour," in C. M. Harris (ed.), *Handbook of Noise Control* (New York: McGraw-Hill Book Co., 1957).

whether this effect of noise is of any practical importance. Furthermore, no matter how prolonged the laboratory experiments, they cannot hope to involve people who are as accustomed to noise as they would be in a real-life working situation. For these reasons it has become very desirable to check the results of the laboratory experiments in an actual working environment.

There are considerable difficulties in finding a suitable situation for a study of this type. On the one hand, since the effect is expected to be in the incidence of human error rather than in output, the task studied needs to be one which will provide sufficient of such errors for statistical analysis. Furthermore, it is well known that any improvement or even change in working conditions may produce improved working efficiency due to improved morale. Consequently it is necessary to make some attempt at control for this factor, and this means at the very least that one should study one set of people whose noise exposure is reduced, and another set of people whose working conditions remain the same throughout the period investigated. Even this comparison is open to some objection since the group who continue to work in high intensity noise may not feel any improvement in morale due to the experiment, while the group working in reduced noise will naturally show any such improvement. The suggestion has been made by Rosenblith *et al*,[2] that ear plugs could be issued to workers, some of the plugs being defective so that they would not in fact reduce the noise to which the wearer was exposed. This would in fact be an investigation similar to that of a drug studied with a placebo, but so far no such investigation appears to have been reported. The reason is probably that ear plugs are not usually industrially acceptable when other methods of noise reduction are available.

Failing this type of control of morale factors, it is possible to draw some conclusions from a study in which the same people work both in noisy and in 'quiet' circumstances. The interest taken by the management in their working conditions as shown by expenditure on acoustic treatment, may lead to a rise in morale. This in turn may lead to an improvement of working efficiency which should be shown as much in the noise as in the quiet. The present study concerns such a comparison. A situation was found in which one work place could be acoustically treated while another, in which the same people sometimes worked, was not. In addition, the type of work was one in which brief failures of perception would produce measurable results, and in which the noise level before sound treatment was above 90 db, but might be expected to fall below that level after treatment. Thus the situation provided an unusually suitable opportunity of studying the effects of noise reduction, and an investigation was initiated.

---

[2] W. A. Rosenblith *et al.*, Vol. II, U.S.A.F. WADC Technical Report 52–204, 1953.

PROCEDURE: THE SITUATION STUDIED

In the production of movie film, the perforations down the sides of the film are inserted at a stage after the film has been coated with emulsion and cut into its final width. The operation is carried out by machines which are loaded rather in a similar way to the loading of a cine projector with film; that is, a reel is placed on the machine and the film threaded through a moderately complex pathway. The machine is then started and proceeds to make the perforations until the whole reel has been finished. While the operation is proceeding, the operator loads other machines. An incentive payment scheme is used, so that he attempts to keep all machines under his charge running as much of the time as possible. For the purposes of payment, the rate of work is recorded. The task is, however, sensitive to any momentary lapses of attention on the operator's part since, if he makes a mistake in threading the film, he is likely to have a breakage of the film, or other breakdown of the machine. These stoppages also are recorded. The operation is carried out in a reduced and controlled illumination, because of the need to protect the film emulsion. The temperature also is controlled.

In the particular plant studied, there were two inter-connected rooms, usually involving about five operators, in which there was a dim safe-light. There were also other rooms involving roughly the same number of people in which there was practically no illumination whatever. Acoustic treatment was carried out in one of the former rooms. Noise in this room was measured in a number of positions before treatment was carried out, using a Dawe sound level meter Type 1400B. When all the machines were operating the level was at least 98 db in all parts of the room and 99 db in the middle of the room amongst the machines. Examination of the noise with a Dawe frequency analyser showed that there were peaks in the spectrum at approximately 80, 175, 250, 500, 700, 1,900 and 7,000 c.p.s., all reaching approximately the same level ±2 db.

The room was treated by placing absorbent material on the walls and ceiling and by putting absorbent baffles between the rows of machines. As a result of this treatment, the level fell by about 8 to 10 db in all positions measured, the final level in the position which gave 99 db originally being 89 db after the treatment. Unexpectedly, it was also found that a reduction in noise level had occurred in the interconnected but untreated room, the initial and final levels being 98 and 90 db respectively. This frustrated the original intention of using comparisons of the inter-connected rooms as a principal source of data. However, the other rooms operating with, in effect, no illumination still provided a control in which noise level had remained unchanged.

TYPES OF MEASUREMENT MADE

1. *Communications.* While it is generally accepted among students of hearing that noise interferes with the understanding of speech, one

occasionally meets people in industry who feel that persons accustomed to a particular job in noise are nevertheless able to understand speech in that noise. Although it is usual to attribute this feeling to the development of lipreading and other non-auditory forms of communication by workers in noise, it is perhaps conceivable that under conditions of prolonged exposure a man might come to understand speech by cues which fall outside the frequency band of the particular noise in which he works. It was therefore thought worthwhile to conduct intelligibility tests in the work-place before and after the acoustic treatment. The technique adopted was to use a tape recording of one of the lists of monosyllabic words, compiled by Hirsh *et al.*[3] in two different orders. Groups of five or six operators stood against the wall of the perforating room and listened to the tape recorder playing at a level which was kept constant for each group. They attempted to write down the monosyllables as they heard them. Two of these groups carried out these tests on two occasions before the soundproofing as a check on practice effects. They did no better on the second day, and it therefore appeared that with this type of listener under these conditions, practice was unimportant.

Unfortunately, at this stage, because a valve had to be replaced in the tape recorder, it was not possible to make direct comparisons with further tests. However, another two groups carried out the tests once before soundproofing and their results were compared with another two groups who did the tests after the soundproofing.

2. *Measures of Working Efficiency.* The sound treatment began to be installed during the annual holiday of 1957. Various measures of operator efficiency were extracted from the records for a six-week period following this holiday, and, for comparison, for the six-week period following the holiday in 1956. The period of six weeks was chosen because operators normally shifted from room to room in a systematic cycle of six weeks for reasons quite unconnected with the investigation. Each cycle involved the rooms in which the noise level had remained constant as well as those in which it had declined, so that by taking this period we should eliminate differences in ability between individual workers from any comparisons made between different rooms. Figures were obtained separately for each 'bay' (that is, each group of machines controlled by one operator) for each shift. No very noticeable difference appeared between shifts, and therefore the results for all shifts in each bay were combined.

Succeeding six-week periods were examined in the same way, except that the periods involving Christmas 1956 and Christmas 1957 were excluded. In all four pairs of six-week periods were studied, each pair comprising one before noise reduction and one after. We may thus com-

---

[3] I. J. Hirsh, H. Davis, S. R. Silverman, E. G. Reynolds, E. Eldert, and R. W. Benson, "Development of Materials for Speech Audiometry," *Journal of Speech Dis.*, 1952, pp. 321–37.

pare performance in 1956/7 and 1957/8 for five bays in which a noise reduction of about 10 db occurred at a time immediately before the 1957/8 period. A similar comparison can be made for four other bays in which no noise reduction occurred. The measures of working efficiency taken were as follows:

(a) *Point hour.* This is a measure of rate of work during those times in which no stoppage of work has occurred. It is calculated for purposes of the incentive payment scheme. When a stoppage occurs, the operator is paid on time rate.

(b) *Number of broken rolls of film.* These were divided into those attributed to the operator and those due to some other cause such as the machine. Records of both were examined since it is of course possible that some change in classification might have occurred during the period.

(c) *Number of shutdowns of the process other than for broken rolls.* Here again stoppages attributed to the operator were distinguished from those not so attributed.

(d) *Number of calls for maintenance assistance.* It was considered possible that operator error might cause breakdown in the machines, and this index was therefore examined.

(e) *Time occupied by stoppages for maintenance.* If the curing of faults took longer when working in noise this measure might be expected to show some effects.

(f) *Labour turnover.* This is hardly a measure of working efficiency, but was obtained on the same basis as the other measures mentioned since it seemed probable that it might reflect a change in working conditions.

(g) *Absenteeism.* This also was thought to be a possible index of effects of noise, since one frequently encounters the opinion that noise produces minor illnesses and nervous complaints, and the incidence of absenteeism was therefore determined on the same basis as the other measures.

RESULTS

1. *Communications.* The subjects who listened to the tape recordings after sound treatment correctly identified 69% of the words in the recordings. The separate group of subjects who heard the recordings before treatment identified correctly only 54% of words. The difference is significant at the .05 level by a one-tailed test using the tau method.[4] The difference is also of much the same magnitude as that to be expected from laboratory experiments on intelligibility in noise, so that it suggests that workers used to noise still benefit from the noise reduction.

2. *Measures of Working Efficiency.* The more important measures are shown in Table 1.

---

[4] J. W. Whitfield, "Rank Correlation between Two Variables, One of Which Is Ranked, the Other Dichotomous," *Biometriks,* Vol. 34, 1947, pp. 290–96.

(a) *Point hour.* It will be noted that the point hour, that is, the rate of work, increased following the acoustic treatment. However, it did so in the untreated bays just as much as in the treated ones. The difference between bays is completely insignificant ($p > 0.5$). Thus it does not seem possible to ascribe the improvement to an effect of noise on working efficiency. On the other hand, all the bays, whether treated or untreated, showed improvement in point hour so that there has undoubtedly been some change in the conditions of work between 1956/7 and 1957/8. This might conceivably be due to general factors such as the economic situation of the country, or the flow of orders through the department of which perforation formed a part. However, as a precaution, the point hour was examined for all other workers in the department, excluding the perforators. There had been a significant fall in point hour amongst these other workers; which does not suggest that factors of the sort mentioned could be responsible for the improvement of rate of work in the perforators. A plausible explanation is that the reduction of the noise improved the morale and attitude to work of the group studied, and that this effect naturally appeared in whichever bay they were working. The presence of the control, untreated, bays has however saved us from interpreting this morale effect as one due primarily to noise. From the point of view of the practical management of work it may, of course, be quite helpful to have an increase in rate of work from noise reduction even though this is really due to an improvement of morale.

(b) *Broken rolls of film.* It will be seen that the number of film breakages has also declined since the 1957 holiday. However, in this case the decline has been much greater in the acoustically treated bays than in the untreated ones. The statistical significance of this difference is perhaps best assessed by again examining each individual bay, deciding how many of the treated bays showed bigger reductions than the untreated ones, and calculating tau. By this method the difference is significant ($p < 0.05$). It thus seems clear that momentary inefficiencies on the part of the operators have been reduced by the treatment. In view of the main purpose of this investigation, to study long term trends in working efficiency after noise reduction, the individual six-week periods were examined for any sign of a 'wearing off' of the effect of noise reduction as time went on. There was no sign whatever of such a 'wearing off'; the largest difference between six-week periods was that for the third period, closely followed by the fourth. The second period gave a smaller difference, and the period immediately following the first noise reduction gave the smallest difference of all. (To some extent this tendency for the effect to increase with time may be due to the fact that not all the acoustic treatment was installed during the 1957 shutdown, and some of it was put in after the first six-week period. But this cannot explain the whole trend.)

TABLE 1

COMPARISON OF ACOUSTICALLY TREATED AND UNTREATED WORK PLACES
BEFORE AND AFTER TREATMENT WAS CARRIED OUT

	TREATED BAYS		UNTREATED BAYS	
	1956/7	1957/8	1956/7	1957/8
Broken rolls (attributed to operator)	75	5	25	22
Other shutdowns (attributed to operator)	158	31	75	56
Calls for maintenance (excluding first six week period in each year)	746	597	516	468
Point hour	84.5	89.6	91.2	95.25
Absenteeism (time as % of possible hours worked)	5.18	4.43	2.72	1.56
Labour turnover (Mean % per six weeks)	1956/7 = 6.2%		1957/8 = 0	

It will be noted that the entries in Table 1 are only for those broken rolls which were attributed to the operator rather than to factors outside his control. Figures for the other types of breakage were also examined, and showed a slight but insignificant difference in the same direction. It would be surprising if noise reduction had affected breakages due to factors other than human error. A change in the method of attributing broken rolls to operators and to other causes might have occurred after the acoustic treatment to the bays. The slight effect in the number of breakages is important as it means that the main results cannot be explained as due to a change of this nature.

(c) *Other shutdowns.* Other types of shutdown again showed a greater reduction in the acoustically treated bays than in the untreated ones, although the statistical significance of the difference is not quite so satisfactory using the same test as previously ($p < 0.10$ by a two-tailed test). Thus this finding can only be regarded as established if we feel that the laboratory experiments give us sufficient grounds for expecting reduced human error after noise reduction. As before, the effect increased with increasing time since the beginning of the period studied, and it was slightly in the same direction when shutdowns not attributed to human error were examined.

(d) *Calls for maintenance.* Although there was slightly greater reduction in the number of these calls in the acoustically treated bays than in the untreated ones, which again agrees with expectation, the statistical significance of the difference is quite unsatisfactory ($p > 0.5$).

(e) *Time occupied by stoppages for maintenance.* This did not appear to show any effects.

(f) *Labour turnover.* As will be seen, there has been a reduction in the number of staff leaving, but this is too small to be confidently regarded as more than a chance effect. The data have been examined to make sure that the other findings could not be explained on the basis that more highly skilled workers took the place of those who left.

(g) *Absenteeism.* There has been a slight reduction in time absent from work, but this appears both in the acoustically treated and in the untreated bays. The difference between bays is actually in a most unlikely direction, the reduction being greater in the untreated bays, but this difference is, of course, completely insignificant. It may be of possible importance that the remainder of the department, excluding the perforators, showed a slight increase in absenteeism during the same period. The same morale factor may therefore be at work.

DISCUSSION

The results of this investigation completely agree with those of the laboratory experiments mentioned at the beginning of the paper. The rate of work is not improved by noise reduction, except perhaps by a general morale factor; human error is, however, less frequent when the noise level is less. There is no sign that the effects found with these experienced workers are less than those met on the much shorter time scale of the laboratory. Indeed the actual differences shown in Table 1 are larger than those met in the laboratory experiments to such an extent that enquiry was made to see whether any other factor could possibly be intruding and producing a spurious effect. For example, the acoustic treatment might have been introduced at the same time as a change in lighting sufficient to alter the number of errors. However, no change in other working conditions was found which could, by itself, have caused the results obtained; and the most probable explanation for the very substantial effects in Table 1 is that the effect of the noise interacts with some of the other features of this job such as the low illumination. The effect of noise reduction may therefore have been greater than it would have been with a job performed under more normal conditions. Another point which should be borne in mind when observing the reduction of, for example, broken rolls, is that the breakages attributable to the operator are naturally only a small proportion of the total breakages which occur. Thus one cannot say that noise reduction will produce an economic advantage as great as might appear from this table. Lastly, it must be borne in mind that although we are certain that chance factors are not responsible for producing the reduction in broken rolls, they may have made that reduction appear somewhat larger in these results than it would if another set of observations were to be taken.

While therefore one must not place too much weight on the actual size of the improvement in efficiency achieved by noise reduction, the agreement in the form of improvement found in actual work and in the laboratory experiments is impressive. Noise does produce human error in a real-life situation, even among people who are used to it.

55. Illumination Standards for Effective and Comfortable Vision*

Miles A. Tinker

DURING THE LAST few years a lighting consciousness has been forced upon most of those who perform visual tasks and upon those who control the environments in which visual work is performed. This lighting consciousness has resulted from information derived from many sources. Among these are the popular articles in newspapers and magazines by authors who have interviewed "lighting experts," reports written by educators and medical men for journals in their own fields, and the better light–better sight publicity. The more fundamental information, however, has appeared as experimental reports in the scientific publications. The result is a keen interest in illumination and a sincere desire on the part of the public for sound information concerning hygienic lighting. Consequently, the consulting psychologist will frequently be called upon to furnish advice on proper illumination.

It is obvious that specifications for hygienic lighting should be based upon experimental findings that have been adequately interpreted. The purpose of this paper is to summarize in a critical manner the results of illumination experiments that are pertinent to the needs of the consulting psychologist.

Lighting should be prescribed by impartial persons who have a competent knowledge of hygienic illumination. Available recommended standards[1] are satisfactory in some respects but unreliable in others. Suggestions concerning quality (color) and distribution of light are adequate. Recommendations for the light intensities needed for specific visual tasks, however, are based largely upon misinterpreted data and consequently are not valid. Proof of this will be cited below.

Surveys reveal inadequate illumination in a large majority of homes, offices, schools and factories. Frequently the lighting is either too dim or

---

* From *Journal of Consulting Psychology*, Vol. 3, 1939, pp. 11–20.

[1] *American Recommended Practice of School Lighting*, prepared under joint sponsorship of Illuminating Engineering Society and American Institute of Architects, Washington, 1938; M. Luckiesh and F. K. Moss, *The New Science of Seeing* (Cleveland: General Electric Co., 1934); M. Luckiesh and F. K. Moss, *The Science of Seeing* (New York: D. Van Nostrand Co., 1937); *Recommended Standards of Illumination* (Cleveland: General Electric Co., 1934).

is arranged so that uncomfortable glare is present. Brighter illumination than is needed is also found. These conditions are no longer excusable since the data now available from the researches of psychologists, physiologists and engineers furnish an adequate basis for sound lighting practice. Healthy conditions for visual work may be had without excessive increase in cost or sacrifice of beauty by conscientious application of the basic principles of hygienic illumination. The three aspects of lighting to be considered are (1) quality or color, (2) brightness or intensity, and (3) distribution or diffusion of illumination.

Color of Light

Light from the common illuminants and daylight is complex, *i.e.*, composed of a series of several wave-lengths. It is well known that the focal length of a simple lens like that in the eye varies from one wave-length to another. This produces chromatic aberration. When the eye is focused upon an object, therefore, the retinal image is surrounded by a faint halo of the light rays which are out of focus. The yellow rays, which are dominant (brightest) in mixed light, are focused automatically and the aberration circles producing the halo come from the violet, green, blue and red rays which are slightly out of focus.

Light rays derived from a limited range of the spectrum are relatively uniform in wave-length and produce an approximately pure or monochromatic spectral color, such as spectral yellow. In view of the chromatic aberration present with complex light, we might expect that vision would become clearer as the light waves of the illuminant become more nearly monochromatic and that best vision is achieved with a pure spectral light. This is not entirely confirmed by experimental results.

For practical purposes mercury-arc light, which has been used for illumination in special situations for several years, has been considered monochromatic. Although most of its light comes from the narrow yellow and green sections of the spectrum, there is included a slight amount of blue and violet light. Contrary to earlier findings, recent determinations[2] show no significant difference in visual acuity under mercury light as compared to tungsten-filament light (ordinary bulbs). In another experiment,[3] no significant differences were found in visibility of 8-point (small) type under light from a 400-watt mercury-arc and under a 100-watt tungsten-filament lamp. The same was true for speed of performing a visual test and for visibility of a test object. Similar results have been obtained by other investigators.[4] When subjects are permitted to choose

---

[2] M. Luckiesh and F. K. Moss, "Seeing in Tungsten, Mercury, and Sodium Lights," *Trans. I.E.S.*, 1936, pp. 655–74.

[3] M. Luckiesh and F. K. Moss, *The Science of Seeing, op. cit.*

[4] C. S. Woodside and H. Leinhardt, "Comparison of the Light from High-Intensity Mercury Vapor Lamps and Incandescent-Filament Lamps for Visual Tasks," *Trans. I.E.S.*, Vol. 32, 1937, p. 365.

the intensity of light they like best for reading, they consistently select slightly brighter mercury light than tungsten-filament light.[5] The differences, however, are not significant. In general, therefore, there appears to be no advantage for mercury-arc light over tungsten-filament illumination. It is also important that there is no disadvantage with the mercury light. Bell's results,[6] however, seemed to reveal a greater *apparent distinctness*[7] under mercury light for objects *above* the acuity threshold. In view of these results, and since there are no known deleterious effects upon people working for long periods under mercury light, it is obvious that it is entirely legitimate to employ mercury light wherever there is any *apparent* advantage to be gained by its use. For instance, there might be a subjective impression of clearer details under the mercury light.

Yellow light from sodium-vapor lamps is for all practical purposes truly monochromatic. Luckiesh and Moss[8] have demonstrated that visual acuity is better under sodium light than under tungsten-filament light at all levels of illumination from very dim to relatively bright. Under sodium light color-contrast entirely disappears and Luckiesh and Moss[9] conclude that sodium light has no outstanding advantage in enhancing brightness contrasts.

Visual acuity varies from one monochromatic (colored) light to another. Ferree and Rand[10] found the order yielding greatest to least acuity to be: Yellow, yellow-green, orange, green, red, blue-green and blue. White light (sunlight), composed of rays from all parts of the spectrum, was superior to the yellow when the test object was black on a white background. In practice, therefore, yellow is to be preferred to any other color or combination of colors found in ordinary illuminants for discriminating fine details. Yellow light has the further advantage of being available (sodium-vapor lamps) at the brighter levels. It can find application in practical situations where fine visual discrimination is required, such as in industrial inspection work. Results indicate that no monochromatic color is superior to sunlight. There is ample evidence, however, that these findings have no bearing upon most supraliminal tasks, such as ordinary reading office work and most factory operations. Thus with legible print and adequate intensity of light, there appears to be no appreciable disadvantage from chromatic aberration in

[5] M. Luckiesh, *Light and Work* (New York: D. Van Nostrand Co., 1924).

[6] L. Bell, "Chromatic Aberration and Visual Acuity," *Elec. World*, Vol. 57, 1911, pp. 1163–66.

[7] M. Luckiesh and F. K. Moss, *The Science of Seeing, op. cit.*

[8] M. Luckiesh and F. K. Moss, "Visual Acuity and Sodium-Vapor Light," *Journal Frank. Inst.*, Vol. 215, 1933, pp. 401–10.

[9] M. Luckiesh and F. K. Moss, *The Science of Seeing, op. cit.*

[10] C. E. Ferree and G. Rand, "Visibility of Objects as Affected by Color and Composition of Light, Part I," *Personnel Journal*, Vol. 9, 1931, pp. 475–91; *Ibid.*, "Part II," Vol. 10, 1931, pp. 108–24.

reading with the common artificial illuminants. In general, one may employ whatever color he wishes for special effects and still maintain hygienic lighting, providing the factors of intensity and distribution are controlled.

Light Intensity

Intensity of light is measured in foot-candles. One foot-candle is the brightness of light from a standard candle one foot away. Light meters are now available for quick and accurate measurement of brightness level. These instruments should be calibrated frequently, however, since they tend to become inaccurate with use and to register less than the true values. Table 1 will give some notion of the relative brightness of

TABLE 1
Approximate Intensities of Light from Different Sized Frosted Bulbs

	Distances in Inches between Bulb and Working Surface to Produce Designated Intensities		
Watt Size	10 Foot-Candles	15 Foot-Candles	25 Foot-Candles
25 16	12	9
40 23	19	14
50 27	21	17
60 31	26	20
75 49	40	31
100 52	44	34

illumination from light bulbs of different wattages. These intensities were measured with a recently calibrated General Electric Light Meter for frosted Mazda bulbs in an ordinary bridge lamp with a parchment shade 12 inches in diameter. Thus a 40-watt bulb yields 10 foot-candles intensity at a distance of 23 inches, 15 foot candles at 19 inches and 25 foot-candles at 14 inches. These figures should be considered only as approximations since bulbs and lamp shades vary and the brightness of light from any bulb decreases with use.

The results of numerous investigations are in agreement concerning the relation of light intensity to visual acuity. These experiments have required visual discrimination of very fine details under various intensities of light.[11] The following results are typical. There is a rapid rise in acuity from low intensity up to about 5 foot-candles. From 5 foot-candles on, the rise in acuity becomes slower and slower and almost reaches a maximum at about 20 foot-candles. In fact, the improvement in visual acuity from about 15 foot-candles to higher intensities for

[11] R. J. Lythgoe, *Illumination and Visual Capacities* (London: His Majesty's Stationery Office, 1926).

the normal eye is scarcely noticeable and of doubtful significance. Typical trends are illustrated by the following results: There was a 67.7 per cent increase in acuity from 0.1 to 1.0 foot-candle, a 43.6 per cent increase from 1.0 to 5.0 foot-candles, and only 8.2 per cent increase from 5.0 to 20.0 foot-candles. From 20 to 100 foot-candles the increase in acuity was slight.

The visual tasks encountered in everyday life situations infrequently require the exacting discriminations found in visual acuity tests. The relation found between visual acuity and intensity of light, therefore, is seldom applicable to the ordinary tasks. Adequate standards must be based upon results obtained under conditions that are strictly comparable to ordinary working situations. Several investigations of this sort are summarized below. At the left is given the task involving visual discrimination and at the right, the critical illumination level. The critical level is the brightness beyond which there was found no further increase in efficiency of performance.

1a. Reading 10-point type (speed), 3 foot-candles
1b. Reading 10-point type (fatigue), 3 foot-candles
2. Reading, 4 foot-candles
3. Reading 12-point (large) type, Between 1 and 10 foot-candles
4a. Reading performance in school, 4 to 6 foot-candles
4b. Educational achievement in school, 4 to 6 foot-candles
5. Computing arithmetic problems, Less than 9.6 foot-candles
6. Sorting mail, 8 to 10 foot-candles
7. Setting 6-point type by hand, Between 13 and 25 foot-candles
8. Time to thread a needle, 30 foot-candles

In the first experiment well-diffused illumination intensities ranging from 0.1 to 53 foot-candles were used. The reading was done by about 500 university students.[12] Speed of reading increased from 0.1 to 3 foot-candles, but showed no further improvement with 10, 17 or 53 foot-candles. In the second part of this experiment, an intensive study was made of the visual fatigue induced by reading two consecutive hours under each intensity. Fatigue was measured by the degree to which clear seeing was disturbed. The results were identical with those found with the speed of reading test. Three foot-candles induced no more fatigue than the brighter lights. Although the second experiment[13] was far less pretentious, 4 foot-candles as the critical level is close to the 3 foot-candles of Experiment 1. In Study No. 3,[14] large type was read under 1, 10 and 100 foot-candles. Although there was a gain in efficiency

---

[12] M. A. Tinker, "Illumination and the Hygiene of Reading," *Journal of Educational Psychology*, Vol. 25, 1934, pp. 669–80.

[13] L. T. Troland, "Analysis of the Literature Concerning the Dependency of Visual Functions upon Illumination Intensity," *Trans. I.E.S.*, Vol. 26, 1931, pp. 107–96.

[14] M. Luckiesh and F. K. Moss, "A Correlation between Illumination Intensity and Nervous Muscular Tension Resulting from Visual Effort," *Journal of Experimental Psychology*, Vol. 16, 1933, pp. 540–55.

from 1 to 10, there was no significant change in performance from 10 to 100 foot-candles. Since there were no intensities used between one and ten, we must assume that the critical level falls somewhere in that range. Reading achievement and educational achievement gains were compared under 4 to 6 and under 20 foot-candles in Experiment No. 4.[15] Re-analysis of the data (shown in detail below) revealed no differences in performance from one intensity to the other. In the fifth study,[16] arithmetic problems were computed under several intensities ranging from 9.6 to 118 foot-candles. Achievement was identical at all levels of brightness. Since no intensity below 9.6 foot-candles was employed, we must assume that the critical level is somewhere below this figure. Study 6[17] was an extensive study of the effect of illumination brightness upon efficiency of letter sorting by postoffice employees under actual working conditions. This performance reached its maximum efficiency only when at least 8 foot-candles of light were used. Increase in efficiency was rapid from 2 to 5 foot-candles and slight from 5 to 8 or 10 foot-candles. Setting 6-point type, Experiment No. 7, by hand is an exacting visual task. Performance was measured under various intensities ranging from 1.3 to 24.5 foot-candles.[18] The criterion of maximum performance was achievement under daylight. With artificial light this level was reached somewhere between 13.0 and 24.5 foot-candles. The authors suggest that this most effective level is approximately 20 foot-candles. In the final study,[19] the fine discrimination involved in threading a needle was most efficient at approximately 30 foot-candles.

The above results may be summed up as follows: In reading ordinary book type (10- and 12-point) the critical level of illumination intensity, beyond which further increases in brightness produce no further improvement in performance and no further decrease in visual fatigue, is apparently 3 to 4 foot-candles. This is directly indicated in or inferred from the results of the first five experiments cited above. When the visual task is somewhat more exacting, as in sorting mail, where less than optimum legibility is present, the critical level lies between 8 and 10 foot-candles. Where very fine discrimination is required (studies 7 and 8) the critical level appears to lie between 20 and 30 foot-candles.

[15] W. Allphin, "Influence of School Lighting on Scholarship," *Trans. I.E.S.*, Vol. 31, 1936, pp. 739–45.

[16] E. W. Atkins, "The Efficiency of the Eye under Different Intensities of Illumination," *Journal of Comp. Psychol.*, Vol. 1, 1927, pp. 1–37.

[17] L. R. White, R. H. Britten, J. E. Ives, and L. R. Thompson, "Studies in Illumination: II. Relation of Illumination to Ocular Efficiency and Ocular Fatigue among the Letter Separators in the Chicago Post Office," *Public Health Bulletin No. 18* (Washington, D.C.: Government Printing Office, 1929).

[18] H. C. Weston and A. K. Taylor, *The Relation between Illumination and Efficiency in Fine Work* (typesetting by hand) (London: His Majesty's Stationery Office, 1933).

[19] L. T. Troland, *op. cit.*

Further experimentation will undoubtedly place this latter figure at approximately 20 foot-candles.

Beutell[20] has developed a system for determining the intensity of light desired for specific tasks when certain important factors affecting discrimination are considered. Taking account of size of detail, contrast and emphasis upon details, the indicated intensities for efficient performance were found to be:

Clerical Work, 6 foot-candles
Type setting (very small, 6-point), 24 foot-candles
Surgical operation, 700 foot-candles
Corridors, 2 foot-candles
Tennis court, 24 foot-candles
Bill-board Ads (near), 9 foot-candles
Bill-board Ads (distant), 6.75 foot-candles
Drafting room, 12 foot-candles

The 24 foot-candles for setting 6-point type are somewhat high in view of the performance-test results cited above.

Greater brightness is needed when vision is defective or when print is illegible. Ferree and Rand[21] have shown that the presbyopic eye (poor accommodation) can benefit by relatively high intensities. Other reports[22] indicate the need of increased brightness for reading illegible print.

Luckiesh and Moss,[23] who have been intimately associated with the science of seeing through their extensive research program, recommend what appears to be extremely high intensities for ordinary visual tasks. These suggestions, because of the high prestige of the investigators, have received wide attention. They recommend, for instance, 20 to 50 foot-candles for ordinary reading, 50 to 100 foot-candles for difficult reading and average sewing, and 100 or more foot-candles for tasks such as fine needlework and close inspection work. Furthermore, they consider these recommendations conservative and state that several hundred foot-candles would be best for reading large print on white paper. Their experiment consisted of recording the nervous tension in subjects' fingers

---

[20] A. W. Beutell, "An Analytical Basis for a Lighting Code," *Illum. Eng.* (English), Vol. 27, 1934, pp. 5–11.

[21] C. E. Ferree and G. Rand, "The Effect of Intensity of Illumination on the New Point of Vision and a Comparison of the Effect for Presbyopic and Non-presbyopic Eyes," *Trans. I.E.S.*, Vol. 28, 1933, pp. 590–611; C. E. Ferree, G. Rand, E. F. Lewis, "The Effect of Increase of Intensity of Light on the Visual Acuity of Presbyopic and Non-presbyopic Eyes," *Trans. I.E.S.*, Vol. 29, 1934, pp. 293–313.

[22] C. E. Ferree and G. Rand, "The Ocular Principles in Lighting," *Trans. I.E.S.*, Vol. 20, 1925, pp. 270–95; M. A. Tinker, "Illumination and the Hygiene of Reading," *op. cit.*

[23] M. Luckiesh and F. K. Moss, "A Correlation between Illumination Intensity and Nervous Muscular Tension Resulting from Visual Effort," *op. cit.*; M. Luckiesh and F. K. Moss, *The New Science of Seeing*, *op. cit.*; M. Luckiesh and F. K. Moss, *The Science of Seeing*, *op. cit.*

while they read under 1, 10 and 100 foot-candles of light. Tinker[24] has pointed out that the experimental data from which these recommendations were derived have been misinterpreted. Re-analysis of the data reveals rapid changes in finger tension up to about 5 foot-candles of brightness, slower changes from 5 to 10 or 12 foot-candles, and only slight changes from there on. In other words, the changes that are of practical significance occur at relatively low intensities. In fact, the resulting curve is practically the same as that expressing the relation between visual acuity and illumination intensity. No one has suggested that the latter indicates the need of high intensities for reading. Luckiesh and Moss's conclusions, therefore, cannot be accepted as valid. Furthermore, the recent investigation by McFarland, Knehr and Berens[25] tends to bring in question the Luckiesh and Moss techniques. The former investigators found no relation between either basal metabolism or heart rate and level of illumination (1 and 50 foot-candles) employed for reading. They suggest that studies dealing with the effects of reading under poor illumination will have to be made directly upon the visual mechanism itself, rather than indirectly through changes in oxygen consumption, pulse rate, or muscular tonus. The numerous popular articles based upon Luckiesh and Moss's recommendations are, of course, necessarily invalid.

A new school lighting code, called American Recommended Practice[26] has been issued recently. It suggests 15 foot-candles as the minimum intensity at the desks and tables. The recommendations are apparently derived partly from the work of Luckiesh and Moss, which has been criticised above. In an explanatory article Dates[27] reports that the new recommended practice is based in part upon Allphin's findings.[28] Allphin measured school progress made by children in two schoolrooms. There were 41 fifth-grade children in each room. In one room the light intensity was 4 to 6 foot-candles, in the other 20 foot-candles were maintained as a minimum. Achievement was measured in November and again in June. Allphin claims that the pupils in the brightly lighted room gained 10 per cent more in educational age than the pupils in the 4 to 6 foot-candle room, and 28 per cent more in reading achievement. Examination of the data reveals that the *percentages were erroneously computed*. The pertinent data with percentages computed correctly are given below. Scores are in months.

---

[24] M. A. Tinker, "Cautions Concerning Illumination Intensities for Reading," *American Journal of Optometry*, Vol. 12, 1935, pp. 43–51.

[25] R. A. McFarland, C. A. Knehr, and C. Berens, "Metabolism and Pulse Rate as Related to Reading under High and Low Levels of Illumination" (to be published).

[26] *American Recommended Practice of School Lighting, op. cit.*

[27] H. B. Dates, "New Recommendations on School Lighting for Easier Seeing Based on Research," *Industrial Standardization*, Vol. 9, 1938, pp. 49–54.

[28] W. Allphin, *op. cit.*

Measure	20 Foot-candles	4 to 6 Foot-candles
November school achievement......118.34		118.27
June school achievement..........129.83		128.27
Gain........................... 11.49 (9.7%)		10.49 (8.9%)
Difference in percentage gain = 0.8 of one per cent		
November reading...............121.61		121.10
June reading....................132.76		130.17
Gain........................... 11.15 (9.1%)		9.07 (7.5%)
Difference in percentage gain = 1.6 per cent		

The data show, therefore, only 0.8 per cent greater gain in the 20 foot-candle room for school achievement, and only 1.6 per cent greater gain for reading achievement. These are close to chance differences for the ratio of the difference to the probable error of the difference is only 0.58 for the former and 0.84 for the latter. The only conclusion indicated by the results is that achievement in the 20 foot-candle room is equal to that in the 4 to 6 foot-candle room. Allphin's mistake was that he merely computed the difference between the two gains (*i.e.*, school achievement gain in 4 to 6 foot-candle room and in 20 foot-candle room) and turned this into per cent using the smaller gain as the base from which to compute the percentage. Obviously, this result has no significant bearing on how much the pupils in the brightly illuminated room gained in comparison with the pupils in the 4 to 6 foot-candle room. An example will show the absurdity of computing percentages by Allphin's method: Suppose the pupils in the 20 foot-candle room had gained 1.0 month in reading and in the 4 to 6 foot-candle room, 0.25 month. Then, by Allphin's method, the pupils in the brightly lighted room would have a 300 per cent greater *gain*. The only acceptable method is to turn the gains from November to June into per cent and compare as indicated above.

The National Council on Schoolhouse Construction is withholding approval of the 15 foot-candle recommendation of the new school code until further experimental work has been done. The recommendation of the International Commission on Illumination is more in line with the experimental findings. It suggested (*Sight-Saving Review*, December, 1935, p. 302) that the minimum intensity in schoolrooms be set at 8 foot-candles. Examination of the data from which the new school code was derived, indicates, therefore, that the Recommended Practice of School Lighting is based upon erroneous interpretation of experimental findings. It may be that school children need 15 foot-candles or more of light, but the evidence adduced by Dates[29] in support of the recommendations is shown to be based upon misinterpretation.

The consulting psychologist will need information on hygienic fac-

[29] H. B. Dates, *op. cit.*

tory illumination. Koepke's survey[30] indicates that industrial lighting is frequently prescribed without adequate planning. Experimental results show that it is a paying proposition to furnish adequate factory lighting. The following data show the effect of increased intensity of light on industrial production:

FACTORY	INITIAL FOOT-CANDLE LEVEL	NEW FOOT-CANDLE LEVEL	PER CENT INCREASE IN PRODUCTION
Electrical................3.8		11.4	8.5
Piston Ring...............1.2		6.5	13.0
" " 1.2		9.0	17.9
" " 1.2		14.0	25.8
Roller Bearing............5.0		6.0	4.0
" " 5.0		13.0	8.0
" " 5.0		20.0	12.5

Nineteen sets of figures[31] show a 13.8 per cent increase in production when the initial mean intensity of 2.7 foot-candles was raised to 10.9 foot-candles. In another set of figures furnished by Luckiesh and Moss[32] for six industrial operations, the original mean intensity of 2.4 foot-candles was raised to 11.0 foot-candles with an average increase in production of 15.4 per cent. The accompanying increase in cost of lighting in per cent of payroll was only 2.1. Having thoroughly analyzed the available data, Troland[33] concluded, "The vast majority of industrial operations can be carried out at maximum efficiency with an illumination intensity in the neighborhood of 10 foot-candles." There are data which show that special factory operations which require fine visual discrimination, as certain inspection jobs, will be performed more efficiently with somewhat brighter light. No results indicate, however, that such intensities should be above 20 to 25 foot-candles. Some evidence suggests that factory production is about 10 per cent greater with daylight than with artificial light.[34]

Adams[35] has demonstrated that in tile pressing, which is rough factory work, 3 to 4 foot-candles assure efficient working conditions. In other industrial situations, such as operation of cranes and dock and ware-

---

[30] C. A. Koepke, "A Job Analysis of Manufacturing Plants in Minnesota" (Minneapolis: University of Minnesota Press, 1934).

[31] L. T. Troland, *op. cit.*

[32] M. Luckiesh and F. K. Moss, *The Science of Seeing, op. cit.*

[33] L. T. Troland, *op. cit.*

[34] *Ibid.*

[35] S. Adams, *The Effect of Lighting on Efficiency of Rough Work* (tile pressing) (London: His Majesty's Stationery Office, 1935).

house work, the intensity may be relatively low, but glare spots should be avoided and good diffusion of light maintained.[36]

Distribution of Light

Control of light distribution throughout the work room is of prime importance. Hygienic vision is achieved only when intensity and distribution are adequately balanced. Failure to maintain satisfactory diffusion of light produces lessened visual efficiency and eyestrain. This results from glare due to poor arrangement and type of lighting fixtures, from surface reflection and from alternation of bright areas and shadows in the visual field.

The uncomfortable effects of bright spots of light above or off to the side of the line of vision while reading, doing other visual work, or even when no visual discrimination is involved, is common experience. Elimination of this disturbing peripheral illumination is necessary if hygienic vision is to be maintained. When these side lights become brighter or are moved closer to the line of direct vision, the immediate working surface, the fatiguing effects become greater. Furthermore, the greater the number of such peripheral light sources, the more detrimental is the effect upon vision.

Uncomfortable glare and loss of visual efficiency also result from highly polished or glazed objects within the field of view. Examples are nickel plated metal parts of a typewriter and glazed printing paper. Such glare is reduced by maintaining well-diffused illumination in the work room.

Visual fatigue and lessened efficiency is produced by brightness contrast within that portion of the visual field where critical vision is required and also within the immediate surroundings. When the eyes must shift back and forth from bright to dark areas or when there is a sharp division between dark and bright portions of the working area, the eyes must constantly re-adapt to the different degrees of brightness. Eyestrain soon results. Examples are (1) white paper on a dark desk, and (2) a dark under-surface of an opaque eye shade used in a brightly lighted room.

The following will aid in eliminating glare effects: (1) Avoid peripheral light sources, such as wall brackets and low hanging fixtures which reach down into the field of vision. (2) Avoid as far as possible the use of glazed paper, polished metallic objects and marked contrasts of brightness within the visual field. (3) Avoid strictly local lighting like that produced by most desk lamps with opaque shades. The latter produce a circle of bright light surrounded by dimly illuminated areas and shadows.

[36] J. S. Preston, "Part I: Docks, Warehouses, and Their Approches," *Industrial Lighting* (London: His Majesty's Stationery Office, 1933); *Ibid.*, "Part II: Lighting for Cranes," 1934.

(4) Maintain, in general, as equal a distribution of light as possible over the working surface.

With a consideration both for efficiency and economy, an adequate intensity of light with satisfactory diffusion is best obtained through a combination of general illumination of moderate intensity (3 to 4 foot-candles) and local lighting at the place of work. It is generally accepted that the ratio between the brightness of the local lighting and the general illumination should never be greater than 10 to 1 if fatiguing brightness contrast is to be avoided. General plus local lighting is usually achieved by use of ceiling fixtures supplemented by auxiliary units at work bench in the factory, and by desk or floor lamps in the office and home. A single lighting unit which yields both general and local illumination is the I.E.S. (Illuminating Engineering Society) certified lamp. One may use bulbs of lower wattage than specified for this type of lamp for many of the ordinary visual tasks. Table and floor lamps should be tall enough so that the light source is out of the field of vision while engaged in visual work. Thus the lower edge of a table lamp should be about 20 inches above the table. It is best to place table lamps to the side and floor lamps to the side or back of the worker. This avoids the necessity of looking at the light source when the eyes are raised.

Conclusions[37]

Specific recommendations for light intensities that will insure hygienic vision must be founded upon experimental results. Many factors such as distribution of light, condition of the eye, and size of detail to be discriminated must be considered. Although these considerations limit the scope of recommendations, nevertheless, some specifications that apply to a variety of visual tasks can be made.

Careful consideration should be given to diffusion of light in all working situations. This includes the elimination of glare spots and shadows by the use of proper lighting fixtures adequately arranged.

The critical level for reading is between 3 and 4 foot-candles. To provide a margin of safety, somewhat higher intensities should be employed. Never read with less than 10 foot-candles of light. Where diffusion of light is quite unsatisfactory, use 10 to 15 foot-candles. When the illumination is well distributed, use 20 to 30 foot-candles. If no glare, due to faulty distribution of light or to other factors, is present higher intensities may be employed with safety but without gain in efficiency and comfort.

In schoolrooms the minimum level of light intensity at the desks should probably not be less than about 20 foot-candles. In sight saving classrooms the brightness should probably be 40 to 50 foot-candles.

---

[37] Editor's Note: The figures below have been brought up to date by the author in the light of his most recent research.

Adequate lighting in industry is a paying proposition. It appears that most operations can be done with comfort and with maximum efficiency under approximately 25 foot-candles of light. Tasks requiring fine discrimination, such as certain inspection work, need relatively bright light. Indications are that it should be between 40 and 50 foot-candles.

With defective eyes, such as presbyopia, with poor legibility of print, and in other situations involving small brightness contrast between objects to be discriminated, brighter light is indicated. In the more severe of these situations, the intensity should probably be between 40 and 50 foot-candles. In others it can be somewhat less than 40 foot-candles.

In general we find that the critical level of illumination is slightly less than 5 foot-candles, and in most situations an adequate margin of safety is achieved by about 20 foot-candles. For exacting visual tasks or for persons with defective eyes, however, 40 to 50 foot-candles are required.

56. Music in a Complex Industrial Job*

William McGehee and James E. Gardner

INDUSTRIAL MUSIC has been used widely in American industry. The exact extent of its use is not known but a recent report[1] estimates that there are as many as 6,000 industrial installations in the United States. In spite of the wide use of industrial music there are few control studies of its effect on the workers and on the performance of their jobs. Too often the effect of music on production, absenteeism, turnover, accident rates, and workers' attitudes is "measured" in terms of the optimistic beliefs concerning its effectiveness held by those responsible for its installation and programming.

The majority of investigators agree that the increase in production attributed to music comes not from rhythmic pacing but from the salutary effects music has on workers' attitudes. For example, Smith writes, "Music can increase production only through stimulating changes in the attitudes or behavior of the employees. Improvements in production are by-products of these changes."[2] It is implicit also in much writing on

* From *Personnel Psychology*, Vol. 2, 1949, pp. 405–17.

[1] Ethel M. Spears, *Music in Industry*, National Industrial Conference Board, Studies in Personnel Policy, No. 78, 1947.

[2] Henry C. Smith, *Music in Relation to Employee Attitudes, Piece-work Production, and Industrial Accidents*, Applied Psychology Monographs, No. 14, 1947, p. 54.

the subject of worker productivity that improved attitudes will result in increased worker productivity. Following this line of reasoning, if music improves attitudes towards work, it should also increase production. This study is designed to investigate certain aspects of the following problems:

1. What is the effect of introducing music on the amount of production of industrial workers?
2. What are the opinions of the workers in regard to the effects of music on their work behavior?
3. What relations exist between the effect of music on production and the opinion of workers as to the effect of music on their work behavior?

The writers are aware that the results reported here may be peculiar to the work situation in which this study has been carried on.

This study should be of interest also in that the conditions under which it was conducted differed from those surrounding two of the better controlled studies of industrial music. Both Kerr's[3] and Smith's[4] studies involved workers performing relatively simple industrial tasks. The work required of the subjects in this study is relatively complex as industrial jobs go. Smith's investigation was conducted during a period of industrial expansion, employee training, and war enthusiasm. The present investigation was made in a stable work situation. All employees were experienced workers; production demands were stable; wages were based on an incentive system which had been in operation for several years without modification; there had been no change in supervision for three years. In other words, the study was made in a relatively stable work situation on workers fully familiar with their jobs and reasonably well adjusted to the social environment of the work situation.

Both Kerr and Smith reported increases in the amount of production associated with the use of music. The former, it is true, based his conclusions on consistent rather than statistically reliable differences in favor of music. The findings in this study concerning production are not in agreement with the results obtained by Kerr and Smith. This is not to imply any inaccuracy in their work but rather to point up the fact that a different situation can lead to different results. It may serve as an antidote to the practice of making generalizations from a sample of behavior to a universe.

SUBJECTS AND JOBS

The subjects involved in this study are 142 women workers employed in the occupation known as "setting" in rug manufacturing. Eighty-two of these operators worked on the first shift, 60 on the second shift. The index of production used in this investigation is the average hourly out-

---

[3] W. A. Kerr, *Effects of Music on Factory Production*, Applied Psychology Monographs, No. 5, 1945.

[4] Henry C. Smith, *op. cit.*

put of these workers based on the units established by careful time study.

The task of "setting" is a relatively complex industrial job. It involves the preparation of material for rug looms. The time required to reach the minimum skill where the worker is at a breakeven point between pay and production ranges from six to 15 months. Two to four years of experience are required to become a skilled operator. Without describing the job in detail, its complexity can be indicated by stating that skilled workers must have a high level of mental and manipulative skill; they must be able to attend to numerous job demands; they must possess high visual memory and color discrimination. The job also requires considerable physical endurance since it involves constant standing and walking. It also requires that the workers make an adjustment to a partner, since the work is performed by pairs of operators and pay is based on the output of the pair.

MUSIC AND PRODUCTION

The writers are indebted to both Smith and Kerr for the methods used in studying the effect of music on production in this study. The effect of music on production was studied by the comparison of the amount of production on days on which music was played with the amount of production on no-music days during an experimental five-week period. The following procedure was used in making this comparison. The experimental period was begun one week after the installation of music. This week was used for the purpose of ironing out difficulties in music equipment and in programming. During each of the five weeks of the experimental period, music was played four days and was not played one day.

Four distinct music programs were used on each of the music days in a week. The amount of music played each day during actual work hours was the same, 80 minutes. The type of music played during the work hours, opening period, and lunch period was identical in each music program. It followed recommendations for programming industrial music made by Benson.[5] The programs differed, however, in the amount of music played in individual work music periods and in the use of music for opening, closing, and lunch periods.

There were, therefore, four music programs (A, B, C, D) and one no-music program (E). These programs were rotated during the five-week period so that no one program was played on the same day twice. This rotation was planned to minimize the effect on production arising from possible daily and weekly variations. It allowed, also, for rigid statistical test of any differences found in terms of the effect of

---

[5] Barbara E. Benson, *Music and Sound Systems in Industry* (New York: McGraw-Hill Book Co., 1945).

music, of no music, of weekly variations in production and of daily variations in production. This test is described in the technical section of this report.

Table 1 gives the arrangement of programs and the average hourly production by weeks, days, shifts, and programs during the experi-

TABLE 1

AVERAGE HOURLY PRODUCTION FOR EACH DAY, IN TERMS OF WEEKS, PROGRAMS, AND SHIFTS

WEEK	SHIFT	PRO-GRAM	MONDAY PRO-DUCTION	PRO-GRAM	TUESDAY PRO-DUCTION	PRO-GRAM	WEDNES-DAY PRO-DUCTION	PRO-GRAM	THURS-DAY PRO-DUCTION	PRO-GRAM	FRIDAY PRO-DUCTION
1	1	A	133	B	139	C	140	D	140	E	145
	2		123		114		120		124		111
2	1	B	136	C	141	D	143	E	146	A	139
	2		115		119		119		122		115
3	1	C	140	A	138	E	142	B	139	D	139
	2		114		116		121		120		107
4	1	D	129	E	132	A	137	C	136	B	140
	2		120		126		118		116		114
5	1	E	132	D	144	B	143	A	142	C	142
	2		114		122		123		124		118

mental period. Table 2 gives the average hourly production for weeks, days and programs by shifts. An analysis of these data shows no significant differences in production which can be attributed to any music pro-

TABLE 2

AVERAGE HOURLY PRODUCTION FOR DAYS, WEEKS, SHIFTS, AND MUSIC PROGRAMS

			WEEKS		
Shifts	1	2	3	4	5
1	139.4	141.0	139.6	134.8	142.0
2	118.4	118.0	115.6	118.8	120.2

		DAYS		
	Mondays	Tuesdays	Wednesdays	Thursdays	Fridays
1	136.0	138.8	140.6	140.7	140.4
2	117.2	119.4	120.5	120.1	113.0

			PROGRAMS				
	A	B	C	D	E	Music	No Music
1	138.0	139.0	139.0	139.0	141.0	139.0	141.0
2	119.0	117.0	117.0	118.0	119.0	118.0	119.0

gram, to the lack of music, or to variations in weekly or daily production. In other words, the only possible conclusion is that during the experimental period industrial music had neither a favorable nor unfavorable effect upon the production of these workers as a group. It is possible that the production of the individual workers may have shown greater variation with music than without it. These data, however, have not been analyzed to determine the nature of individual differences. It is doubtful if this would be a fruitful procedure since the employees worked in pairs.

Production considerations made it advisable not to extend the experimental period beyond five weeks. It is possible that a longer period of adjustment might have been necessary before the maximum influence of music on production could be realized. A comparison, however, was made between production during a five-week period subsequent to the experimental period and production during a five-week period immediately preceding the installation of music. While this procedure does not allow for careful statistical control of the effect of daily and weekly variation and other factors influencing production, it is interesting to note that the difference in average production between these two periods is not statistically significant. The average hourly production (both shifts) for the five-week period prior to music was 130.8 while for the five-week period with music subsequent to the experimental period, average hourly production was 131.0. It seems unlikely, therefore, that an extension of the experimental period would have revealed any significant differences in production that could be attributed to the presence or absence of music.

EMPLOYEES' OPINIONS OF THE MUSIC PROGRAM

Music, then, had no favorable or unfavorable effect upon the production of these workers as a group. This failure to have any effect on production might be traceable to the employees' like or dislike of the music program. Accordingly, we developed a questionnaire to be administered to these workers to determine first, their general reaction to the music program and second, to determine how the employees felt that music affected their work. The questions used in the questionnaire were based on data collected from intensive preliminary interviews with 14 members of this department. These workers who were interviewed were selected at random.

The questionnaire was administered to the entire group. However, due to absenteeism and to a few returned questionnaires which were unusable, there were only 130 questionnaires which could be analyzed. In other words, the results which are to be reported represent the opinion of slightly over 90% of the workers in this department. The results of this questionnaire indicate clearly that the workers were favorably disposed towards the music program. In reply to a question "Do you want us to continue playing music in this department?," 84.5% answered in the affirmative. Only 1% answered in the negative, while 14.5% indicated that it made no difference to them whether or not we continued the music.

When asked about the specific aspects of the music programs such as the type of music used and its programming, the answers in the main were favorable. The major complaint that we received regarding the type of music played was that we were playing too much semi-classical and Latin music, and not enough hymns.

The music program, then, was received favorably by the majority of the workers. Yet, as indicated above, it had no effect on the amount of production. We, therefore, asked on the questionnaire the specific question, "What effect does music have on your work?" The checklist which was submitted to the group was again based on our preliminary interviews. Table 3 gives a summary of how music seemed to affect the job

TABLE 3

WORKER RESPONSES TO QUESTION "WHAT EFFECT DOES MUSIC HAVE ON YOUR WORK?"—*N* = 130

	PER CENT RESPONDING		
REPORTED EFFECTS	Yes	No	Can't Tell
A. Makes time pass	90	3	7
B. Takes your mind off other things	74	14	12
C. Gives you a lift when you're tired	86	4	10
D. Makes you feel more like coming in	74	6	20
E. If you come in feeling bad, music helps	82	5	13
F. Music keeps work from getting on nerves	73	6	21
G. Music gives you something to look forward to	75	5	19
H. The hard patterns seem to come easier with music	49*	14	37
I. You get more work done with music	59	7	34
J. Music lets you know how much time has passed	65	6	28
K. Music helps you know if you're behind or ahead in your work	49*	10	41
L. You move in time with the music	54*	18	28
M. Music breaks monotony	73	4	23
N. You do less talking with music	80	5	15
O. You seem to have more pep with music	77	6	17
P. Interferes with your work	4	74	21
Q. Makes you nervous	6	75	19

* Differences between percentage answering "yes" and combined percentage answering "no" and "can't tell" are *not* statistically significant. Remaining differences between "yes" and other responses are statistically significant.

performance of these workers. In general, music seemed to reduce monotony, to make time pass more rapidly, and to make the work easier. It is interesting to note, further, that 59 per cent of the group said they got more work done with music as compared with a negative response of seven per cent. The opinion of the workers that music helps them to produce more is extremely interesting in view of the fact that there was no increase in measured production.

As indicated, the rank and file employees in this department were favorably disposed toward the music program and felt that it helped their work. We secured a similar reaction to the music from the supervisors. This was secured through a questionnaire issued separately to supervisors at the same time we issued the questionnaire to the workers. The items in this questionnaire were based again on information secured in informal interviews with these men.

Returns were secured from the total supervisory force in the Setting Department, five foremen and assistant foremen. In addition, returns were received from two supervisors in a small department adjacent to the Setting Department in which the same music was played. Since it was desired to give these supervisors complete anonymity in making their replies to the questionnaire, no attempt was made to keep the two departments separate. These responses indicated that the supervisors believed that the music improved employee attitudes, gave the employees' morale a lift, created better interpersonal relations, and increased job satisfaction among the supervisors themselves. The supervisors believed further that music had made their duties easier to handle. All of them wanted music continued; all except one of the supervisors believed that music was a worthwhile investment in their department. In other words, these supervisors believed that music had definitely improved the attitude of their workers as well as their own attitude toward their job.

IMPLICATIONS

As shown above, there is evidence that the employees in this study were favorably disposed towards music. We have, further, evidence that they believed that music not only made the work more pleasant but, also, that it increased their actual production. On the other hand, within the limitation of the experimental design, we have evidence that there was no statistically significant change in the amount of production.

As indicated earlier, it has been implicitly assumed by most writers on the problems of workers' attitudes, that an improvement in the attitudes of workers and a reduction in the monotony of the task would tend to increase production. Music, as a non-financial incentive, is assumed to increase production by bringing about changes in the attitudes or behavior of the employees.[6]

Smith further has suggested that "the more complex and varied the job, the less likely music is to increase production on it."[7] The reasoning here is that if the job is so complex that it requires the full attention of the employee, he will not attend to the music and the music will have no effect on his production. It might also be implied that if the job is so complicated that it requires the full attention of an employee music might serve as a distracting element and thus reduce production.

The task which the employees in this study performed is a complex one. It is possible that the failure of music, in this study, to increase production can be attributed to the fact that the entire attention of these

---

[6] Henry C. Smith, *op. cit.*, p. 54.
[7] *Ibid.*, p. 55.

workers was devoted to the job demands. This does not seem, however, to be the case. Both through observation and interviews with employees we have evidence that, in spite of the complexity of the task, workers were strongly aware of the music and that they sometimes hummed the tunes or sang the words of the music. The answer to the questionnaire items themselves indicate that music received considerable attention from the workers. It seems, therefore, that the failure of music, in this study, to increase production cannot be attributed to the failure of the employees to attend to the music due to the complexity of their tasks. Further, attention to music did not result in any significant loss in production.

It seems to us, therefore, that an alternate hypothesis must be advanced to explain the failure of music within the limits of this study to increase or decrease production. The workers in this study over a long period of time have reached relatively stable levels of production. They have developed definite habit patterns of work and tempo of work. Further, they have developed a fairly adequate adjustment to the social and task demand of this work situation. It seems, therefore, in this very stable situation that the effect of music was not sufficiently strong in spite of its other salutary aspects to break up these well established habit patterns. While some of the workers used music as a pacing device, i.e., as a means of knowing whether they were behind or ahead in their work, the music did not change their production goals. These workers, therefore, seem after long experience on this complex job to have reached a stable level of production. This level may have been arbitrarily established by the workers or may represent a physiological limit. In any case, it is apparently so strongly established that it was not affected by music despite the favorable reactions of the workers toward the music. Moreover, it seems that workers' opinions regarding the effect of music on their own output cannot be taken as evidence of the actual effect.

As indicated earlier, the production of individual workers may have been favorably or unfavorably affected by the music. Due to the nature of the task, it is impossible to determine whether or not this is so. If it were so, favorable effects on one worker are masked or cancelled by unfavorable effects on other workers.

Section Eight

ACCIDENTS AND SAFETY

Introduction

A RECENT REPORT of the National Safety Council indicated that industrial work accidents cost $3.2 billion a year with an average cost to industry of $50 a worker. Regardless of how this figure is computed, it points up the tremendous need to learn more about the causes of accidents in order to reduce their frequency and severity. The problem of accident causation is a complex one. Some accidents are attributable to mechanical failures, some to human elements, and some to chance factors. Even the mechanical or engineering aspects are not independent of human elements. Thus, some workers will circumvent the best designed mechanical safety devices. And, in the next section, we will see how psychologists are developing principles by which machines can be designed to minimize the human errors made in operating them. In the present section, we will examine some of the issues and research on human factors in accidents and safety. In turn, we will focus on the contribution to accidents of personal factors in the individual, training and experience, and factors in the work situation.

First of all, it is frequently reported that a small proportion of workers are responsible for a large proportion of the accidents in particular jobs. This has led to the notion of "accident proneness" as a trait which is more pronounced in some individuals than in others. In "A Re-examination of the Accident Proneness Concept," Mintz and Blum describe the evidence on the probable contributions of these "personal factors" to industrial accidents. They clarify the important distinction between "accident proneness" and "accident liability" and provide a method for evaluating the accident liability of different jobs.

Next, the study by Van Zelst focuses on "The Effect of Age and Experience upon Accident Rate." The study also presents evidence on the importance of safety training on subsequent accident records.

In "Psychological Climate and Accidents," Keenan, Kerr, and Sherman focus on certain factors in the work situation which might be related to accidents. These include production pressures, promotion probabilities, shop environment, amount of individual responsibility, job prestige, pay systems, type of job, and degree of obvious danger.

Finally, Kerr's article, "Complementary Theories of Safety Psychology," serves as a summary and an attempted resolution of much of the current evidence on accident behavior. Kerr emphasizes situational or "industrial climate" factors as major determinations of accidents, and this leads to recommendations for better control of the accident problem.

57. A Re-examination of the Accident Proneness Concept*

Alexander Mintz and Milton L. Blum

It is generally accepted that certain individuals consistently have many accidents while others do not. This is commonly known as the principle of accident proneness. A critical examination of the data reported in the literature points to the desirability of reconsidering the significance attached to the principle of accident proneness.

This article has two objectives: (1) To indicate that one of the methods to substantiate the principle of accident proneness is unsound and to show that its use has led in some instances to exaggerated views of differences in accident proneness; and (2) To propose a method whereby quantitative estimates of differences in accident liability[1] may be obtained and to point out the conditions when it may be used.

The statistical evidence for the principle of accident proneness was presented by Greenwood and Woods[2] in 1919. These authors compared the distribution of accidents in a given population with a simple chance distribution for the same number of accidents in a population of the same size. Evidence of differences in accident proneness was obtained: It was discovered that more people had no accidents than might have been expected "by chance." Conversely, it was discovered that more people had many accidents than would have been expected in accordance with a simple chance distribution. In other words, Greenwood and Woods demonstrated that the obtained distributions of accidents differed significantly from chance expectancy. Furthermore, they showed that most of their distributions agreed with theoretically computed distributions based on the assumption that people differed from each other in their likelihood to have accidents.

Newbold[3] further investigated this problem and pointed out that the

---

* From *Journal of Applied Psychology,* Vol. 33, No. 3, 1949, pp. 195–211.

[1] In the subsequent discussions we shall use the expression "accident proneness" in referring to personal characteristics of people contributing to the likelihood of their having accidents. The expression "accident liability" will refer to both personal characteristics and stable environmental conditions contributing to accidents records.

[2] M. Greenwood and H. M. Woods, "The Incidence of Industrial Accidents upon Individuals with Specific Reference to Multiple Accidents" (London: Industrial Fatigue Research Board, Report 4, 1919).

[3] E. M. Newbold, "A Contribution to the Study of the Human Factor in the Causation of Accidents" (London: Industrial Fatigue Research Board, Report 34, 1926).

differences in accident liabilities could not be entirely explained simply in terms of different job hazards. In addition Newbold, in some of her work, compared the accident rates for the same people in two successive periods and reported that significant correlations existed.

Both Greenwood and Woods, and Newbold were primarily interested in the establishment of the existence of a difference between accident records and chance expectancy. In this they were successful and accordingly the principle of accident proneness was established.

However, another method has been used to support the principle of accident proneness. A number of investigators and writers of books on industrial psychology have pointed out that small percentages of people have large percentages of accidents and have presented data accordingly. In this method the obtained accident distribution is presented as evidence for the principle of accident proneness without a comparison to the distribution that would be normally expected "by chance," i.e., if all individuals were equally liable to accidents. This method is fallacious.

THE METHOD OF PERCENTAGES

The method of percentages of people and accidents implies an incorrect assumption, viz., that chance expectation requires that all people in a population should have the same number of accidents. This is not the case. An obvious limitation that has often been overlooked is the fact that very often the reported total number of accidents in a population is smaller than the number of people in the population. For example, if a group of one hundred factory workers had fifty accidents in one year, then a maximum of fifty people could have contributed to the accident record and accordingly a maximum of 50% of the population would have contributed to 100% of the accidents. Obviously a small percentage of the population in this case does not establish the principle of accident proneness. However, the number of employees having accidents is almost certain to be less than fifty since there is no reason to believe that each one should have had only one accident. Such an assumption would imply that an accident immunizes its victim against further accidents. If one makes the assumption of equal liability, the people who had one accident should be just as liable to have future accidents as those who have not had any. Thus if accident liability is unchanged by accidents already had, some people should have two accidents before others have had any. In fact, in accordance with chance expectancy some people should have had three or more accidents before another had a single accident. In dealing a deck of cards it is not improbable that a person will receive more or less than the three or four cards in a suit that seem to be his share. He may get six, seven or more such cards without any laws of probability being violated. Similarly, a person may have more accidents than seems to be his share in a given population without being more accident prone than the average.

Thus the assumption of equal accident liability results in different accident totals for the individuals within the group. The resulting distribution can be readily derived from the statement, "the current rate at which accidents occur per person is identical in groups of people with different numbers of accidents in the past." It follows directly from this statement that as the number of people who have had no accidents decreases, fewer people are likely to have first accidents per unit of time; as the number of people who have had first accidents increases, the rate of occurrence of second accidents increases proportionately. These and other similar statements can be reformulated as a set of differential equations, and the solution of this set of equations gives the terms of the Poisson distribution. Greenwood and Yule[4] first demonstrated its applicability to the accident problem. The Poisson is a discrete distribution rather than a continuous one. As applied to the accident problem, its consecutive terms give the predicted numbers of people who had no accidents, one accident, two accidents, etc. The terms are Ne^{-m}, $Ne^{-m}m$, $N - e^m \dfrac{m^2}{2!}$, $Ne^{-m} \dfrac{m^3}{3!}$, etc., where N is the number of people, e is the constant $2.71828 \ldots$, m is the mean number of accidents per person.

A number of sets of data will now be discussed in order to illustrate the inadequacy of the method of percentages of people and accidents.

Based upon original records obtained by the authors from a foundry it was found that 1.8% of the 280 men in the day shift had 11.4% of the accidents; 10% of the men had 44.3% of the accidents. In the night shift 5.8% of the 120 men had 12.5% of the accidents and 37.5% of the men had all of the accidents. A computation of the distribution of accidents in accordance with chance expectancy (equal liability distribution) indicated that the differences between the obtained and expected distributions were not significant. In accordance with the theoretical distribution, 1.4% of the people should have had 8.3% of the accidents and 8.9% of the people should have had 38.8% of the accidents. These percentages obtained from a theoretically computed equal liability distribution show that the accident distribution actually obtained is in accordance with chance expectancy and does not establish the existence of accident proneness.

A study that is often referred to in discussions of accident proneness is that of the National Association of Taxicab Owners and the Metropolitan Life Insurance Company.[5] These data deal with the records of 1294 drivers employed by several taxicab companies. Viteles[6] states that

---

[4] M. Greenwood and C. V. Yule, "An Enquiry into the Nature of Frequency Distributions Representative of Multiple Happenings, with Particular Reference to the Occurrence of Multiple Attacks of Disease or of Repeated Accidents," *J. Roy. Statist. Soc.*, Vol. 83, 1920, pp. 255–79.

[5] *Preventing Taxicab Accidents* (New York: Metropolitan Life Insurance Co., 1931).

[6] M. S. Viteles, *Industrial Psychology* (New York: W. W. Norton & Co., 1932).

"the incidence of accident proneness in the operation of motor vehicles has been well demonstrated in this study." "It is interesting to note that the data obtained in accident prone studies in other types of industries if plotted would closely conform to the curve shown. . . ."

Neither the authors of the report nor the author of the textbook compared the data with the simple chance distribution. Such computations have been made and are presented in Figure 1.

FIGURE 1

RELATIONSHIP BETWEEN CUMULATIVE PERCENTAGE OF TAXI DRIVERS AND OF ACCIDENTS

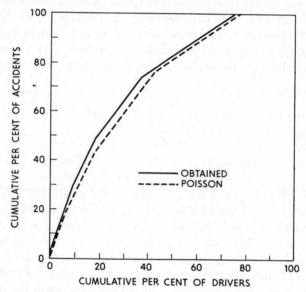

The solid line in the figure represents the cumulative percentages of accidents corresponding to cumulative percentages of drivers, based on the data as quoted in the original report. The dotted line represents the corresponding cumulative percentages from an equal liability distribution.

The two lines are obviously very similar in shape. The argument[7] could be repeated verbatim with percentages from the chance distribution substituted for obtained percentages, with very little loss in apparent persuasiveness. In the chance distribution, 23.5% of the people would have had no accidents instead of the obtained 25.2%. The best and the worst 50% would have had 18.3% and 81.7% of the accidents respectively, instead of the actually obtained 17.2% and 82.8%. The worst third of the drivers would have had 63.9% of the accidents (instead of 69.3%); the worst 10% would have had 24.7% instead of 31.9% of the accidents.

---

[7] M. S. Viteles, *op. cit.*

In spite of the fact that the two distributions are very similar in shape, the difference between them is statistically significant, the chi square being 122.77 $(d.f. = 6, P < .0001)$. In other words, factors other than so called chance factors are definitely present but do not markedly change the general shape of the chance distribution.

Another often referred to study on accident proneness is the one reported by Slocombe and Brakeman.[8] Their data are based upon accident records of 2300 men employed by the Boston Elevated Railway Company.

In discussing their data as indicative of differences in accident proneness, Slocombe and Brakeman classified the men with four or less accidents as "low accident men" and those with five or more accidents as "high accident men." This arbitrary division placed 1828 men in the first category and 472 men in the latter division. The "low accident" men averaged 2.1 accidents while the "high accident" men averaged 7 accidents. Slocombe and Brakeman did not compute the chance expectancy of the number of men having four accidents or less. Actually, in a simple chance distribution, 1824 men should be expected to be in this category and so only four more men of the total 2300 are in the "low accident" group than obtained by chance. According to chance expectancy, the "low accident" and "high accident" men should have averaged 2.4 accidents per man and 5.8 accidents per man respectively. The difference is not much smaller than the one actually obtained. This does not mean that there is no evidence for differences in accident proneness in the data. It merely means that Slocombe and Brakeman's line of argumentation is inconclusive.

More recent data based upon a random sample of licensed drivers in the state of Connecticut[9] have been analyzed by Cobb.[10] He computed the amount by which the variance of accident records exceeds the variance of the Poisson distribution and thus determined that these accidents records cannot correlate with a perfect test of accident proneness to a degree higher than $+.44$.

DeSilva[11] refers to these data and uses as argument for the principle of accident proneness mainly the fact that 4% of the drivers were responsible for 36% of the accidents. In a simple chance distribution 2.4% of the drivers would be responsible for 21.2% of the accidents. Again a comparison of percentages of people and of accidents is inconclusive. The figures just quoted based on the assumption of a simple chance

---

[8] C. S. Slocombe and E. E. Brakeman, "Psychological Tests and Accidents Proneness," *British Journal of Psychology*, Vol. 26, 1930, pp. 29–38.

[9] H. R. De Silva, *Why We Have Automobile Accidents* (New York: John Wiley & Sons, 1942).

[10] P. W. Cobb, "The Limit of Usefulness of Accident Rate as a Measure of Accident Proneness," *Journal of Applied Psychology*, Vol. 24, 1940, pp. 154–59.

[11] H. R. De Silva, *op. cit.*

distribution look almost as impressive as the figures in the actually obtained distribution.

QUANTITATIVE ESTIMATE OF DIFFERENCES IN ACCIDENT LIABILITY

It is possible to arrive at an estimate of the magnitude of differences in accident liability (as distinguished from differences in accident records) in the case of many populations. The procedure has been previously used by Cobb[12] as a step in estimating the maximum correlation between accident records and psychological tests. This procedure can be used in many instances to estimate the magnitude of differences in accident liability, but it is also necessary to mention that this procedure is not universally applicable.

The presence of differences in accident liability of individuals in a population results in a composite of Poisson distributions of the accident records. The reason for this is as follows: Each particular degree of accident liability present in a population should result in a Poisson distribution of the accident records. When two or more degrees of accident liability are present the resulting distribution is the sum of the two or more corresponding Poisson distributions. If the distribution of accident liability is a continuous function the resulting probability function of accidents is a composite of Poisson distributions which can be determined by integration.

When a given distribution of accident records is found to conform closely to a composite of Poisson distributions the evidence is consistent with the assumption that the differences between the accident records of different people are due partly to differences in their accident reliability and partly to "chance" factors not predictable in terms of knowledge of the people or of their accident records. In this assumption, the "chance" factors produce the variability within the constituent Poisson distributions while the differences in accident liability are responsible for the differences between their means. In accordance with such an assumption, one may analyze the obtained variance of a set of accident records into two constituent variances and view one of them as representing the operation of the "chance" factors, the other as characterizing the differences in accident liability. The former is the weighted arithmetic average of the variances of the Poisson distributions. As Cobb has shown, its value can be readily estimated as equal to the mean number of accidents per person.[13] Thus the residual variance representing the operation of differences in accident liability may be estimated if one subtracts the mean number of accidents per person from the obtained variance of accident records. We have performed this com-

---

[12] P. W. Cobb. *op. cit.*

[13] This follows from the fact that in a simple Poisson distribution the variance is always equal to the mean. Hence, in a composite of such distributions, the mean of the variances is equal to the mean of the means.

putation for a considerable number of accident distributions and have expressed the resulting variances attributable to unequal accident liabilities as percentages of the corresponding total variances of accident records.

The argument of the last paragraph pre-supposes that the obtained accident distribution approximates a composite Poisson distribution. Theoretically, an infinite variety of such distributions could be computed, depending on the assumed form of the distribution of the means of the Poisson distributions. Actually only one kind of such composites seems to have been used in research, viz., Greenwood and Yule's[14] "unequal liability distribution" ("UD"). This distribution is based on the assumption that accident liability of people is distributed along a Pearson Type III curve, a continuous skewed unimodal curve. Its equation may be found in several sources.[15] Many sets of accident data can be actually approximated by composite Poisson distributions based on such assumed distributions of accident liability. It should be noted however, that Greenwood and Yule's "UD" distribution is by no means the only possible unequal liability (composite Poisson) distribution. Greenwood and Yule[16] report a set of equations for a different type of composite Poisson distribution, based on the assumption that accident liability is normally distributed. This distribution does not seem to have been used in research. The possibility should not be overlooked that this distribution or still another composite Poisson distribution, based on some other assumed distribution of accident liability, might prove to be useful in research. In this paper, composite Poisson distributions based on the Pearson III curve were used most of the time. In a few instances another possibility was explored to some extent; some sets of data suggested discontinuous distributions of accident liability, the discontinuity being due to the presence of small numbers of deviant individuals. On the other hand, the presented analysis of the sample variance into two components is not legitimate if the obtained distribution deviates significantly from any composite Poisson distribution.

The line of reasoning just developed will now be applied to the more widely known studies of accident proneness.

The Greenwood and Woods study[17] presents fourteen sets of data. The majority of their findings agree rather well with the composite Poisson distributions computed according to Greenwood and Yule.[18] In other words, the obtained figures are in accord with the assumptions:

[14] M. Greenwood and C. V. Yule, *op. cit.*

[15] W. P. Elderton, *Frequency Curves and Correlation* (London: Layton, 1906); M. G. Kendall, *The Advanced Theory of Statistics* (Philadelphia: J. B. Lippincott, 1943).

[16] M. Greenwood and C. V. Yule, *op. cit.*

[17] M. Greenwood and H. M. Woods, *op. cit.*

[18] M. Greenwood and C. V. Yule, *op. cit.*

1. Accident proneness varies from person to person and its distribution is represented by a unimodal continuous skewed curve known as Pearson Type III.

2. Accident proneness of a person is unaltered by accidents he may have.

Twelve of the fourteen sets of data do not differ significantly from the corresponding theoretically computed figures. The *P*'s reported by Greenwood and Woods obtained from the chi square technique range from 0.15 to 0.93.[19] The sum of the chi squares for these 12 sets of data, based upon our computations, is 35.33, which for 30 degrees of freedom results in a *P* equal to about .23. The two deviant distributions will be discussed later.

Thus it is possible to approximate closely the majority of Greenwood and Woods' tables by theoretically computed distributions based on the assumptions that accident proneness is constant for each person and distributed in different people in accordance with a Pearson III curve. This finding is one of the principal ones in favor of the existence of differences in accident proneness.

How large then are these differences in accident proneness if we take the findings at their face value and assume that variations in "chance" and differences in accident proneness are the only factors accounting for these distributions of accident records. Table 1 presents the data per-

TABLE 1

PERCENTAGES OF VARIANCE ATTRIBUTABLE TO DIFFERENCES IN ACCIDENT LIABILITY, FROM GREENWOOD AND WOODS ORIGINAL DATA

GREENWOOD AND WOODS TABLE NO.	NUMBER OF CASES	MEAN (m)	OBTAINED VARIANCE (m'_2)	$\dfrac{m'_2 - m}{m'_2} \times 100$
I (A)	750	0.576	0.540	—
I (B)	580	0.478	0.491	—
II (A)	647	0.465	0.691	32.7%
II (B)	584	0.433	0.521	16.9%
III	100	3.040	6.938	56.2%
IV	414	0.483	1.008	52.1%
V	201	0.473	0.508	7.0%
VI	198	1.318	1.873	29.6%
VII (A)	59	0.983	1.203	19.3%
VII (B)	136	0.794	0.928	14.4%
VIII (A)	50	2.800	6.720	58.3%
VIII (B)	50	1.920	3.313	42.1%
IX (A)	55	2.473	3.704	33.2%
IX (B)	61	0.705	0.897	21.4%

taining to the relative size of these differences in the Greenwood and Woods study.

---

[19] The computations do not appear to be accurate in all cases. It is to be noted that the paper appeared in 1919 prior to Fisher's pointing out the procedure for determining degrees of freedom.

For each one of Greenwood and Woods' tables the estimated percentage of the variance of accident records attributable to differences in accident liability is given. As stated on a preceding page, the estimated variance of accident liability is the difference between the obtained variance of accident records and the mean number of accidents. Dividing this difference by the variance of accident records we obtain the percentage of the variance attributable to differences in accident liability. In addition, the following data are also given: the number of cases, the mean and the variance of accident records.

The median percentage of the total variance, attributable to differences in accident liability is 31.15. The percentages range from 7% to 58.3%. In nine of the twelve cases the percentage is less than 50. These figures hardly correspond to the impressions one is likely to derive from textbook accounts. The share of differences in accident liability in the variance of accident records is very variable; it exceeds 30% in only half of the cases while the rest of the variance which is more than twice as large must be attributed to unpredictable "chance" factors.

Newbold[20] collected a large number of sets of data from a number of factories. The factories were chosen on the basis of uniformity of the work performed, completeness of accident recording and opportunities for many minor accidents. The large majority of the accidents were trivial in nature, the author stating that the serious injuries were too few for correlational work. The findings differ in some respects from those of Greenwood and Woods.

A large variety of results can be found in Newbold's material. Nevertheless, in general the ratio $\dfrac{m'_2 - m}{m'_2} \times 100$ tends to be considerably larger than in the data of Greenwood and Woods. It also tends to be larger than in the other studies we have examined. This difference between Newbold's data and those of the other investigators is due in part to the fact that the mean numbers of accidents per person are rather large as compared to those of most of the other distributions. The irregularly variable factors should become relatively less and less important in the long run. Still, this is not the whole explanation. The ratios computed for Newbold's material remain large even when compared to ratios from distributions with similar means. Table 2 presents these ratios as computed from the statistics given in Newbold's paper; the number of cases and mean numbers of accidents as given by Newbold and the variances (squares of Newbold's standard deviations) are also given. The figures may be compared to the corresponding ones in Table 1.

The median percentages are 71.6 and 56.05 for the men and women respectively. The range is very great, the largest figure being 90% while at the other extreme there is an obtained variance which is actually

[20] E. M. Newbold, *op. cit.*

TABLE 2

ANALYSIS OF NEWBOLD'S DATA

NEWBOLD'S TABLE NO.	NUMBER OF CASES	MEAN (m)	VARIANCE (m_2)	$\dfrac{m'_2 - m}{m'_2} \times 100$
EIII	226	.18	.59	68.0
FI	22	.27	.20	—
EIV	256	.41	.69	40.5
FII	81	.43	.45	4.2
MIV	106	.48	.59	19.1
EII	281	.51	.94	43.8
BII	299	.57	.81	29.6
I	190	.68	1.72	60.5
P	50	1.04	1.99	48.7
GI	47	1.47	3.76	60.9
GII	82	1.61	5.66	71.6
BI	148	1.81	5.11	64.6
MVI	218	1.95	7.13	72.6
MIII	181	2.50	6.60	62.1
AIII	304	2.56	10.56	75.8
EVI	93	2.66	12.53	78.8
EV	77	2.73	18.84	85.0
N	284	2.90	23.33	87.6
EI	440	3.64	13.76	73.1
AII	352	3.78	17.14	77.9
MI	301	3.94	14.90	73.3
MII	376	3.98	14.06	72.7
MV	92	4.07	18.15	78.6
EVII	57	5.60	56.25	90.0
AI	204	6.44	41.86	84.4
MI	380	.37	.53	30.6
GII	50	.52	1.04	50.0
GI	120	.63	1.64	61.5
MV	110	.65	1.46	53.5
I	161	.70	1.21	42.1
H	346	.79	1.35	41.3
MIII	142	1.06	1.77	40.1
BI	145	1.06	2.04	48.2
K	125	1.34	3.24	58.6
DII	98	1.39	3.39	58.9
BII	100	2.12	5.57	61.9
MII	161	2.30	8.58	73.2
C	58	2.43	7.88	68.7
DI	28	5.43	15.52	65.0

slightly smaller than that of the corresponding Poisson distribution; this distribution closely approximates a simple chance distribution. These percentages do not accurately represent the share of differences in accident liability in the variance of accident records in all cases. Inspection of Newbold's curves suggests that many of the obtained accident distributions deviate significantly from composite Poisson distributions. This matter was only partially investigated. The amount of work involved in the computation of composite Poisson distributions for thirty nine sets of data would have been prohibitive, particularly because these data are given by Newbold in the form of graphs rather than tables.

Many of these graphs appear to have been inaccurately drawn, inasmuch as there are discrepancies between the totals of workers and accidents as read off from the graphs and as given in Newbold's Table. Nevertheless, it can be shown that in some of Newbold's sets of data composite Poisson distributions are appropriate and the percentage of the variance attributable to differences in accident liability is large.

Some of Newbold's sets of data suggest that the distribution of accident liability was a discontinuous one; in these sets of data the great bulk of the cases fit either a simple or a composite Poisson distribution, but there are also a few deviant cases which lie outside of such distributions. Most of the obtained variance of accident records due to accident liability may be due to the presence of these deviant cases; in other

TABLE 3

COMPARISON OF TWO OF NEWBOLD'S SETS OF DATA WITH THEORETICALLY COMPUTED DISTRIBUTIONS

ACCIDENTS PER MAN	SET EIII*		SET EV	
	Actual	Equal Liability Distribution (omitting 1 case)	Obtained	Unequal Liability Distribution (Composite Poisson) (omitting 9 cases)
0	201	197	24	22
1	21	26	22	19
2	2	2	8	12
3	1	0	5	7
4	0	0	6	4
5	0	0	1	2
6	0	0	1	1
7	0	0	1	0
8	0	0	3	0
9	0	0	2	0
10	1	0	1	0
11	0	0	0	0
12	0	0	0	0
13	0	0	0	0
14	0	0	0	0
15	0	0	1	0
16	0	0	1	0
Total	226	225	76	67

* The discrepancy between the "actual" and the "equal liability" accident totals is due to a similar discrepancy between the totals as given in a table in Newbold's paper, and as obtained from her curve.

words, large deviations from the average accident liability appear only in a very small minority of cases. Thus Newbold's set EIII is essentially a distribution of the simple Poisson type, plus one markedly deviant worker. Set EV may be viewed as a distribution of the composite Poisson type (excess variance = 41%) plus 9 deviant workers. Table 3 presents these data.

The differences between Newbold's findings and those of Greenwood and Woods, and of other investigators whose material is examined in this paper may possibly be attributed to the fact that her material consisted almost entirely of minor accidents. In spite of Newbold's statement, the reporting of accidents may not have been complete. It is difficult to ascertain the degree of completeness with which minor accidents were reported and there may have been individual differences in the reporting of accidents, producing the illusion of large differences in accident liability. On the other hand, constant personal characteristics may play a more direct role in the causation of minor accidents than in that of major accidents. Psychonanalysts generally believe that many accidents are unconscious self-injuries. It is possible that such unconscious self-injuries usually result in minor damage, just as in hysteria, in which minor self-injuries are common while major injuries are unusual. Minor accidents in industry may be often due to psychological mechanisms of the hysterical type.[21]

The distribution of the Connecticut licensed car drivers is essentially a composite Poisson distribution. A Greenwood and Yule "unequal liability" distribution fits the data rather well, except at the upper end. The results can be accounted for if one assumes that the distribution of accident liability deviates slightly from a Pearson III curve. The estimated portion of the variance of accident records attributable to differences in accident liability is 21.2%.

There is corroborative information from other sources, indicating that differences in accident liability often account for only a relatively small portion of the variance of accident records. The correlations between accident records in different periods of time reported by Newbold[22] and more recently by Ghiselli and Brown[23] are in most instances not high. Newbold's correlations range from −.01 to +.71, with a median of +.36. Ghiselli and Brown's correlations range from +.15 to +.80 with a median of +.42; we omit the intercorrelations between different kinds of accidents presented in both papers which are considerably lower. Such correlations justify inferences which are similar to those we arrived at by the use of a different method.

It should also be noted that the differences between automobile insurance rates for people with different accident records are nonexistent. This practice is in conformity with our findings. The usual textbook discussions of accident proneness would suggest very different insurance rates for different accident records.

When no composite Poisson distribution conforms to a set of accident data the suggested procedure is not applicable. The existence of factors

---

[21] This hypothesis was suggested to the writers by E. Emmons.
[22] E. M. Newbold, *op. cit.*
[23] E. E. Ghiselli and C. W. Brown, "Accident Proneness among Street Car Motormen and Motor Coach Operators," *Journal of Applied Psychology*, Vol. 32, 1948, pp. 20–23.

must be assumed, which alter the shapes of the constituent Poisson curves. Changes in accident liability of people as a function of previous accidents encountered suggest a possible explanation of such results. We did not attempt to verify this possibility inasmuch as there seemed to be no way of arriving at a reasonably plausible hypothesis about the course of these changes in terms of information available at present. The only hypothesis suggested so far in the literature seems to have been the one implied in Greenwood and Yule's "Biassed distribution," and it is untenable theoretically and therefore unsuitable for research. This distribution is simply a Poisson distribution with a different first term. If there were no initial differences in accident liability, but the first accident changed the accident liability of its participants which would subsequently remain constant, the resulting distribution would not be an incomplete Poisson distribution, because the one accident class would not grow as in the "simple chance" case. An incomplete Poisson distribution could be produced only by continuing changes in accident liability with successive accidents, and it would be a strange coincidence if these changes should be so graded as to produce a tail end of a Poisson distribution which has a completely different derivation.

The distributions which deviate significantly from any composite Poisson distributions are two of Greenwood and Woods' distributions (their Table 1A and 1B), the distributions of taxicab accidents and the distribution of street car accidents. Inspection of the data indicates that the obtained distributions are more leptokurtic than Poisson distributions, and compounding several of the latter can only flatten out the resulting shape. Several of Newbold's distributions may be in the same category; they were not examined in detail for reasons stated earlier. The share of differences in accident liability in the total variance cannot be determined in such cases. The existence of other factors than differences in accident liability and unpredictable "chance" factors must be assumed.

DISCUSSION

It must be remembered that not all differences in accident liability are differences in accident proneness viewed as an individual characteristic. This point is not a new one; it has been made among others by Newbold and by Cobb. It is disregarded by investigators who combine data about street car accidents or taxi accidents from different cities. In factory work, different jobs differ in conditions of safety. In automobile or other vehicle driving, the safety conditions are not necessarily the the same from route to route, in city compared with city. The amount of mileage driven, necessary driving in adverse weather, etc., must contribute more opportunities for accidents and these are not functions of accident proneness defined as an individual trait. For example, only 21.2% of the variance of the accident records of the Connecticut drivers was due to differences in constant accident rates. When one considers the hazards of driving just mentioned, it seems logical to state that there is not much room for differences in accident proneness as a psychological characteristic, insofar as these data are concerned.

We have pointed out that in many instances the portion of the variance of accident records attributable to differences in all forms of accident liability is relatively small as compared to the residual variance attributable to the operation of factors which are not predictable in terms of either the constant characteristics of people or of their previous accident records. These unpredictable or "chance" factors when operating alone give a so-called simple chance or equal liability or Poisson distribution. The expression "chance factors" should not be misunderstood. They are not necessarily unpredictable in terms of changing features of the life situation. Thus a well known psychoanalyst spoke to one of the writers about a man he knew who had a temporary period of accident proneness as a result of marital trouble, during which time he had several near-accidents in rapid succession. "Chance" refers only to lack of predictability in terms of constant characteristics of the individual.

There are many kinds of such "chance" factors. One kind does not seem to have received enough attention in the literature. Even when a person is clearly at fault in causing an accident, the accident might not have occurred if the circumstances had been different. One of the writers was once in a car driven by a man who did badly enough to have caused a very serious accident: the driver became frightened by a wasp on his leg and stopped looking at the road; shortly afterwards the car travelled into a ditch at the bottom of an embankment to the left of the highway. There had been no cars in the other traffic lane at the moment he crossed it, the embankment was not steep and there was no accident. About half a mile further there was a steep drop into a river on the left side. The expression "luck" seems to be quite appropriate here.

As Cobb pointed out, the correlation between accident records and a perfect test of accident proneness need not be high. One cannot use any arbitrary criterion for classifying people as excessively accident-prone. For example, Poffenberger[24] states that "accident prone drivers are those who have two or three times as many accidents as the average driver . . . the term need not be restricted to auto accidents . . . for it covers equally well accident repeaters in industry." In many distributions examined here the number of accidents per person is one-half an accident or less. According to Poffenberger then, this would mean that persons with one or more accidents are to be considered as accident prone. This is obviously unfair. It is legitimate to select for study those

---

[24] A. T. Poffenberger, *Principles of Applied Psychology* (New York: D. Appleton-Century Co., 1942).

people who have more than the average number of accidents but they should not be automatically classified as excessively accident prone without further evidence. Actually within a simple chance distribution some people are likely to have two to three times as many accidents as the average person. One can verify this by referring to the Poisson distributions in our tables. In most published distributions only a very small minority have accident records which lie completely above the point at which the Poisson distribution gives negligible values. As one approaches this point, one finds additional cases of more than average accident proneness, but some people with only average accident proneness who have had bad luck or temporary difficulties are also included in the group of people who have had many accidents. The problem of the exact estimation of the relative number of accident-prone individuals and bad luck individuals in any particular group of accident records is complicated. One should not attempt to make rough estimates without a comparison of obtained frequencies with the corresponding Poisson frequencies.

SUMMARY

1. A commonly used method of comparing percentages of men and of accidents proves nothing about the existence of differences in accident proneness. Examples proving the inconclusive nature of the method are cited.

2. Comparison of obtained accident distributions with simple chance (Poisson) distributions establishes that there are differences in accident liability but does not indicate whether these differences are large or small and does not exclude the simultaneous operation of unpredictable "chance" factors.

3. Different accident records do not necessarily represent different degrees of accident liability. A method for analysis of the variances of accident records of people into two component variances is suggested, one component attributable to differences in accident liability, the other to unpredictable "chance factors." It is pointed out that the method is only applicable when the obtained distribution resembles a composite of Poisson distributions.

4. A number of published distributions of accidents are examined by the use of the above method. The variance attributable to differences in accident liability varies considerably.

In the distributions which are examined in this paper and which do not involve primarily minor accidents, the variance attributable to differences in accident liability is in most cases between twenty and forty per cent of the total variance of accident records. Although differences in accident liability should not be overlooked as a factor in the different accident records of people, the effect of this factor is rather small as compared to the residual 60 to 80 per cent attributable to unpredictable factors. It is therefore apparent that in many instances personal accident proneness, which is but one of the components of accident liability, has been an overemphasized factor.

58. The Effect of Age and Experience upon Accident Rate*

R. H. Van Zelst

INDUSTRIAL ACCIDENTS, their prediction and control and the various factors related to and affecting them have long been a subject of study for the psychologist in industry. One of the specific topics of interest has been the relationships existing between the age and experience of the worker and his accident frequency.

Most research studies in this area have demonstrated the existence of some relationship between accidents and both experience and age. Though by no means universal the general conclusion arrived at in these experiments is that accident frequency tends to decline with increasing age and/or experience.

Many of the studies of experience suffer, however, from a procedural error. The most common method applied in this type of study appears to be to divide the men in a given organization into experience groups and then to calculate the accident rate of each group. The application of this method of necessity assumes that if no differences in experience exist, all of these different groups would have the same average number of accidents. However, it is also reasonable to assume that in many jobs the high-accident employees will tend to drop out either through retirement due to injury, separation or voluntarily leaving employment. Such a natural selection process tends to retain on the job only those persons who have maintained a certain safety standard in their operations.

The usually discovered decrease in accident frequency with experience may be due then to this natural selection process. What would then appear to be necessary in order that the effects of experience may be properly evaluated is to follow the accident history of the same group of workers over a period of time. Several studies[1] have done

* From *Journal of Applied Psychology*, Vol. 38, 1954, pp. 313–17.

[1] C. W. Brown, E. E. Ghiselli, and E. W. Minium, *Experience and Age in Relation to Proficiency of Street Car Motormen*, Report to Municipal Railway System of San Francisco, 1946; L. W. Chaney and H. S. Hanna, *Safety Movement in the Iron and*

this. Unfortunately, in most instances these studies either follow the employee's accident history for only a relatively short duration or fail to remove possible influences due to the operation of the age variable.

The study of the relationship between age and accident frequency presents a somewhat similar picture to the experience problem. The typical procedure here again is to subdivide employees into differing age groups and to compute the mean number of accidents for each age group. In most instances, however, age is highly correlated with experience, thus confusing the issue and making it difficult, if not impossible, clearly to ascribe any discovered relationship either to age or to experience.

Attempts have been made to minimize the effect of the experience variable through the utilization of partial correlational methods.[2] However, these methods are also subject to question in that it is not certain that experience may be held constant by using partial correlation methodology in view of the safety selection process previously mentioned. It seems probable that the operation of these selective factors prevents compliance with certain basic assumptions inherent in this statistical method.

It is the author's purpose therefore to present material obtained in a different manner from most of the previous studies in this field in an attempt to provide more information and gain further insight into the existence of the relationships between age and experience with accident frequency.

SUBJECTS

The subjects used in this study are employees of a copper plant in Indiana. These subjects were selected from six sections comprising a single large department operating metal forming mills. Work tasks were identical for the members of all groups and no unusual differences in pressures of production were observed for the different groups during the periods of data collection.

Conditions of work, light, heat, ventilation were also highly similar for all subjects as were the number of hours worked. Only employees working on the same shift were used in this experiment.

Conditions and methods of work, together with type of equipment, remained virtually constant throughout the five-year experimental period.

A total of 1,237 employees who remained with the company in the above mentioned department for the experimental period had their accident records carefully traced and charted for each month of the period. In addition other members of the work force hired at the same time

---

Steel Industry, Bur. Labor Statistics, Report 234, 1918; A. Hewes, "Study of Accident Records in a Textile Mill," *Journal of Industrial Hygiene*, Vol. 3, 1921, p. 187; H. M. Vernon, "Prevention of Accidents," *British Journal of Ind. Med.*, Vol. 2, 1945, p. 3.

[2] C. W. Brown, E. E. Ghiselli, and E. W. Minium, *op. cit.;* A. Hewes, *op. cit.*

(when the plant was first opened) but who dropped out or were separated also had their records carefully tabulated and recorded. These workers at the onset of the experimental period totaled an additional 1,317 workers.

The number of accidents experienced by each man was readily traced through employee history data which contained carefully detailed records of dispensary visits and their reason and cause. It is felt that this criterion is valid since it is a compulsory policy of the company to have all employees who are injured on the job, regardless of how slight the injury might be, visit the dispensary for medical clearance, treatment, and report. No distinctions as to severity of accident were made in this study. Only accidents occurring during working hours and in actual performance of the job were used.

Accident frequency data were reported on the basis of mean number of accidents per 1,000 man hours of operation. Payroll records of the subjects provided the necessary data for computation.

RESULTS

Figure 1 displays graphically the mean number of accidents per 1,000 man hours of operation for both of the experimental groups and also

FIGURE 1

THE RELATIONSHIP BETWEEN EXPERIENCE ON THE JOB AND THE AVERAGE MONTHLY
ACCIDENT RATE PER 1,000 HOURS OF OPERATION FOR A
NON-TURNOVER GROUP AND A TURNOVER GROUP

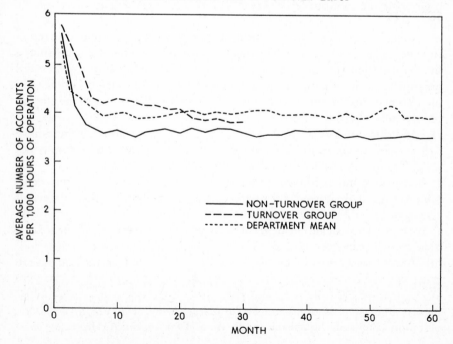

the entire departmental mean accident rate. Accident rate figures are reported on a monthly basis for a period of 60 months or 5 years. Accident rates for the turnover group are not reported after the first 30
months because of the small number of workers remaining in that group
beyond this period of time. (The number of workers in the turnover
group was reduced to 243 members at the end of thirty months.)

It can readily be seen from the presented data that in this particular instance the accident rate for these workers declines rapidly during the first five months of operation for both of the groups. The entire
department mean accident rate closely approximates the rate curves of
the two experimental groups. This is readily explained by the fact that
the two experimental groups, particularly in the early phases of the experimental period, comprised a majority of the entire work force.

The tendency for the departmental rate curve to be higher during
the latter phases of the experimental period can be attributed to the in-
corporation of newly hired employees into the work force.

The consistency with which the accident rate curve of the turnover
group remains higher than that of their fellow-workers tends to support
the hypothesis that a natural selection process does exist. The higher rate
and more gradual decline in accident frequency for this group of turnover employees apparently is indicative of an informal and perhaps to
some extent a formal weeding out of high accident workers.

In studying these accident rate graphs the effect of job experience
upon the accident rate of these workers appears to be considerable for
their first five months of employment, but seems to be of little significance beyond the fifth month of employment. The general leveling off
in accident rate after five months on the job seems to point up the thesis
that experience makes its contribution towards accident rate reduction
by familiarizing the employee with proper work and safety habits. Apparently five months of on-the-job duties is sufficient for these workers
on this particular type of operation to become well enough trained to
reduce accident rate to what may be considered normal expectancy. It
should be pointed out that these workers did not receive the benefit of
any formalized pre-job assignment training and so actual experience was
called upon to substitute for this formalized training.

These initially high accident rates would appear to lend further support to the often stressed necessity for proper immediate training in correct work methodology and safety habits.

In order to provide an experimental test of this conclusion the accident rates of another 872 workers were charted. These men had been
hired at various times after the company was better established and so
received the benefit of formal training in correct job procedure and
safety methods. These men also performed the same work tasks under
highly similar conditions. Data on this group for their first fifteen months
of employment are graphically presented in Figure 2.

FIGURE 2

THE RELATIONSHIP BETWEEN EXPERIENCE ON THE JOB AND THE AVERAGE MONTHLY
ACCIDENT RATE PER 1,000 HOURS OF OPERATION FOR A GROUP OF TRAINEES

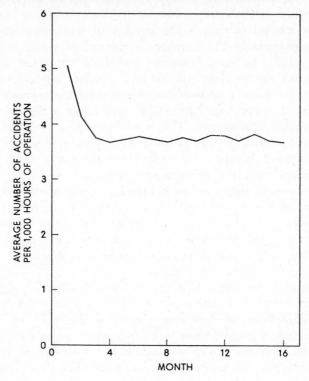

Results here follow the same general pattern found for the previous groups. There is an almost identical sharp decline in accident frequency for the early on-the-job period followed by the same leveling off pattern. Of note, however, is the fact that the initial accident frequency rate is markedly lower for this group. Furthermore, the level which approximates what has been termed normal expectancy for the previous groups is reached after the third month of on-the-job performance rather than after the fifth.

In view of the strong similarity between the work tasks and work environment of this and the other two previous groups, this reduction in the frequency of accidents amongst these workers for this formative period can in the author's opinion be traced only to the benefits derived from the formal training program.

However, the observed decline, still sharp, for these trained workers during the early phases of their employment still suggests the importance of actual accumulated on-the-job experience in bringing accident rates down to what might be considered normal.

Still untested is the effect of age upon accident frequency. To study this relationship two other groups were formed. These groups were matched on the experience variable. Group A was a young group (Mean Age = 28.7 years, S.D. = 1.4, N = 639) with approximately three years of experience (Mean experience = 2.9 years, S.D. = .45). Group B was composed of older workers (Mean Age = 41.1, S.D. = 2.9, N = 552) also with approximately three years of experience (Mean experience = 3.2 years, S.D. = .63).

Accident frequency rate for these groups (Figure 3) differs markedly throughout the eighteen month experimental period. Although both groups have the same amount of experience, the younger group has what appears to be a significantly higher accident rate than their older work companions.

As might be expected the younger group's (Group A) accident rate is above the department level while the mean accident rate of the older group (Group B) is below the department's level for these particular periods of time.

To further pursue this study of the effects of age upon accident frequency rate a third group (Group C) was used. These workers were similar to Group B in that they too were an older group (Mean Age = 39.2, S.D. = 3.1, N = 297), but unlike either of the two previous experimental groups these men were inexperienced at the onset of the experimental period. They did, however, receive the benefit of training prior to actual job assignment and performance.

As can be seen from Figure 3, the accident frequency rate for this group again as in past instances shows the same early sharp decline followed by a general leveling off to a position approximating that of the older group (Group B). The accident rate of Group C follows also the pattern of the previous trainee group although mean accident frequency is somewhat lower throughout the period.

It is to be noted that from the third month onward and practically from the second month onward the accident rate for this group of workers is lower than that of their younger and much more experienced fellow workers (Group A). It is also to be noted that this older group functions below the mean departmental level after what might be termed the three-month breaking-in period.

The greater strength of the relationship between age and accident frequency rate as compared with experience and accident frequency rate becomes even more noticeable as the experience level differences begin to disappear with the passage of time spent on the job.

It would appear then from these data that age is definitely related to accident frequency. Older employees in this study even when less experienced maintain better safety records than do the younger men. The accident rate of these younger workers exceeds slightly the mean accident rate level of the entire department despite the disparity in job experience. Their rate, in fact, appears from the data to be exceeded only

FIGURE 3

The Relationship between the Age of the Employee
and Average Monthly Accident Rate per 1,000 Hours of Operation

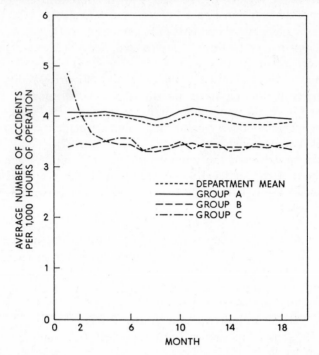

by those employees who are currently in the breaking-in stage of
development.

SUMMARY AND CONCLUSIONS

The results obtained in this experiment seem to indicate that at least
for these groups of men and for this particular type of operation the
effect of experience upon the frequency rate of accidents apparently is
limited to a three to five month period of initial on-the-job performance.
This particular period of time may be termed a breaking-in period and it
is characterized by a sharp decline in the number of accidents. Following
this period there is a leveling off in accident rate throughout the employee's work history. This rather level period may be considered to be
normal expectancy.

When the workers are given formal training prior to actual job
performance there is a considerable reduction in early accident frequency rate, which is manifested in lower initial accident frequency
and also in what may be regarded as a faster developmental period in
that the amount of time required for the trained work groups to level off
at the normally expected frequency is significantly reduced.

It would appear that age in this instance apparently exerts a greater influence upon accident rate than does experience once the breaking-in stage is passed. From the comparisons made between the matched work groups it has been found that older workers tend to have fewer accidents than their younger co-workers. This appears to be true throughout the employee's work history when similar groups are compared. Lower accident rates are remarkably characteristic of these older men from their earliest job performance on.

It is the author's opinion, although no conclusive evidence is presented, that since age exerts the stronger influence upon accident frequency rate, beyond initial employment, it is necessary to explain accidents in part on the basis of immaturity of employees. Furthermore, the usually found reduction in accident rate with increasing age and experience can also be attributed to some extent to the operation of a natural selection process which results in the weeding out of workers less fit for the job. It is also felt that little importance can be attached to the effect of experience upon accident rate for periods other than that of initial employment particularly when the effects of age and the natural selection process are eliminated. Proper training in correct work methodology and safety habits can further reduce the effect of experience upon accident rate but cannot apparently substitute completely for actual job performance in helping the worker to internalize fully the correct procedures and habits necessary to efficient operation from the safety standpoint.

59. Psychological Climate and Accidents*

Vernon Keenan, Willard Kerr, and William Sherman

IN THE BELIEF that certain factors of psychological climate and physical environment may be of great importance in the causation of accidents in heavy industry, the authors formulated a series of hypotheses concerning correlates of accidents and subjected each to an experimental design for testing. The hypotheses were:

1. Excessive variation in pressure to "get out production" induces stress and tension contributing to accidents.
2. Intensity of normal production schedules contribute to accidents.

* From "Psychological Climate and Accidents in an Automotive Plant," *Journal of Applied Psychology*, Vol. 35, No. 2, 1951, pp. 108–11.

The authors gratefully acknowledge the indispensable aid and original suggestions of Mr. Howard M. Huntington, Safety Supervisor, International Harvester Tractor Works.

3. High promotion probability encourages alertness which reduces accidents.

4. A comfortable shop environment reduces accidents by minimizing physical annoyances and distractions.

5. Emphasis on individual responsibility (rather than upon crew work) acts to reduce accidents.

6. A reasonable level of job prestige is required for safe behavior.

7. Heavy manual work induces stress, fatigue, and weariness, which increase probability of accident.

8. Incentive pay systems encourage alertness which in turn promotes safe behavior.

9. Relative adequacy-predictability of work space is essential for avoidance of distraction-worry and safety.

10. Presence of an obvious and threatening danger has a semi-hypnotic effect upon the worker and increases accidents which are unrelated to the obvious danger.

SUBJECTS

Lost-time accident records of 7,103 (average) personnel of a tractor factory for the 1944–48 five-year period were tabulated for each of the 44 shop departments of the plant, and accident rate per 100 personnel was computed for each department. The enterprise experienced 1,943 lost-time accidents during this period, and departmental rates per hundred personnel per year ranged from 1.5 to 13.2.

PROCEDURE

Five-point continuum ratings on each of the variables shown in Table 1 were collected independently from each member of a "best-informed" panel of judges. This panel of eight judges, all individuals with at least ten years of diversified experience in the plant, includes the staff assistant to the works manager, the assistant works manager, the general superintendent, the plant engineer, the chief of methods and rates, the planning engineer, the safety supervisor, and the industrial relations manager. Split-half (odd-versus-even judges) reliability coefficients corrected via the Spearman-Brown prophecy formula for these ratings are indicated in Table 1.

Mean judge ratings on each department, on each of the ten variables, then were computed and the departmental means on each variable were correlated with departmental accident rates. Intercorrelations among all variables also are shown in Table 1.

RESULTS

Results of these correlational studies between accident rates and certain psychological characteristics of organizational units are displayed in Table 1. A summary inspection of the table suggests that several of the ten hypotheses stated receive enough confirmation to continue them as tenable into more rigorous future researches.

TABLE 1

PEARSONIAN INTERCORRELATIONS AMONG ACCIDENT RATE AND EACH OF TEN OTHER VARIABLES IN 44 DEPARTMENTS OF A TRACTOR FACTORY (7,103 PERSONNEL)*

VARIABLE	1	2	3	4	5	6	7	8	9	10	11
1. Variation in Pressure to Get Things Done	*-.42*	.27	.00	-.60	.56	-.30	.24	.55	.78	.11	.11
2. Constant Pressure to Get Things Done	.27	*.26*	.23	-.94	.42	-.08	.84	.67	.50	.65	-.06
3. Promotion Probability	.00	.23	*.92*	-.67	-.28	.94	-.11	.00	.56	.43	-.01
4. Comfortable Shop Environment	-.60	-.94	-.67	*.82*	-.50	.44	-.46	-.59	-.11	-.53	-.70
5. Degree of Crew Work	.56	.42	-.28	-.50	*.91*	.00	.58	.46	.13	.37	.33
6. Job Prestige	-.30	-.08	.94	.44	.00	*.99*	-.30	-.34	.05	.18	-.23
7. Manual Effort Involved	.24	.84	-.11	-.46	.58	-.30	*.83*	.68	.36	.64	.47
8. Degree of Operational Congestion	.55	.67	.00	-.59	.46	-.34	.68	*.70*	.49	.47	.45
9. Degree of Incentive Work	.78	.50	.56	-.11	.13	.05	.36	.49	*.76*	.43	.28
10. Degree of Obvious Danger Factor	.11	.65	.43	-.53	.37	.18	.64	.47	.43	*.95*	.35
11. Accident Rate	.11	-.06	-.01	-.70	.33	.23	.47	.45	.28	.35	*.73*

* Coefficients in boldface type are statistically significant at the five per cent level of confidence or better. Coefficients in italics represent odd-even–corrected reliability coefficients, except for accident rate which is not corrected.

Variation and Volume of Production Pressure. Neither of these variables seem to be significantly related to accident rate. The extraordinary fact of a negative (−.42) reliability coefficient suggests the chance identification of two "schools of thought" as to what constitutes "pressure to get things done." Since each of these variables correlate substantially with at least one other variable in Table 1, it is obvious that the split-half reliability coefficients in these two instances are gross underestimates.

Partial correlations of $r_{1,11.9} = -.18$ and $r_{1,11.4} = -.55$ help estimate possible effects of incentive work and comfort of shop environment on the relationship between accidents and rated variation in production pressure. When comfort of shop environment is held constant by partial correlation, the relationship increases to statistical significance, suggesting *fewer* accidents in departments with above average variation in production pressure. While all statistics in this study which pertain to production pressure are somewhat questionable in interpretation because of the apparently divided opinions of raters, it is possible that variation in production pressure tends to reduce accidents by reducing monotony and encouraging alertness.

Similarly, when comfort of shop environment is held constant, the partial correlation between constant production pressure and departmental accident rate attains (inverse) a value of unity. If this result is not artifactual, it may be that production pressure even when constant encourages alertness which in turn makes for safe behavior.

Promotion Probability. Although the zero order correlation between departmental promotion probability and accident rate is insignificant, the relationship becomes significant (−.90) when comfort of shop environment is held constant by partial correlation. This result is consistent with the finding of a significant correlation of $-.40$ between these same two variables in a New Jersey electronics plant.[1]

Comfortable Shop Environment. Most significant of the findings in this research is the discovery of a correlation of $-.70$ between accident rate and mean-rated comfort of the shop environment. Partial correlations holding constant degree of operational congestion ($-.60$), manual effort involved ($-.55$), constant pressure ($-.96$), and degree of crew work ($-.66$) sustain the original correlation. The psychological implication of this result is that approximately half of the variance in departmental accident rates is accounted for by variance in the comfort factor. Heavy industries in which forges and foundries are essential operations inevitably experience great difficulty in making some job environment physically comfortable. Heat radiating from molten metals, violent sound vibrating from drop forges, and gritty earth particles from foundry "molds" are vivid examples of the practical obstacles to comfortable adjustment of the worker to the job.

Workers with low "physical frustration tolerance" under conditions of heat, noise, etc., probably have somewhat higher accident frequency than their co-workers. An accumulation of physical frustration tensions leads easily to "distractive" behavior which often results simultaneously in reduced quality of work and accident. It should be emphasized, however—and this qualification is supported by the evidence of Mintz and Blum[2]—that variance in such accident proneness of individuals probably accounts for a minority of the variance in accident rates. In other words, the "normal" worker as well as the "prone" worker is prone to these same unsafe behaviors under identical frustrating conditions, but at a slightly better threshold of tolerance. A reasonable conclusion under such evidence appears to be that *major preventative effort can most profitably be expended in working to alleviate as much as possible the overall physical frustrations which impinge on all personnel.* Such effort can reasonably be expected to reduce the accident rates of both the more-prone and less-prone personnel.

Degree of Crew Work. Departments in which the typical job performance is in a "crew" often have above-average accident rates. Crew work in difficult operations (e.g., moving a hot ingot to position in a drop forge and later removal of the shaped part calls not only for reasonably synchronous action and cooperation of the crew members, but constant vigilance for the continous accepting and relinquishing of responsibility as well as the development of any unusual circumstances. Less stringent cooperative work sometimes has greater accident probability also in large part perhaps because of the occasional transition moments in which

---

[1] W. A. Kerr, "Accident Proneness of Factory Departments," *Journal of Applied Psychology*, Vol. 34, 1950, pp. 167–70.

[2] A. Mintz, and M. L. Blum, "A Re-examination of the Accident-Proneness Concept," *Journal of Applied Psychology*, Vol. 33, 1949, pp. 195–211. (See Article 57.)

responsibility for consequences is vague or suspended but operations nevertheless continue, from momentum if nothing else. In those brief seconds, accidents are made. In individual-type work the individual rarely is uncertain about responsibility for consequences.

Job Prestige. It is interesting to note that while this correlation of $-.23$ with accidents is not statistically significant, it is highly consistent with the value of $-.30$ found in the 53 departments of the Camden Works of RCA.[3] Combining the two plants makes a total of 97 departments with a total of 18,000 personnel, and the relationship between job prestige and accident rate is established as highly significant. Partial correlation evidence, however, suggests that the relationship is at least in part artifactual. When comfort of shop environment is held constant, the coefficient declines to .12, and when manual effort is held constant it declines to $-.10$. High accident departments are characterized by less physical comfort and a demand for greater manual effort; incidentally, they are of lower average prestige value, but this fact seems to have little causal bearing upon accident rate.

Manual Effort. The greater the degree of manual effort involved in successful performance of the typical job, the greater the tendency toward accidents ($r = .47$). This relationship persists ($r_{7,11.2} = .96$) when "pressure to get things done" is held constant by partial correlation. As in the demand for constant vigilance in crew work, the demand for physical energy sometimes exceeds efficiently directed supply. Workers trained in economical expenditure of effort as well as in control of physical forces may reduce the frequency of such accidents.

Operational Congestion. "Degree of operational congestion" implies frequency-proximity of moving objects and persons. Such activities in the psychological periphery of the immediate task may connote greater annoyance-distraction value than actual physical threat to the worker, but may contribute ($r = .45$) to unsafe behavior of personnel. A limitation to this interpretation is the fact that the correlation declines to .06 when comfort of shop environment is held constant by partial correlation. In view of this limitation, a causal interpretation of the zero order r is not warranted.

Incentive Work. Departments with incentive work may on the average incur a few more accidents than do departments on the "straight-time" payment system. This is suggested by the original correlation of .28 (not significant) which is increased to .35 when promotion probability is held constant. While evidence is not available to test the point, it is possible that when more work is being performed (as it usually is under an incentive system) more accidents will occur. Thus, an increase in accidents under incentive conditions might be a function of increased productivity or productive activity ("motionless bodies" rarely have

---

[3] W. A. Kerr, *op. cit.*

accidents). On the other hand, this finding barely borders on statistical significance and similar study of another factory yielded a correlation of .00 between incentive system and departmental accident rate.[4]

Obvious Danger Factor. Departments with a constant obvious danger present such as glowing molten metal have significantly higher accident rates ($r = .35$) than do other departments. An arresting finding by Mr. Huntington, the Safety Supervisor, on the nature of the accidents in these departments is that the accidents usually are not physically involved with the obvious hazard factor. For example, in molten metal operation departments, accident rates are above average but they rarely include burns. The obvious hazard seems to exercise an almost hypnotic effect upon personnel, delimiting their attention too much and facilitating their involvement in other hazards. When comfort of shop environment is held constant (this is a questionable procedure in this instance because "comfort" and "danger factor" may be regarded as almost synonomous in certain key departments), the zero order r declines to a partial r of $-.04$ between obvious danger factor and departmental accident rate.

SUMMARY

Against a criterion of five years of lost-time accident rates in the 44 shop departments of a tractor factory, ten possible explanatory hypotheses were evaluated by means of data from a special rating panel. Until more exacting and precise data are obtained, all conclusions of this research must be considered tentative; however, within these limitations, certain trends appear.

1. Results obtained on variation in production pressure and constant production pressure are inconclusive.

2. The hypothesis that promotion probability encourages safe behavior appears to be supported by this study.

3. Comfortable shop environment appears from this research to be a major determinant of safe behavior.

4. Degree of crew work is positively correlated with accident rates of the factory departments in this study. This is believed to be the result of more complete and continuous acceptance of individual responsibility in the noncooperative work situation.

5. Job prestige of typical job fails to correlate significantly with departmental accidents when certain other variables are held constant.

6. The greater the degree of manual effort involved, the higher, on the average, is the departmental accident rate.

7. Both degree of operational congestion and degree of incentive work fail to predict departmental accident rates when certain other variables are held constant.

---

[4] W. A. Kerr, *op. cit.*

8. The effects of an "obvious danger factor" on departmental accident rates are somewhat uncertain, although observational evidence indicates that where an obvious danger factor exists, the accidents which occur tend *not* to be identified with the obvious danger. Existence of an impressive obvious hazard seems to contribute to "unrelated" accidents by delimiting attention and encouraging proneness to involvement in the non-obvious hazards.

60. Complementary Theories of Safety Psychology*

Willard Kerr

PROBABLY THE most universally ignored area of safety psychology is that pertaining to the psychological climate of the workplace. A devotion to safety gadgets on the one hand and concern for the alleged proneness factors within the accident repeater on the other hand has led to the almost total neglect of the situational factors which help shape work personality and help manufacture accident-free or accident-liable employees.

Many investigators[1] have shown that becoming a safe worker is a typical learning function. The decline in accidents from date of employment in the typical job is a representative learning curve. But like other learning curves, the decline in error performance can be obstructed by a multitude of other factors. It now appears that a chief obstruction to the rapid decline in error performance is defective psychological climate. This conclusion, to be supported in this paper, stands in sharp contrast to past emphasis upon the accident proneness theory.

THE ACCIDENT PRONENESS THEORY

Before presenting the crucial evidence on this theory, the term "accident proneness" should be defined. *Accident proneness* is a constitutional (i.e., permanent) tendency within the organism to engage in unsafe behavior within some stated field of vocational activity. A temporary tendency to have accidents is not proneness; it is liability. And proneness is not general; that is, its referrent to an activity field must be

---

* From *Journal of Social Psychology*, Vol. 45, 1957, pp. 3–9.

[1] R. H. Van Zelst. "The Effect of Age and Experience upon the Accident Rate," *Journal of Applied Psychology*, Vol. 38, 1954, pp. 313–17. (See Article 58.)

limited to be meaningful, for, obviously, *everyone* is "accident prone" in a general sense because there are potential tasks that no human being can perform without accident (e.g., climb the outside walls of the Empire State Building to the top with one's bare hands).

Professors Mintz and Blum[2] and Maritz[3] have shown that the accident proneness theory has been explaining entirely too much of the industrial accident rate. The research of Cobb,[4] Johnson,[5] Whitlock and Crannell,[6] Forbes,[7] Farmer and Chambers,[8] and Harris[9] point toward the same conclusion. Mintz and Blum showed that the frequency of "repeater" accidents approximates a pure chance (Poisson) distribution. Maritz then suggested that the final crucial test of variance in the industrial accident rate accounted for by proneness is the correlation between one's accidents experienced over two different periods of accident exposure—such as the last two years and the next two years. Ghiselli and Brown[10] have collated 18 such coefficients from the literature, and the present author has computed their median; it is .38. This typical value suggests that only about 15 per cent of the variance in individual accidents is accounted for by variance in individual accident proneness; furthermore, this even may be spuriously high because such coefficients are contaminated by the correlation of the worker's position hazard with the consistency of his accidents over split time periods. In fact, it is almost certain that much, if not most, of this 15 per cent of potential variance due to accident proneness actually is due to environmental factors (temperature differences, fumes, congestion-space-threat differences, etc.) left uncontrolled and hence correlated with each other in the 18 coefficients cited.

---

[2] A. Mintz and M. L. Blum, "A Re-examination of the Accident Proneness Concept," *Journal of Applied Psychology*, Vol. 33, 1949, pp. 195–211. (See Article 57.)

[3] J. S. Maritz, "On the Validity of Inferences Drawn from the Fitting of Poisson and Negative Binomial Distributions to Observed Accident Data," *Psychological Bulletin*, Vol. 47, pp. 434–43.

[4] P. W. Cobb, unpublished reports to Highway Research Board, Washington, D.C., 1938–39 (summarized in H. M. Johnson, "The Detection and Treatment of Accident-Prone Drivers," *Psychological Bulletin*, Vol. 43, 1946, pp. 489–532).

[5] H. M. Johnson, *op. cit.*

[6] J. B. Whitlock and C. W. Crannell, "An Analysis of Certain Factors in Serious Accidents in a Large Steel Plant," *Journal of Applied Psychology*, Vol. 33, 1949, pp. 494–98.

[7] T. W. Forbes, "The Normal Automobile Driver as a Traffic Problem," *Journal of General Psychology*, Vol. 20, 1939, pp. 471–74.

[8] E. Farmer and E. G. Chambers, "A Study of Personal Qualities in Accident Proneness and Proficiency" (London: Industrial Health Research Board, Report No. 55, 1929).

[9] F. J. Harris, "A Comparison of the Personality Characteristics of Accident and Non-accident Industrial Population" (abstract), *American Psychologist*, Vol. 4, 1949, p. 279.

[10] E. E. Ghiselli and C. W. Brown, *Personnel and Industrial Psychology* (New York: McGraw-Hill, 1948).

Even allowing the unreasonable assumption that these 18 coefficients were not influenced by fatigue and stress differences in different job locations, the 15 per cent of variance in accidents "accounted for" by proneness still leaves 85 per cent of the variance in accident rates unaccounted for.

It is interesting that an earlier study of automobile drivers by Forbes[11] arrived independently at the similar conclusion that the accident repeater contributes not more than three or four per cent to the accident problem. Both Johnson[12] and Thorndike[13] who later surveyed the entire research literature on automobile safety likewise found that such constitutional factors as basic aptitudes yielded negligible relationships with accident records. Relevant, also, is the fact that Hunt, Wittson, and Burton[14] computed the psychiatric discharge rate at Naval induction stations and subsequently during World War II to vary between four and nine per cent (such dischargees were, of course, those individuals regarded as "prone" to behavior unsafe to themselves and/or their country).

Two situational or climatic theories may explain the remaining non-chance variance.

THE GOALS FREEDOM ALERTNESS THEORY

Plainly, both management and union training activities, policies, and leaderships are responsible for some interference with the normal decline of error performance.

In stating this theory now, we hold that *great freedom to set reasonably attainable goals is accompanied typically by high quality work performance*. This theory regards an accident merely as a low-quality work behavior—a "scrappage" that happens to a person instead of to a thing. Raising the level of quality involves raising the level of alertness; such high alertness cannot be sustained except within a rewarding psychological climate. The more rich, therefore, the climate in diverse (economic and non-economic) reward opportunities, the higher the level of alertness—and the higher the level of work quality. Obviously, the rewards system must be geared to support high quality work behavior.

In business practice some training interferes by too much "telling what to do and what not to do" and too little encouragement to the new worker to do his own thinking and "stand on his own feet." Union leadership likewise often is guilty of too much propagandizing and not enough "asking" in relations with new workers. Such initial climate for

---

[11] T. W. Forbes, *op. cit.*

[12] H. M. Johnson, *op. cit.*

[13] R. L. Thorndike, "The Human Factor in Accidents," *USAF School of Aviation Medical Reports*, Randolph Field, Texas, Feb., 1951.

[14] W. A. Hunt, C. L. Wittson, and H. W. Burton, "Further Validation of Naval Neuropsychiatric Screening," *Journal of Consulting Psychology*, Vol. 14, 1950, pp. 485–88.

the new worker is less conducive to alertness than to a relatively un-motivated, resigned, passive conformity to the apparently already-structured total situation.

Accidents, of course, show that the total situation is *not* firmly structured and from them the worker gradually accepts more self responsibility in order to survive. But an accident is an expensive teaching device. Furthermore, if it occurs in a climate in which the employee is expected to supply his energy but not his opinions or ideas, the accident is misunderstood as a foreign intruder which does not belong in the scheme of events. In such circumstances, it rarely occurs to management, union, or worker that an accident is made necessary and inevitable in order to teach the employee his own individuality and essential personal dignity.

Even the teaching efficiency of the accident itself is interfered with, however, if most aspects of the total psychological climate in effect deny that the individual's own mental content is important.

If the climate encourages the individual to set up long-term and short-term goals with reasonable probability of attainment, the *Gestalt* of the work situation seems less fixed and the worker feels himself to be a significant participant. Significant participation makes for habits of alertness, problem-raising, and problem-solving. The psychological work environment must reward the worker emotionally for being alert, for seeking to contribute constructive suggestions, for passing a tip to a co-worker on how best to do something or how not to get hurt, and for achievement out of the ordinary. The worker must feel free to exercise influence over his environment.

Considerable evidence supports this theory. Factory departments with more movement of personnel among departments, that is, intra-company transfer mobility, have fewer accidents[15]; the same is true of departments with greater promotion probability for the typical employee (r is $-.40$).[16] Departments with the best suggestion records (rewarded) tend to have fewer accidents.[17] Additional evidence of the influence of the stimulating individual climate on safety is found in the tendency toward fewer accidents in individual-type than in crew-type jobs at the International Harvester Works.[18] In individual-type work, the employee rarely is uncertain about his responsibility for consequences; he better knows his immediate work goals. Another interesting bit of evidence is that in two

---

[15] W. A. Kerr, "Accident Proneness of Factory Departments," *Journal of Applied Psychology*, Vol. 34, 1950, pp. 167–70.

[16] *Ibid.*

[17] *Ibid.*

[18] V. Keenan, W. A. Kerr, and W. E. Sherman, "Psychological Climate and Accidents in an Automotive Plant," *Journal of Applied Psychology*, Vol. 35, 1951, pp. 108–11. (See Article 59.)

different studies[19] the factory departments with incentive pay systems, although problem departments in regards to monotony, lower job prestige, and lower promotion probability, still have no more accidents than departments without incentive pay systems. This seems in such defiance of expectations as to suggest that incentive pay systems restrict accidents by encouraging greater individual initiative and alertness.

Accidents are more frequent in jobs of lower-rated prestige[20]; one interpretation of this finding is that climatically the job must seem worthy enough to the worker to sustain his euphoria level. This interpretation is supported by the finding of Hersey[21] that out of 400 accidents which were studied clinically, more than half took place when the worker was in a worried, apprehensive, or some other low emotional state.

This individual goals-freedom-alertness theory suggests the climatic need for providing emotional reward opportunities for alertness—such as special economic incentives, prestige-building honors, extra privileges, machine and work space decoration contest participation, and representation on special committees and councils. These rewards held as attainable goals by workers in relatively "dead end" jobs should operate to raise the average level of alertness, not just to hazards but to everything.

THE ADJUSTMENT STRESS THEORY

The individual goals opportunity alertness theory of safety seems to cover much of the variance not covered by the proneness theory, but some variance still remains and it appears necessary to verbalize a third theory. Probably almost all of the remaining variance can be explained by a third theory—*an adjustment stress theory. It holds that unusual, negative, distracting stress upon the organism increases its liability to accident or to other low quality behavior.* This too is a climatic theory, because environment is internal as well as external, and this theory refers to distractive negative stresses imposed upon the individual organism either by internal environment (such as disease organisms, alcohol, or toxic items) or by external environment (such as temperature excesses, poor illumination, excessive noise level, excessive physical work strain). Its stresses are different from those experienced by the accident prone; their stresses result from a *constitutional* inadequacy. Ordinary adjustment stress is *not* the result of constitutional inadequacy but of temporary conditions.

What often appears at first to be constitutional accident proneness may be shown very clearly upon more careful examination to be the operation

---

[19] *Ibid.*; W. A. Kerr, "Accident Proneness of Factory Departments," *op. cit.*

[20] *Ibid.*

[21] R. B. Hersey, "Emotional Factors in Accidents," *Personnel Journal*, Vol. 15, 1936, pp. 59–65.

of *temporary* stress factors. The most sobering example of this is found in the curve of accident rates of successive age groups of industrial workers.[22] This curve shows high rates in the first 10 years of the worklife and a secondary increase in rates between the ages of 40 and 55. These age periods also are the great stress periods in the typical worklife; this is suggested by the fact that the accident rate curve and the turnover rate curve[23] superimpose almost perfectly upon each other when plotted through successive age groups of the industrial population. The alleged proneness within the young accident repeater is largely dissipated when one considers that most of the stress is environmental—and associated with adjustment to work discipline, attaining self-sufficiency away from parental ties, courtship, marriage, assumption of family economic responsibilities, and the struggle for a foothold on a vocational ladder that seems to lead somewhere worthwhile. Another set of obvious stress explanations comes to mind to account for the "middle-age boom" in accident rate.

Temporary stress factors which already have been found significantly correlated with accident rates include employee age,[24] workplace temperature,[25] illumination,[26] mean rated comfort of the shop (r is $-.70$),[27] degree of operational congestion,[28] obvious danger factor threateningly present,[29] manual effort involved in job (r is .47),[30] weight of parts handled,[31] frequency of parts handled,[32] alcohol consumption,[33] and influence of disease organisms.[34]

COMPLEMENTARY LIMITATIONS AND INTERPRETATIONS

It seems wise to emphasize that both of these new theories of safety complement each other as well as existing proneness theory. In the

---

[22] W. A. Kerr, "Psychological Climate and Safety" (address, Midwest Safety Show, National Safety Council, Chicago, Hotel Sherman, May 4, 1950).

[23] H. D. Kitson, "A Critical Age as a Factor in Labor Turnover," *Journal of Industrial Hygiene*, Vol. 4, 1922, pp. 199–203.

[24] W. A. Kerr, "Psychological Climate and Safety," *op. cit.*

[25] J. W. Griffith, "The Time Factor in a Psychological Analysis of Accidents" (unpublished master's thesis) (Chicago: Illinois Institute of Technology, June, 1950).

[26] H. M. Vernon, T. Bedford, and C. G. Warner, "A Study of Absenteeism in Certain Scottish Collieries" (London: Industrial Health Research Board, Report No. 62, 1931).

[27] V. Keenan, W. A. Kerr, and W. E. Sherman, *op. cit.*

[28] *Ibid.*

[29] *Ibid.*

[30] *Ibid.*

[31] *Ibid.*

[32] *Ibid.*

[33] H. M. Vernon, *Accidents and Their Prevention* (New York: Macmillan, 1937).

[34] E. M. Newbold, "A Contribution to the Study of the Human Factor in the Causation of Accidents" (London: Industrial Fatigue Research Board, Report No. 34, 1919).

goals-freedom-alertness theory it must be recognized that (*a*) even under an optimal opportunity climate, individuals who lack the characteristics necessary for the work probably will continue to have accidents; (*b*) excessive physical stresses can cause accidents in any psychological climate; and (*c*) psychological stresses relative to adjustment to changing life aspirations, family and marital affairs, etc., still will carry over into the workplace psychological climate and cause accidents.

In the adjustment stress theory it must be admitted that individual differences do exist in ability to withstand what ordinarily would be stress-inducing situations. Yet, such individual differences account for less than one-fifth of the variance in individual accident rates; therefore, the limitations on the accident proneness theory appear to be much more severe than those on the adjustment stress theory. The fact is that both employer judgment and job applicant judgment operate to prevent the operation of any great amount of accident proneness. While all of us are accident prone for one task or another, we don't ordinarily apply for or allow ourselves to be engaged in such tasks—and we probably couldn't get hired for such tasks if we tried.

On the basis of the evidence summarized and the author's own estimates, the variance in accident rates among industrial personnel probably distributes in terms of theoretical causation according to the following pattern:

Accident proneness	1% to 15%
Individual goals-opportunity-alertness	30% to 40%
Adjustment stress	45% to 60%
Total Variance	100%

Constructive thinking about the individual goals opportunity climate and about adjustment stresses should assist industry to escape the defeatism of the overly-emphasized proneness theory and better understand and control accidents.

Section *Nine*

ENGINEERING
PSYCHOLOGY

Introduction

THE GROWING AWARENESS that man and machines function in relation to each other has led to a branch of applied science known as "engineering psychology." This field deals with ways of designing machines, operations, and work environments so that they match human capacities and limitations. Various other terms have been used, more or less interchangeably, to label this field, including *human engineering, applied experimental psychology, biomechanics,* and *ergonomics*.

Much of the recent research in this field grew out of military necessity, since the development of increasingly complex weapon and support systems required better information on the human capacities needed to perform them. Today, engineering psychology is prominent in many diverse fields in industry. Psychologists contribute to the design of household appliances, guided-missile control panels, radar scopes, artificial limbs, telephone sets, electronic computers, semiautomatic post office equipment, jet aircraft cockpits, and numerous other industrial machines.

The articles in this section require little introduction since they include the best statements available on the concepts, definition, scope, and typical problems in the field. The article by Mead, "A Program of Human Engineering," gives some of the history in the development of the field, offers a definition which distinguishes it from related areas, and outlines some typical problems and results obtained in human engineering research on displays, controls, systems, and optimal environment.

In Taylor's article, "Psychology and the Design of Machines," we get a highly sophisticated treatment of the *man-machine systems concept*. Taylor's article represents the "new look" in engineering psychology with its emphasis on man as "an organic data transmission and processing link" inserted between the mechanical or electronic displays and controls of a machine. Here we encounter the notions of man as an information channel, a multipurpose computer, and a feedback control system. This article also describes the role of the engineering psychologist in basic research, in designing machines, and in evaluating man-machine systems.

The next article brings us face to face with the study of a specific, highly complex man-machine system. The problem is a very topical one—the design of a safe and efficient system of aircraft control in airport terminal areas. In "Some Concepts and Methods for the Conduct of Man-Machine System Research in a Laboratory Setting," Fitts, Schipper, Kidd, Shelly, and Kraft describe how research on this important problem was planned, the methodological and conceptual issues which had to be solved, the variables studied, and the procedures for evaluating the system developed.

The final three articles deal with specific research representative of "display," "information processing," and "control" problems in equipment design. The term "display" refers to various means of providing information to people. A whole set of display problems is represented in the area of instrument and dial design. The article by Norah Graham, entitled "The Speed and Accuracy of Reading Horizontal, Vertical, and Circular Scales," illustrates one such problem.

Karlin's article, "Human Factors Evaluation of a New Telephone Numerical Dialing System," gives us an advance look into a probable change in telephone dial design. The article illustrates that there are all kinds of "common sense" reasons in support of each of two alternative designs, but that research on differences in accuracy, speed, "memory" and preference seems to favor the new design. The article also illustrates the not infrequent relation between consumer psychology and engineering psychology.

The final article is entitled "The Tactual Identification of Shapes for Coding Switch Handles," by Green and Anderson. They show how it is possible to design equipment with control handles which will be least subject to confusion by the human operator.

61. A Program of Human Engineering*

Leonard C. Mead

HUMAN ENGINEERING problems seem to arise whenever man is confronted with technological advancements. Perhaps the primitive cave dweller would have profited if his tools and weapons had been shaped and weighted so as to fit his psychophysiological capacities. The need for such modifications, however, does not seem to have been very pressing; it resembles giving Aristotle a telephone. Not until the machine age was well advanced in the 19th century did anyone do any systematic worrying about the fact that man was actually the weak sister in mechanized production. The time-study work of Taylor in the 80's, followed by the motion-study contribution of the Gilbreths, represent the first organized attempts to make a man a more efficient partner in the modern industrial scene.

During this same period the notion was being developed in the new field of psychology that individuals are constituted differently and that some people are naturally better suited than others for particular types of jobs. The mental testing movement led to the development of intelligence and aptitude tests. World War I gave both impetus and status to personnel selection. Thus, during the early decades of the 20th century we find both engineers and psychologists attempting to adapt human beings to the demands of a technological society.

Meanwhile another group of scientists, the experimental psychologists, were developing their field by the discovery of new facts and techniques concerning man's sensory and perceptual processes. It was a long time before this group became enmeshed in the practical problems of matching man with the technical appurtenances of his civilization. In fact, the leading experimentalists took pride in divorcing themselves from the applied aspects of their research and a number of psychological publications made the point that this psychology must remain "pure." The stress of a World War II, however, brought this group of specialists into the human engineering field. Early in the war it was observed that the potentialities of modern weapons and equipment, despite superior engineering achievements, were not yielding the performance that their advanced design seemed to merit. It was recognized, too late in many instances, that the human operator remained as an essential link in military

* From *Personnel Psychology*, Vol. 1, 1948, pp. 303–17.

tasks and procedures, and that special effort is required to design the equipment so that it fits the natural characteristics of the average man. It was the experimental psychologist who seemed to know the most about these normal capabilities of man. What World War I did for the mental testing movement, World War II seems to have done for experimental psychology. In tracing the history of this movement, it is interesting to note that engineers first invaded the domain of psychology by recommending certain behavioral procedures on the basis of their time and motion studies. Psychologists have now returned the favor by specifying the manner in which equipment should be designed.

DEFINITION OF HUMAN ENGINEERING

Our definition of the field goes like this: human engineering is that endeavor which seeks to match human beings with modern machines so that their combined output will be comfortable, safe and more efficient. Obviously, this kind of effort is not specific to any one professional group but rather requires the special aptitudes of many professions and individuals. In addition to the engineers who devise a particular type of equipment there may be the need in some cases for motion-and-time study men, physicians, psychologists, physiologists or other specialists from the field of the biological sciences. The problems of human engineering present great diversity. Many industrial situations involve particular environmental problems of heat, noise, lighting, humidity, noxious gases and so forth. Modern aircraft, both commercial and military, repeat and add to this list of the physical factors which may affect the human being adversely. Military equipment has confronted us with the necessity for the design of instrument indicators which can be quickly interpreted without error and controls which are conveniently arranged and have physical characteristics which match the muscular capabilities of the operator. The design and use of prosthetic devices is another area which has brought the engineer, medical man and psychologist together.

The examples of human engineering endeavor just cited seem to constitute a unique and coherent set of problems. Some individuals prefer to call this general area "engineering psychology," a phrase which is acceptable to the writer. However, the line must be drawn somewhere. It is proposed that we do not attempt to include in this field the problems of human relations, personnel management or labor relations. The term "human engineering" has been applied to all three of these fields during the past few months. There is no objection, naturally, to these types of activity, but it is believed that the term "human engineering" will lose much of its value if it is applied indiscriminately to all attempts to fit the individual into his social and economic, as well as his machine, environment. Let us confine ourselves, therefore, to that area of scientific endeavor which seeks an optimal rapprochement between the human individual and the mechanized tasks which he is required to perform in our society. Some are undoubtedly of the opinion that this laboring over the matter of definition is merely a bit of definitional hair-splitting. As one from a very small number of people who are actually called human engineers, and one who sincerely believes that the events of the past few years have produced a unique opportunity and need for the engineering and biological professions to work together, I am convinced that the recognition and delimitation of this biomechanical field is essential to its success.

A PROGRAM OF HUMAN ENGINEERING

The writer's experience is primarily with military problems and, naturally, the general trends and outlines which are to be mentioned stem from this experience. Obviously, there are parallel phenomena and problems in industrial civilian life. The application of military research results to such industrial problems will be apparent.

The proposed definition of human engineering gave as a goal the man-machine combination which was efficient, comfortable and safe. So far as efficiency is concerned, the objective is to have a given operation accurate, rapid and without error. One way of eliminating human error is to automatize the operation and thereby eliminate the operating personnel. This commendable objective frequently backfires, however, by leading to a situation where some men are eliminated but others are left with tasks which are more complicated than ever. Meanwhile our technology continues to produce machines, gadgets, equipment and vehicles which require of the user novel and difficult skills. Since man does not undergo evolutionary changes as rapidly as the field of engineering advances, it behooves us to persuade the engineer to design his contributions so as to take account of what the normal individual is naturally fitted to do.

Thus the first requirement of a human engineering program is the acquisition of information about man's natural capabilities and limitations. Although a great deal of this knowledge has already been provided by the biological sciences, most of it was not gathered with our present objectives in view. There is the need, therefore, for a careful review and analysis of psychophysiological data already in existence in the professional journals, and in other reports so that those who are concerned with equipment design problems may use the knowledge which already has been gathered. Because of the interdisciplinary skills which human engineering engenders, this kind of literature survey is regarded as of about equal importance with new research efforts.

The types of experimental studies which also are required in an ideal program may be grouped as follows:

1. *Studies of the optimal environment.* Investigations are needed to specify the effects of physical factors having deleterious or favorable influence on operator behavior. Great progress has been made in recent

years by the engineering profession on the manner in which temperature, humidity and ventilation interact to affect employee productivity. Other variables which are encountered in industrial situations are noxious gases, noise (sonic and ultrasonic), vibration and illumination. Commercial aviation has given us the additional complications of oxygen deficiency, air pressure, acceleration and motion.[1] Military circumstances make it even more difficult to obviate the undesirable effects of these physical factors. Continued cooperation between members of the engineering, medical and psychological sciences will be required to protect the human individual while working in environments which offer hazards to his safety and efficiency.

2. *Studies of equipment display.* This area has been under attack for an appreciable period of time and many general principles are now available for application. As these data become more widely known we can anticipate more functional designs of dials, scales, meters, graphs and other types of instrument and tabular indicators. Included in this problem of the display of machine information is the layout and arrangement of the working place. Frequently a simple rearrangement or redesign of the machine indicators and layout greatly simplifies the sensory requirements of the job.

3. *Studies of equipment controls.* This is an area which has been neglected by psychological and medical investigators. Present information has come from the engineering side of the ledger and is expressed in the general principles of motion-and-time study. The rules of motion economy have been appraised by the practical yardstick of greater and faster production. But is this the best criterion for making recommendations on man's motor performance? The old controversy as to whether there is "one best way" to perform an operation still needs to be resolved. Fortunately the cooperative efforts, begun during World War II, are now in progress on the physical design of machine controls. In the near future we may expect definitive recommendations for the optimal size, shape, gearing, direction of motion, speed of motion, inertia, and friction of different types of controls in a variety of machine situations. The problem of control design is associated closely with the specification of the ideal controls to be combined with the equipment display. An important consideration in this regard is the extent to which a control knob, wheel or lever can serve as an instrument display and provide additional information to the operator. More data are needed on the extent to which the muscle sense can be utilized in keeping the operator informed of the progress of the task and the conditions of the machine.

4. *Studies of man-machine systems.* This area is probably not as significant in civilian industrial situations as it is in military operations. In the

---

[1] R. A. McFarland, *Human Factors in Air Transport Design* (New York: McGraw-Hill, 1946).

latter case there are many instances where large groups of men must coordinate their individual efforts so as to meet a single common objective. Many instances of crew coordination are demanded in the control of vehicles such as ships and airplanes. Communication networks also illustrate the fact that the human factor may determine whether a complex physical system will or will not function properly.

In summary, the first requirement of a program of human engineering is the acquisition of knowledge which will specify what the normal working man can do naturally and effectively. This objective can be attained by the collection and dissemination of published facts, and the conduct of further research on the working environment, equipment display, machine controls and man-machine systems. Much valuable information can be found in the stockpile of knowledge possessed by the engineering profession and the biological scientists. Without cooperative effort on the part of these groups the solution to many present-day problems will remain one-sided or unsatisfactory.

While speaking of the requirement for interdisciplinary effort, a further detail of explanation is appropriate. During a recent meeting of engineers, physicians and psychologists, who were discussing problems of aeronautics, the medical men and the psychologists spent considerable time in announcing what was wrong about cockpit design from the point of view of physical safety and ease of operation. To this some engineers took offense and pointed out, justly, that they made their airplanes according to design specifications furnished by others. The point is that the engineers are not basically responsible for machine designs which neglect biomechanical considerations. As suggested above, the ideal human engineering program will not only gather the basic data but will also disseminate them to those who can use them. The study of the human being is within the province of biological investigators and they must accept the responsibility of translating this knowledge into a useful form and then cooperate with the engineering profession in its application. A reversal of this experience has occurred in the development of prosthetic devices. In this field it was found that the medical men were in dire need of engineering information. This is merely another instance wherein professional teamwork is required to satisfy the needs. Group endeavor implies that each member will contribute his special skill for common benefit. At the same time each partner should attempt to understand the contributions of the other members of the diverse professional group.

In concluding the presentation of a human engineering program, there remains one additional item. Thus far the discussion has centered about the modification of equipment, machines, vehicles, and prosthetic devices to take account of human characteristics. An alternative procedure is to modify the individual through training procedures and devices. The best human engineering endeavors will undoubtedly still leave *homo sapiens* in behavior situations which are complex and difficult. Therefore, to round out an adequate program, the writer believes that personnel training is a part, or at least a necessary adjunct, of the total project.

SOME RECENT FINDINGS IN HUMAN ENGINEERING

In this section of the paper some results of specific research investigations will be cited to illustrate the kind of information that will be forthcoming as the program outlined above becomes effective.

The first area of problems mentioned was the fitting of the individual into atypical environments. A most striking example of this type of problem has been brought about by the development of high speed, piloted aircraft. It is difficult to imagine the visual, acoustic and vibrational environment for the pilot who flies straight and level at more than 600 miles per hour. Insofar as he uses visual contact reference, his whole visual field moves at much greater rates than in traditional flights so that he approaches the limits of ordinary reaction time in observing and responding to stimuli. What was a mild bump at 160 miles per hour now becomes a violent jar so that the pilot must wear crash gear to keep from being knocked unconscious. If the pilot wants to do a turn he is now in danger of blacking out due to angular acceleration.

In order to study the effects of centrifugal acceleration and to develop protective measures, there are several human centrifuges now in operation. Data from studies employing a centrifuge show that when the pilot is exposed to a force of no more than 2 g in the direction of head to feet there is a marked feeling of pressure as he is forced into his seat and that the extremities become difficult to lift.[2] Response time is increased accordingly. At 3–4 g the heaviness of the extremities is exaggerated and great effort is required to move the hands and feet; erect posture is maintained with difficulty. Between 5 and 8 g unconsciousness or coma develop; this state is preceded by blacking out of the field of vision, probably due to the loss of blood from the head and face. The pilot's value in controlling his machine is practically nil at this point. Yet the accelerative forces about which we have been speaking are well within the stress limits of the aircraft structures. Whether it will be possible to bring the man's tolerance up to the tolerance limits of his aircraft is difficult to say. It may be that here we have a true instance of engineering possibility not being realized because of human weakness.[3]

Illustrative research in the field of instrument displays will now be cited. A large percentage of visual indicators are of the clock-face type. A question which faces the designer of such instruments is the number of graduation marks to put around the scale. One might guess that it would be extremely easy to ascertain the answer to this question. As a matter of

---

[2] H. G. Armstrong, *Principles and Practice of Aviation Medicine* (New York: Houghton Mifflin, 1946).

[3] R. A. McFarland, *op. cit.*; L. C. Mead, "Application of Human Engineering to Flight Problems," *Journal of Aviation Medicine*, Vol. 19, 1948, pp. 45–51.

fact, it has taken a number of years and several comprehensive experiments to begin to see a general solution to this problem.

One of the first experiments was done during World War II by Loucks[4] who used aircraft tachometer dials with various numbers of markings. On the basis of short exposures, he showed that the percentage of errors was greatest for the dial with the largest number of graduations. He concluded that the cleanest dial from the standpoint of design gave the most accurate readings. Grether and Williams[5] measured speed and accuracy of reading dials ranging from 1 to 4 inches in diameter and from 5 to 40 degrees in angular separation of graduations. They found an increase in accuracy of dial reading as the dial diameter increased, except for the case with 40 degrees angular separation of graduation marks. In the latter case there was a decrease in accuracy when dial diameter exceeded 2 inches. They then plotted all their data on a single curve relating accuracy to length (*not* degrees) of graduation interval. Regardless of diameter of the dial and the angular separation between graduation marks, the error was found to decrease as the linear distance between intervals increased up to ¼ inch with little improvement thereafter. The most recent relevant experiment is that of Kappauf[6] who employed a different method of measurement and found, contrary to Loucks,[7] that accuracy increased with an increase in the number of graduation marks. A 5-unit dial was better in terms of error and speed of reading than a 10-unit dial; a 1-unit dial was only slightly better than the 5-unit dial.

Grether[8] explains these diverse findings by noting that quantitative dial reading errors may be of two kinds, interpretation errors and interpolation errors. Interpretation errors would be *increased* by an increase in the number of graduations because of the greater ambiguity as to which of the markings the pointer is over. Interpolation errors, on the other hand, are *decreased* by an increment in number of dial markings because the reader has less difficulty in deciding how far along the pointer is between the scale divisions.

The third major area of human engineering is the specification of the characteristics of machine controls. One of the most significant problems

[4] R. B. Loucks, "Legibility of Aircraft Instrument Dials: A Further Investigation of the Relative Legibility of Tachometer Dials," AAF School of Aviation Medicine, Randolph Field, Texas, Project No. 265, October, 1944.

[5] W. F. Grether and A. C. Williams, Jr., "Speed and Accuracy of Dial Reading as a Function of Dial Diameter and Angular Separation of Scale Divisions," in R. M. Fitts (ed.), *Psychological Research on Equipment Design*, Report No. 19, AAF Aviation Psychology Program Research Reports, U.S. Government Printing Office, 1947.

[6] W. E. Kappauf, "Design of Instrument Dials for Maximum Legibility: I. Development of Methodology and Some Preliminary Results," USAF, AMC, Aero-Medical Laboratory Memorandum Report No. TSEAA-694-1L, 1947.

[7] R. B. Loucks, *op. cit.*

[8] W. F. Grether, "The Design of Instrument Dials for Ease of Reading," paper presented before SAE National Aeronautic and Air Transport Meeting, April, 1948.

here is the basic motor capacity of the average individual. The Therblig notation system of the motion-and-time study engineer has long been a standard method for classifying the different elements of work performance. In 1947, however, Brown and Jenkins[9] proposed a new classification which may serve as an impetus for further research. In brief, they separate motor reactions into three distinct classes:

1) Static reactions, which include all instances where a body member is required to be held in a fixed position in space;
2) Positioning reactions, wherein the members of the body are moved from a position of rest to a specified position in space, the terminal accuracy being of primary significance; and
3) Movement reactions, which are movements of the bodily members at given rates, in given directions, along specific paths.

Subsequent to this analysis of motor reactions, Brown[10] completed several investigations on discrete and positioning responses. Mention of some of these results is warranted both because of their novelty and their significance. One of these studies[11] was to ascertain the accuracy with which individuals could perform positioning reactions in the absence of visual corrective cues. The subjects were required to move the right arm and hand from a point of rest to a terminal position located either 0.6, 2.5, 10 or 40 cm. distant. After an exposure of 2.5 seconds to one of these four extents the reactions were made in total darkness. Movements were made in both horizontal and vertical planes in various directions. It was found that there was a tendency to overshoot the intended mark at shorter distances and to fall short at longer distances. One exception, attributed to the effects of gravity, was noted for all distances in the vertical plane when the direction of movement was downward. The per cent error decreased and the variability increased with each increment in distance. A plot relating speed of movement to distance was found to be of the exponential form $y = ax^b$.

Because of the possible significance of speed of bodily movements to equipment design and job performance, Brown[12] completed a follow-up study to determine the effects of speed-up instructions on positioning reactions. The motions were all in the horizontal plane. Despite the emphasis on speed in the instructions to the subjects, there was no increase in the average reaction time. Although primary-movement time was de-

---

[9] J. S. Brown and W. O. Jenkins, "An Analysis of Human Motor Abilities Related to the Design of Equipment and a Suggested Program of Research," in P. M. Fitts (ed.), *Psychological Research on Equipment Design*, Report No. 19, AAF Aviation Psychology Program Research Report, U.S. Government Printing Office, 1947.

[10] J. S. Brown and A. T. Slater-Hammel, "The Effect of Speed-up Instructions upon the Performance of Discrete Movements in the Horizontal Plane," ONR Report No. 57-2-3, 1948; A. T. Slater-Hammel and J. S. Brown, "Discrete Movements in the Horizontal Plane as a Function of Their Length and Direction," ONR Report No. 57-2-2, 1947.

[11] A. T. Slater-Hammel and J. S. Brown, *op. cit.*

[12] J. S. Brown and A. T. Slater-Hammel, *op. cit.*

creased, the total-movement time was not. There was an increase in the time spent in making the fine, secondary adjustments following the initial gross approaches to the terminal point. Brown concludes that attempts to speed one's movements may produce apparent increases in speed which, in terms of over-all efficiency, yield little genuine improvement.

The last area in the program of biomechanics was designated as the study of man-machine systems.[13] Rather than present an illustrative sample of results obtained in this field, it seems preferable to outline briefly a method of attack on such problems which has been proposed by the Systems Research Laboratory of the Johns Hopkins University. A paper by Dr. Chapanis represents one phase of the Hopkins' attack on the over-all efficiency of man-machine combinations. Methodology is one of the main determinants of progress and this project's contributions to methods are of far-reaching significance.

The objective of psychophysical systems analysis is to specify (1) the most efficient number of human operators, (2) the number and characteristics of the equipment components, and (3) the best arrangement and layout of the men and their gear.

To say unequivocally that such appraisals can now be made would be to exaggerate the facts. What has actually been accomplished is the formulation of a systematic approach, that is, a theoretical scheme for attacking problems of this nature.

The tentative nature of this theoretical structure prevents presentation of more than a skeleton outline of the procedure. The first step is to analyze and itemize all the connections between all of the components of the system; thus all connections between men and machines, men and men, and machines and machines are listed. These connections, which are termed "links," will be found in a majority of cases to be "visual," "auditory" or "control" in nature. After determining what these "links" are it is then necessary to estimate the importance of each one. There are two criteria for determining importance or "link value." One is the "frequency" with which each link is used and the other is the "importance" of the link when it is used. In the case of a system which already exists, the link value as measured by "frequency" can be determined merely by tabulating the number of times that a particular link is employed. For determining the link "importance" value measures of a more qualitative sort involving psychological rating scale techniques must be used. These techniques may be applied to existing systems or to proposed systems not yet constructed. When "link use value" and "link importance value" of an existing system have been estimated, the two measures are then combined into a single score which is used in the final rearrangement of the whole system. This last step consists in arranging the over-all link values in order of size and importance. By using a

[13] L. C. Mead, "Human Factors in Engineering Design," *Soc. Auto. Eng. J.*, Vol. 55, No. 12, 1947, pp. 40–46.

graphical plot and juggling the link values around in proper manner, a proposed solution to the particular systems problem is obtained.

This approach to systems design is admittedly qualitative in some respects and not rigorously scientific. Whether or not we have here the essence of a basic and valid theoretical construct is not yet clear. On the other hand this approach has been used in a number of military circumstances and has been found to increase the over-all efficiency of complicated men-machine linkages. Further research and application by motion-and-time engineers and psychologists is needed to demonstrate both its generality and its limitations.

62. Psychology and the Design of Machines*

Franklin V. Taylor

PSYCHOLOGISTS HAVE been helping engineers design machines for more than fifteen years. It all began during World War II with the rapid development of radars, sonars, aircraft control systems, and other similar devices. Previous to this time, the only role played by psychologists relative to military mechanisms was that of doing research and giving advice on the selection and training of the operators. However, very early in the war, it became apparent that these Procrustean attempts to fit the man to the machine were not enough. Regardless of how much he could be stretched by training or pared down through selection, there were still many military equipments which the man just could not be moulded to fit. They required of him too many hands, too many feet, or in the case of some of the more complex devices, too many heads.

Sometimes they called for the operator to see targets which were close to invisible, or to understand speech in the presence of deafening noise, to track simultaneously in three coordinates with the two hands, to solve in analogue form complex differential equations, or to consider large amounts of information and to reach life-and-death decisions in split seconds and with no hope of another try. Of course the man often failed in one or another of these tasks. As a result, bombs and bullets often missed their mark, planes crashed, friendly ships were fired upon and sunk. Whales were depth-charged.

*Selected portions from "Psychology and the Design of Machines," *American Psychologist*, Vol. 12, No. 5, 1957, pp. 249–56.

Because of these "human errors," as they were called, psychologists were asked to help the engineers produce machines which required less of the man and which, at the same time, exploited his special abilities. The story of what happened is sufficiently well known not to require any lengthy retelling here. In brief, the psychologists went to work, and with the help of anatomists, physiologists, and, of course, engineers they started a new inter-discipline aimed at better machine design and called variously human engineering, biomechanics, psychotechnology, or engineering psychology. The new field has developed rapidly in the seventeen or eighteen years of its existence.

FIGURE 1

THE MAN-MACHINE SYSTEM

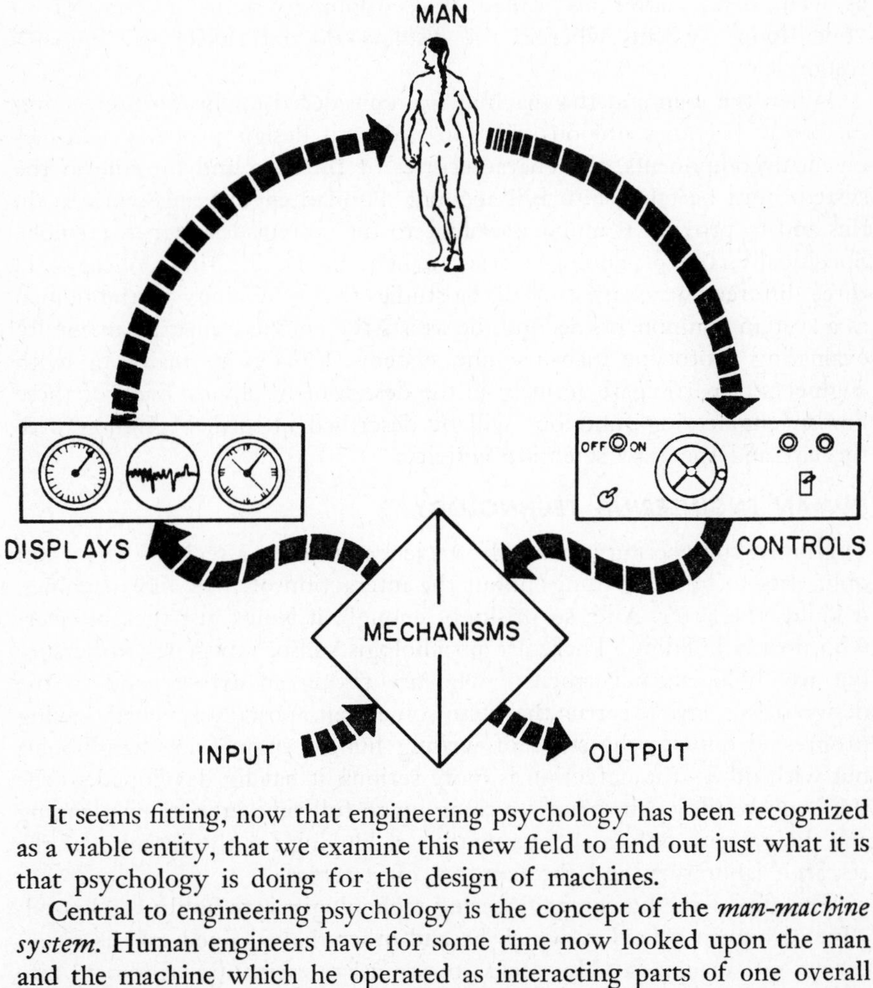

It seems fitting, now that engineering psychology has been recognized as a viable entity, that we examine this new field to find out just what it is that psychology is doing for the design of machines.

Central to engineering psychology is the concept of the *man-machine system*. Human engineers have for some time now looked upon the man and the machine which he operated as interacting parts of one overall system. In Figure 1 is shown a paradigm of the concept. This may be viewed as a radar device, a pilot-aircraft control system, a submarine diving control station, the captain's station on the bridge of his ship, or, in fact, any man-machine system at all.

In essence, it represents the human operator as an organic data transmission and processing link inserted between the mechanical or electronic displays and controls of a machine. An input of some type is transformed by the mechanisms into a signal which appears on a display. Perhaps it is shown as a pointer reading, a pattern of lights, or a pip on a cathode ray tube. However it appears, the presented information is read by the operator, processed mentally, and transformed into control responses. Switches are thrown, buttons are pushed, or force is applied to a joy stick. The control signal, after transformation by the mechanisms, becomes the system output, and in some devices it acts upon the displays as well. These latter are called "closed-loop" systems in contrast to "open-loop" systems wherein the displays do not reflect the human's response.

When the man and the machine are considered in this fashion, it immediately becomes obvious that, in order to design properly the mechanical components, the characteristics of the man and his role in the system must be taken into full account. Human engineering seeks to do this and to provide as much assistance to the system designer as possible. Specifically, the psychologist tries to help his engineering colleague in three different ways. First of all, he studies the psychology of the human as a system component. Second, he assists the engineer in experimentally evaluating prototype man-machine systems. Finally, he teams up with engineers to participate actively in the design of machines. Each of these human engineering functions will be described in turn, beginning with the last and the least scientific activity.

HUMAN ENGINEERING TECHNOLOGY

Human engineering is not only a science, it is also a technology; it not only tries to find out things about the interaction of men and machines, it builds the latter. And, surprisingly enough, it is not just the engineers who do the building. There are psychologists also, renegades to be sure but psychologists nevertheless, who are taking an active hand in the design of systems. It is true that with some their apostasy is venial, having progressed only to the stage of writing human engineering handbooks; but with others the defection is more serious, it having developed to the stage where they can spend anything up to full time in systems planning and design with only a twinge or two of longing for the serenity of the research laboratory and the comfort of statistics.

The aim of the human engineering technologist is to apply the knowledge of human behavior, which he and others have gained, to the structuring of machines. He seeks to translate scientific findings into electronic circuits and "black boxes" which in specific situations will compensate for the human's limitations or complement his abilities. Specifically, the practicing engineering psychologist works on an engineering team and participates in the design of man-machine systems. Using procedural analysis techniques, drawing upon his psychological knowledge and attitudes, and employing his common sense and creative ability, the human engineer proceeds to contribute to system development at three levels of complexity.

At the simplest, he designs individual displays, controls, or display-control relationships. At a somewhat more complex level, the human engineering technologist contributes to the design of consoles and instrument panels. At the highest level of complexity, he assists in structuring large systems composed of many mechanical elements and frequently several human beings. In this capacity he helps to determine what information must flow through the system, how it must be processed, how many men are required, what tasks they will perform, and what type of information each one will need. In short, the enginering psychologist helps at this level to determine the configuration of the system.

Human engineering technology is much more extensively practiced by psychologists than is generally recognized by those who are not closely identified with the field. The specific nature of each accomplishment and the difficulty of assigning individual credit for team effort conspire with security and proprietary considerations to keep the lay and psychological public in almost complete ignorance of the technological products of human engineering. However, literally hundreds of devices and systems have been affected to a greater or less extent during the last ten years by the efforts of engineering psychologists. Every major type of military equipment has received some attention, as have also certain nonmilitary products such as aircraft instruments and cabins, flight control towers, artificial limbs, semiautomatic post office sorting equipment, telephone sets, theodolites, experimental equipment for the earth satellite program, control panels for an atomic reactor, and numerous industrial machines.

MAN-MACHINE SYSTEMS EVALUATION

The second way in which the engineering psychologist assists in the design of machines is by taking part in systems evaluations. Like human engineering technology, evaluation studies require a sizeable effort yet receive scarcely any publicity. Evaluations have been performed on headphones, range finders, gunsights, fire control and missile control systems, radar sets, information plotting systems, combat information centers, aircraft control towers, and numerous assorted display and control components. In some instances, the experiments have been carried out in the laboratory with the system inputs being simulated. In other cases, the tests are conducted in the field. But in both situations, the attendant complexities and difficulties of statistical control make this necessary variety of research as trying as any in which psychologists are likely to participate.

The reason that psychologists were called upon in the first place to assist in these evaluations was that they possessed methods for dealing with human variability. In contrast, the engineers generally had worked only with time-stationary components and, therefore, found themselves at somewhat of a loss when they were called upon to assess the performance of devices which were being operated by men.

ENGINEERING PROPERTIES OF THE MAN

The third and final way in which psychologists help in the design of machines is through studying, by conventional means, the behavior of the man as a machine operator. They have undertaken to study selected aspects of the behavior of the man as a system component. The intent here is to provide the engineers or the technologically oriented psychologists with information concerning certain of the characteristics of the man in order that the properties of the machine may be made to harmonize with them. This class of responses may be characterized in a number of different ways:

1. First off, as was pointed out at the very beginning, the human in a man-machine system can be considered as an information transmission and processing link between the displays and the controls of the machine. When so viewed, his behavior consists of reading off information, transforming it mentally, and emitting it as action on the controls. Thus, the performance may be described as of the type in which the operator's responses image in some way the pattern or sequence of certain of the input events. For example, the S signals when a tone comes on and withholds his response when he hears nothing, or he presses one key when he sees a red light and a different key when he sees a green one, he perceives the range and bearing of a radar target and identifies its location verbally, he moves a cursor to follow the motion of a target image. In all these cases, the essential interest in the behavior focuses upon the correlation in space and time between events in a restricted and predefined stimulus "space" and corresponding events in a preselected response "space."

2. Another way to characterize the behaviors studied in engineering psychology is to indicate that they are voluntary and task-directed or purposive. The operator of a man-machine system is always consciously trying to perform some task. Perhaps it is to follow on a keyboard the successive spatial positions of a signal light, perhaps to see a visual target imbedded in "noise" and to signal its position, possibly it is to watch a bank of displays in order to determine malfunction and to take action where necessary. In all cases, the operator is voluntarily trying to accomplish something specific; he is not just free associating, or living.

3. A third characteristic of the human operator's behavior emerges as

a corollary of voluntary control. The class of human responses of interest to the engineering psychologist involves chiefly the striate muscles. Because it is through the action of this type of effector that men speak and apply force to levers and handwheels, it is these muscles which play the dominant role in the human's control of machines.

4. Finally, practical considerations dictate that vision and audition be the sense modalities most often supplying the input to the human transmission channel. Because of the nature and location of the eyes and ears and because of their high informational capacity, they are ideal noncontact transducers for signal energies emitted by the mechanical or electronic displays of machines.

These four characteristics define some of the human reactions investigated in engineering psychology. The concepts and models of orthodox psychology are beginning to be replaced by physical and mathematical constructs and engineering models. We have already encountered the notion of the man as an information channel. Systems psychologists also view him as a multipurpose computer and as a feedback control system. The virtue of these engineering models is that they furnish ready-made a mathematics which has already proved itself of value when applied to the inanimate portions of the man-machine system and which may turn out to be useful for the human element as well. In addition, they provide the behavioral scientist with a new set of system-inspired hypothetical constructs and concepts which may redirect his research and stimulate entirely novel lines of inquiry.

Whereas orthodox psychology still speaks in a construct language consisting of terms like stimulus, response, sensation, perception, attention, anticipation, and expectancy, the new "hardware" school is rapidly developing a concept argot which, although quite unintelligible to outsiders, is providing considerable inspiration to the initiates. Human behavior for this psychological avant-garde is a matter of inputs, outputs, storage, coding, transfer functions, and bandpass.

And this is far more than a matter of language. The research itself is changing. Questions about human behavior are now being asked experimentally which were literally inconceivable a few years ago. Yet they are the very questions to which engineers desire answers. How stationary and linear is the man? What frequencies can he pass and how many bits per second can he transmit under a variety of different conditions? How does the human's gain change with different system dynamics? How well can he perform as a single integrator, or double integrator, or triple integrator? How effectively can he act as the surrogate for different computer functions? These are some of the experimental questions which engineering psychologists are beginning to ask and which, no doubt, will be asked with increasing frequency as the new field develops.

It is probably not too much to expect that one day soon we will have a completely revised textbook of human engineering, perhaps entitled *The Engineering Properties of the Man*, which will present to engineers in a form which is useful to them the system-relevant facts of psychology as then known. Instead of conventional chapter headings like "Seeing," "Hearing," "Speaking," "Moving," and "Working," it might contain such rubics as "Mechanical Properties of the Man," "Transduction," "Informational Capacity and Bandwidth," "Linear Properties of the Man" (including analogue addition, integration, differentiation, and multiplication by constants), and "Nonlinear Properties of the Man" (including, it must be confessed, most everything else). Such a treatise, when it is written, will certainly be welcomed by the system designer, and he will waste no time in putting the information to use.

63. Some Concepts and Methods for the Conduct of Man-Machine System Research in a Laboratory Setting*

Paul M. Fitts, Lowell Schipper, Jerry S. Kidd, Maynard Shelly, and Conrad Kraft

GENERAL ACCEPTANCE has recently been gained for the idea that human-factor specialists can make an important contribution to the design of man-machine systems. This contribution lies in helping to decide such important questions as those pertaining to the allocation of functions between men and machines, planning for the work loads on individual operators, and the optimum coupling of men and machines. However, few efforts have been made to bring such system-design problems into the laboratory where they can be subjected to controlled experimental study. This lack of work has been due chiefly to lack of the necessary simulation equipment, and of appropriate methods. The present paper reviews the concepts and methods, and some selected results of an experimental

* The project was initiated in 1950, work being done for the National Research Council with funds provided by the Air Navigation Development Board. Since 1952 the research program has been supported by contracts [AF 33 (616)–43 and AF 33 (616)–3612] between the Wright Air Development Center and the Ohio State University Research Foundation.

From "Some Concepts and Methods for the Conduct of System Research in a Laboratory Setting," *Air Force Human Engineering, Personnel, and Training Research*, G. Finch and F. Cameron (eds.) (Washington, D.C.: National Academy of Science—National Research Council), publication 516, 1958.

program that has been investigating such system-design problems for the past two and a half years. The specific system under study has as its function the safe and efficient control of aircraft in the terminal (approximately 50-mi. radius) area around an airport.

THE PLANNING PHASE

The Laboratory of Aviation Psychology of Ohio State University is now completing its sixth year of experimental work on human engineering aspects of air traffic control. Earlier, one of the authors together with Dr. George Long conducted a human engineering analysis of air traffic control on the Berlin Airlift[1] and some of the background for the current work goes back to that study.

The first step in initiating the current research program was a one year study phase which was carried out under the auspices of the NRC Committee on Aviation Psychology. Eleven psychologists from eight different universities and Government laboratories participated in preparing a report of this project.[2]

THE RESEARCH PHASE

The research phase of the program began a short while later. A major initial task was to develop suitable simulation equipment and methodology for the study of system-design problems in the laboratory; pending these developments, initial research emphasis was placed on the study of specific display problems. Following an unsuccessful attempt to adapt existing simulation equipment for use in system experiments, an electronic analog simulator was designed specifically to meet our research needs (by Prof. C. E. Warren of the Ohio State University Department of Electrical Engineering and several of his students) and constructed in the laboratory. This device[3] is capable of generating 30 independently-controlled simulated aircraft (or target "blips"), which can be displayed on simulated radar scopes. A photograph of the "pilot" room, and a photograph of a typical simulated radar scope in the "radar control" room, with identity coded targets, are shown in Figures 1 and 2, respectively.

At the present time our system experimentation is planned around two general goals: (*a*) to solve some of the specific human engineering problems of air-traffic-control system design, and at the same time (*b*) to provide a contribution to the development of a general theory of the capacities and proficiencies of small groups of people in performing the

---

[1] G. E. Long and P. M. Fitts, "Human Engineering Aspects of the Berlin Airlift," USAF Air Material Command, Memo. Rep., 1949, No. MCREXD–694–23.

[2] P. M. Fitts (ed.), *Human Engineering for an Effective Air-Navigation and Traffic-Control System* (Washington, D.C.: National Research Council, 1951).

[3] W. C. Hixson, G. A. Harter, C. E. Warren, and J. D. Cowan, Jr., "An Electronic Radar Target Simulator for Air Traffic Control Studies," *USAF WADC Technical Report*, No. 54–569, 1954.

FIGURE 1

A view of part of the simulation equipment, showing the panels used to control the positions of the radar blips representing the simulated aircraft in the system.

kinds of perceptual, memory, and decision-making functions required by complex tasks which must be solved continuously in real time.

In this paper we discuss some of the basic concepts which have guided the formulation of the research program, review critical aspects of the methodology we have developed, and present a few illustrations of typical results. For the most part we shall confine the discussion to system research, with only brief reference to related research projects. Although all examples refer to a specific system, many of the methodological problems encountered in studying this system are believed to be quite general.

OBJECTIVES AND CONCEPTS

Objectives. The major objectives of the research program are indicated in Table 1. One goal is to provide human engineering principles that can be used by the engineers who will design future air traffic control systems, and by the operational personnel who will devise the procedures to be employed in operating these systems. We attempt to anticipate future problems and to provide sufficient lead time for our research so that there will be maximum opportunity for findings to be used in the critical planning and development phases of new systems. As an example, we may study the effects of displaying types of information

FIGURE 2

A view of one of the simulated radar scopes showing radar blips that are identity-coded by means of two electronic arms.

that cannot yet be obtained with current electronic devices, but that may be attainable in five or ten years.

From a psychological viewpoint, another goal of the research is to provide quantitative estimates of human capacity for performing the different types of functions which may characterize future air traffic control and similar complex man-machine systems.

In planning any particular study we first decide what functions must be performed in the general type of system under study. We then allocate certain functions to people and assume that other functions will be performed by automatic or semi-automatic equipment. We next design an experiment which will permit us to measure man's ability to carry out those functions which may have been allocated to him, such as to perceive and handle information, to make decisions, and/or to communicate instructions, as indicated by criteria of system performance.

We are interested in determining human performance capacities under both normal conditions and under unexpected or "emergency" conditions. In some experiments performance is measured under intermediate

TABLE 1

<small>OBJECTIVES OF THE SYSTEM-RESEARCH PROGRAM</small>

1. To provide human engineering principles for use in the design and operation of future Air Traffic Control systems.
2. To provide measures of human capacity and reliability relative to future Air Traffic Control systems.
   a) When men perform different functions in the system,
   b) Under both emergency and normal conditions,
   c) With different traffic control procedures, and
   d) With various types and rates of aircraft inputs.

levels of task difficulty and later human breakdown characteristics are noted when the load is increased to the point where controllers cannot do all that the task demands.

Since human capacity is also a function of the procedures employed by individuals and by groups in solving on-going problems, one of the objectives of our research has been to determine human capacity as a function of procedural or organizational variables. We also have evaluated human capacity as a function of the inputs to the system, i.e., the types of problems which the man-machine system is required to handle. These load variables have to do with the number of stimuli, the similarity of stimuli, and the nature of stimulus changes—for example, aircraft entry rate, heterogeneity of aircraft types, and aircraft speeds.

Concepts. Several concepts or directing tenets have been formulated as guides to our research planning. Several of these concepts are listed in Table 2.

TABLE 2

<small>CONCEPTS USED TO GUIDE SYSTEM-RESEARCH PLANNING</small>

1. Human Engineering should include the study of
   a) *Existing* systems,
   b) *Simulated future* systems, and
   c) *Subsystems* or specific technical problems.
2. Human operator capabilities should be determined for
   a) *Optimized* as well as *degraded* information, and for
   b) Control *teams* as well as for *individuals*.

The scope of our general research probram includes (a) field studies of existing systems, (*b*) laboratory experiments on simulated future systems, and (*c*) supporting basic research on specific display- and information-handling problems. Emphasis is placed on the last two topics; we consider here only the system experiments.

One of the major tenets that we have followed is that human capabilities should first be determined under optimized system conditions (e.g., with "idealized" displays and reliable information) and then determined for nonoptimal or degraded systems. Only data obtained under idealized conditions permit an estimate to be made of the upper limits of system performance that could result from future improvements in the machine aspects of the man-machine system. One of the gratifying results of our policy of first studying human performance under idealized conditions is that on several occasions it has been unnecessary to go on to the study of degraded systems. In each case, by the time a series of human factor research studies has been completed, engineering progress had made it possible to eliminate many of the deficiencies of existing systems, and hence had rendered unnecessary the study of the effects of such deficiencies on human performance.

Another of the tenets is that human capacities should be determined for groups of controllers who are collaborating in the solution of a common problem, as well as for individuals working singly. We are interested for example, in the question of how much two men working together can accomplish in comparison with what one man can do when working alone. By studying group-performance capabilities we hope to discover methods of displaying information, and procedures for the division of responsibilities, that will make possible efficient group effort, and to provide estimates of the number of people required to perform particular functions. We also hope to make a contribution to the theory of small-group proficiency.

A further tenet concerns the importance of maintaining the realism of the total environment in which the research is conducted. Some degree of realism is necessary, and its achievement requires careful attention to details. The environment in our control room is especially conducive to the creation of a realistic attitude on the part of the controllers since many of the characteristics of an actual radar control center are faithfully replicated.

THE EXPERIMENTAL PROGRAM

Experimental Study of System Variables. Most of our system experiments have been conducted through the use of the OSU electronic

TABLE 3

AREAS INCLUDED IN THE SYSTEM-RESEARCH PROGRAM

---

1. System Experiments, covering
   a) *Display* variables,
   b) *Load* variables, and
   c) *Procedural* variables.
2. Related Technical Research, including
   a) Visibility and lighting,
   b) Specific display principles,
   c) Information coding, and
   d) Information-handling ability.

---

air traffic control simulator.[4] This equipment permits us to investigate three types of system variables. These are shown at the top of Table 3.

Display variables may alternatively be called information variables. They involve the type of information made available to controllers,

---

[4] *Ibid.*

the degree of precision in the information, and the way in which the information is encoded and displayed. An example of a display variable is the method of indicating identity.

Load variables define the input to the air-traffic-control system, such as the traffic conditions with which the controller must cope. Traffic variables can be manipulated by predetermining the characteristics of aircraft and the times at which aircraft enter the system.

Procedural variables involve the methods employed by the team that solves the air-traffic-control problem. These variables include communication procedures, procedures by means of which two or more individuals make joint or complementary decisions, and procedures governing the types of instructions that controllers are permitted to issue to aircraft pilots. An important subclass of procedural variables is the way in which two or more men divide responsibilities. As an illustration, a division of responsibility can be based on either geographic or temporal factors, each controller accepting responsibility for different parts of the air space or for different blocks of time; or it can be based on the types of functions to be performed by each man.

Areas of Supporting Basic Research on Specific Display Problems. Supporting research is conducted with two objectives in mind: (*a*) the establishment of basic principles of information transmission, and (*b*) the provision of principles in support of the system-research program. Supporting research is divided into the four phases shown in the lower half of Table 3.

Problems of *visibility* and *lighting* arise because of the unusual visual environment that must be provided in a radar control center. As a part of our work in this area Mr. Kraft has developed the OSU Broad-Band Blue Lighting System.[5] This lighting has now been in use at Wright-Patterson AFB for three years, and has recently been adopted with only minor modification by several national agencies.

In the area of *specific displays*, special emphasis has been given to the problem of identity and altitude coding.[6] Much of this basic research

---

[5] C. L. Kraft, "A Broad-Band Blue Lighting System for Radar Approach Control Centers: Evaluations and Refinements Based on Three Years of Operational Use," *USAF WADC Technical Report*, No. 56-71, 1956; C. L. Kraft and P. M. Fitts, "A Broad-Band Blue Lighting System for Radar Air Traffic Control Centers," *USAF WADC Technical Report* No. 53-416, 1954.

[6] E. A. Alluisi and P. F. Muller, "*Rate of Information Transfer with Seven Symbolic Visual Codes: Motor and Verbal Responses,*" *USAF WADC Technical Report*, No. 56-226, 1956; E. A. Alluisi, P. F. Muller, and P. M. Fitts, "Rate of Handling Information and the Rate of Information Presentation," *USAF WADC Technical Note*, No. 55-745, 1955; D. B. Learner and E. A. Alluisi, "Comparison of Four Methods of Encoding Elevation Information with Complex Line-Inclination Symbols," *USAF WADC Technical Note*, No. 56-485, 1956; P F. Muller, Jr., R. C. Sidorsky, A. J. Slivinske, E. A. Alluisi and P. M. Fitts, "The Symbolic Coding of Information on Cathode Ray Tubes and Similar Display," *USAF WADC Technical Report*, No. 55-375, 1955.

has made use of information measures as a criterion of performance. In particular, we have been interested in *coding for efficient handling of information*. Usually our first procedure is to scale the stimulus by means of absolute information transmitted. Next, we study the rate at which this information can be transmitted.

METHODOLOGY FOR SYSTEM RESEARCH

During the past two and a half years, eight major system experiments have been completed. The methodology for these studies is constantly evolving so that we shall summarize chiefly the current procedures.

The Types of Control Tasks That Have Been Investigated. The focus of most activity in the simulated system is a plan position (PPI) display showing the ground positions of all aircraft in a 50-mi. radius from the simulated radar site. In some cases additional information is provided on secondary displays. All of the displays have been idealized to the extent that available knowledge and present techniques permit. A good quality air-ground communication system has been simulated. Standard, but abbreviated, voice procedures have been used.

The most typical problem studied in the laboratory is that of a group of military aircraft returning from a combat-type mission. No airborne or ground-navigation equipment other than radar is simulated.

Experiments usually involve a series of 30 to 60 discrete problems, with from 20 to 30 aircraft included in a single problem. These simulated aircraft are given flight characteristics similar to current advanced types such as the B-47 and F-86, or are made to represent possible future types. The mean temporal and spatial separation of aircraft as they enter the control zone has been one of the variables studied.

In most cases the output point of the system has been a hypothetical GCA gate near the center of the PPI display, where aircraft are turned over to a final (GCA) controller. Outgoing aircraft leave the system at designated points around the periphery. The last 10 mi. of the landing approach has not been explicitly studied, but this part of the system has usually been simulated by a GCA controller who had used realistic criteria for determining whether or not aircraft turned over to him could be landed. If any airplane cannot be accepted for landing, a "go-around" is initiated by the GCA controller and the aircraft is returned to the previous controller who must return it to the GCA gate for a second time.

Plans for future studies call for the simulation of other types of terminal operations, such as simultaneous landings on different landing fields, and the delegation of certain responsibilities from controllers to pilots, with controllers assuming a greater degree of monitor activity.

Level of Experience of Controllers and Pilots. In most system experiments, experienced Air Force personnel have been used as controllers. The pilots who operate the other portion of the simulator have been

OSU students, selected for previous aviation experience, and thoroughly pretrained before the beginning of an experiment.

The Research Environment. Although we conduct research in a laboratory setting we have devoted a good deal of effort to the creation of a realistic environment, one which produces a high level of motivation and allows individuals to develop sets similar to those that characterize actual field situations. The controllers work under environmental conditions approximating those of an actual radar center. The radar displays are realistic, standard voice procedures are followed precisely, and familiar aircraft types are employed with realistic flight characteristics.

The choice of which variables to treat experimentally and which to treat as fixed parameters is perhaps more of a problem in studying complex man-machine systems than it is in simpler experiments. In each case, the choice has been a compromise between the desire to simulate a realistic situation and the necessity for obtaining unambiguous results. For continuity, we try to carry the same values of parameters through several experiments.

CRITERIA OF SYSTEM PERFORMANCE

If the results of research on man-machine systems are to exercise a significant influence on the design of future systems, the effects of human engineering variables of the type described above must be measured in terms of their effects on over-all man-machine system performance. Provided such meaningful system measures are available, however, then specific measures of the behavior of the people in the system take on added importance because these intervening measures can be related to the performance of the total system. Both types of measures have been employed in our experiments, but we have concentrated initially on the development of system criteria. The most important of these are listed in Table 4.

Listed first in Table 4 are several over-all measures of system efficiency. *Average control time* in the terminal area is the average amount of time required to bring an aircraft from 50 mi. away to the GCA gate, or (for a departing aircraft) to take it to a point 50 mi. from take-off. *Accumulated delay in landing* is the average of the control times for the first few (usually three) aircraft, compared with the average control time for the last few (usually three) aircraft handled during a problem. *Average fuel consumption* is a measure somewhat analogous to average control time, but is computed from altitude and speed as well as time. *Excess fuel consumption* is the amount of fuel used in excess of a theoretical minimum amount. These three are related measures, and have self-evident validity. In addition, several other efficiency measures are taken. *Final heading at the GCA gate and deviation from the runway extension* are measures of the amount of deviation from the heading of the runway when the aircraft arrives at the GCA gate. *Average separa-*

TABLE 4

CRITERIA OF SYSTEM PERFORMANCE

1. Measures of efficiency
   a) Average control time
   b) Accumulated delay in landing
   c) Average fuel consumption
   d) Excess fuel consumption
   e) Final heading at the GCA gate
   f) Deviation from runway extension
   g) Average separation at GCA gate
2. Measures of safety
   a) Number of conflicts enroute
   b) Number of conflicts at GCA gate
3. Measures of communication load
   a) Regarding heading
   b) Regarding altitude
   c) Regarding speed

tion at the GCA gate is a measure in time of the separation of aircraft as they arrive at the gate. Also listed in Table 4 are several measures of safety and of communications. As most communications in our system are concerned with determinations of or changes in such aircraft characteristics as heading, altitude, and speed, the frequencies of each of these categories are included when a content analysis is made of communications. We use two principal criterion measures of safety. These are *number of midair conflicts enroute*, and *number of conflicts near the GCA gate*. A conflict is defined arbitrarily as a failure to maintain a certain minimal separation measured in units of flying time.

In system research we feel that it is necessary to establish criteria which reflect over-all system performance. Once this is accomplished, it may then be profitable to examine intermediate measures. We are now beginning to use criterion measures which reflect the functioning of parts of the total system. To a certain extent communication measures are of this sort.

THE POWER OF A TYPICAL EXPERIMENT

The development of experimental methods appropriate to system experiments must include the determination of the power of these designs in respect to alternative hypotheses which specify differences of practical significance. As an illustration, in a recent experiment[7] an analysis of the power of the design indicated that the experiment provided better than 90% probability of rejecting the null hypothesis of the independent variables under consideration contributed an actual difference of as much as 10% in such characteristics as control time or fuel consumption. In this experiment there were 64 separate traffic problems of the type studied,

---

[7] L. M. Schipper, C. L. Kraft, A. F. Smode, and P. M. Fitts, "The Use of Displays Showing Identity versus No-Identity; A Study in Human Engineering Aspects of Radar Air Traffic Control," *USAF WADC Technical Report*, No. 57-21, 1957.

and the handling of a total of 1280 simulated aircraft movements. Although a typical experiment is not sufficiently sensitive to detect very small effects reliably, nevertheless sufficient power is available for us to feel relatively confident that we will not reject as unimportant any variables that produce large effects on over-all system performance.

Perhaps the most serious limitation of the experimental designs that we have employed is the use of small numbers of experienced controllers. In many of our studies we have used as few as four controllers. Thus, strictly speaking, we are unable to generalize with much confidence to controllers in general. On the other hand, the use of experienced controllers gives us greater confidence in making statements about the maximum performance that can be expected of human operators.

REVIEW OF RESULTS FROM SEVERAL SYSTEM EXPERIMENTS

As had been pointed out earlier, system variables can be grouped into three classes. These are (*a*) load or input variables, (*b*) information or display variables, and (*c*) procedural or organizational variables. We now will summarize some typical experimental findings for each of these major classes of variables, drawn from the series of studies conducted during the past two years.[8]

In Figure 3 are shown some results for a traffic variable, rate of aircraft entry. As rate of entry (number of aircraft entering the terminal area per unit of time) is increased beyond some point, measures of system efficiency have uniformly been found to decline. Thus, in Figure 3, average control time showed a marked upward trend as the average time separation between successive entries decreased beyond one aircraft every 90 sec. for the condition of no identity, and as it decreased beyond one entry every 75 sec. for the condition in which identity was given. The number of conflicts also increased as a function of increased entry rate. These data are for a system in which a single controller was required to handle all aircraft, and entries deviated randomly around the

---

[8] L. M. Schipper and J. Versace, "Human Engineering Aspects of Radar Air Traffic Control: I. Performance in Sequencing Aircraft for Landings as a Function of Control Time Availability," *USAF WADC Technical Report*, No. 56-67, 1956; L. M. Schipper, J. S. Kidd, M. Shelly, and A. F. Smode, "Terminal System Effectiveness as a Function of the Method Used by Controllers to Obtain Altitude Information: A Study in Human Engineering Aspects of Radar Air Traffic Control," *USAF WADC Technical Report*, in preparation; L. M. Schipper, C. L. Kraft, A. F. Smode, and P. M. Fitts, *op. cit.*; L. M. Schipper, J. Versace, C. L. Kraft, J. C. McGuire, "Human Engineering Aspects of Radar Air Traffic Control: II. and III. Experimental Evaluations of Two Improved Identification Systems under High-Density Traffic Conditions," *USAF WADC Technical Report*, No. 56-68, 1956; L. M. Schipper, J. Versace, C. L. Kraft, and J. C. McGuire, "Human Engineering Aspects of Radar Air Traffic Control: IV. A Comparison of Sector and In-Line Control Procedures," *USAF WADC Technical Report*, No. 56-69, 1956; J. Versace, "The Effect of Emergencies and Communications Availability with Differing Entry Rates: A Study in Human Engineering Aspects of Radar Air Traffic Control," *USAF WADC Technical Report*, No. 56-70, 1956.

FIGURE 3

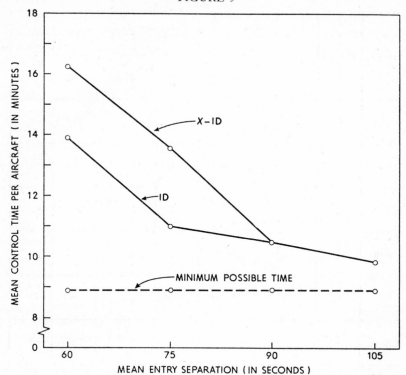

System performance at four entry rates under identity and no-identity conditions. Data are based on the performance of single controllers. ID indicates identity; X-ID, no identity.

mean temporal separation and appeared anywhere within a 90° sector of the periphery. Each problem consisted of blocks of 20 military-type aircraft. All aircraft were inbound, and had to be moved through a 50-mi. zone in order to reach the GCA gate.

Our most recent experiment[9] was concerned with a more detailed analysis of the load variable, the effect of the degree of spatial and temporal organization upon control efficiency and safety.

A display variable which has been found to have pronounced effect on system efficiency is the addition of an effective means of identifying the blips which appear on the primary display. In Figure 4 is shown the visual code used in most of the system experiments as a means of providing the controllers with knowledge of the identity of incoming aircraft. This coding system is based on the results of several supporting research

---

[9] M. W. Shelly, J. S. Kidd, G. Jeantheau, and P. M. Fitts, "Effect of Enroute Air Traffic Regulation on Radar Air Traffic Control Systems Employing Partially Optimized Displays: A Study in Human Engineering Aspects of Radar Air Traffic Control," *USAF WADC Technical Report,* in preparation.

FIGURE 4

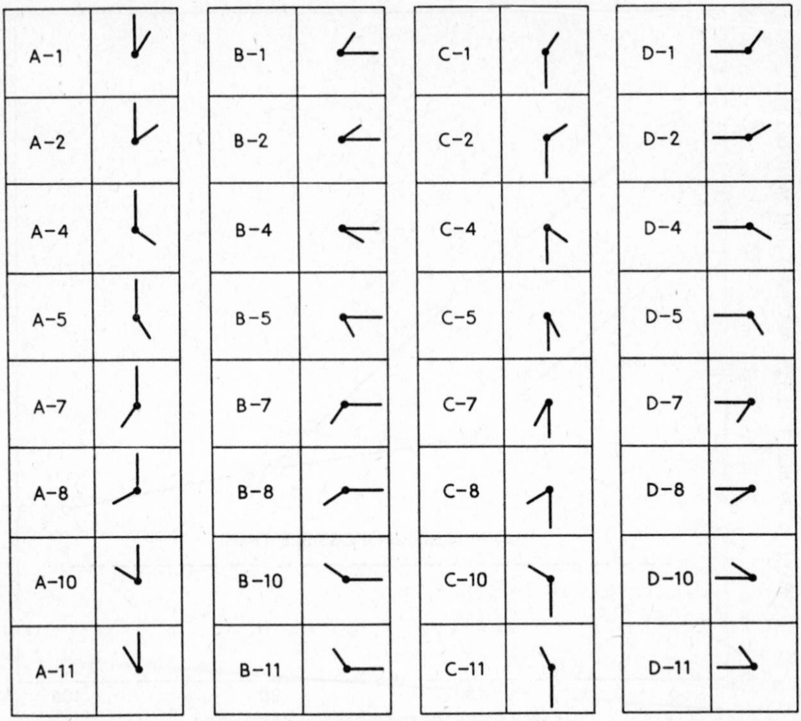

The clock-code identification system. The longer arm is read as Alpha, Bravo, Charlie, or Delta; the shorter arm is read as the corresponding clock numeral.

studies.[10] The effect of the use of this identity code on accumulated delay in landing in one of our experiments was shown in Figure 3. Except for the slowest rate, the landing delay was found to be greater for the condition in which there was no identity.[11] These data are for single controllers who were asked to handle random-entry problems.

The provision for aircraft identity, however, did not reduce the number of requests for information directed by controllers to pilots, as can be seen in Table 5.

The number of requests for altitude, speed, and heading information were found to be about the same under conditions of identity and of no identity. In this experiment the number of requests for altitude were about three times as great as requests for heading information. However, when a secondary altitude display was introduced in a subsequent experiment,[12] a dramatic change in the number of requests for altitude

[10] P. F. Muller, Jr., R. C. Sidorsky, A. J. Slivinske, E. A. Alluisi, and P. M. Fitts, *op. cit.*

[11] L. M. Schipper, C. L. Kraft, A. F. Smode, and P. M. Fitts, *op. cit.*

[12] L. M. Schipper, J. S. Kidd, M. Shelly, A. F. Smode, *op. cit.*

TABLE 5

SUMMARY OF THE FREQUENCIES OF DIFFERENT TYPES OF
COMMUNICATIONS BETWEEN CONTROLLERS AND PILOTS
AS A FUNCTION OF THE PRESENCE OR ABSENCE
OF AN IDENTITY CODE

(Data Are Frequencies per Aircraft Movement)

TYPE OF COMMUNICATION	COMMANDS TO PILOTS		INFORMATION REQUESTED	
	Identity	No Identity	Identity	No Identity
Heading	3.13	3.55	0.56	0.72
Airspeed	2.38	2.31	0.28	0.30
Altitude	2.20	2.18	1.60	1.59

information occurred, as might be expected. Such a reduction in the number of altitude requests directly reduces the load on the communication channel, i.e., reduces voice radio time, and this in itself may be an important gain in certain situations. However, in this particular experiment the availability of an altitude display, and the accompanying reduction in radio time, had no appreciable effect on total system performance as measured by such criteria as control time and fuel consumption.

Organizational variables will be a major focal point of much of our future system research. The largest number of directly cooperating controllers we have used to date, however, is two, supplemented by two additional men who provided contacts at the input and output points. In one investigation the effects of permitting two controllers to work in a face-to-face situation was compared with the effects of a condition in which they were assigned to separate semi-isolated work stations.[13] Under conditions of free and direct voice communications between the two controllers (face-to-face situation) not only did the controllers talk more frequently with each other, but the amount of time each spent in communication with pilots also increased. However, measures of system performance, such as fuel economy and control time, showed small changes, and the differences that did occur most often favored the condition of separate work stations.

Another organizational variable that has been investigated concerns the division of control responsibility between two men. Some results from an experiment on this topic[14] are shown in Table 6. The data shown permit an assessment of the effect of the use of two different ways of dividing the work between controllers. Both procedures used a geographic basis for the division of labor. One procedure employed an *in-line* principle in which control zones were determined by the distance from the GCA gate. One controller handled those aircraft farther from the gate, and the second controller handled those nearer to the gate.

---

[13] J. Versace, *op. cit.*

[14] L. M. Schipper, J. Verace, C. L. Kraft, and J. C. McGuire, *op. cit.*

TABLE 6

RESULTS ON SYSTEM PERFORMANCE OF THE USE OF SECTOR VS.
IN-LINE PROCEDURES BY TWO COOPERATING CONTROLLERS
(Data Based on 832 Aircraft Movements)

Criterion of System Performance	Average Time between Successive Entries			
	60 Sec.		90 Sec.	
	Sector	In-Line	Sector	In-Line
Mean Control Time (in min.)	10.12	10.42	10.16	10.21
Mean Fuel Used per Aircraft (in lbs.)	862	903	876	846
	Sector	In-Line	60 Sec.	90 Sec.
No. of Conflicts	22	19	30	11

The other procedure employed a *sector-control* principle. One controller handled all aircraft entering the terminal area north of the GCA gate, and the other controller, all aircraft entering south of the gate. The results indicated that the sector procedure might be slightly superior in efficiency for the faster rates, but the difference was not statistically reliable. In most respects the two controllers used the two procedures about equally well, even though very different modes of cooperation were required.

It is worth noting that negative findings, such as have been obtained in several of the studies we have completed (e.g., little or no effect of a visual altitude display, little difference between sector and in-line division of responsibility, little difference between an omnipresent identity code and use of a light-pencil interrogation device), are often very valuable since they permit system engineers to exercise much greater freedom of choice in designing the over-all system.

LINES OF FUTURE RESEARCH

The content direction of future system research in the Ohio State University Laboratory of Aviation Psychology will emphasize (*a*) the study of simulated automatic control systems in which people will be asked to monitor the system and to handle emergencies, (*b*) the study of different kinds of procedures for attaining a high level of effectiveness from a group of men who are working together, (*c*) the development of displays, work stations, and communication nets suitable for use by groups of three or more controllers, and (*d*) the study of the optimum numbers of controllers for performing different functions and handling various loads. Continued emphasis will be given to the general problem of the optimum allocation of functions to men and to machines in complex systems, and of optimum allocation of functions among the several men in such systems.

The theoretical and methodological direction of future research will place increasing emphasis on the topic of small-group proficiency, in the setting of a complex man-machine system which must solve externally paced problems in real time. More use will be made of measures of controller interactions and individual behavior in an effort to relate these theoretically to system performance.

Unfortunately, currently there is no effective framework or theoretical model for dealing with system research. The concepts, terminology, and models of present-day social psychology and personality theory are of little use for our present purposes. Thus, in our further investigations of complex systems we are faced with the development of theory in a relatively new area of psychology, an area lying between traditional experimental psychology, which centers its interest on the study of single subjects under carefully controlled conditions, and social psychology, which studies the behavior of individuals in groups, but only infrequently has been able to bring the environment and the tasks to which these groups are subjected under adequate experimental control. During the past two years, we have succeeded in creating a realistic task in the laboratory, we have developed meaningful and relatively highly reliable measures of group proficiency in problem solving, and we have been able to determine empirically the effects of several important input, display, and procedural variables. Our current major effort is to develop more effective theory for relating the empirical findings to more specific aspects of individual behavior on the one hand, and to a wider type of group problems on the other hand.

64. The Speed and Accuracy of Reading Horizontal, Vertical, and Circular Scales*

Norah E. Graham

A SERIES OF experiments has been designed to compare the human response to numerical information displayed on horizontal, vertical, and

* From *Journal of Applied Psychology*, Vol. 40, No. 4, 1956, pp. 228–32.

Acknowledgments are due to Professor R. C. Browne for his advice in this work, and to Mr. H. Campbell, B.A., F.S.S., for statistical help; also to the Department of Photography, Medical School, King's College, Newcastle upon Tyne, for their cooperation in making the films.

circular scales. It has already been shown[1] that if an operator has to control a moving pointer on a scale by turning a knob, then speed and accuracy are greatest when the horizontal scale is used. This suggests that clockwise rotation of the control knob is naturally associated with pointer movement from left to right when the control is vertically below the display. The principal value of this work lies, therefore, in the information which it gives about display-control relations: the subjects could have ignored all the scale markings except the one on which the pointer was to be kept. The comparison of the three types of display is not complete without some measure of the speed and accuracy of making scale readings and this is the purpose of the experiments described here.

METHOD

The subjects (Ss) read the scales from a projected cinefilm. Horizontal, vertical, and circular scales, identical to those used in the previous experiments (Figure 1) were drawn in white ink on black paper. The pointer, which was cut out of aluminum foil and painted white, was placed opposite the appropriate number as each scale was photographed. A 16-mm. cinecamera was used and the timing regulated by the successive-frame exposure technique. The camera was fitted with an accurate frame counter worked from the shutter shaft so that each frame was counted as it was exposed. The speed of projection was 24 frames per sec., so that, for example, a setting which the Ss were to see for ½ sec. was exposed for 12 frames. Each exposure was followed by 8 sec. of black spacing which allowed Ss to write down the scale reading. The word "READY" then appeared on the screen, for 2 sec., to prepare Ss for the next scale.

The projected circular scale was 5.1 in. in diameter and the horizontal and vertical scales were 16 in. in length. The intervals between scale markings were therefore the same on all three displays. The scales were viewed from a distance of 40 in. and appeared approximately at eye level. The angle subtended at the eye by the image of a scale on the screen was comparable to that subtended by the displays in the tracking experiments.

The film started with one example of each scale, which remained on the screen for 10 sec.; the correct reading appearing alongside the scale after the first 5 sec. This was followed by 9 practice readings, three on each scale, and then by the test itself. In both practice and test, the exposure time was ½ sec., this value having been chosen as the result of a pilot experiment.

When choosing the test numbers, the scales were considered as being made up of five major segments—0–2, 2–4, 4–6, 6–8, and 8–10—and on each scale two readings were chosen in each segment. The subdivisions within the major segments were divided into two groups:

1. .1, .4, .6, and .9, all of which are next to an extra long graduation mark, and:

2. .2, .3, .7, and .8, all of which are two subdivisions away from such a well-defined scale marking.

On each scale five readings were chosen in the first of these two groups and

[1] N. E. Graham, I. G. Baxter, and R. C. Browne, "Manual Tracking in Response to the Display of Horizontal, Vertical, and Circular Scales," *British Journal of Psychology* (Gen. Sec.), Vol. 42, 1951, pp. 155–63; N. E. Graham, "Manual Tracking on a Horizontal Scale and in the Four Quadrants of a Circular Scale," *British Journal of Psychology* (Gen. Sec.), Vol. 43, 1952, pp. 70–77.

FIGURE 1

HORIZONTAL, VERTICAL, AND CIRCULAR SCALES

five in the second. Thus, with only three scales, five major segments and two types of subdivisions to be considered, it was only necessary for each subject to make $3 \times 5 \times 2 = 30$ readings in order for a complete analysis of the results to be possible.

Sixty male university students, all studying some branch of engineering, acted as Ss.

RESULTS

The Ss' responses were scored as follows:

Correct readings scored 0.

Readings in error by ±0.1 scale units scored 1.

All other errors and omissions scored 2.

The resulting distribution of scores was approximately normal. Marked improvement in performance occurred during the practice exposures, but the scores obtained during the experiment proper show no systematic improvement.

The error score for each segment of the three scales is shown in Table 1. The high incidence of mistakes at the ends of the scales is very noticeable. This is to be expected on the linear scales as it may take longer to find the pointer in these positions, but it is surprising to find a similar trend on the circular scale.

It was also found that the position on the scale in which the pointer

TABLE 1

THE TOTAL ERROR SCORE FOR EACH SEGMENT OF THE THREE DISPLAYS

Major Segment	Scale			Total Error
	Horizontal	Vertical	Circular	
0–2	80	72	78	230
2–4	33	58	38	129
4–6	44	48	40	132
6–8	18	64	41	123
8–10	53	123	64	240
Total error	228	365	261	854

lies has more effect on the accuracy of reading on one type of scale than on another. This was due to the very high error at the top of the vertical scale. Many more mistakes were made between 8 and 10 on this scale than in any other region of the three displays.

It was also shown that the errors are significantly greater on the vertical scale than on the horizontal or the circular scale, but the difference between the latter two may be attributed to chance.

Another significant variable is the unit or section of the scale in which the pointer lies. In this case the t test shows that the liability to make mistakes is significantly greater at the ends of the scales in sections 0–2 and 8–10 than in the three middle sections, 2–4, 4–6, and 6–8.

A more detailed analysis of the results showed that the position of the subdivision within the major segment (i.e., the tenths) had no significant effect on the accuracy of reading. The total error score for the group of readings ending in .1, .4, .6, or .9 was 457, while the total score for those ending in .2, .3, .7, or .8 was 397.

When compared with the residual variance the differences between Ss are highly significant. The best S read 29 out of the 30 scales correctly, while the poorest made 21 mistakes.

Table 2 shows the frequency with which different types of error occurred on the three scales. The number of correct readings was greatest on the horizontal scale, and even if the readers had been allowed a margin of error of ±0.1 scale units, this display would still have ranked first in order of accuracy. Readings on the circular scale, on the other hand, were nearly always correct to within 0.2 scale units and only one reading on this display was missed altogether.

When the direction of the errors is taken into account it is seen that there is a tendency to overestimate a reading by 0.1 or 0.2 scale units on the circular scale. This was particularly true of the four readings 0.2, 8.6, 1.4, and 4.6. For example, 11 Ss read 1.4 as 1.6 and 13 read it as 1.5. Only four Ss underestimated and called it 1.3. Or again, 8.6 was read as 8.8 by nine Ss, and as 8.7 by 17 Ss, whereas only two mistook it for 8.5. This accounts for the high error score at the extremities of the circular

TABLE 2

THE FREQUENCY WITH WHICH ERRORS OF DIFFERENT MAGNITUDE WERE MADE ON
EACH SCALE

	HORIZONTAL		VERTICAL		CIRCULAR	
	Number	%	Number	%	Number	%
Correct readings	413	69.0	324	54.0	390	65.0
Errors						
+1.0	4	1.0	3	1.2	2	0.3
−1.0	2		4		0	
+0.2	6	2.0	8	2.6	34	6.0
−0.2	6		8		2	
+0.1	66	24.3	110	31.2	102	26.7
−0.1	80		77		58	
Other errors	11	3.7	23	11.0	11	2.0
Missed readings	12		43		1	
Total	600	100.0	600	100.0	600	100.0

scale, particularly between 0 and 2, though it does not explain it. Such a tendency to overestimate is not peculiar to the circular scale, however. On the vertical scale errors of +0.1 occur much more frequently than those of −0.1.

Discussion

The gross errors of +1.0 scale unit which occurred in the present experiment were all associated with readings in the second half of a numbered division. Kappauf[2] remarks that under these conditions the scale number read is apt to be that nearest to the pointer. The tendency noted by the same author to "round out" readings, particularly in the first numbered interval of scales which start at zero, is not apparent in the present experiment, presumably because of instructions to record the zero in such cases; it may, however, occur in practical situations. Vernon[3] considers that gross mistakes are also liable to occur near the zero on circular scales, but the present results confirm the finding of Sleight[4] that gross errors at the ends of a scale are less frequent on scales without a clearly defined break.

The mistakes which do happen at the ends of the circular scale are principally local, that is to say, of less than one numbered scale division. Local errors in any part of the scale display a tendency to overestimation. This was also noted by Sleight and seems to have no obvious explanation.

[2] W. E. Kappauf, "A Discussion of Scale-Reading Habits," *USAF WADC Technical Report*, No. 6569, 1951.

[3] M. D. Vernon, "Scale and Dial Reading," *Flying Personnel Research Committee Report*, No. 668, 1946.

[4] R. B. Sleight, "The Effect of Instrument Dial Shape on Legibility," *Journal of Applied Psychology*, Vol. 32, 1948, pp. 170–88.

Sleight attributes the differences between the scales used in his experiment to the variation in their "effective" area: the larger the area to be scanned the less accurate the reading. Such an explanation does not account, however, for the difference between the horizontal and vertical scales which he also found to be significant and which the present work suggests is the more important difference. From a physiological point of view, an explanation can be based on the shape of the visual field and the mechanics of eye movements. Objects that subtend an angle of more than ½° at the eye can be detected if they lie within a field whose boundaries are approximately 100° to the right or left of the point of fixation, 70° above it and 80° below it. The width of the visual field is thus considerably greater than its height, which is one factor that might favor the reading of horizontal scales. This is simply another way of saying that the eyes are set in the head in a horizontal line. The linear displays as they appeared in this experiment subtended an angle of approximately 10° at the eye. No difficulty should have been experienced, therefore, in finding the pointer even at the top of the vertical scale. The region of foveal vision, however, only subtends an angle of about 3° at the eye and, in order to read the scale, it is necessary to focus on the pointer itself. During very short exposures the accuracy of reading therefore depends upon the speed with which eye movements can be made. Scanning along a horizontal line is a relatively simple action involving the use of the lateral and medial recti muscles only. Raising or lowering the eyes, on the other hand, involves the joint action of the superior and inferior recti and the inferior and superior obliques. According to Duke-Elder[5] it has been shown by photographic studies that the eyes can follow lines in the horizontal plane more easily than in any other. It has been found, moreover, that horizontal eye movements are the most rapid and vertical ones the slowest. When the fact that people are accustomed, when reading, to scanning along a horizontal line is added to this evidence, it is not difficult to explain the superiority of the horizontal scale.

SUMMARY

1. The speed and accuracy of reading comparable horizontal, vertical, and circular scales has been studied by means of a film. Pictures of the scales were flashed on a screen at 10-sec. intervals, the exposure time being ½ sec.

2. The vertical scale is clearly less easy to read than either of the other two displays, particular difficulty being experienced near its ends.

3. The success of the circular scale may be attributed to the fact that it presents a smaller area to be scanned. The shape of the visual field and the relative ease of moving the eyes from side to side, rather than up and

---

[5] W. S. Duke-Elder, *Textbook of Ophthalmology* (London: Kimpton, 1932).

down, are thought to account for the greater accuracy on the horizontal scale.

65. Human Factors Evaluation of a New Telephone Numerical Dialing System*

J. E. Karlin

WHEN A NEW item of telephone equipment is designed at Bell Laboratories, its technical aspects are put to an exhaustive series of tests before it is placed in the hands of the customer or of a Telephone Company employee. Characteristically, a new item is thoroughly tested in the laboratory and later is used in a field trial before it is recommended for general use. In this way, the Bell System guards against unforeseen circumstances which could lead to costly failures.

It has long been recognized, of course, that other factors besides those of a purely technical nature help to determine the success or failure of a new design. Specifically, since all equipment is at one point or another used, installed, or maintained by human beings, the Bell System has always considered the preferences and performance of users as one of the crucial groups of facts to be determined in any extensive trial of telephone equipment.

As outlined in a previous article (*Bell Laboratories Record*, May, 1954), Bell Laboratories makes an organized effort to study user characteristics, and this raises the question as to how effectively human factors important in the telephone situation can be measured under laboratory conditions with Laboratories employees as test subjects. Clearly, both the "users" and the conditions may, in any given instance, vary widely from their counterparts in a real residence or business telephone situation. The value of human-factors testing, however, is seen by drawing an analogy with engineering testing. Large-scale field trials of equipment are expensive and are never undertaken unless technical facts determinable in the laboratory are known. A field trial could also be an inconvenience to customers if a major technical fault were found, and this is another reason that laboratory testing, even if it cannot uncover *all* the facts, ensures that the more inclusive trials under actual field conditions are worth their expense and effort. The same is true of human-factors test-

---

* From "All-Numeral Dialing—Would Users Like It," *Bell Laboratories Record*, Vol. 36, 1958, pp. 284–88.

ing. Much information can be accumulated in the laboratory, and this information is of great value in the subsequent steps in the process by which a laboratory idea becomes a reality of the telephone industry.

These observations about users and the extent to which their preferences and performance can be determined in the laboratory are illustrated by some recent studies of all-numeral dialing. All-numeral dialing, or AND, involves the use of numerals in place of the office-name letters of the present letter-numeral dialing or LND system. For instance, the office letters UN of the telephone number UNiversity 4–5271 would be replaced by their numeral equivalents on the telephone dial to result in the AND number 864–5271. The telephone dial would thus contain only the digits 1–9 and zero, and the telephone directory would list all numbers by numerals alone.

AND offers certain advantages, some of them rather obvious and some perhaps less so. AND eliminates the confusion between "oh" (letter O)

FIGURE 1

Telephone numbers can be found with less effort because of uncluttered face of all-numeral dial.

and "oh" (number zero), and also between "I" and "1"—features that are especially important for direct-distance dialing of long-distance calls, in which the second digit is always a "zero" or a "one." In addition, the space saved by deleting letter designations would be advantageous in looking ahead to possible designs of pushbutton telephone sets: one number on a small button would be read more easily than three letters and one number. Similarly, elimination of letters would be helpful in any future reduction in size of the present telephone and dial, for example in the "dial-in-handset" where the dial is placed around the transmitter.

One other advantage of AND has to do with international dialing. In anticipation of the time when we may see dialing of calls to other countries, AND would simplify international dialing codes, since foreign telephones frequently have the letters in different finger-holes. As desirable as these advantages might be, however, they are secondary to the fundamental question of the acceptability of AND to customers, and it was to this question that the Laboratories experiments were directed.

In a matter such as this, we would all tend to have our own opinions as to whether AND would be good, bad, or indifferent. In fact, the most common reaction is that AND would not work, and the principal objections expressed are that AND numbers would be hard to dial and to remember. Specifically, four issues are involved. With AND, would telephone users dial numbers faster, slower, or at the same speed? Would dialing be more or less accurate? Are AND numbers actually harder to remember? And, beyond other considerations, would customers *like* the AND system?

All-numeral dialing has from time to time been considered by people at the Laboratories and by many others in the Bell System, and a number of limited but valuable investigations have been carried out. The present investigation, carried out in 1954 and 1955 by the Human Factors Engineering Group at the Laboratories, was intended to be more comprehensive and to carry the laboratory type of study as far as it could go. Four separate experiments were conducted, and it will be seen that they proceeded in a progressive order, each growing out of the previous results and attempting to answer a new phase of the problem.

The first experiment was designed to simulate the dialing aspects of a cutover from LND to AND and to determine users' reactions to it. Nine employees of Bell Laboratories were selected for the experiment, and care was taken that insofar as possible, these employees were more nearly representative of the range of telephone users than other employees who might have specialized interests in techniques of using the telephone instrument. Each person was asked to go to a special test room once a day for 22 days, and while in the test room place a list of calls. The list consisted of names of people and places to call, rather than numbers. For the first 10 of these 22 days, each person used the regular Manhattan Telephone Directory to look up LND numbers and place the calls. For the other 12 days the Manhattan Directory was so modified that the number found appeared on the page in its AND form, and the person placing the calls had to use a telephone with an all-numeral dial. In such Laboratory experiments, it has been found that dialing speeds and errors are quite close to the values observed in the field.

The calls actually terminated in a nearby room and were answered by the experimenter. "Busy's" and "Don't answer's" were introduced with appropriate frequencies; these calls were repeated until successful. Mechanical aspects of dialing that could be observed from the receiving end—such as dialing speed and dialing accuracy—were measured and tabulated. To reduce the "guinea pig" effect to a minimum, there was no contact between the user and experimenter until the entire experiment was finished, at which time each user was interviewed.

What were the results of this experiment? It was found that AND was about 10 per cent faster (Figure 2) and also was slightly more ac-

FIGURE 2

When nine Laboratories users were "cut over" to AND, their dialing performance improved.

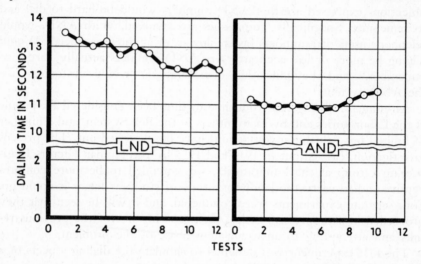

curate than LND. Five of the nine users preferred AND and four thought both systems equally acceptable. All nine, however, strongly preferred AND once a number was fixed in mind, for the reason that it was easier to place the call using the large, uncluttered symbols of the AND dial. All nine felt that it was just as easy to memorize AND numbers long enough to dial.

It turned out, however, that this experiment fell short of realistic dialing in one respect: with a telephone directory always at hand, users had little incentive to memorize the AND numbers, even though certain of these numbers were dialed every day. In fact it was known that users in the first experiment almost never dialed from memory, because the times between successive calls from the lists clearly indicated that users consistently consulted the directory.

The second experiment was therefore conducted in a different manner. A second group of nine employees was selected. Each was a resident of Manhattan who, in his or her normal LND telephoning, had already memorized several frequently-called numbers. Instead of dialing from a test room, each user placed calls from his own desk. He was given a specially prepared directory page containing both his memorized numbers and many unfamiliar ones. Each day the experimenter called the user at his desk and asked him to place a certain series of calls. For three days all numbers were in LND form and for 16 or more days were in AND form.

As before, all calls terminated in the same Laboratories building, and dialing performance was measured. In this case, the user had an incentive (but was not instructed) to rememorize familiar numbers in their new AND form. Whether he rememorized them at all, and if so, how rapidly and how completely, was observed by the experimenter.

Of the nine users in the second experiment, eight found AND as acceptable as LND, but one expressed a general dislike of AND. Dialing speed and accuracy were again superior, and within the month following cutover to AND, six of the nine had rememorized all the numbers they had previously dialed from memory with LND, and two felt that they could memorize all their numbers given more time.

In both of these two experiments, it was difficult to isolate memory difficulties from dialing errors; when a wrong number was dialed, it was not always possible to tell whether the subject had memorized incorrectly or had merely made a mistake in dialing. The third experiment was therefore designed as a straight "memory test," with no actual dialing of calls. One hundred employees were involved in this experiment, fifty being tested for ability to memorize unfamiliar LND numbers and fifty for their ability to memorize the equivalent AND numbers. The experimenter called each person at his desk and gave him a number. If the person were in the LND group, for example, he might be told that "The Sears Roebuck number is Foxcroft 9–2675." Similarly, another person in the AND group would be told that "The Sears Roebuck number is 369–2675." (All numbers were made up specially for the experiment and were therefore equally unfamiliar to all participants.) The experimenter then called back daily to ask what the number was. If the person had forgotten it, he was given it again on consecutive days until he succeeded in memorizing it. When he had memorized it he was given a second number, and when he had memorized *both* numbers he was given a third. This test of long-term memory ended when all three numbers were memorized.

In addition to these daily calls, the experimenter tested *short-term memory* by sometimes calling back soon after a number was given, to determine whether the person remembered it. The situation was such that he was not expecting to be called back. This short-term memory is the type used in going from a directory to a dial; it was tested in this fashion over a range up to fifteen minutes.

As indicated in Figure 3 the experiment showed that it was just as easy to remember AND numbers for short periods of time as it is for LND numbers. This experiment also demonstrated, however, that it takes a little longer to memorize AND numbers for greater periods of time. In quantitative terms, if a person dials an LND number once each day

FIGURE 3

After using a new telephone number people at the Laboratories remembered all-numeral numbers about as well as letter-numeral numbers.

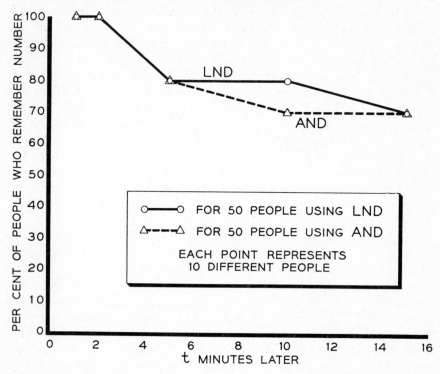

and succeeds in memorizing it on the third day, he would on the average require about one extra day to memorize the equivalent AND number. The importance of this aspect of AND dialing of course depends partially upon how much memory is involved in real telephone situations, and it should therefore be noted that the average telephone user "permanently" memorizes only about four or five numbers.

The three studies yielded rather definite results, but there could always remain some doubt about their value because of the possibility that user dialing in real homes would be different from employee dialing under laboratory conditions. The final experiment was therefore conducted in the homes of telephone users. Seventy-three Laboratories employees and relatives of employees participated in the test. About half were in New York City and half in various small towns in New Jersey. In each home, telephone numbers in the ready-reference directory were changed to the equivalent AND forms, an all-numeral dial was put on the telephone, and a "card translator" for converting LND to AND numbers was supplied (ABC = 2, DEF = 3, *etc.*). The participants then used AND for ten weeks, and their reactions to it were determined at various times during the trial.

The results of this home experiment were not as objectively measurable as in the previous three in the laboratory, but they nevertheless were of great value because this experiment approached most nearly to an actual AND cutover. Of the 73 users, 31 preferred AND, 17 found AND and LND equally acceptable, and 24 preferred LND. Of the 24 who preferred LND, only 8 felt strongly about retaining it. The reasons given were chiefly the reluctance to change from the LND habits acquired over many years, and the difficulty of discussing telephone information when everybody around them was still using LND. Of the 73 users, 58 stated that they found no difference between memorizing AND and LND numbers, and no one felt that remembering numbers would be a serious handicap. There was little difference in reaction between users in small towns and those users who live in New York City.

It should be noted that in this experiment, and to a certain extent in experiments 1 and 2, certain factors tended to make the test AND cutovers more troublesome to the user than they would be in actual practice. Since it is impracticable in laboratory experiments to reprint entire telephone directories, users had to depend on modified directories, typed "directory" pages, or, in experiment 4, on card translators for determining AND numbers. Second, users were dialing AND numbers in an isolated environment. That is, unlike a real AND cutover where a whole community would be involved, test users were subjected to AND while everyone else was dialing LND. This meant that an AND user could not discuss telephone information with his neighbor; for example, he could not give anybody his home number without first mentally translating it back to LND. It was therefore felt that these disadvantages would tend to act as a conservative factor in the final results.

How helpful are the results of such laboratory experiments on human beings for predicting field results? On the basis of Laboratory results alone, no one can say definitely that telephone users would surely accept or reject AND. On the other hand, one can see that when more extensive field trials are conducted, the preliminary laboratory results will be of great value in deciding how to conduct the trials and what facts to determine.

The most one would want to say at this point is that with AND, dialing speed should increase and the error rate should be about the same or slightly lower. There should be little strong feeling against AND, and there is a good chance that it would be widely accepted. With field trials,[1] it will be possible to compare the results with those obtained in

---

[1] The foregoing analysis was prepared prior to a field trial of AND which was begun in Wichita Falls, Texas, in January of this year. On the basis of the first three months of this trial, indications are that AND performance compares quite favorably with LND. This seems to verify some of the conclusions reached as a result of laboratory studies. It should be emphasized, however, that the Wichita Falls numbering change is a trial only, and that the Bell System has reached no conclusion that a change in present numbering is desirable. Wichita Falls results are still under study,

the laboratory. A study of any discrepancies should be helpful in improving laboratory testing methods.

66. The Tactual Identification of Shapes for Coding Switch Handles*

Bert F. Green and Lois K. Anderson

CONTROL PANELS for complex electronic equipment often contain many switches. In many applications the operator could work more efficiently if he could select the appropriate switch without looking at it. Coding the switches by spacing them in groups or by using switch handles of different shapes should help the operator to locate a particular switch without visual cues. Weitz[1] has shown that accuracy of performance is significantly affected by the shape of aircraft-type control knobs when visual cues are restricted. We might expect similar effects in the case of electronic control panels.

The major purpose of the experiments reported here was to select a set of differently shaped switch handles that could be identified easily. Jenkins[2] has reported a very similar investigation of shapes for aircraft-type controls. He selected sets of 8 and 11 knobs from sets of 25 and 22 knobs. The selected knobs were almost never confused in his studies. We adapted some of his shapes for the lever-switch handles, although most of the handles we studied are our own designs. In addition to selecting a set of easily discriminable shapes, we investigated the rela-

---

and substantial advantages must be demonstrated to justify a change in numbering for millions of our customers. If such advantages seem indicated when Wichita Falls studies are complete, other more stringent trials of the all-numeral type of numbering plan would have to be undertaken in larger cities before any firm conclusions could be drawn. Many factors outside the scope of this article are involved in numbering plans and dialing procedures.

* From *Journal of Applied Psychology*, Vol. 39, No. 4, 1955, pp. 219–26.

This research was supported jointly by the Army, Navy, and Air Force under contract with the Massachusetts Institute of Technology.

[1] J. Weitz, "The Coding of Aircraft Control Knobs," in P. M. Fitts (ed.), *Psychology of Equipment Design*, AAF Aviation Psychology Program Research Representatives, Report No. 19 (Washington: U.S. Government Printing Office, 1947), pp. 187–98.

[2] W. O. Jenkins, "The Tactual Discrimination of Shapes for Coding Aircraft-Type Controls," in P. M. Fitts (ed.), *Psychology of Equipment Design*, AAF Aviation Psychology Program Research Representatives, Report No. 19 (Washington: U.S. Government Printing Office, 1947), pp. 199–205.

tion between two experimental procedures for measuring the confusability of the handles. We also compared the relative discriminability of two different handle sizes.

Experiment I

In the first experiment we measured the confusions among the 16 handles shown in Figure 1. The handles were made of black Lucite and were ⅞ in. long, and either ⅜ in. square or ⅜ in. in diameter. Although most of the handles were designed to be maximally discriminable from the others, we deliberately included some similar pairs of handles in order to check our measurement techniques. Specifically, we expected *square* and *diamond, half moon* and *groove,* and *cross* and *triple groove* to be confused more often than the other handles.

Two methods, which we have called the learn method and the find method, were used to measure confusability. In the learn method, S learned to associate a number from 1 through 16 with each of the handles in a typical paired-associates procedure. The numbers were assigned to the handles in a different random order for each S.

The presentation device for the learn method consisted of a circular disk mounted so that it rotated in the vertical plane. The handles were mounted, near the periphery, with their axes perpendicular to the face of the disk. By rotating the disk behind a shield, E could position any handle near an aperture so that S could reach through to feel it, but could not see it. No attempt was made to control the manner in which Ss felt the handles, although they typically used the thumb and the index and middle fingers of their favored hand. Trials were arranged in blocks of 16, each handle being presented once in random order in each block. On each trial S was allowed approximately two seconds to feel the handle and report its number. The S was required to respond with some number on each trial, after which E announced the correct number. The handles were said to be learned when S responded correctly on all trials in one block.

For the find method, a complete set of handles was mounted in a linear array on each of the four long sides of a rectangular box 2 in. × 2 in. × 18 in. Successive handles were one inch apart. The handles were arranged in a balanced random order in each of the four arrays. For each trial, E presented a "target" handle on the rotary device used in the learn method. The blindfolded S felt the target, and then tried to locate the handle with the same shape in one of the four arrays, which was placed directly to the left of the rotary device. The S was instructed to begin at the right of the array and to feel each handle in turn until he either found the target shape or reached the end of the array. He could then skip around, if necessary, but he was required to select a handle on each trial. Four blocks of 16 trials were given; each handle was presented once in each block, and once in each array.

The Ss were 20 U.S. Army enlisted men with AGCT scores in the range 80–100. All Ss were run in both the learn and the find methods. Ten Ss were tested with the learn method first; the others were tested with the find method first.

RESULTS

We first examined the differences between the two groups of 10 Ss. The group which learned after they found required an average of 24.4 blocks to reach the criterion, while the group who learned first required an aver-

FIGURE 1

Handle Shapes Used in These Experiments

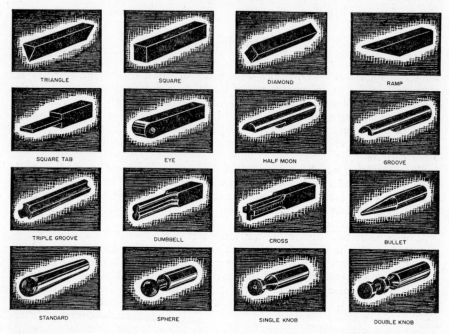

age of 18.1 blocks. This difference is not statistically significant. Likewise, the average number of learning errors was not significantly different for the two groups. (These statistics adequately describe the learning data since all individual learning curves were virtually linear.) In the find method, the average number of errors was significantly smaller for the group which learned first, presumably because they were familiar with the shapes.

Finally, we wanted to compare the pattern of confusions among handles in the two groups. The learning data for each S were tallied in a confusion matrix that showed the number of times S made each possible response to each of the stimuli. A pooled matrix was obtained by summing the corresponding cells in the individual matrices and dividing by the total number of responses made to each stimulus. Each cell entry is then an estimate of the conditional probability of a specific response, given a particular stimulus.

Using the term "confusion" for such matrices in the learn method seems to imply that all errors made during the learning process are being called confusions. We would prefer to distinguish conceptually between two sources of error: random guessing and specific perceptual confusions. We have no way to classify any particular error as a guess or a confusion, but we can find the specific confusions, on the average, from the relative sizes of entries in the confusion matrix. If all errors were random guesses, the off-diagonal entries would all be equal, except for statistical fluctuations. Thus a matrix with uniform off-diagonal entries indicates a homogeneous set of stimuli, while departures from uniformity indicate the presence of specific perceptual confusions. Since we had no precise statistical test of deviations from uniformity, we arbitrarily defined the largest 5% of the entries to be "predominant confusions."

When the confusion matrices were tallied for the two groups in the learn method, six of the twelve predominant confusions in each matrix were the same, indicating a moderate degree of agreement. We also computed the correlations of the corresponding off-diagonal cells and of the diagonal cells in the two matrices. The correlations were .70 and .63, respectively. They indicate, in a general way, how well the matrices agree. In order to evaluate the extent of individual differences, we split each group into two subgroups and obtained correlations between subgroups. These correlations are of about the same magnitude as the correlations between groups, which suggests that any differences between groups are due to differences between individuals.

The data from the find method were also tallied in pooled confusion matrices for the two groups. The five largest confusions were common; the other predominant confusions did not overlap. The correlations for the find confusion matrices were .92 for diagonals, .93 for off-diagonals, indicating a high degree of agreement. Thus, although the group who learned first made fewer errors in the find method, their pattern of confusions was very similar to that of the other group.

These results made it reasonable to pool all 20 Ss. The pooled matrices for the two methods are shown in Tables 1 and 2. The predominant confusions are shown in boldface type. Eight of these are common to the two matrices, indicating moderately good agreement between the two methods. The correlations between these tables are .50 for diagonals and .83 for off-diagonals. We can safely conclude that both methods will find the same important confusions, although the fine structure of the confusion matrices may differ somewhat.

The *square-diamond* and *cross-triple groove* confusions predominate. These were two of the three pairs deliberately put in to show confusion. The third pair that we expected to be confused often was *half-moon groove;* this pair also ranks among the top 12. Tables 1 and 2 show that *sphere, single knob,* and *double knob,* all of which have round, specially shaped heads, were frequently confused with one another. The similarities in the other shapes that were often confused are equally obvious.

The confusion between *square* and *diamond* is especially interesting since the two handles actually have the same shape but differ in orientation. Our Ss were not warned to pay attention to the orientation, and apparently had difficulty in learning to make this distinction. In fact, many Ss did not learn to distinguish between these two handles, but appeared

TABLE 1

Confusion Matrix in Experiment 1—Learn Method*

Stimulus		Response																Total
		1	2	3	4	5	6	7	8	9	10	11	12	13	14	15	16	
1	triangle	62.1	3.1	3.1	4.2	2.4	1.4	2.4	1.4	1.9	2.4	1.9	2.4	2.6	4.2	0.5	4.2	100.2
2	square	4.5	57.7	21.2	1.6	2.4	0.7	1.9	1.2	1.9	0.7	2.4	0.7	0.2	1.2	0.7	1.2	100.2
3	diamond	4.5	26.8	48.7	1.2	3.5	1.2	1.2	0.9	3.1	1.2	2.1	1.2	0.5	1.9	0.9	1.2	100.1
4	ramp	7.8	2.4	4.0	63.5	2.8	0.9	2.1	2.4	1.4	2.8	0.9	3.5	0.7	1.6	1.6	1.4	99.8
5	square tab	2.1	1.4	0.7	2.6	52.7	0.7	7.3	3.5	4.9	4.9	1.4	1.9	3.3	4.0	3.3	5.2	99.9
6	eye	0.9	2.6	2.6	0.5	2.8	72.7	0.9	2.6	1.2	4.5	0.9	1.2	0.2	3.3	1.2	1.9	100.0
7	half moon	2.1	1.9	1.2	4.9	9.4	1.6	40.5	8.2	5.9	5.4	1.6	1.6	3.5	6.6	1.2	4.2	99.8
8	groove	1.9	0.9	0.7	2.6	4.0	3.1	8.7	53.9	4.0	4.2	1.2	1.6	3.1	5.2	1.6	4.0	100.0
9	triple groove	1.9	1.2	2.1	1.4	2.1	1.6	2.6	7.1	39.3	7.1	18.4	0.9	3.1	7.3	1.6	3.1	100.0
10	dumbbell	2.1	1.4	1.9	1.2	4.9	2.1	4.7	3.3	6.4	48.9	5.9	2.4	2.4	5.4	1.4	5.7	100.1
11	cross	2.1	1.2	1.9	1.9	4.0	0.9	3.8	1.9	15.5	5.7	49.7	1.9	0.9	4.7	0.9	3.1	100.1
12	bullet	2.6	1.9	2.6	3.1	2.1	1.9	2.6	1.6	1.2	0.9	1.2	66.8	3.5	2.6	3.3	3.1	100.0
13	standard	1.6	2.1	1.9	1.9	2.8	2.1	0.9	3.3	1.9	1.9	1.2	8.7	56.9	4.2	5.7	2.8	99.9
14	sphere	1.4	2.8	2.1	3.5	4.7	3.1	4.2	4.2	3.5	2.1	1.6	3.8	7.3	40.2	10.8	4.5	99.8
15	single knob	2.4	2.1	0.7	2.8	3.1	1.2	5.4	3.5	2.1	2.8	2.6	2.4	4.5	8.9	48.5	7.1	100.1
16	double knob	1.6	1.9	0.9	2.6	3.8	2.4	3.5	4.9	1.9	4.2	1.9	1.9	4.7	7.8	4.0	52.0	100.0
	Total	101.6	111.4	96.3	99.5	107.5	97.6	92.7	103.9	96.1	99.7	94.9	102.9	95.9	109.1	87.2	103.7	1600.0

* Twenty Ss were given a total of 425 trials per handle. Entries in any row show the proportion of presentations of the given stimulus that resulted in each response.

TABLE 2
Confusion Matrix in Experiment 1—Find Method*

Stimulus	1	2	3	4	5	6	7	8	9	10	11	12	13	14	15	16	Total
1 triangle	**91.2**	2.5	3.8	2.5													100.0
2 square		**63.8**	33.8			2.5											100.1
3 diamond	2.5	38.8	**52.5**	1.2		3.8				1.2							100.0
4 ramp				**98.8**	1.2												100.0
5 square tab					**95.0**		1.2	1.2		2.5							99.9
6 eye			1.2			**96.2**		1.2		1.2							99.8
7 half moon	2.5				1.2		**81.2**	12.5	1.2				1.2				99.8
8 groove						1.2	3.8	**88.8**	2.5	2.5	1.2						100.0
9 triple groove	1.2							2.5	**65.0**		28.8					2.5	100.0
10 dumbbell							1.2		7.5	**80.0**	6.2		2.5	1.2		1.2	99.8
11 cross									26.2	2.5	**71.2**						99.9
12 bullet												**100.0**					100.0
13 standard									1.2				**96.2**	2.5			99.9
14 sphere													2.5	**91.2**	3.8	2.5	100.0
15 single knob														5.0	**87.5**	7.5	100.0
16 double knob										1.2	1.2			1.2	6.2	**90.0**	99.8
Total	97.4	105.1	91.2	102.5	97.4	103.7	87.4	106.2	103.6	91.1	108.6	100.0	102.4	101.1	97.5	103.7	1599.0

* Twenty Ss were given four trials on each handle. Entries in any row show the proportion of presentations of the given stimulus that resulted in each response. Cells with no entries are indicated by blanks rather than zeroes. Predominant confusions are shown by boldface type.

to reach the criterion of one perfect block by chance. This can be seen by comparing the *square-diamond* confusion made by the two groups of Ss in the find method. If S was not noting the orientation, then he would probably pick the first of the two that he reached. The "find first" group picked the first of the two on 75% of the presentations of square or diamond, of which 40% were correct. The "learn first" group picked the first of the two on 60% of the presentations, of which 38% were correct. Clearly the former group was rarely responding to orientation, and in the latter group some of the Ss were still not aware of the orientation cue.

Experiment II

In the second experiment we compared the 16 handles used in the first experiment with a set of 16 handles having the same shapes, but one-third smaller (¼ in. in diameter, rather than ⅜ in.). The shapes were identical except for some slight alterations in the base to facilitate mounting the handles. Only the learning method was used in this experiment. One group of seven Ss learned the small handles, and was then tested on the large handles. Another group of seven Ss learned the large handles and then transferred to the small size.

RESULTS

The results of this experiment can be summarized very simply. The groups did not differ significantly in the number of learning errors, the number of blocks to reach criterion, or the number of errors on the

TABLE 3

PREDOMINANT CONFUSIONS IN POOLED CONFUSION MATRIX
(Based on 27 Ss)

MATRIX ENTRY*	STIMULUS	RESPONSE
25.2	3 diamond	2 square
22.6	2 square	3 diamond
20.6	9 triple groove	11 cross
15.0	11 cross	9 triple groove
10.4	14 sphere	15 single knob
9.5	7 half moon	5 square tab
9.0	7 half moon	8 groove
9.0	8 groove	7 half moon
8.8	4 ramp	1 triangle
8.1	15 single knob	14 sphere
7.8	16 double knob	14 sphere
7.6	9 triple groove	10 dumbbell

* Proportion of presentations of the stimulus that resulted in the specific confusion.

transfer trials. An average of 2.4 errors was made on the first block of transfer trials, indicating that Ss can transfer very easily. Six of the predominant confusions overlap. The correlation of the off-diagonal entries in the confusion matrices of the two groups was .66; the correlation of the diagonal entries was .63. These correlations are about as large as those obtained between the two groups on the first experiment, and seem to be about as large as individual differences permit.

Experiment III

In the third experiment we tested two subsets of ten handles that were chosen from the 16 original large-sized handles. In order to increase the stability of the confusion pattern, we pooled the seven Ss in Experiment II who learned the large handles first with the 20 Ss from the first experiment to obtain a "learn" confusion matrix based on 27 Ss. This matrix is very similar to Table 1 and will not be presented here. The 12 most prevalent confusions of the pooled matrix are listed in Table 3. We selected two subsets of ten handles in such a way that most of these confusions were avoided. The sets are shown in Tables 4 and 5.

TABLE 4

Confusion Matrix for Subset 1*

	RESPONSE										
STIMULUS	1	2	4	5	6	7	9	12	13	15	TOTAL
1 triangle	62.3	8.2	3.4	5.5	2.1	6.9	2.7	1.4	1.4	6.2	100.1
2 square	4.1	61.6	5.5	3.4	3.4	5.5	5.5	4.1	2.7	4.1	99.9
4 ramp	6.9	7.5	54.8	4.8	2.1	6.2	1.4	4.8	6.9	4.8	100.2
5 square tab	2.7	7.5	6.9	44.5	3.4	13.0	2.7	4.8	9.6	4.8	99.9
6 eye	2.1	6.2	3.4	3.4	72.6	2.7	3.4	0.7	2.7	2.7	99.9
7 half moon	2.7	4.8	8.9	9.6	4.1	52.7	4.1	2.7	4.1	6.2	99.9
9 triple groove	4.1	2.7	2.1	2.7	2.7	6.2	70.6	3.4	0.7	4.8	100.0
12 bullet	2.7	4.8	3.4	9.6	4.1	4.8	1.4	57.5	8.2	3.4	99.9
13 standard	2.7	2.7	2.1	9.6	2.7	3.4	0.0	12.3	58.9	5.5	99.9
15 single knob	0.7	5.5	3.4	3.4	6.2	3.4	3.4	0.0	4.1	69.9	100.0
Total	91.0	111.5	93.9	96.5	103.4	104.8	95.2	91.7	99.3	112.4	999.7

* Fifteen Ss were given a total of 146 trials per handle. Entries in any row show the proportion of presentations of the given stimulus that resulted in each response.

TABLE 5

Confusion Matrix for Subset 2*

	RESPONSE										
STIMULUS	1	3	4	5	6	8	11	12	13	14	TOTAL
1 triangle	67.9	7.3	4.4	2.9	0.7	2.2	7.3	2.9	2.2	2.2	100.0
3 diamond	8.0	59.9	1.5	4.4	2.9	1.5	7.3	0.7	8.8	5.1	100.1
4 ramp	8.0	9.5	40.9	13.1	5.8	7.3	8.0	0.7	3.6	2.9	99.8
5 square tab	7.3	8.0	5.8	58.4	4.4	2.2	3.6	2.9	4.4	2.9	99.9
6 eye	0.7	5.8	5.1	2.2	71.5	2.9	1.5	0.7	6.6	2.9	99.9
8 groove	1.5	6.6	5.8	13.9	5.8	49.6	6.6	2.2	4.4	3.6	100.0
11 cross	2.2	2.9	2.9	6.6	2.2	5.8	71.5	0.7	4.4	0.7	99.9
12 bullet	1.5	1.5	4.4	2.9	0.0	1.5	2.9	79.6	3.6	2.2	100.1
13 standard	5.1	2.9	3.6	7.3	4.4	2.2	0.7	5.1	59.9	8.8	100.0
14 sphere	1.5	2.9	3.6	4.4	1.5	1.5	4.4	2.9	4.4	73.0	100.1
Total	103.7	107.3	78.0	116.1	99.2	76.7	113.8	98.4	102.3	104.3	999.8

* Fifteen Ss were given a total of 137 trials per handle. Entries in any row show the proportion of presentations of the given stimulus that resulted in each response.

We tested each subset by the "learn" method. Thirty USAF airmen served as Ss, 15 learning each subset. In this experiment we also determined how accurately the Ss could identify the handles visually after they had learned them tactually. Thus, when S reached criterion (one perfect block) on the tactual trials, the apparatus was placed so he could see the handles but not feel them. Learning trials were continued with the visual identification until he reached criterion.

RESULTS

We first inspected the learning data for the two subsets. Neither the difference between the average number of learning errors nor the difference in the average number of blocks required to each criterion was significant.

The transfer data show that the visual imagery of our *S*s was good. Both the *S*s who learned Subset 1 and the *S*s who learned Subset 2 were able to identify an average of 8.7 of the ten handles on the first block of trials after the tactual learning, although they had never seen the handles before. They reached criterion in an average of 2.2 blocks for Subset 1, 1.8 blocks for Subset 2, which suggests that the shapes can easily be discriminated visually as well as tactually.

The confusion matrices for the two subsets are shown in Tables 4 and 5, and are more homogeneous than the matrix for the complete set in that the off-diagonal entries are more similar, and the largest entries are less extreme. The average size of the entries in the subset matrices is greater than in the complete matrix because of the reduced number of response alternatives. In both subsets it appears that if a smaller subset were wanted, it would be better to omit *square tab* and *standard* than any other two handles. However, we must remember that there is always a largest entry. If we were to omit the *square tab* and *standard*, other confusions would become largest. Actually, each subset was learned quickly: an average of 9.7 blocks was required to learn Subset 1, an average of 9.1 blocks for Subset 2.

Discussion

These experiments strongly suggest that tactual coding of switch handles can aid an operator materially in many applications. Since the *S*s quickly learned to identify these shapes tactually it is clear that differences in shape are useful cues for distinguishing switches. The utility of shape cues is also indicated by the ease with which subjects transferred to handles of different sizes and by the apparent ease of changing from tactual to the visual identification.

Most of our handles are not radially symmetric; that is to say, they can be mounted in different orientations. In practice it is often difficult to set the handle at the desired orientation. The prominent confusion of *square* and *diamond* suggests that *S*s could easily learn to disregard orientation cue, so that different orientations should not be troublesome. In fact, it suggests that orientation should not be used as part of a coding scheme. Two handles of the same shape but in different orientation should signify the same thing, not two different things.

Experiment I indicates that the find and learn methods will discover the same important confusions, although the fine structure of the confusion matrices may differ somewhat. Neither method is completely satisfactory. The results of the find method, which has been used by other investigators, depend on S's familiarity with the set of stimuli. The S makes very few errors when he knows the stimulus alternatives, so the find method does not clearly show differences in the degree of perceptual confusion. The learning method provides a distribution with a greater range, but random guesses cannot be distinguished from specific confusions.

Summary

The three experiments are reported concerning the tactual identification of 16 differently shaped lever-switch handles. In Experiment I, two methods for measuring confusability were compared: the find method, in which S searched through a set of 16 handles to find a particular handle, and the learn method, in which S learned to associate a number with each of the 16 handles. The methods agreed moderately but not perfectly in specifying the predominant confusions and in measuring their extent. Significantly fewer errors were made in the find method by Ss who had first been tested on the learn method, indicating that familiarity with the stimuli is an important factor.

Experiment II showed that a set of 16 small handles (¼-in. diameter), was learned as quickly as a corresponding set of large handles (⅜-in. diameter), and that Ss transferred from one size to the other with few errors.

Two subsets of ten handles were selected in such a way that most of the prediminant confusions were avoided. In Experiment III these subsets were tested by the learn method and found to be more homogeneous than the present set of 16 handles. Each subset was learned quickly. When Ss first saw the handles they had previously learned tactually, they could identify the handles with very few errors.